lonely planet

D0405189

London

"All you've got to do is decide to go
and the hardest part is over.

So go!"

TONY WHEELER, COFOUNDER – LONELY PLANET

THIS EDITION WRITTEN AND RESEARCHED BY

Peter Dragicevich, Steve Fallon, Emilie Filou, Damian Harper

Contents

Plan Your Trip · 4

Welcome to London 4
London's Top 16 6
What's New 17
Need to Know 18
First Time London 20
Getting Around 22
Top Itineraries 24

If You Like 26
Month by Month 29
With Kids 33
Like a Local 36
For Free 38
**Museums &
Galleries** **40**

Eating **44**
Drinking & Nightlife **52**
Entertainment **56**
Shopping **61**
Sports & Activities **65**
Gay & Lesbian **68**

Explore London · 70

**Neighbourhoods
at a Glance** **72**
The West End 76
The City 134
The South Bank 156
Kensington &
Hyde Park 174

Clerkenwell, Shoreditch
& Spitalfields 196
East London 213
Camden &
North London 230
Notting Hill &
West London 255

Greenwich &
South London 268
Richmond, Kew
& Hampton Court 288
**Day Trips from
London** **303**
Sleeping **318**

Understand London · 335

London Today 336
History 338
Architecture 356

Literary London 361
Theatre & Dance 365
Art & Fashion 368

The Music Scene 372
Film & Media 375

Survival Guide · 379

Transport 380
Directory A–Z 387
Index 395

London Maps · 403

(left) **Changing of the Guard p86** A must-see attraction.

(above) **Leadenhall Market p147** Take a step back in time.

(right) **Big Ben p87** A London icon at the Houses of Parliament.

Camden & North London p230

East London p213

Clerkenwell, Shoreditch & Spitalfields p196

Notting Hill & West London p255

The West End p76

The City p134

The South Bank p156

Kensington & Hyde Park p174

Greenwich & South London p268

Richmond, Kew & Hampton Court p288

Welcome to London

One of the world's most visited cities, London has something for everyone: from history and culture to fine food and good times.

Time Travel

London is immersed in history, with more than its share of mind-blowing antiquity. London's buildings are eye-catching milestones in the city's unique and compelling biography, and a great many of them – the Tower of London, Westminster Abbey, Big Ben – are instantly familiar landmarks. There's more than enough innovation (the Shard, the London Eye, the planned Garden Bridge) to put a crackle in the air, but it never drowns out London's well-preserved, centuries-old narrative. Architectural grandeur rises all around you in the West End, ancient remains dot the City and charming pubs punctuate the banks of the Thames. Take your pick.

Art & Culture

A tireless innovator of art and culture, London is a city of ideas and the imagination. Londoners have always been fiercely independent thinkers (and critics), but until not so long ago people were suspicious of anything they considered avant-garde. That's all in the past now, and the city's creative milieu is streaked with left-field attitude, from theatrical innovation to contemporary art, pioneering music, writing and design. Food in all its permutations has become almost an obsession in certain circles.

Ethnic Diversity

This city is very multicultural, with a third of all Londoners foreign born, representing 270 different nationalities. What unites them and visitors alike is the English language, for this is both our tongue's birthplace and its epicentre. These cultures season the culinary aromas on London's streets, the often exotic clothing people wear and the music they listen to. London's diverse cultural dynamism makes it among the world's most international cities. And diversity reaches intrinsically British institutions too; the British and Victoria & Albert Museums have collections as varied as they are magnificent, while flavours at centuries-old Borough Market now run the full gourmet and cosmopolitan spectrum.

A Tale of Two Cities

London is as much about wide-open spaces and leafy escapes as it is high-density, sight-packed exploration. Central London is where you will find the major museums, galleries and most iconic sights, but visit Hampstead Heath or the new Queen Elizabeth Olympic Park to escape the crowds and view the city's greener hues up close. Or venture even further out to Kew Gardens, Richmond or Hampton Court Palace for excellent panoramas of riverside London.

Why I Love London

By Steve Fallon, Author

Like most Londoners, I revel in all our familiar landmarks – Big Ben, Tower Bridge, the murky Thames, the London Eye. I still thank the former government that made some of the greatest museums and art galleries in the world free to one and all. The choice of restaurants, bars and clubs is legion, and what's not to love about a city with more lush parkland than any other world capital? But the one thing that sets my adopted city apart from any other is its amazing tolerance. 'As long as you don't scare the horses, mate, you'll be all right here,' I was told when I arrived here more than 20 years ago. Guess what? It still hasn't happened.

For more about our authors, see p448.

Top: Tower Bridge (p145) and the Shard (p164)

London's
Top 16

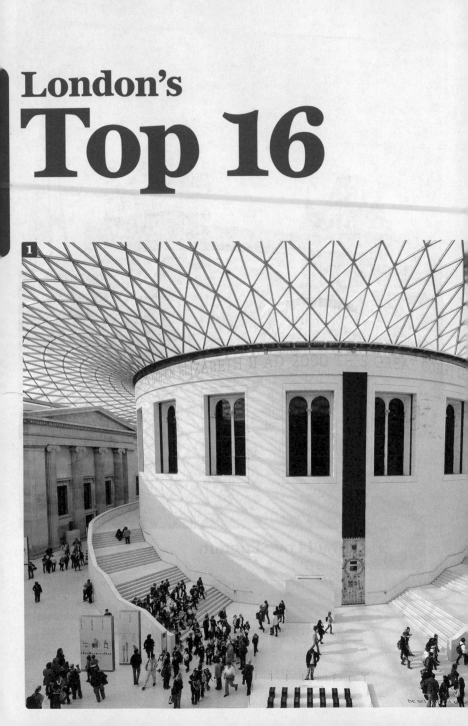

1

British Museum *(p81)*

1 With six million visitors trooping through its doors annually, the British Museum in Bloomsbury is Britain's most visited attraction. You could spend a lifetime in this vast and hallowed collection of artefacts, art and age-old antiquity, and still make daily discoveries (admission is free, so you could do just that, if so inclined). Otherwise, join everyone else on the highlights tours (or eyeOpener tours) for a précis of the museum's treasures.

◉ *The West End*

National Gallery *(p89)*

2 This superlative collection of (largely pre-modern) art at the heart of London is one of the largest anywhere, and a roll-call of some of the world's most outstanding artistic compositions. With highlights including work from Leonardo da Vinci, Michelangelo, Gainsborough, Constable, Turner, Monet, Renoir and Van Gogh, it's a bravura performance and one not to be missed. The onsite restaurants and cafes are also exceptional, rounding out a terrific experience and putting the icing on an already eye-catching cake.

◉ *The West End*

CHRIS HEPBURN / GETTY IMAGES ©

KIMBERLEY COOLE / GETTY IMAGES ©

London Pubs (p52)

3 London minus its pubs would be like Paris sans cafes or Beijing shorn of its charming *hutong*. Pub culture is an indispensable element of London DNA and the pub is the place to be if you want to see local people in their hop-scented element. Longer hours for many pubs have only cemented them as the cornerstone for a good night out across the capital. They're also a favourite for family-friendly long weekend lunches. Once no-go zones for discerning foodies, pubs long ago upped their game: standout gastropubs dot London's culinary cosmos and rival great restaurants.

Drinking & Nightlife

Tate Modern (p158)

4 The favourite of Londoners (and quite possibly the world), this contemporary art collection enjoys a triumphant position right on the River Thames. Housed in the former Bankside Power Station, the Tate Modern is a vigorous statement of modernity, architectural renewal and accessibility. The permanent collection is free and the gallery's much-anticipated extension, scheduled to open in 2016, will give it more space to display its treasures. New exhibition spaces will push the conceptual envelope too with installation and performance art.

The South Bank

Tower of London (p136)

5 Few parts of the UK are as steeped in history or as impregnated with legend and superstition as the titanic stonework of this fabulous fortress. Not only is the tower an architectural odyssey but there's also a diamond almost as big as the Ritz, free tours from magnificently attired 'Beefeaters', a dazzling array of armour and weaponry, and a palpable sense of ancient history at every turn. Because there is simply so much to see, it's well worth getting here early as you will need at least half a day of exploration.

The City

Culinary London (p44)

6 Don't let anybody tell you that the food in England isn't good: London has long been a shining light in culinary excellence, with a kaleidoscope of cuisines unrivalled in Europe. The capital is particularly strong in Indian and other Asian food (such as Chinese, Japanese and Thai), but don't miss the opportunity of trying traditional or Modern British cuisine, either in a good gastropub or the finer restaurants. For those with a sweet tooth, an afternoon tea or a treat from the capital's many cake shops is a must.

✗ *Eating*

Camden Town (p240)

7 A foray into trendy North London, away from the central sights, is a crucial part of the London experience. Camden's market – actually four markets in one great melange – may be a hectic and tourist-oriented attraction, but snacking on the go from the international food stalls is a great way to enjoy browsing the merchandise, while Camden's terrific dining scene, throbbing nightlife and well-seasoned pub culture is well known to night owls citywide. CAMDEN MARKET

🔒*Camden & North London*

6

Victoria & Albert Museum (p176)

8 You could spend a whole day in this huge museum and still be astounded at its variety and depth. Located in stylish South Kensington, the world's leading collection of decorative arts has something for everyone, from Islamic textiles to antique Chinese ceramics, photography, fashion, works by Raphael and modern design classics from iMacs to Nike shoes. And don't overlook the fabulous architecture of the museum, a major attraction in itself.

⊙ *Kensington & Hyde Park*

Hampton Court Palace (p290)

9 It may not be a royal residence any more but Hampton Court hasn't lost any of its splendour – inside or out. The magnificent Tudor palace, so coveted by Henry VIII that he coaxed it out of Cardinal Thomas Wolsey in 1515, was extended in the 17th century by Christopher Wren, and visitors will be able to delight in the different architectural styles in the various 'apartments'. Don't miss the Tudor kitchens, which once churned out meals for up to 1200 people for Henry's court, and make sure you leave plenty of time for the sumptuous gardens – you might get lost in the maze...

⊙ *Richmond, Kew & Hampton Court*

West End Performances (p56)

10 The West End is synonymous with musicals and no trip to London would be complete without an evening of *Mama Mia!*, *Les Misérables* or *Phantom of the Opera*. If musicals don't float your boat, there are more alternatives than you'll have evenings to fill: theatre, dance, opera, small gigs, big-ticket concerts or live jazz. London truly is the capital of the arts. The trick is to book either far in advance if you have a particular show in mind or last minute for bargains. QUEEN'S THEATRE

☆ *Entertainment*

Hyde Park & Kensington Gardens (p182)

11 London's urban parkland is virtually second to none and is *the* place to see locals at ease and in their element. Hyde Park alone ranges across a mighty 142 hectares; throw in Kensington Gardens and you have even more space to roam and everything you could want: a central London setting, a royal palace, extravagant Victoriana, boating opportunities, open-air concerts, an art gallery, magnificent trees and a tasteful granite memorial to Princess Diana. HYDE PARK

⊙ *Kensington & Hyde Park*

9

London Eye *(p161)*

12 You may have eyed up London from altitude as you descended into Heathrow, but your pilot won't have lingered over the supreme views of town that extend in every direction from London's great riverside Ferris wheel. The queues move as slowly as the Eye rotates (there are ways to fast-track your way on), but that makes the occasion even more rewarding once you've lifted off and London unfurls beneath you. Avoiding grey days is the top tip – but with London's notoriously overcast skies, that might be a tall order. If you've only a few days in the capital, make this your first stop and you can at least say you've seen the sights.

LONDON EYE DESIGNED BY DAVID MARKS AND JULIA BARFIELD

⊙ *The South Bank*

14

Notting Hill Carnival (p257)

13 Every August, trendy Notting Hill throws a big, long and loud party. Europe's leading street festival is a vibrantly colourful three-day celebration of Afro-Caribbean music, culture and food. Over a million people visit every year, taking part in the celebrations, thronging the streets and letting their hair down. The festival is a must if you want a spirited glimpse of multicultural London and its cross-pollination of music, food, clothing, language and culture.

✿Notting Hill & West London

Westminster Abbey (p78)

14 Adorers of medieval ecclesiastic architecture will be in seventh heaven at this sublime abbey, hallowed place of coronation for England's sovereigns. Almost every nook and adorable cranny has a story attached to it but few sights in London are as beautiful, or as well preserved, as the Henry VII chapel. Elsewhere you will find the oldest door in the UK, Poet's Corner, the Coronation Chair, 14th-century cloisters, a 900-year-old garden, royal sarcophagi and much more. Be warned that the crowds are almost as solid as the abbey's unshakeable stonework, so aim to join the queue first thing in the morning.

◉The West End

East End Nightlife *(p225)*

15 While you can party pretty much anywhere in London, the East End has had the edge over everywhere else for a few years now. There are grungy clubs, rooftop bars carpeted with astroturf, retro-chic Victorian pubs, 500-year old pubs, a lively gay and lesbian scene, and bars of every description. And you won't have to party on an empty stomach: the food offering is as diverse as the area's population, from curry houses to modern British cuisine and cafes serving the finest coffees.

🍷*East London*

Natural History Museum *(p180)*

16 With its thunderous, animatronic Tyrannosaurus Rex, fascinating displays about Planet Earth, outstanding Darwin Centre and architecture straight from a Gothic fairy tale, the Natural History Museum is quite simply a work of great curatorial imagination. Kids are the target audience but, looking around, you'll see adults equally mesmerised. Winter brings its own magic, when the glittering ice rink by the east lawn swarms with skaters.

⊙*Kensington & Hyde Park*

What's New

Round-the-Clock Tube

We didn't think we'd live to see the day, but 24-hour service at the weekend (only) has begun on five of **London Underground**'s nine lines, with night-time departures averaging every 10 minutes. (p383)

Underground Spreads South

As if that wasn't enough good news, the Northern line is being extended and gaining two stations in Battersea by 2020, with a southern extension of the Bakerloo line under discussion. (p277)

Tasteful Views from on High

Two of the new additions to the London skyline – the Shard (p164) and the Walkie Talkie (p147) – now feature a number of restaurants and cafes from which to enjoy the city on high.

Garden Bridge Oasis

A bridge covering 2500 sq metres of garden, including 270 trees and 2000 bushes, will link the South Bank with Temple Underground station and open to the public around 2018.

A New Park for London

The southern half of the 2012 Olympic site has opened as Queen Elizabeth Olympic Park (p221), with the Aquatics Centre (p229) now available for swimming, the Velodrome for cycling and the Arcelor-Mittal Orbit for abseiling.

First World War Galleries

To mark the centenary of the start of WWI, the Imperial War Museum opened what is arguably the finest new permanent exhibition in a London museum. (p275)

More Room at the British Museum

A long-awaited £135 million new extension called the World Conservation and Exhibitions Centre has opened at the august institution. (p81)

All Change in Trafalgar Square

Katharina Fritsch's *Hahn/Cock*, a huge, cobalt-blue sculpture of a rooster, has made way on the Fourth Plinth for Hans Haacke's *Gift Horse*, a skeletal, riderless equine with live stock exchange ticker. We don't know either. (p105)

Harry Potter Pilgrims

Warner Bros Studios (p237) near Watford in north London has become the new mecca for Harry Potter fans, with its tour of the film sets and original Hogwarts Express steam engine.

Sir John Soane's Museum

The 2nd floor of the building next door to this wonderful museum, which contains the architect's private apartments and model room, has opened to the public for the first time ever. (p96)

For more recommendations and reviews, see **lonelyplanet. com/london**

Need to Know

For more information, see Survival Guide (p379)

Currency
Pound sterling (£). 100 pence = £1.

Language
English (and more than 300 others).

Visas
Not required for US, Canadian, Australian, New Zealand or South African visitors for stays of up to six months. European Union nationals can stay indefinitely.

Money
ATMs are widespread. Major credit cards are accepted everywhere. The best place to change money is in post office branches, which do not charge a commission.

Mobile Phones
Buy local SIM cards for European and Australian phones, or a pay-as-you-go phone. Set other phones to international roaming.

Time
London is on GMT; during British Summer Time (BST; late March to late October), London clocks are one hour ahead of GMT.

Tourist Information
Visit London (☑0870 156 6366; www.visitlondon.com) can fill you in on everything from attractions and events to tours and accommodation.

Daily Costs

Budget: Less than £85
➡ Dorm bed: £10–32
➡ Market-stall lunch: £5, supermarket sandwich £3.50–4.50
➡ Many museums: free
➡ Standby theatre tickets: £5–25
➡ Santander Cycles daily rental fee: £2

Midrange: £85–185
➡ Double room: £90–160
➡ Two-course dinner with glass of wine: £35
➡ Theatre ticket: £15–60

Top End: More than £185
➡ Four-star/boutique hotel room: £200
➡ Three-course dinner in top restaurant with wine: £60–90
➡ Black cab trip: £30
➡ Top theatre ticket: £65

Advance Planning

Three months before Book weekend performances of top shows; make dinner reservations for renowned restaurants with celebrity chefs; snatch up tickets for must-see temporary exhibitions; book accommodation at boutique properties.

One month before Check listings on entertainment sites such as Time Out (p57) for fringe theatre, live music and festivals, and book tickets.

A few days before Check the weather on the Met Office (www.metoffice.gov.uk/public/weather/forecast) website.

Useful Websites

Lonely Planet (www.lonelyplanet.com/london) Bookings, traveller forum and more.

Time Out London (www.timeout.com/london) Up-to-date and comprehensive listings.

Londonist (www.londonist.com) A website about London and everything that happens in it.

Transport for London (www.tfl.gov) Essential tool for staying mobile in the capital.

BBC London (www.bbc.co.uk/news/england/london) All the news that's fit to print.

WHEN TO GO

Summer is peak season: days are long and festivals are afoot, but expect crowds. Spring and autumn are cooler, but delightful. Winter is cold but quiet.

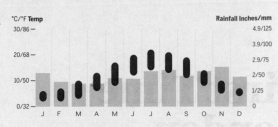

°C/°F Temp
30/86 —
20/68 —
10/50 —
0/32 —
J F M A M J J A S O N D

Rainfall Inches/mm
4.9/125
3.9/100
2.9/75
2/50
1/25
0

Arriving in London

Heathrow Airport Trains, London Underground (tube) and buses to central London from just after 5am to before midnight (night buses run later) £5.70 to 21.50; taxi £45 to 85.

Gatwick Airport Trains to central London from 4.30am to 1.35am £10 to 20; hourly buses to central London around the clock from £5; taxi £100.

Stansted Airport Trains to central London from 5.30am to 1.30am £23.40; round-the-clock buses to central London from £12; taxi from £130.

Luton Airport Trains to central London from 7am to 10pm from £14; round-the-clock buses to central London £10; taxi £110.

London City Airport DLR trains to central London from 5.30am to 12.30am Monday to Saturday, 7am to 11.15pm Sunday from £2.80; taxi around £30.

St Pancras International Train Station In Central London (for Eurostar train arrivals from Europe) and connected by many underground lines to other parts of the city.

For much more on **arrival** see p380

Digital London

There are scores of cool apps for travellers. Here are some of our favourite free ones – from inspirational to the downright practical. Many museums and attractions also have their own.

➡ **Streetmuseum** Historical images (photographs, paintings, drawings etc) superimposed on modern-day locations.

➡ **Street Art Tours London** Hand-picked graffiti and other street-art locations.

➡ **Soho Stories** Social history of London's most Bohemian neighbourhood, told through poems and extracts from novels and newspapers.

➡ **Hailo** Summons the nearest black cab right to the curb.

➡ **Uber** A taxi, private car or rideshare at competitive prices.

➡ **London Bus Live** Real-time route finder and bus arrivals for a stop of your choice.

➡ **Santander Cycles** Find a 'Boris Bike', a route and a place to return it.

➡ **ToiletFinder** Where to find one when you need it most.

Sleeping

Hanging your hat (and anything else you care to remove) in London can be painfully expensive, and you'll almost always need to book your room well in advance. Decent, central hostels are easy enough to find and also offer reasonably priced double rooms. Bed and breakfasts are a dependable and inexpensive, if rather simple, option. Hotels range from cheap, no-frills chains through boutique choices to luxury five-star historic hotels.

Useful Websites

➡ **Lonely Planet** (www.lonelyplanet.com/london) Hundreds of properties, from budget hostels to luxury apartments.

➡ **London Town** (www.londontown.com) Excellent last-minute offers on boutique hotels and B&Bs.

➡ **Alastair Sawdays** (www.sawdays.co.uk) Hand-picked selection of boltholes in the capital.

➡ **Visit London** (www.visitlondon.com) Huge range of listings from the city's official tourism portal.

For much more on **sleeping** see p318

First Time London

For more information, see Survival Guide (p379)

Checklist

➡ Make sure your passport is valid for at least six months past your arrival date

➡ Check airline baggage restrictions (liquids and fresh products in particular)

➡ Arrange travel insurance and, if you're from the EU, a European Health Insurance Card

➡ Inform your debit/credit card company of your travel plans

➡ Book tickets for popular plays, shows or festivals to avoid disappointment

What to Pack

➡ An umbrella (yes, the rumours about the weather are true)

➡ Good walking shoes – the city is best explored on foot

➡ UK plug adaptor

➡ A few extra layers – it can be cool, even in summer

➡ A small day pack

Top Tips for Your Trip

➡ London is huge – work by neighbourhood to avoid wasting time (and money) on transport.

➡ An Oyster Card is a cheaper and convenient way to use public transport, but you can also pay by credit or debit card provided it has a contactless function indicated by a symbol of four wavy lines.

➡ Walk – it's cheaper than transport and the best way to discover central London.

➡ For West End performances at bargain prices, opt for standby tickets (which you buy on the day at the venue) or last-minute ticket-booth tickets on Leicester Sq.

➡ To treat yourself to fine dining without breaking the bank, opt for lunch rather than dinner, or try for pre- or post-theatre dinner deals.

What to Wear

Fashion is big in London but very eclectic so you're unlikely to stand out, whatever your sartorial choice.

Dress codes are rare (although you'll need smart shoes for some restaurants and clubs), but many Londoners make an effort in the evening, whether they're kitted out in cool T-shirts or more formal gear.

The weather has a mind of its own, regardless of the season: always carry an umbrella or a jacket that can repel a shower or two. And do wrap up warm in winter, the wind can be punishing.

Be Forewarned

➡ London is open for business every day of the year, except Christmas Day (25 December) when absolutely everything shuts down, including the transport network. Hotel restaurants are about the only thing you'll find open.

➡ Most shops in central London are open seven days a week, though they can only trade for six hours (usually noon to 6pm) on Sunday.

➡ London is a relatively safe city, though common sense applies: avoid deserted streets at night and be mindful of pickpockets in crowded areas or even at outdoor cafes.

➡ Be discreet with your tablet/smartphone – snatching happens.

➡ Always use black cabs or licensed minicabs.

Money

ATMs are widespread. Major credit cards are accepted everywhere. The best place to change money is in post office branches, which do not charge a commission.

Taxes & Refunds

Value-added tax (VAT) is a 20% sales tax levied on most goods and services. Restaurants must always include VAT in their prices, but the same requirement does not apply to hotel room prices, so double-check when booking.

It's sometimes possible for visitors to claim a refund of VAT paid on goods (p390).

Market stalls at Covent Garden Piazza (p104)

Tipping

➡ **Hotels** Pay a porter £1 per bag; gratuity for room staff is at your discretion.

➡ **Pubs** Not expected unless table service is provided, then £1 for a round of drinks is sufficient.

➡ **Restaurants** Service charge often included in the bill. If not, 10% for decent service, up to 15% if exceptional.

➡ **Taxis** Round fare up to nearest pound only.

Etiquette

Although largely informal in their everyday dealings, Londoners do observe some (unspoken) rules of etiquette.

➡ **Strangers** Most Londoners would no more speak to a stranger in the street than fly to the moon. If you're a tourist in need of directions, there's no problem. But try starting a general conversation at a bus stop or on a tube platform and people will react as if you were mad.

➡ **Queues** The English are happy to break many rules they consider silly but lining up is not one of them. Any attempt to 'jump the queue' will result in an outburst of tutting.

➡ **Tube** An unbreakable rule involves where to stand (on the right) and where to pass (on the left) while riding an Underground escalator.

➡ **Bargaining** Haggling over the price of goods (but not food) is okay in markets, but nonexistent in shops.

Staying Connected

Smartphone users can turn their expensive data-roaming off: there are numerous ways to get online for free in London (outside your hotel or hostel):

➡ Chains such as Pret a Manger, McDonalds or Starbucks and most cafes all have free wi-fi.

➡ The City of London is one giant hotspot as is Upper St in Islington.

➡ Public buildings such as the Barbican, the Southbank Centre and the British Library all offer free wi-fi.

➡ Wi-fi is also available in some Overground stations (free) and some Underground stations (fees may apply).

➡ Check out *Time Out*'s useful free wi-fi guide (www.timeout.com/london/things-to-do/where-to-find-free-wi-fi-in-london-9).

Getting Around

For more information, see Transport (p380)

Underground (Tube)
The quickest (but most expensive) form of public transport; trains run from 5.30am to 12.30am (7am to 11.30pm Sunday). Selected lines run all night Friday and Saturday.

Bus
Slow-going but cheap, with ace views from double-deckers. Large number of night buses.

Bicycle
Santander Cycles are the ideal way to get around central London on a dry day. Cheap, fast and scenic.

Walking
Free, healthy and immersive, you can't beat it for neighbourhood exploration.

Overground
Runs all the way around London across Zones 2 and 3. Similar operating hours to the Underground but less frequent trains (every five to 20 minutes).

Taxi
Available everywhere and round-the-clock. Hail in the street (black cabs) or book ahead (minicabs).

Train
Best to get to/from the airport, go to Hampton Court or on day trips to places further afield, such as Oxford or Windsor.

Key Phrases

Black Cab London's signature clunky taxi, which can be hailed anywhere in the city. Note that despite the name, they are not all black!

Boris Bike A colloquialism for the red Santander-branded bikes for hire all over London. Named after mayor Boris Johnson (who served between 2008 and 2016), although the initiative was set in motion by previous mayor Ken Livingstone.

Contactless Payment card (debit or credit) that can be used to make quick payments without signature or chip and pin; used in the same way as an Oyster Card.

DLR Docklands Light Railway, an overground, driverless train in East London, almost as frequent as the tube.

Minicab A taxi that cannot be hailed in the street and must be pre-booked over the phone, in person with the dispatcher (offices can generally be spotted by an orange flashing light outside) or, increasingly, through apps such as Uber.

Oyster Card Smart card ticket for London's transport network.

The Tube London's underground metro system.

Key Routes

Bus: Route 15 This 'heritage' bus route uses the classic London Routemaster double-decker buses and takes in the Tower of London, St Paul's, the Strand and Trafalgar Sq.

Bus: Route RV1 Links all the sights along the South Bank with Covent Garden across the river.

DLR: Bank to Greenwich Bag the seats at the front of this driverless, overground train for an amazing sightseeing trip through the Docklands and Canary Wharf.

Tube: Piccadilly Line This tube line stops at some of London's key sights and neighbourhoods – Piccadilly Circus, Covent Garden, Hyde Park and Knightsbridge.

How to Hail a Taxi

➡ To hail a black cab, look for a stationary or approaching cab with its 'For Hire' sign lit up.

➡ If the car is approaching, stand in a prominent place on the side of the road and stick out your arm.

➡ Alternatively, find them at the numerous taxi ranks dotting the city (at stations, airports, outside big hotels etc).

➡ Use a smartphone app such as Hailo, which uses your phone's GPS to find the nearest available black cab.

TOP TIPS

➡ As a general rule, eschew the tube within Zone 1 unless going from one end to the other: cycling, walking or the bus will be cheaper/quicker.

➡ Check www.tfl.gov.uk or advanced notices in tube stations for planned engineering works and line closures at weekends.

➡ Get an Oyster Card – and return it when you leave to get the £5 deposit back, along with any remaining credit.

➡ Santander Cycles are good for short trips – you pay £2 for the day and can cycle for up to 30 minutes for free, as many times as you like. Just leave five minutes between each rental.

When to Travel

➡ Travelling during rush hour (6.30am to 9.30am and 4pm to 7pm) can be uncomfortably crowded: think stealthy seat races, face-in-armpit standing and toe-treading. Tube fares are also more expensive at rush hour and tempers easily fray.

➡ Weekends are notorious for engineering works, when entire tube lines or sections of lines shut down. Replacement bus services are usually in place, but they often take longer so try to plan around these restrictions.

➡ On weeknights, the tube stops running around 12.30am; selected lines run all night Friday and Saturday night. Night buses cover all corners of London, but note that some services only run every half-hour, so check times before leaving lest you fancy hanging around at a bus stop at 3am.

Travel Etiquette

➡ Have your ticket or card ready before you go through the gate. Londoners are well-practiced at moving through ticket barriers without breaking stride.

➡ On escalators, stand on the right-hand side and use the left if you want to walk down. Failure to observe this can cause consternation among other users, especially during rush hour.

➡ Take your rucksack off at rush hour to avoid sweeping off somebody's newspaper, tablet or child.

➡ Give up your seat for people less able to stand than you – people with reduced mobility have priority over the seats closest to the doors on the tube.

➡ Cars will usually stop for pedestrians at zebra crossings without a traffic light; remember to look right first, however!

Tickets & Passes

➡ The cheapest and most convenient way to pay for public transport is to buy an Oyster Card, a smart card on which you can store credit. The card works on the entire transport network and can be purchased from all tube and train stations and some shops.

➡ Oyster Cards will work out whether to charge you per journey, for a return or for a day travelcard.

➡ You need to pay a £5 deposit per Oyster Card, which you will get back when you return the card, along with any remaining credit.

➡ If you're staying for more than just a few days, consider getting a weekly or monthly pass (which can be loaded on the Oyster card).

➡ Paper tickets are still available but are more expensive than Oyster fares.

➡ Contactless cards can be used instead of Oyster Cards (they benefit from the same 'smart fare' system); just check for international fees with your card issuer.

For much more on **getting around** see p382 ➡

Top Itineraries

Day One

The West End (p76)

 First stop, **Trafalgar Sq** for its architectural grandeur and photo-op views down Whitehall and of **Big Ben**. Art lovers will make an instant break for the **National Gallery** and its unrivalled collection of European paintings. Alternatively, if you're here during **Buckingham Palace's** summer opening, visit the royal residence.

 Lunch Inn the Park (p111) for the leafy surroundings of St James's Park.

The South Bank (p156)

With your pre-booked ticket for the **London Eye**, walk across the pedestrian Hungerford Bridge to the South Bank and enjoy a revolution in the city skies and unrivalled views, notably of the **Houses of Parliament**. Afterwards, sashay along the river and head down the ramp into the bowels of the **Tate Modern** for some grade-A art. Aim your camera at **St Paul's Cathedral** on the far side of the elegant **Millennium Bridge**.

Dinner Elaborate Italian at Zucca (p169).

The South Bank (p156)

Depending what mood you're in, you could watch a performance at **Shakespeare's Globe**. Standing tickets can be bought last minute (but book in advance for seats). Otherwise, join the post-work crowds in the **pubs** around London Bridge for real ales and historical surroundings.

Day Two

The City (p134)

London's finance-driven Square Mile is home to the **Tower of London**. Spend the morning following the **Beefeaters** and marvelling at the **Crown Jewels**. When you're finished, take a minute to admire the iconic **Tower Bridge** on the Thames.

 Lunch Wine Library (p153) for good wine and platters.

The West End (p76)

Hop on a double-decker bus for city views and head to the **British Museum** for a shot of world culture. Choose one of the excellent introductory tours so as not to feel overwhelmed. Round off the afternoon with a recuperative pint at a local **pub**.

Dinner Yauatcha (p115) for excellent Chinese food in the heart of Soho.

The West End (p76)

There are literally dozens of pubs, bars and cocktail bars to choose from. If you fancy soaking up the atmosphere, stroll through **Chinatown** and **Soho** and make your way to **Leicester Sq** for some people watching.

Day Three

Greenwich & South London (p268)

Hop on a boat in central London and make your way down to Greenwich with its world-renowned architecture. Start your visit at the legendary **Cutty Sark**, a star clipper during the tea-trade years.

> **Lunch** Greenwich Market (p280) for a culinary tour of world cuisine.

Greenwich & South London (p268)

Stroll through **Greenwich Park** all the way up to the **Royal Observatory**. The views of **Canary Wharf**, the business district across the river, are stunning. Inside the Observatory, straddle the **Greenwich Meridian** and find out about the incredible quest to solve the longitude problem. At the **planetarium**, join another quest: finding extra-terrestrial life. Walk back down to Greenwich and settle down for a pint at the **Trafalgar Tavern**.

> **Dinner** St John (p202) for high-brow, nose-to-tail British cuisine

Clerkenwell, Shoreditch & Spitalfields (p196)

Head back to central London on the DLR from Greenwich and treat yourself to dinner in one of the fine restaurants dotting this part of town. There are plenty of clubs if you fancy a boogie after dinner, otherwise opt for a beautifully crafted cocktail at **Zetter Townhouse Cocktail Lounge** or **Worship St Whistling Shop**.

Day Four

Kew, Richmond & Hampton Court (p288)

Head to **Kew Gardens** bright and early to make the most of the morning: this is so much more than a botanical garden! Families shouldn't miss the treetop walkway, while plant lovers will go weak at the knees in the Palm House and Conservatory.

> **Lunch** Glasshouse (p301) for fine gastronomy.

Kensington & Hyde Park (p174

Hop on the tube to **Kensington**. Keen shoppers will want to stroll along Old Brompton Rd and pop into **Harrods**, the famous department store. Culture vultures should save their energy for the **Victoria & Albert Museum** or the **Natural History Museum**.

> **Dinner** Dinner by Heston Blumenthal (p191) for theatrical English cuisine.

Notting Hill & West London (p255)

If the pubs around Kensington are too staid for you, hop over to **Notting Hill** where the crowds are livelier and the nightlife more eclectic. If you just fancy sitting down with a good film, you're in luck: Notting Hill has some of the coolest independent **cinemas** in London.

If You Like...

Royalty

Tower of London Castle, tower, prison, medieval execution site and home of the dazzling Crown Jewels. (p136)

Buckingham Palace The Queen Mother of all London's royal palaces, with lovely gardens and – the popular drawcard – the Changing of the Guard. (p85)

Hampton Court Palace Magnificent Tudor palace, located within beautiful grounds on the Thames. (p290)

Kensington Palace Princess Diana's former home, this stately and stunning royal palace is the highlight of Kensington Gardens. (p187)

Windsor Castle Magnificent and ancient royal fortress within easy reach of London. (p304)

Views

London Eye For gently rotating, tip-top views of London – but choose a fair-weather day. (p161)

View from the Shard The highest – and most expensive – views in London. (p164)

Parliament Hill Skyscraping views across London from Hampstead Heath. (p242)

Greenwich Park Clamber up to the statue of General Wolfe for superlative views of Canary Wharf, the Thames and the O2. (p271)

Sky Pod Phenomenal views of London, a roof garden and not a sight of the awkward Walkie Talkie, since you're in it! (p153)

DANITA DELIMONT / GETTY IMAGES ©

National Gallery (p89) and St Martin-in-the-Fields (p106)

Madison For a full-frontal view of St Paul's elegant dome in alfresco settings, you can't beat this cocktail bar. (p155)

ArcelorMittal Orbit Ideal for a bird's eye view of the Queen Elizabeth Olympic Park. (p221)

Parks & Gardens

Hampstead Heath Woods, hills, meadows and top scenic views, all rolled into one sublime sprawl. (p242)

Richmond Park Europe's largest urban parkland has everything from herds of deer to tranquil pockets of woodland, seemingly infinite wild tracts and beautiful vistas. (p296)

St James's Park Feast on some sublime views in one of London's most attractive royal parks. (p100)

Kew Gardens A botanist's paradise, a huge expanse of greenery and a great day out with the kids. (p294)

Chelsea Physic Garden A tranquil and particularly tidy botanical enclave just a stone's throw from the Thames. (p189)

Greenwich Park A delightful mix of views, expansive lawns, beautiful trees and home of the Meridian. (p271)

Cemeteries

Highgate Cemetery Gothic and sublimely overgrown 20-hectare Victorian place of the dead, including Karl Marx. (p243)

Abney Park Cemetery Tangled with weeds, reclaimed by nature, with moments of magic. (p247)

Brompton Cemetery Some of this cemetery's dead found immortality in the names of Beatrix Potter's animal characters. (p258)

Tower Hamlets Cemetery Park Another specialist in the wild and sublime Victorian ruin look. (p219)

Kensal Green Cemetery Distinctive Greek Revival architecture and illustrious residents including Isambard Kingdom Brunel and Charles Babbage. (p259)

Squares

Trafalgar Square London's iconic central square, lorded over by Lord Nelson – and four magnificent felines. (p94)

Soho Square Serene spot for a sandwich in the sun in the heart of the West End. (p103)

Trinity Square Gardens Picturesque and well-tended one-time location of the notorious Tower Hill scaffold. (p146)

Squares of Bloomsbury Elegant, historic and tranquil squares dotted around literary Bloomsbury. (p98)

Covent Garden Piazza Fine-looking West End square originally laid out in the 17th century, and now popular with street performers. (p104)

Leicester Square Unbeatable for people watching and celebrity spotting on film premiere nights. (p105)

Music

Wireless Festival London's big-ticket music festival (held in July), with an emphasis on R&B and dance. (p30)

Wigmore Hall One of the best and most active classical-music concert venues in the capital. (p126)

Royal Festival Hall Fantastic acoustics and an excellent programme of music across the aural spectrum. (p171)

For more top London spots, see the following:

➡ Eating (p44)
➡ Drinking & Nightlife (p52)
➡ Entertainment (p56)
➡ Shopping (p61)
➡ Sports & Activities (p65)

PLAN YOUR TRIP IF YOU LIKE…

Church recitals Take a pew at one of the many free afternoon church recitals around town. (p39)

Indie rock gigs Playing in one of North London's numerous grungy bars is a rite of passage for aspiring acts. (p251)

Royal Opera House London's world-famous opera in Covent Garden is second to none for lavish opera productions. (p125)

Cultural Diversity

Chinatown At the heart of London and the place to be for dim sum dining or the Chinese New Year. (p103)

Brick Lane Take a wander and a gander and go shopping around this vibrant neighbourhood, shaped by migration over the centuries. (p210)

Brixton Village Great dining and shopping converge in South London's most famous multicultural neighbourhood. (p276)

Whitechapel Road Lively, vibrant and cacophonous tangle of cultures and languages. (p215)

Rivers & Canals

Regent's Canal Amble along the historic trade route and take a shortcut across North London at the same time. (p246)

Richmond Home to some spectacular views of the Thames with enchanting pastoral shade in Petersham Meadows. (p296)

Greenwich Pop into a riverside pub and toast the fine views of the river with a pint. (p284)

South Bank Hop on our South Bank Stroll and walk from County Hall to City Hall, past some outstanding waterside sights. (p168)

Hampton Court Palace Take a riverboat up the Thames to Henry VIII's spectacular palace. (p290)

Village Charms

Primrose Hill With lovely restaurants, boutiques and pubs, this North London village has genuine appeal (and celebrity-spotting ops). (p238)

Richmond Perhaps the archetypal London village, with village green, a river perspective, a fabulous bridge and gorgeous parkland. (p296)

Dulwich Village After viewing the Dulwich Picture Gallery, wander around Dulwich Village with its towering horse chestnut trees to experience some of London's easy-going and tranquil charms. (p280)

Walking

Hampstead Heath Wild, hilly, carefree heathland and woodland with some excellent views from London's highest open space. (p242)

Regent's Canal Take a canalside hike across North London. (p246)

Putney to Barnes Amble along the delightful riverside on this doable segment of the Thames Path. (p289)

The West End Jump on our highlights tour from Covent Garden to Trafalgar Sq. (p129)

Wimbledon Common Follow the nature trail or just branch off in any direction for woodland, heath, grassland and bracing exploration. (p299)

Churches

St Paul's Cathedral Sir Christopher Wren's 300-year-old domed masterpiece and London's most iconic historic church. (p142)

Westminster Abbey Ancient and sublime site of coronation for English monarchs since William the Conqueror. (p78)

Westminster Cathedral The gaunt interior sparkles fitfully with dazzling Byzantine mosaics. (p97)

All Saints An extraordinarily beautiful example of lavish High Victorian Gothic architecture. (p99)

St Stephen Walbrook Sir Christopher Wren's finest City church, and his first experience with a dome, a precursor to St Paul's. (p148)

Modern Architecture

30 St Mary Axe Colloquially dubbed 'the Gherkin', this is the City's most iconic modern edifice. (p146)

Shard A crystalline spike dominating the South Bank, with views of the city to die for. (p164)

London Eye Unsurprisingly visible from many remote parts of town. (p161)

City Hall Does it look like a woodlouse or Darth Vader's helmet? Your call. (p166)

Serpentine Sackler Gallery A former 19th century gunpowder depot, with an undulating modern extension by architect Zaha Hadid. (p183)

History

Tower of London Spanning almost 1000 years of history, from fortress to home of the Crown Jewels. (p136)

Churchill War Rooms Ground zero of London's war effort during WWII, left pretty much as it was in 1945. (p95)

Museum of London From Anglo-Saxon village to 21st century metropolis, retrace the history of the capital. (p151)

Museum of London Docklands See how the Thames and the Docklands have shaped London's history. (p220)

Geffrye Museum A fascinating insight into the daily lives of London residents through the ages. (p198)

Month by Month

TOP EVENTS
....

Notting Hill Carnival,
August

Chelsea Flower Show,
May

Trooping the Colour,
June

Guy Fawkes Night,
November

**Wimbledon Lawn Tennis
Championships**, June

January

January in London kicks off with a big bang at midnight. London is in the throes of winter, with short days: light appears at 8am and is all but gone by 4pm.

✷ New Year's Celebration

On 31 December, the famous countdown to midnight with Big Ben is met with terrific fireworks from the London Eye and massive crowds.

◉ London Art Fair

More than 100 major galleries participate in this contemporary art fair (www.londonartfair.co.uk), now one of the largest in Europe, with thematic exhibitions, special events and the best emerging artists.

February

February is usually chilly, wet and even snow-encrusted. The Chinese New Year (Spring Festival) is fun, and Londoners lark about with pancakes on Shrove Tuesday.

✷ Chinese New Year

In late January or early February, Chinatown fizzes, crackles and pops in this colourful street festival, which includes a Golden Dragon parade, eating and partying.

✷ BAFTAs

The British Academy of Film and Television Arts (BAFTA; www.bafta.org) rolls out the red carpet on Leicester Sq in early February to hand out its annual cinema awards, the BAFTAs (the British Oscars if you will). Expect plenty of celebrity glamour.

☆ Pancake Races

On Shrove Tuesday, in late February/early March, you can catch pancake races and associated silliness at various venues around town (Spitalfields Market in particular).

March

March sees spring in the air and trees beginning to flower, most colourfully in parks and gardens. London is getting in the mood to head outdoors again.

✷ Head of the River Race

Some 400 crews take part in this colourful annual boat race (p65), held over a 7km course on the Thames, from Mortlake to Putney.

✷ St Patrick's Day Parade & Festival

Top festival for the Irish in London, held on the Sunday closest to 17 March, with a colourful parade through central London and other festivities in and around Trafalgar Sq.

☆ Flare

This LGBT film festival, organised by the British Film Institute (www.bfi.org.uk/flare), runs a packed programme of film screenings, along with parties, talks and events for schools and families.

April

April sees London in bloom with warmer days and a spring in everyone's step. British summer time starts late March, so it's now light until 7pm. Some sights previously shut for winter reopen.

🏃 London Marathon

Some 35,000 runners – most running for charity – pound through London in one of the world's biggest road races (www.virgin moneylondonmarathon. com), heading from Greenwich Park to the Mall.

🏃 Oxford & Cambridge Boat Races

Crowds line the banks of the Thames for the country's two most famous universities going oar-to-oar from Putney to Mortlake (p65). Dates vary, due to each university's Easter breaks, so check the website (www.theboatraces.org).

☆ Udderbelly Festival

Housed in a temporary venue in the shape of a purple upside-down cow on the South Bank, this festival of comedy, circus and general family fun (www.udderbelly.co.uk) has become a spring favourite. Events run from April to July.

May

A delightful time to be in London: days are warming up and Londoners begin to start lounging around in parks, popping sunshades on and enjoying two bank holiday weekends (the first and the last in May).

☆ Chelsea Flower Show

The world's most renowned horticultural event (www.rhs.org.uk/chelsea) attracts the cream of London's green-fingered and flower-mad gardeners.

◉ Museums at Night

For one weekend in May, numerous museums across London open after-hours (www.culture24.org.uk/museumsatnight), with candle-lit tours, spooky atmospheres, sleep-overs and special events such as talks and concerts.

June

The peak season begins with long, warm days (it's light until 10pm), the arrival of Wimbledon and other alfresco events.

☆ Trooping the Colour

The Queen's official birthday (www.trooping-the-colour.co.uk) is celebrated with much flag-waving, parades, pageantry and noisy flyovers.

🏃 Wimbledon Lawn Tennis Championships

For two weeks, the quiet South London village of Wimbledon falls under a sporting spotlight as the world's best tennis players gather to battle for the championships (p299).

☆ London Festival of Architecture

This month-long celebration of London's built environment (www.londonfestival ofarchitecture.org) explores the significance of architecture and design and how London has become a centre for innovation in those fields.

◉ Open Garden Squares Weekend

Over one weekend, more than 200 gardens in London that are usually inaccessible to the public fling open their gates for exploration (www.opensquares.org).

☆ Pride London

The gay community paints the town pink in this annual extravaganza (www.pride inlondon.org), featuring a smorgasbord of experiences, from talks to live events and culminating in a huge parade across London.

July

This is the time to munch on strawberries, drink in beer gardens and join in the numerous outdoor activities, including big music festivals.

◉ Royal Academy Summer Exhibition

Beginning in June and running through August, this exhibition at the Royal Academy of Arts (p101) showcases works submitted by artists from all over Britain, distilled to a thousand or so pieces.

☆ Wireless

One of London's top music festivals, with an emphasis on dance and R&B, Wireless (www.wirelessfestival.co.uk) takes place in Finsbury Park in northeast London. It is extremely popular, so book in advance.

☆ Lovebox

This three-day music extravaganza (www.mamacolive.com/lovebox) in Victoria Park in East London was

(Top) Pancake race competitor, Spitalfields

(Bottom) Lord Mayor's state coach, Lord Mayor's Show (p327)

MICHAELPUCHE / SHUTTERSTOCK ©

ED NORTON / GETTY IMAGES ©

created by dance duo Groove Armada in 2002. Although its raison d'être is dance music, there are plenty of other genres, too, including indie, pop and hip-hop.

August

Schools have broken up for summer, families are holidaying and the hugely popular annual Caribbean carnival dances into Notting Hill.

☆ BBC Promenade Concert (the Proms)

Starting in mid-July and ending in early September, the Proms offer two months of outstanding classical concerts (www.bbc.co.uk/proms) at various prestigious venues, centred on the Royal Albert Hall.

🍷 Great British Beer Festival

Organised by CAMRA (Campaign for Real Ale), this boozy festival (www.gbbf.org.uk) cheerfully cracks open casks of ale from the UK and abroad at Olympia (an exhibition centre).

☆ Summer Screen at Somerset House

For a fortnight every summer, Somerset House turns its stunning couryard into an open-air cinema (p107) screening an eclectic mix of film premieres, cult classics and popular requests.

🎊 Notting Hill Carnival

Europe's biggest – and London's most vibrant – outdoor carnival (p257) is a celebration of Caribbean London, featuring music, dancing and costumes over the summer bank-holiday weekend.

September

The end of summer and start of autumn is a lovely time to be in town, with comedy festivals and a chance to look at London properties normally shut to the public.

TotallyThames

Celebrating the River Thames, this cosmopolitan festival (www.totallythames. org) sees fairs, street theatre, music, food stalls, fireworks and river races, culminating in the superb Night Procession.

Greenwich Comedy Festival

This week-long laugh fest – London's largest comedy festival (www.greenwichcome dyfestival.co.uk) – brings big names and emerging acts to the National Maritime Museum.

Open House London

For a weekend in late September, the public is invited in to see more than 700 heritage buildings throughout the capital that are normally off-limits (www. openhouselondon.org.uk).

Great Gorilla Run

It looks bananas, but this gorilla-costume charity run (www.greatgorillarun.org) along an 8km route from the City to Bankside, and back again, is all in aid of gorilla conservation.

October

The weather is getting colder, but London's parklands are splashed with gorgeous autumnal colours. Clocks go back to winter time the last weekend of the month.

Dance Umbrella

London's annual festival of contemporary dance (www.danceumbrella.co.uk) features five weeks of performances by British and international dance companies at venues across London.

London Film Festival

The city's premier film event (www.bfi.org.uk/lff) attracts big overseas names and you can catch more than 100 British and international films before their cinema release. Masterclasses are given by world-famous directors.

Affordable Art Fair

For four days in March and October, Battersea Park turns into a giant art fair (www.affordableartfair. com/battersea), where more than 100 galleries offer works of art from just £50. There are plenty of talks and workshops too.

November

London nights are getting longer, but they crackle with fireworks in the first week of November.

Guy Fawkes Night (Bonfire Night)

Bonfire Night commemorates Guy Fawkes' foiled attempt to blow up Parliament in 1605. Bonfires and fireworks light up the night on 5 November. Primrose Hill, Highbury Fields, Alexandra Palace, Clapham Common and Blackheath have some of the best firework displays.

Lord Mayor's Show

In accordance with the Magna Carta of 1215, the newly elected Lord Mayor of the City of London travels in a state coach from Mansion House to the Royal Courts of Justice to take an oath of allegiance to the Crown. The floats, bands and fireworks that accompany the Mayor were added later (www. lordmayorsshow.london).

London Jazz Festival

Musicians from around the world swing into town for 10 days of jazz (www.efg londonjazzfestival.org.uk). World influences are well represented, as are more conventional strands.

December

London may see snow and a festive mood reigns as Christmas approaches and shops are dressed up to the nines. Days are increasingly shorter.

Lighting of the Christmas Tree & Lights

A celebrity is normally carted in to switch on all the festive lights that line Oxford, Regent and Bond streets, and a towering Norwegian spruce is set up in Trafalgar Sq.

Ice-skating

From mid-November until January, open-air ice-rinks pop up across the city, including one in the exquisite courtyard of Somerset House (p107) and another one in the grounds of the Natural History Museum (p180).

With Kids

London is a fantastic place for children. The city's museums will fascinate all ages, and you'll find theatre, dance and music performances ideal for older kids. Playgrounds and parks, city farms and nature reserves are perfect for either toddler energy-busting or relaxation.

Gloucestershire Old Spots pig, Mudchute (p220)

ISABELLE PLASSCHAERT / GETTY IMAGES ©

Museums

London's museums are nothing if not child friendly. There are dedicated children or family trails in virtually every museum. Additionally, you'll find plenty of activities such as storytelling at the National Gallery (p89), thematic backpacks to explore the British Museum (p81) and the Natural History Museum (p180), pop up performances at the Victoria & Albert Museum (p176), family audioguides at the Tate Modern (p158), or art and crafts workshops at Somerset House (p107). Even better, many of these activities are free (check websites for details).

Museum Sleepovers

What better fun than sleeping at the feet of a dinosaur? Museum sleepovers are very popular and must be booked at least a couple of months in advance.

Dino Snores at the Natural History Museum (p180; held monthly; for ages seven to 11) offers the opportunity to snooze under the watchful eye of the 150-million-year-old diplodocus, having first explored the museum's darkest nooks and crannies with only a torch to light your way. Or head for the stars at the Science Museum (p184), for a night of hands-on workshops, science shows and an IMAX 3D film. Held monthly; ages seven to 13.

Best for Babies & Toddlers

London's parks and gardens are manna from heaven for parents of young children.

St James's Park (p100)

Admiring the ducks and squirrels and watching the pelicans' teatime is a must.

Hyde Park & Kensington Gardens (p182)

Row your boat on the Serpentine Lake or hire a pedalo. Otherwise, take little ones to splash about the Diana, Princess of Wales Memorial Fountain (p183) or play at the excellent Diana, Princess of Wales Memorial Playground (p186).

NOT FOR PARENTS

For an insight into London aimed directly at kids, pick up a copy of Lonely Planet's *Not for Parents: London*. Perfect for children aged eight and up, it opens up a world of intriguing stories and fascinating facts about London's people, places, history and culture.

Science Museum (p184)

Really! Head down to the basement where **The Garden** is a dedicated interactive play-zone for under fives. The water area is especially popular (waterproofs are available).

Queen Elizabeth Olympic Park (p221)

From the sprouting fountain patio in which kids frolic to the amazing **Tumbling Bay Playground** (complete with tree houses, sand pit and wobbly bridge), the park will keep kids busy for hours.

Mudchute (p220)

This working farm near Canary Wharf has lots of animals, meadows and plenty of activities for kiddies.

Best for Kids

Where do you start? There is so much to see and do!

V&A Museum of Childhood (p216)

Dressing-up boxes, toys from times gone-by and interactive play areas.

Warner Bros Harry Potter Studio Tour (p237)

Need we say more? If your kids love the books and the films, they'll be in seventh heaven.

Natural History Museum (p180)

Dinosaurs, animals, more dinosaurs, Planet Earth, the role of scientific research – all fascinating stuff.

London Transport Museum (p105)

Twenty London Transport buses and trains are on display and available for touching, climbing on and general child-handling.

Royal Observatory & Greenwich Park (p270)

First there is the park, which you need to gambol through to get to the Observatory; then there are the Astronomy galleries and the Planetarium, which kids will marvel at.

Golden Hinde (p164)

Kids go wild for the treasure hunts, the tall tales of pirates and mutinies, and the incredibly evocative interior of this 16th century galleon.

Horniman Museum (p277)

An aquarium, a hands-on music room, natural history galleries and huge grounds – endless fun.

Best for Teenagers

Teenagers can be hard to please but London punches above its weight when it comes to entertaining blasé teens.

Science Museum (p184)

The sensational displays about space, information technology, flying and more will have teenagers enthralled.

Madame Tussauds (p109)

With its celebrity waxworks, this is selfie heaven, be it with Katniss Everdeen, David Beckham or One Direction.

London Film Museum (p105)

The James Bond car collection steals the show but there is plenty more film memorabilia to enjoy.

London Dungeon (p163)

The gory anecdotes, the rides, the unexpected scares...the dungeon was made for teenagers.

LONELY PLANET / GETTY IMAGES ©

London Transport Museum (p105)

West End matinee (p56)

There are plenty of plays and musicals children will love, from the *Lion King* to *The Curious Incident of the Dog in the Night Time*. Tickets are often available on the day.

Best for Outdoor Fun

Xstrata Treetop Walkway at Kew Gardens (p294)

Go underground and then 18m high into the canopy for an unforgettable encounter with nature.

London RIB Voyages (p386)

Tear through the Thames like Bond on a high-speed boat.

Thames river cruise (p386)

Less thrill but definitely more sightseeing than the RIB tours!

Maze at Hampton Court Palace (p291)

It takes the average visitor 20 minutes to find the centre – can your kids beat that?

HMS Belfast (p165)

A real light cruiser that served in WWII and the Korean War, with amazing displays to bring those history lessons to life.

Changing of the Guard (p86)

Soldiers in bearskin hats, red uniforms, military orders and all the pomp; kids will gape.

Best for Rainy Days (Other than Museums)

Plans rain-checked by London's famously unpredictable weather? As well as myriad museums and galleries, here are some ideas to stay warm and dry.

BFI IMAX Cinema (p172)

Documentaries and blockbusters in 3D for a different cinema experience.

Thermae Bath Spa (p314)

After visiting Bath's Roman Baths, plunge into a warm pool at the spa.

NEED TO KNOW

➡ Under 11s travel free on all public transport (except National Rail train services); children aged 11 to 15 years pay half price; they must be registered on an accompanying adult's Oyster Card (up to four children per adult). Registration can be done at tube stations in Zone 1 or Heathrow.

➡ Get a babysitter or nanny at www. findababysitter.com; top end establishments may also have some recommendations.

➡ If you are a new London resident, check your local council for information on child-friendly activities in your area.

Like a Local

Local life envelops you in London, but you might notice it only in glimpses. Londoners know how to avoid the tourist crowds – waiting until late-opening nights before slipping into museums or galleries, swarming to parks as soon as the sun pops out – so go where they go and be surprised.

Brixton Village (p276)

Drinking Like a Local

Londoners, and the British in general, get bad press for binge drinking. But most drinking in London is actually warmly sociable, gregarious and harmless fun. Londoners drink at the 'local', shorthand for the 'pub around the corner'. Prices may be high but generosity is commonplace and drinkers always step up to buy the next round. Despite the fickle weather, alfresco drinking is commonplace, be it in beer gardens, or on patios or pavements.

Dining Like a Local

As a rule of thumb, Londoners will dine at their local fish and chip shop or enjoy Sunday roast at their local gastropub rather than trek across town for dinner, but they'll readily go out for a meal further afield for special occasions. You'll also find them piling on the peri-peri sauce at Nando's, enjoying a fry-up (full English breakfast) at a 'greasy spoon' (a no-frills cafe) or grabbing a sandwich from Marks & Spencer to lunch outside in Hyde Park. Food markets are incredibly popular, be they the gourmet likes of Borough Market (p162) or smaller farmers markets across town.

Idiosyncratic delicacies you'll find Londoners tucking into include chip butty (fries in a sandwich), marmite (a yeast extract spread) on toast and jellied eel (often served with pies).

Shopping Like a Local

They are on home turf, so Londoners know precisely where to shop. They'll be in charity shops hunting for overlooked first editions and hard-to-find clothing, skimming market stalls for vintage togs off Brick Lane, browsing along Portobello Rd (p258), rifling through Brixton Village (p276) or retreating to small, independent bookshops for peace, quiet and old-school service. But you'll also find them in their droves in high-street franchises in Kensington High St, Oxford St or shiny malls such as Westfield (p266).

GERARD PUIGMAL / GETTY IMAGES ©

Taking to the Park

London has some of the world's most beautiful urban green spaces and locals swarm en masse to the park the minute the sun pops out to read a book, play football, lord over a picnic or BBQ, or just chat with friends on the grass. Join them at lunch time when office workers come out for their fix of sunlight or at weekends for fun and games.

Sightseeing Like a Local

Londoners are habitually off the beaten track, taking the back route into their local park, exploring London's wilder fringes or making short cuts like following Regent's Canal across North London. Go exploring in zones 2 and 3 and see what you find. Many Londoners bide their time until late-night openings for central London museums, when there are less crowds, and save 'regular hour' visits for special exhibitions.

Local Obsessions

Property

Owning a property is a national obsession in the UK but is made particularly difficult in London where prices are stratospheric. Talks of unaffordable housing, renting versus buying, mortgage deals, putting an offer and being gazumped, DIY and grand renovations are classic Sunday lunch fodder.

North v South

The existential divide between 'Norff' and 'Saff' of the river remains as wide as ever. Each camp swears by its side. For Londoners, the main difference is that South London lacks access to the tube (which means that house prices are lower). But for visitors, the debate is moot: London is London, with the same amazing array of sights, restaurants, bars and markets.

The Weather (& Whether It'll Hold Out for Saturday's BBQ)

More than wet, cold or grey, London's weather is unpredictable, which causes

> **NEED TO KNOW**
>
> Everyone's getting about town on two wheels these days, so why not hop on a Santander Cycle (p67): it's fun, cheap, practical, definitively local and there are docking stations everywhere. All Londoners who travel by public transport invest in an Oyster Card (p383), which nets excellent discounts and avoids queues for tickets. On the buses, Routemaster heritage line 15 is excellent for sightseeing, so grab a seat upstairs.

PLAN YOUR TRIP LIKE A LOCAL

Londoners any amount of angst about their BBQ/picnic/beer garden plans from April to September, when it's supposed to be spring/summer but you may still get hit by unseasonal showers/cold snap/high winds.

Public Transport

London has a world-class public transport network but Londoners like nothing more than a good old moan about their commute to work. Grievances range from delays due to improbably long red lights/signal failure/leaves on track/the wrong kind of snow (these are all real life examples by the way) to the horribly high fares. Londoners can also argue endlessly about the definitive route from A to B.

Politics

Traditional rabble-rousers (cue the rather combative style of debate in the House of Commons), the British always talk about politics. Once their teeth are truly stuck in, they won't let a political debate go; so if you like politics, you'll find company.

Football

Passions run high when it comes to the beautiful game and rivalries between London's three major teams (Arsenal, Chelsea and Tottenham Hotspur) are real. The capital has several other clubs in the Premier League, each with equally devoted supporters.

For Free

London may be one of the world's most expensive cities, but it doesn't always cost the earth. Many sights and experiences are free or cost next to nothing.

Temple Church (p152)

Free Sights

Houses of Parliament

When parliament is in session, it's free to attend and watch UK parliamentary democracy in action (p87).

Changing of the Guard

London's most famous open-air freebie, the Changing of the Guard in the forecourt of Buckingham Palace (p85) takes place at 11.30am from April to July (and alternate days, weather permitting, August to March). Alternatively, catch the changing of the mounted guard at Horse Guard's Parade (p107) at 11am (10am on Sundays).

Unlocking the Tower of London

Daily ritual performed at the Tower (p136) at 9am (10am on Sundays). The more elaborate closing Ceremony of the Keys daily at 9.30pm is also free, but you'll have to apply in writing months in advance.

Architecture & Interiors

For one weekend in September, Open House London (p357) opens the doors to some 850 buildings for free.

Day in Court

All legal proceedings – even celebrated murder trials – are open to the public (space permitting) on weekdays at the Old Bailey, otherwise known as the Central Criminal Court (p150).

Free Museums & Galleries

The permanent collections of all state-funded museums and galleries are open to the public free of charge; temporary exhibitions cost extra.

Victoria & Albert Museum

The spectacular V&A (p176) can easily consume a day of exploration.

National Gallery

This magnificent art collection (p89) contains more than 2000 European chefs-d'oeuvre.

JULIAN LOVE / GETTY IMAGES ©

Tate Modern
The art in this gallery (p158) will perplex and enthral.

Saatchi Gallery
Exceptionally well-presented displays of contemporary art works here (p188).

British Library
The Ritblat Gallery (p232) exhibits many of the world's most precious manuscripts, spanning three millennia.

Free Activities

Guided Tours
Some museums, galleries and churches, such as the National Gallery (p89), Tate Britain (p92), Brompton Cemetery (p258) and All Hallows by the Tower (p146), offer free guided tours (on top of free admission). Other attractions such as the Churchill War Rooms (p95) or St Paul's Cathedral (p142) offer free audio guides, but general admission charges apply.

A number of attractions, such as the Courtauld Gallery (p107) and the Natural History Museum (p180), host free talks and lectures.

Walking in London
Walking around town is possibly the best way to get a sense of the city and its history. Try our walking tours (see the neighbourhood chapters) or check **London Footprints** (www.london-footprints.co.uk) for ideas. Note that guided walks advertised as 'free' in London are not that at all; substantial tips will be expected at the end.

Views From the Top
It's free to look around Kensington Roof Gardens (p264) when they are not being used for a function or to enjoy the views from the Sky Garden atop the Walkie Talkie (p147) providing you have a (free) ticket.

> **NEED TO KNOW**
> ➡ **Websites** Click on London for Free (www.londonforfree.net) for ideas.
> ➡ **Discount cards** The London Pass (p387) can be a good investment if you want to see a lot in a short time.
> ➡ **Wi-fi access** Many cafes and bars offer free wi-fi to customers.
> ➡ **Newspapers** The *Evening Standard* and *Metro* are both free.
> ➡ **Children** Under 11s travel free on buses and the Underground, under fives on trains.

Free Music
A number of churches in London, especially the City ones, offer free lunchtime classical-music concerts.

St Martin-in-the-Fields
This magnificent church (p106) hosts free concerts at 1pm on Monday, Tuesday and Friday.

St James's Piccadilly
Free 50-minute recitals (donation suggested) on Monday, Wednesday and Friday at 1.10pm (p100).

Temple Church
Free half-hour organ concerts at 1.15pm on Wednesday in this iconic round church (p152).

St Alfege Church
Free recital at 1.05pm on Thursdays courtesy of the students from Trinity Laban Conservatoire of Music and Dance (p273).

Low-Cost Transport
The Santander Cycles access fee is £2 for 24 hours; bike hire is then free for the first 30 minutes. Use a one-day Travelcard or an Oyster Card to travel as much as you can on London Transport.

Dulwich Picture Gallery (p280)

Museums & Galleries

London's museums and galleries top the list of the city's must-see attractions – and not just for rainy days. Many display incomparable collections that make them acknowledged leaders in their field. A trinity of top-name museums awaits in South Kensington, and there is a similar concentration in the West End, especially around Trafalgar Sq.

Science Museum (p184)

NEED TO KNOW

Tickets

➜ Permanent collections at national museums (eg British Museum, National Gallery, Victoria & Albert Museum) are free; temporary exhibitions cost extra and should be booked ahead.

➜ Smaller museums will charge an entrance fee, typically £5 to £8.

➜ Private galleries are usually free or have a small admission fee.

Opening Hours

National collections are generally open 10am to about 6pm, with one or two late nights a week; evenings are an excellent time to visit museums as there are far fewer visitors.

Dining

Many of the top museums also have fantastic restaurants (eg National Portrait Gallery, Wallace Collection, Royal Academy), worthy of a visit in their own right.

Useful Websites

Most London museums – especially the most visited ones such as the British Museum, the National Gallery and the Victoria & Albert Museum – have sophisticated and comprehensive websites.

➜ **Culture 24** (www.culture24.org.uk) Reams of museum and gallery info.

➜ **London Galleries** (www.london-galleries.co.uk) A to Z of all London's galleries, with web links.

The Big Hitters

London's most famous museums are all central, easy to get to and – best of all – free. The National Gallery (p89) on Trafalgar Sq displays masterpieces of Western European art from the 13th to the early 20th centuries, with everyone represented from Leonardo da Vinci and Rembrandt to Turner and Van Gogh. Just behind the gallery, the National Portrait Gallery (p93) celebrates famous British faces through a staggering collection of 4000 paintings, sculptures and photographs from the 16th century to the present day. A 20-minute walk to the north is the British Museum (p81) in Bloomsbury, housing an astonishing assembly of antiquities representing 7000 years of human civilisation.

South Kensington is the home of three of London's leading museums: the Victoria & Albert Museum (p176), with its vast range of historical exhibits from the decorative arts, and the kid-friendly Natural History (p180) and Science Museums (p184).

Modern and contemporary art lovers will enjoy the Tate Modern (p158) on the South Bank. The Tate Britain (p92), venue of the annual Turner Prize, is home to British artworks across the centuries.

Private Art Galleries

London's vibrant artistic scene (p259) finds expression in private galleries, which number 1500 – more than any other city in the world. Mayfair has long been strong on private galleries in the more highbrow, traditional schools of art, while more cutting-edge art finds its way into Spitalfields and Hoxton and even now south of the river with the White Cube Bermondsey (p166).

Museums at Night

Many museums open late once or even twice a week, but several museums organise special nocturnal events to extend their range of activities and to present the collection in a different light. Some museums arrange night events only once a year, in May.

Museums with special nocturnal events or late-night opening hours include:

➜ British Museum (p81) Open to 8.30pm on Friday.

➜ British Library (p232) Open to 8pm Tuesday, Wednesday and Thursday.

➡ National Portrait Gallery (p93) Open to 9pm Thursday and Friday.

➡ Sir John Soane's Museum (p96) Evenings (6pm to 9pm) of the first Tuesday of each month are illuminated by candlelight.

➡ Tate Britain (p92) Open to 10pm first Friday of the month.

➡ Tate Modern (p158) Open to 10pm Friday and Saturday.

Courses, Talks & Lectures

Museums and galleries are excellent places to pick up specialist skills from qualified experts in their field. If you'd like to learn a new skill, brush up on an old one, or attend a fascinating lecture, there are many to choose from. Venues include the British Library, British Museum, Courtauld Gallery (p107), Dulwich Picture Gallery (p280), National Gallery, National Portrait Gallery, Tate Britain, Tate Modern and Victoria & Albert Museum.

Museums & Galleries by Neighbourhood

➡ **The West End** British Museum, National Gallery, National Portrait Gallery, Tate Britain, Charles Dickens Museum, Queen's Gallery, Churchill War Rooms, Royal Academy of Arts, Wallace Collection and many smaller museums and galleries. (p81)

➡ **The City** Tower of London, Museum of London, Guildhall Art Gallery, Barbican, Bank of England Museum and Dr Johnson's House. (p136)

➡ **The South Bank** Tate Modern, Hayward Gallery, Shakespeare's Globe, Design Museum (until late 2016), Fashion & Textile Museum and many other smaller museums and galleries. (p158)

➡ **Kensington & Hyde Park** Victoria & Albert Museum, Natural History Museum, Science Museum and others. (p176)

➡ **Clerkenwell, Shoreditch & Spitalfields** Geffrye Museum, Dennis Severs House, St John's Gate. (p198)

➡ **East London** Museum of London Docklands, Ragged School Museum, V&A Museum of Childhood, Whitechapel Gallery. (p215)

➡ **Camden & North London** Wellcome Collection, London Canal Museum, Kenwood House, British Library and others. (p236)

➡ **Notting Hill & West London** Museum of Brands, Packaging & Advertising, Leighton House, 18 Stafford Terrace. (p257)

➡ **Greenwich & South London** National Maritime Museum, Royal Observatory, Imperial War Museum, Fan Museum, Horniman Museum, Dulwich Picture Gallery. (p270)

Imperial War Museum (p275)

Lonely Planet's Top Choices

British Museum (p81) Supreme collection of international artefacts and an inspiring testament to human creativity over seven millennia, now expanded into a new wing.

Victoria & Albert Museum (p176) Very eclectic collection of decorative arts and design in what is affectionately known as 'the nation's attic'.

National Portrait Gallery (p93) Put a face to a name in this shrine to British portraiture.

Tate Modern (p158) A feast of modern and contemporary art, housed within a transformed riverside power station.

Imperial War Museum (p275) The new First World War Galleries have turned the IWM into a must-see attraction.

Museum of London (p151) Get a firm handle on the history of the city at this fantastic museum.

Best Large Museums & Galleries

National Gallery (p89) Treasury of European artwork from the 13th to 20th centuries.

Tate Britain (p92) The best of British (Turner, Constable, Reynolds, Gainsborough) rehung and renovated.

Churchill War Rooms (p95) The nerve centre of Britain's war effort during WWII.

Museum of London Docklands (p220) The story of the river and the trade that made London prosper.

Natural History Museum (p180) A cathedral to the natural world.

Wallace Collection (p108) An aristocrat's collection in a stunning mansion.

Science Museum (p184) Spellbinding A to Z of gizmos, devices, contraptions and thingamabobs.

Best Small Museums

Geffrye Museum (p198) A fascinating journey through British households from the 17th century onward.

Old Operating Theatre Museum & Herb Garret (p165) Delve into the pre-anaesthetic, pre-antiseptic days of modern medicine.

Sir John Soane's Museum (p96) The atmospheric home of the 19th-century architect now includes his private apartments and model room.

Shakespeare's Globe (p160) As much as you'll ever need to know about the Bard and his work.

Brunel Museum (p166) Discover how the world's first-ever underwater tunnel was built.

Best Small Galleries

Guildhall Art Gallery (p149) Eclectic City of London collection above a Roman amphitheatre.

Courtauld Gallery (p107) Probably the best collection of impressionist art in London.

Kenwood House (p241) Stunning collection of greats from the 17th to 19th century in equally stunning settings.

Whitechapel Gallery (p215) A groundbreaking gallery that continues to challenge with excellent exhibitions.

Saatchi Gallery (p188) Cutting-edge, ultra-cool shrine to contemporary art.

Serpentine Sackler Gallery (p183) The Serpentine's new gallery, housed in a former 19th century gunpowder depot daringly extended by Zaha Hadid.

Best House Museums

Charles Dickens Museum (p99) The Victorian novelist's only London house.

18 Stafford Terrace (p257) A comfortable middle-class Victorian family brought back to life.

Dennis Severs' House (p200) A quirky time capsule that sends you back to an 18th-century Huguenot house.

Carlyle's House (p189) Victorian essayist's home and workspace frozen in time.

Leighton House (p257) Byzantine gem on the cusp of Holland Park.

Red House (p285) Arts & Craft designer William Morris' charmingly decorated home.

Best Specialist Museums

Fan Museum (p274) Tortoiseshell, ivory, bone, feather and paper – fans in all their glory.

Ragged School Museum (p219) Reading, writing and 'rithmatic in an original Victorian setting.

Hunterian Museum (p109) Vast collection of innards, both grisly and educational.

Wimbledon Lawn Tennis Museum (p299) Everything tennis, with ace views of centre court.

London Film Museum (p105) Newly relocated exhibition focuses on James Bond, his films and flashy motors.

National Maritime Museum (p274) Model ships, a real ship simulator and a pirate gallery.

Full English breakfast

Eating

Once the laughing stock of the cooking world, London has got its culinary act together in the last 20 years and is today an undisputed dining destination. There are plenty of top-notch, Michelin-starred restaurants, but it is the sheer diversity on offer that is head-spinning: from Afghan to Vietnamese, London is a virtual A to Z of world cuisine.

Borough Market (p162)

Specialities
ENGLISH FOOD

England might have given the world baked beans on toast, mushy peas and chip butties (French fries between two slices of buttered and untoasted white bread), but that's hardly the whole story. When well prepared – be it a Sunday lunch of roast beef and Yorkshire pudding (light batter baked until fluffy, eaten with gravy) or a cornet of lightly battered fish and chips sprinkled with salt and malt vinegar – English food can be excellent. And nothing beats a fry-up (or full English breakfast) with bacon, sausages, beans, eggs and mushrooms the morning after a big night out.

Modern British food has become a cuisine in its own right, by championing traditional (and sometimes underrated) ingredients such as root vegetables, smoked fish, shellfish, game, sausages and black pudding (a kind of sausage stuffed with oatmeal, spices and blood). Dishes can be anything from game served with a traditional vegetable such as Jerusalem artichoke, to seared scallops with orange-scented black pudding, or roast pork with chorizo on rosemary mash.

SEAFOOD

Many visitors to England comment that for islanders, Brits seem to make surprisingly little of their seafood, with the exception of the ubiquitous – and institutionalised – fish and chips. But modern British restaurants have started to cast their nets and many offer local specialities such as Dover sole, Cornish oysters, Scottish scallops, smoked Norfolk eel, Atlantic herring, and mackerel. Top-of-the-line restaurants specialising in

NEED TO KNOW

Opening Hours

As a rule, most restaurants serve lunch between noon and 2.30pm and dinner between 6pm and 11pm. Brasserie-type establishments and chains tend to have continuous service from noon to 11pm.

Price Ranges

These symbols indicate the average cost per main course at the restaurant in question.

£ less than £10

££ £10–20

£££ more than £20

Reservations

➡ Make reservations for weekends if you're keen on a particular place or if you're in a group of more than four people.

➡ Top-end restaurants often run multiple sittings, with allocated time slots (generally two hours); pick a late slot if you don't want to be rushed.

Tipping

Most restaurants automatically tack a 'discretionary' service charge (usually 12.5%) onto the bill; this should be clearly advertised. If you feel the service wasn't adequate, you can tip separately (or not tip at all). If there is no service charge on your bill and you would like to tip, 10% is about right.

Haute Cuisine, Low Prices

➡ Top-end restaurants offer set lunch menus that are great value. À la carte prices are also sometimes cheaper for lunch than dinner.

➡ Many West End restaurants offer good-value pre- or post-theatre menus.

➡ The reliable internet booking service **Open Table** (www.opentable.co.uk) offers substantial discounts (up to 50% off the food bill) at selected restaurants.

BYO

➡ BYO is common among budget establishments; some charge corkage (£1 to £1.50 per bottle of wine).

➡ **Wine Pages** (www.wine-pages.com) keeps a useful directory of BYO restaurants.

Eating by Neighbourhood

Camden & North London
Gourmet choices, gastropubs
and ethnic eats (p244)

Clerkenwell, Shoreditch & Spitalfields
Famous, creative restaurants
and great bargains (p201)

Notting Hill & West London
Eclectic, from vegetarian
to Eastern European
(p260)
(1mi)

East London
Curry houses,
traditional caffs,
cool restaurants
(p222)
(1mi)

The City
Geared towards
the business
lunch (p152)

The West End
Great for Asian,
European and
fusion (p110)

Kensington & Hyde Park
Chic, cosmopolitan
and often pricey
(p189)

London Eye

The South Bank
Chains on the river,
culinary gems 'inland'
(p166)

Richmond, Kew & Hampton Court
Sophisticated restaurants,
with style and substance
(p300)
(2mi)

Greenwich & South London
Fine gastronomy,
trendy markets
and eateries
(p280)

seafood abound and fish-and-chips counters trading in battered cod, haddock and plaice are ubiquitous.

WORLD FOOD

One of the joys of eating out in London is the profusion of choice. For historical reasons Indian cuisine is widely available (curry has been labelled a national dish), but Asian cuisines in general are very popular. You'll find dozens of Chinese, Thai, Japanese and Korean restaurants, as well as elaborate fusion establishments blending flavours from different parts of Asia. Middle Eastern cuisine is also well covered.

Food from continental Europe – French, Italian, Spanish, Greek, Scandinavian – is another favourite, with many excellent modern European establishments. Restaurants serving these cuisines tend to congregate where their home community is based: Eastern European in Shepherd's Bush, Turkish in Dalston, Korean in New Malden, Bengali in Brick Lane, African Caribbean in Brixton, Vietnamese around Kingsland Rd etc.

DESSERTS

England does a mean dessert, and establishments serving British cuisine revel in these indulgent treats. Favourites include bread-and-butter pudding, sticky toffee pudding (a steamed pudding containing dates and topped with a divine caramel sauce), the alarmingly named spotted dick (a steamed suet pudding with currants and raisins), Eton mess (meringue, cream and strawberries mixed into a gooey, heavenly mess), and seasonal musts such as Christmas pudding (a steamed pudding with candied fruit and brandy) and fruity crumbles (rhubarb, apple etc).

Gastropubs

While not so long ago the pub was where you went for a drink, with maybe a packet of potato crisps to soak up the alcohol, the birth of the gastropub in the 1990s means that today just about every establishment serves full meals. But the quality varies widely, from defrosted-on-the-premises to Michelin-star worthy.

Breakfast

The Brits were always big on breakfast – they even invented one, the full English breakfast. It's something of a protein overload but there's nothing quite like it to mop up the excesses of a night on the tiles. A typical plate will include bacon, sausages, baked beans in tomato sauce, eggs (fried or scrambled), mushrooms, tomatoes and toast (maybe with Marmite). You'll find countless brightly-lit, grotty cafes – nicknamed 'greasy spoons' – serving these monster plates. They're also a must in gastropubs.

Making a comeback on the breakfast table is porridge (boiled oats in water or milk, served hot), sweet or savoury. Top-end restaurants serving breakfast, such as Balthazar (p117), have played a big part in glamming up what was essentially poor folk's food. It's great with banana and honey, fruit compote or even plain with some chocolate powder.

Vegetarians & Vegans

London has been one of the best places for vegetarians to dine out since the 1970s, initially due mostly to its many Indian restaurants, which, for religious reasons, always cater for people who don't eat meat. A number of dedicated vegetarian restaurants have since cropped up, offering imaginative, filling and truly delicious meals. Most nonvegetarian places generally offer a couple of dishes for those who don't eat meat; vegans, however, will find it harder outside Indian or dedicated establishments.

Celebrity Chefs

London's food renaissance was partly led by a group of telegenic chefs who built food empires around their names and their TV programs. Gordon Ramsay is the most (in)famous of the lot but his London venues are still standard-bearers for top-quality cuisine. Other big names include Jamie Oliver, whose restaurant Fifteen (p205) trains disadvantaged young people, and Heston Blumenthal, whose mad-professor-like experiments with food (molecular gastronomy, as he describes it) have earned him rave reviews.

Coffee & Cafes

Tea may be the quintessential English beverage, but it's coffee that keeps the city moving and the urban pulse throbbing. Home to an incredibly vibrant and varied coffee culture and an army of skilled baristas, London has an abundance of coffee shops and cafes, from busy chains to small independent affairs, classic operations, artisan cafes and designer spots. To catch London's coffee obsession in full swing, pitch up during the **London Coffee Festival** (www.londoncoffeefestival.com) in spring. And if it's just coffee beans you're after, swing by the fantastic Algerian Coffee Stores (p130).

Food Markets

The boom in London's eating scene has extended to its markets, which come in three broad categories: food stalls that are part of a broader market and appeal to visitors keen to soak up the atmosphere (eg Spitalfields (p211), Borough (p162) or Camden (p240)); farmers markets, which sell pricey local and/or organic products (check out www.lfm.org.uk for a selection of the best, such as Broadway (p228) and Marylebone

HOWARD SHOOTER / GETTY IMAGES ©

Yorkshire pudding

(p118)); and the many colourful food markets, where the oranges and lemons come from who knows where and the barrow boys and girls speak with perfect Cockney accents (Brixton (p287), Ridley Road (p216) and Berwick Street (p118)).

Food Trends & Fads

Just like with fashion and music, Londoners like to keep up with the Joneses when it comes to eating. Here are some of the current food obsessions in the capital:

Going regional It's no longer plain old Chinese but Dōngběi or Xīnjiāng; Indian is now Gujarati, Goan or Punjabi.

Food trucks Whether part of a market or just occupying a chain-free corner, food trucks have become a feature of the capital's eating scene. Office workers in particular love them.

Smokehouse The growing fad for flame-seared flavours, glowing charcoals and red coals has hatched a host of restaurants across town.

Late night dining The weekend night tube service is only going to give this trend a further shot in the arm.

Burgers Everyone loves a burger, and London remains fixated with meat-and-bun combos from independents to mushrooming local chains.

Peruvian food Having come out of left field, ceviche and Peruvian food is still trendy.

Ramen Still going strong to the slurping masses, the Japanese noodle broth is quickly served, swiftly consumed and perfect to snackers on the move.

Supper Clubs

Half-restaurant, half-dinner-party, supper clubs combine the quality of the former with the informality of the latter. Run by average Joes with a penchant for cooking and

generally catering for 10 to 20 people, meals are set three- or four-course menus (£20 to £40), with an eclectic clientele as standard.

Recommending a supper club can be tricky as it's a transient business, but the following will help:

Ms Marmite (www.supperclubfangroup.ning.com) An excellent directory of London supper clubs set up by a supper club host.

London Foodie (www.thelondonfoodie.co.uk) This food blog features regular supper club reviews.

Facebook & Twitter Forthcoming events are widely publicised on social media.

Chain Gang

While the usual bleak offerings of US-based chain restaurants are to be found all over the capital, London also boasts some excellent homegrown chains. They're all good value and made even cheaper by regular voucher offers: check out www.vouchercodes.co.uk and www.myvouchercodes.co.uk for the latest offers.

The following are some of the offerings; check their websites for a full list of outlets.

Benugo (www.benugo.com) Deli chain serving good but expensive sandwiches.

Busaba Eathai (www.busaba.com) Divine Thai food, served without fuss among beautiful, modern Asian decor.

Byron (www.byronhamburgers.com) Simple but excellent burgers accompanied by the bare essentials (lettuce, tomato, red onion).

Jamie's Italian (www.jamieoliver.com) Good (but not gastronomic) Italian food in modern settings.

Le Pain Quotidien (www.lepainquotidien.com) A simple, French-style chain of cafes that serves salads, baguettes and cakes.

Masala Zone (www.masalazone.com) An excellent Indian chain that specialises in *thalis* (a meal made of several small dishes).

Nando's (www.nandos.co.uk) Ever-popular for its peri-peri chicken and off-the-scale trademark spicy sauces; order at the till.

Pret a Manger (www.pret.com) Affordable sandwich chain, with good selection of sandwiches and chunky soups.

Real Greek (www.therealgreek.com) Beautifully presented mezze and souvlaki, perfect for sharing between friends.

PIE & MASH

From the middle of the 19th century until just after WWII, the staple lunch for many Londoners was a spiced-eel pie (eels were once plentiful in the Thames) served with mashed potatoes and liquor (a parsley sauce). Pies have been replaced by sandwiches nowadays, although they remain popular in the East End. A popular modern-day filling is beef and mashed potato (curried meat is also good), with eel served smoked or jellied as a side dish.

Tas (www.tasrestaurants.co.uk) An established chain of good Turkish restaurants with a roll-call of stews, grills and mezze.

Wagamama (www.wagamama.com) Fusion noodle place with rapid turnover, ideal for a quick meal.

Wahaca (www.wahaca.com) Working the Mexican street-food angle in fresh, colourful settings.

Wasabi (www.wasabi.uk.com) Superb sushi and bento chain, with fantastic rice sets, noodles, rolls and salads.

Food Festivals

Because just eating never seems enough, London has whole festivals dedicated to food. They generally have tastings galore and are always good for inspiration.

Feast London (www.wefeast.co.uk; ⊘Mar) A tip-top event bringing together top chefs and the best street-food stalls in the capital for four days, with music and entertainment on the side.

London Chocolate Festival (www.festival-chocolate.co.uk; ⊘Mar/Apr) Everyone's favourite, for obvious reasons, generally in time for Easter.

London Coffee Festival (www.londoncoffee festival.com; ⊘Apr) If you know your robusta from your arabica, this is the place for you. Host of the UK Barista Championship.

Taste of London (www.tastefestivals.com/london; Regent's Park, NW1; ⊘Jun) This festival turns Regent's Park into a haze of Michelin stars, with top chefs competing for your palate's attention.

BBC Good Food Show (www.bbcgoodfood showlondon.com; London Olympia, Hammersmith Rd, W14; ⊘Nov) Masterclasses, recipes, tastings – this is very hands-on and very delicious.

KRZYSZTOF SLUSARCZYK / GETTY IMAGES ©

RICHARD I'ANSON / GETTY IMAGES ©

Top: Eton mess
Middle: Old Spitalfields Market (p211)
Bottom: Fish and chips

JOE FOX / GETTY IMAGES ©

Lonely Planet's Top Choices

Gymkhana (p119) Outstanding Indian cuisine in a Raj gentleman's club setting.

Clove Club (p206) From Dalston supper club to stupendous Michelin star restaurant.

Dinner by Heston Blumenthal (p191) Not just for supper, lunch is top tier, as is the setting.

Brasserie Zédel (p114) Buzzing brasserie atmosphere, good looks and surefire menu.

Tom's Kitchen (p189) The perfect combination of sunny service, ambience and a knockout European menu.

Best by Budget

£

Shoryu (p116) Perfectly executed bowls of *tonkotsu ramen*.

Café Below (p152) One of London's most atmospheric locations with excellent value to boot.

Pimlico Fresh (p192) Perky cafe with an accent on good value fine food.

Kerbisher & Malt Classic fish and chips, no-nonsense good looks.

Polpo (p201) Addictive selection of Italian tapas.

Watch House (p167) Ace sandwiches, fine coffee and a lovely setting.

££

10 Greek St (p115) Top-quality British produce with a Med accent.

Tom's Kitchen (p189) Relaxing ambience, warm staff, excellent food: you can't go wrong.

Palomar (p114) Excellent Jerusalem food for sharing with a foodie friend.

Angels & Gypsies Authentic Spanish products and cuisines, with a Mexican wild card thrown in.

Santa Maria del Sur (p282) Excellent Argentine grilled meats, rounded off with some stunning pancakes.

£££

Dinner by Heston Blumenthal (p191) A supreme fusion of perfect British food, eye-catching design and celeb stature.

Greenhouse (p119) Amongst the most imaginative menus in Mayfair.

Le Boudin Blanc (p120) For ace French food, this place has no rival.

Chez Bruce (p282) Timeless elegance and gastronomy on the edge of Wandsworth Common.

Best by Cuisine

Modern European

Ledbury (p260) Still causing a gastronomic stir in Notting Hill.

Andrew Edmunds (p114) Perennial favourite with a handwritten menu.

Naughty Piglets (p282) Inventive Brixton bistro, low on tables, high on popularity.

10 Greek St (p115) Fab Soho choice, still at the top of its game.

Tom's Kitchen (p189) Frontrunner with bags of panache, but affordable.

Indian

Tayyabs (p222) Long-standing Punjabi favourite in the East End.

Potli (p262) Steeping Hammersmith in authentic Indian aromas.

Dishoom (p116) Bombay caff food as it really is served and eaten.

Gymkhana (p119) Splendid club-style Raj environment, top cuisine.

Kennington Tandoori (p281) Sound and stylish, south of the river.

Chinese

Yauatcha (p115) Glamorous dim sum and great for people watching.

Bar Shu (p114) Authentic Sichuān that will sear your tastebuds.

Min Jiang (p192) Peking duck meets glorious views.

Dragon Castle (p281) Off-the-beaten track Kennington spot with sure-footed Cantonese menu.

Vegetarian

Gate (p263) Meat-free but full of flavours.

Mildreds (p113) Soho stalwart with vegan dishes too.

Orchard (p111) Excellent-value lunch spot with above-average soups.

Sagar (p111) South Indian vegetarian food as light as it is tasty.

Italian

Union Street Cafe (p167) Gordon Ramsay's Italian bistro venture hits all the right notes.

Cafe Murano (p110) Italian cuisine of the highest quality.

Polpo (p113) *Ciccheti* 'tapas' as the Venetians make them – in casual surrounds.

Rotorino (p223) Sharp-looking Kingsland Rd arrival and instant success.

British

St John (p202) The restaurant that inspired the revival of British cuisine.

Launceston Place (p191) Magnificent food, presentation and service.

Rules (p117) London's oldest restaurant serves classic game dishes.

Rabbit (p192) Make it to King's Rd for some of the best British food in London.

Dinner by Heston Blumenthal (p191) Seriously good-looking Knightsbridge choice with a triumphant menu.

Best for Eating Like a Local

A Cooke's (p262) Shepherd's Bush pie 'n mash stalwart with no pretensions whatsoever.

Rosie's Deli Café (p282) Grab lunch or a slice of cake after a morning pottering about Brixton Village.

M Manze (p167) If David Beckham can dine here, you can too.

Goddards at Greenwich (p281) Pie 'n mash institution for classic London fare.

Best Gastropubs

Anchor & Hope (p167) Flying the gastropub flag on the South Bank for the best part of a decade.

White Swan (p153) Wonderful City venue open weekdays only.

Perkin Reveller (p153) Fantastically named Thames-side top spot with classic British menu.

Empress (p224) Choice East End spot with an excellent modern British menu.

Best for Views

Duck & Waffle (p152) Hearty British dishes from the top of Heron Tower, round the clock.

Min Jiang (p192) Breathtaking panoramas over Kensington Gardens.

City Social (p153) Wow factor views of the City.

Portrait (p116) Classic views to Nelson's Column and beyond, down Whitehall to Big Ben.

Best Afternoon Teas

Foyer at Claridge's (p120) The last word in classic art deco elegance.

Orangery (p192) Sit with tea and cake in the shadow of Kensington Palace.

Portrait (p116) The tea and accompaniments are second to the views.

Best Food Markets

Borough Market (p162) Foodscapes, free tastings and glorious takeaways.

Portobello Road Market (p258) A global atlas of street food.

Maltby Street Market (p173) Perfect for lazing an afternoon away at quirky food stalls.

Broadway Market (p228) The East End foodies' weekly event.

Marylebone Farmers Market (p118) A posh offering reflecting the neighbourhood make-up.

Best Gourmet Shops

Fortnum & Mason (p127) Elegant Piccadilly shop with no end of fine comestibles.

Algerian Coffee Stores (p130) Beans and more beans for sale at this historic Soho shop.

Harrods (p194) The Food Hall is an epicurean paradise.

Lina Stores (p131) Yummy-looking prewar delicatessen selling Italian goods.

Best Celebrity-Chef Restaurants

Dinner by Heston Blumenthal (p191) Molecular gastronomy at its very best.

Tom's Kitchen (p189) Tom Aiken's relaxed Chelsea brasserie remains ever popular.

Nobu (p120) Nobuyuki Matsuhisa's Japanese eatery still reigns supreme.

Dabbous (p112) Chef Ollie Dabbous' celebrated Fitzrovia restaurant keeps earning plaudits.

Best Ice Cream

Chin Chin Labs (p245) Liquid nitrogen ice cream: weird and utterly wonderful.

Gelupo (p113) All natural ingredients, right in central London.

Black Vanilla (p281) Cupcakes, comfy seats and gorgeous gelato, Greenwich way.

Gelateria Danieli (p300) Hand-made ice cream with seasonal flavours, such as Christmas pudding.

Drinking & Nightlife

You need only glance at William Hogarth's Gin Lane prints from 1751 to realise that Londoners and alcohol have more than a passing acquaintance. The metropolis offers a huge variety of venues to wet your whistle in – from neighbourhood pubs to all-night clubs, and everything in between.

The Pub

The pub (public house) is at the heart of London life and is one of the capital's great social levellers. Virtually every Londoner has a 'local' and looking for your own is a fun part of any visit to the capital.

Pubs in central London are mostly after-work drinking dens, busy from 5pm onwards with the postwork crowd during the week and revellers at weekends. But in more residential areas, pubs come into their own at weekends, when long lunches turn into sloshy afternoons and groups of friends settle in for the night. Many also run popular quizzes on weeknights. Other pubs entice punters through the doors with live music or comedy. Some have developed such a reputation for the quality of their food that they've been dubbed 'gastropubs'.

You'll be able to order almost anything you like in a pub, from beer to wine, soft drinks, spirits and sometimes hot drinks too. Some specialise in craft beer, offering drinks from local microbreweries, including real ale, fruit beers, organic ciders and other rarer beverages. Others, particularly the gastropubs, have invested in a good wine list.

In winter, some pubs offer mulled wine; in summer the must-have drink is Pimm's and lemonade (if it's properly done it should have fresh mint leaves, citrus, strawberries and cucumber).

BEER

The raison d'être of a pub is first and foremost to serve beer – be it lager, ale or stout in a glass or a bottle. On draught (drawn from the cask), it is served by the pint (570mL) or half-pint (285mL) and, more occasionally, third-of-a-pint for real ale tasting.

Pubs generally serve a good selection of lager (highly carbonated and drunk cool or cold) and a smaller selection of real ales or 'bitter' (still or only slightly gassy, drunk at room temperature, with strong flavours). The best-known British lager brand is Carling, although you'll find everything from Foster's to San Miguel.

Among the multitude of ales on offer in London pubs, London Pride, Courage Best, Burton Ale, Adnams, Theakston (in particular Old Peculiar) and Old Speckled Hen are among the best. Once considered something of an old man's drink, real ale is enjoying a renaissance among young Londoners. Staff at bars serving good selections of real ales and craft beers (small-batch beers from independent brewers) are often hugely knowledgeable, just like a sommelier in a restaurant with a good cellar, so ask them for recommendations if you're not sure what to order.

Stout, the best known of which is Irish Guinness, is a slightly sweet, dark beer with a distinct flavour that comes from malt that is roasted before fermentation.

Numerous microbreweries have sprouted throughout London in recent years. Names to look out for include Meantime, Sambrook's, Camden Town Brewery, London Fields Brewery, the Five Points Brewing Co, Redchurch, Beavertown, Crate Brewery, Hackney Brew-

Beer on tap

NEED TO KNOW

Opening Hours

Traditionally pubs opened at 11am or midday and closed at 11pm, with a slightly earlier closing on a Sunday. A 2005 law change enabled longer opening hours and although most still close at around midnight, some bars and pubs remain open to around 2am or 3am. Clubs generally open at 10pm and close between 3am and 7am.

Club Costs

Many clubs are free or cheaper midweek. If you want to go to a famous club on a Saturday night (*the* night for clubbing), expect to pay around £20. Some places are considerably cheaper if you arrive earlier in the night.

Tickets & Guest Lists

Queuing in the cold at 11pm can be frustrating; get there early and/or book tickets for bigger events if you can't bear being left in limbo.

Some clubs allow you to sign up on their guest list beforehand; check ahead on their websites.

Dress Code

London's clubs are generally relaxed. Posh clubs in areas such as Kensington will want a glam look, so dress to impress (no jeans or trainers); the further east, the more laid-back and edgy the fashion.

What's On?

Check the listings in *Time Out* or the *Evening Standard*. Part of the charm of London's nightlife is that it's always changing, so keep your eyes peeled.

ery, Pressure Drop, Anspach & Hobday, Partizan, the Kernel and Brew by Numbers.

Bars

In the large party space left between pubs and clubs, bars are a popular alternative for a London night out. Generally staying open later than pubs but closing earlier than clubs, they tempt those keen to skip bedtime at 11pm but not keen enough to pay a hefty cover charge and stay out all night. Many have DJs on weekends and sometimes a small dance floor too. Drinks tend to be more expensive than pub prices, and some dance bars charge a small cover charge later in the night.

Cocktail bars are undergoing a renaissance, so you'll find lots of upmarket options serving increasingly interesting concoctions. Specialist wine, whisky, craft beer and cider bars have also been sprouting in profusion. A romantic attachment to the US prohibition era has seen a scattering of speakeasies hiding themselves in basements and down back lanes.

Clubs

When it comes to clubbing, London is up there with the best of them. You'll probably know what you want to experience – it might be big clubs such as Fabric (p207) or the Ministry of Sound (p284), or sweaty shoebox clubs with the freshest DJ talent – but there's plenty to tempt you to branch out from your usual tastes and try something new. Whether thumping techno, indie rock, Latin, ska, pop, dubstep, grime,

minimal electro, R&B or hip hop, there's something going on every night.

Thursdays are loved by those who want to have their fun before the office workers mob the streets on Friday. Saturdays are the busiest and best if you're a serious clubber, and Sundays often see surprisingly good events throughout London, popular with hospitality workers who tradionally have Mondays off.

There are clubs across town, though it has to be said that the best of them are moving further out of the centre by the

Drinking by Neighbourhood

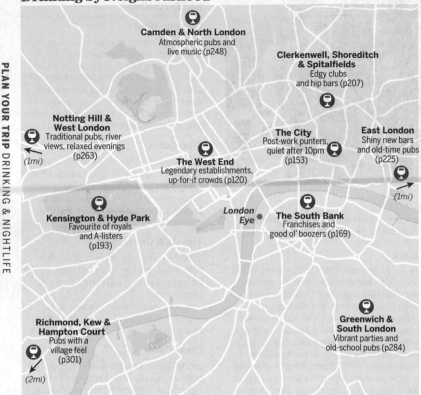

Camden & North London
Atmospheric pubs and
live music (p248)

**Clerkenwell, Shoreditch
& Spitalfields**
Edgy clubs
and hip bars (p207)

**Notting Hill &
West London**
Traditional pubs, river
views, relaxed evenings
(p263)
(1mi)

The City
Post-work punters,
quiet after 10pm
(p153)

East London
Shiny new bars
and old-time pubs
(p225)
(1mi)

The West End
Legendary establishments,
up-for-it crowds (p120)

*London
Eye*

Kensington & Hyde Park
Favourite of royals
and A-listers
(p193)

The South Bank
Franchises and
good ol' boozers (p169)

**Richmond, Kew &
Hampton Court**
Pubs with a
village feel
(p301)
(2mi)

**Greenwich &
South London**
Vibrant parties and
old-school pubs (p284)

year, so be prepared to take a hike on a night bus. The East End is the top area for cutting-edge clubs, especially Shoreditch. Dalston and Hackney are popular for makeshift clubs in restaurant basements and former shops – so it's great for night-fun hunters. Camden Town still favours the indie crowd, while King's Cross has a bit of everything. The gay party crowd mainly gravitates to the south of the river, especially Vauxhall, although they still maintain a toehold in the West and East End.

Cabaret

After years of low-profile parties with high-glitter gowns, the cabaret scene burst into the mainstream in the noughties, showering London with nipple tassels, top hats, sexy lingerie and some of the best parties in town. Subsequently, the 'alternative' cabaret scene became overwhelmingly mainstream,

and some club-night organisers raised prices to ward off those who wouldn't buck up and dress up. So prepare to pay up to £25 for some (but not all) of the city's best cabaret nights, and make sure you look like a million dollars.

Expect anything from male burlesque contests to girls on roller skates hosting tea parties on a good burlesque night. Venues and events to look out for include:

➡ **Bethnal Green Working Men's Club** (p226) A true working men's club that nonetheless hosts quirky cabaret nights.

➡ **RVT** (p286) Home to the legendary Duckie and Sunday Social, the Royal Vauxhall Tavern is the kooky kingpin of London's queer cabaret scene.

➡ **Soho Theatre** (p125) This acclaimed comedy venue lets the freaks off the leash in their Downstairs bar.

Lonely Planet's Top Choices

Princess Louise (p123) A stunner of a Victorian pub with snugs and a riot of etched glass.

Worship St Whistling Shop (p208) Fine-dining sophistication in liquid form.

Cat & Mutton (p227) Simultaneously traditional and hip, and always up for a party.

Holly Bush (p250) A cosy Georgian pub tucked away in leafy Hampstead.

Wine Pantry (p170) Showcasing the best of British wine.

Trafalgar Tavern (p284) Riverside tavern oozing history.

Best Clubs

Ministry of Sound (p284) The original superclub is back on top form.

Fabric (p207) A huge venue (literally) for fans of drum-and-bass, dubstep, house, techno and electronica.

Egg LDN (p249) Flit between indoor and outdoor spaces at this multistorey megaclub.

Corsica Studios (p284) A not-for-profit underground club that hosts some of London's best EDM (Electronic Dance Music) nights.

XOYO (p209) Excellent and varied gigs, club nights and art events.

Best Pubs

Jerusalem Tavern (p207) Tiny but crammed with antique atmosphere.

Lamb & Flag (p122) Just about everyone's favourite, so expect a scrum.

Mayflower (p170) Venerable riverside pub with an American connection.

French House (p122) Not exactly a pub, but still Soho's best boozer, with a steady supply of local eccentrics.

Edinboro Castle (p250) A huge beer garden and a refined atmosphere inside.

Jamaica Wine House (p155) Hidden down a City lane, but well worth seeking out.

Best Cocktail Bars

Worship St Whistling Shop (p208) Molecular cocktails at a Victorian-style drinking den.

Happiness Forgets (p208) Mixed drinks and mischief in Hoxton.

LAB (p121) Bespoke cocktails at a long-standing Soho favourite.

London Cocktail Club (p121) Inventive concoctions in a basement bar.

Madison (p155) Views and drinks from a perch overlooking St Paul's.

Best Wine Bars

Gordon's Wine Bar (p123) A classic and long-standing London institution in darkened vaults.

Bar Pepito (p249) A delightful, pocket-sized Andalucian bar dedicated to lovers of sherry.

Sager + Wilde (p226) Stylish supping in the heart of the East End.

Wine Pantry (p170) Challenging perceptions of British wine, one drinker at a time.

Best for Views

Galvin at Windows (p124) Fabulous cocktails and views west across Hyde Park.

Madison (p155) Look into the heart of St Paul's and beyond from One New Change.

Oblix (p170) It's not even halfway up the Shard, but the views are legendary.

Rumpus Room (p170) Dress to impress in this swanky 12th-floor hotel bar.

Sky Pod (p153) Sip a cocktail on an open air terrace, 35 floors above the City.

Best Beer Gardens

Windsor Castle (p264) Come summer, regulars abandon the Windsor's historic interior for the chilled out garden.

Edinboro Castle (p250) A festive place to stretch out on a summer evening.

Garden Gate (p250) Sip on a Pimm's amid the greenery.

Greenwich Union (p284) Work your way through the Meantime brews from a garden table.

People's Park Tavern (p227) The sunny garden backs right onto Victoria Park.

BBC's Proms concert, Royal Albert Hall (p185)

☆ Entertainment

Whatever it is that sets your spirits soaring or your booty shaking, you'll find it in London. The city's been a world leader in theatre ever since a young man from Stratford-upon-Avon set up shop here in the 16th century. And if London started swinging in the 1960s, its live rock and pop scene has barely let up since.

Royal Opera House (p105)

Theatre

A night out at the theatre is as much a must-do London experience as a trip on the top deck of a double-decker bus. London's Theatreland in the dazzling West End – from Aldwych in the east, past Shaftesbury Ave to Regent St in the west – has a concentration of theatres only rivalled by New York's Broadway. It's a thrillingly diverse scene, encompassing Shakespeare's classics performed with old-school precision, edgy new works, raise-the-roof musicals and some of the world's longest-running shows.

There are around 40 theatres in the West End alone, but Theatreland is just the brightest facet of London's sparkling theatre world, where venues range from highbrow theatrical institutions to tiny fringe stages tucked away above pubs.

London's cosmopolitan DNA and multicultural roots nourish a great flowering of theatrical creativity. Even Hollywood stars are willing to abandon their pampered lives for a season treading the boards in London. The celebrated National Theatre is the regular home of innovative new shows, creative directing and much-loved classics that often migrate to other West End theatres. The Barbican (p155) hosts foreign drama companies to massive acclaim. Traditional stagecraft is also on offer, particularly at the re-creation of Shakespeare's Globe (p171), a wonderful venue where the focus is on the authentic Shakespearean experience.

The theatrical fringes are busy with peripheral, subsidised shows from experimental groups, where conceptual ideas find expression to sometimes bewildered audi-

ences. In summer, open-air theatres avail themselves of balmy days (punctuated with sudden showers) to entertain crowds in parks, most famously in Regent's Park.

NEED TO KNOW

Tickets

➡ Book well ahead for live performances and if you can, buy directly from the venue.

➡ Enquire at the theatre's own box office about cut-price standby tickets or limited late releases for otherwise sold-out-shows.

➡ Student standby tickets are sometimes available one hour or so before performances start. Some theatres have cheap tickets or cheap student/youth tickets on certain days.

➡ Shakespeare's Globe offers 700 standing tickets (£5) for each performance. Four 10p standing tickets are available for performances at the Jerwood Theatre Downstairs at the Royal Court Theatre.

➡ Midweek matinees at such venues as the Royal Opera House are usually much cheaper than evening performances; restricted-view seats can be cheap.

➡ At gigs, be wary of touts outside the venue on the night. Tickets may be counterfeit or stolen.

➡ Most mainstream and art-house cinemas offer discounts all day Monday (or Tuesday) and most weekday afternoon screenings.

➡ On the day of performance, you can buy discounted tickets, sometimes up to 50% off, for West End productions from **Tkts Leicester Sq** (www.tkts.co.uk/leicester-square).

Useful Magazines

The free weekly **Time Out** (www.timeout.com/london) has current theatre and entertainment listings.

Useful Websites

➡ **London Theatre** (www.londontheatre.co.uk) Comprehensive overview of London theatre.

➡ **London Dance** (www.londondance.com) Handy listing for dance events.

Classical Music

With multiple world-class orchestras and ensembles, quality venues, reasonable ticket prices and performances covering the whole musical gamut from traditional crowd-pleasers to innovative compositions, London will satisfy even the fussiest classical music buff. The Southbank Centre (p171), Barbican and Royal Albert Hall (p194) all maintain an alluring programme of performances, further gilding London's outstanding reputation as a cosmopolitan centre for classical music. The Proms is the festival calendar's biggest event.

Opera

With one of the world's leading opera companies at the Royal Opera House (p124) in Covent Garden, the English National Opera based at the London Coliseum (p126) and plenty of other smaller players and events, London will keep opera lovers busy. It's not just the classics that get attention, as new productions are regularly staged which grapple with a host of contemporary themes. In summer, Holland Park is the venue for opera under the stars. Opera is expensive to produce and, consequently, tickets can be pricey.

Dance

London is home to five major dance companies and a host of small and experimental ones. The **Royal Ballet** (www.roh.org.uk), the best classical-ballet company in the land, is based at the Royal Opera House in Covent Garden. The English National Ballet (p367) often performs at the London Coliseum, especially at Christmas and in summer. Sadler's Wells (p210) is excellent for experimental dance. Also worth investigating is the Laban Theatre (p286), which features performances by students of the Trinity Laban Conservatoire of Music and Dance.

Dance Umbrella (www.danceumbrella.co.uk) is a contemporary dance festival which takes place in late October.

Live Rock, Pop, Jazz & Blues

Musically diverse and defiantly different, London is a hotspot of musical innovation and talent. It leads the world in articulate indie rock, in particular, and tomorrow's guitar heroes are right-this-minute paying their dues on sticky-floored stages in Camden Town, Shoreditch and Dalston.

Monster international acts see London as an essential stop on their transglobal stomps, but be prepared for tickets selling out faster than you can find your credit card. The city's beautiful old theatres and music halls play host to a constant roster of well-known names in more intimate settings. In summer, giant festivals take over the city's parks, while smaller, more localised events such as the **Dalston Music Festival** (www.dalstonmusicfestival.com) showcase up-and-comers in multiple spaces.

Londoners are more musically aware than most – perhaps it's got something to do with all that time spent on the tube with their headphones on. The beauty about catching a gig in London is that its sheer size means that there's always enough totally devoted fans who know all the words to all the songs to fill any venue – whether it's Blur at Hyde Park or John Grant at the Hammersmith Apollo.

If jazz or blues are your thing, London has some truly excellent clubs and pubs where you can catch classics and contemporary tunes. The city's major jazz event is the **London Jazz Festival** (www.londonjazzfestival.org.uk) in November.

Comedy

They may look a miserable bunch on the underground – and the winter drizzle and summer wash-outs don't help – but Londoners have a solid sense of humour and comedy is flourishing in the capital. On any given night, you can pitch up at any one of the 20-plus major comedy clubs or countless other venues (including pubs) to roll in the aisles or snort your drink down the wrong way.

Most acts have both eyes on the critical Edinburgh Festival season. From April to July, new acts are being tried out on audiences. August is the cruellest month for comedy in London, because everyone's shifted up north for the festival itself. Come winter, London's stages are full of comedians performing the stuff that went down well in Edinburgh. Check the winners list of the **Edinburgh Comedy Awards** (www.comedyawards.co.uk) for the brightest new stars.

Some of the world's most famous modern comedians hail from, or made their names in, London, including Ben Elton, Alexei Sayle, Victoria Wood, Julian Clary, Rowan Atkinson, Reeves & Mortimer, Eddie Izzard, Jo Brand, Sacha Baron Cohen, Ricky Gervais, Matt Lucas, David Walliams, Russell Brand, Josie Long, Russell Howard and Alan Carr.

Film

Londoners have a passion for film, with movie buffs filling venues large and small all across the city. For back-catalogue classics, turn to the BFI (p172) at South Bank, but keep an eye out for film festivals at independent cinemas, which bring in reels of foreign movies.

For more eclectic tastes, shorts and foreign cinema, as well as mainstream movies, London's independent cinemas allow you to put your feet up, sip a glass of wine and feel right at home. You can often catch monthly seasons and premieres, as well as actors and directors chatting about their work and answering questions. Cinemas such as the Prince Charles (p125) have cheap tickets, run mini-festivals and screen popular sin-galong classics.

Many major premieres are held in Leicester Sq, the priciest part of London for cinema tickets. Look out also for the *Summer Screen* at Somerset House (p107), movies on the lawn at Fulham Palace (p188) and other open-air cinema screenings.

Entertainment by Neighbourhood

➡ **The West End** Packed with theatres, opera houses, classical-music concert halls, small live-music venues, comedy clubs and cinemas.

➡ **The City** Barbican Arts Centre and church concerts.

➡ **The South Bank** A major concentration of some of London's best known and prestigious theatres.

➡ **Kensington & Hyde Park** Royal Albert Hall and the Royal Court Theatre.

➡ **Clerkenwell, Shoreditch & Spitalfields** Sadler's Wells, live music bars and comedy.

➡ **East London** Theatres, independent cinemas and live music venues.

➡ **Camden & North London** The works: indie rock, jazz, blues, traditional music, folk dancing, comedy and theatre.

➡ **Notting Hill & West London** Tremendous independent cinemas, live music, summer opera.

➡ **Greenwich & South London** Live music, dance, theatre and cinema.

➡ **Richmond, Kew & Hampton Court** Live jazz, open-air concerts and live-music pubs.

PLAN YOUR TRIP ENTERTAINMENT

Performance of the *Tempest*, Shakespeare's Globe (p160)

Lonely Planet's Top Choices

Royal Opera House (p124) London's preeminent stage for opera and classical dance.

Shakespeare's Globe (p171) Experience the Bard's work as it was first performed.

Southbank Centre (p171) Concerts, recitals, musicals – you name it – the Southbank Centre has it.

Barbican (p155) A powerhouse of culture, from music and dance to theatre and film.

Wilton's (p227) The Victorian music hall tradition lives on in the East End.

Sadler's Wells (p210) Modern dance at its most immediate.

Best for Theatre

Shakespeare's Globe (p171) Shakespeare, as it would have been 400 years ago.

National Theatre (p171) Contemporary theatre on the South Bank.

Old Vic (p172) A heavy-hitter in London's theatrical scene.

Donmar Warehouse (p126) Consistently delivers thought-provoking productions.

Royal Court Theatre (p194) Forward-thinking, promoting new voices.

Young Vic (p172) Dramatic productions from new writers, actors and directors.

Best for Classical Music

Royal Opera House (p124) One of the world's great opera venues, with classical ballet too.

Royal Albert Hall (p194) The Grand Dame of classical music venues.

Wigmore Hall (p125) London's most important chamber music venue.

Southbank Centre (p171) Classical music from around the world in the wonderful Royal Festival Hall.

Cadogan Hall (p194) Chelsea home of the Royal Philharmonic Orchestra.

Best Church Venues for Classical Music

St Martin-in-the-Fields (p106) Excellent classical music concerts, many by candlelight.

Westminster Abbey (p78) Evensong and the city's finest organ concerts.

St Paul's Cathedral (p142) Evensong at its most evocative.

St Alfege Church (p273) Free lunchtime concerts on Thursdays.

Best for Dance

Sadler's Wells (p210) Top-drawer international and UK dance.

London Coliseum (p126) Home to the English National Ballet.

Southbank Centre (p171) From Bollywood to break-dancing, and all things in between.

Place (p125) The very birth-place of modern English dance.

Laban Theatre (p286) A pioneering dance school hosting new and emerging talent.

Best Live Rock & Pop Venues

Royal Albert Hall (p194) Gorgeous, grand and spacious, yet strangely intimate.

Union Chapel (p252) One of London's most atmospheric venues.

O2 Arena (p286) A massive venue for the biggest gigs.

KOKO (p251) Fabulously glitzy venue, showcasing original indie rock.

Barfly (p252) Camden Town's seminal indie rock venue, as grotty and brilliant as ever.

Best for Live Jazz

Ronnie Scott's (p125) Still the best jazz club in Britain.

Pizza Express Jazz Club (p125) Top-class jazz in the basement of a chain restaurant.

606 Club (p194) Legendary Chelsea basement jazz outfit.

Vortex Jazz Club (p228) Tiny but packing a punch with superb programming.

Best for Comedy

Soho Theatre (p125) Attracts local and foreign talent.

Comedy Store (p125) Hosts the most famous improvisation outfit in town.

Angel Comedy (p252) Free shows every night of the week.

Union Chapel (p252) Giggle in church at the monthly *Live at the Chapel*.

Up the Creek (p286) Longstanding comedy favourite south of the river.

Amused Moose Soho (p126) Comedy routines without the heckling.

Shoppers at Harrods department store (p194)

🛍 Shopping

From charity-shop finds to designer bags, there are thousands of ways to spend your hard-earned cash in London. Many of the big-name shopping attractions, such as Harrods, Hamleys, Camden Market and Old Spitalfields Market, have become must-sees in their own right. Chances are that with so many temptations, you'll give your wallet a full workout.

NEED TO KNOW

Opening Hours

➡ Shops generally open from 9am or 10am to 6pm or 7pm Monday to Saturday.

➡ The majority of stores in the most popular shopping strips also open on Sunday, typically from noon to 6pm but sometimes 10am to 4pm.

➡ Shops in the West End open late (to 9pm) on Thursday; those in Chelsea, Knightsbridge and Kensington open late on Wednesday.

➡ If there's a major market on a certain day – say, Columbia Road Flower Market on a Sunday morning – it's a good bet that neighbouring stores will also fling their doors open.

Taxes & Refunds

In certain circumstances visitors from non-EU countries are entitled to claim back the 20% value-added tax (VAT) they have paid on purchased goods. The rebate applies only to items purchased in stores displaying a 'tax free' sign (there are plenty of these along Bond St).

The retailer should provide you with a VAT 407 form, which you'll need to complete and present at Customs, along with the receipt and goods, as you're leaving the country. For more information, see www.gov.uk/tax-on-shopping/taxfree-shopping.

Markets

Perhaps the biggest draw for visitors are the capital's famed markets. A treasure trove of small designers, unique jewellery pieces, original framed photographs and posters, colourful vintage pieces and bric-a-brac, they are the antidote to impersonal, carbon-copy shopping centres.

The most popular markets are Camden (p240), Old Spitalfields (p211) and Portobello Road (p258), which operate most days, but there are dozens of others, such as Brick Lane's excellent Sunday Upmarket (p210), which only pop up on the weekend. Camden and Old Spitalfields are both mainly covered, but even the outdoor markets are busy, rain or shine.

Cheese, Broadway Market (p228)

Designers

British designers are well established in the fashion world and a visit to Stella Mc-Cartney, Vivienne Westwood, Paul Smith, Burberry or Mulberry is an experience in its own right. The fashion house started by the late Alexander McQueen is now under the creative direction of Sarah Burton, perhaps most famous as the designer of Princess Catherine's wedding dress.

Vintage Fashion

The realm of vintage apparel has moved from being sought out by those looking for something off-beat and original, to an all-out mainstream shopping habit. Vintage designer garments and odd bits and pieces from the 1920s to the 1980s are all gracing the rails in some surprisingly upmarket boutique vintage shops.

The less self-conscious charity shops – especially those in areas such as Chelsea, Kensington and Islington – are your best bets for real bargains on designer wear (usually, the richer the area, the better the secondhand shops).

Chain Stores

Many bemoan the fact that chains have taken over the main shopping centres, leaving independent shops struggling to balance the books. But since they're cheap, fashionable and always conveniently located, Londoners (and others) keep going back for more. As well as familiar overseas retailers, such as Gap, H&M, Urban Outfitters and Zara, you'll find plenty of home-grown chains, including luxury womenswear brand Karen Millen

Shopping by Neighbourhood

Camden & North London
It's all about Camden
Market (p252)

**Clerkenwell, Shoreditch &
Spitalfields**
Vintage, vintage, vintage,
fashion and jewellery (p211)

**Notting Hill &
West London**
Famous market, vintage stores
and lovely boutiques
(p266)
(1mi)

The City
Good for suits but
little else (p155)

East London
Wonderful markets,
discounted fashion
(p228)
(1mi)

The West End
Shopping galore,
from franchises to
boutiques (p126)

Kensington & Hyde Park
High fashion and
glamorous shopping
(p194)

*London
Eye*

The South Bank
Fabulous food and
small designer shops
(p173)

**Greenwich &
South London**
Eclectic markets,
up-and-coming fashion
(p287)

(p132) and global giant Topshop (p130). Some of the best UK chains to look out for include:

Ben Sherman (www.bensherman.com) Fashionable menswear with a particularly British, 1960s Mod vibe.

French Connection UK (www.frenchconnection.com) FCUK is good for party outfits, girly frills and cool men's clothing.

Jigsaw (www.jigsaw-online.com) Classic yet slightly boho clothes for women and men, with an emphasis on tweeds and knits.

Marks & Spencer (www.marksandspencer.co.uk) After years of being synonymous with 'quality knickers', M&S continues to produce some fabulous fashion lines.

Oasis (www.oasis-stores.com) Good catwalk copies for women that are sure to keep you on trend.

Reiss (www.reiss.co.uk) A classic English label of understated fashion with a good dose of class.

Lonely Planet's Top Choices

Sunday Upmarket (p210) Up-and-coming designers, cool tees and terrific food.

Silver Vaults (p155) The world's largest collection of silver, from cutlery to jewellery.

Fortnum & Mason (p127) The world's most glamorous grocery store.

Camden Market (p253) Every shade of exotic and alternative: steampunk fashion, navel jewellery, Moroccan lamps.

Harrods (p194) Garish, stylish, kitsch, yet perennially popular department store.

Sister Ray (p130) A top independent music shop, with an ever-changing selection of vinyls and CDs.

Best for Fashion

Selfridges (p133) Everything from streetwear to high fashion under one roof.

Dover Street Market (p133) An indoor market that's a shrine to fine fashion labels.

Burberry Outlet Store (p229) A slightly cheaper take on the classic Brit brand.

Present (p211) Top-end Shoreditch style for men.

Start (p212) Denim fittings for women, directional designer labels and personal tailoring for men.

Folk (p128) Simple but striking Scandinavian style for men and women.

Best Markets

Broadway Market (p228) ocal market known for its food ⸱t with plenty else besides.

Brixton Market (p287) It's bright, fun and keeps evolving – and keeps getting better all the time.

Camden Market (p253) Authentic antiques to tourist tat – and everything in between.

Portobello Road Market (p258) Classic Notting Hill sprawl, perfect for vintage everything.

Greenwich Market (p287) Food, food, glorious food, with shopping to be had, too.

Old Spitalfields Market (p211) One of London's best for young fashion designers.

Best Vintage

Blitz London (p211) A massive selection of just about everything.

Beyond Retro (p229) London vintage empire with a rock 'n' roll heart.

Absolute Vintage (p212) Great for vintage shoes, in particular.

Bang Bang Clothing Exchange (p128) On-trend vintage designer pieces.

Retrobates Vintage (p287) Duds for a dinner at Downton.

British Red Cross (p194) Kensington castoffs of exceptional quality.

Best Bookshops

Foyles (p127) A brilliant selection covering most bases.

Daunt Books (p127) Guides, maps and tales from every corner of the world.

Slightly Foxed on Gloucester Road (p195) Well-stocked bibliophile's hunting ground.

Peter Harrington (p133) First editions and rare books.

Lutyens & Rubinstein (p266) Curated selections of exceptional writing.

Housmans (p254) Specialises in all manner of leftie tomes.

Best Music Shops

Rough Trade East (p211) Excellent selection of vinyl and CDs, plus in-store gigs.

Sister Ray (p130) Just what you'd expect from a store whose name references the Velvet Underground.

Honest Jon's (p267) For reggae, jazz, funk, soul, dance and blues junkies.

Sounds of the Universe (p130) Soul, reggae, funk and dub CDs and vinyl and some original 45s.

Phonica (p130) Dance music specialist but more besides.

Casbah Records (p287) Classic vinyl and memorabilia.

Best Department Stores

Selfridges (p133) Over 100 years of retail innovation.

Liberty (p131) Fabric, fashion and much, much more.

Harrods (p194) Enormous, overwhelming and indulgent, with a world-famous food hall.

Fortnum & Mason (p127) A world of food in luxuriously historic surroundings.

Harvey Nichols (p195) Fashion, food, beauty and lifestyle over eight floors.

Sports & Activities

The 2012 Olympic Games put a spring in London's step and left the city with a sudden embarrassment of world-class sports facilities in the east of town, some of which are now open to the public. The rest of London boasts a well-developed infrastructure for participatory and spectator sports to get your heart racing and the endorphins flowing.

Health & Fitness

London parks and commons swarm with joggers, but when the skies open overhead runners hit the treadmill. For a rather large organised run, check out the **Virgin Money London Marathon** (www.virginmoneylondonmarathon.com) in spring.

Fitness First (☑0844 571 3400; www.fitnessfirst.co.uk) Branches all over the city.

La Fitness (☑01302-892455; www.lafitness.co.uk) With over 25 gyms in town.

Virgin Active (☑020-7717 9000; www.virginactive.co.uk) One of the largest chains in the UK; top end.

Football

Football is at the very heart of English culture, with about a dozen league teams in London and usually around five or six in the Premier League. Tickets for Premier League fixtures (August to mid-May) can be impossible to secure for visitors. Stadiums where you can watch matches (or, more realistically, take tours) include the city's landmark national stadium, **Wembley** (☑0844 980 8001; www.wembleystadium.com; tours adult/child £19/11; ⊖Wembley Park); Arsenal Emirates Stadium (p241); **Chelsea** (☑0871 984 1955; www.chelseafc.com; Stamford Bridge, Fulham Rd, SW6; tours adult/child £20/13; ⊗museum 9.30am-5pm; ⊖Fulham Broadway); and **West Ham United** (www.whufc.com; Boleyn Ground, Green St, Upton Park, E13; ⊖Upton Park), who are making the Olympic Stadium their new ground from 2016.

Athletics

Major international athletics events are staged at the Olympic Stadium in the Queen Elizabeth Olympic Park (p221), the site of the Olympic Games in 2012. Other athletics meets are staged at the Crystal Palace National Sports Centre in Crystal Palace Park.

Cricket

On a long summer's day, you could do a lot worse than packing up a picnic and enjoying

---

THAMES BOAT RACES

The top fixture on the Thames rowing calendar is the **Oxford & Cambridge Boat Race** (www.theboatrace.org) – otherwise known as the Boat Race – usually held in late March or early April. Surging upstream between Putney and Mortlake, the event (which included a female crew boat race for the first time in 2015) draws huge crowds along the river. The other major date on the rowing calendar is the **Head of the River Race** (www.horr.co.uk), held along the same course (but in the opposite direction and with international crews) in March.

NEED TO KNOW

Opening Hours

As a rule, most gyms open very early, usually from 6.30am, to ensure early risers get their workout on time. Equally, they are open until at least 9pm. Parks are generally open dawn to dusk.

Tickets

Finding tickets for Premier League matches during the August to mid-May football season in London is tricky, as seats are snapped up by season-ticket holders. Tickets for all other enclosed sporting events need to be booked well in advance. The free entertainment weekly **Time Out** (www.timeout.com/london) has the best information on fixtures, times, venues and ticket prices.

the thwack of leather on willow. The **English Cricket Board** (☏020-7432 1200; www.ecb.co.uk) has complete details of match schedules and tickets. Test matches are regularly played at Lord's (p238) and the **Oval** (☏0844 375 1845; www.kiaoval.com; Kennington, SE11; international match £20-350, county £20-35; ⊜Oval).

Cycling

Santander Cycles are a sloth-busting inducement to pedal your way around London. The city is carpeted with dedicated cycle paths and the choice of cycle routes around London is breathtaking, from breezy canal-side towpaths to criss-crossing parks and commons. The velodrome and attached BMX park at the Lee Valley Velopark (p229) in the Olympic Park are open to cyclists, from amateur to hardcore.

Horse Racing

If you fancy a flutter, several racecourses are within striking distance of London. The flat racing runs from April to September, while you can see the gee-gees jumping fences from October to April. Famous venues include **Ascot** (☏0844 346 3000; www.ascot.co.uk; admission from £10; ®Ascot), **Epsom**

(☏01372 726311; www.epsomdowns.co.uk; admission from £10; ®Epsom Downs), **Royal Windsor Racecourse** (☏01753 498400; www.windsorracecourse.co.uk; admission from £9; ®Windsor) and **Sandown Park** (☏01372 464348; www.sandown.co.uk; admission from £16; ®Esher).

Ice Skating

A combined ice rink and bowling venue, Queens Ice & Bowl (p267) has skating year-round and disco nights on ice. In winter months, outside ice rinks sparkle at Somerset House (p107), the Natural History Museum (p180), the Tower of London (p136) and other venues.

Rugby Union

Between January and March, England competes against Scotland, Wales, Ireland, France and Italy in the Six Nations Championship. Three games take place at Twickenham Stadium (p302).

Skateboarding

The most famous skateboarding area is in the fantastic graffiti-splodged undercroft of the Southbank Centre (p163), but there are skateparks all over town. See www.london skateparks.co.uk for a full list.

Swimming

With two 50m pools and a 25m diving pool, the London Aquatics Centre (p229) at the Queen Elizabeth Olympic Park (p221) is a magnet for swimmers. London also has some lovely 1930s art-deco lidos, while swimming pools and public baths can be found across town. Hotels with pools are all indicated in this book with a swimming pool icon.

Tennis

Wimbledon (www.wimbledon.com; ⊜Wimbledon) becomes the centre of the sporting universe for a fortnight in June/July when the thrilling grass tennis tournament gets underway, but obtaining tickets (p299) is far from straightforward. To look out onto or visit Centre Court at other times of the year, head to the Wimbledon Lawn Tennis Museum (p299). Numerous parks around London have tennis courts, many free.

SANTANDER CYCLES

Like Paris and other European cities, London has its own cycling-hire scheme called **Santander Cycles** (☎0343 222 6666; www.tfl.gov.uk), also variously referred to as 'Barclays Bikes' after their former sponsor, or 'Boris Bikes' after the city's mayor, Boris Johnson (2008–2016), who launched the initiative. The bikes have proved as popular with visitors as with Londoners.

The idea is simple: pick up a bike from one of the 700 docking stations dotted around the capital. Cycle. Drop it off at another docking station.

The access fee is £2 for 24 hours. All you need is a credit or debit card. The first 30 minutes are free. It's then £2 for any additional period of 30 minutes.

You can take as many bikes as you like during your access period (24 hours), leaving five minutes between each trip.

The pricing structure is designed to encourage short journeys rather than longer rentals; for those, go to a hire company. You'll also find that although easy to ride, the bikes only have three gears and are quite heavy. You must be 18 to buy access and at least 14 to ride a bike.

Hiring a Bike

➡ Insert your debit or credit card in the docking station to pay your access fee (only once for the access period).

➡ Request a cycle release code slip at the docking station every time you want to take a bike during your access period.

➡ Enter the release code at your chosen bike dock; wait for the green light to release the bike.

➡ If you find it difficult to pull the bike free from its dock, bounce the back wheel up and down first.

➡ Ride!

➡ Return the bike at any free dock; wait for the green light to make sure the bike is locked.

➡ If the docking station is full, consult the terminal to find available docking points nearby. Smartphone users may also want to download the free Santander Cycles app, which locates nearby docking stations and shows you how full they are.

Gay & Lesbian

The city of Oscar Wilde, Quentin Crisp and Elton John does not disappoint its queer visitors, proffering a fantastic mix of brash, camp, loud and edgy parties, bars, clubs and events year-round. A world gay capital on par with New York and San Francisco, London's gay and lesbian communities have turned good times into an art form.

Gay Rights

Protection from discrimination is enshrined in law. Civil partnerships allowed gay couples the same rights as straight ones from 2005 and bona-fide gay marriage came into force here in 2014. That's not to say homophobia does not exist.

Drinking

The queer drinking scene in London is wonderfully varied. Whether you fancy a quiet pint in a traditional boozer that just happens to be gay, or want a place to wet your whistle before going out dancing, you'll be spoiled for choice.

Clubbing

London has some fun and very varied gay clubs, from Fire London (p286) in Vauxhall to White Swan (p227) in the East End. But it's a moveable feast, as the clubbing scene is about club nights rather than venues, meaning a club that was fantastic and full of hunks one night might well be straight and full of goths the next.

Lesbian Venues

The lesbian scene in London is far less in your face than the flamboyant gay one, though there's now very central She Soho (p122), the first lesbian bar on overwhelmingly gay Old Compton St. Some clubs have lesbian nights such as Ruby Tuesdays at Ku Klub Lisle St (p123) and Clam Jam on Thursday at Dalston Superstore (p226). Check out the **Ginger Beer** (www.gingerbeer.co.uk) website for the full low-down.

Gay & Lesbian Events

The renamed **BFI Flare** (www.bfi.org.uk/flare) is a renowned gay and lesbian film festival hosted by the British Film Institute in March, with screenings, premieres, awards and talks. Highly recommended.

In late June, **Pride in London** (http://prideinlondon.org), one of the world's largest gay parades, complete with floats, stalls and performers sails across town.

Gay & Lesbian by Neighbourhood

➡ **East End** London's more alternative gay scene, often very well mixed in with local straights, is spread across the East End in Shoreditch, Bethnal Green, Dalston and Limehouse. Here you'll find arty parties, hip bars and clubs and the odd bit o' rough.

➡ **Soho** The long-established gay village of Soho in the West End, once so central to any gay experience here, has somewhat lost its pre-eminence to the edgy East End.

➡ **Vauxhall** The erstwhile bleak concrete jungle that was Vauxhall is now home to London's mainstream muscle-boy venues.

Best Gay Bars

Edge (p122) London's largest gay bar, with something for everybody on four floors.

Yard (p122) Laidback venue off Old Compton St with alfresco courtyard.

Dalston Superstore (p226) New York warehouse in gritty East London.

Eagle (p286) A bastion of gay blokedom south of the river.

Best Gay Clubs

Fire London (p286) Vauxhall's leading light, with regular all-nighters and big names.

Heaven (p124) The point on the map for most gay weekend clubbers.

RVT (p286) Cabaret, drag shows, open stage, crazy bingo, and never a dull night.

White Swan (p227) East End stalwart with great dancefloor.

Best Gay Club Nights

Popcorn at Heaven (p124) A fun and cheap Monday night out, Popcorn is an Ibiza-style club night with a great selection of music and refreshingly priced drinks offers.

Orange at Fire London (p286) Regularly hosting some of the best gay club nights in London, Fire is best known for its infamous Sunday all-nighter, Orange. Pure hedonism.

G-A-Y at Heaven (p124) Love it or hate it, G-A-Y is a centre of gravity for the gay scene and seemingly where half of Soho is headed on a Saturday night.

Duckie at RVT (p286) Tagged 'London's Authentic Honky Tonk', this is the club's signature queer performance night.

NEED TO KNOW

Free Listings

London has a lively gay online press charting the ever-changing scene. Check out any of these publications, available both online and in hard copy; their listings are the most up-to-date available.

➡ **Boyz** (www.boyz.co.uk)

➡ **QX** (www.qxmagazine. com)

➡ **Pride Life** (http:// pridelife.com)

Magazines

Along with the above free-bies, the following are for sale at most newsagents in Soho.

➡ *Gay Times* (www. gaytimes.co.uk)

➡ *Diva* (www.divamag. co.uk)

➡ *Attitude* (www. attitude.co.uk)

Blogs & Other Resources

➡ **60by80** (www. 60by80.com/london)

➡ **Ginger Beer** (www. gingerbeer.co.uk)

➡ **Jake** (www.jaketm.com)

➡ **Time Out London LGBT** (www.timeout. com/london/lgbt)

➡ **Me Me Me** (www.me-me-me.tv)

Help

➡ Always report homophobic crimes to the **police** (☑999).

➡ **London Lesbian & Gay Switchboard** (☑0300 330 0630; www llgs.org.uk; ☺10am-11pm) offers counselling, free advice and other help to anyone who needs a sympathetic ear.

PLAN YOUR TRIP GAY & LESBIAN

Explore London

Neighbourhoods at a Glance 72

The West End. 76
Top Sights 78
Sights. 97
Eating. 110
Drinking & Nightlife 120
Entertainment 124
Shopping. 126

The City 134
Top Sights 136
Sights. 146
Eating. 152
Drinking & Nightlife 153
Entertainment 155
Shopping. 155

The South Bank 156
Top Sights 158
Sights. 163
Eating. 166
Drinking & Nightlife 169
Entertainment 171
Shopping. 173

Kensington & Hyde Park 174
Top Sights 176
Sights. 185
Eating. 189
Drinking & Nightlife 193

Entertainment 194
Shopping. 194

Clerkenwell, Shoreditch & Spitalfields 196
Sights. 198
Eating. 201
Drinking & Nightlife 207
Entertainment 210
Shopping. 211

East London 213
Sights. 215
Eating. 222
Drinking & Nightlife 225
Entertainment 227
Shopping. 228
Sports & Activities. 229

Camden & North London 230
Top Sights 232
Sights. 235
Eating. 244
Drinking & Nightlife 248
Entertainment 251
Shopping. 252
Sports & Activities. 254

Notting Hill & West London 255
Sights. 257
Eating. 260

Drinking & Nightlife 263
Entertainment 266
Shopping. 266
Sports & Activities. 267

Greenwich & South London 268
Top Sights 270
Sights. 273
Eating. 280
Drinking & Nightlife 284
Entertainment 286
Shopping. 287
Sports & Activities. 287

Richmond, Kew & Hampton Court. 288
Top Sights 290
Sights. 296
Eating. 300
Drinking & Nightlife 301
Sports & Activities. 302

Day Trips from London 303
Top Sights 304
Oxford 307
Cambridge. 311
Bath 314

Sleeping. 318

LONDON'S
TOP SIGHTS

Westminster Abbey 78

British Museum.................81

Buckingham Palace..........85

Houses of Parliament.......87

National Gallery 89

Tate Britain 92

National Portrait Gallery ...93

Trafalgar Square...............94

Churchill War Rooms........95

Sir John Soane's
Museum 96

Tower of London.............136

St Paul's Cathedral 142

Tower Bridge...................145

Tate Modern 158

Shakespeare's Globe......160

London Eye 161

Borough Market..............162

Victoria & Albert
Museum 176

Natural History
Museum 180

Hyde Park 182

Science Museum 184

British Library.................232

London Zoo.....................234

Royal Observatory &
Greenwich Park 270

Old Royal Naval College...272

Hampton Court Palace...290

Kew Gardens 294

Windsor Castle...............304

Left: The Shard (p164), designed by
architect Renzo Piano

Neighbourhoods at a Glance

❶ The West End p76

With many of London's premier postcodes, and superlative restaurants, hotels and shops, the West End should be your first port of call. Iconic sights (Trafalgar Sq, Piccadilly Circus), buildings and museums (Buckingham Palace, Westminster Abbey, British Museum), nightlife (Soho), shopping (Oxford St, Covent Garden, Regent St), parks (St James's Park) and theatres – they are all here.

❷ The City p134

London's historic core is a tale of two cities: all go during the week and eerily quiet at weekends. But there are ancient streets and spectacular architecture, with history awaiting at every turn. St Paul's Cathedral and the Tower of London are hallmark sights, as are the daring and amusingly named skyscrapers – the Gherkin, the Walkie Talkie and the Cheese Grater.

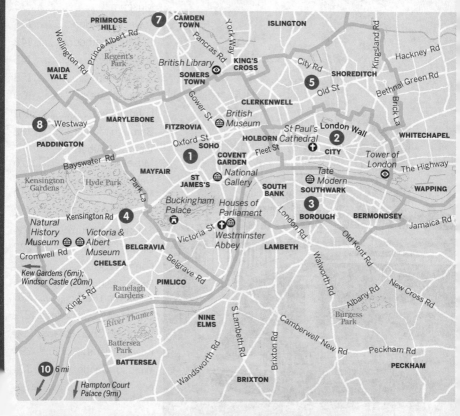

③ The South Bank p156

The Tate Modern has done much to re-energise the South Bank, a must-visit area for art lovers, theatre-goers and culture hounds. There are also iconic Thames views, great food markets, first-rate pubs, dollops of history, striking examples of modern architecture and a sprinkling of fine bars and restaurants.

④ Kensington & Hyde Park p174

Splendidly well groomed, Kensington is one of London's most pleasant neighbourhoods. You'll find three fine museums here – the V&A, the Natural History Museum and the Science Museum – as well as excellent dining and shopping and graceful parklands.

⑤ Clerkenwell, Shoreditch & Spitalfields p196

This redeveloped area boasts top sights (Geffrye Museum, Georgian Spitalfields), excellent markets (Exmouth, Spitalfields, Brick Lane) and a creative frisson. It truly comes alive at night.

⑥ East London p213

Anyone with an interest in multicultural London needs to visit the East End. There's standout Asian cuisine, great galleries, excellent pubs, canal-side eating and drinking, and clubbing in Dalston, but it's the Queen Elizabeth Olympic Park that will entice.

⑦ Camden & North London p230

With its famous market, unrivalled music scene and excellent pubs, Camden keeps North London in check when it comes to good times. But there's plenty for quiet enjoyment too – from gorgeous green spaces (Hampstead Heath, Regent's Park), to overgrown Victorian cemeteries and canal walks.

⑧ Notting Hill & West London p255

Portobello Market, fabulous cinemas, canal-side charms, superb pubs and clubs, swish parkland and mansions, varied shopping and ethnic eats all make Notting Hill and West London an eclectic must-see.

⑨ Greenwich & South London p268

Regal riverside Greenwich complements its village feel with some grand architecture, grassy parkland and riverside pubs. Brixton has the creative edge in its glorious food-and-shop Village, Clapham and Battersea are full of hidden gems, while Dulwich Village is all leafy charm.

⑩ Richmond, Kew & Hampton Court p288

Wander by the Thames, explore Tudor palaces (Hampton Court), get lost in Kew Gardens, go deer-spotting in Richmond Park and down a pint by the river at sunset.

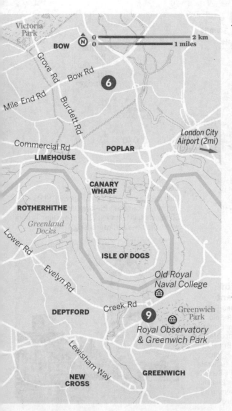

NEIGHBOURHOODS AT A GLANCE

The River Thames

A FLOATING TOUR

London's history has always been determined by the Thames. The city was founded as a Roman port nearly 2000 years ago and over the centuries since then many of the capital's landmarks have lined the river's banks. A boat trip is a great way to experience the attractions.

There are piers dotted along both banks at regular intervals where you can hop on and hop off the regular services to visit places of interest. The best place to board is Westminster Pier, from where boats head downstream, taking you from the City of Westminster, the seat of government, to the original City of London, now the financial district and dominated by a growing band of skyscrapers. Across the river, the once shabby and neglected South Bank now bristles with as many top attractions as its northern counterpart, including the slender Shard.

In our illustration we've concentrated on the top highlights you'll enjoy from a waterborne vessel.

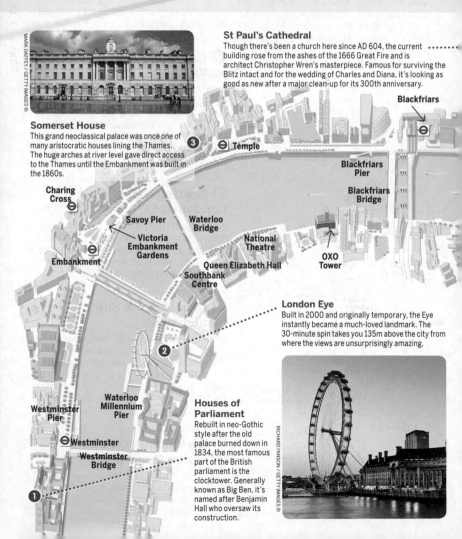

St Paul's Cathedral
Though there's been a church here since AD 604, the current building rose from the ashes of the 1666 Great Fire and is architect Christopher Wren's masterpiece. Famous for surviving the Blitz intact and for the wedding of Charles and Diana, it's looking as good as new after a major clean-up for its 300th anniversary.

Somerset House
This grand neoclassical palace was once one of many aristocratic houses lining the Thames. The huge arches at river level gave direct access to the Thames until the Embankment was built in the 1860s.

Blackfriars

Temple

Blackfriars Pier

Blackfriars Bridge

Charing Cross

Savoy Pier

Waterloo Bridge

Victoria Embankment Gardens

National Theatre

Embankment

OXO Tower

Queen Elizabeth Hall

Southbank Centre

London Eye
Built in 2000 and originally temporary, the Eye instantly became a much-loved landmark. The 30-minute spin takes you 135m above the city from where the views are unsurprisingly amazing.

Westminster Pier

Waterloo Millennium Pier

Houses of Parliament
Rebuilt in neo-Gothic style after the old palace burned down in 1834, the most famous part of the British parliament is the clocktower. Generally known as Big Ben, it's named after Benjamin Hall who oversaw its construction.

Westminster

Westminster Bridge

MARK DAFFEY / GETTY IMAGES ©

RICHARD l'ANSON / GETTY IMAGES ©

These are, from west to east, the **Houses of Parliament ❶**, the **London Eye ❷**, **Somerset House ❸**, **St Paul's Cathedral ❹**, **Tate Modern ❺**, **Shakespeare's Globe ❻**, the **Tower of London ❼** and **Tower Bridge ❽**.

Apart from covering this central section of the river, boats can also be taken upstream as far as Kew Gardens and Hampton Court Palace, and downstream to Greenwich and the Thames Barrier.

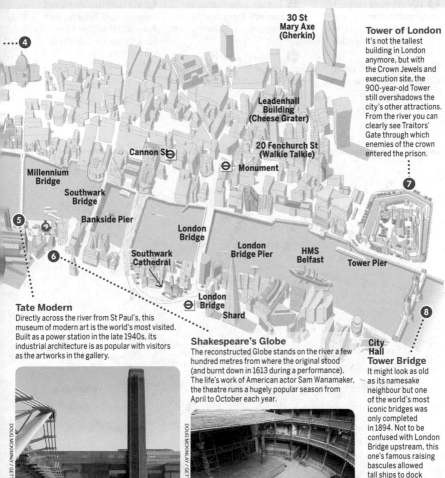

30 St Mary Axe (Gherkin)

Tower of London
It's not the tallest building in London anymore, but with the Crown Jewels and execution site, the 900-year-old Tower still overshadows the city's other attractions. From the river you can clearly see Traitors' Gate through which enemies of the crown entered the prison.

Leadenhall Building (Cheese Grater)

Cannon St⊖

20 Fenchurch St (Walkie Talkie)

⊖ **Monument**

Millennium Bridge

Southwark Bridge

Bankside Pier

London Bridge

London Bridge Pier

HMS Belfast

Tower Pier

Southwark Cathedral

⊖ **London Bridge**

Shard

City Hall

Tate Modern
Directly across the river from St Paul's, this museum of modern art is the world's most visited. Built as a power station in the late 1940s, its industrial architecture is as popular with visitors as the artworks in the gallery.

Shakespeare's Globe
The reconstructed Globe stands on the river a few hundred metres from where the original stood (and burnt down in 1613 during a performance). The life's work of American actor Sam Wanamaker, the theatre runs a hugely popular season from April to October each year.

Tower Bridge
It might look as old as its namesake neighbour but one of the world's most iconic bridges was only completed in 1894. Not to be confused with London Bridge upstream, this one's famous raising bascules allowed tall ships to dock at the old wharves to the west and are still lifted up to 1000 times a year.

DOUG MCKINLAY / GETTY IMAGES ©

DOUG MCKINLAY / GETTY IMAGES ©

The West End

WESTMINSTER | BLOOMSBURY & FITZROVIA | ST JAMES'S | SOHO & CHINATOWN | COVENT GARDEN & LEICESTER SQUARE | WHITEHALL | HOLBORN & THE STRAND | MARYLEBONE | MAYFAIR

Neighbourhood Top Five

1 Paying your respects to **Westminster Abbey** (p78), church of coronations, royal burials and weddings.

2 Enjoying a fabulous night out in all singin', all dancin' **Soho** (p102).

3 Hiring a deckchair in **St James's Park** (p100) and enjoying regal views of London.

4 Exploring the history of ancient civilisations at the excellent (and free) **British Museum** (p81).

5 Hitting the shops and boutiques of **Covent Garden** (p104) before stopping to watch the street performers.

For more detail of this area see Maps p406, p408, p412, p414 and p416 ➡

Explore: The West End

It may be a compact area, but the West End packs in a lot when it comes to sights. You'll need to allow half a day for each of the big museums (the British Museum and the National Gallery), and at least a couple of hours for places like Westminster Abbey and Buckingham Palace.

One of the delights of the West End is its energy and there is no better way to enjoy it than by walking around and taking it all in. Atmospheric places for a breather include Covent Garden, Trafalgar Sq and St James's Park.

Westminster and Whitehall are deserted in the evenings, with little in the way of bars and restaurants. It's a similar story in St James's. Instead, head to vibrant Soho for fantastic bars and restaurants, or the streets surrounding Covent Garden.

Local Life

→**Eating out** Soho is unrivalled when it comes to eating out. Andrew Edmunds (p114) and Mildreds (p113) never seem to go out of fashion, while hip new places such as Yalla Yalla (p118), Chiltern Firehouse (p119) and 10 Greek St (p115) open all the time.

→**Late-night openings** Be it catching the latest exhibition or simply enjoying the permanent collections without the weekend crowds, many Londoners make the best of late-night openings at the National Gallery (p89), the National Portrait Gallery (p93) and the British Museum (p81).

→**Shopping** Love it or loathe it, most Londoners will hit crowded Oxford St at some stage to shop; it's smack bang in the centre of town and has every franchise under the sun, as well as good department stores such as Selfridges (p133) and John Lewis (p133).

Getting There & Away

→**Underground** Almost every tube line goes through the West End, so wherever you're staying in London, you'll have no difficulty getting here. The tube is also good for getting from one end of the West End to the other.

→**Walking** The West End is relatively compact, so it'll be cheaper and generally more enjoyable to walk from one place to another rather than take public transport.

→**Santander Cycles** There are docking stations everywhere within the West End and cycling is your best bet for short journeys.

Lonely Planet's Top Tip

London – the West End especially – can be expensive, but there are plenty of tricks to make your pennies last. Many of the top museums are free, so give them priority. The West End is compact, so walk or take the bus (cheaper than the tube).

THE WEST END

✗ Best Places to Eat

→ Brasserie Zédel (p114)

→ Palomar (p114)

→ Dabbous (p112)

→ Bar Shu (p114)

→ Shoryu (p116)

For reviews, see p110 →

☕ Best Places to Drink

→ Lamb & Flag (p122)

→ Dukes Bar (p120)

→ London Cocktail Club (p121)

→ Rivoli Bar (p120)

→ Gordon's Wine Bar (p123)

→ Queen's Larder (p121)

For reviews, see p120 →

◉ Best Free Sights

→ British Museum (p81)

→ National Gallery (p89)

→ National Portrait Gallery (p93)

→ Houses of Parliament (p87)

→ Wallace Collection (p108)

→ Sir John Soane's Museum (p96)

For reviews, see p81 →

TOP SIGHT
WESTMINSTER ABBEY

Westminster Abbey is such an important commemoration site that it's hard to overstress its symbolic value or imagine its equivalent anywhere else in the world. With the exception of Edward V (murdered) and Edward VIII (abdicated), every English sovereign has been crowned here since William the Conqueror in 1066, and most of the monarchs from Henry III (died 1272) to George II (died 1760) – a total of 17 – are buried here.

There is an extraordinary amount to see at the Abbey. The interior is chock-a-block with ornate chapels, elaborate tombs of monarchs and grandiose monuments to sundry luminaries throughout the ages. First and foremost however, it is a sacred place of worship. Be warned: it can get very busy, with tiring queues.

A Regal History

Though a mixture of architectural styles, the Abbey is considered the finest example of Early English Gothic (1190–1300). The original church was built in the 11th century by King (later Saint) Edward the Confessor, who is buried in the chapel behind the sanctuary and main altar. Henry III (r 1216–72) began work on the new building but didn't complete it; the French Gothic nave was finished by Richard II in 1388. Henry VII's huge and magnificent Lady Chapel was added in 1519.

The Abbey was initially a monastery for Benedictine monks, and many of the building's features attest to this collegial past (the octagonal Chapter House, the Quire and four cloisters). In 1536, Henry VIII separated the Church of

DON'T MISS...

➡ Coronation Chair
➡ Henry VII's Lady Chapel
➡ Cosmati marble pavement
➡ College Garden
➡ Chapter House
➡ Westminster Abbey Museum

PRACTICALITIES

➡ Map p416, D4
➡ ☎020-7222 5152
➡ www.westminster-abbey.org
➡ 20 Dean's Yard, SW1
➡ adult/child £20/9, verger tours £5, cloister & gardens free
➡ ⊙9.30am-4.30pm Mon, Tue, Thu & Fri, to 7pm Wed, to 2.30pm Sat
➡ ⊖Westminster

England from the Roman Catholic Church and dissolved the monastery. The king became head of the Church of England and the Abbey acquired its 'royal peculiar' status, meaning it is administered directly by the Crown and exempt from any ecclesiastical jurisdiction.

North Transept, Sanctuary & Quire

Entrance to the Abbey is via the Great North Door. The North Transept is often referred to as Statesmen's Aisle: politicians and eminent public figures are commemorated by large marble statues and imposing marble plaques.

At the heart of the Abbey is the beautifully tiled **sanctuary** (or sacrarium), a stage for coronations, royal weddings and funerals. George Gilbert Scott designed the ornate **high altar** in 1873. In front of the altar is the **Cosmati marble pavement** dating back to 1268. It has intricate designs of small pieces of marble inlaid into plain marble, which predicts the end of the world in AD 19,693! At the entrance to the lovely **Chapel of St John the Baptist** is a sublime Virgin and Child bathed in candle light.

The **Quire**, a magnificent structure of gold, blue and red Victorian Gothic by Edward Blore, dates back to the mid-19th century. It sits where the original choir for the monks' worship would have been but bears no resemblance to the original. Nowadays, the Quire is still used for singing but its regular occupants are the Westminster Choir – 22 boys and 12 'lay vicars' (men) who sing the daily services.

Chapels & Chair

The sanctuary is surrounded by chapels. **Henry VII's Lady Chapel**, in the easternmost part of the Abbey, is the most spectacular with its fan vaulting on the ceiling, colourful banners of the Order of the Bath and dramatic oak stalls. Behind the chapel's altar is the elaborate sarcophagus of Henry VII and his queen, Elizabeth of York.

Beyond the chapel's altar is the **Royal Air Force Chapel**, with a stained-glass window commemorating the force's finest hour, the Battle of Britain (1940), and 1500 RAF pilots who died. A stone plaque on the floor marks the spot where Oliver Cromwell's body lay for two years (1658) until the Restoration, when it was disinterred, hanged and beheaded. Two bodies, believed to be those of the child princes allegedly murdered in the Tower of London in 1483, were buried here almost two centuries later in 1674.

There are two small chapels either side of Lady Chapel with the tombs of famous monarchs: on the left (north) is where **Elizabeth I** and her half-sister **Mary I** (AKA Bloody Mary) rest. On the right

REFRESHMENTS

You can get drinks and snacks at the Coffee Club in the Cloister. For a proper sit-down meal head for the **Cellarium** (Map p416; ☎020-7222 0516; www.cellariumcafe. com; Westminster Abbey, 20 Dean's Yard, SW1; mains £10.50-14.50; ☉8am-6pm Mon-Fri, 9am-5pm Sat, 10am-4pm Sun), part of the original 14th-century Benedictine monastery with stunning views of the Abbey's architectural details.

On 29 April 2011, Prince William married his fiancée Catherine Middleton at Westminster Abbey. The couple had chosen the Abbey for the relatively intimate setting of the sanctuary. Unusually, the couple decided to decorate the Abbey with trees; less controversial was the bride's decision to opt for a gown by a British designer, Sarah Burton (of Alexander McQueen). And in a tradition started by the future Queen Mother in 1923, Kate left her bridal bouquet on the Tomb of the Unknown Warrior.

(south) is the tomb of **Mary Queen of Scots**, beheaded on the orders of her cousin Elizabeth.

The vestibule of the Lady Chapel is the usual place for the rather ordinary-looking **Coronation Chair**, upon which every monarch since the early 14th century has been crowned.

Shrine of St Edward the Confessor

The most sacred spot in the Abbey lies behind the high altar; access is generally restricted to protect the 13th-century flooring. St Edward was the founder of the Abbey and the original building was consecrated a few weeks before his death. His tomb was slightly altered after the original was destroyed during the Reformation but still contains Edward's remains – the only complete saint's body in Britain. Ninety-minute **verger-led tours** of the Abbey include a visit to the shrine.

Outer Buildings & Gardens

The oldest part of the cloister is the East Cloister (or East Walk), dating to the 13th century. Off the cloister are three museums. The octagonal **Chapter House** has one of Europe's best-preserved medieval tile floors and retains traces of religious murals on the walls. It was used as a meeting place by the House of Commons in the second half of the 14th century. To the right of the entrance to Chapter House is what is claimed to be the oldest door in Britain – it's been there for 950 years.

The adjacent **Pyx Chamber** is one of the few remaining relics of the original Abbey and holds the Abbey's treasures and liturgical objects. It contains the pyx, a chest with standard gold and silver pieces for testing coinage weights in a ceremony called the Trial of the Pyx.

Next door in the vaulted undercroft, the **museum** (Map p416; Westminster Abbey; ◷10.30am-4pm) exhibits the death masks of generations of royalty, wax effigies representing Charles II and William III (who is on a stool to make him as tall as his wife, Mary II), armour and stained glass. Highlights are the graffiti-inscribed Mary Chair (used for the coronation of Mary II) and the Westminster Retable, England's oldest altarpiece, from the 13th century.

To reach the 900-year-old **College Garden** (Map p416; ◷10am-6pm Tue-Thu Apr-Sep, to 4pm Tue-Thu Oct-Mar), enter Dean's Yard and the Little Cloisters off Great College St.

Nave & South Transept

The south transept contains **Poets' Corner**, where many of England's finest writers are buried and/or commemorated (including Ted Hughes) by monuments or memorials.

In the nave's north aisle is **Scientists' Corner**, where you will find **Sir Isaac Newton's tomb** (note the putto holding a prism to the sky while another feeds material into a smelting oven). Just ahead of it is the north aisle of the Quire, known as **Musicians' Aisle**, where baroque composers Henry Purcell and John Blow are buried, as well as more modern music-makers like Benjamin Britten and Edward Elgar.

The two towers above the west door are the ones through which you exit. These were designed by Nicholas Hawksmoor and completed in 1745. Just above the door, perched in 15th-century niches, are the additions to the Abbey unveiled in 1998: 10 stone statues of international 20th-century martyrs who died for their Christian faith. These include American pacifist Dr Martin Luther King, the Polish priest St Maximilian Kolbe, who was murdered by the Nazis at Auschwitz, and Wang Zhiming, publicly executed during the Chinese Cultural Revolution.

TOP SIGHT
BRITISH MUSEUM

Britain's most visited attraction, the British Museum, draws in over six million visitors each year. The museum was founded in 1753 when royal physician Hans Sloane sold his 'cabinet of curiosities' for the then-princely sum of £20,000, raised by national lottery. The collection opened to the public for free in 1759, and the museum has since kept expanding its collection through judicious acquisitions, bequests and the controversial plundering of imperialism. It's an exhaustive and exhilarating stampede through world cultures over 7000 years, with galleries devoted to ancient civilisations, from Egypt to western Asia, the Middle East, Rome and Greece, India, Africa, prehistoric and Roman Britain, and medieval antiquities.

The museum is huge, so make a few focused visits if you have time, and consider the tours. There are 15 free 30- to 40-minute **eyeOpener tours** of individual galleries per day. The museum also has free daily gallery talks, a highlights tour (adult/child £12/free, 11.30am and 2pm Friday, Saturday and Sunday) and excellent **multimedia iPad tours** (adult/child £5/3.50), offering six themed one-hour tours, and a choice of 35-minute children's trails.

Great Court

Covered with a spectacular glass-and-steel roof designed by Norman Foster in 2000, the Great Court is the largest covered public square in Europe. In its centre is the world-famous **Reading Room**, formerly the British Library, which has been frequented by all the big brains of history, from Mahatma Gandhi to Karl Marx. It is currently used for temporary exhibits.

DON'T MISS...

➡ Rosetta Stone
➡ Mummy of Katebet
➡ Parthenon Sculptures
➡ Winged Bulls from Khorsabad
➡ Sutton Hoo Ship-Burial artefacts
➡ Mildenhall Treasure
➡ Lewis Chessmen

PRACTICALITIES

➡ Map p412, D6
➡ 020-7323 8000
➡ www.britishmuseum.org
➡ Great Russell St, WC1
➡ admission free
➡ ⊙10am-5.30pm Sat-Thu, to 8.30pm Fri
➡ Ⓔ Russell Sq, Tottenham Court Rd

The British Museum

A HALF-DAY TOUR

The British Museum, with almost eight million items in its permanent collection, is so vast and comprehensive that it can be daunting for the first-time visitor. To avoid a frustrating trip – and getting lost on the way to the Egyptian mummies – set out on this half-day exploration, which takes in some of the museum's most important sights. If you want to see and learn more, join a tour or hire a multimedia iPad.

A good starting point is the **Rosetta Stone ❶**, the key that cracked the code to ancient Egypt's writing system. Nearby treasures from Assyria – an ancient civilisation centred in Mesopotamia between the Tigris and Euphrates Rivers – including the colossal **Khorsabad Winged Bulls ❷**, give way to the **Parthenon Sculptures ❸**, highpoints of classical Greek art that continue to influence

Winged Bulls from Khorsabad
This awesome pair of alabaster winged bulls with human heads once guarded the entrance to the palace of Assyrian King Sargon II at Khorsabad in Mesopotamia, a cradle of civilisation in present-day Iraq.

Parthenon Sculptures
The Parthenon, a white marble temple dedicated to Athena, was part of a fortified citadel on the Acropolis in Athens. There are dozens of sculptures and friezes with models and interactive displays explaining how they all once fitted together.

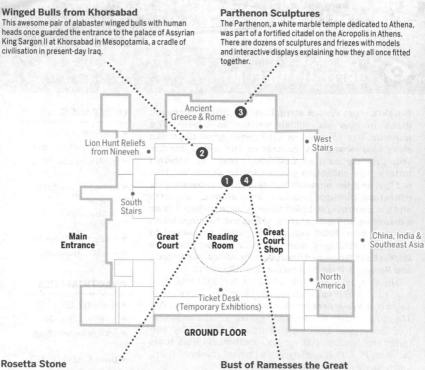

Ancient Greece & Rome

❸

Lion Hunt Reliefs from Nineveh

West Stairs

❷

South Stairs

❶ ❹

Main Entrance

Great Court

Reading Room

Great Court Shop

China, India & Southeast Asia

North America

Ticket Desk (Temporary Exhibtions)

GROUND FLOOR

Rosetta Stone
Written in hieroglyphic, demotic (cursive ancient Egyptian script used for everyday use) and Greek, the 762kg stone contains a decree exempting priests from tax on the first anniversary of young Ptolemy V's coronation.

Bust of Ramesses the Great
The most impressive sculpture in the Egyptian galleries, this 7.5-tonne bust portrays Ramesses II, scourge of the Israelites in the Book of Exodus, as great benefactor.

us today. Be sure to see both the sculptures and the monumental frieze celebrating the birth of Athena. En route to the West Stairs is a huge bust of **Pharaoh Ramesses II** ❹, just a hint of the large collection of **Egyptian mummies** ❺ upstairs. (The earliest, affectionately called Ginger because of wispy reddish hair, was preserved simply by hot sand.) The Romans introduce visitors to the early Britain galleries via the rich **Mildenhall Treasure** ❻. The Anglo-Saxon **Sutton Hoo Ship Burial** ❼ and the medieval **Lewis Chessmen** ❽ follow.

EATING OPTIONS

» **Court Cafes** At the northern end of the Great Court; takeaway counters with salads and sandwiches; communal tables

» **Gallery Cafe** Slightly out of the way near Room 12; quieter; offers hot dishes

» **Court Restaurant** Upstairs overlooking the former Reading Room; sit-down meals

Lewis Chessmen
The much-loved 78 chess pieces portray faceless pawns, worried-looking queens, bishops with their mitres turned sideways and rooks as 'warders', gnawing away at their shields.

Egyptian Mummies
Among the rich collection of mummies and funerary objects is 'Ginger', who was buried at the site of Gebelein, in Upper Egypt, more than 5000 years ago, and Katebet, a one-time chantress (ritual performer) at the Amun temple in Karnak.

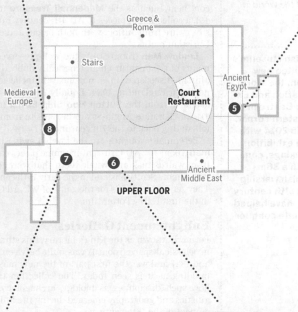

Greece & Rome

Stairs

Medieval Europe

Ancient Egypt

Court Restaurant

❺

❽

❼

❻

Ancient Middle East

UPPER FLOOR

Sutton Hoo Ship Burial
This unique grave of an important (but unidentified) Anglo-Saxon royal has yielded drinking horns, gold buckles and a stunning helmet with face mask.

Mildenhall Treasure
Roman gods such as Neptune and Bacchus share space with early Christian symbols like the *chi-rho* (short for 'Christ') on the find's three dozen silver bowls, plates and spoons.

A HISTORY OF THE WORLD IN 100 OBJECTS

In 2010, the British Museum launched an outstanding radio series on BBC Radio 4 called *A History of the World in 100 Objects*. The series, presented by British Museum director Neil MacGregor, retraces two million years of history through 100 objects from the museum's collections. Each object is described in a 15-minute program, its relevance and significance analysed. Podcasts of the series are available from www.bbc.co.uk/podcasts/series/ahow. Neil MacGregor also wrote a book on the topic, *A History of the World in 100 Objects*.

The British Museum's long-awaited new extension, the World Conservation and Exhibitions Centre in its northwestern corner, opened in 2014 with a special exhibition on the Vikings, complete with a 36m-long Danish warship from the 11th century that may have helped King Canute conquer the seas.

Ancient Egypt, Middle East & Greece

The star of the show here is the Ancient Egypt collection. It comprises sculptures, fine jewellery, papyrus texts, coffins and mummies, including the beautiful and intriguing **Mummy of Katebet** (room 63). The most prized item in the collection (and the most popular postcard in the shop) is the **Rosetta Stone** (room 4), the key to deciphering Egyptian hieroglyphics. In the same gallery is the enormous bust of the pharaoh **Ramesses the Great** (room 4).

Assyrian treasures from ancient Mesopotamia include the 16-tonne **Winged Bulls from Khorsabad** (room 10), the heaviest object in the museum. Behind it are the exquisite **Lion Hunt Reliefs from Ninevah** (room 10) from the 7th century BC, which influenced Greek sculpture. Such antiquities are all the more significant after the Islamic State's bulldozing of Nimrud in 2015.

A major highlight of the museum is the **Parthenon sculptures** (room 18). The marble frieze is thought to be the Great Panathenaea, a blow-out version of an annual festival in honour of Athena.

Roman & Medieval Britain

Upstairs are finds from Britain and the rest of Europe (rooms 40 to 51). Many go back to Roman times, when the empire spread across much of the continent, such as the **Mildenhall Treasure** (room 49), a collection of pieces of AD 4th-century Roman silverware from Suffolk with both pagan and early-Christian motifs.

Lindow Man (room 50) is the well-preserved remains of a 1st-century man (comically dubbed Pete Marsh) discovered in a bog near Manchester in northern England in 1984. Equally fascinating are artefacts from the **Sutton Hoo Ship-Burial** (room 41), an elaborate Anglo-Saxon burial site from Suffolk dating back to the 7th century.

Perennial favourites are the lovely **Lewis Chessmen** (room 40), AD 12th-century game pieces carved from walrus tusk and whale teeth that were found on a remote Scottish island in the early 19th century. They served as models for the game of Wizard Chess in the first Harry Potter film.

Enlightenment Galleries

Formerly known as the King's Library, this stunning neoclassical space (room 1) was built between 1823 and 1827 and was the first part of the new museum building as it is seen today. The collection traces how such disciplines as biology, archaeology, linguistics and geography emerged during the Enlightenment of the 18th century.

TOP SIGHT
BUCKINGHAM PALACE

Built in 1705 as Buckingham House for the duke of the same name and then purchased by George III, the palace has been the Royal Family's London lodgings only since 1837, when Queen Victoria moved in from her childhood home at Kensington Palace. St James's Palace was judged too old-fashioned and insufficiently impressive, although Buckingham Palace underwent a number of modifications until it was deemed fit.

The palace's first resident is commemorated in great pomp outside with the 25m-high **Queen Victoria Memorial** (Map p416; Queen's Gardens; ⊖St James's Park) by Thomas Brock on a spot where Marble Arch once stood. The memorial was dedicated by her grandson George V in 1911 and got a nose job for the Royal Wedding a century later. Commoners can now get a peek of the State Rooms, a mere 19 of the palace's 775 rooms, and only during August and September, when Her Majesty is holidaying in Scotland. The Queen's Gallery is open year-round, and the Royal Mews from April to December.

State Rooms

The tour starts in the **Grand Hall** at the foot of the monumental **Grand Staircase**, commissioned by George IV in 1828. It takes in John Nash's Italianate **Green Drawing Room**, the **State Dining Room** (all red damask and Regency furnishings), the **Blue Drawing Room** (which has a gorgeous fluted ceiling by Nash) and the **White Drawing Room**, where foreign ambassadors are received.

The **Ballroom**, where official receptions and state banquets are held, was built between 1853 and 1855 and opened with a ball a year later to celebrate the end of the Crimean War.

DON'T MISS...

➡ Picture Gallery
➡ Royal Mews
➡ Palace Gardens
➡ Changing of the Guard
➡ Queen's Gallery
➡ Throne Room

PRACTICALITIES

➡ Map p416, A4
➡ ☎020-7766 7300
➡ www.royalcollection.org.uk
➡ Buckingham Palace Rd, SW1
➡ adult/child £20.50/11.80
➡ ⏰9.30am-7.30pm late Jul–Aug, to 6.30pm Sep
➡ ⊖St James's Park, Victoria, Green Park

CHANGING OF THE GUARD

At 11.30am daily from April to July, and on alternate days, weather permitting, from August to March, the old guard (Foot Guards of the Household Regiment) comes off duty to be replaced by the new guard on the forecourt of Buckingham Palace. Crowds come to watch the carefully choreographed marching and shouting of the guards in their bright red uniforms and bearskin hats. It lasts about 40 minutes and is very popular, so arrive early if you want to get a good spot.

At the centre of Royal Family life is the Music Room, where four royal babies have been christened – the Prince of Wales (Prince Charles), the Princess Royal (Princess Anne), the Duke of York (Prince Andrew) and the Duke of Cambridge (Prince William) – with water brought from the River Jordan.

The **Throne Room** is rather anticlimactic, with his-and-hers pink chairs initialled 'ER' and 'P', sitting under a curtained theatre arch.

Picture Gallery & Gardens

The most interesting part of the tour is the 47m-long **Picture Gallery**, featuring splendid works by such artists as Van Dyck, Rembrandt, Canaletto, Poussin, Claude Lorrain, Rubens, Canova and Vermeer.

Wandering the 18 hectares of **gardens** is another highlight – as well as admiring some of the 350 or so species of flowers and plants and listening to the many birds, you'll get beautiful views of the palace and a peek of its famous lake.

Queen's Gallery

Since the reign of Charles I, the Royal Family has amassed a priceless collection of paintings, sculpture, ceramics, furniture and jewellery. The splendid **Queen's Gallery** (Map p416; www.royalcollection.org. uk; Southern wing, Buckingham Palace, Buckingham Gate, SW1; adult/child £10/5.20, with Royal Mews £17.10/9.60; ⊙10am-5.30pm; ⊜St James's Park, Victoria, Green Park) showcases some of the palace's treasures on a rotating basis.

The gallery was originally designed as a conservatory by John Nash. It was converted into a chapel for Queen Victoria in 1843, destroyed in a 1940 air raid and reopened as a gallery in 1962. A £20-million renovation for Elizabeth II's Golden Jubilee in 2002 added three times as much display space.

Royal Mews

Southwest of the palace, the **Royal Mews** (Map p416; www.royalcollection.org.uk; Buckingham Palace Rd, SW1; adult/child £9/5.40, with Queen's Gallery £17.10/9.60; ⊙10am-5pm daily Apr-Oct, to 4pm Mon-Sat Nov & Dec; ⊜Victoria) started life as a falconry but is now a working stable looking after the royals' three dozen immaculately groomed horses, along with the opulent vehicles – motorised and horse-driven – the monarch uses for transport. The Queen is well known for her passion for horses; she names every horse that resides at the mews and still rides every weekend. Nash's 1820 stables are stunning.

Highlights for visitors include the enormous and opulent Gold State Coach of 1762, which has been used for every coronation since that of George III; the 1911 Glass Coach used for royal weddings and the Diamond Jubilee in 2012; Queen Alexandra's State Coach (1893), used to transport the Imperial State Crown to the official opening of Parliament, and a Rolls-Royce Phantom VI from the royal fleet.

⊙ TOP SIGHT
HOUSES OF PARLIAMENT

Both the House of Commons and the House of Lords sit in the sumptuous Palace of Westminster, a neo-Gothic confection dating from the mid-19th century. The House of Commons is where Members of Parliament (MPs) meet to propose and discuss new legislation and to grill the prime minister and other ministers. The House of Lords contains Lords Spiritual, linked with the established church, and Lords Temporal, who are both appointed and hereditary.

When Parliament is in session, visitors are welcome to attend the debates in the House of Commons and the House of Lords. Enter via Cromwell Green Entrance. It's not unusual to have to wait up to two hours to access the chambers (but waiting times have improved). The best time to watch a debate is during Prime Minister's Question Time at noon on Wednesday, but it's also the busiest.

Towers

The most famous feature of the Houses of Parliament is the Clock Tower, officially named Elizabeth Tower to mark the Queen's Diamond Jubilee in 2012 but commonly known as **Big Ben**. Big Ben is actually the 13.5-tonne bell hanging inside and is named after Benjamin Hall, the over 6ft-tall first Commissioner of Works when the tower was completed in 1858. At the base of the taller **Victoria Tower** at the southern end is the Sovereign's Entrance, which is used by the Queen.

Westminster Hall

One of the most stunning features of the Palace of Westminster, seat of the English monarchy from the 11th to the early 16th centuries, is Westminster Hall. Originally built in 1099, it is the oldest surviving part of the complex; the awesome hammerbeam roof was added around 1400. It has been described as 'the greatest surviving achievement of medieval English carpentry'. The only other part of the original palace to survive a devastating 1834 fire

DON'T MISS...
→ Westminster Hall's hammer-beam roof
→ Palace's Gothic Revival interior
→ Big Ben striking the hours
→ Sovereign's Entrance
→ Jewel Tower

PRACTICALITIES
→ Map p416, E4
→ www.parliament.uk
→ Parliament Sq, SW1
→ admission free
→ ⊚Westminster

DEBATES

To find out what's being debated on a particular day, check the notice board beside the entrance, or check online at www.parliament.uk. The debating style in the Commons is quite combative, but not all debates are flamboyant argumentative duelling matches. In fact, many are rather boring and long-winded, although they are an essential feature of British democracy.

Astonishingly, until 2015 the Houses of Parliament was home to the Palace of Westminster Rifle Club, a shooting range. The club was open to club members from Mondays to Thursdays when the House of Commons was sitting. Before 1997, handguns could be discharged, but this was changed to only permit the use of .22 calibre rifles.

is the **Jewel Tower** (Map p416; ☑020-7222 2219; www. english-heritage.org.uk/daysout/properties/jewel-tower; Abingdon St, St James's Park, SW1; adult/child £4/2.40; ⊙10am-5pm daily Apr-Oct, 10am-4pm Sat & Sun Nov-Mar; ⊜Westminster), built in 1365 and used to store the monarch's valuables.

Westminster Hall was used for coronation banquets in medieval times, and also served as a courthouse until the 19th century. The trials of William Wallace (1305), Thomas More (1535), Guy Fawkes (1606) and Charles I (1649) all took place here. In the 20th century, monarchs and Sir Winston Churchill lay in state here after their deaths.

House of Commons

The layout of the **Commons Chamber** (Map p416; www. parliament.uk/business/commons; Parliament Sq, SW1; ⊙2.30-10pm Mon & Tue, 11.30am-7.30pm Wed, 10.30am-6.30pm Thu, 9.30am-3pm Fri; ⊜Westminster) is based on St Stephen's Chapel in the original Palace of Westminster. The chamber, designed by Giles Gilbert Scott, replaced the one destroyed by a 1941 bomb.

Although the Commons is a national assembly of 650 MPs, the chamber has seating for only 437. Government members sit to the right of the Speaker and Opposition members to the left.

House of Lords

The **House of Lords** (Map p416; www.parliament.uk/business/lords; Parliament Sq, SW1; ⊙2.30-10pm Mon & Tue, 3-10pm Wed, 11am-7.30pm Thu, 10am-close of session Fri; ⊜Westminster) is visited via the amusingly named Strangers' Gallery. The intricate Gothic Revival interior led its poor architect, Pugin (1812–52), to an early death from overwork and nervous strain.

Most of the 780-odd members of the House of Lords are life peers (appointed for their lifetime by the monarch); there is also a small number – 92 at the time of research – of hereditary peers and a group of 'crossbench' members (numbering 179, not affiliated to the main political parties), and 26 bishops.

Tours

On Saturdays year-round and on most weekdays during Parliamentary recesses, including Easter, summer and Christmas, visitors can join a 90-minute **guided tour** (Map p416; ☑020-7219 4114; www.parliament.uk/guided-tours; Parliament Sq, SW1; adult/child £25/10), conducted by qualified Blue Badge Tourist Guides in seven languages, of both chambers, Westminster Hall and other historic buildings. Afternoon Tea in the Terrace Pavilion overlooking the River Thames is a popular add-on to the tours. Tour schedules change with every recess and are occasionally subject to variation or cancellation due to the State Opening of Parliament and other Parliamentary business, so check ahead and book.

TOP SIGHT
NATIONAL GALLERY

With some 2300 European paintings on display, this is one of the world's richest art collections, with seminal paintings from every important epoch in the history of art — from the mid-13th to the early 20th century, including works by Leonardo da Vinci, Michelangelo, Titian, Van Gogh and Renoir.

The modern Sainsbury Wing on the gallery's western side houses paintings from 1250 to 1500. Here you will find largely religious paintings commissioned for private devotion (eg the *Wilton Diptych*), as well more unusual masterpieces such as Botticelli's *Venus and Mars* and Van Eyck's *Arnolfini Portrait*. Leonardo Da Vinci's *Virgin of the Rocks*, in room 57, is a stunning masterpiece.

Works from the High Renaissance (1500–1600) embellish the West Wing where Michelangelo, Titian, Raphael, Correggio, El Greco and Bronzino hold court; Rubens, Rembrandt and Caravaggio grace the North Wing (1600–1700). Notable are two self-portraits of Rembrandt (age 34 and 63) and the beautiful *Rokeby Venus* by Velázquez.

Many visitors flock to the East Wing (1700–1900), where works by 18th-century British artists such as Gainsborough, Constable and Turner, and seminal Impressionist and post-Impressionist masterpieces by Van Gogh, Renoir and Monet await. Don't, however, overlook the astonishing floor mosaics in the main vestibule inside the entrance to the National Gallery.

The comprehensive audio guides (£4) are highly recommended, as are the free one-hour taster tours that leave from the information desk in the Sainsbury Wing daily at 11.30am and 2.30pm, and at 7pm Friday. There are also special trails and activity sheets for children.

The National Dining Rooms (p116) have high-quality British food, an all-day bakery and splendid afternoon teas.

DON'T MISS...

➡ *Venus and Mars* by Botticelli
➡ *Virgin of the Rocks* by Leonardo da Vinci
➡ *Wilton Diptych*
➡ *Rokeby Venus* by Velázquez

PRACTICALITIES

➡ Map p406, B7
➡ www.nationalgallery.org.uk
➡ Trafalgar Sq, WC2
➡ admission free
➡ ⊙10am-6pm Sat-Thu, to 9pm Fri
➡ ⊖Charing Cross

1. *Sunflowers* by Van Gogh 2. *Venus and Mars* by Botticelli
3. *Hay Wain* by Constable 4. *Fighting Temeraire* by Turner

National Gallery Masterpieces

The National Gallery's collection spans seven centuries of European painting in a whirl of 2000-odd tableaux displayed in sumptuous, airy galleries. All are masterpieces, but some stand out for their iconic beauty and brilliance.

Venus and Mars, Botticelli

Venus, goddess of love, upright and alert, stares intently at Mars, god of war, fast asleep after they've made love. The message: make love not war because love conquers all.

Sunflowers, Van Gogh

This instantly recognisable masterpiece, one of four by the great Dutch Post-Impressionist, depicts 14 sunflowers at different stages of life. The main colour – yellow – is applied thickly, a bold new 'sculptural' approach to painting.

Rockeby Venus, Velázquez

A rare subject during the Spanish Inquisition, a self-absorbed Venus is gazing at herself – and us – in a mirror held by her son Cupid.

Arnolfini Portrait, Van Eyck

This is history's first bourgeois portrait, an early example of the use of oils and a revolutionary way to create space by painting light. It shows a rich Bruges merchant and his wife, who, despite looking pregnant, is actually making a fashion statement.

Hay Wain, Constable

A horse-drawn wagon in the middle of a river is a romantic portrayal of England on the eve of the Industrial Revolution. Flecks of white paint (`Constable snow') reflect and create movement – a foretaste of Impressionism.

Fighting Temeraire, Turner

Painted by Turner in his 60s, this magnificent painting shows the sailing ship *Temeraire*, a hero of Trafalgar, being towed to a ship-breaking yard in Rotherhithe. The sun goes down, the moon comes up; her world is ending and the age of steam and industrialisation approaches.

TOP SIGHT
TATE BRITAIN

Splendidly refurbished with a stunning new art-deco inspired staircase and a rehung collection, the more elderly and venerable of the two Tate siblings – in a riverside Portland stone edifice – celebrates British paintings from 1500 to the present, with works from Blake, Hogarth, Gainsborough, Barbara Hepworth, Whistler, Constable and Turner, as well as vibrant modern and contemporary pieces from Lucian Freud, Francis Bacon, Henry Moore and Tracey Emin.

The star of the show at Tate Britain is, however, the light infused visions of JMW Turner. After he died in 1851, his estate was settled by a decree declaring that whatever had been found in his studio – 300 oil paintings and about 30,000 sketches and drawings – would be bequeathed to the nation. The collection at Tate Britain constitutes a grand and sweeping celebration of his work, including classics like *The Scarlet Sunset* and *Norham Castle, Sunrise*.

There are also seminal works from Constable, Gainsborough and Reynolds, as well as the pre-Raphaelites, including William Holman Hunt's *The Awakening Conscience*, John William Waterhouse's *The Lady of Shalott*, *Ophelia* by John Everett Millais and Edward Burne-Jones' *The Golden Stairs*. Look out also for Francis Bacon's *Three Studies for Figures at the Base of a Crucifixion*. Tate Britain hosts the prestigious and often controversial Turner Prize for contemporary art from October to early December every year.

Among several tours and talks are free 45-minute **thematic tours** (⊙11am, noon, 2pm & 3pm) and free 15-minute **Art in Focus** (⊙1.15pm Tue, Thu & Sat) talks on specific works. Audio guides (£3.50) are also available.

DON'T MISS...

➡ *The Scarlet Sunset* by JMW Turner

➡ *Three Studies for Figures at the Base of a Crucifixion* by Francis Bacon

➡ *Ophelia* by John Everett Millais

➡ *The Awakening Conscience* by William Holman Hunt

PRACTICALITIES

➡ Map p416, E7

➡ www.tate.org.uk

➡ Millbank, SW1

➡ admission free

➡ ⊙10am-6pm, to 10pm 1st Fri of month

➡ ⊜Pimlico

TOP SIGHT
NATIONAL PORTRAIT GALLERY

What makes the National Portrait Gallery, the only such museum in Europe, so compelling is its familiarity; in many cases you'll have heard of the subject (royals, scientists, politicians, celebrities) or the artist (Andy Warhol, Annie Leibovitz, Sam Taylor-Wood).

The collection is organised chronologically (starting with the early Tudors on the 2nd floor), and then by theme. A highlight is the famous 'Chandos portrait' of William Shakespeare, the first artwork the gallery acquired (in 1856); believed to be the only one to have been painted during the playwright's lifetime. Other highlights include the 'Ditchley' portrait of Queen Elizabeth I displaying her might by standing on a map of England, and a touching sketch of novelist Jane Austen by her sister.

The 1st-floor portraits illustrate the rise and fall of the British Empire through the Victorian era and the 20th century. Don't miss the high-kitsch statue of Victoria and Albert in Anglo-Saxon dress in room 21.

The ground floor is dedicated to modern figures and celebrities, employing various media, including sculpture, photography and video. Among the most popular are the iconic Blur portraits by Julian Opie and Sam Taylor-Wood's *David*, a (low-res by today's standards) video-portrait of David Beckham asleep after football training. Don't miss *Self* by Mark Quinn, a frozen, refrigerated sculpture of the artist's head, made from 4.5l of his own blood and recast every five years.

The excellent audio guide (£3; ID required) highlights 200 portraits and allows you to hear the voices of some of the subjects. The Portrait (p116) restaurant has superb views towards Westminster and does wonderful food.

DON'T MISS...

➜ *Self* by Mark Quinn

➜ Shakespeare 'Chandos' portrait attributed to John Taylor

➜ *Jane Austen* by Cassandra Austen

➜ *Queen Elizabeth I* by Marcus Gheeraerts the Younger

PRACTICALITIES

➜ Map p406, B6

➜ www.npg.org.uk

➜ St Martin's Pl, WC2

➜ admission free

➜ ⏱10am-6pm Sat-Wed, to 9pm Thu & Fri

➜ ⊖Charing Cross, Leicester Sq

⊙ TOP SIGHT
TRAFALGAR SQUARE

In many ways Trafalgar Sq is the centre of London, where tens of thousands congregate for anything from communal open-air cinema and Christmas and New Year celebrations to political protests.

The great square was neglected over many years, ringed with traffic and given over to flocks of feral pigeons fed by tourists and locals alike. In 2000, a scheme was launched to transform the square into the kind of space John Nash had intended when he designed it in the early 19th century. Traffic was banished from the northern flank in front of the National Gallery and a new pedestrian plaza built, making way for cohorts of living statues, 'levitating' Yodas and other street artistes.

DON'T MISS...
→ Nelson's Column
→ Bronze lions
→ Fourth Plinth
→ Admiralty Arch

PRACTICALITIES
→ Map p406, B7
→ ⊜ Charing Cross

Square
The square commemorates the 1805 victory of the British navy at the Battle of Trafalgar against the French and Spanish navies during the Napoleonic wars. The main square contains two beautiful fountains, which are dramatically lit at night. At each corner of the square is a plinth, three topped with statues of military leaders and the fourth, in the northeast corner, now an ubiquitous art space called the Fourth Plinth (p105).

Note the much overlooked, if not entirely ignored, 19th century brass plaques recording the precise length of imperial units – including the yard, the perch, pole, chain and link – set into the stonework and steps below the National Gallery.

Nelson's Column
Standing in the centre of the square since 1843, the 52m-high Dartmoor granite Nelson's Column honours Admiral Lord Horatio Nelson, who led the fleet's heroic victory over Napoleon. The good (sandstone) admiral gazes down Whitehall towards the Houses of Parliament, his column flanked by four enormous bronze statues of lions sculpted by Sir Edwin Landseer and only added in 1867. The battle plaques at the base of the column were cast with seized Spanish and French cannons. Adolf Hitler planned to move the column, along with the admiral, to Berlin in the event of a successful Nazi invasion of Great Britain!

Buildings Around Trafalgar Square
The splendid buildings ringing the square are, clockwise from 12 o'clock (north): National Gallery (and National Portrait Gallery behind it); St Martin-in-the-Fields; and three commissions – South Africa House, Malaysia House and Canada House, designed by Robert Smirke in 1827. If you look southwest down Whitehall, past the equestrian statue of Charles I (which gazes to the point where he was beheaded at Banqueting House in Whitehall), you'll also get a glimpse of Big Ben at the Houses of Parliament.

Admiralty Arch
To the southwest of Trafalgar Sq stands Admiralty Arch, from where the ceremonial Mall leads to Buckingham Palace. It is a grand Edwardian monument, a triple-arched stone entrance designed by Aston Webb in honour of Queen Victoria in 1910 and earmarked for transformation into a five-star hotel. The large central gate is opened only for royal processions and state visits. About 2m up the wall of the northernmost (right) arch is a curious porcelain nose. Urban myth attributes it to the Duke of Wellington and guards would stroke it for luck as they rode by (but it's more likely to be the work of artist Rick Buckley, from 1997).

DAVID BANK / GETTY IMAGES ©

TOP SIGHT
CHURCHILL WAR ROOMS

In late August 1939, with war seemingly imminent, the British cabinet and chiefs of the armed forces decided to move underground into a converted basement below what is now the Treasury. On 3 September Britain was at war.

The bunker served as nerve centre of the war cabinet until the end of WWII in 1945: here chiefs of staff ate, slept and plotted Hitler's downfall, believing they were protected from Luftwaffe bombs (it turns out the 3m slab of cement above them would have crumpled had the area taken a direct hit).

Cabinet War Rooms

The Cabinet War Rooms have been left much as they were on 15 August 1945. Many rooms have been preserved, including the room where the War Cabinet met 115 times; the **Transatlantic Telegraph Room**, with a hotline to President Roosevelt; the converted broom cupboard that was **Churchill's office-bedroom** (though he slept here only three times), and the all-important **Map Room**, which was the operational centre.

The free audio guide is very informative and entertaining and features plenty of anecdotes, including some from people who worked here in the war.

Churchill Museum

This superb multimedia museum doesn't shy away from its hero's foibles – it portrays the heavy-drinking Churchill as having a legendary temper, being a bit of a maverick and, on the whole, a pretty lousy peace-time politician. It does focus on his strongest suit: his stirring speeches. Churchill's orations are replayed for each goose-bumped visitor who steps in front of the interactive displays.

DON'T MISS...
- → Map Room
- → Anecdotes from former War Rooms staff
- → Extracts from Churchill's famous speeches
- → Churchill's office-bedroom

PRACTICALITIES
- → Map p416, D3
- → www.iwm.org.uk
- → Clive Steps, King Charles St, SW1
- → adult/child £18/9
- → ⊘9.30am-6pm, last entry 5pm
- → ⊜Westminster

TOP SIGHT
SIR JOHN SOANE'S MUSEUM

This little museum is one of the most atmospheric and fascinating in London. The building is the bewitching home of architect Sir John Soane (1753–1837), which he left brimming with surprising personal effects and curiosities, and the museum represents his exquisite and eccentric taste.

Soane was a country bricklayer's son, most famous for designing the Bank of England. In his work and life, he drew on ideas picked up while on an 18th-century grand tour of Italy. He married a rich woman and used the wealth to build this house and the one next door at No 12, which now serves as an exhibition and education space. The 2nd floor of No 13, including Soane's private apartment and model room, has been recently restored.

The heritage-listed house is largely as it was when Soane died and is itself a big part of the attraction. It has a canopy dome that brings light right down to the crypt, a colonnade filled with statuary and a picture gallery where paintings are stowed behind each other on folding wooden panes. This is where Soane's choicest artwork is displayed, including *Riva degli Schiavoni, looking West*, by Canaletto, architectural drawings by Christopher Wren and Robert Adam, and the original *Rake's Progress,* William Hogarth's set of satirical cartoons of late-18th-century London low-life. Among Soane's more unusual acquisitions are an Egyptian hieroglyphic sarcophagus, a mock-up of a monk's cell and slaves' chains.

Mobile phones must be switched off and photography is not allowed. Tours (£10) depart at 11.30am Tuesday and Friday, at 3.30pm Wednesday and Thursday, and at 11am Saturday. The evening of the first Tuesday of each month, when the house is lit by candles, is very popular and sees long queues.

DON'T MISS...

➜ *Rake's Progress* by William Hogarth
➜ Sarcophagus of King Seti I
➜ *Riva degli Schiavoni, looking West* by Canaletto
➜ Candlelit tours

PRACTICALITIES

➜ Map p406, E2
➜ www.soane.org
➜ 13 Lincoln's Inn Fields, WC2
➜ admission free
➜ ⊙10am-5pm Tue-Sat & 6-9pm 1st Tue of month
➜ ⊖Holborn

◉ SIGHTS

The West End is a vague term – any Londoner you meet will give you their own take on which neighbourhoods it does and doesn't include – but what is striking is its variety: from reverentially quiet in Bloomsbury and Holborn, to bustling with revellers and shoppers 24/7 in Soho, Piccadilly Circus and Oxford St. The best way to get to know the West End is on foot. Most sights are within walking distance of one another, and you'll get a much better sense of the area's atmosphere that way.

◉ Westminster

WESTMINSTER ABBEY CHURCH
See p78.

HOUSES OF PARLIAMENT HISTORIC BUILDING
See p87.

CHURCHILL WAR ROOMS MUSEUM
See p95.

SUPREME COURT LANDMARK
Map p416 (☎020-7960 1900/1500; www.supreme court.uk; Parliament Sq, SW1; ⊗9.30am-4.30pm Mon-Fri; ⊖Westminster) **FREE** The Supreme Court, the highest court in the UK, was the Appellate Committee of the House of Lords until 2009. It is now housed in the neo-Gothic Middlesex Guildhall (1913), and members of the public are welcome to observe cases when the court is sitting (Monday to Thursday).

For who or what's on trial, ask for a list at reception, or go to the Current Cases page of the court's website. On the lower ground floor there's a permanent exhibition looking at the work and history of the UK's highest court as well as the building's history. The self-guided tour booklet is £1; tours are also available on Fridays (£5; 11am, 2pm and 3pm).

WESTMINSTER CATHEDRAL CHURCH
Map p416 (www.westminstercathedral.org.uk; Victoria St, SW1; tower adult/child £6/3; ⊗9.30am-5pm Mon-Fri, to 6pm Sat & Sun; ⊖Victoria) With its distinctive candy-striped red-brick and white-stone tower features, John Francis Bentley's 19th-century cathedral, the mother church of Roman Catholicism in England and Wales, is a splendid example of neo-Byzantine architecture. Although construction started here in 1896 and worshippers began attending services seven years later,

the church ran out of money and the gaunt interior remains largely unfinished.

The application of colour is a painfully slow process. The **Chapel of the Blessed Sacrament** and elsewhere are ablaze with Eastern Roman mosaics and ornamented with 100 types of marble; the arched ceiling of the **Lady Chapel** is also richly presented, while other areas of the church remain just bare brick.

The highly regarded stone bas-reliefs of the **Stations of the Cross** (1918) by Eric Gill and the marvellously sombre atmosphere make this a welcome haven from the traffic outside. The views from the 83m-tall **bell tower** – thankfully, accessible by lift – are impressive. The **Treasures of the Cathedral exhibition** is rewarding and there's a cafe near the Baptistry. Several masses are said daily (including one in Latin, and one with singing from the Cathedral's Choir); check the website for the full schedule.

ST JOHN'S, SMITH SQUARE CHURCH
Map p416 (☎020-7222 2168; www.sjss.org.uk; Smith Sq, Westminster, SW1; ⊖Westminster, St James's Park) In the heart of Westminster, this eye-catching church was built by Thomas Archer in 1728 under Queen Anne's Fifty New Churches Act (1711), which aimed to build that many new churches for London's rapidly growing metropolitan area. After receiving a direct hit during WWII, it was rebuilt in the 1960s as a classical music venue, and is renowned for its excellent acoustics.

LOCAL KNOWLEDGE

THE HOUSES OF PARLIAMENT

Joanna Freeman is an in-house guide at the Houses of Parliament. We caught up with her to pose some questions:

What is your favourite part of the Houses of Parliament, and why?
Westminster Hall, especially early in the morning or late in the evening when fewer people are around. To walk in a space where incredible episodes in history have taken place and still do, as well as following in the footsteps of the famous and infamous, for example the diarist Samuel Pepys, who was a frequent visitor, and Nelson Mandela who addressed both Houses from the steps, fills me with an enormous sense of the continuity of existence.

Any fascinating facts associated with the Palace of Westminster?
Before the Queen travels to Parliament from Buckingham Palace, certain traditional precautions are observed. A detachment of The Queen's Body Guard of the Yeomen of the Guard searches the cellars of the Houses of Parliament. This tradition dates back to the Gunpowder Plot of 1605, when Guy Fawkes was arrested whilst preparing to blow up Parliament. Today, the Yeomen of the Guard continue this historic search, in addition to the security checks by police.

Another tradition is the 'hostage' MP, a Government whip who is held at Buckingham Palace to guarantee the safe return of the monarch. The custom dates back to centuries when the monarch and Parliament were on less cordial terms.

Once these precautions have been taken, the Queen travels from Buckingham Palace in a State coach to the Palace of Westminster, usually accompanied by The Duke of Edinburgh.

Spencer Perceval, the only Prime Minister to be assassinated, was shot dead near the entrance to the former House of Commons Chamber by businessman John Bellingham, on 11 May 1812.

Any legends or myths visitors should know of?
It is illegal to die in the Houses of Parliament because the person would be entitled to a State Funeral. Apparently, a law to this effect has yet to be traced but the myth that it exists still persists.

Any events, beyond tours, you can recommend?
Every September the Houses of Parliament participates in the 'Open House' weekend. On the Saturday, Portcullis House, the newest building on the Parliamentary Estate, is opened to the public and visitors can enjoy browsing the contemporary portraiture exhibition on the first floor. On the Sunday, visitors have the opportunity to book a place on a tour of St Mary Undercroft, a little-known medieval gem hidden beneath St Stephen's Hall and not normally open to the public.

Though they never did build all 50 churches, St John's, along with about a dozen others, saw the light of day. Unfortunately, with its four corner towers and monumental facades, the structure was much maligned for the first century of its existence thanks to rumours that Queen Anne likened it to a footstool. Nonetheless, it's generally agreed now that the church is a masterpiece of English baroque. The brickvaulted **Smith Square Cafe & Restaurant** (Map p416; ☎020-7222 2779; http://www.sjss.org.uk/footstool; St John's Smith Square, SW1; mains £12.95-22.95; ☺8.30am-5pm Mon-Fri; ⊖St James's Park or Westminster) in the crypt is a delightful choice for sustenance or a coffee.

⊙ Bloomsbury & Fitzrovia

BRITISH MUSEUM   MUSEUM
See p81.

SQUARES OF BLOOMSBURY   SQUARE
The Bloomsbury Group, they used to say, lived in squares, moved in circles and loved in triangles. **Russell Square** (Map p412; ⊖Russell Square) sits at the very heart of the district. Originally laid out in 1800, a striking facelift a decade ago spruced it up and gave the square a 10m-high fountain. The centre of literary Bloomsbury was **Gordon Square** (Map p412; ⊖Russell Sq, Euston Sq), where some of

the buildings are marked with blue plaques. Lovely **Bedford Square** (Map p412; ⊖Tottenham Court Rd) is the only completely Georgian square still surviving in Bloomsbury.

At various times, Bertrand Russell (No 57), Lytton Strachey (No 51) and Vanessa and Clive Bell, Maynard Keynes and the Woolf family (No 46) lived in Gordon Square, while Strachey, Dora Carrington and Lydia Lopokova (the future wife of Maynard Keynes) all took turns living at No 41.

NEW LONDON ARCHITECTURE   EXHIBITION
Map p412 (☑020-7636 4044; www.newlondonarchitecture.org; Building Centre, 26 Store St, WC1; ⊙9am-6pm Mon-Fri, 10am-5pm Sat; ⊖Goodge St) FREE A large, constantly updated model of the capital highlights planned and new buildings, as well as various neighbourhood regeneration programs. There's an excellent Royal Institute of British Architects bookshop and cafe here too. It's an excellent place to see which way London's architectural development is going, and the frequently changing exhibitions will capture the imagination.

ALL SAINTS   CHURCH
Map p412 (www.allsaintsmargaretstreet.org.uk; 7 Margaret St, W1; ⊙7am-7pm; ⊖Oxford Circus) In 1850, architect William Butterfield fashioned one of the country's most supreme examples of High Victorian Gothic architecture, enclosing an interior of lavish ornamentation, extraordinary nave tiling and sumptuous stained glass. The breathtakingly beautiful church was selected by the head of English Heritage in 2014 as one of the top 10 buildings in the UK that have changed the face of the nation.

CHARLES DICKENS MUSEUM   MUSEUM
Map p412 (www.dickensmuseum.com; 48 Doughty St, WC1; adult/child £8/4; ⊙10am-5pm, last admission 4pm; ⊖Chancery Lane, Russell Sq) A £3.5 million renovation made this museum, located in a handsome four-storey house that was the great Victorian novelist's sole surviving residence in London, bigger and better than ever. A period kitchen in the basement and a nursery in the attic were added, and newly acquired 49 Doughty St increased the exhibition space substantially.

Not that the prolific writer stayed here very long – a mere 2½ years (1837–39) – but this is where his work really flourished: he dashed off *The Pickwick Papers, Nicholas Nickleby* and *Oliver Twist,* despite anxiety over debts, the death of his beloved sister-in-law, Mary Hogarth, and his ever-growing family. The house was saved from demolition and the museum opened in 1925, showcasing the family drawing room (restored to its original condition) and a dozen rooms containing various memorabilia. Audio guides are £3 (or download the free app).

POLLOCK'S TOY MUSEUM   MUSEUM
Map p412 (☑020-7636 3452; www.pollocks toys.com; 1 Scala St, enter from 41 Whitfield St, W1; adult/child £6/3; ⊙10am-5pm Mon-Sat; ⊖Goodge St) Aimed at adults as much as kids, this museum is simultaneously creepy and mesmerising. You walk in through its shop, laden with excellent wooden toys and various games, and start your exploration by climbing up a rickety narrow staircase, where displays begin with mechanical toys, puppets and framed dolls from Latin America, Africa, India and Europe.

Upstairs is the museum's collection of toy theatres, many made by Benjamin Pollock himself, the leading Victorian manufacturer of the popular sets, as well as tin toys, teddy bears and weird-looking dolls in cotton nighties.

PETRIE MUSEUM OF EGYPTIAN ARCHAEOLOGY   MUSEUM
Map p412 (UCL; ☑020-7679 2884; www.ucl.ac.uk/museums/petrie; University College London, Malet Pl, WC1; ⊙1-5pm Tue-Sat; ⊖Goodge St) FREE Counting some 80,000 artefacts, this is one of the most impressive collections of Egyptian and Sudanese archaeology in the world. The old-fashioned dusty displays in glass cases don't really do much to highlight them, though. The museum is named after Professor William Flinders Petrie (1853–1942), who uncovered many of the items during his excavations and donated them to the university in 1933. Torches are available to pierce the gloomier recesses of the collection.

ST GEORGE'S, BLOOMSBURY   CHURCH
Map p412 (☑020-7242 1979; www.stgeorges bloomsbury.org.uk; Bloomsbury Way, WC1; ⊙church 1-4pm daily, service 10.30am Sun; ⊖Holborn, Tottenham Court Rd) Designed by Nicholas Hawksmoor, this superbly restored church (1730) is distinguished by its classical portico of Corinthian capitals and a steeple (visible in William Hogarth's satirical painting *Gin Lane*) inspired by the Mausoleum of Halicarnassus. The statue atop the steeple is of King George I in Roman dress, while lions and unicorns scamper about its

base. Phone ahead, as the church depends on volunteers and may not be open.

Guided tours of the church can be booked at a cost of £5 per person.

BROADCASTING HOUSE   HISTORIC BUILDING

Map p414 (☑0370 901 1227; www.bbc.co.uk/showsandtours; Portland Pl, W1; adult/child £15.00/10.00; ⊙tour days & times vary; ⊖Oxford Circus) The iconic building from which the BBC began radio broadcasting in 1932 and from where all TV and radio broadcasting in London has taken place since early 2013 is open to the public on 1½-hour tours, departing up to nine times per day (but check the website for details).

The tour takes in the huge, state-of-the-art newsroom (where you can have a go at reading the news). You can also produce your own radio play and, on some tours, get a look at the Radio Theatre and also peek behind the scenes at the studios of the various BBC channels. Pre-booking is essential; no children under nine are allowed on the tour.

ALL SOULS CHURCH   CHURCH

Map p414 (☑020-7580 3522; www.allsouls.org; 2 All Souls Pl, off Langham Pl, W1; ⊙9.30am-5.30pm Mon-Fri, 9am-2pm & 5.30-8.30pm Sun; ⊖Oxford Circus) Designed by John Nash in golden-hued Bath stone as an eye-catching monument for Regent Street, All Souls features a circular columned porch and a distinctive needle-like spire, reminiscent of an ancient Greek temple.

⊙ St James's

BUCKINGHAM PALACE   PALACE
See p85.

TATE BRITAIN   GALLERY
See p92.

ST JAMES'S PARK   PARK

Map p416 (www.royalparks.org.uk; The Mall, SW1; deckchairs per hr/day £1.50/7; ⊙5am-midnight, deckchairs daylight hrs Mar-Oct; ⊖St James's Park, Green Park) At just 23 hectares, St James's is one of the smallest but best-groomed of London's royal parks. It has brilliant views of the London Eye, Westminster, St James's Palace, Carlton Tce and the Horse Guards Parade; the sight of Buckingham Palace from the footbridge spanning the central lake is photo-perfect and the best you'll find.

The lake brims with different types of ducks, geese, swans and general fowl, and

the rocks on its southern side serve as a rest stop for a half-dozen pelicans (fed at 2.30pm daily). Some of the technicolour flowerbeds were modeled on John Nash's original 'floriferous' beds of mixed shrubs, flowers and trees. You can rent deckchairs to make lounging around more comfortable.

At the junction of Horse Guards Rd and The Mall stands the **National Police Memorial** (Map p416), one column of marble and another of glass. Conceived by film director Michael Winner (*Death Wish*) and designed by architect Norman Foster and artist Per Arnoldi, it pays tribute to around 4000 policemen and women who have lost their lives in the line of duty. Note also the ivy-choked concrete bastion nearby, the **Admiralty Citadel** (Map p416; Horse Guards Rd, SW1; ⊖Charing Cross), a heavily fortified, bomb-proof command and control fortress built for the Royal Navy in 1941 to prepare for a German invasion. Sitting over a network of tunnels, the building sports 20-foot thick concrete and steel walls (making it impossible to demolish) and a lawn roof to render it invisible from an overhead perspective.

BURLINGTON ARCADE   HISTORIC BUILDING

Map p416 (www.burlington-arcade.co.uk; 51 Piccadilly, W1; ⊙10am-9pm Mon-Fri, 9am-6.30pm Sat, 11am-5pm Sun; ⊖Green Park) Flanking Burlington House, home to the Royal Academy of Arts, is this delightful arcade, built in 1819. Today it is a shopping precinct for the wealthy, and is most famous for the Burlington Berties, uniformed guards who patrol the area keeping an eye out for such offences as running, chewing gum, whistling, opening umbrellas or anything else that could lower the tone.

The fact that the arcade once served as a brothel finds no mention. Running perpendicular to it between Old Bond and Albemarle Sts is the more recent (1880) **Royal Arcade** (Map p416; between 28 Old Bond & 12 Albemarle Sts, W1; ⊖Green Park).

ST JAMES'S PICCADILLY   CHURCH

Map p416 (☑020-7734 4511; www.sjp.org.uk; 197 Piccadilly, W1; ⊙8am-8pm; ⊖Piccadilly Circus) The only church Christopher Wren (1684) built from scratch and one of a few established on a new site (most of the other London churches are replacements for those razed in the Great Fire), this simple building substitutes what some might call the pompous flourishes of Wren's most famous churches with a warm and elegant accessibility. The baptismal font portraying Adam and Eve on the shaft and the altar reredos are by Grinling Gibbons.

This is a particularly sociable church; it houses a counselling service, provides a night shelter for the homeless in the winter months (note the laminex signs saying 'Please do not sleep in this pew'), stages lunchtime and evening concerts, and provides shelter for an antiques market (10.30am to 5pm Tuesday) and an arts and crafts fair (10am to 6pm Wednesday to Saturday) out front. Note the arresting bronze Statue of Peace, in the garden.

ST JAMES'S PALACE   PALACE
Map p416 (www.royal.gov.uk; Cleveland Row, SW1; ⊖Green Park) The striking Tudor gatehouse of St James's Palace, the only surviving part of a building initiated by the palace-mad Henry VIII in 1530, is best approached from St James's St to the north of St James's Park. This was the official residence of kings and queens for more than three centuries and was built on the grounds of a famous leper hospital. The palace is not open to the public, but you can appreciate the architecture from the outside.

Foreign ambassadors are still formally accredited to the Court of St James, although they are actually received at Buckingham Palace. Princess Diana, who hated this place, lived here until her divorce from Charles in 1996, when she moved to Kensington Palace. Prince Charles and his sons stayed on at St James's until 2004, before decamping next door to Clarence House, leaving St James's Palace as the London residence of his sister Anne, the Princess Royal, and nieces the Princesses Beatrix and Eugenie.

CLARENCE HOUSE   PALACE
Map p416 (☑020-7766 7300; www.royalcollection.org.uk/visit/clarence-house; Cleveland Row, SW1; adult/child £9.80/5.80; ⊙10am-4.30pm Mon-Fri & 10am-5.30pm Sat & Sun Aug; ⊖Green Park) Five ground-floor rooms of Clarence House, the official residence of Charles, the Prince of Wales, Camilla, the Duchess of Cornwall, and Prince Harry, are open to the public on guided tour for one month in summer.

The highlight of the 45-minute tour is the late Queen Mother's small art collection, including one painting by playwright Noël Coward and others by WS Sickert and Sir James Gunn. The house was originally designed by John Nash in the early 19th century, but has been modified much since. Book in advance.

TOP SIGHT
ROYAL ACADEMY OF ARTS

Britain's oldest society devoted to fine arts was founded in 1768 and the organisation moved to Burlington House exactly a century later. The collection contains drawings, paintings, architectural designs, photographs and sculptures by past and present Academicians such as Joshua Reynolds, John Constable, Thomas Gainsborough, JMW Turner, David Hockney and Norman Foster. Highlights are displayed in the **John Madejski Fine Rooms** on the 1st floor, which are accessible on **free guided tours** (⊙1pm & 3pm Wed-Fri, 1pm Tue, 11.30am Sat).

The famous **Summer Exhibition** (⊙Jun–mid-Aug), which has showcased contemporary art for sale by unknown as well as established artists for nearly 250 years, is the academy's biggest annual event.

Burlington House's courtyard features a stone-paved piazza with choreographed lights and fountains arranged to display the astrological star chart of Joshua Reynolds, the RA's first president, on the day he was born. His statue stands in the centre. The courtyard is also the venue for temporarily installed statues and outdoor works by contemporary artists. The academy has grown its exhibition space by expanding into 6 Burlington Gardens and is undergoing an ambitious redevelopment through to 2018.

DON'T MISS...
➡ Summer Exhibition
➡ John Madejski Fine Rooms
➡ Forecourt piazza

PRACTICALITIES
➡ Map p416, B1
➡ www.royalacademy.org.uk
➡ Burlington House, Piccadilly, W1
➡ adult/child £10/6, prices vary for exhibitions
➡ ⊙10am-6pm Sat-Thu, to 10pm Fri
➡ ⊖Green Park

SPENCER HOUSE
HISTORIC BUILDING

Map p416 (020-7514 1958; www.spencerhouse. co.uk; 27 St James's Pl, SW1; adult/child £12/10; ☺10am-4.45pm Sun Feb-Jul & Sep-Dec; ☻Green Park) Just outside Green Park is Spencer House, completed in the Palladian style in 1766 for the first Earl Spencer, an ancestor of Princess Diana. The Spencers moved out in 1927 and their grand family home was used as an office, until Lord Rothschild stepped in and returned it to its former glory in 1987 with an £18-million restoration.

Visits to the eight lavishly furnished rooms of the house are by guided tour only. The 18th-century gardens are open only between 2pm and 5pm on a couple of Sundays in summer.

QUEEN'S CHAPEL
CHURCH

Map p416 (Marlborough Rd, SW1; ☺services 8.30am & 11.15am Sun Easter-Jul; ☻Green Park) This small chapel is where contemporary royals such as Princess Diana and the Queen Mother have lain in their coffins in the run-up to their funerals. The church was originally built by Inigo Jones in the Palladian style for the French wife of Charles I and was the first post-Reformation Roman Catholic church erected in England.

The simple interior, illuminated by light streaming through the large windows above the altar, has exquisite 17th-century fittings. It was once part of St James's Palace but was separated after a fire.

GREEN PARK
PARK

Map p416 (www.royalparks.gov.uk; ☺24hr; ☻Green Park) Less manicured than adjoining St James's, 19-hectare Green Park has huge oaks and hilly meadows, and it's never as crowded as its neighbour. It was once a duelling ground and, like Hyde Park, served as a vegetable garden during WWII.

It famously has no flowers beds as they were banned by Queen Catherine of Braganza after she learned her philandering husband Charles II had been picking posies for his mistresses. Or so the story goes (others blame diseased soil from a plague pit beneath the park).

GUARDS MUSEUM
MUSEUM

Map p416 (020-7414 3428; www.theguardsmuseum.com; Wellington Barracks, Birdcage Walk, SW1; adult/child £5/free; ☺10am-4pm; ☻St James's Park) Take stock of the history of the five regiments of foot guards (Grenadier, Coldstream, Scots, Irish and Welsh Guards) and their role in military campaigns from Waterloo onwards at this little museum in Wellington Barracks. There are uniforms, oil paintings, medals, curios and memorabilia that belonged to the soldiers. Perhaps the biggest draw is the huge collection of toy soldiers for sale in the shop.

If you found the crowds at the Changing of the Guards tiresome and didn't see a thing, get here 10.50am on any day from April to July (alternate days the rest of the year) to see the soldiers of the new guard get into formation outside the museum, be inspected 20 minutes later, and depart just before 11.30am for their march over to Buckingham Palace to relieve the old guard.

INSTITUTE OF CONTEMPORARY ARTS
ARTS CENTRE

Map p416 (ICA; 020-7930 9493; www.ica.org. uk; Nash House, The Mall, SW1; ☺11am-11pm Tue-Sun, exhibition times vary; ☏; ☻Charing Cross) FREE Housed in a John Nash building along the Mall, the untraditional ICA is where Picasso and Henry Moore had their first UK shows. Since then, the ICA has been on the cutting (and controversial) edge of the British arts world, with an excellent range of experimental and progressive films, music nights, photography, art, lectures, multimedia works and book readings.

There's also the licensed **ICA Cafe Bar**. The complex includes an excellent bookshop.

FARADAY MUSEUM
MUSEUM

Map p408 (www.rigb.org/visit-us/faraday-museum; 21 Albemarle St, W1; ☺9am-6pm Mon-Fri; ☻Green Park) FREE Buried in the basement of the Royal Institution of Great Britain, this low-key and low-fi, neon-purple-lit museum is a tranquil escape from the bustle at street level. The exhibits themselves commemorate the work of scientist Michael Faraday, including his isolation of benzene, his 'condenser' and glass 'egg'. Learn the Periodic Table by heart using the fun automated wall chart.

☉ Soho & Chinatown

SOHO
NEIGHBOURHOOD

Map p408 (☻Tottenham Court Rd, Leicester Sq) In a district that was once pastureland, the name Soho possibly evolved from a rabbit hunting cry. While the centre of London nightlife has shifted east and Soho has recently seen landmark clubs and music venues shut down in a process of gentrification, the neighbourhood definitely comes into its

ST GILES-IN-THE-FIELDS, A LITANY OF MISERIES

St Giles Church (Map p406; 60 St Giles High St, WC2; ⊙9am-4pm Mon-Fri; ⊜Tottenham Court Rd) Built in what used to be countryside between the City of London and Westminster, St Giles-in-the-Fields isn't much to look at but its history is a chronicle of London's most miserable inhabitants. The current structure (1733) is the third to stand on the site of an original chapel built in the 12th century to serve as a hospital for lepers.

Until 1547, when the hospital closed, prisoners on their way to be executed at Tyburn stopped at the church gate and sipped a large cup of soporific ale – their last refreshment – from St Giles's Bowl. From 1650, the prisoners were buried in the church grounds. It was also within the boundaries of St Giles that the Great Plague of 1665 took hold.

In Victorian times, it was London's worst slum, often mentioned in Dickens' novels. Today the drug users who hang out around the area make it feel like things haven't changed much.

An interesting relic in the church (north side) is the plain white pulpit that was used for 40 years by John Wesley, the founder of Methodism.

own in the evenings and remains a proud gay neighbourhood. During the day you'll be charmed by the area's bohemian side and its sheer vitality.

At Soho's northern end, leafy **Soho Square** (Map p408; ⊜Tottenham Court Rd, Leicester Sq) is the area's back garden. It was laid out in 1681, and originally named King's Sq; a statue of Charles II stands in its northern half. In the centre is a tiny mock-Tudor house – the gardener's shed – whose lift was a passage to underground shelters during WWII.

South of the square is **Dean Street**, lined with bars and restaurants. No 28 was the home of Karl Marx and his family from 1851 to 1856; they lived here in extreme poverty as Marx researched and wrote Das Kapital in the Reading Room of the British Museum. **Old Compton Street** is the epicentre of Soho's gay village. It's a street loved by all, gay or other, for its great bars, risqué shops and general good vibes.

Seducer and heart-breaker Casanova and opium-addicted writer Thomas de Quincey lived on nearby Greek St, while the parallel **Frith Street** housed Mozart at No 20 for a year from 1764.

CHINATOWN
NEIGHBOURHOOD

Map p408 (www.chinatownlondon.org; ⊜Leicester Sq) Immediately north of Leicester Sq – but a world away in atmosphere – are Lisle and Gerrard Sts, a focal point for London's Chinese community. Although not as big as Chinatowns in many other cities – it's just two streets really – this is a lively quarter with fake oriental gates, Chinese street signs, red lanterns, restaurants, great Asian

supermarkets and shops. Do be aware that the quality of food here varies enormously.

To see it at its effervescent best, time your visit for Chinese New Year in late January/early February. London's original Chinatown was further east at Limehouse but moved here after heavy bombardments in WWII.

PICCADILLY CIRCUS
SQUARE

Map p408 (⊜Piccadilly Circus) John Nash had originally designed Regent St and Piccadilly in the 1820s to be the two most elegant streets in town but, curbed by city planners, couldn't realise his dream to the full. He may be disappointed, but suitably astonished, with Piccadilly Circus today: a traffic maelstrom, deluged with visitors and flanked by flashing advertisement panels. A seething hubbub, 'it's like Piccadilly Circus', as the expression goes, but it's certainly fun.

Piccadilly Circus has become a postcard for the city, buzzing with the liveliness that makes it exciting to be in London. 'Piccadilly' was named in the 17th century for the stiff collars (picadils) that were the sartorial staple of the time (and were the making of a nearby tailor's fortune), while 'Circus' comes from the Latin word meaning ring or circle.

At the centre of the circus stands the famous aluminium statue, Anteros, twin brother of Eros, dedicated to the philanthropist and child-labour abolitionist Lord Shaftesbury. The sculpture was at first cast in gold, but was later replaced by newfangled aluminium, the first outdoor statue in that metal. Down the years, the angel has been mistaken for Eros, the God of Love, and the misnomer has stuck (you'll even see signs for 'Eros' from the Underground).

REGENT STREET   STREET

Map p408 (◉Piccadilly Circus, Oxford St) The handsome border dividing the hoi polloi of Soho from the Gucci-two shoed of Mayfair, Regent Street was designed by John Nash as a ceremonial route linking the Prince Regent's long-demolished city dwelling with the 'wilds' of Regent's Park. Nash had to downscale his plan but Regent Street is today a well-subscribed shopping street and a beautiful curve of listed architecture.

Its most famous tenant is undoubtedly Hamleys, London's premier toy and game store. Regent Street is also famous for its Christmas light displays, which get glowing with great pomp earlier and earlier (or so it seems) each year (usually around mid-November). The street is closed to traffic for one day a year during the Regent Street Festival.

PHOTOGRAPHERS' GALLERY   GALLERY

Map p408 (✆020-7087 9300; thephotographersgallery.org.uk; 16-18 Ramillies St, W1; ◷10am-6pm Mon-Wed, Fri & Sat, to 8pm Thu, 11.30am-6pm Sun; ◉Oxford Circus) FREE With seven galleries over three floors, an excellent cafe (weekdays only) and a shop brimming with prints and photography books, the refurbished Photographers' Gallery is London's largest public gallery devoted to photography. It awards the prestigious Deutsche Börse Photography Prize annually, which is of major importance for contemporary photographers; past winners include Richard Billingham, Luc Delahaye, Andreas Gursky, Boris Mikhailov and Juergen Teller.

◉ Covent Garden & Leicester Square

NATIONAL GALLERY   GALLERY

See p89.

NATIONAL PORTRAIT GALLERY   GALLERY

See p93.

TRAFALGAR SQUARE   SQUARE

See p94.

COVENT GARDEN PIAZZA   SQUARE

Map p406 (◉Covent Garden) London's first planned square is now the preserve of visitors, who flock here to shop among the quaint old arcades, browse through eclectic market stalls and shops, cast coins at street performers pretending to be statues and traipse through the fun London Transport Museum (p105).

On the square's west side rises handsome **St Paul's Church** (Map p406; www.actorschurch.org; Bedford St, WC2; ◷8.30am-5pm Mon-Fri, varies Sat, 9am-1pm Sun; ◉Covent Garden), built in 1633. When the Earl of Bedford commissioned Inigo Jones to design the piazza, he asked for a simple church 'not much better than a barn'; the architect responded by producing 'the handsomest barn in England'. It has long been regarded as the actors'

COVENT GARDEN IN A NUTSHELL

Covent Garden was originally pastureland that belonged to a 'convent' associated with Westminster Abbey in the 13th century. The site became the property of John Russell, the first Earl of Bedford, in 1552. His descendants employed the architect Inigo Jones to convert a vegetable field into a square in the 17th century. He built the elegant Italian-style piazza, and its tall terraced houses soon started to draw rich socialites who coveted the central living quarters. The bustling fruit and veg market – immortalised in *My Fair Lady* where it was a flower market – dominated the piazza. London society, including such writers as Pepys, Fielding and Boswell, gathered here in the evenings, looking for some action among the coffee houses, theatres, gambling dens and brothels.

Lawlessness became commonplace, leading to the formation of a volunteer police force known as the Bow Street Runners. In 1897 Oscar Wilde was charged with gross indecency in the now-closed Bow St Magistracy. A flower market designed by Charles Fowler was added at the spot where London's Transport Museum now stands.

During the 1970s, the city traffic made it increasingly difficult to maintain the fruit and veg market so it was moved to Nine Elms in South London in 1974. Property developers loomed over the space and there was even talk of the market being demolished for a road but, thanks to the area's dedicated residential community who demonstrated and picketed for weeks, the piazza was saved.

FOURTH PLINTH

Three of the four plinths at Trafalgar Sq's corners are occupied by notables: King George IV on horseback, and military men General Sir Charles Napier and Major General Sir Henry Havelock. One, originally intended for a statue of William IV, has largely remained vacant for the past 150 years (although some say it is reserved for an effigy of Queen Elizabeth II, on her death). The Royal Society of Arts conceived the unimaginatively titled **Fourth Plinth Project** (Map p406; www.london.gov.uk/fourthplinth) in 1999, deciding to use the empty space for works by contemporary artists. They commissioned three works: *Ecce Homo* by Mark Wallinger (1999), a life-size statue of Jesus, which appeared tiny in contrast to the enormous plinth; Bill Woodrow's *Regardless of History* (2000); and Rachel Whiteread's *Monument* (2001), a resin copy of the plinth, turned upside down.

The Mayor's office has since taken over what's now called the Fourth Plinth Programme, declaring it 'the most talked about contemporary art prize in the UK'. Most recently, the plinth was occupied by Katharina Fritsch's *Hahn/Cock*, a huge, cobalt blue sculpture of a cockerel, itself making way for Hans Haacke's *Gift Horse* depicting a skeletal, riderless horse. Each artwork will be exhibited for 18 months.

church for its associations with all the nearby theatres, and contains memorials to the likes of Charlie Chaplin, Noël Coward, Peter O'Toole and Vivien Leigh. The first Punch and Judy show took place in front of St Paul's in 1662, while Gwen Stefani married Gavin Rossdale inside the church in 2002.

ROYAL OPERA HOUSE HISTORIC BUILDING
Map p406 (📞020-7304 4000; www.roh.org. uk; Bow St, WC2; adult/child general tours £9.50/7.50, backstage tours £12/8.50; ☉general tour 4pm daily, backstage tour 10.30am, 12.30pm & 2.30pm Mon-Fri, 10.30am, 11.30am, 12.30pm & 1.30pm Sat; ⊖Covent Garden) On the northeastern flank of Covent Garden piazza is the gleaming Royal Opera House. The 'Velvet, Gilt & Glamour Tour' is a general 45-minute turn around the auditorium; more distinctive are the 1¼-hour backstage tours taking you through the venue – a much better way to experience the preparation, excitement and histrionics before a performance.

LONDON TRANSPORT MUSEUM MUSEUM
Map p406 (www.ltmuseum.co.uk; Covent Garden Piazza, WC2; adult/child £16/free; ☉10am-6pm Sat-Thu, 11am-6pm Fri; ⊖Covent Garden) This entertaining and informative museum looks at how London developed as a result of better transport and contains everything from horse-drawn omnibuses, early taxis, underground trains you can drive yourself, a forward look at Crossrail (a high-frequency rail service linking Reading with east London, southeast London and Essex, due to open in 2018), plus everything in between. Check out the museum shop for imaginative souvenirs, including historical tube posters and 'Mind the Gap' socks.

LONDON FILM MUSEUM MUSEUM
Map p406 (www.londonfilmmuseum.com; 45 Wellington St, WC2; adult/child £14.50/9.50; ☉10am-5pm; ⊖Covent Garden) Recently moved from County Hall south of the Thames, this museum's star attraction is its signature 'Bond In Motion' exhibition. Get shaken and stirred at the largest official collection of 007 vehicles, including Bond's submersible Lotus Esprit (*The Spy Who Loved Me*), the iconic Aston Martin DB5, Goldfinger's Rolls Royce Phantom III and Timothy Dalton's Aston Martin V8 (*The Living Daylights*).

LEICESTER SQUARE SQUARE
Map p406 (⊖Leicester Sq) Although Leicester Sq was very fashionable in the 19th century, more recent decades won it associations with antisocial behaviour, rampant pickpocketing, outrageous cinema ticket prices and the nickname 'Fester Square' during the 1979 Winter of Discontent strikes, when it was filled with refuse. As part of the Diamond Jubilee and 2012 Olympics celebrations, the square was given an extensive £15.5 million makeover to turn it once again into a lively plaza.

Today a sleek, open-plan design replaces the once-dingy little park. It retains its many cinemas and nightclubs, and as a glamorous premiere venue it still attracts celebrities and their spotters. The much beloved Shakespeare Fountain (1874) has been steam-cleaned and decorated with new water features.

INNS OF COURT

Clustered around Holborn and Fleet St are the Inns of Court, with quiet alleys, open spaces and a serene atmosphere. All London barristers work from within one of the four inns, and a roll-call of former members ranges from Oliver Cromwell and Charles Dickens to Mahatma Gandhi and Margaret Thatcher. It would take a lifetime working here to grasp the intricacies of the protocols of the inns; they're similar to the Freemasons – both are 13th-century creations with centuries of tradition. It's best to just soak in the dreamy atmosphere and relax.

Lincoln's Inn (Map p406; www.lincolnsinn.org.uk; Lincoln's Inn Fields, Newmans Row, WC2; ⊗grounds 7am-7pm Mon-Fri, chapel noon-2.30pm Mon-Fri; ⊜Holborn) The attractive Lincoln's Inn has a chapel, pleasant square and picturesque gardens that invite a stroll, especially early or late in the day. The court itself, although closed to the public, is visible through the gates and is relatively intact, with original 15th-century buildings, including the Tudor Lincoln's Inn Gatehouse on Chancery Lane.

Inigo Jones helped plan the well-preserved chapel, which was built in 1623.

Inner Temple (Map p406; www.innertemple.org.uk; King's Bench Walk, EC4; ⊗grounds 10am-4pm Mon-Fri, gardens 12.30-3pm Mon-Fri; ⊜Temple) Duck under the archway next to Prince Henry's Room (17 Fleet St) and you'll find yourself in the Inner Temple, a sprawling complex of some of the finest buildings on the river, including **Temple Church** (p152).

Middle Temple (Map p406; www.middletemple.org.uk; Middle Temple Lane, EC4; ⊗grounds 10-11.30am & 3-4pm Mon-Fri; ⊜Temple) From the Strand, look for a studded black door labelled 'Middle Temple Lane', opposite the Royal Courts building, and you'll find yourself in the sprawling complex surrounding the Temple Church and the Elizabethan Middle Temple Hall. The church was originally planned and built by the secretive Knights Templar in the mid-12th century; the hall was pieced together bit by bit after being blown to smithereens during WWII. There are wonderful gardens and courtyards at every turn. At the weekend enter from the Victoria Embankment.

Gray's Inn (Map p406; www.graysinn.org.uk; Gray's Inn Rd, WC1; ⊗grounds 10am-4pm Mon-Fri, chapel 10am-6pm Mon-Fri; ⊜Chancery Lane) This inn was destroyed during WWII, rebuilt and expanded; its peaceful gardens are still something of a treat. The walls of the original hall absorbed the first ever performance of Shakespeare's *Comedy of Errors*.

ST MARTIN-IN-THE-FIELDS   CHURCH
Map p406 (☏020-7766 1100; www.stmartin-in-the-fields.org; Trafalgar Sq, WC2; ⊗8.30am-6pm Mon, Tue, Thu & Fri, 8.30am-5pm Wed, 9.30am-6pm Sat, 3.30-5pm Sun; ⊜Charing Cross) The 'royal parish church' is a delightful fusion of classical and baroque styles. It was completed by James Gibbs in 1726 and serves as a model for many churches in New England. The church is well known for its excellent classical music concerts, many by candlelight, and its links to the Chinese community (services in English, Mandarin and Cantonese). It usually closes for one hour at 1pm.

The wonderful **Cafe in the Crypt** hosts jazz evenings at 8pm on Wednesdays; there's brass rubbing in the shop for kids and you can visit the church with an audioguide (£3.50). Refurbishment excavations in the last decade unearthed a 1.5-tonne limestone Roman sarcophagus in the churchyard; the yard also holds the graves of 18th-century artists Joshua Reynolds and William Hogarth.

⊙ Whitehall

NO 10 DOWNING STREET   HISTORIC BUILDING
Map p416 (www.number10.gov.uk; 10 Downing St, SW1; ⊜Westminster) The official office of British leaders since 1732, when George II presented No 10 to Robert Walpole, this has also been the Prime Minister's London residence since refurbishment in 1902. For such a famous address, No 10 is a small-looking building on a plain-looking street, hardly warranting comparison with the White House, for example. Yet it is actually three houses joined into one and boasts roughly 100 rooms plus a garden covering 2000 sqm.

The street was cordoned off with a rather large iron gate during Margaret Thatcher's time, so you won't see much. After an IRA mortar attack in 1991, the stout wooden door was replaced with a blast-proof steel version (which cannot be opened from the outside).

HORSE GUARDS PARADE
HISTORIC SITE

Map p416 (www.changing-the-guard.com/london-programme.html; Horse Guards Parade, off Whitehall, W1; ☺11am Mon-Sat, 10am Sun; ⊜Westminster, St James's Park) In a more accessible version of Buckingham Palace's Changing of the Guard, the mounted troops of the Household Cavalry change guard here daily, at the official vehicular entrance to the royal palaces. A slightly less pompous version takes place at 4pm when the dismounted guards are changed. On the Queen's official birthday in June, the Trooping of the Colour is staged here.

The parade ground and its buildings were built in 1745 to house the Queen's so-called Life Guards. During the reigns of Henry VIII and his daughter Elizabeth, jousting tournaments were staged here.

BANQUETING HOUSE
PALACE

Map p416 (☏020-3166 6155; www.hrp.org.uk/banquetinghouse; Whitehall, SW1; adult/child £6.60/free; ☺10am-5pm; ⊜Westminster) After the Holbein Gate was demolished in 1759, this is the sole surviving part of the Tudor Whitehall Palace (1532) that once stretched most of the way down Whitehall before going skywards in a 1698 conflagration. Designed by Inigo Jones in 1622 and controversially refaced in Portland stone in the 19th century, Banqueting House was England's first purely Renaissance building and resembled no other structure in the country at the time. The English apparently loathed it for over a century.

A bust outside commemorates 30 January 1649, when Charles I, accused of treason by Oliver Cromwell after the Civil War, was executed on a scaffold built against a 1st-floor window here. When the monarchy was reinstated with his son, Charles II, it inevitably became something of a royalist shrine. Look to the clock tower opposite at Horse Guards Parade. The number 2 (the time of the execution) is blacked out. In a huge, virtually unfurnished hall on the 1st floor there are nine ceiling panels painted by Peter Paul Rubens in 1635. They were commissioned by Charles I and celebrate the 'benefits of wise rule' and the Union of England and Scotland Act (1603). Call ahead as Banqueting House occasionally shuts at 1pm for functions and events.

CENOTAPH
MEMORIAL

Map p416 (Whitehall, SW1; ⊜Westminster, Charing Cross) The Cenotaph, completed in 1920 by Edwin Lutyens, is Britain's main memorial to the men and women of Britain and the

TOP SIGHT
SOMERSET HOUSE

Passing beneath the arched entrance before this Palladian masterpiece, it's hard to believe that the magnificent Safra Fountain Court, with its 55 dancing fountains, was a car park until a spectacular refurbishment in 2000. William Chambers designed the house in 1775 – the first purpose-built office block – and it now contains two galleries.

The **Courtauld Gallery** (Map p406; www.courtauld.ac.uk; Somerset House, The Strand, WC2; adult/child Tue-Sun £7/free, temporary exhibitions an additional £1.50 ; ☺10am-6pm; ⊜Charing Cross, Embankment or Temple) is near the Strand entrance, with masterpieces by Rubens, Botticelli, Cézanne, Degas, Renoir, Seurat, Manet, Monet, Leger and others. There are free, 15-minute lunchtime talks on specific works or themes from the collection at 1.15pm every Monday and Friday and sometimes on Wednesday. The **Embankment Galleries** focus on contemporary fashion, architecture, photography and design. Somerset House hosts **London Fashion Week** in February and September.

The courtyard is a popular **ice rink** in winter and is used for concerts and events in summer. Particularly popular is the **Film4 Summer Screen**, an outdoor cinema in the Great Court in early August. Behind the house, there's a sunny terrace and cafe overlooking the embankment.

DON'T MISS...
➡ Courtauld Gallery
➡ Skating in winter
➡ Movies in summer
➡ London Fashion Week

PRACTICALITIES
➡ Map p406, E5
➡ www.somersethouse.org.uk
➡ The Strand, WC2
➡ ☺galleries 10am-6pm, Safra Courtyard 7.30am-11pm
➡ ⊜Charing Cross, Embankment, Temple

Commonwealth killed during the two world wars. The Queen and other public figures lay poppies at its base on Remembrance Sunday, the second Sunday in November.

⊙ Holborn & the Strand

SIR JOHN SOANE'S MUSEUM   MUSEUM
See p96.

STRAND   STREET
Map p406 (⊖Charing Cross, Temple) Built in the 12th century, the Strand (from the Old English word for 'shore') runs by the Thames. Over the centuries its grandiose stone houses counted as some of the most prestigious places to live, sitting as they did on a street that connected the City and Westminster. Some of these buildings are now the Savoy Hotel, Simpson's, King's College and Somerset House. But modern times haven't treated the Strand with much respect; the street is overrun by offices, cheap restaurants and odd souvenir shops.

Other interesting addresses include **Twinings** (Map p406; www.twinings.co.uk; 216 The Strand; ⊙9.30am-7.30pm Mon-Fri, 10am-5pm Sat, 10.30am-4.30pm Sun; ⊖Temple) at No 216 – a teashop opened by Thomas Twining in 1706 and thought to be the oldest company in the capital still trading on the same site and owned by the same family – and the stamp- and coin-collectors' mecca **Stanley Gibbons** (Map p406; www.stanleygibbons.com; 339 The Strand; ⊙9am-5.30pm Mon-Fri, 9.30am-5.30pm Sat; ⊖Covent Garden or Embankment) at No 339.

ROYAL COURTS OF
JUSTICE   HISTORIC BUILDING
Map p406 (www.justice.gov.uk; 460 The Strand, WC2; ⊙9am-4.30pm Mon-Fri; ⊖Temple) FREE Where the Strand joins Fleet St, you'll see the entrance to this gargantuan melange of Gothic spires, pinnacles and burnished Portland stone, built in 1874. It is a public building and you're allowed to sit in on court proceedings; the list of cases to be heard is both on the website and available at reception in the Great Hall.

ST CLEMENT DANES   CHURCH
Map p406 (☏020-7242 8282; www.raf.mod.uk/stclementdanes; The Strand, WC2; ⊙9am-4pm; ⊖Temple) Christopher Wren designed the original church here in 1682, but only the walls and a steeple added by James Gibbs in 1719 survived WWII bombing, after which

---

👁 TOP SIGHT
WALLACE COLLECTION

Arguably London's finest smaller gallery, the Wallace Collection is an enthralling glimpse into 18th-century aristocratic life. The sumptuously restored Italianate mansion shelters a treasure-trove of 17th- and 18th-century paintings, porcelain and furniture collected by one family. It was bequeathed to the nation by the widow of Sir Richard Wallace (1818–90) on the condition it should always be on display in the centre of London and the paintings hung as specified in his will.

Among the many highlights are paintings by Rembrandt, Delacroix, Titian, Rubens, Poussin, Velázquez and Gainsborough in the stunning **Great Gallery**; look out for the *Laughing Cavalier* by Frans Hals. Particularly rich is its collection of Rococo paintings and furniture, and porcelain that belonged to Queen Marie-Antoinette of France. There's also an astonishing array of armour and weapons, both medieval and Renaisance European and Oriental. The sweeping staircase is deemed one of the best examples of French interior architecture anywhere. The excellent audio guide costs £3.

The fabulous glass-roofed courtyard restaurant **Wallace** (p116) is in the heart of the museum.

DON'T MISS...

➜ Great Gallery

➜ Marie-Antoinette's furniture, paintings and porcelain

➜ The *Laughing Cavalier* by Frans Hals

➜ Medieval and Renaissance armour

PRACTICALITIES

➜ Map p414, C3

➜ www.wallacecollection.org

➜ Hertford House, Manchester Sq, W1

➜ admission free

➜ ⊙10am-5pm

➜ ⊖Bond St

TOP SIGHT
MADAME TUSSAUDS

It may be kitschy and pricey (book online for much cheaper rates), but Madame Tussauds makes for a fun-filled day. There are photo ops with your dream celebrity at the A-List Party (Daniel Craig, Lady Gaga, George Clooney, the Beckhams), the Bollywood gathering (studs Hrithik Roshan and Salman Khan) and the Royal Appointment (the Queen, Harry, William and Kate). If you're into politics, get up close and personal with Barack Obama, Vladimir Putin or even London Mayor Boris Johnson with his signature mop haircut. In 2015, a *Star Wars* experience, featuring a host of its key heroes and villains, won top billing.

The whole place is pretty commercial, with shops and spending opportunities in every room. But the Spirit of London taxi ride through the city's history is great, educational fun, the Chamber of Horrors as scary as ever and the 3-D Super Heroes extravaganza very high-tech.

The museum has a long and interesting history since the French artist and model-maker Marie Tussaud (1761–1850) started making death masks of people guillotined during the French Revolution. She came to London in 1803 and exhibited around 30 wax models in nearby Baker St, providing visitors with their only glimpse of the famous and infamous before photography was widespread.

DON'T MISS...
➡ Lady Gaga
➡ The Queen
➡ David & Victoria Beckham
➡ Barack Obama
➡ Daniel Craig

PRACTICALITIES
➡ Map p414, B1
➡ ☎0870 400 3000
➡ www.madame-tussauds.com/london
➡ Marylebone Rd, NW1
➡ adult/child £30/26
➡ ◷9.30am-5.30pm
➡ ⊖Baker St

THE WEST END SIGHTS

---

the church was rebuilt as a memorial to Allied airmen. An 'island church' named after the Danes who colonised Aldwych in the 9th century, St Clement Danes today is the chapel of the Royal Air Force (RAF), and there are some 800 slate badges of different squadrons set into the pavement of the nave.

The statue in front of the church quietly and contentiously commemorates the RAF's Sir Arthur 'Bomber' Harris, who led the bombing raids that obliterated Dresden and killed up to 25,000 civilians during WWII. Should you pass the church at 9am, noon or 3pm, you may hear the bells chiming a distantly familiar tune. It's the 18th-century English nursery rhyme that incorporates the names of London churches starting: 'Oranges and lemons, say the bells of St Clements', with the soothing final lines: 'Here comes a chopper to chop off your head/Chop, chop, chop, chop, the last man's dead!'.

★TWO TEMPLE PLACE   GALLERY
Map p406 (☎020-7836 3715; www.twotempleplace.org; 2 Temple Pl, WC2; ◷10am-4.30pm Mon & Thu-Sat, to 9pm Wed & 11am-4.30pm Sun mid-Jan–mid-Apr; ⊖Temple) FREE This neo-Gothic house built in the late 1890s for William

Waldorf Astor, of hotel fame and once the richest man in America, showcases art from UK museum collections outside the capital. Visit as much to see the opulent house (it's astonishing) as the collections on display, but note it's only open for a few months each year for the Winter Exhibition Programme (see the website). Check out the bronze putti chatting on old telephones on the steps!

HUNTERIAN MUSEUM   MUSEUM
Map p406 (☎020-7869 6560; www.hunterian-museum.org; Royal College of Surgeons, 35-43 Lincoln's Inn Fields, WC2; ◷10am-5pm Tue-Sat; ⊖Holborn) FREE The collection of anatomical specimens of pioneering surgeon John Hunter (1728–93) inspired this fascinating, slightly morbid, yet little-known museum. Among the more bizarre items on display are the skeleton of a 2.3m Irish giant named Charles Byrne, half of mathematician Charles Babbage's brain (the other part is in the Science Museum) and, incongruously, Winston Churchill's dentures.

The atmosphere is less gory than it once was but remains transfixing, with an impressive array of internal organs in a state of atrophy and disease, and explanations on trepanation and other medical curiosities. There's the bloated skull of a 25-year old victim of hydrocephalus and the model of a Chinese patient with a parasitic twin (1820). The art gallery contains Hunter's own paintings of 'exotics': Qing dynasty Chinese with queues (a plait worn at the back) and the original Siamese twins, Chang and Eng, with, well, each other. Upstairs there's a display on surgery techniques, which will impress and repel in equal measure. The museum was bombed by the Luftwaffe in 1941, putting paid to two thirds of its collection. There's a free curatorled guided tour at 1pm on Wednesday. The excellent audioguide costs £3.50.

⊙ Marylebone

SHERLOCK HOLMES MUSEUM   MUSEUM
Map p414 (☑020-7224 3688; www.sherlock-holmes.co.uk; 221b Baker St, NW1; adult/child £10/8; ⊙9.30am-6pm; ⊜Baker St) The growing army of fans of Arthur Conan Doyle's classic detective novels may enjoy these three floors of reconstructed Victoriana, complete with deerstalkers, costumed staff, burning candles and flickering grates, but may baulk at the tiring queues and the dearth of information on the author himself.

For years there was a dispute over the famous address, since the occupant of 221b Baker St, the fictional abode of Sherlock Holmes, was the Abbey National Bank. A bank secretary even had the full-time job of responding to fan mail. When the bank moved out in 2005, the Royal Mail recognised the museum's exclusive right to receive post addressed to 'Sherlock Holmes'.

⊙ Mayfair

HANDEL HOUSE MUSEUM   MUSEUM
Map p414 (☑020-7399 1953; www.handelhouse.org; 25 Brook St, W1; adult/child £6.50/2; ⊙10am-6pm Tue, Wed, Fri & Sat, 10am-8pm Thu, noon-6pm Sun; ⊜Bond St) George Frederick Handel lived in this 18th-century Mayfair building for 36 years until his death in 1759. This is where he composed some of his finest works, including *Water Music*, *Messiah*, *Zadok the Priest* and *Fireworks Music*. Following extensive restorations, the house looks as it would have when the great German-born composer was in residence. Enter from Lancashire Court (current work underway on the house aims to restore the entrance to that on Brook St).

Early editions of Handel's operas and oratorios, portraits of musicians and singers who worked with Handel, and musical instruments are on the 1st floor; musicians regularly come to practise so you may be treated to a free concert. On the 2nd floor there are more exhibits and quite a good film with music. The staff attending the rooms are all Handel enthusiasts and wonderfully knowledgeable. Children are admitted free on Saturdays and Sundays. Ticketed events at the house include plays, concerts and recitals.

The house at No 23 (now part of the museum) was home to a musician cut from a different piece of musical cloth: American guitarist Jimi Hendrix (1942–70), who lived there from 1968 until his death. A blue plaque on the exterior attests to his residency; the flat he lived in is currently being authentically restored and will be open in 2016.

✗ EATING

Many of the city's best and most eclectic and fashionable restaurants are dotted around the West End. As with most things in London, it pays to be in the know: while there's a huge concentration of mediocre places to eat along the main tourist drags, the best eating experiences are frequently tucked away on backstreets and not at all obvious.

✗ Westminster & St James's

VINCENT ROOMS   MODERN EUROPEAN £
Map p416 (☑020-7802 8391; www.centrallondonvenues.co.uk/?page_ID=3; Westminster Kingsway College, Vincent Sq, SW1; mains £8-12; ⊙noon-2pm Mon-Fri, 6.30-9pm Wed & Thu; ⊜Victoria) Care to be a guinea pig for student chefs at Westminster Kingsway College, where celebrity chefs Jamie Oliver and Ainsley Harriott were trained? Service is eager to please, the atmosphere in both the Brasserie and the Escoffier Room smarter than expected, and the food (including veggie options) ranges from wonderful to exquisite – at prices that put other culinary stars to shame.

★CAFE MURANO   ITALIAN ££
Map p416 (☑020-3371 5559; www.cafemurano.co.uk; 33 St James's St, SW1; mains £9-40, 2-/3-course set meal £18/22; ⊙noon-3pm & 5.30-

11pm Mon-Sat; ⊖Green Park) The setting may be somewhat demure (but busy) at this superb restaurant, but with such a sublime North Italian menu on offer, it sees no need to make nods to being flash and of-the-moment. You get what you come for, and the beef carpaccio, crab linguine and lamb ragu are as close to culinary perfection as you can get. Reserve.

INN THE PARK   BRITISH ££
Map p416 (🖉020-7451 9999; www.innthepark. com; St James's Park, SW1; mains £14.50-29; ◷8am-9pm; ☎; ⊖Charing Cross, St James's Park) This stunning wooden cafe and restaurant in St James's Park is run by Irish wonderchef Oliver Peyton and offers cakes and tea as well as excellent British food, with the menu changing monthly. The terrace, which overlooks one of the park's fountains and views of Whitehall's grand buildings, is wonderful in warm weather.

✗ Bloomsbury

ORCHARD   VEGETARIAN £
Map p406 (www.orchard-kitchen.co.uk; 11 Sicilian Ave, WC1; mains £6.50-7; ◷8am-4pm Mon-Fri; 🖉; ⊖Holborn) A boon for vegetarians in central London is this delightful retro-style cafe on a quiet pedestrian street. Mains include specialities like broccoli and Yorkshire blue cheese pie, a sarnie (that's a sandwich to Londoners) and mug of soup is just £4.95 and desserts are unusual – try the toasted oat and currant cake with Horlicks icing.

LADY OTTOLINE   GASTROPUB ££
Map p412 (🖉020-7831 0008; www.theladyotto-line.com; 11a Northington St, WC1; mains £11.50-18; ◷noon-11pm Mon-Sat, to 5pm Sun; ⊖Chancery Lane) Bloomsbury can sometimes seem a culinary wasteland, but this buzzy gastropub (named after a patron of the Bloomsbury Group) is a pleasant exception. You can eat in the noisy pub downstairs, but the cosy dining room above is more tempting. Favourites like beer-battered fish and chips and pork and cider pie are excellent.

ABENO   JAPANESE ££
Map p412 (🖉020-7405 3211; www.abeno.co.uk; 47 Museum St, WC1; mains £7.95-25.80; ◷noon-10pm; ⊖Tottenham Court Rd) This Japanese restaurant specialises in *okonomiyaki*, a savoury pancake from Osaka. The pancakes consist of cabbage, egg and flour combined with the ingredients of your choice (there

are more than two dozen varieties, including anything from sliced meats and vegetables to egg, noodles and cheese), cooked on the hotplate at your table. There are also more familiar teppanyaki and yakisoba dishes.

NORTH SEA FISH
RESTAURANT   FISH & CHIPS ££
Map p412 (www.northseafishrestaurant.co.uk; 7-8 Leigh St, WC1; mains £8.95-20; ◷noon-2.30pm & 5.30-10.30pm Mon-Sat, 1-6pm Sun; ⊖Russell Sq) The North Sea sets out to cook fresh fish and potatoes – a simple ambition in which it succeeds admirably. Look forward to jumbo-sized plaice or halibut fillets, deep-fried or grilled, and a huge serving of chips. There's takeaway next door if you can't face the rather austere dining room.

✗ Fitzrovia

BUSABA EATHAI   THAI £
Map p412 (🖉020-7299 7900; www.busaba.com; 22 Store St, WC1; mains £7.90-14.50; ◷noon-11pm Mon-Thu, to 11.30pm Fri & Sat, to 10pm Sun; ☎; ⊖Goodge St) The Store St branch of this hugely popular minichain is slightly less hectic than some of the other West End outlets, but it retains all the features that have made the chain a roaring success. Think sleek Asian interior, large communal wooden tables, and heavenly cheap and tasty Thai dishes, like *pad thai* noodles, green and red curries, and fragrant noodle soups.

SAGAR   VEGETARIAN £
Map p412 (🖉020-7631 3319; www.sagarveg. co.uk; 17a Percy St, W1; mains £5.25-8.95; ◷noon-3pm & 5.30-10.45pm Mon-Thu, to 11pm Fri & Sat, to 10pm Sun; 🖉; ⊖Tottenham Court Rd) This branch of a minichain specialises in vegetarian dishes from the southern Indian state of Karnataka. It's cheap, filling and of a fine standard. Try the paper masala dosa, an enormous lentil pancake with spicy potato filling. Thalis – steel trays with a selection of small dishes – are £13.95 to £15.95.

FRANCO MANCA   PIZZA £
Map p412 (www.francomanca.co.uk; 98 Tottenham Court Rd, W1; mains £4.50-6.95; ◷11.30am-11pm Mon-Thu, 11.30am-11.30pm Fri & Sat, noon-10pm Sun; ⊖Goodge St) It's first come, first served at Franco Manca, which has come a long way since first feeding Brixton on slow-rising sourdough pizzas several years back. The six-pizza choice menu may seem

lightweight, but you really don't need to look any further, it's the real deal.

RAGAM
SOUTH INDIAN £

Map p412 (www.ragamindian.co.uk; 57 Cleveland St, W1; mains £5.95-9.95; ⊘noon-3pm & 6-11pm; ⊜Goodge St) If it ain't broke, don't fix it, and tiny Ragam hasn't been messing with the fundamentals – affordable, excellent dishes – for three decades. It hardly merits a glance from the outside – suggesting a rather grubby hole-in-the-wall with a rather cheesy interior, which it is – but never judge a book by its cover: the dosas are supreme.

DABBOUS
MODERN EUROPEAN ££

Map p412 (✆020-7323 1544; www.dabbous. co.uk; 39 Whitfield St, W1; set lunch/dinner £35/56; ⊘noon-3pm & 5.30-11.30pm Tue-Sat; ☏; ⊜Goodge St) This award-winning eatery is the creation of Ollie Dabbous, everyone's favourite new chef, so book ahead for dinner or come for lunch (four courses £28). The combination of flavours is inspired – squid with buckwheat, pork with mango, rhubarb with lavender – and at first seems at odds with the industrial, hard-edged decor. But it all works exceedingly well. Reservations essential.

FINO
SPANISH ££

Map p412 (✆020-7813 8010; www.finorestaurant. com; 33 Charlotte St, enter from Rathbone St, W1; tapas £3-13; ⊘noon-2.30pm Mon-Fri, 6-10.30pm Mon-Sat; ⊜Goodge St) Set in a glamorous basement with a fabulous bar, Fino is a tapas restaurant with a difference. The menu changes daily, but expect to find *morcilla* (blood sausage), *presa iberica* (tender Iberian pork), prawn and piquillo pepper tortilla and other delightful and innovative Spanish dishes. For groups, consider the whole slow roast suckling pig (but give 48 hours notice).

BARNYARD
BRITISH ££

Map p412 (✆020-7580 3842; www.barnyard-london.com; 18 Charlotte St, W1; mains £7-15; ⊘noon-10.30pm Mon-Wed, noon-11pm Thu & Fri, 11am-11pm Sat, 11am-9pm Sun; ☏; ⊜Goodge St) Ollie Dabbous' second London restaurant greets arrivals with hip enamel dishware, walls clad in corrugated iron and reclaimed wood, and a workman-style British/American menu of cornbread, homemade sausage roll, cauliflower cheese, bubble and squeak and black pudding that does little to suggest the exciting flavours within. It's tiny, with no reservations, so pitch up and join the queue.

ROKA
JAPANESE ££

Map p412 (✆020-7580 6464; www.rokarestaurant. com; 37 Charlotte St, W1; mains £8-36; ⊘noon-3.30pm & 5.30-11.30pm Mon-Sat, to 10.30pm Sun; ☏; ⊜Goodge St) This stunner of a Japanese restaurant mixes casual dining (wooden benches) with savoury titbits from the *robatayaki* (grill) kitchen in the centre. It has modern decor, the dominating materials being grey steel and floor-to-ceiling windows.

PIED-À-TERRE
FRENCH £££

Map p412 (✆020-7636 1178; www.pied-a-terre. co.uk; 34 Charlotte St, W1; 2 courses £27.50, 10-course tasting menu £105; ⊘12.15–2.30pm Mon-Fri & 6-11pm Mon-Sat; ☏; ⊜Goodge St) Gratifying diners since 1991, this petite, elegant and recently refurbished Michelin-starred gourmet French choice pins its long-standing and ever popular success to a much-applauded menu, with sensationally presented dishes from award-winning chef Marcus Eaves.

LIMA
SOUTH AMERICAN £££

Map p412 (✆020-3002 2640; www.limalondon. com; 31 Rathbone Place, W1; mains £20-29; ⊘noon-2.30pm & 5.30-10.30pm Mon-Sat, noon-3.15pm Sun; ☏; ⊜Tottenham Court Rd) Sublimely zestful and piquant Peruvian flavours percolate at the heart of this fantastic and unassuming Fitzrovia restaurant. The stunningly presented cuisine has pulled a Michelin star, while helpful staff take pride in their work.

HAKKASAN HANWAY PLACE
CHINESE £££

Map p412 (✆020-7927 7000; www.hakkasan.com; 8 Hanway Place, W1; mains £13.50-100; ⊘noon-3pm Mon-Fri, to 4pm Sat & Sun & 5.30-11pm Sun-Wed, to 12.15am Thu-Sat; ☏; ⊜Tottenham Court Rd) This basement Michelin-starred restaurant – hidden down a back alleyway – successfully combines celebrity status, stunning design, persuasive cocktails and sophisticated Chinese food. The low, nightclub-style lighting makes it a good spot for dating or a night out with friends (the bar serves seriously creative cocktails). Book far in advance or come for lunch (three courses for £35, also available from 6pm to 7pm).

✕ Soho & Chinatown

★KOYA
NOODLES £

Map p408 (www.koya.co.uk; 49 Frith St, W1; mains £7-15; ⊘noon-3pm & 5.30-10.30pm; ⊜Tottenham Court Rd, Leicester Sq) Arrive early or late if you don't want to queue at this excellent

Japanese eatery. Londoners come for their fill of authentic udon noodles (served hot or cold, in soup or with a cold sauce), the efficient service and very reasonable prices. The *saba* udon noodles with generous chunks of smoked mackerel and topped with watercress is a gorgeous dish.

On a roll, Koya has opened the Koya Bar next door at No 50 Frith St.

NORDIC BAKERY
SCANDINAVIAN £

Map p408 (www.nordicbakery.com; 14a Golden Sq, W1; snacks £4-5; ⏰7.30am-8pm Mon-Fri, 8.30am-8pm Sat, 9am-7pm Sun; ⦵Piccadilly Circus) This is the perfect place to escape the chaos that is Soho and relax in the dark-wood-panelled space on the south side of a delightful 'secret' square. Lunch on Scandinavian smoked-fish sandwiches or goat's cheese and beetroot salad, or have an afternoon break with tea/coffee and rustic oatmeal cookies.

MILDREDS
VEGETARIAN £

Map p408 (www.mildreds.co.uk; 45 Lexington St, W1; mains £8.20-10.50; ⏰noon-11pm Mon-Sat; 📶🍴; ⦵Oxford Circus, Piccadilly Circus) Central London's most inventive vegetarian restaurant, Mildred's heaves at lunchtime so don't be shy about sharing a table in the sky-lit dining room. Expect the likes of Sri Lankan sweet potato and cashew nut curry, pumpkin and ricotta ravioli, Middle Eastern meze, wonderfully exotic (and filling) salads and delicious stir-fries. There are also vegan and gluten-free options.

CEVICHE
SOUTH AMERICAN £

Map p408 (www.cevicheuk.com; 17 Frith St, W1; mains £6-13; ⏰noon-11.30pm Mon-Sat, to 10.30pm Sun; 📶; ⦵Leicester Sq) Peruvian food is the new black in London, and this colourfully decorated *bodega* serves some of the most authentic. Start with *cancha* (large crunchy corn kernels) and move onto one of the signature dishes of *ceviche* (fish or shellfish marinated in lime juice with chillies, onion and coriander). Salads made with quinoa (a type of grain) and palm hearts are excellent.

BAIWEI
CHINESE £

Map p406 (8 Little Newport St, WC2; mains from £8.95; ⏰noon-11pm; ⦵Leicester Square) Expect dishes such as spicy *dàn dan* noodles and *yúxiāng ròusī* (fish-flavoured pork strips) and Mao-era propaganda art work on the walls. Celebrated Sìchuān culinary expert Fuschia Dunlop served as consultant on this cafe-style restaurant and the menu rarely falters in its fiery exploration of Sìchuān and Húnán tastes.

HONEST BURGERS
BURGERS £

Map p408 (www.honestburgers.co.uk; 41 Meard St, W1; mains from £8.50; ⏰noon-11pm Mon-Wed, 11.45am-11pm Thu-Sat, noon-10pm Sun; 📶; ⦵Tottenham Court Rd, Piccadilly Circus) The burgers – from Ginger Pig dry aged beef – rather than ambience are the pull at this Soho branch of the mushrooming Honest Burgers empire. Served in glazed buns on distressed white enamel plates with a scattering of rosemary salted chips, the burgers are (just about) worth the long wait for a table (an hour when its busy). No reservations.

SPUNTINO
AMERICAN £

Map p408 (www.spuntino.co.uk; 61 Rupert St, W1; mains £6-10; ⏰11am-midnight Mon-Wed, noon-1am Thu-Sat, noon-11pm Sun; ⦵Piccadilly Circus) Offering an unusual mix of speakeasy decor and surprisingly creative fusion American-Italian food, Spuntino is a delight at every turn. Try old favourites such as macaroni cheese, cheese burger with jalapeno chillis and, as a dessert, peanut butter and jelly sandwich. Seating is at the bar or counters at the back.

POLPO
ITALIAN £

Map p408 (📞020-7734 4479; www.polpo.co.uk; 41 Beak St, W1; mains £6-10; ⏰noon-11pm Mon-Sat, noon-10pm Sun; ⦵Oxford Circus, Piccadilly Circus) *Cicheti* – 'Italian tapas', for want of a better word – are all the rage in backstreet *bàcari* (wine bars) in Venice and rustic Polpo serves a lovely selection. More substantial are the half-dozen types of flavourful meatballs and the mini pizzette. The Venetian painter Canaletto lived here.

BONE DADDIES RAMEN BAR
NOODLES £

Map p408 (www.bonedaddiesramen.com; 21 Peter St, W1; dishes £9-12; ⏰noon-3pm & 5.30-10pm Mon, noon-3pm & 5.30-11pm Tue-Wed, noon-midnight Thu-Sat, noon-9.30pm Sun; ⦵Tottenham Court Rd) For a bowl of sustaining ramen noodles, you couldn't do better than Bone Daddies (and we'll come back just for the name). Choose your 'foundation' – be it noodles in broth or a salad – and then add a topping or two (*chāshū* pork, pulled chicken, bean sprouts etc).

GELUPO
ICE CREAM £

Map p408 (www.gelupo.com; 7 Archer St, W1; pot £3-5; ⏰11am-11pm Mon-Thu, to midnight Fri & Sat,

THE WEST END EATING

noon-11pm Sun ; ⊜Piccadilly Circus) The queue outside Gelupo can stretch down the street on summer weekends, and it's no wonder: this is central London's most authentic gelateria. All the ingredients are natural and the servings are generous. Go for traditional flavours such as pistachio or bitter chocolate or try original creations such as *marron glacé* (candied chestnut) or bergamot.

FERNANDEZ & WELLS
CAFE £

Map p408 (www.fernandezandwells.com; 73 Beak St, W1; dishes £4.50-6; ◷7.30am-6pm Mon-Fri, 9am-6pm Sat & Sun; ⊜Piccadilly Circus) A wonderful taste of Spain in Soho, Fernandez serves simple lunches of *jamón* (ham) and cured meats and cheese platters. Grilled chorizo sandwiches are perfect for quick lunchtime bites. The place is usually busy, with a relaxed atmosphere. Excellent coffee.

BAOZI INN
CHINESE £

Map p406 (25 Newport Ct, WC2; mains £5-7.50; ◷noon-10.30pm; ⊜Leicester Sq) Decorated in a vintage style that plays at kitsch communist pop, Baozi Inn serves quality Běijīng- and Chéngdū-style street food, such as *dan dan* noodles with spicy pork and *bāozi* buns (steamed buns with stuffing) handmade daily. It's authentic, delicious and cheap food in often-unreliable Chinatown.

THE BREAKFAST CLUB
BREAKFAST £

Map p408 (✆020-7434 2571; 33 D'Arblay St; mains £5-12.50; ◷8am-10pm Mon-Sat, 8am-7pm Sun; 🖝; ⊜Oxford Circus) A scowling Judd Nelson may not be in the queue out front, but this fun and friendly original branch of The Breakfast Club has been successfully frying up for over a decade. Full/half Monty/All American brekkies are the natural temptation, but chorizo hashbrowns, pancakes and delights of the El Butty also await once you forge your way to the front of the line.

YOOBI
JAPANESE £

Map p408 (www.loveyoobi.com; 38 Lexington St, W1; mains £3.20-5; ◷11.30am-9pm Mon-Sat; 🖝; ⊜Piccadilly Circus) 'London's first temakeria', Yoobi's speciality is fresh and scrummy *temaki* (sushi rolled up in a crispy seaweed – *nori* – cone) for devouring in a trice. For fillings (*neta*), select from Scottish salmon, wasabi tuna, spicy tuna, avocado and asparagus, sun-kissed tomatoes and other tasty flavours. There's also maki rolls and sashimi boxes on the menu.

★BRASSERIE ZÉDEL
FRENCH ££

Map p408 (✆020-7734 4888; www.brasseriezedel.com; 20 Sherwood St, W1; mains £8.75-30; ◷11.30am-midnight Mon-Sat, to 11pm Sun; 🖝; ⊜Piccadilly Circus) This brasserie in the renovated art deco ballroom of a former Piccadilly hotel is the French-est eatery west of Calais. Choose from among the usual favourites, including *choucroute alsacienne* (sauerkraut with sausages and charcuterie, £14) and duck leg confit with Puy lentils. The set menus (£8.95/11.75 for two/three courses) and *plats du jour* (£12.95) offer excellent value, in a terrific setting.

★PALOMAR
JEWISH ££

Map p408 (✆020-7439 8777; 34 Rupert St, W1; mains £6.50-19; ◷noon-2.30pm Mon-Sat & noon-3.30pm Sun, 5.30-11pm Mon-Wed, 5.30-11.30pm Thu-Sat; 🖝; ⊜Piccadilly Circus) The buzzing vibe at this good-looking celebration of modern-day Jerusalem cuisine (in all its inflections) is infectious, but we could enjoy the dishes cooked up here in a deserted warehouse and still come back for more. The polenta Jerusalem style and aubergine and feta *bourekas* (flaky pastry parcels) were fantastic, but portions are smallish, so sharing is the way to go. Reservations essential.

★BAR SHU
CHINESE ££

Map p408 (✆020-7287 6688; www.barshurestaurant.co.uk; 28 Frith St, W1; mains £10-31; ◷noon-11pm Sun-Thu, noon-11.30pm Fri & Sat; ⊜Piccadilly Circus, Leicester Sq) The restaurant that introduced London to the joys of fiery Sìchuān cuisine remains more authentic than much of the competition. Dishes are steeped in the flavours of smoked chillies and the all-important *huājiāo* peppercorn. Service can be a little brusque, but the food is delicious and the portions huge.

ANDREW EDMUNDS
MODERN EUROPEAN ££

Map p408 (✆020-7437 5708; www.andrewedmunds.com; 46 Lexington St, W1; mains £12-19.50; ◷noon-3.30pm & 5.30-10.45pm Mon-Fri, 12.30-3.30pm & 5.30-10.45pm Sat, 1-4pm & 6-10.30pm Sun; ⊜Oxford Circus, Piccadilly Circus) This cosy little place, in situ since 1986, is exactly the sort of restaurant you wish you could find everywhere in Soho. Two floors of wood-panelled bohemia with a hand-written menu of French (confit of duck) and European (beetroot and goat's cheese tart) country cooking – it's a real find and reservations are essential.

YAUATCHA
CHINESE ££

Map p408 (⏰020-7494 8888; www.yauatcha. com; 15 Broadwick St, W1; dishes £4-30; ⊙noon-11.30pm Mon-Sat, to 10.30pm Sun; ⊖Piccadilly Circus, Oxford Circus) This most glamorous of dim sum restaurants has a Michelin star and is divided into two: the upstairs dining room offers a delightful blue-bathed oasis of calm from the chaos of Berwick St Market, while downstairs has a smarter, more atmospheric feel with constellations of 'star' lights. Both serve exquisite dim sum and have a fabulous range of teas.

BOCCA DI LUPO
ITALIAN ££

Map p408 (⏰020-7734 2223; www.boccadilupo. com; 12 Archer St, W1; mains £8-28; ⊙12.30-3pm & 5.30-11pm Mon-Sat, 12.15-3.15pm & 5.15-9.30pm Sun; ⊖Piccadilly Circus) Hidden in a dark Soho backstreet, Bocca radiates elegant sophistication. The menu has dishes from across Italy (and informs you which region they're from), and every main course can be ordered as a large or small portion. There's a good choice of Italian wines and fantastic desserts. It's often full, so make sure to book.

BARRAFINA
SPANISH ££

Map p408 (⏰020-7813 8016; www.barrafina. co.uk; 54 Frith St, W1; tapas £6-19; ⊙noon-3pm & 5-11pm Mon-Sat, 1-3.30pm & 5.30-10pm Sun; ⊖Tottenham Court Road) Tapas are always better value in Spain but the quality of this food just justifies the prices. Along with *gambas al ajillo* (prawns in garlic; £8.50), there are more unusual things such as tuna tartare and grilled quail with aioli. Customers sit along the bar so it's not a good choice for groups. No reservations, so prepare to queue.

10 GREEK ST
MODERN EUROPEAN ££

Map p408 (⏰020-7734 4677; www.10greekstreet. com; 10 Greek St, W1; mains £8-22; ⊙noon-11.30pm Mon-Sat; ☎; ⊖Tottenham Court Rd) This understated bistro, which takes bookings at lunch but not dinner, is making quite a splash with a menu that takes top-quality British produce and puts a Mediterranean spin on it (hake with pickled grapes, lamb with roasted artichokes). Desserts are especially fine and service is seamless.

GAUTHIER SOHO
FRENCH ££

Map p408 (⏰020-7494 3111; www.gauthiersoho. co.uk; 21 Romilly St, W1 ; 2-/3-course set lunch £18/25, with wine £26/33; ⊙noon-2.30pm Tue-Sat & 6.30-10.30pm Mon-Sat; ⊖Leicester Sq) Alexis Gauthier's temple of gastronomy – a find if there ever was one – is housed over two floors of a discreet Georgian townhouse where you have to buzz to be let in. Evening meals are a delight but pricey at £40/50/60 for three/four/five courses. Do what we do and treat yourself to a luxurious weekday lunch for half the price.

BURGER & LOBSTER SOHO
AMERICAN ££

Map p408 (www.burgerandlobster.com; 36-38 Dean St, W1; mains £20; ⊙noon-10.30pm Mon-Wed, to 11pm Thu-Sat, to 10pm Sun; ⊖Leicester Sq, Piccadilly Circus) London's seemingly insatiable appetite for burgers has taken a slight detour at this branch of an award-winning minichain. The concept is simple: £20 gets you a burger, a 1.5lb lobster or a lobster roll as well as a carton of chips and salad. Seating is in bright-red banquettes and the atmosphere is buzzing, almost party-like.

PITT CUE CO
BARBECUE ££

Map p408 (www.pittcue.co.uk; 1 Newburgh St, W1; mains £11.50-16.50; ⊙noon-3pm & 5.30-11pm Mon-Sat, noon-4pm Sun; ⊖Oxford Circus) With only 30 seats jammed into this titchy upstairs-bar, downstairs-dining-room affair, prepare to line up (no reservations) for a table and tin trays loaded with slow-cooked meats (pulled pork, beef ribs), classic American BBQ-style. Tuck your elbows in, and enjoy.

BÓ DRAKE
KOREAN ££

Map p408 (www.bodrake.co.uk; 6 Greek St, W1; ⊙6-11pm Tue-Sat; ⊖Tottenham Court Rd) 'Asian BBQ' is the ballpark region, but the specific zone at Bó Drake is the culinary continental collision of 'Korexican' (Korean-Mexican), which actually makes considerable fusion sense, once the flavours of the kimchi quesedillas and rib tips in bourbon sauce start washing over your tongue. No reservations.

POLLEN STREET SOCIAL
MODERN EUROPEAN £££

Map p408 (⏰020-7290 7600; www.pollenstreet-social.com; 8-10 Pollen St, W1; mains £33-37.50; ⊙noon-2.45pm & 6-10.45pm Mon-Sat; ⊖Oxford Circus) Jason Atherton's cathedral to haute cuisine would be beyond reach of anyone not on a hefty expense account, but the excellent-value set lunch (£29.50/34.50 for two/three courses) makes it accessible to all. A generous two-hour slot allows ample time to linger over such delights as lime-cured salmon, braised ox 'tongue 'n' cheek' and a choice from the dessert bar.

MUSEUM RESTAURANTS

National Dining Rooms (Map p406; ☑020-7747 2525; www.peytonandbyrne.co.uk; 1st fl, Sainsbury Wing, National Gallery, Trafalgar Sq, WC2; mains £12.50-17.50; ⊙10am-5.30pm Sat-Thu, to 8.30pm Fri; ⊜Charing Cross) Chef Oliver Peyton's restaurant at the National Gallery styles itself as 'proudly and resolutely British', and what a great idea. The menu features an extensive and wonderful selection of British cheeses for a light lunch. For something more filling, go for the monthly changing County Menu, honouring regional specialities from across the British Isles. Set lunch is £19.50/23.50 for two/three courses.

Portrait (Map p406; ☑020-7312 2490; www.npg.org.uk/visit/shop-eat-drink.php; 3rd fl, National Portrait Gallery, St Martin's Pl, WC2; mains £17.50-26, 2-/3-course menu £26.50/31.50; ⊙10-11am, 11.45am-2.45pm & 3.30-4.45pm daily, 5.30-8.15pm Thu, Fri & Sat; ⊜Charing Cross) This stunningly located restaurant above the excellent National Portrait Gallery – with views over Trafalgar Square and Westminster – is a great place to relax after a morning or afternoon at the gallery. The brunch (10am to 11.30am) and afternoon tea (3.30pm to 4.45pm) come highly recommended. Booking is advisable.

Wallace (Map p414; ☑020-7563 9505; www.wallacecollection.org/visiting/thewallacerestaurant; Hertford House, Manchester Sq , W1; mains £14-26; ⊙10am-5pm Sun-Thu, to 11pm Fri & Sat ; ⊜Bond St) There are few more idyllically placed restaurants than this brasserie in the enclosed courtyard of the Wallace Collection. The emphasis is on seasonal French-inspired dishes, with the daily menu offering two- or three-course meals for £22/26. Afternoon tea is £17.

ARBUTUS
MODERN EUROPEAN £££

Map p408 (☑020-7734 4545; www.arbutusrestaurant.co.uk; 63-64 Frith St, W1; mains from £19; ⊙noon-2.30pm & 5-11pm Mon-Sat, noon-3pm & 5.30-10.30pm Sun; ☎; ⊜Tottenham Court Rd) This Michelin-starred brainchild of Anthony Demetre does great British food, focusing on seasonal produce. Try such inventive dishes as pigeon, sweet onion and beetroot tart, squid and mackerel 'burger' or *pieds et paquets* (lamb tripe parcels with pig trotters). Don't miss the bargain 'working lunch' set menu at £17.95 for two courses and £19.95 for three. Booking essential.

✕ Covent Garden & Leicester Square

★SHORYU
NOODLES £

Map p416 (www.shoryuramen.com; 9 Regent St, SW1; mains £9-15; ⊙11.15am-midnight Mon-Sat, to 10.30pm Sun; ⊜Piccadilly Circus) Compact, well-mannered noodle parlour Shoryu draws in reams of noodle diners to feast at its wooden counters and small tables. It's busy, friendly and efficient, with informative staff. Fantastic tonkotsu ramen is the name of the game here, sprinkled with *nori* (dried, pressed seaweed), spring onion, *nitamago* (soft-boiled eggs) and sesame seeds. No bookings.

DISHOOM
INDIAN £

Map p406 (☑020-7420 9320; www.dishoom.com; 12 Upper St Martin's Lane, WC2; mains £5-16.50; ⊙8am-11pm Mon-Thu, 8am-midnight Fri, 9am-midnight Sat, 9am-11pm Sun; ☎; ⊜Covent Garden) This laid back eatery takes the fast-disappearing old-style 'Bombay cafe' and gives it the kiss of life. Distressed with a modern twist (all ceiling fans and Bollywood photos), you'll find favourites like *sheekh kabab* and *haleem* (slow-cooked lamb, cracked wheat, barley and lentils), okra fries and snack foods like *bhel* (Bombay mix and puffed rice with pomegranate and lime).

WAHACA
MEXICAN £

Map p406 (www.wahaca.com; 66 Chandos Pl, WC2; mains £7-10.50; ⊙noon-11pm; ☎; ⊜Covent Garden) ⦿ This delightful cantina, a branch of an ever-expanding chain, styles itself as a 'Mexican market eating' experience. You can choose to share a selection of street snacks (tacos, tostadas, *quesadillas*) or go for more traditional mains such as grilled fish a la Pimienta or a seafood salad. Wash it down with one of a dozen tequilas. It can get very busy.

ROCK & SOLE PLAICE
FISH & CHIPS £

Map p406 (www.rockandsoleplaice.com; 47 Endell St, WC2; mains £10-11.50; ⊙11.30am-10.30pm Mon-Sat, noon-9.30pm Sun; ⊜Covent Garden) This no-nonsense chippie dating back to Victorian times is simplicity itself: basic wooden tables under the trees in summer, simple decor inside and delicious cod, haddock or skate in batter served with a generous portion of chips. Eat in or take away.

FOOD FOR THOUGHT VEGETARIAN £

Map p406 (http://foodforthought-london.co.uk; 31 Neal St, WC2; mains £5-8.70; ⊙noon-8.30pm Mon-Sat, to 5.30pm Sun; ⊅; ⊖Covent Garden) Earthy, unpretentious, deservedly packed and in situ for four decades, this tiny vegetarian cafe is big on sociability and flavour, and small on price and space. Brimming over with soups, salads, stews and stir-fries with brown rice, dishes span the vegan, organic and/or gluten-free fold.

DELAUNAY BRASSERIE ££

Map p406 (⊅020-7499 8558; www.thedelaunay.com; 55 Aldwych, WC2; mains £6.50-27.50; ⊙7am-midnight Mon-Fri, 8am-midnight Sat, 9am-11pm Sun; ⊖Temple, Covent Garden) This smart brasserie across from Bush House is a kind of Franco-German hybrid, where schnitzels and wieners sit happily beside croque-monsieurs and *choucroute alsacienne* (Alsace sauerkraut). Even more relaxed is the adjacent **Counter** (Map p406; ⊙7am-8pm Mon-Wed, 7am-10.30pm Thu & Fri, 10.30am-10.30pm Sat, 11am-5.30pm Sun; ⊖Temple, Covent Garden), where you can drop in for chicken noodle soup and a New York–style hot dog.

Brunch is from 11am to 5pm at the weekend and tea (£23.75, or £33.50 with champagne) is daily from 3pm.

GREAT QUEEN STREET BRITISH ££

Map p406 (⊅020-7242 0622; 32 Great Queen St, WC2; mains £14-20; ⊙noon-2.30pm & 6-10.30pm Mon-Sat, 1-4pm Sun; ⊖Holborn) The menu at what is one of Covent Garden's best places to eat is seasonal (and changes daily), with an emphasis on quality, hearty dishes and good ingredients – there are always delicious stews, roasts and simple fish dishes. The atmosphere is lively, with a small cellar bar (open 5pm to midnight Tuesday to Saturday) for cocktails and drinks. The staff are knowledgeable about the food and wine they serve and booking is essential.

CANELA PORTUGUESE ££

Map p406 (www.canelacafe.com; 33 Earlham St, WC2; mains £10-12.50; ⊙8am-11pm Mon-Sat, 8am-9pm Sun; ⊛; ⊖Covent Garden) This small cafe in Seven Dials at the heart of Covent Garden serves tasty Portuguese and Brazilian dishes. Try the classic dish of the day, opt for the Portuguese national dish *feijoada*, a bean stew with smoked meat, or call in early for a rustic brekkie. There's a good selection of vegetarian dishes too, as well as a strong Portuguese wine list.

J SHEEKEY SEAFOOD £££

Map p406 (⊅020-7240 2565; www.j-sheekey.co.uk; 28-32 St Martin's Ct, WC2; mains £16-44; ⊙noon-3pm daily, 5.30pm-midnight Mon-Sat, 6-11pm Sun; ⊛; ⊖Leicester Sq) A jewel of the local dining scene, this incredibly smart restaurant, whose pedigree stretches back to the closing years of the 19th century, has four elegant, discreet and spacious wood-panelled rooms in which to savour the riches of the sea, cooked simply and exquisitely. The oyster bar, popular with pre- and post-theatre goers, is another highlight. The three-course weekend lunch is £28.75.

BALTHAZAR BRASSERIE £££

Map p406 (⊅020-3301 1155; www.balthazar.com; 8 Russell St, WC2; mains £18-43; ⊙7.30am-midnight Mon-Fri, 9am-midnight Sat, 9am-11pm Sun; ⊛; ⊖Covent Garden) Few diners have been disappointed by the mostly French fare on offer (mussels, bouillabaisse, duck confit) at this handsome brasserie (with yummy bakery treats at the adjacent *boulangerie*), where there's the odd nod to *les rosbifs* ('roast beefs', or Britons) in the way of shepherd's pie.

HAWKSMOOR SEVEN DIALS STEAKHOUSE £££

Map p406 (⊅020-7420 9390; www.thehawksmoor.com; 11 Langley St, WC2; steak £18-34, 2-/3-course express menu £24/27; ⊙noon-3pm & 5-10.30pm Mon-Sat, noon-9.30pm Sun; ⊛; ⊖Covent Garden) ⌀ Legendary among London carnivores for its mouth-watering and flavour-rich steaks from British cattle breeds, Hawksmoor's sumptuous Sunday roasts, burgers and well-executed cocktails are show-stoppers. Book ahead.

RULES BRITISH £££

Map p406 (⊅020-7836 5314; www.rules.co.uk; 35 Maiden Lane, WC2; mains £17.95-29.95; ⊙noon-11.30pm Mon-Sat, to 10.30pm Sun; ⊛; ⊖Covent Garden) Established in 1798, this posh and very British establishment is London's oldest restaurant. The menu is inevitably meat-oriented – Rules specialises in classic game cookery, serving up thousands of birds between mid-August and January from its own estate – but fish dishes are also available. Puddings are traditional: tarts, crumbles, sticky toffees and treacles with lashings of custard.

CANTINA LAREDO

MEXICAN £££

Map p406 (020-7420 0630; www.cantinalaredo.co.uk; 10 Upper St Martin's Lane, WC2; mains £15-30; noon-11.30pm Mon-Thu, to midnight Fri & Sat, to 10.30pm Sun; Covent Garden) This colourful and upbeat cantina serves modern, enlightened versions of all the favourites (fajitas, enchiladas) as well as some more inspired dishes like lamb rump in a pumpkin-seed crust with pistachio pipian sauce.

✗ Holborn

KANADA-YA

NOODLES £

Map p406 (www.kanada-ya.com; 64 St Giles High St, WC2; mains £10-12.50; noon-3pm & 5-10pm Mon-Sat; Tottenham Court Rd) With no reservations, queues can get impressive outside Kanada-ya, where *tonkutsu* (pork bone broth) ramen draws in fans for its three types of noodles that arrive in steaming bowls, steeped in a delectable broth and highly authentic flavours. The restaurant also serves up *onigiri* (dried seaweed-wrapped rice balls).

✗ Marylebone

GOLDEN HIND

FISH & CHIPS £

Map p414 (73 Marylebone Lane, W1; mains £6-11.50; noon-3pm Mon-Fri, 6-10pm Mon-Sat; Bond St) This 100-year-old chippie offers a classic interior, vintage fryer, chunky wooden tables, plus builders sitting elbow-to-elbow with folks in suits, tucking into ace fish and chips.

MONOCLE CAFE

CAFE £

Map p414 (http://cafe.monocle.com/; 18 Chiltern St, W1; mains from £5; 7am-7pm Mon-Fri, 8am-7pm Sat & Sun; Baker St) A small and cool ground floor and basement hideout for the Marylebone hipster set, Monocle Cafe (from the eponymous magazine) is a delightful addition to buzzing Chiltern St. It offers eclectic flavours from Swedish pastries to Japanese breakfasts, Bircher muesli with strawberries or shrimp katsu (breaded shrimp) sandwiches.

ROTI CHAI

INDIAN £

Map p414 (www.rotichai.com; 3 Portman Mews South, W1; mains from £5-16; noon-10.30pm Mon-Sat, 12.30-9pm Sun; Marble Arch) With a refreshing street kitchen menu from India, colourful Roti Chai cooks up a roaring trade in *bel puris* (puffed rice with tamarind), *papri chaat* (wheat crisps and sweet yoghurt) and railway lamb curries (lamb and potato) for upstairs snackers, with a more expansive dining room menu down below.

LOCANDA LOCATELLI

ITALIAN ££

Map p414 (020-7935 9088; www.locandalocatelli.com; 8 Seymour St, W1; mains from £13.50; noon-3pm daily, 6.45-11pm Mon-Sat, to 10.15pm Sun; Marble Arch) This dark but quietly glamorous restaurant in an otherwise unremarkable Marble Arch hotel remains one of London's hottest tables, and you're likely to see some famous faces being greeted by celebrity chef Giorgio Locatelli. The restaurant is renowned for its pasta dishes, and the mains include five fish and five meat dishes. Booking is essential.

YALLA YALLA

LEBANESE ££

Map p412 (12 Winsley St, W1; mains £4.25-14.50; ; Oxford Circus) A funky pit-stop for lunch, this bright, buzzing and brisk restaurant specialises in Beirut street food, welcoming droves of customers who fill the communal counters and individual tables. Dishes are delightful, from the smooth, olive-oil drizzled hummus, to the scrummy *arayes* (grilled pitta filled with minced lamb), grills, light lunch platters and cooling puddings, tarts, pastries and desserts.

WEST END FRUIT & VEG MARKETS

Berwick Street Market (Map p408; www.berwickstreetlondon.co.uk/market; Berwick St, W1; 9am-6pm Mon-Sat; Piccadilly Circus, Oxford Circus) South of Oxford St and running parallel to Wardour St, this fruit-and-vegetable market has managed to hang onto its prime location since about 1830. It's a great place to put together a picnic or shop for a prepared meal, and to hear Cockney accents straight out of Central Casting.

Marylebone Farmers Market (Map p414; www.lfm.org.uk/markets/marylebone; Cramer St , W1; 10am-2pm Sun; Baker St) This weekly farmers market is the largest in town with 30 to 40 producers coming from within a 100-mile radius of the M25. It's expensive but charming, reflecting the local demographic.

LA FROMAGERIE
CAFE ££

Map p414 (www.lafromagerie.co.uk; 2-6 Moxon St, W1; mains £8.50-18; ⊙8am-7.30pm Mon-Fri, 9am-7pm Sat, 10am-6pm Sun; ⏣; ⊖Baker St) This deli-cafe has bowls of delectable salads, antipasto, peppers and beans scattered about the long communal table. Huge slabs of bread invite you to tuck in, while the heavenly waft from the cheese room beckons. Cheese boards come in small and large (£8.95 and £13.75).

CHILTERN FIREHOUSE
MODERN EUROPEAN £££

Map p414 (✆020-7073 7676; www.chilternfire-house.com; 1 Chiltern St, W1; mains £21-75; ⊙8-10.30am, noon-2.30pm & 5.30-10.30pm Mon-Fri, 11am-3pm & 6-10.30pm Sat & Sun; ⏣; ⊖Baker St, Bond St) When they can secure a table, diners come to this splendidly dapper Marylebone Fire Station to celeb-spot and bask in its glorious setting as much as to dine. Chef Nuno Mendes has worked some considerable culinary flair into his menu, but the hype and overarching trendiness guarantee an outlay almost as high as the red-brick chimneys aloft.

✖ Mayfair

BRICIOLE
ITALIAN £

Map p414 (✆020-7723 0040; www.briciole.co.uk; 20 Homer St, W1; mains £6-12.50; ⊙11am-11pm Mon-Sat, to 10.30pm Sun; ⊖Edgware Rd) This trattoria fronted by a cafe and a deli is tiny but perfectly formed. It serves pretty basic stuff: Palermo-style sweet-and-sour meatballs, Tuscan barbecue and all kinds of pasta. But it's very tasty and excellent value, especially for this part of town.

EMBER YARD
TAPAS £

Map p408 (http://emberyard.co.uk; 60 Berwick St, W1; mains £7-9; ⊙noon-midnight Mon-Sat, to 10.30pm Sun; ⊖Oxford Circus) Infused with beautiful flavours that capture the culinary aromas of the Basque country and Tuscany, many of Ember Yard's tapas are fired up on the Basque-style grill. The atmosphere is lively, warm and buzzing, while staff are thoughtful and informative. Expect dishes such as steamed, chargrilled octopus and spiced lamb burger with piquillo peppers, aubergine and garrotxa cheese.

★GYMKHANA
INDIAN ££

Map p416 (✆020-3011 5900; www.gymkhanalon-don.com; 42 Albemarle St, W1; mains £8-28, 2-/3-course lunch £25/30; ⊙noon-2.30pm &

5.30-10.30pm Mon-Sat; ⏣; ⊖Green Park) The rather sombre setting is all British Raj: ceiling fans, oak ceiling, period cricket photos and hunting trophies, but the menu is lively, bright and inspiring. Game gets its very own menu, but for lovers of variety, the seven course tasting menu (£65) is the way to go. The bar is open to 1am.

TIBITS
VEGETARIAN ££

Map p408 (www.tibits.ch; 12-14 Heddon St, W1; lunch £2.30 per 100g, dinner £2.60 per 100g; ⊙9am-10.30pm Mon-Wed, 9am-midnight Thu-Sat, 11.30am-10.30pm Sun; ⏣; ⊖Piccadilly Circus, Oxford Circus) This cool, bright and casual vegetarian buffet, pay-by-weight restaurant on the corner of Heddon St (of Ziggy Stardust fame) sees a regular stream of West End grazers. The eclectic menu is light, breezy and eclectic, with Middle Eastern *mejadra* (basmati rice, lentils and fried onion) elbow-to-elbow with Malaysian udon-noodles with tofu and pak choi, and sticky toffee pudding. Seats are strewn outside for sunbathers.

GREENHOUSE
MODERN EUROPEAN £££

Map p414 (✆020-7499 3331; www.greenhouser-estaurant.co.uk; 27a Hay's Mews, W1; 2-/3-course set lunch £35/40; ⊙noon-2.30pm Mon-Fri & 6.30-11pm Mon-Sat; ⏣; ⊖Green Park) Located at the end of a wonderful sculpted 'garden', Greenhouse offers some of the best food in Mayfair, served with none of the attitude commonly found in restaurants of this class. The tasting menu (£90) is only for the intrepid and truly hungry. Greenhouse doles out so many dishes, from *amuses-gueule* (appetisers) and inter-course sorbets to petits fours, you'll never get up.

MOMO
MOROCCAN £££

Map p408 (✆020-7434 4040; www.momoresto.com; 25 Heddon St, W1; mains £13.50-24.95; ⊙noon-2.30pm Mon-Fri, 11am-3pm Sat & Sun, 6.30pm-1am Mon-Sat, 6.30pm-midnight Sun; ⏣; ⊖Piccadilly Circus) Stuffed with cushions and lamps, and staffed by tambourine-playing waiters, this atmospheric Moroccan restaurant has warm service and dishes as exciting as you dare to be. After the meze, eschew the traditional and ordinary *tagine* (stew cooked in a traditional clay pot) and couscous, and tuck into the splendid Moroccan speciality *pastilla* (wood pigeon pie).

There's outside seating in this quiet back-street (where Bowie's *The Rise and Fall of Ziggy Stardust and the Spiders from Mars* cover was shot) in the warmer months.

BRASSERIE CHAVOT
BRASSERIE £££

Map p414 (www.brasseriechavot.com; 41 Conduit St, W1; mains £19.50-28; 🐾; ⊖Oxford Circus) A feast of sparkling chandeliers, mirrors and a gorgeous mosaic floor, this classically styled Parisian brasserie is a dining occasion even before you reach for the menu. Excitement awaits in its perfectly prepared dishes including *cassoulet de canard et cochon* (duck and pork casserole) and roasted cod with lentils and lardons. Reserve (and avoid the expensive nibbles.)

NOBU
JAPANESE £££

Map p414 (📞020-7447 4747; www.noburestaurants.com; 1st fl, Metropolitan Hotel, 19 Old Park Lane, W1; mains £14-48; ⊘noon-2.15pm Mon-Fri, 12.30-2.30pm Sat & Sun, 6-10.15pm Mon-Thu, 6-11pm Fri & Sat, 6-10pm Sun; 🐾; ⊖Hyde Park Corner) You'll have to book a month in advance to eat here (or resign yourself to 6pm or 10pm if you book just a few days before), but you'll get to chew at and view one of the greatest celebrity restaurant magnets in town. Signature dishes include the black cod with miso at an eye-watering £42. Decor is understated, service discreet and efficient.

FOYER AT CLARIDGE'S
BRITISH £££

Map p414 (www.claridges.co.uk; 49-53 Brook St, W1; afternoon tea £55, with champagne £65; ⊘tea served 2.45-5.30pm; 🐾; ⊖Bond St) Extend your pinkie finger to partake in afternoon tea within the classic art deco–style foyer of this landmark hotel. The gentle clinks of fine porcelain and champagne glasses may be a highlight of your trip to London. The setting is gorgeous and dress is elegant, smart casual (no ripped jeans or baseball caps).

LE BOUDIN BLANC
FRENCH £££

Map p414 (📞020-7499 3292; www.boudinblanc. co.uk; 5 Trebeck St, W1; mains £16-30; ⊘noon-3pm & 6-11pm Mon-Sat, to 10.30pm Sun; 🐾; ⊖Green Park) Surely one of the best French brasseries in the capital, with meat cooked to perfection, sauces mouth-wateringly good and portions huge. The *frites* (French fries) are the best you'll find this side of La Manche. And with a whopping 500 wines to choose from, no wonder it's always full.

WILD HONEY
MODERN EUROPEAN £££

Map p414 (📞020-7758 9160; www.wildhoneyrestaurant.co.uk; 12 St George St, W1; mains £24-30; ⊘noon-2.30pm Mon-Fri, noon-3pm Sat, 6-10.30pm Mon-Sat; ⊖Oxford Circus) Wild Honey receives consistently good reviews for its food and wine, stunning wood-panelled dining room and professional service. The French-slanted menu is seasonal and inspiring; you'll generally discover a combination of inventive dishes, such as Lincolnshire smoked eel lacquered with Asian spice, and classic mains like grilled rib-eye of beef with bone marrow and young spring vegetables.

🍷 DRINKING & NIGHTLIFE

Over the last decade or so, the East End has trumped the West End as the coolest place in town. But this is still a wonderful place for a night out – Friday and Saturday nights buzz with excitement and decadence, particularly the areas around Soho, Leicester Sq and Covent Garden where people, booze and rickshaws fill the streets till the early hours. Here, bars and clubs range from the swanky to the skanky – with everything in between.

🍸 St James's

RIVOLI BAR
COCKTAIL BAR

Map p416 (www.theritzlondon.com/rivoli-bar; Ritz, 150 Piccadilly, W1; ⊘11.30am-midnight Mon-Sat, noon-10pm Sun; 🐾; ⊖Green Park) You may not quite need a diamond as big as the Ritz to drink at this art deco marvel, but it always helps. This gorgeous little jewel box of a bar is all camphor wood, illuminated glass, golden ceiling domes and stunning cocktails. Unlike in some other parts of the Ritz, dress code at the Rivoli is smart-casual.

DUKES BAR
COCKTAIL BAR

Map p416 (📞020-7491 4840; www.dukeshotel. com; 35 St James's Pl, SW1; ⊘2-11pm Mon-Sat, 4-10.30pm Sun; 🐾; ⊖Green Park) Sip to-die-for martinis like royalty in a gentleman's club-like ambience at this tidily tucked away classic bar where white-jacketed masters mix up some awesomely good preparations. Ian Fleming used to drink here, perhaps perfecting his 'shaken, not stirred' Bond maxim.

🍸 Bloomsbury & Fitzrovia

LAMB
PUB

Map p412 (www.thelamblondon.com; 94 Lamb's Conduit St, WC1; ⊘noon-11pm Mon-Wed, to midnight Thu-Sat, to 10.30pm Sun; ☺Russell Sq) The Lamb's central mahogany bar with beautiful Victorian dividers (also called 'snob screens' as they allowed the well-to-do to drink in private) has been a favourite with locals since 1729. Nearly three centuries later, its popularity hasn't waned, so come early to bag a booth and sample its decent selection of Young's bitters and genial atmosphere.

QUEEN'S LARDER
PUB

Map p412 (www.queenslarder.co.uk; 1 Queen Sq, WC1; ☺11.30am-11pm Mon-Sat, noon-10.30pm Sun; ☺Russell Sq) In a lovely square southeast of Russell Sq is this pub, so called because Queen Charlotte, wife of 'Mad' King George III, rented part of the pub's cellar to store special foods for her husband while he was being treated nearby. It's a tiny but wonderfully cosy pub; there are benches outside for fair-weather fans and a dining room upstairs.

MUSEUM TAVERN
PUB

Map p412 (49 Great Russell St, WC1; ☺11am-11.30pm Mon-Thu, 11am-midnight Fri & Sat, 10am-10pm Sun; ☺Holborn, Tottenham Court Rd) Karl Marx used to retire here for a well-earned pint after a hard day inventing communism in the British Museum's Reading Room; it was also where George Orwell boozed after his literary musings. A lovely traditional pub set around a long bar, it has friendly staff and is popular with academics and students alike.

BRADLEY'S SPANISH BAR
PUB

Map p412 (www.bradleysspanishbar.co.uk; 42-44 Hanway St, W1; ☺noon-11.30pm Mon-Thu, noon-midnight Fri & Sat, 3-10.30pm Sun; ☺Tottenham Court Rd) Bradley's is only vaguely Spanish in decor, but much more authentic in its choice of booze: Estrella, Cruzcampo, *tinto de verano* (red wine with rum and lemonade) and tequila sangrita. Squeeze in under low ceilings in the basement bar (open from 5pm Monday to Saturday), while a vintage vinyl jukebox plays rock tunes.

LONDON COCKTAIL CLUB
COCKTAIL BAR

Map p412 (www.londoncocktailclub.co.uk; 61 Goodge St, W1; ☺4.30pm-11.30pm Mon-Thu, to midnight Fri & Sat; ☺Goodge St) There are cocktails and then there are cocktails. The guys in this slightly tatty ('kitsch punk') subterranean bar will shake, stir, blend and smoke (yes, smoke) you some of the most inventive, colourful and punchy concoctions in creation. Try the smoked apple martini

or the squid ink sour. And relax. You'll be staying a lot longer than you thunk (errr, make that thought).

FITZROY TAVERN
PUB

Map p412 (16 Charlotte St, W1; ☺noon-11pm Mon-Sat, to 10.30pm Sun; ☺Goodge St) In the years before and after WWII, the Fitzroy was a hangout of literary giants like George Orwell and Dylan Thomas. Today it's a typical downtown boozer – though a bit rough round the edges – and part of the popular Sam Smith's chain, which means plenty of ales and specialist beers at rock-bottom prices.

TEA AND TATTLE
TEAHOUSE

Map p412 (☎07722-192703; www.apandtea.co.uk; 41 Great Russel St, WC1; afternoon tea £15; ☺9am-6.30pm Mon-Fri, noon-4pm Sat; ☎; ☺Tottenham Court Rd) This sweet six-table tearoom in the basement of a bookstore is a lovely spot to recuperate for some afternoon tea, sandwiches, cake and scones with clotted cream and jam after legging it around the British Museum opposite. Tea for one is £15; tea for two is £29.50.

♟ Soho & Chinatown

LAB
COCKTAIL BAR

Map p408 (☎020-7437 7820; www.labbaruk.com; 12 Old Compton St, W1; ☺4pm-midnight Mon-Sat, to 10.30pm Sun; ☺Leicester Sq, Tottenham Court Rd) A long-standing Soho favourite for almost two decades, the London Academy of Bartenders (to give it its full name) has some of the best cocktails in town. The list is the size of a small book but, fear not, if you can't make your way through it, just tell the bartenders what you feel like and they'll concoct something divine.

EXPERIMENTAL COCKTAIL CLUB
COCKTAIL BAR

Map p408 (www.experimentalcocktailclublondon.com; 13a Gerrard St, W1; ☺6pm-3am Mon-Sat, to midnight Sun; ☎; ☺Leicester Sq, Piccadilly Circus) The three-floor Experimental is a sensational cocktail bar in Chinatown with an unmarked, shabby door (it's next to the Four Seasons restaurant). The interior, with its soft lighting, mirrors, bare brick wall and elegant furnishings, matches the sophistication of the cocktails: rare and original spirits, vintage champagne and homemade fruit syrups. Booking not essential; there's a £5 cover charge after 11pm.

FRENCH HOUSE   BAR

Map p408 (www.frenchhousesoho.com; 49 Dean St, W1; ☺noon-11pm Mon-Sat, to 10.30pm Sun; ⊜Leicester Sq) French House is Soho's legendary boho boozer with a history to match: this was the meeting place of the Free French Forces during WWII, and De Gaulle is said to have drunk here often, while Dylan Thomas, Peter O'Toole and Francis Bacon all ended up on the wooden floor at least once.

Come to sip on Ricard, French wine or Kronenbourg and check out the quirky locals. Be warned: beer is served by the half-pint only. Above-average pub grub (mains £6.50 to £14.50) is served upstairs noon to 4pm weekdays.

APE & BIRD   PUB

Map p406 (www.apeandbird.com; 142 Shaftesbury Ave, WC2; ☺noon-11.30pm Mon-Sat, to 10.30pm Sun; ⊜Leicester Square) Right on Cambridge Circus, where Covent Garden abuts Soho and Chinatown, this excellent pub offers a comprehensive craft beer, spirit and wine selection. Ranged around a large copper bar, it has artfully distressed walls and exposed pipes, with large windows lined with terracotta-potted herbs. There's top-quality pub grub too, finer dining in the upstairs restaurant and cocktails in the downstairs Dive bar.

EDGE   GAY

Map p408 (www.edgesoho.co.uk; 11 Soho Sq, W1; ☺4pm-1am Mon-Thu, noon-3am Fri & Sat, 4-11.30pm Sun; ☎; ⊜Tottenham Court Rd) Overlooking Soho Sq in all its four-storey glory, the Edge is London's largest gay bar and heaves every night of the week. There are dancers, waiters in skimpy outfits, good music and a generally super friendly vibe. There's a heavy straight presence, as it's so close to Oxford St. So much the better.

VILLAGE   GAY

Map p408 (www.village-soho.co.uk; 81 Wardour St, W1; ☺4pm-1am Mon-Sat, to 11.30pm Sun; ⊜Piccadilly Circus) The Village is always up for a party, whatever the night of the week. There are karaoke nights, 'discolicious' nights, go-go dancer nights – take your pick. And if you can't wait to strut your stuff until the clubs open, there is a dance floor downstairs, complete with pole, of course.

YARD   GAY

Map p408 (☎020-7437 2652; www.yardbar.co.uk; 57 Rupert St, W1; ☺4-11.30pm Mon-Wed, 3-11.30pm Thu, 2pm-midnight Fri & Sat, 2-10.30pm Sun; ⊜Piccadilly Circus) This old Soho favourite attracts a cross-section of the great and the good. It's fairly attitude-free, perfect for preclub drinks or just an evening out. There are DJs upstairs in the Loft most nights as well as a friendly crowd in the al fresco (heated in season) Courtyard Bar below.

DOG AND DUCK   PUB

Map p408 (www.nicholsonspubs.co.uk/thedog-andducksoholondon; 18 Bateman St, W1; ☺10am-11pm; ⊜Tottenham Court Rd) With a fine array of real ales, some stunning Victorian glazed tiling and garrulous crowds spilling onto the pavement, the Dog and Duck has attracted a host of famous regulars, including painters John Constable and pre-Raphaelite Dante Gabrielle Rossetti, dystopian writer George Orwell and Madonna.

SHE SOHO   LESBIAN

Map p408 (☎0207 437 4303; www.she-soho.com; 23a Old Compton St, W1D; ☺4-11.30pm Mon-Thu, to 12.30am Fri & Sat, to 10.30pm Sun; ⊜Leicester Square) Soho has lost a lesbian bar (Candy Bar) but gained another with this intimate and dimly lit place with DJs at weekends, comedy, live music and quiz nights.

DUKE OF WELLINGTON   GAY

Map p408 (77 Wardour St, W1; ☺noon-midnight Mon-Fri, 11am-midnight Sat, noon-11.30pm Sun; ⊜Leicester Sq) This pub off Old Compton St is often busy but has few pretensions, attracting a more beardy, fun-loving gay crowd, many of whom gather outside in warmer months.

Covent Garden & Leicester Square

LAMB & FLAG   PUB

Map p406 (www.lambandflagcoventgarden.co.uk; 33 Rose St, WC2; ☺11am-11pm Mon-Thu, 11am-11.30pm Fri & Sat, noon-10.30pm Sun; ⊜Covent Garden) The Lamb & Flag is pocket-sized but brimful of charm and history, squeezed into an alley (where poet John Dryden was mugged in December 1679) on the site of a pub that dates to at least 1772. Rain or shine, you'll have to elbow your way to the bar through the merry crowd drinking outside. Inside, it's all brass fittings and creaky wooden floors.

The main entrance is on top of a tiny cobbled street, but you can also reach it from the backstreet donkey path called Lazenby Court that'll transport you to Victorian England. First Sunday of the month is jazz night.

KU KLUB LISLE ST GAY

Map p406 (www.ku-bar.co.uk; 30 Lisle St, WC2; ☺10am-3am Mon-Sat, to midnight Sun; ⊜Leicester Sq) With its smart interior and busy events schedule (disco, cabaret, DJ sets etc) in the basement, the Lisle St branch of this gay minichain attracts a young, fun-loving crowd. Sunday is retro night.

CROSS KEYS PUB

Map p406 (www.crosskeyscoventgarden.com; 31 Endell St, WC2; ☺11am-11pm Mon-Sat, noon-10.30pm Sun; ⊜Covent Garden) Frequented by loyal locals who come for pints and spicy fry-ups, the Cross Keys is Covent Garden's tourist-free local pub. Eccentric landlord Brian has displayed his pop purchases as bar decorations (such as his £500 Elvis Presley napkin), and punters spill onto the pavement and outside tables on summer days.

TERROIRS WINE BAR

Map p406 (www.terroirswinebar.com; 5 William IV St, WC2; ☺noon-11pm Mon-Sat; 🛜; ⊜Charing Cross Road) Fab two-floor spot for a pre-theatre glass or some expertly created charcuterie, with informative staff, affordable £10 lunch specials, a lively, convivial atmosphere and a breathtaking list of organic wines.

FREUD BAR BAR

Map p406 (198 Shaftesbury Ave, WC2; ☺11am-11pm Mon-Wed, to 1am Thu & Sat, to 2am Fri, noon-10.30pm Sun; ⊜Covent Garden) Make this the first stop on your crawl because there's no way you'll make it down (or up) the stairs (not much more than a ladder) after a few drinks. It's a small basement bar/gallery with works from up-and-coming artists on the walls, with plans to convert the ground floor space by 2016. The decor and locals are suitably scruffy, and the cocktail list (40-plus) is extensive.

📍 Holborn & the Strand

HOLBORN WHIPPET PUB

Map p406 (www.holbornwhippet.com; 25-29 Sicilian Ave, WC1; ☺noon-11.30pm Mon-Sat, noon-10.30pm Sun; ⊜Holborn) Tiny, all wood, and at the end of a pedestrian-only street, this hideaway stocks a commendable range of draft ales (we counted two dozen) from small craft breweries. Staff are more than keen to offer a taste from the spouts on the 'brick wall' to help you decide. Food is of the sandwich/salad variety (£6 to £9).

PRINCESS LOUISE PUB

Map p406 (http://princesslouisepub.co.uk; 208 High Holborn, WC1; ☺11am-11pm Mon-Fri, noon-11pm Sat, noon-6.45pm Sun; ⊜Holborn) This late-19th-century Victorian pub is spectacularly decorated with a riot of fine tiles, etched mirrors, plasterwork and a stunning central horseshoe bar. The old Victorian wood partitions give drinkers plenty of nooks and alcoves to hide in. Beers are Sam Smith's only but cost just under £3 a pint, so it's no wonder many elect to spend the whole evening here.

GORDON'S WINE BAR BAR

Map p406 (www.gordonswinebar.com; 47 Villiers St, WC2; ☺11am-11pm Mon-Sat, noon-10pm Sun; ⊜Embankment) Gordon's is a victim of its own success; it is relentlessly busy and unless you arrive before the office crowd does (generally around 6pm), you can forget about getting a table. It's cavernous and dark, and the French and New World wines are heady and reasonably priced. You can nibble on bread, cheese and olives. Outside garden seating in summer.

SEVEN STARS PUB

Map p406 (53-54 Carey St, WC2; ☺11am-11pm Mon-Fri, noon-11pm Sat, to 10pm Sun; ⊜Holborn, Temple) Even though it's packed with lawyers in the after-office booze rush hour, the tiny Seven Stars is still a relative secret to many Londoners. Sitting between Lincoln's Inn Fields and the Royal Courts of Justice, and originally a sailors' hang-out, this is the place to come for real ale and ravishing game dishes.

The eccentric landlady and chef, Roxy Beaujolais, is a former TV chef and raconteur.

HEAVEN CLUB, GAY

Map p406 (www.heavennightclub-london.com; Villiers St, WC2; ☺11pm-5am Mon, Thu & Fri, 10pm-5am Sat; ⊜Embankment, Charing Cross) This 36-year old, perennially popular gay club under the arches beneath Charing Cross station has always been host to excellent live gigs and club nights. Monday's Popcorn (mixed dance party, all-welcome door policy) has to be one of the best weeknight's clubbing in the capital. The celebrated G-A-Y takes place here on Thursday (G-A-Y Porn Idol), Friday (G-A-Y Camp Attack) and Saturday (plain ol' G-A-Y).

DRAFT HOUSE BAR

Map p412 (www.drafthouse.co.uk; 43 Goodge St, W1; ☺noon-11pm Mon-Sat; 🛜; ⊜Goodge Street) Although you can line your tummy with good food here, Draft House is largely about the beer choice it crams into its pea-sized premises. This is a public house for ale aficionados, where you can happily corner a Flying Dog Gonzo Imperial Porter or a head-spinning Samichlaus 14%.

POLSKI BAR
BAR

Map p406 (11 Little Turnstile, WC1; ☺4-11pm Mon, 12.30-11pm Tue-Thu, 12.30-11.30pm Fri, 6-11pm Sat; ⊜Holborn) With around 60 different types of vodka – from hazelnut to wheat-flavoured, simple old *slivowica* (plum brandy) to ko-sher – everyone should find something that tickles their taste buds. There's great Polish food like *bigos* (hunter's stew) and *pierogis* (dumplings), too, but the bare and cold inte-rior leaves something to be desired.

🍽 Marylebone

ARTESIAN
BAR

Map p414 (📞020-7636 1000; www.artesian-bar.co.uk; Langham Hotel, 1c Portland Pl, W1; ☺11am-2am Mon-Sat, to midnight Sun; ⊜Oxford Circus) For a dose of colonial glamour with a touch of the Orient, the sumptuous bar at the Langham hits the mark. Rum is the speci-ality here – award-winning cocktails (£17) are concocted from the 60 varieties on offer.

PURL
COCKTAIL BAR

Map p414 (📞020-7935 0835; www.purl-london.com; 50-54 Blandford St, W1; ☺5-11.30pm Mon-Thu, to midnight Fri & Sat; ⊜Baker St, Bond St) A 'purveyor of fine matches and alcoholic libations', Purl is a fabulous underground drinking den. Decked out in vintage fur-niture, it serves original and intriguingly named cocktails (What's Your Poison? or Mr Hyde's No 2) and a punch of the day. It's all subdued lighting and hushed-tone con-versations, which only adds to the mysteri-ous air. Booking recommended.

🍽 Mayfair

PUNCH BOWL
PUB

Map p414 (www.punchbowllondon.com; 41 Farm St, W1; ☺noon-11pm Mon-Sat, to 10.30pm Sun; ⊜Green Park) The Punch Bowl attracts a young and happening crowd sipping cask ales, fine wines and whisky rather than run-of-the-mill pints. The pub retains many of its original 18th-century features (wood panels, cornicing etc), although the dining room at the back has a more modern feel to it.

GUINEA
PUB

Map p414 (www.theguinea.co.uk; 30 Bruton Pl, W1; ☺11.30am-10.30pm Mon-Fri, 5.30-11pm Sat; 📷; ⊜Green Park, Bond St) This quiet, friendly pub in London's most exclusive neighbour-hood has something of a gentlemen's club feel about it, with shiny brass fittings, heavy upholstery and a good selection of ales. There are very few places to sit, but if you do manage to bag a seat, you could order one of the celebrated sirloins, grills or pies from the rear restaurant.

The Guinea dates to 1675, although an inn has been on this site since 1423.

GALVIN AT WINDOWS
BAR

Map p414 (www.galvinatwindows.com; London Hilton on Park Lane, 28th fl, 22 Park Lane, W1; ☺11am-1am Mon-Wed, to 2am Thu-Fri, 3pm-2am Sat, 11am-11.30pm Sun; 📷; ⊜Hyde Park Corner) This swish bar on the edge of Hyde Park opens onto stunning views, especially at dusk. Mocktail and cocktail prices reach similar heights (£11.50 to £15.25) but the leather seats are comfortable and the mar-ble bar is gorgeous. The restaurant (same views, one Michelin star) offers a giveaway two- and three-course lunch menu for £25 and £29. Dress code is smart casual.

☆ ENTERTAINMENT

ROYAL OPERA HOUSE
OPERA

Map p406 (📞020-7304 4000; www.roh.org.uk; Bow St, WC2; tickets £7-250; ⊜Covent Garden) The £210 million redevelopment for the millennium gave classic opera a fantastic setting in London, and coming here for a night is a sumptuous – if pricey – affair. Although the program has been fluffed up by modern influences, the main attrac-tions are still the opera and classical ballet – all are wonderful productions and feature world-class performers.

Midweek matinees are usually cheaper than evening performances and restricted-view seats cost as little as £7. There are same-day tickets (one per customer avail-able to the first 67 people in the queue) from 10am for £8 to £44 and student standby tickets for £10. Half-price standby tickets four hours before the performance are only occasionally available. Free lunchtime re-citals are held on Mondays, when possible, in the Crush Room or Paul Hamlyn Hall, depending on the programme.

COMEDY STORE
COMEDY

Map p408 (📞0844 871 7699; www.thecomedy-store.co.uk; 1a Oxendon St, SW1; admission £8-23.50; ⊖Piccadilly Circus) One of the first (and still one of the best) comedy clubs in London. Wednesday and Sunday night's Comedy Store Players is the most famous improvisation outfit in town, with the wonderful Josie Lawrence; on Thursdays, Fridays and Saturdays Best in Stand Up features the best on London's comedy circuit.

PRINCE CHARLES
CINEMA

Map p408 (www.princecharlescinema.com; 7 Leicester Pl, WC2; tickets £8-16; ⊖Leicester Sq) Leicester Sq cinema ticket prices are brutal, so wait until the first-runs have moved to the Prince Charles, central London's cheapest cinema, where non-members pay only £8 to £10 for new releases. Also on the cards are mini-festivals, Q&As with film directors, classics, sleepover movie marathons and exuberant sing-along screenings of *Frozen, The Sound of Music* and *Rocky Horror Picture Show.*

PIZZA EXPRESS JAZZ CLUB
JAZZ

Map p408 (📞0845 602 7017; www.pizzaex-presslive.com; 10 Dean St, W1; admission £10-35; ⊖Tottenham Court Rd) Pizza Express has been one of the best jazz venues in London since opening in 1969. It may be a bit of a strange arrangement, in a basement beneath the main chain restaurant, but it's highly popular. Lots of big names perform here and promising artists such as Norah Jones, Jamie Cullum and the late Amy Winehouse played here in their early days.

RONNIE SCOTT'S
JAZZ

Map p408 (📞020-7439 0747; www.ronniescotts.co.uk; 47 Frith St, W1; ⊘7pm-3am Mon-Sat, to midnight Sun; ⊖Leicester Sq, Tottenham Court Rd) Ronnie Scott originally opened his jazz club on Gerrard St in 1959 under a Chinese gambling den. The club moved to its current location six years later and became widely known as Britain's best jazz club. Gigs are at 8.15pm (8pm Sunday) with a second act at 11.15pm Friday and Saturday, and are followed by a late, late show until 2am. Expect to pay between £20 and £50.

Ronnie Scott's has hosted such luminaries as Miles Davis, Charlie Parker, Thelonious Monk, Ella Fitzgerald, Count Basie and Sarah Vaughan. The club continues to build upon its formidable reputation by hosting a range of big names and new talent. The at-mosphere is great, but talking during music is a big no-no.

SOHO THEATRE
COMEDY

Map p408 (📞020-7478 0100; www.sohotheatre.com; 21 Dean St, W1; admission £10-25; ⊖Tottenham Court Rd) The Soho Theatre has developed a superb reputation for showcasing new comedy-writing talent and comedians. It's also hosted some top-notch stand-up or sketch-based comedians including Alexei Sayle and Doctor Brown, plus cabaret.

BORDERLINE
LIVE MUSIC

Map p408 (www.mamacolive.com/theborderline; Orange Yard, off Manette St, W1; ⊖Tottenham Court Rd) Through the Tex-Mex entrance off Orange Yard and down into the basement you'll find a packed, 275-capacity venue that really punches above its weight. Read the gig list: Ed Sheeran, REM, Blur, Counting Crows, PJ Harvey, Lenny Kravitz, Pearl Jam, plus many anonymous indie outfits, have all played here. The crowd's equally diverse but can be full of music journos and record-company talent spotters.

PLACE
DANCE

Map p412 (www.theplace.org.uk; 17 Duke's Rd, WC1; ⊖Euston Sq) One of London's most exciting cultural venues, this was the birthplace of modern British dance; it still concentrates on challenging and experimental choreography. Behind the late-Victorian facade you'll find a 300-seat theatre, an arty, creative cafe atmosphere and a dozen training studios. The Place sponsors an annual Place Prize, which awards new and outstanding dance talent. Tickets usually cost from £15.

CURZON SOHO
CINEMA

Map p408 (www.curzoncinemas.com; 99 Shaftesbury Ave, W1; tickets £8-14; ⊖Leicester Sq, Piccadilly Circus) The Curzon Soho is one of London's best cinemas. It has a fantastic program lineup with the best of British, European, world and American indie films; regular Q&As with directors; shorts and mini-festivals; a Konditor & Cook cafe upstairs; cakes to die for; and an ultracomfortable bar.

WIGMORE HALL
CLASSICAL MUSIC

Map p414 (www.wigmore-hall.org.uk; 36 Wigmore St, W1; ⊖Bond St) This is one of the best and most active (400 events a year) classical-music venues in town, not only because of its fantastic acoustics, beautiful art nouveau hall and great variety of concerts and recitals, but also because of the sheer standard of the performances. Built in 1901, it has remained one of the world's top places for chamber music.

The Sunday coffee concerts at 11.30am and the lunchtime ones at 1pm on Monday (both adult/concession £13/11) are excellent value. Evening concerts cost between £15 and £35.

AMUSED MOOSE SOHO   COMEDY

Map p408 (✍box office 020-7287 3727; www. amusedmoose.com; Sanctum Hotel cinema, 20 Warwick St, W1; ⊖Piccadilly Circus, Oxford Circus) One of the city's best clubs, the peripatetic Amused Moose (Moonlighting is just one of its hosting venues) is popular with audiences and comedians alike, perhaps helped along by the fact that heckling is 'unacceptable' and all of the acts are 'first-date friendly' (ie unlikely to humiliate the front row).

LONDON COLISEUM   OPERA

Map p406 (✍020-7845 9300; www.eno.org; St Martin's Lane, WC2; ⊖Leicester Sq) The London Coliseum is home to the English National Opera (ENO), celebrated for making opera modern and more relevant, as all productions are sung in English. The building, built in 1904 and lovingly restored 100 years later, is very impressive. The English National Ballet also does regular performances at the Coliseum. Tickets range from £12 to £99.

After several years in the wasteland, the ENO has been receiving better reviews and welcoming much bigger audiences under the tutelage of music director Edward Gardner (his tenure, at the time of research, was due to end soon).

100 CLUB   LIVE MUSIC

Map p412 (✍020-7636 0933; www.the100club. co.uk; 100 Oxford St, W1; admission £8-20; ⊙check website for gig times; ⊖Oxford Circus, Tottenham Court Rd) This legendary London venue has always concentrated on jazz, but also features swing and rock. It's showcased Chris Barber, BB King and the Stones, and was at the centre of the punk revolution and the '90s indie scene. It hosts dancing swing gigs and local jazz musicians, the occasional big name and where-are-they-now bands.

DONMAR WAREHOUSE   THEATRE

Map p406 (✍0844 871 7624; www.donmarwarehouse.com; 41 Earlham St, WC2; ⊖Covent Garden) The cosy Donmar Warehouse is London's 'thinking person's theatre'. Current artistic director Josie Rourke has staged some intriguing and successful productions, including the well-received comedy *My Night with Reg.*

But some think it has taken a step back from the days when Nicole Kidman administered 'theatrical Viagra' nightly by peeling off her clothes in Sam Mendes' production of *The Blue Room,* and Michael Grandage framed blue-eyed Jude Law as *Hamlet.*

ICA CINEMA   CINEMA

Map p416 (www.ica.org.uk; Nash House, The Mall, SW1; 🐦; ⊖Charing Cross, Piccadilly Circus) The Institute of Contemporary Arts (ICA) is a treasure for lovers of indie cinema – its program always has material no one else is showing, such as the latest independents from the developing world, films showing out of season, all-night screenings and rare documentaries. The two cinemas are quite small, but comfortable enough. Tickets usually cost £11 (concessions £8).

🛍 SHOPPING

The West End's shopping scene hardly needs a formal introduction. Oxford St is heaven or hell, depending on what you're after. It's all about chains, from Marks & Spencer to H&M, Top Shop to Gap. Covent Garden is also beset with run-of-the-mill outlets, but they tend to be smaller and counterbalanced by independent boutiques, vintage ones in particular. As well as fashion, the West End is big on music. There are some great independent record shops, especially in Soho.

🛍 Westminster & St James's

PENHALIGON'S   ACCESSORIES

Map p416 (www.penhaligons.com; 16-17 Burlington Arcade, W1; ⊙10am-6pm Mon-Fri, to 6.30pm Sat, 11am-5pm Sun; ⊖Piccadilly Circus, Green Park) Ensconced within stunningly historic Burlington Arcade, Penhaligon's is a classic British perfumery. Attendants inquire about your favourite smells, take you on an exploratory tour of the shop's signature range and help you discover new scents in their traditional perfumes, home fragrances and bath and body products. Everything is made in Cornwall.

BOOKWORM PARADISE: THE WEST END'S BEST BOOKSHOPS

Daunt Books (Map p414; www.dauntbooks.co.uk; 83 Marylebone High St, W1; ⊙9am-7.30pm Mon-Sat, 11am-6pm Sun; ⊜Baker St) An original Edwardian bookshop, with oak panels and gorgeous skylights, Daunt is one of London's loveliest travel bookshops. It has two floors and stocks general fiction and nonfiction titles as well.

London Review Bookshop (Map p412; www.londonreviewbookshop.co.uk; 14 Bury Pl, WC1; ⊙10am-6.30pm Mon-Sat, noon-6pm Sun; ⊜Holborn) The flagship bookshop of the *London Review of Books* literary magazine doesn't believe in piles of books, taking the clever approach of stocking wide-ranging titles in one or two copies only. It often hosts high-profile author talks (tickets £10, unless otherwise stated); and there is a charming cafe where you can peruse your new purchases.

Foyles (Map p408; www.foyles.co.uk; 107 Charing Cross Rd, WC2; ⊙9.30am-9pm Mon-Sat, 11.30am-6pm Sun; ⊜Tottenham Court Rd) This is London's most legendary bookshop, where you can bet on finding even the most obscure of titles. In 2014, the store moved just down the road into the spacious former home of Central St Martins. Thoroughly redesigned, its stunning new home is a joy to explore.

The cafe is on the 5th floor, where you can also find the Gallery at Foyles (for art exhibitions); **Grant & Cutler** (Map p408; www.grantandcutler.com; 4th fl, 107 Charing Cross Rd, WC2; ⊜Oxford Circus), the UK's largest foreign-language bookseller, is on the 4th floor while **Ray's Jazz** (p130) is on the 2nd floor.

Hatchards (Map p416; 187 Piccadilly, W1; ⊙9.30am-7pm Mon-Sat, noon-6pm Sun; ⊜Green Park, Piccadilly Circus) London's oldest bookshop dates to 1797. Holding three royal warrants (hence the portrait of the Queen), it's a stupendous independent book-store, with a solid supply of signed editions and bursting at its smart seams with very browseable stock. There's a strong selection of first editions on the ground floor as well as regular literary events.

Stanford's (Map p406; www.stanfords.co.uk; 12-14 Long Acre, WC2; ⊙9am-8pm Mon-Fri, 10am-8pm Sat, noon-6pm Sun; ⊜Leicester Sq, Covent Garden) As a 160-year-old seller of maps, guides and literature, the granddaddy of travel bookshops is a destination in its own right. Ernest Shackleton and David Livingstone and, more recently, Michael Palin and Brad Pitt have all popped in here.

Waterstones (Map p416; www.waterstones.com; 203-206 Piccadilly, W1; ⊙9am-10pm Mon-Sat, noon-6pm Sun; ⊜Piccadilly Circus) The chain's megastore is the largest book-shop in Europe, boasting knowledgeable staff and regular author readings and sign-ings. The store spreads across four floors, and there is a cafe in the basement and a fabulous rooftop bar–restaurant, **5th View** (Map p416; ⌕020-7851 2433; www.5thview.co.uk; 5th fl, Waterstone's Piccadilly, 203-206 Piccadilly, W1; mains £9-15; ⊙9am-10pm Mon-Sat, noon-5pm Sun; ⊜Piccadilly Circus).

Gosh! (Map p408; www.goshlondon.com; 1 Berwick St, W1; ⊙10.30am-7.30pm; ⊜Pic-cadilly Circus) Draw up here for graphic novels, manga, newspaper-strip collections and children's books, such as the Tintin and Asterix series. It's also perfect for finding presents for kids and teenagers.

Skoob Books (Map p412; ⌕020-7278 8760; www.skoob.com; 66 The Brunswick, off Mar-mont St, WC1; ⊙10.30am-8pm Mon-Sat, to 6pm Sun; ⊜Russell Sq) Skoob (you work out the name) has got to be London's largest second-hand bookshop, with some 55,000 titles spread over 2000 sq ft of floor space. If you can't find it here, it probably doesn't exist.

FORTNUM & MASON DEPARTMENT STORE

Map p416 (www.fortnumandmason.com; 181 Pic-cadilly, W1; ⊙10am-9pm Mon-Sat, noon-6pm Sun; ⊜Piccadilly Circus) With its classic eau de nil colour scheme, London's oldest grocery store (into its fourth century), refuses to yield to modern times. Its staff still clad in old-fashioned tailcoats, its glamorous food hall supplied with hampers, cut marma-lade, speciality teas and so forth.

PAXTON & WHITFIELD FOOD & DRINK

Map p416 (www.paxtonandwhitfield.co.uk; 93 Jermyn St, W1; ⊕9.30am-6pm Mon-Sat, 11am-5pm Sun; ⊜Piccadilly Circus, Green Park) With modest beginnings as an Aldwych stall in 1742 and purveying a dizzying range of fine cheeses, this black- and gold-fronted shop holds a royal warrant and won over Winston Churchill, who observed: 'A gentleman buys his hats at Locks, his shoes at Lobbs, his shirts at Harvie & Hudson, his suits at Huntsman and his cheese at Paxton & Whitfield'.

Whatever your cheese leanings, you'll find the shop well-supplied, from Caerphilly Gorwydd to Spanish Picos Blue or French Mothais Sur Feuille.

JAMES J. FOX ACCESSORIES

Map p416 (www.jjfox.co.uk; 19 St James's St, SW1; ⊕9.30am-5.45pm Mon-Wed & Fri, to 9.30pm Thu, to 5pm Sat; ⊜Green Park) James J. Fox has been in business for over 225 years and any cigar merchant that kept Winston Churchill well-supplied with maduro cigars has to be a reliable choice for enthusiasts of the Cuban tobacco leaf. Prices start at about £5.50 for a Quorum Short Robusto and head into the (smokey) clouds. The shop is *not* no-smoking.

TAYLOR OF OLD BOND STREET BEAUTY

Map p416 (www.tayloroldbondst.co.uk; 74 Jermyn St, SW1; ⊕8.30am-6pm Mon-Sat; ⊜Green Park, Piccadilly Circus) Plying its trade since the mid-19th century, this shop supplies the 'well-groomed gentleman' with every sort of razor, shaving brush and scent of shaving soap imaginable – not to mention oils, soaps and other bath products.

🔒 Bloomsbury & Fitzrovia

BANG BANG CLOTHING
EXCHANGE VINTAGE

Map p412 (www.bangbangclothingexchange.com; 21 Goodge St, W1; ⊕10am-6.30pm Mon-Fri, 11am-6pm Sat; ⊜Goodge St) Got some designer or high-street or vintage pieces you're tired of? Bang Bang exchanges, buys and sells. As the exchange says of itself, 'think of Alexander McQueen cocktail dresses rubbing shoulders with Topshop shoes and 1950s jewellery'.

JAMES SMITH & SONS ACCESSORIES

Map p412 (www.james-smith.co.uk; 53 New Oxford St, WC1; ⊕10am-5.45pm Mon-Fri, to 5.15pm Sat; ⊜Tottenham Court Rd) 'Outside every silver lining is a big black cloud', claim the cheerful owners of this quintessential English shop. Nobody makes and stocks such elegant umbrellas, walking sticks and canes like this place. It's been fighting the British weather from this address since 1857 and, thanks to London's notorious downpours, will hopefully do great business for years to come.

Prices start at around £40 for a pocket umbrella and go up to over £2000.

DARKROOM JEWELLERY

Map p412 (www.darkroomlondon.com; 52 Lamb's Conduit St, WC1; ⊕11am-7pm Mon-Fri, to 6pm Sat, noon-5pm Sun; ⊜Holborn, Russell Sq) This – well – very dark room on one of London's top shopping streets displays and sells stylish, carefully chosen and boldly-patterned designer jewellery, accessories and handbags. There's also glassware and ceramics and its own line of prints and cushions.

BLADE RUBBER STAMPS ARTS & CRAFTS

Map p412 (www.bladerubberstamps.co.uk; 12 Bury Pl, WC1; ⊕10.30am-6pm Mon-Sat, 11.30am-4.30pm Sun; ⊜Holborn) Just south of the British Museum, this specialist shop stocks just about every wooden-handled rubber stamp you care to imagine: from London icons like post boxes, Beefeaters and the Houses of Parliament to landscapes, planets, rockets and Christmas stamps. They can make you one to your design or you can have a go yourself with a stamp-making kit.

FOLK FASHION

Map p412 (www.folkclothing.com; 49 & 53 Lamb's Conduit St, WC1; ⊕11am-7pm Mon-Fri, 10am-6pm Sat, noon-5pm Sun; ⊜Holborn) Simple but strikingly styled casual clothes, often in bold colours and with a hand-crafted feel. Head for No 49 for Folk's own line of menswear and to No 53 for womenswear.

GAY'S THE WORD BOOKS

Map p412 (www.gaystheword.co.uk; 66 Marmont St, WC1; ⊕10am-6.30pm Mon-Sat, 2-6pm Sun; ⊜Russell Sq) This London gay institution has been selling books nobody else stocks for 35 years, with a superb range of gay- and lesbian-interest books and magazines plus a real community spirit. Used books available as well.

🔒 Soho & Chinatown

JOY FASHION

Map p408 (www.joythestore.com; 162-170 Wardour St, W1; ⊕10.30am-8pm Mon-Fri, 10am-7pm

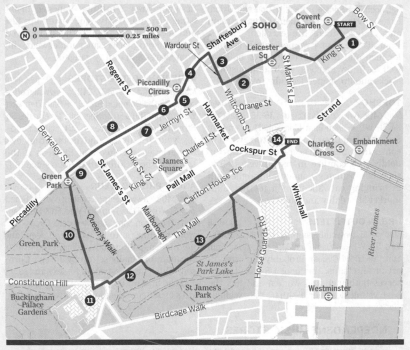

🏃 Neighbourhood Walk
The West End

START COVENT GARDEN TUBE STATION
END TRAFALGAR SQ
LENGTH 2.5 MILES; 1½ HOURS

This walk takes you through the heart of the West End, from Covent Garden's chic shopping streets to Trafalgar Sq, via Chinatown and leafy St James's Park.

First, head to busy ❶ **Covent Garden Piazza** (p104) and enjoy the street performers outside St Paul's Church. Continue along King and Garrick Sts; turn left on Long Acre and you'll arrive at renovated ❷ **Leicester Square** (p105), where many international blockbuster films premiere. Turn right on Wardour St; you'll soon come to the Oriental gates of ❸ **Chinatown** (p103) on your right. The area is especially attractive around Chinese New Year, when hundreds of lanterns adorn the streets.

Turn left on ❹ **Shaftesbury Avenue**, where you'll find some of the West End's most prestigious theatres. At the end of the avenue is hectic ❺ **Piccadilly Circus**

(p103), 'London's Times Square', full of flashing ads, shops and tourists.

Make your way west along ❻ **Piccadilly**; this avenue gives just a hint of the aristocratic St James's and Mayfair neighbourhoods. Pop into ❼ **St James's Piccadilly** (p100), Wren's only original church. Further along on the right, you'll see stately Burlington House, home of the ❽ **Royal Academy of Arts** (p101), before passing the famous ❾ **Ritz Hotel**.

Turn left into ❿ **Green Park** (p102), a quiet space with stunning oak trees and old-style street lamps. ⓫ **Buckingham Palace** (p85) is at the bottom of the park, past the beautiful Canada Gates.

Walk down the grandiose ⓬ **Mall**; on the right is the lovely ⓭ **St James's Park** (p100). Views of Buckingham Palace and Whitehall are stunning from the footbridge over the lake. At the end of the Mall is ⓮ **Trafalgar Square** (p94), dominated by Nelson's Column and the National Gallery. There are also great views of Big Ben and the Houses of Parliament from its south side.

Sat, noon-7pm Sun; ◉Tottenham Court Rd, Oxford Circus) Joy is an artistic blend of mainstream and vintage: there are excellent clothes, from silk dresses for women, fabulous shirts for men and timeless T-shirts for both, as well as funky gadgets, such as moustache clocks and lip-shaped ice cube trays.

TOPSHOP
CLOTHING

Map p408 (www.topshop.co.uk; 36-38 Great Castle St, W1; ◷9am-9pm Mon-Sat, 11.30am-6pm Sun; ◉Oxford Circus) The 'It'-store when it comes to clothes and accessories, venturing boldly into couture in recent years, Topshop encapsulates London's supreme skill at bringing catwalk fashion to the youth market affordably and quickly.

URBAN OUTFITTERS
FASHION

Map p408 (www.urbanoutfitters.co.uk; 200 Oxford St, W1; ◷10am-8pm Mon-Sat, noon-6pm Sun; ◉Oxford Circus) Probably the trendiest of all chains, this cool US-based store serves both men and women and has the best young designer T-shirts, an excellent designer area (stocking Vanessa Bruno Athé, Vivienne Westwood, Something Else and See by Chloé, among others), 'renewed' second-hand pieces, saucy underwear, silly homewares and quirky gadgets.

ALGERIAN COFFEE STORES
FOOD & DRINK

Map p408 (☑020-7437 2480; www.algcoffee. co.uk; 52 Old Compton St, W1; ◷9am-7pm Mon-Wed, to 9pm Thu & Fri, to 8pm Sat; ◉Leicester Sq) Stop for a shot of espresso (£1) while choosing your freshly ground beans from over 80 varieties of coffee and 120 teas at this fantastic shop, caffeinating Soho since 1887.

AGENT PROVOCATEUR
CLOTHING

Map p408 (www.agentprovocateur.com; 6 Broadwick St, W1; ◷11am-7pm Mon-Wed, Fri & Sat, 11am-8pm Thu, noon-5pm Sun; ◉Oxford Circus) For women's lingerie to be worn and seen, and *not* hidden, pull up to wonderful Agent Provocateur, originally set up by Joseph Corré, son of Vivienne Westwood. Its sexy and saucy corsets, bras and nighties for all shapes and sizes exude confident and positive sexuality.

INDEPENDENT MUSIC STORES

Britons buy more music per head than any other nation. Independent music stores find it difficult to keep going, especially in central London, but they still exist . Here are the West End's best:

Sister Ray (Map p408; www.sisterray.co.uk; 75 Berwick St, W1; ◷10am-8pm Mon-Sat, noon-6pm Sun; ◉Oxford Circus, Tottenham Court Rd) If you were a fan of the late, great John Peel on the BBC/BBC World Service, this specialist in innovative, experimental and indie music is just right for you.

Ray's Jazz (Map p408; www.foyles.co.uk; 2nd fl, 107 Charing Cross Rd, WC2; ◷9.30am-9pm Mon-Sat, 11.30am-6pm Sun; ◉Tottenham Court Rd) Quiet and serene with friendly and helpful staff, this shop on the 2nd floor of Foyles bookshop has one of the best jazz selections in London.

Sounds of the Universe (Map p408; www.soundsoftheuniverse.com; 7 Broadwick St, W1; ◷11am-7.30pm Sat, 11.30am-5.30pm Sun; ◉Oxford Circus, Tottenham Court Rd) Outlet of Soul Jazz Records label (responsible for so many great soul, reggae, funk and dub albums), this place stocks CDs and vinyl plus some original 45s.

Harold Moore's Records (Map p408; www.hmrecords.co.uk; 2 Great Marlborough St, W1; ◷10am-7pm Mon-Sat; ◉Oxford Circus, Tottenham Court Rd) London's finest classical-music store stocks an extensive range of vinyl, CDs and DVDs, plus jazz in the basement. It can source hard-to-find music for you

Reckless Records (Map p408; www.reckless.co.uk; 30 Berwick St, W1; ◷10am-7pm; ◉Oxford Circus, Tottenham Court Rd) Despite its numerous name changes, this outfit hasn't really changed in spirit. It still stocks new and secondhand records and CDs, from punk, soul, dance and independent to mainstream.

Phonica (Map p408; www.phonicarecords.co.uk; 51 Poland St, W1; ◷11.30am-7.30pm Mon-Wed & Sat, 11.30am-8pm Thu-Fri, noon-6pm Sun; ◉Tottenham Court Rd, Oxford Circus) A cool and relaxed shop that stocks a lot of house, electro, hip hop and punk funk, but you can find just about anything from reggae to dub, jazz and rock.

HAMLEYS TOYS
Map p408 (www.hamleys.com; 188-196 Regent St, W1; ⏰10am-9pm Mon-Fri, 9.30am-9pm Sat, noon-6pm Sun; ⊖Oxford Circus) Claiming to be the world's oldest (and some say, the largest) toy store, Hamleys moved to its address on Regent Street in 1881. From the ground floor – where staff glide UFOs and foam boomerangs through the air with practised nonchalance – to Lego World and a cafe on the 5th floor, it's a layercake of playthings.

LIBERTY DEPARTMENT STORE
Map p408 (www.liberty.co.uk; Great Marlborough St, W1; ⏰10am-8pm Mon-Sat, noon-6pm Sun; ⊖Oxford Circus) An irresistible blend of contemporary styles in an old-fashioned mock-Tudor atmosphere, Liberty has a huge cosmetics department and an accessories floor, along with a breathtaking lingerie section, all at very inflated prices. A classic London souvenir is a Liberty fabric print, especially in the form of a scarf.

LINA STORES FOOD
Map p408 (www.linastores.co.uk; 18 Brewer St, W1; ⏰8.30am-7.30pm Mon & Tue, to 8.30pm Wed-Fri, 9am-7.30pm Sat, 11am-5pm Sun ; ⊖Piccadilly Circus) This delightful Italian delicatessen in the heart of Soho, here since 1944, is so gorgeous in its cream and pastel green that you could almost imagine eating it. Come here for picnic cheeses, charcuterie, bread and olives.

BEYOND RETRO VINTAGE
Map p408 (www.beyondretro.com; 58-59 Great Marlborough St, W1; ⏰10.30am-7.30pm Mon, Tue & Sat, to 8.30pm Wed-Fri, 11am-6pm Sun; ⊖Oxford Circus) A more central basement outlet of an enormous warehouse just off Brick Lane in East London, Beyond Retro sells vintage and some repro clothes for men and women, with the requisite stilettos, bowler and top hats and satin wedding dresses.

🛍 Covent Garden & Leicester Square

NEAL'S YARD DAIRY FOOD
Map p406 (www.nealsyarddairy.co.uk; 17 Shorts Gardens, WC2; ⏰10am-7pm Mon-Sat; ⊖Covent Garden) A fabulous, fragrant cheese house that would fit in rural England, this place is proof that the British can do just as well as the French when it comes to big rolls of ripe cheese. There are more than 70 varieties that the shopkeepers will let you taste, including

independent farmhouse brands. Condiments, pickles, jams and chutneys are also on sale.

CAMBRIDGE SATCHEL COMPANY ACCESSORIES
Map p406 (www.cambridgesatchel.com; 31 James St, WC2; ⏰10am-7pm Mon-Sat, 11am-7pm Sun; ⊖Covent Garden) The classic British leather satchel concept morphed into a trendy and colourful him-or-her array of backpacks, totes, clutches, tiny satchels, work bags, music bags, mini satchels, two-in-one satchels and more.

MOLTON BROWN BEAUTY
Map p406 (www.moltonbrown.co.uk; 18 Russell St, WC2; ⏰10am-7pm Mon-Sat, 11am-6pm Sun; ⊖Covent Garden) A fabulously fragrant British natural beauty range, Molton Brown is *the* choice for boutique hotels, posh restaurants and 1st-class airline bathrooms. Its skin-care products offer plenty of pampering for both men and women. In this store you can also have a facial as well as pick up home accessories.

WATKINS BOOKS
Map p406 (www.watkinsbooks.com; 19-21 Cecil Court, WC2; ⏰10.30am-6.30pm Mon-Wed & Fri, 11am-7.30pm Thu & Sat, noon-7pm Sun; ⊖Leicester Square) More books than you can shake a dreamcatcher at on the afterlife, Taiji Quan, divination, fairies, tarot, Kabbalah, Shamanism, religious spirituality, astrology, Indian philosophy, Tibetan Buddhism, conspiracy theories and more. If you've even the mildest interest in the esoteric, you could find yourself here for hours (if not days).

MONMOUTH COFFEE COMPANY FOOD & DRINK
Map p406 (www.monmouthcoffee.co.uk; 27 Monmouth St, WC2; pastry & cakes from £2.50; ⏰8am-6.30pm Mon-Sat; ⊖Tottenham Court Rd, Leicester Sq) Essentially a shop selling beans from just about every coffee-growing country, Monmouth, here since 1978, has a few wooden alcoves at the back where you can squeeze in and savour blends from around the world as well as cakes from local patisseries.

TED BAKER FASHION
Map p406 (www.tedbaker.com; 9-10 Floral St, WC2; ⏰10.30am-7.30pm Mon-Wed, Fri & Sat, to 8pm Thu, 10am-7pm Sat, noon-6pm Sun; ⊖Covent Garden) The one-time Glasgow-based tailor shop has grown into a superb brand of clothing, with elegant men's and womenswear.

Ted's forte is its formal wear, with beautiful dresses for women (lots of daring prints and exquisite material) and sharp tailoring for men. The casual collections (denim, beachwear etc) are excellent too.

PAUL SMITH
FASHION

Map p406 (www.paulsmith.co.uk; 40-44 Floral St, WC2; ☉10.30am-6.30pm Mon-Wed, to 7pm Thu & Fri, 10am-7pm Sat, 12.30-5.30pm Sun ; ◉Covent Garden) Paul Smith represents the best of British classics with innovative twists. Super-stylish menswear, suits and tailored shirts are all laid out on open shelves in this walk-in closet of a shop. Smith also does womenswear, with sharp tailoring for an androgynous, almost masculine, look.

BENJAMIN POLLOCK'S TOY SHOP
TOYS

Map p406 (www.pollocks-coventgarden.co.uk; 1st fl, 44 Market Bldg, Covent Garden, WC2; ☉10.30am-6pm Mon-Wed, to 6.30pm Thu-Sat, 11am-6pm Sun; ◉Covent Garden) Here's a traditional toyshop stuffed with the things that kids of all ages love. There are Victorian paper theatres, wooden marionettes and finger puppets, and antique teddy bears that might be too fragile to play with.

KAREN MILLEN
FASHION

Map p406 (www.karenmillen.com; 2-3 James St, WC2; ☉10am-8pm Mon-Sat, 11am-6pm Sun; ◉Covent Garden) An upmarket womenswear store, with glam suit-trousers, voluptuous knits, shiny trench coats and evening frocks.

DO SHOP
HOMEWARES

Map p406 (do-shop.com; 34 Shorts Gardens, WC2; ☉10am-6.30pm Mon-Wed, Fri & Sat, to 8pm Thu, noon-6pm Sun; ◉Covent Garden) A highly imaginative collection of functional furniture, kitchenware and home accessories from independent designers, including students from the Royal College of Art and other art schools. From tables and bookshelves, to bento boxes, innovative porcelain and ornaments, it's perfect for presents (to self, as well).

🔒 Marylebone

CATH KIDSTON
HOMEWARES, CLOTHING

Map p414 (www.cathkidston.com; 51 Marylebone High St, W1; ☉10am-7pm Mon-Sat, 11am-5pm Sun; ◉Baker St) If you favour the preppy look, you'll love Cath Kidston with her signature floral prints and 1950s fashion (dresses above the knee and cinched at the waist, cardigans, shawls and old-fashioned pyjamas). There is also a range of homewares.

CADENHEAD'S WHISKY & TASTING SHOP
DRINK

Map p414 (www.whiskytastingroom.com; 26 Chiltern St, W1; ◉Baker St) Scotland's oldest independent bottler of pure, non-blended whisky from local distilleries, this excellent shop is a joy for anyone with a passion for *uisge* (the gaelic word for 'water'). All bottled whiskies derive from individually selected casks, without any filtrations, additions or colouring, guaranteeing purity. Regular whisky tastings are held downstairs (maximum 12 people).

MONOCLE SHOP
ACCESSORIES

Map p414 (☎020-7486 8770; www.monocle. com; 2a George St, W1; ☉11am-7pm Mon-Sat, noon-5pm Sun; ◉Bond St) Run by the people behind the design and international current affairs magazine *Monocle,* this shop is pure understated heaven. Costly stuff but if you're a fan of minimalist quality design (clothes, bags, umbrellas and so on), you'll want to stop by. Beautifully bound first editions too. There's the Monocle Cafe (p118) not far away too, on Chiltern St.

BEATLES STORE
SOUVENIRS

Map p414 (www.itsonlyrocknrolllondon.com; 230 Baker St, NW1; ☉10am-6.30pm; ◉Baker St) Fab Four Guitar picks, Abbey Road fridge magnets, Ringo T-shirts, mop top mugs, *Magical Mystery Tour* bags, *Yellow Submarine* Christmas lights, *Help!* posters, alarm clocks...the whole Beatles shebang.

🔒 Mayfair

STING
FASHION

Map p408 (www.thesting.nl; 55 Regent St, W1; ☉10am-10pm Mon-Sat, noon-6pm Sun; ◉Piccadilly Circus) This Dutch chain is a 'network of brands': most of the clothes it stocks are European labels that are little known in the UK. Spread over three floors are anything from casual sweatpants and fluoro T-shirts to elegant dresses, frilly tops and handsome shirts.

ABERCROMBIE & FITCH
FASHION

Map p408 (www.abercrombie.com; 7 Burlington Gardens, W1; ☉10am-7pm Mon-Sat, noon-6pm Sun; ◉Piccadilly Circus) All tall wood doors, bling chandeliers, hip sounds, low lighting and two floors of stylish casual wear, A & F is one cool customer that hasn't waned in popularity. The shop is busy from the minute it opens its doors, and at weekends queues snake through the ground floor.

DOVER STREET MARKET   CLOTHING

Map p416 (www.doverstreetmarket.com; 17-18 Dover St, W1; ⊘11am-7pm Mon-Sat, noon-5pm Sun; ⊜Green Park) Showcasing the colourful creations of Tokyo fashion darlings Comme des Garçons (among other labels), Dover Street Market is the place to come for that shirt you only wear on special occasions. There are four floors of clothing for men and women, all artfully displayed.

BROWNS FOCUS   CLOTHING

Map p414 (24 South Molton St, W1; ⊘10am-6.30pm Mon-Wed, Fri & Sat, 10am-7pm Thu; ⊜Bond St) Edgy and exciting Browns Focus is full of natty and individual clothing ideas and shoes from American Retro, Asish, Stella Jean, Natasha Zinko and other creative designers.

POSTCARD TEAS   FOOD & DRINK

Map p414 (www.postcardteas.com; 9 Dering St, W1; ⊘10.30am-6.30pm; ⊜Bond St) If you know your *longjing* from your *pu'er*, or your nokcha from your Lotus Lake Green – or wish to know – Postcard Teas could well be your cup of tea. This small shop specialises in carefully provenanced teas and small producers (15 acres or less) from China, Japan, Vietnam, Korea, Taiwan and India.

SELFRIDGES   DEPARTMENT STORE

Map p414 (www.selfridges.com; 400 Oxford St, W1; ⊘9.30am-9pm Mon-Sat, 11.30am-6pm Sun; ⊜Bond St) Selfridges loves innovation – it's famed for its inventive window displays by international artists, gala shows and, above all, its amazing range of products. It's the trendiest of London's one-stop shops, with labels such as Boudicca, Luella Bartley, Emma Cook, Chloé and Missoni; an unparalleled food hall; and Europe's largest cosmetics department.

GINA   SHOES

Map p414 (www.gina.com; 119 Mount St, W1; ⊘10am-6pm Mon-Sat, to 7pm Thu, noon-5pm Sun; ⊜Bond St) Beyond the quality of leathers and fabrics and gorgeously chic styling, a frequent motif of these beautifully-made and elegant British couture women's sling backs, stilettos, court shoes, flat sandals, peep toes

and platorms is their glittering Swarovski crystals. Prices start from around £425.

MULBERRY   ACCESSORIES

Map p414 (www.mulberry.com; 41-42 New Bond St, W1; ⊘10am-7pm Mon-Sat, 11am-5pm Sun; ⊜Bond St) Mulberry bags are voluptuous, soft and a massive style statement. The brand has followed in the footsteps of its other British design titans like Burberry and Pringle and modernised itself in recent years.

BURBERRY   FASHION

Map p414 (www.burberry.com; 21-23 New Bond St, SW1; ⊘10am-9pm Mon-Sat, 11.30-6pm Sun; ⊜Bond St) The first traditional British brand to reach the heights of fashion, Burberry is known for its innovative take on classic pieces (eg bright-coloured trench coats, khaki pants with large and unusual pockets), its brand check pattern and a tailored, groomed look.

JOHN LEWIS   DEPARTMENT STORE

Map p414 (www.johnlewis.co.uk; 300 Oxford St, W1; ⊘9.30am-8pm Mon-Wed, Fri & Sat, to 9pm Thu, 11.30am-6pm Sun ; ⊜Oxford Circus) 'Never knowingly undersold' is the motto of this store, whose range of household goods, fashion and luggage is better described as reliable rather than cutting edge. And for that reason it's some people's favourite store in the whole wide world.

STELLA MCCARTNEY   FASHION

Map p414 (www.stellamccartney.co.uk; 30 Bruton St, W1; ⊘10am-7pm Mon-Sat; ⊜Bond St) ⊘ Stella McCartney's sharp tailoring, floaty designs, accessible style and 'ethical' approach to fashion (no leather or fur) is very of-the-moment. This three-storey terraced Victorian home is a minimalist showcase for the designer's current collections. Depending on your devotion and wallet, you'll feel at ease or like a trespasser.

PETER HARRINGTON   BOOKS

Map p416 (www.peterharrington.co.uk; 43 Dover St, W1; ⊘10am-7pm Mon-Fri, 10am-6pm Sat; ⊜Green Park) Fine purveyors of first editions and rare books, Peter Harrington is a delightful and extremely well-presented shop, devoid of clutter but stocking a fabulous range of titles from a fine signed first edition of *Harry Potter and the Half-Blood Prince* (£2750), to Dr Seuss' *The Lorax* (£1000), Sylvia Plath's *Winter Trees* (£150) and beyond. Staff are knowledgeable, helpful and friendly but leave you well alone to browse.

The City

Neighbourhood Top Five

1 Walking through that treasury of history, the **Tower of London** (p136), past the colourful Yeoman Warders (or Beefeaters), the spectacular Crown Jewels, the soothsaying ravens and armour fit for a *very* large king.

2 Listening in on whispering neighbours in the dome of **St Paul's** (p142), before enjoying its far-reaching views.

3 Getting below the surface – literally – of the City at the extensive **Museum of London** (p151).

4 Imagining the tragedy of medieval London ablaze as you climb the **Monument** (p148) to the Great Fire of 1666.

5 Marvelling at the City's ultramodern new buildings from what is perhaps its least admired building, **20 Fenchurch St** (p147), aka the 'Walkie Talkie'.

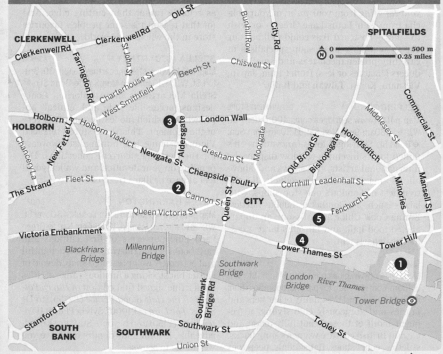

CLERKENWELL
Clerkenwell Rd
Clerkenwell Rd
Old St
Bunhill Row
City Rd
SPITALFIELDS

Farringdon Rd
St John St
Charterhouse St
Beech St
Chiswell St
0   500 m
0   0.25 miles

Holborn La
HOLBORN
New Fetter La
Holborn Viaduct
West Smithfield
3
Aldersgate
London Wall
Moorgate
Old Broad St
Bishopsgate
Houndsditch
Middlesex St
Commercial St

Chancery La
Newgate St
Gresham St

The Strand
Fleet St
Cheapside
Poultry
Cornhill
Leadenhall St
Mansell St
Minories

2
Cannon St
Queen St
CITY
Fenchurch St

Queen Victoria St

Victoria Embankment
5

Blackfriars
Bridge
Millennium
Bridge
4
Lower Thames St
Tower Hill

Southwark
Bridge
1

London
Bridge
River Thames

Stamford St
Southwark Bridge Rd
Tower Bridge

SOUTH
BANK
SOUTHWARK
Southwark St
Tooley St

Union St

For more detail of this area see Map p418 ➡

Explore: The City

For its size – just one square mile (about 2.6 sq km) – the City punches well above its weight for attractions. Start with the heavyweights – the Tower of London and St Paul's – allowing at least a half-day for each. It's worth arriving early to avoid the queues in season. You can combine the other top sights with explorations of the City's lesser-known delights and quieter corners – Christopher Wren's dozens of churches make peaceful stops along the way.

While more than 350,000 people work in the City of London, fewer than 8000 actually live here. To appreciate its frantic industry and buzz, come during the week, when you'll find everything open. It largely empties in the evening as its workers retreat to the suburbs, and weekends have traditionally been quiet. But in recent years, the One New Change shopping mall and the new bars and restaurants atop the City's flashiest skyscrapers have begun attracting people at off-peak times.

Local Life

➡ **Culture Vulture Nest** A powerhouse of culture (though not the prettiest kid in class), people flock to the Barbican (p149) for its innovative dance, theatre, music, films and art.

➡ **Meals with a View** There's nothing like getting a taste of the high life, trying to spot your hotel and watching the sun go down over the capital at Tower 42's City Social (p153).

➡ **Old-Style Drinking** Though they tend to keep bankers' hours, the City's pubs are some of the most atmospheric and historic – the Jamaica Wine House (p155) once did time as London's first coffee house.

Getting There & Away

➡ **Underground** There's a tangle of tube lines under the City. The handiest stations are Bank (Central, Northern, DLR and Waterloo & City) and St Paul's (Central Line), but Blackfriars (Circle and District), Barbican (Circle, Metropolitan and Hammersmith & City) and Tower Hill (Circle and District) are useful for sights further afield.

➡ **Bus** For a west-to-east sweep from Tottenham Court Rd past St Paul's, Bank and Liverpool St, hop on the 8. From Trafalgar Sq via Fleet St and the Tower, the 15. The 11 sets off from Liverpool St and passes Bank, Mansion House and St Paul's on its way to Chelsea. The 26 follows a similar route through the City but branches off for Waterloo.

Lonely Planet's Top Tip

Designed by Jean Nouvel, **One New Change** (Map p418; www.onenewchange.com; 1 New Change, EC4M; ⏰10am-7pm Mon-Wed & Fri, to 8pm Thu, to 6pm Sat, noon-6pm Sun; ⊜St Paul's, Blackfriars) – called the 'Stealth Bomber' by some because of its distinctive shape – is a shopping mall housing mainly high-street brands, but take the lift to its 6th floor and a great open viewing platform will reward you with up-close views of the dome of St Paul's Cathedral and out over London.

THE CITY

🍴 Best Places to Eat

➡ City Social (p153)
➡ White Swan (p153)
➡ Miyama (p153)
➡ Wine Library (p153)
➡ Perkin Reveller (p153)

For reviews, see p152 ➡

🍷 Best Places to Drink

➡ Sky Pod (p153)
➡ Blackfriar (p155)
➡ Madison (p155)
➡ Jamaica Wine House (p155)
➡ Counting House (p155)

For reviews, see p153 ➡

⊙ Best Churches

➡ St Bartholomew-the-Great (p150)
➡ All Hallows by the Tower (p146)
➡ Temple Church (p152)

For reviews, see 146 ➡

JOHN AND TINA REID / GETTY IMAGES ©

TOP SIGHT
TOWER OF LONDON

The absolute kernel of London, with a history as bleak and bloody as it is fascinating, the Tower of London should be at the top of everyone's list of London's sights. Begun during the reign of William the Conqueror (1066–87), the Tower is in fact a castle containing 22 towers and has served over the years as a palace, observatory, armoury, mint and even a zoo. Most famously, it has been a a prison and site of execution.

Tower Green

The buildings to the west and the south of this verdant patch have always accommodated Tower officials. Indeed, the current constable has a flat in Queen's House built in 1540. But what looks at first glance like a peaceful, almost village-like slice of the Tower's inner ward is actually one of its bloodiest.

Scaffold Site

Those 'lucky' enough to meet their fate here (rather than suffering the embarrassment of execution on Tower Hill observed by tens of thousands of jeering and cheering onlookers) numbered but a handful and included two of Henry VIII's wives (and alleged adulterers), Anne Boleyn and Catherine Howard; 16-year-old Lady Jane Grey, who fell foul of Henry's daughter Mary I by attempting to have herself crowned queen; and Robert Devereux, Earl of Essex, once a favourite of Elizabeth I. Just west of the scaffold site is brick-faced **Beauchamp Tower**, where high-ranking

DON'T MISS...
➡ Crown Jewels
➡ Scaffold Site
➡ White Tower and its armour collection
➡ A Yeoman Warder's tour
➡ The ravens

PRACTICALITIES
➡ Map p418, G4
➡ ☑ 0844 482 7777
➡ www.hrp.org.uk/toweroflondon
➡ Tower Hill, EC3
➡ adult/child £22/10, audioguide £4/3
➡ ⏲ 9am-5.30pm Tue-Sat, 10am-5.30pm Sun & Mon Mar-Oct, 9am-4.30pm Tue-Sat, 10am-4.30pm Sun & Mon Nov-Feb
➡ ⊖ Tower Hill

prisoners left behind unhappy inscriptions and other graffiti.

Chapel Royal of St Peter ad Vincula

Just north of the site is the 16th-century Chapel Royal of St Peter ad Vincula (St Peter in Chains), a rare example of ecclesiastical Tudor architecture and the place where those beheaded on the scaffold outside – most notably Anne Boleyn, Catherine Howard and Lady Jane Grey – were reburied in the 19th century. The church can be visited on a Yeoman Warder tour, or during the first and last hour of normal opening times.

Crown Jewels

To the east of the chapel and north of the White Tower is **Waterloo Barracks**, the home of the Crown Jewels, which are said to be worth up to £20 billion but are in a very real sense priceless. Here, you file past film clips of the jewels and their role through history, and of Queen Elizabeth II's coronation in 1953, before you reach the vault itself.

Once inside you'll be greeted by lavishly bejewelled sceptres, church plate, orbs and, naturally, crowns. A moving walkway takes you past the dozen or so crowns and other coronation regalia, including the platinum crown of the late Queen Mother, Elizabeth, which is set with the 106-carat Koh-i-Noor (Mountain of Light) diamond, and the State Sceptre with Cross topped with the 530-carat First Star of Africa (or Cullinan I) diamond. A bit further on, exhibited on its own, is the centrepiece: the Imperial State Crown, set with 2868 diamonds (including the 317-carat Second Star of Africa, or Cullinan II), sapphires, emeralds, rubies and pearls. It's worn by the Queen at the State Opening of Parliament in May/June. Note the bizarrely shaped boxes at the exit used to transport the baubles from the Tower to state functions.

White Tower

Built in stone as a fortress in 1078, this was the original 'Tower' of London – its name arose after Henry III whitewashed it in the 13th century. Standing just 30m high, it's not exactly a skyscraper by modern standards, but in the the Middle Ages it would have dwarfed the wooded huts surrounding the castle walls and intimidated the peasantry.

Apart from St John's Chapel, most of its interior is given over to a **Royal Armouries** collection of cannons, guns and suits of mail and armour for men and horses. Among the most remarkable exhibits on the entrance floor are Henry VIII's two suits of armour, one made for him when he was a dashing

YEOMAN WARDERS

A true icon of the Tower, the Yeoman Warders have been guarding the fortress since at least the early 16th century. There can be up to 40 – they number 37 at present – and, in order to qualify for the job, they must have served a minimum of 22 years in any branch of the British Armed Forces. They all live within the Tower walls and are known affectionately as 'Beefeaters', a nickname they dislike. The origin of this name is unknown, although it's thought to be due to the rations of beef – then a luxury food – given to them in the past. There is currently just one female Yeoman Warder, Moira Cameron, who in 2007 became the first woman to be given the post. While officially they guard the Tower and Crown Jewels at night, their main role is as tour guides (and to pose for photographs with eager tourists). Free tours leave from the Middle Tower every 30 minutes from 10am to 3.30pm (2.30pm in winter).

The red-brick New Armouries Cafe in the southeastern corner of the inner courtyard offers hot meals and sandwiches.

THE CITY TOWER OF LONDON

Tower of London

TACKLING THE TOWER

Although it's usually less busy in the late afternoon, don't leave your assault on the Tower until too late in the day. You could easily spend hours here and not see it all. Start by getting your bearings on one of the Yeoman Warder (Beefeater) tours; they are included in the cost of admission, entertaining and the easiest way to access the **Chapel Royal of St Peter ad Vincula** ❶, which is where they finish up.

When you leave the chapel, the **Scaffold Site** ❷ is directly in front. The building immediately to your left is Waterloo Barracks, where the **Crown Jewels** ❸ are housed. These are the absolute highlight of a Tower visit, so keep an eye on the entrance and pick a time to visit when it looks relatively quiet. Once inside, take things at your own pace. Slow-moving travelators shunt you past the dozen or so crowns that are the treasury's centrepieces, but feel free to double-back for a second or even third pass. Allow plenty of time for the **White Tower** ❹, the core of the whole complex, starting with the exhibition of royal armour. As you continue onto the 1st floor, keep an eye out for **St John's Chapel** ❺. The famous **ravens** ❻ can be seen in the courtyard south of the White Tower. Head next through the towers that formed the **Medieval Palace** ❼, then take the **East Wall Walk** ❽ to get a feel for the castle's mighty battlements. Spend the rest of your time poking around the many other fascinating nooks and crannies of the Tower complex.

Chapel Royal of St Peter ad Vincula

This chapel serves as the resting place for the royals and other members of the aristocracy who were executed on the small green out front. Several other historical figures are buried here too, including Thomas More.

Dry Moat

Scaffold Site

Seven people, including three queens (Anne Boleyn, Catherine Howard and Jane Grey), lost their heads here during Tudor times, saving the monarch the embarrassment of public executions on Tower Hill. The site features a rather odd 'pillow' sculpture by Brian Catling.

Beauchamp Tower

Main Entrance

Middle Tower

Byward Tower

Bell Tower

White Tower

Much of the White Tower is taken up with an exhibition on 500 years of royal armour. Look for the virtually cuboid suit made to match Henry VIII's bloated 49-year-old body, complete with an oversized armoured codpiece to protect, ahem, the crown jewels.

BEAT THE QUEUES

» **Buy** your fast-track ticket in advance online or at the City of London Information Centre in St Paul's Churchyard.

» **Become a member** An annual Historic Royal Palaces membership allows you to jump the queues and visit the Tower (and four other London palaces) as often as you like.

St John's Chapel

Kept as plain and unadorned as it would have been in Norman times, the White Tower's 1st-floor chapel is the oldest surviving church from 1080.

Crown Jewels

When they're not being worn for ceremonies of state, Her Majesty's bling is kept here. Among the 23,578 gems, look out for the 530-carat 1st Star of Africa diamond at the top of the Sovereign's Sceptre with cross, the largest part of what was then the largest diamond ever found.

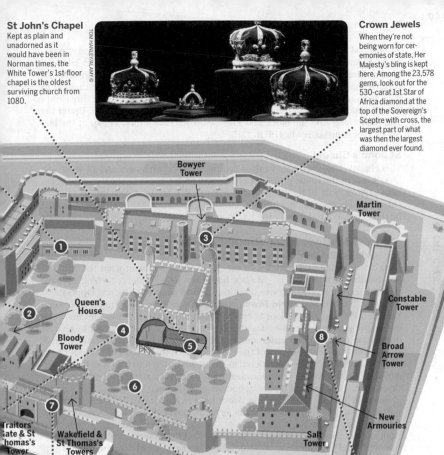

Bowyer Tower

Martin Tower

Constable Tower

Broad Arrow Tower

New Armouries

Salt Tower

Queen's House

Bloody Tower

Traitors' Gate & St Thomas's Tower

Wakefield & St Thomas's Towers

River Thames

Medieval Palace

This part of the Tower complex was begun around 1220 and was home to England's medieval monarchs. Look for the recreations of the bedchamber of Edward I (1272–1307) in St Thomas's Tower and the throne room of his father, Henry III (1216–72) in the Wakefield Tower.

Ravens

This stretch of green is where the Tower's half-dozen ravens are kept, fed on raw meat and blood-soaked biscuits. According to legend, if the birds were to leave the Tower, the kingdom would fall.

East Wall Walk

Follow the inner ramparts, starting from the 13th-century Salt Tower, passing through the Broad Arrow and Constable Towers, and ending at the Martin Tower, where the Crown Jewels were stored till the mid-19th century.

24-year-old and the other when he was a bloated 50-year-old with a waist measuring 129cm. You won't miss the oversized codpiece. Also here is the fabulous **Line of Kings**, a late-17th-century parade of carved wooden horses and heads of historic kings. On the 1st floor, check out the 2m suit of armour once thought to have been made for the giant-like John of Gaunt and, alongside it, a tiny child's suit of armour designed for James I's young son, the future Charles I. Up on the 2nd floor you'll find the block and axe used to execute Simon Fraser at the last public execution on Tower Hill in 1747.

St John's Chapel

This chapel (1080), with its vaulted ceiling, rounded archways and 12 stone pillars, is one of the finest examples of Norman architecture in the country. Elizabeth of York, wife of the grief-stricken Henry VII, lay in state here for 12 days, surrounded by candles, having died after complications in childbirth on her 37th birthday in 1503. Enter from the 1st floor.

Medieval Palace & the Bloody Tower

The Medieval Palace is composed of three towers: St Thomas's, Wakefield and Langthorn. Inside **St Thomas's Tower** (1279) you can look at what the hall and bedchamber of Edward I might once have been like. Here, archaeologists have peeled back the layers of newer buildings to find what went before. Opposite St Thomas's Tower is **Wakefield Tower**, built by Edward's father, Henry III, between 1220 and 1240. Its upper floor is entered from St Thomas's Tower and has been even more enticingly furnished with a replica throne and other decor to give an impression of how, as an anteroom in a medieval palace, it might have looked. During the 15th-century Wars of the Roses between the Houses of York and Lancaster, King Henry VI was murdered as (it is said) he knelt in prayer in this tower. A plaque on the chapel floor commemorates this Lancastrian king. The Langthorn Tower, residence of medieval queens, is to the east.

Below St Thomas's Tower along Water Lane is the famous **Traitors' Gate**, the portal through which prisoners transported by boat entered the Tower. Opposite Traitors' Gate is the huge portcullis of the Bloody Tower, taking its nickname from the 'princes in the Tower' – Edward V and his younger brother, Richard – who were held here 'for their own safety' and later murdered to annul their claims to the throne. The blame is usually laid (notably by Shakespeare) at the feet of their uncle, Richard III, whose remains were unearthed beneath a car park in Leicester in late 2012, but that idea is now being reexamined. An exhibition inside looks at the life and times of Elizabethan adventurer Sir Walter Raleigh, who was

---

THE RAVENS

Common ravens, scavengers on the lookout for scraps chucked from the Tower's windows (and feasting on the corpses of beheaded traitors displayed as a deterrent), have been here for centuries. Tower tradition tells us that when it was proposed they be culled after the Restoration, someone remembered the old legend that should the ravens depart, a great calamity would befall England. Having lived through the plague, the Great Fire *and* the execution of his father, Charles II clearly wasn't going to take any chances and let the birds remain in residence. There are always at least six ravens in residence at the Tower, and their wing feathers are clipped to keep them around. The birds all have names and live charmed, well-fed (170g of raw beef, biscuits soaked in blood, the odd egg and so on) lives. Don't miss the 'raven hotel', where the birds spend the night.

St John's Chapel

CEREMONY OF THE KEYS

The elaborate locking of the main gates has been performed daily without fail for more than 700 years. The ceremony begins at 9.53pm precisely, and it's all over by 10pm. Even when a bomb hit the Tower of London during the Blitz, the ceremony was only delayed by 30 minutes – some say that displays the essence of the famed British stiff upper lip, others their sheer lunacy. Entry to the ceremony begins at 9.30pm and is free, but you must book in advance online (www. hrp.org.uk).

imprisoned here three times by the capricious Elizabeth I and her successor James I.

East Wall Walk

The huge inner wall of the Tower was added to the fortress in 1220 by Henry III to improve the castle's defences. It is 36m wide and is dotted with towers along its length. The East Wall Walk allows you to climb up and tour its eastern edge, beginning in the 13th-century **Salt Tower**, probably used to store saltpetre for gunpowder. The walk also takes in **Broad Arrow Tower** and **Constable Tower**, each containing small exhibits. It ends at the **Martin Tower**, which houses an exhibition about the original coronation regalia. Here you can see some of the older crowns, with their precious stones removed. The oldest surviving crown (1715) is that of George I, which is topped with the ball and cross from the crown of James II. It was from this tower that Colonel Thomas Blood attempted to steal the Crown Jewels in 1671 disguised as a clergyman. He was caught but – surprisingly – Charles II gave him a full pardon.

More accessible is the official unlocking of the Tower, which takes place daily at 9am. The keys are escorted by a military guard and the doors are unlocked by a Yeoman Warder. With fewer visitors around, this is a great time to arrive (although you'll have to wait until 10am on a Sunday or Monday to begin your visit). Everyone can see the Ceremony of the Word at 2.45pm daily; this is when the Queen's Guard on duty at Waterloo Barracks marches to the Byward Tower to collect the secret password for after-hours entry to the Tower from the Chief Yeoman Warder.

TOP SIGHT
ST PAUL'S CATHEDRAL

Towering over Ludgate Hill, one of just three tiny hills in the pancake-flat City of London, and in a position that's been a place of Christian worship for more than 1400 years, St Paul's Cathedral is one of London's most majestic buildings. For Londoners the vast dome, which still manages to dominate the skyline despite the far higher skyscrapers of the Square Mile, is a symbol of resilience and pride, standing tall for more than 300 years (at least in this incarnation).

Officially completed in 1711 and sporting the capital's largest church dome, this is the fifth Christian church to dominate on this site.

The easiest way to explore the cathedral is by joining a free 1½-hour guided tour, which grants you access to the Geometric Staircase, the Chapel of St Michael and St George and the quire. These *usually* take place four times a day (10am, 11am, 1pm and 2pm) Monday to Saturday – head to the desk just past the entrance to check times and book a place. You can also enquire here about the shorter introductory 15- to 20-minute talks. Or pick up one of the free 1½-hour iPod tours available at the entrance.

Dome

Despite the cathedral's rich history and impressive (and uniform) English Baroque interior, many visitors are more interested in climbing the dome for one of the best views of London. It actually consists of three parts: a plastered brick inner dome, a nonstructural lead outer dome visible on the skyline and a brick cone between them holding it all together, one inside the other. This unique structure, the first triple

DON'T MISS...

→ Climbing the dome

→ Quire ceiling mosaics

→ Tombs of Admiral Nelson and Duke of Wellington

→ American Memorial Chapel

→ *Martyrs (Earth, Air, Fire, Water)* video installation

PRACTICALITIES

→ Map p418, C2

→ ☏020-7246 8350

→ www.stpauls.co.uk

→ St Paul's Churchyard, EC4

→ adult/child £18/8

→ ⊗8.30am-4.30pm Mon-Sat

→ ⊜St Paul's

dome ever built and second only in size to St Peter's in the Vatican, made the cathedral Christopher Wren's tour de force. It all weighs 59,000 tonnes.

Some 528 stairs take you to the top, but it's a three-stage journey. Through a door on the western side of the southern transept, and some 30m and 257 steps above, you reach the interior walkway around the dome's base. This is the **Whispering Gallery**, so called because if you talk close to the wall it carries your words around to the opposite side, 32m away. Climbing even more steps (another 119) you reach the **Stone Gallery**, an exterior viewing platform 53m above the ground, obscured by pillars and other suicide-preventing measures. The remaining 152 iron steps to the **Golden Gallery** are steeper and narrower than below but are really worth the effort. From here, 85m above London, you can enjoy superb 360-degree views of the City.

Interior

Just beneath the dome is an **epitaph** written for Wren by his son: *Lector, si monumentum requiris, circumspice* (Reader, if you seek his monument, look around you). In the north aisle you'll find the grandiose **Duke of Wellington Memorial** (1912), which took 54 years to complete – the Iron Duke's horse Copenhagen originally faced the other way, but it was deemed unfitting that a horse's rear end should face the altar.

In the north transept chapel is William Holman Hunt's celebrated painting, **The Light of the World**, which depicts Christ knocking at a weed-covered door that, symbolically, can only be opened from within. Beyond, in the cathedral's heart, you'll find the spectacular **quire** (or chancel) – its ceilings and arches dazzling with green, blue, red and gold mosaics telling the story of creation – and the **high altar**. The ornately carved choir stalls by Dutch-British sculptor Grinling Gibbons on either side of the quire are exquisite, as are the ornamental wrought-iron gates, separating the aisles from the altar, by French Huguenot Jean Tijou (both men also worked on Hampton Court Palace).

Walk around the altar, with its massive gilded oak **baldacchino**, a kind of canopy with barley-twist columns, to the **American Memorial Chapel**, commemorating the 28,000 Americans based in Britain who lost their lives during WWII. Note the Roll of Honour book turned daily, the state flags in the stained glass and American flora and fauna in the carved wood panelling.

In the south quire aisle, Bill Viola's new and very poignant **video installation** *Martyrs (Earth, Air, Fire, Water)* depicts four figures being overwhelmed

REFRESHMENTS & FACILITIES

In the crypt you'll find the **Crypt Café** (Map p418; dishes £5.65-8.25; ⊙9am-5pm Mon-Sat, 10am-4pm Sun) for light meals, and the excellent **Restaurant at St Paul's** (Map p418; ☑020-7248 2469; www.restaurantatstpauls.co.uk; 2/3-course lunch £21.50/25.95, tea from £15.95; ⊙breakfast 9-11am Thu & Fri, lunch noon-2.15pm, tea 3-4.15pm Mon-Sat; ☎), in addition to a **shop** (⊙9am-5pm Mon-Sat, 10am-4pm Sun).

As part of its 300th-anniversary celebrations in 2011, St Paul's underwent a £40-million, decade-long renovation project that cleaned the cathedral inside and out – a painstakingly slow process that has been likened to carefully applying and removing a face mask. To the right as you face the enormous Great West Door (opened only on special occasions), there's a section of unrestored wall under glass that shows the effects of centuries of pollution and failed past restoration attempts.

by natural forces. A bit further on is an **effigy of John Donne** (1573–1631), metaphysical poet and one-time dean of Old St Paul's, that survived the Great Fire.

Crypt

On the eastern side of both the north and south transepts are stairs leading down to the crypt and the **OBE Chapel**, where services are held for members of the Order of the British Empire. The crypt has memorials to around 300 of the great and the good, including Florence Nightingale, TE Lawrence (of Arabia) and Winston Churchill, while both the Duke of Wellington and Admiral Nelson are actually buried here. On the surrounding walls are plaques in memory of those from the Commonwealth who died in various conflicts during the 20th century, including Gallipoli and the Falklands War.

Wren's tomb is also in the crypt and many others, notably painters such as Joshua Reynolds, John Everett Millais, JMW Turner and William Holman Hunt, are remembered here, too.

The **Oculus**, in the former treasury, projects four short films onto its walls (you'll need the iPad audio tour to hear the sound). If you're not up to climbing the dome, experience it here audiovisually.

Exterior

Just outside the north transept, there's a simple **monument to the people of London**, honouring the 32,000 civilians killed (and another 50,000 seriously injured) in the City during WWII. Also to the north, at the entrance to Paternoster Sq, is **Temple Bar**, one of the original gateways to the City of London. This medieval stone archway once straddled Fleet St at a site marked by a silver dragon, but was removed to Middlesex in 1877. It was placed here in 2004.

....

ST PAUL'S CATHEDRAL

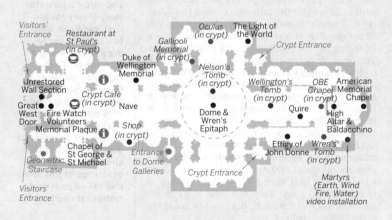

Cathedral Floor & Crypt

TOP SIGHT
TOWER BRIDGE

One of London's most familiar sights, Tower Bridge doesn't disappoint up close. There's something about its neo-Gothic towers and blue suspension struts that make it quite enthralling.

Built in 1894 by Horace Jones (who designed many of London's markets) as a much-needed crossing point in the east, it was equipped with a then-revolutionary bascule (see-saw) mechanism that could clear the way for oncoming ships in just three minutes. Although London's days as a thriving port are long over, the bridge still does its stuff, lifting largely for pleasure craft around 1000 times a year, and as often as 10 times a day in summer.

Housed within is the **Tower Bridge Exhibition** (Map p430; ☏020-7403 3761; www.towerbridge.org.uk; SE1; adult/child £9/3.90, incl Monument £10.50/4.70; ⊙10am-6pm Apr-Sep, 9.30am-5.30pm Oct-Mar), which explains the nuts and bolts of it all. If you're not technically minded, it's still fascinating to get inside the bridge and look along the Thames from its two walkways. A lift takes you to the top of the structure, 42m above the river, from where you can walk along the east- and west-facing walkways, lined with information boards.

A new, wow-inducing addition is the 11m-long glass floor with a dozen see-through panels – acrophobes can take solace in knowing that each weighs a load-bearing 530kg. There are a couple of stops on the way down before you exit and continue on to the **Victorian Engine Rooms**, which house the beautifully maintained steam engines that powered the bridge lifts, as well as some excellent interactive exhibits and a couple of short films.

DON'T MISS...

➡ Bridge lifting
➡ Victorian Engine Rooms
➡ View from top
➡ New glass floor

PRACTICALITIES

➡ Map p418, G4
➡ ⊖Tower Hill

◉ SIGHTS

TOWER OF LONDON CASTLE
See p136.

ST PAUL'S CATHEDRAL CHURCH
See p142.

TOWER BRIDGE BRIDGE
See p145.

ALL HALLOWS BY THE TOWER CHURCH
Map p418 (☑020-7481 2928; www.ahbtt.org.uk;
Byward St, EC3; ⊗8am-5pm Mon, Tue, Thu & Fri, to
7pm Wed, 10am-5pm Sat & Sun; ⊖Tower Hill) All
Hallows (meaning 'all saints'), which dates to
AD 675, survived virtually unscathed by the
Great Fire, only to be hit by German bombs
in 1940. Come to see the church itself, by all
means, but the best bits are in the atmospheric undercroft (crypt), where you'll the discover
a pavement of 2nd-century Roman tiles and
the walls of the 7th-century Saxon church.

In the nave, note the pulpit taken from
a Wren church on Cannon St that was destroyed in WWII and, by the south door, a
Saxon archway and a beautiful 17th-century
font cover decorated by the master wood-
carver Grinling Gibbons. The church has
two strong American connections: William
Penn, founder of Pennsylvania, was baptised
here in 1644 and schooled in what is now the
Parish Room; and John Quincy Adams, sixth
president of the USA, was married here in
1797. Free 20-minute tours depart at 2pm
Monday to Friday from April to October.

TRINITY SQUARE GARDENS GARDENS
Map p418 (⊖Tower Hill) Trinity Square Gardens, just west of Tower Hill tube station,
was once the **Tower Hill scaffold site**,
where a confirmed 125 people met their fate,
the last in 1747. Now it's a much more peaceful place, ringed with important buildings
and bits of the wall enclosing the Roman
settlement of Londinium.

To the north is **Trinity House** (1795), topped
with a ship's weathervane and housing the
General Lighthouse Authority for England
and Wales. To the west is the massive former
Port of London Authority building (1922),
lorded over by Father Thames – it is now
being converted into a residential block and
100-room hotel called Ten Trinity Square. To
the south is Edwin Lutyens' **Tower Hill Memorial** (1928), dedicated to the almost 24,000
merchant sailors who died in both world wars
and have no known grave. On a grassy area

next to the tube's main exit there's a stretch
of the **medieval wall** built on Roman foundations, with a modern **statue of Emperor Tra-
jan** (r AD 98–117) standing in front of it. You
can see more of the 2nd-century **Roman wall**
around the corner from the tube station, in
the courtyard of the Grange Hotel.

ST OLAVE'S CHURCH
Map p418 (☑020-7488 4318; www.sanctuary-
inthecity.net; 8 Hart St, EC3; ⊗9am-5pm Mon-Fri;
⊖Tower Hill) Tucked at the end of quiet Seething Lane, St Olave's was built in the mid-15th
century and is one of the few churches to
have survived the Great Fire. It was bombed
in 1941 and restored in the 1950s. The diarist
Samuel Pepys was a parishioner and is buried here – see the tablet on the south wall.
Dickens called the place 'St Ghastly Grim'
because of the skulls above the east doorway.

30 ST MARY AXE NOTABLE BUILDING
Map p418 (Gherkin; www.30stmaryaxe.info; 30
St Mary Axe, EC3; ⊖Aldgate) Nicknamed 'the
Gherkin' for its unusual shape, 30 St Mary
Axe is arguably the City's most distinctive
skyscraper, dominating the skyline despite
actually being slightly smaller than the
neighbouring NatWest Tower. Built in 2003
by award-winning Norman Foster, the
Gherkin's futuristic exterior has become an
emblem of modern London – as recognisable as Big Ben and the London Eye.

The building is closed to the public,
though in the past it has opened its doors
over the Open House London (p357) weekend in September.

BEVIS MARKS SYNAGOGUE SYNAGOGUE
Map p418 (☑020-7626 1274; http://bevismarks.
org.uk; 4 Heneage Lane, EC3; adult/child £5/2.50;
⊗10.30am-2pm Mon, Wed & Thu, to 1pm Tue & Fri,
to 12.30pm Sun; ⊖Aldgate) Completed in 1701
and the first synagogue built after Oliver
Cromwell allowed the return of the Jews to
Britain in 1657, this is a Sephardic temple
and is sometimes referred to as the Spanish
and Portuguese Synagogue. Its resemblance
to a Protestant church is not coincidental.
The architect, Joseph Avis, was a Quaker and
took his cue from the City's Wren churches.

LLOYD'S OF LONDON NOTABLE BUILDING
Map p418 (www.lloyds.com/lloyds/about-us/the-
lloyds-building; 1 Lime St, EC3; ⊖Aldgate, Monument) While the world's leading insurance
brokers are inside underwriting everything
from astronauts' lives to Mariah Carey's legs

LOCAL KNOWLEDGE

JOHN SCHOFIELD: CATHEDRAL ARCHAEOLOGIST

John Schofield has been Cathedral Archaeologist at St Paul's since 1990.

An archaeologist...in a cathedral?
About 25 years ago the Care of Cathedrals Measure decreed that each of the 42 cathedrals in England and Wales should have a consultant archaeologist. St Paul's is the City's greatest asset, but it's a baroque structure standing on a pedestal of strata going back to the Romans. My job is to elucidate this and to see that the right thing is done.

Do you dig?
When the cathedral wants to repair or alter any part of its fabric or the ground outside, we record and excavate the parts to be affected. Sometimes what we find is larger than the hole we're digging. People say, 'A Roman mosaic has been found, chase it further'. But it might extend into another property. Instead, we record and archive the discovery. There's a good chance the site will be dug up and examined in a half-century, since the average life of a building in the City is now just 30 years.

Tell me something I didn't know about St Paul's.
Members of the Fire Watch (volunteers who extinguished incendiary devices during the Blitz) saved the cathedral. But the second bomb to hit the cathedral (falling on the north transept in April 1941) would have destroyed it were it not for the stout metal corset that had been put in place after having been served a dangerous structures notice on Christmas Day 1925.

Did I miss anything in the cathedral?
There are stones in the walls of the crypt dating from the medieval cathedral. Wren reused such stones, but usually turned them inward. One opposite the cafe cashier and another in the crypt's north entrance staircase have mouldings facing outward. Graffiti uncovered after cleaning around the west portal dates to as early as 1712 – a year after the cathedral opened. There's shrapnel damage from WWII on the exterior wall opposite the original site of Pauls' Cross in the north churchyard. And a bit further west, next to a statue of John Wesley, is the top of a medieval well discovered in 1970.

and Tom Jones' chest hair, people outside still stop to gawp at the stainless-steel external ducting and staircases of this 1986 postmodern building designed by Richard Rogers, one of the architects of Paris' Pompidou Centre.

LEADENHALL MARKET MARKET
Map p418 (www.leadenhallmarket.co.uk; Whittington Ave, EC3; ⊙10am-6pm Mon-Fri; ⊖Bank, Monument) A visit to this covered mall off Gracechurch St is a step back in time. There's been a market on this site since the Roman era, but the architecture that survives is all cobblestones and late-19th-century Victorian ironwork. Leadenhall Market appears as Diagon Alley in *Harry Potter and the Philosopher's Stone* and an optician's shop was used for the entrance to the Leaky Cauldron wizarding pub in *Harry Potter and the Goblet of Fire.*

20 FENCHURCH ST NOTABLE BUILDING
Map p418 (Walkie Talkie; ☎0333-772 0020; www.skygarden.london; 20 Fenchurch St, EC3; ⊖Monument) The City's fifth-tallest building didn't get off to a good start when it opened in spring 2014. The in-your-face shape of the so-called 'Walkie Talkie' riled many Londoners, and its highly reflective windows damaged the bodywork of several cars parked below. But since the opening of the three-level rooftop **Sky Garden**, with its brasserie, restaurant, verdant Sky Pod (p153) cafe-bar and 360-degree views, all has been forgiven. Entry is free, but unless you've a restaurant reservation you'll need to book a slot in advance.

BANK OF ENGLAND MUSEUM MUSEUM
Map p418 (www.bankofengland.co.uk/museum; Bartholomew Lane, EC2; ⊙10am-5pm Mon-Fri; ⊖Bank) **FREE** The centrepiece of this museum, which explores the evolution of money and the history of the venerable Bank of England, founded in 1694 by a Scotsman, is a reconstruction of architect John Soane's original Bank Stock Office, complete with original mahogany counters. A series of rooms leading off the office are packed with exhibits ranging from silverware and coins to a 13kg gold bar you can lift up.

ROYAL EXCHANGE
HISTORIC BUILDING

Map p418 (www.theroyalexchange.co.uk; Royal Exchange, EC3; ⊘shops 10am-6pm, restaurants 8am-11pm Mon-Fri; ⊜Bank) The Royal Exchange was founded by Thomas Gresham in 1564, and this imposing, colonnaded building at the juncture of Threadneedle St and Cornhill is the third building on the site – the first was officially opened by Elizabeth I in 1570. It ceased functioning as a financial institution in the 1980s and now houses posh shops, cafes and restaurants.

MANSION HOUSE
HISTORIC BUILDING

Map p418 (☑020-7397 9306; www.cityoflondon. gov.uk/about-the-city/the-lord-mayor/mansion-house; btwn King William St & Walbrook; tours adult/concession £7/5; ⊘guided tour 2pm Tue; ⊜Bank) Opposite the Bank of England stands porticoed Mansion House, the official residence of the Lord Mayor of London since 1752. Built by George Dance the Elder, its magnificent interiors, including an impressive art collection and stunning banqueting hall, can be visited on a weekly tour, which leaves from the porch entrance on Walbrook. The 40 tickets are sold on a first-come-first-served basis. Check the website for advance closure notices.

ST STEPHEN WALBROOK
CHURCH

Map p418 (☑020-7626 9000; www.ststephen-walbrook.net; 39 Walbrook, EC4; ⊘10am-4pm Mon-Thu, to 3pm Fri; ⊜Bank) Just south of Mansion House, St Stephen Walbrook (1679) is considered to be the finest of Wren's City churches and, as it was his first experiment with a dome, a forerunner to St Paul's Cathedral. Sixteen pillars with Corinthian capitals support the dome, and the modern travertine marble altar, nicknamed 'the Camembert', is by sculptor Henry Moore.

ST MARY-LE-BOW
CHURCH

Map p418 (☑020-7248 5139; www.stmarylebow. co.uk; Cheapside, EC2; ⊘7.30am-6pm Mon-Wed, to 6.30pm Thu, to 4pm Fri; ⊜St Paul's, Bank) One of Wren's great churches, St Mary-le-Bow (1673) is famous as the church with the bells that still dictate who is – and who is not – a true cockney – it's said that a true cockney has to have been born within earshot of Bow Bells. The church's delicate steeple showing the four classical orders is one of Wren's finest works.

GUILDHALL
HISTORIC BUILDING

Map p418 (☑020-7606 3030; www.guildhall.city-oflondon.gov.uk; Gresham St, EC2; ⊜Bank) FREE

◉ TOP SIGHT
MONUMENT

This huge 1677 column, known simply as the Monument, is a memorial to the Great Fire of London of 1666, whose impact on London's history cannot be overstated. The Doric column made of Portland stone is 4.5m wide and 60.6m tall – the exact distance it stands from the bakery in Pudding Lane where the fire is thought to have started.

Much of medieval London was destroyed in the fire, with 13,200 houses reduced to rubble and an estimated 70,000 people made homeless (though only a half-dozen died). A relief at the base shows Charles II directing the fire-fighting operations.

The Monument was designed by Sir Christopher Wren and Dr Robert Hooke and is topped with a gilded bronze urn of flames that some think looks like a big gold pincushion. Although Lilliputian by today's standards, the 'Fish St Pillar' (as Hooke called it) would have towered over London when it was built.

Climbing up the column's 311 spiral steps rewards you with some of the best 360-degree views over London (due to its central location as much as to its height). And after your descent, you'll also be the proud owner of a certificate that commemorates your achievement.

DON'T MISS...

➜ Fantastic views
➜ Relief of Charles II
➜ Claiming your certificate

PRACTICALITIES

➜ Map p418, E3
➜ www.themonument. info
➜ Fish Street Hill, EC3
➜ adult/child £4/2, incl Tower Bridge Exhibition £10.50/4.70
➜ ⊘9.30am-6pm Apr-Sep, to 5.30pm Oct-Mar
➜ ⊜Monument

Bang in the centre of the Square Mile, the Guildhall has been the City's seat of government for more than 800 years. The present building dates from the early 15th century, making it the only existing secular stone structure to have survived the Great Fire of 1666, although it was severely damaged both then and during the Blitz of 1940.

Check in at reception to visit the impressive **Great Hall**, where you can see the banners and shields of London's 12 principal livery companies, or guilds, which used to wield absolute power throughout the City. The lord mayor and two sheriffs are still elected annually in the vast open hall. Among the monuments to look out for are statues of Winston Churchill, Admiral Nelson, the Duke of Wellington and Prime Minister William Pitt the Elder. In the upper gallery, at the western end, are statues of the biblical giants Gog and Magog, traditionally considered to be guardians of the City – today's figures replaced similar 18th-century statues destroyed in the Blitz. The Guildhall's stained glass was also blown out during the Blitz, but a modern window in the southwestern corner depicts the City's history – look out for a picture of London's most famous lord mayor, Richard 'Dick' Whittington, with his famous cat, a scene of the Great Fire and even the Lloyd's of London building.

GUILDHALL GALLERIES & ROMAN AMPHITHEATRE GALLERY

Map p418 (☏020-7332 3646; www.cityoflondon. gov.uk/guildhallgalleries; Guildhall Yard, EC2; ◷10am-5pm Mon-Sat, noon-4pm Sun; ◉Bank) FREE The **Guildhall Art Gallery** provides a fascinating look at the politics of the Square Mile over the past few centuries, with a great collection of paintings of London in the 18th and 19th centuries, while the new **City of London Heritage Gallery** displays documents from the archives. Below the gallery is **London's Roman Amphitheatre** dating back to the early 2nd century AD.

Among the art gallery's works is *The Defeat of the Floating Batteries* (1791) by the the American artist John Singleton Copley, which depicts the British victory at Gibraltar in 1782. This huge oil painting was removed to safety just a month before the gallery was hit by a German bomb in 1941 – it spent 50 years rolled up before restoration in 1999.

Sharing the same space, the heritage gallery displays such documents as a 1967 charter from William the Conqueror and a 1297 copy of the Magna Carta.

The archaeological remains of the long-sought Roman amphitheatre (or coliseum) were only discovered in 1988 when work finally began on a new gallery after the original's destruction in the Blitz. While only a few remnants of the stone walls lining the eastern entrance still stand, they're imaginatively fleshed out with a black-and-fluorescent-green trompe l'oeil of the missing seating, and computer-meshed outlines of spectators and gladiators. Markings on the square outside the Guildhall indicate the original extent and scale of the amphitheatre, which could seat up to 6000 spectators.

ST LAWRENCE JEWRY CHURCH

Map p418 (☏020-7600 9478; www.stlawrencejewry.org.uk; Guildhall Yard, EC2; ◷8am-5pm Mon-Fri; ◉Bank) The Corporation of London's well-preserved official church was built by Christopher Wren in 1677, but almost completely destroyed during WWII bombing. Its immaculate alabaster walls and gilt trimmings do its restorers proud. Free piano recitals are held each Monday at 1pm; organ recitals are at the same time on Tuesday.

The first part of the church's name refers to a 3rd-century Christian martyr executed on a sizzling gridiron. The second part tells us that this was once part of the Jewish quarter – the centre being Old Jewry, the street to the southeast. The Jews were expelled from England by Edward I in 1290 and did not return until the late 17th century.

BARBICAN ARCHITECTURE

Map p418 (☏020-7638 4141; www.barbican. org.uk; Silk St, EC2; architectural tours adult/child £12.50/10; ◷arts centre 9am-11pm Mon-Sat, from 10am Sun, architectural tours 6pm or 7pm Tue & Thu, 2pm, 3pm & 4pm Sat & Sun; ☎; ◉Barbican, Moorgate) Londoners remain fairly divided about the architectural value of this vast complex built after WWII, but the Barbican remains the City's preeminent cultural centre, counting the main Barbican Hall, two theatres, a state-of-the-art cinema complex and two well-regarded art galleries: the 3rd-floor **Barbican Gallery** (◷10am-6pm Sat-Wed, to 9pm Thu & Fri) and the **Curve** (◷11am-8pm Sat-Wed, to 9pm Thu & Fri) on the ground floor.

Built on a huge bomb site abandoned since WWII and opened progressively between 1969 and 1982, the vast housing and cultural complex is named after a Roman fortification that once stood here protecting ancient Londinium. It incorporates Joh

Milton's parish church, **St Giles Cripplegate** (☎020-7638 1997; www.stgilescripplegate.com; Fore St, EC2; ⊙11am-4pm Mon-Fri; ☻Barbican), into its avant-garde (for the time) design and embellishes its public areas with lakes and ponds ringed with benches. Apartments in the three high-rise towers that surround the cultural centre are some of the City's most sought-after living spaces. Guided architectural tours are fascinating and the best way to make sense of the purpose and beauty of the estate.

Getting around the Barbican can be frustratingly difficult. There are stairs from Barbican tube station that take you up onto the elevated walkways, from where a yellow line on the floor guides you to the arts complex. More straightforward is to walk through the Beech St road tunnel to the Silk St entrance.

ST BARTHOLOMEW-THE-GREAT CHURCH

Map p418 (☎020-7606 5171; www.greatstbarts. com; West Smithfield, EC1; adult/concession £4/3.50; ⊙8.30am-5pm Mon-Fri, 10.30am-4pm Sat, 8.30am-8pm Sun; ☻Farringdon, Barbican) Dating to 1123 and adjoining one of London's oldest hospitals, St Bartholomew-the-Great is worth more than a fleeting visit. The authentic Norman arches and other details lend this holy space an ancient calm. Approaching from nearby Smithfield Market through the restored 13th-century half-timbered archway is like walking back in time.

The church was originally part of the monastery of Augustinian Canons, but became the parish church of Smithfield in 1539 when King Henry VIII dissolved the monasteries. William Hogarth was baptised here and the young American statesman Benjamin Franklin worked in the yard as an apprentice printer. The church has been used as a setting for many films and TV productions, including *Four Weddings and a Funeral*, *Shakespeare in Love* and *Sherlock Holmes*. The **Cloister Cafe** (⊙8.30am-5pm Mon-Fri, 9.30am-6.30pm Sun; ☻Barbican) is great for a meal or snack.

SMITHFIELD MARKET MARKET

Map p418 (www.smithfieldmarket.com; West Smithfield, EC1; ⊙2-10am Mon-Fri; ☻Farringdon) Smithfield is central London's last surviving meat market. Its name derives from 'smooth field', where animals could graze, although its history is far from pastoral as this was once a place where public executions were held. Visit the market by 7am at the latest to see it in full swing.

Built on the site of the notorious St Bartholomew's Fair, where witches were burned at the stake, this is where Scottish independence leader William Wallace was executed in 1305 (there's a plaque on the wall of St Bart's Hospital, south of the market, ending with the Gaelic words *'Bas agus Buaidh'* or 'Death and Victory'), as well as the place where one of the leaders of the Peasants' Revolt, Wat Tyler, met his end in 1381. Described in terms of pure horror by Dickens in *Oliver Twist,* this was once the armpit of London, where animal excrement and entrails created a sea of filth. The market itself is a colourful building designed in 1868 by Horace Jones, who also designed Leadenhall Market and Tower Bridge.

GOLDEN BOY OF PYE CORNER MONUMENT

Map p418 (cnr Cock Lane & Giltspur St, EC1; ☻St Paul's, Barbican) This small statue of a corpulent boy opposite St Bartholomew's Hospital has a strange dedication: 'In memory put up for the fire of London occasioned by the sin of gluttony 1666'. All becomes clear, however, when you realise the Great Fire started in a bakery on Pudding Lane and burned itself out in what was once called Pye (Pie) Corner. This was interpreted as a sign the fire was an act of God as punishment for the gluttony of Londoners.

POSTMAN'S PARK PARK

Map p418 (btwn King Edward & St Martin's-le-Grand Sts, EC1; ☻St Paul's) This peaceful patch of greenery, just north of what was once London's General Post Office on St Martin's-le-Grand St, contains the unusual **Memorial to Heroic Self-Sacrifice**, a loggia with 54 ceramic plaques describing deeds of bravery by ordinary people who died saving the lives of others and who might otherwise have been forgotten.

The memorial was the brainchild of the artist George Frederic Watts (1817-1904) and was unveiled in 1900. His wife, Mary, oversaw the ongoing project after his death but the memorial was all but abandoned when she died in 1938. Only two plaques have been added since that time, most recently in 2009. It is dedicated to Leigh Pitt, a print technician who died in 2007 while trying to rescue a nine-year-old boy who was drowning in a canal in southeast London.

CENTRAL CRIMINAL COURT (OLD BAILEY) HISTORIC BUILDING

Map p418 (☎020-7248 3277; www.cityoflondon. gov.uk; cnr Newgate & Old Bailey Sts; ⊙9.45am-

1pm & 2-4pm Mon-Fri; ⊖St Paul's) FREE Taking in a trial in what's nicknamed the Old Bailey leaves watching a TV courtroom drama for dust. Even if you end up sitting in on a fairly run-of-the-mill trial, simply being in the court where such people as the Kray brothers and Oscar Wilde (in an earlier building on this site) once appeared is memorable.

The daily register of cases is outside, to the right of the main doorway on Old Bailey St; the public-gallery entrance is via Warwick Ct a few steps to the south. Choose from among 18 courts, of which the oldest – courts one to four – usually have the most interesting cases. As cameras, video equipment, mobile phones, large bags and food and drink are all forbidden inside, and there are no cloakrooms or lockers, it's important not to take these with you. If you're interested in a high-profile trial, get here early.

The Central Criminal Court gets its nickname from the street on which it stands: *baillie* was Norman French for 'enclosed courtyard'. The current building opened in 1907 on the combined site of a previous court and Newgate Prison. Intriguingly the figure of justice holding a sword and scales in her hands above the building's copper dome is not blindfolded (against undue influence, as is traditionally the case).

HOLBORN VIADUCT
BRIDGE

Map p418 (⊖St Paul's, Farringdon) This fine iron bridge was built in an effort to smarten up the area, as well as to link Holborn and Newgate St above what had been a valley created by the River Fleet. The four bronze statues represent commerce and agriculture (on the southern side) and science and fine art (on the north).

DR JOHNSON'S HOUSE
MUSEUM

Map p418 (www.drjohnsonshouse.org; 17 Gough Sq, EC4; adult/child £4.50/1.50, audioguide £2; ⊙11am-5.30pm Mon-Sat May-Sep, to 5pm Oct-Apr; ⊖Chancery Lane) This wonderful house, built in 1700, is a rare surviving example of a Georgian mansion in the City. It was the home of the great Georgian wit Samuel Johnson, the author of the first serious dictionary of the English language and the man who famously proclaimed, 'When a man is tired of London, he is tired of life'.

The house contains antique furniture and artefacts from Dr Johnson's life, including a chair from his local pub, the Old Cock Tavern on Fleet St, and numerous paintings of

THE CITY SIGHTS

TOP SIGHT
MUSEUM OF LONDON

One of the capital's best museums, this is a fascinating walk through the City's various incarnations from Anglo-Saxon village to 21st-century metropolis.

The first gallery, **London Before London**, brings to life the ancient settlements that predated the capital and is followed by the Roman era, which is full of excellent displays, models and archaeological finds. The rest of the floor takes you through the Saxon, medieval (don't miss the 1348 Black Death video), Tudor and Stuart periods, culminating in the Great Fire of 1666.

After a glimpse of the real Roman wall from the window, head down to the modern galleries where, in **Expanding City**, you'll find exquisite fashion and jewellery, the graffitied walls of a prison cell (1750) and the *Rhinebeck Panorama*, a detailed watercolour of London in 1806–07. After the re-created Georgian Pleasure Gardens, you emerge onto a glorious Victorian street. Highlights include a 1908 taxi cab, a 1928 art-deco lift from Selfridges and costumes worn by East End Pearly Kings and Queens. The testimonies of ordinary people from WWII are particularly moving. Highlights tours depart daily at 11am, noon, 3pm and 4pm.

DON'T MISS...

➡ Victorian walk
➡ *Rhinebeck Panorama*
➡ Wellclose Square prison cell
➡ Roman London
➡ 1348 Black Death video

PRACTICALITIES

➡ Map p418, D1
➡ www.museumoflondon.org.uk
➡ 150 London Wall, EC2
➡ admission free
➡ ⊙10am-6pm
➡ ⊖Barbican

the lexographer and his associates, including his black manservant Francis Barber and his clerk and biographer James Boswell.

On the upper floors there are leaflets describing how Dr Johnson and six clerks (Boswell wasn't among them yet) developed the first English dictionary in the house's attic during the period he lived here from 1748 to 1759, as well as a copy of the first edition of the dictionary from 1755. Children will love the Georgian dress-up clothes, and there are also temporary exhibits.

ST BRIDE'S, FLEET STREET
CHURCH

Map p418 (☑020-7427 0133; www.stbrides.com; Bride Lane, EC4; tours £6; ☺8.30am-5pm Mon-Fri, hours vary Sat, 11am-5.30pm Sun; ⊜St Paul's, Blackfriars) Printing presses fell silent on Fleet St in the 1980s, but St Bride's, designed by Christopher Wren in 1672 and his tallest (and most expensive) church after St Paul's Cathedral, is still referred to as the 'journalists' church'. There's a moving chapel in the north aisle honouring journalists who've died or been injured in the course of their work.

The spire, added in 1703, is said to have inspired the design of the tiered wedding cake. The church was hit by bombs in December 1940, and the interior layout is wood-panelled, modern and not particularly attractive.

In the 11th-century crypt, however, there's a well-presented history of the church, its surrounding areas and the printing industry – don't miss the Roman pavement from the 2nd century AD. Guided tours depart at 3pm on Tuesday, but check the website for details.

TEMPLE CHURCH
CHURCH

Map p406 (☑020-7353 3470; www.temple-church.com; adult/child £5/free; ☺10am-1pm & 2-4pm Mon-Fri, hours & days vary; ⊜Temple) This magnificent church was built by the secretive Knights Templar, an order of crusading monks founded in the 12th century to protect pilgrims travelling to and from Jerusalem. Today the sprawling oasis of fine buildings and pleasant, traffic-free green space is home to two Inns of Court: Inner Temple and Middle Temple. A key scene of The Da Vinci Code was set here.

The Temple Church has a distinctive design and is in two parts: the Round (consecrated in 1185 and modelled after the Church of the Holy Sepulchre in Jerusalem) adjoins the Chancel (built in 1240), which is the heart of the modern church. Both parts were severely damaged by a bomb in 1941 and have been completely reconstructed.

Its most obvious points of interest are the life-size stone effigies of nine 13th-century knights lying on the floor of the Round. Some of them are cross-legged, but contrary to popular belief this doesn't necessarily mean they were crusaders. It's one of just four round churches left in England.

✖ EATING

The financial heart of London unsurprisingly caters for a well-heeled crowd and it can be a tough place to find a meal at the weekend, if not on a weekday evening. You'll find plenty of places to choose from, however, in One New Change (p135). During the week, Leadenhall Market (p147) stalls offer a delicious array of food, from steaming noodles to mountains of sarnies (sandwiches) at lunchtime.

CAFÉ BELOW
CAFE £

Map p418 (☑020-7329 0789; www.cafebelow.co.uk; St Mary-le-Bow, Cheapside, EC2; mains £8.75-11.25, 3-course set dinner £20; ☺7.30am-2.30pm Mon & Tue, to 9.15pm Wed-Fri; ☑; ⊜Mansion House, St Paul's) This atmospheric cafe-restaurant, in the crypt of one of London's most famous churches offers excellent value and such tasty dishes as pan-fried sea bream with chermoula (spicy North African sauce) and aubergine Parmigiana. There are as many vegetarian choices as meat ones. Summer sees tables outside in the shady courtyard.

BEA'S OF BLOOMSBURY
CAFE £

Map p418 (☑020-7242 8330; www.beasofblooms-bury.com; 83 Watling St, EC4; teas £9-24; ☺7.30am-7pm Mon-Fri, from 10.30am Sat & Sun; ⊜St Paul's) Bea's made its name with its signature cupcakes, so it was only natural for it to offer a full afternoon tea, too. This branch of the Bloomsbury institution is tiny but original, with great cake displays and boutique decor. It's at One New Change and is an excellent place to refuel after visiting St Paul's.

DUCK & WAFFLE
BRASSERIE ££

Map p418 (☑020-3640 7310; www.duckandwaffle.com; 40th fl, Heron Tower, 110 Bishopsgate, EC2; mains £10-19; ☺24hr; ⊜Liverpool St) If you like your views with sustenance round the clock, this is the place for you. Perched atop Heron Tower, just down from Liverpool St Station, it serves European and British dishes (shellfish, roast chicken, some unusual seafood concoctions such as pollack meatballs) in small and large sizes by day, waffles by night, and round-the-clocktails.

WINE LIBRARY
MODERN EUROPEAN ££

Map p418 (☎020-7481 0415; www.winelibrary. co.uk; 43 Trinity Sq, EC3; set meal £18; ☺11.30am-3pm Mon, to 8pm Tue-Fri; ☻Tower Hill) This is a great place for a light but boozy lunch opposite the Tower. Buy a bottle of wine at retail price (no mark-up, £8 corkage fee) from the large selection on offer at the vaulted-cellar restaurant and then snack on a set plate of delicious pâtés, cheeses and salads. Reservations are recommended at lunch.

FOLLY
INTERNATIONAL ££

Map p418 (☎0845 468 0102; www.thefollybar. com; 41 Gracechurch St, EC3; mains £9-25; ☺7.30am-late Mon-Fri, from 10am Sat & Sun; ☻Monument) Love, love, love this 'secret garden' cafe-restaurant-cum-bar on two levels filled with greenery (both real and faux) and picnic-table seating. The aptly named Folly has a full menu on offer, with a strong emphasis on burgers and steaks, and its desserts are positively sinful. It has an excellent wine and champagne selection, too.

MIYAMA
JAPANESE ££

Map p418 (☎020-7489 1937; www.miyama-restaurant.co.uk; 17 Godliman St, EC4; mains £13.50-23; ☺11.30am-2.30pm & 5.45-9.30pm Mon-Fri; ☻St Paul's) Always one of our favourite Japanese restaurants, and virtually in the shadow of St Paul's Cathedral, Miyama offers something for everyone from soba and udon noodles to sushi and bento boxes. But find us for the most part in the teppan bar in the basement, where the teppanyaki (from £30) offers some of the best value in the City.

CAMINO MONUMENTO
SPANISH ££

Map p418 (☎020-7841 7335; www.camino. uk.com; 15 Mincing Lane, EC3; mains £13.50-22.50; ☺noon-11pm Mon-Fri; ☻Monument) With an enormous map of the Iberian peninsula on one wall and its illustrative name, there's no doubt you're in a Spanish restaurant. Stick with the tapas (£4 to £13.50), which might be *del asador* (from the grill) such as Rioja chorizo with roasted *piquillo* peppers or more prosaic *bodega* (cellar) ones such as manchego cheese with quince jelly.

★PERKIN REVELLER
BRASSERIE ££

Map p418 (☎020-3166 6949; www.perkinreveller. co.uk; The Wharf, Tower of London, EC3; mains £15.50-25.50; ☺10am-9pm Mon-Sat, to 5pm Sun;

☻Tower Hill) The location of this minimalist new build on the Thames, at the foot of Tower Bridge, is hard to beat – indeed, the restaurant's bar actually spreads into an arch under Tower Bridge. The food – mostly classic British (Morecambe Bay potted shrimp, fish and chips, high-end pies) – matches the A-list spot.

The restaurant's odd name comes from a character in the *Canterbury Tales* by Geoffrey Chaucer who, as comptroller of the customs for the port of London (his day job), oversaw the construction of Tower Wharf in the late 14th century.

WHITE SWAN
GASTROPUB ££

Map p418 (☎020-7242 9696; www.thewhiteswan-london.com; 108 New Fetter Lane, EC4; mains £14-24; ☺noon-3pm & 6-10pm Mon-Fri; ☻Chancery Lane) Though it may look like just another City pub from the street, the White Swan is anything but typical – a smart downstairs bar that serves excellent pub food (mains £13 to £19) under the watchful eyes of animal prints and trophies, including a swan, and an upstairs dining room with a classic, meaty British menu (two-/three-course meal £29/34).

CITY SOCIAL
MODERN BRITISH £££

Map p418 (☎020-7877 7703; http://citysociallondon.com; Tower 42, 25 Old Broad Dt, EC2; mains £18-38; ☺noon-3pm & 6-11.30pm Mon-Sat; ☻Liverpool St) Should you need to impress someone – even yourself – bring him, her and/or said self to this glamour puss on the 24th floor of Tower 42. Come for the stunning City views (including ones from the toilets), the art-deco decor, the chef's table with room for 10 soon-to-be-new best friends and Jason Atherton's Michelin-starred dishes.

There are lots of safe-as-houses pasta and grill choices, but we'll go every time for the superb Lancashire saddle of rabbit, Romney Marsh lamb fillet, or one of the three or four fish dishes.

🍷 DRINKING & NIGHTLIFE

★SKY POD
BAR, CAFE

Map p418 (☎0333-772 0020; http://skygarden. london/sky-pod-bar; 20 Fenchurch St, EC3; ☺7am-2am Mon-Fri, 8am-2am Sat, 9am-9pm Sun; ☻Monument) One of the best places in the City to get high is the Sky Pod in the Sky Garden on level 35 of the so-called Walkie Talkie. The views are nothing short of phenomenal – especially

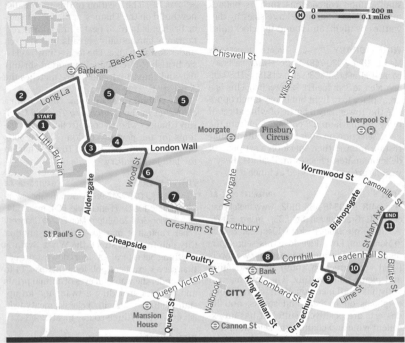

Neighbourhood Walk
A Taste of the City

START ST BARTHOLOMEW-THE-GREAT
END 30 ST MARY AXE (THE GHERKIN)
LENGTH 1.5 MILES; THREE HOURS

The City of London has as much history in its Square Mile as the rest of London put together, and this walk picks out just a few of its highlights. Start by exploring 12th-century **①St Bartholomew-the-Great** (p150), whose atmospheric interior has been used frequently as a film set. Head through the Tudor gatehouse and turn right towards the colourful Victorian arches of **②Smithfield Market** (p150). Take a right down Long Lane and another at Aldersgate St. Follow the roundabout to the right and nip up the stairs (or take the lift) to the **③Museum of London** (p151). Explore the museum's excellent galleries or head to the right to the ruins of the **④Roman City Walls** and behind them the distinctive towers of the **⑤Barbican** (p149). Turn right at Wood St to find the remaining **⑥Tower of St Alban** (1698), all that's left of a

Wren-designed church destroyed in a WWII bombing in 1940. Turn left into Love Lane and right into Aldermanbury – the impressive 15th-century **⑦Guildhall** (p148) is on your left. Crossing its courtyard – note the black outline of the Roman amphitheatre – continue east onto Gresham St, taking a right into Prince's St and emerging onto the busy Bank intersection lined with neoclassical temples to commerce. Behind the Duke of Wellington statue is a metal pyramid detailing the many significant buildings here. From the **⑧Royal Exchange** (p148), follow Cornhill and take a right down Gracechurch St. Turn left into wonderful **⑨Leadenhall Market** (p147), roughly where the Roman forum once stood. As you leave the market's far end, **⑩Lloyd's of London** (p146) displays its innards for all to see. Once you turn left onto Lime St, **⑪30 St Mary Axe** (p146), or 'the Gherkin', looms before you. Built nearly 900 years after St Bartholomew-the-Great, it's tangible testimony to the City's ability to constantly reinvent itself.

from the open-air South Terrace – the gardens are lush and it's the only place where this obstructive building won't be in your face.

Enjoy a cocktail or a light meal (breakfast £5.50, sandwiches and salads from £4.75). More substantial meals are available above in the Sky Garden's **Darwin Brasserie** (level 36) and the **Fenchurch Seafood Bar & Grill** (level 37). But we prefer this cafe and bar where the seating is free and the atmosphere relaxed. The only drawback is that without a restaurant reservation, entry is ticketed (see website) from 10am to 6pm weekdays and 11am to 9pm on Saturday and Sunday. Outside those hours, be prepared to queue (and perhaps be disappointed).

JAMAICA WINE HOUSE   PUB

Map p418 (www.shepherdneame.co.uk/pubs/london/jamaica-wine-house; 12 St Michael's Alley, EC3; ⊘11am-11pm Mon-Fri; ⊜Bank) Not a wine bar at all, but a historic Victorian pub, the 'Jam Pot' stands on the site of what was London's first coffee house (1652), places that were often just fronts for brothels. At the end of a narrow alley, this is a difficult place to find but well worth it.

MADISON   COCKTAIL BAR

Map p418 (☑020-3693 5160; www.madison-london.net; Roof Terrace, One New Change, EC4; ⊘8am-midnight Mon-Wed, to 2am Thu-Sat, 9am-9pm Sun; ⊜St Paul's) Perched atop One New Change with a full-frontal view of St Paul's and beyond, Madison offers one of the largest public open-air roof terraces you'll ever encounter. There's a full restaurant and bar on one side and a cocktail bar with outdoor seating on the other. We come for the latter.

BLACKFRIAR   PUB

Map p418 (☑020-7236 5474; www.nicholsons-pubs.co.uk/theblackfriarblackfriarslondon; 174 Queen Victoria St, EC4V; ⊘10am-11.30pm Mon-Fri, 11am-11.30pm Sat, noon-11pm Sun; ⊜Blackfriars) It may look like the corpulent friar above the entrance just stepped out of this olde-worlde pub just north of Blackfriars station, but the interior is actually an art-nouveau makeover from 1905. Built on the site of a monastery of Dominicans (who wore black robes), the theme is appealingly celebrated throughout the pub. Good selection of ales.

COUNTING HOUSE   PUB

Map p418 (www.the-counting-house.com; 50 Cornhill, EC3; ⊘11am-11pm Mon-Fri; 📶; ⊜Bank, Monument) With its counters and basement vaults, this award-winning pub certainly looks and feels comfortable in the former headquarters of NatWest Bank (1893) with its domed skylight and beautifully appointed main bar. This is a favourite of City boys and girls, who come for the good range of real ales and the speciality pies (from £11.25).

YE OLDE CHESHIRE CHEESE   PUB

Map p418 (☑020-7353 6170; Wine Office Court, 145 Fleet St, EC4; ⊘11.30am-11pm Mon-Fri, noon-11pm Sat; ⊜Chancery Lane) The entrance to this historic pub is via a narrow alley off Fleet St. Over its long history, locals have included Dr Johnson, Thackeray and Dickens. Despite (or possibly because of) this, the Cheshire feels today like a bit of a museum. Nevertheless it's one of London's most famous pubs and well worth popping in for a pint.

SHIP   PUB

Map p418 (☑020-7702 4422; www.shipec3.co.uk; 3 Hart St, EC3; ⊘11.30am-11pm Mon-Fri; ⊜Tower Hill) This small and now very smart pub with a nautical theme is a short walk from Tower Hill and an oasis of calm away from the hubbub of the Tower. The Upper Deck dining room looks like a film set and serves better-than-average pub grub.

☆ ENTERTAINMENT

BARBICAN   PERFORMING ARTS

Map p418 (☑0845 121 6823, box office 10am-8pm Mon-Sat, from 11am Sun 020-7638 8891; www.barbican.org.uk; Silk St, EC2; ⊜Barbican) Home to the wonderful London Symphony Orchestra and its associate orchestra, the less-known BBC Symphony Orchestra, the arts centre also hosts scores of other leading musicians, focusing in particular on jazz, folk, world and soul artists. Dance is another strong point here.

🛍 SHOPPING

★SILVER VAULTS   CRAFT

Map p418 (☑020-7242 3844; http://silvervaults-london.com; 53-63 Chancery Lane, WC2; ⊘9am-5.30pm Mon-Fri, to 1pm Sat; ⊜Chancery Lane) The 30-odd shops that work out of these secure subterranean vaults make up the largest collection of silver under one roof in the world. The different businesses tend to specialise in particular types of silverware – from cutlery sets to picture frames and lots of jewellery.

The South Bank

WATERLOO | BANKSIDE & SOUTHWARK | LONDON BRIDGE | BERMONDSEY | ROTHERHITHE

Neighbourhood Top Five

1 Finding out what all the fuss is about by exploring the magnificent modern-art collection at the peerless **Tate Modern** (p158).

2 Revolving in leisurely fashion above London's panoramic cityscape in the iconic **London Eye** (p161).

3 Stimulating your taste buds on a gastronomic tour of discovery at **Borough Market** (p162).

4 Sipping a coffee or cocktail at **Oblix** (p170) in the Shard for riveting views of the city.

5 Getting a Bard's-eye view of Elizabethan theatrics at the magnificent **Shakespeare's Globe** (p160).

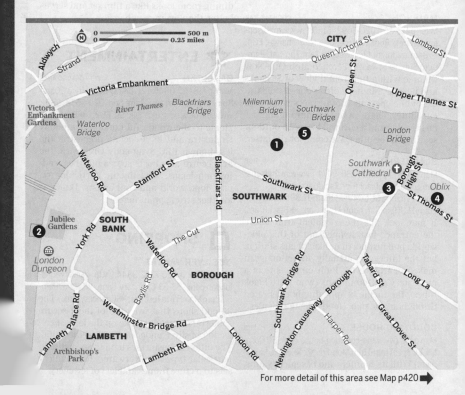

For more detail of this area see Map p420 ➡

Explore: The South Bank

Once neglected beyond its arts venues, the South Bank has transformed into one of London's must-see neighbourhoods. A roll call of riverside sights stretches along the Thames, commencing with the London Eye, running past the cultural enclave of the Southbank Centre and on to the Tate Modern, the Millennium Bridge and Shakespeare's Globe. It continues: waterside pubs, a cathedral, one of London's most-visited food markets, London's tallest building, a handful of fun diversions for kids and irrepressible kidults and the increasingly hip neighbourhood of Bermondsey. A stunning panorama unfolds on the far side of the Thames, as head-swivelling architecture rises up on either bank.

The drawcard sights stretch west–east in a manageable riverside melange, so doing it on foot is the best way. Located roughly halfway between the London Eye and Tower Bridge, the Tate Modern is by far the most time-intensive sight, and can easily hollow out a day's sightseeing; two to three days for the South Bank is optimum but if you're in a rush, one day may do for a (frazzling) whistle-stop look at the main sights.

Local Life

➡**Hang-outs** Cool Londoners love Maltby Street Market (p173) for its gourmet sandwiches, crazy cocktails and rollicking atmosphere.

➡**Museums** Locals earmark Friday and Saturday late-night opening (till 10pm) at the Tate Modern (p158), when the art crowds have thinned.

➡**Artisan food & drink** Be it for their next dinner party or just a treat, Londoners love buying delicious products at Borough Market (p162), trying English wines at the Wine Pantry (p170) or craft beers from the Bermondsey Beer Mile (p171).

Getting There & Away

➡**Underground** The South Bank is lashed into the tube system by stations at Waterloo, Southwark, London Bridge and Bermondsey, all on the Jubilee Line; the Northern Line runs through London Bridge and Waterloo (the Bakerloo line runs through the latter).

➡**On Foot** Cross to South Bank from the City over Tower Bridge or the Millennium Bridge, or from the West End across Waterloo Bridge. Each offers sublime views of the city.

➡**Bicycle** Jump on a Santander Bike and wheel it!

➡**Bus** The Riverside RV1 runs around the South Bank and Bankside, linking all the main sights (running between Covent Garden and Tower Gateway).

Lonely Planet's Top Tip

To collect the main sights, trace the Silver Jubilee Walk and the South Bank section of the Thames Path along the southern riverbank, but do venture further inland for the best eating and drinking.

✗ Best Places to Eat

➡ Arabica Bar & Kitchen (p167)

➡ Union Street Cafe (p167)

➡ Skylon (p167)

➡ Baltic (p167)

➡ Watch House (p167)

For reviews, see p166 ➡

🍺 Best Places to Drink

➡ Wine Pantry

➡ Scootercaffe (p169)

➡ 40 Maltby Street (p170)

➡ Oblix (p170)

➡ Mayflower (p170)

For reviews, see p169 ➡

⦿ Best Theatres

➡ Shakespeare's Globe & Sam Wanamaker Playhouse (p171)

➡ National Theatre (p171)

➡ Young Vic (p172)

➡ Old Vic (p172)

For reviews, see p171 ➡

THE SOUTH BANK

TOP SIGHT
TATE MODERN

The public's love affair with this phenomenally successful modern-art gallery shows no sign of cooling more than 15 years after it opened. In fact, so enraptured are art goers with the Tate Modern that over 60 million visitors have flocked to the former power station since it opened in 2000. To accommodate this exceptional popularity, the Tate is expanding: the museum is converting the power station's three huge subterranean oil tanks and building a daring 11-storey geometric extension at the back. Grand opening planned for 2016.

Power Station

The 200m-long Tate Modern is an imposing sight. The conversion of the empty Bankside Power Station – all 4.2 million bricks of it – into an art gallery was a masterstroke of design. The 'Tate Modern effect' is clearly as much about the building and its location (cue the ever popular balconies on level 3 with magnificent views of St Paul's) as the mostly 20th-century art inside. The new Tate Modern Project extension will similarly be constructed of brick, but artistically devised as a lattice through which interior lights will be visible at eventide.

Turbine Hall

The first thing to greet you as you pour down the ramp off Holland St (the main entrance) is the astounding 3300-sq-metre Turbine Hall (enter from the river entrance and you'll end up on more-muted level 2). Originally housing the power station's humungous electricity generators, this vast space has become the commanding venue for large-scale installation art and temporary exhibitions. Some art critics swipe at its populism, particularly the 'participatory art' (Carsten Höller's funfair-like slides *Test Site;* Doris Salcedo's enormous

JOHN HARPER / GETTY IMAGES ©

DON'T MISS...

- ➡ Turbine Hall
- ➡ Special Exhibitions
- ➡ Views of St Paul's from level 3 balconies

PRACTICALITIES

- ➡ Map p420, D3
- ➡ www.tate.org.uk
- ➡ Queen's Walk, SE1
- ➡ admission free
- ➡ ⊙10am–6pm Sun-Thu, to 10pm Fri & Sat
- ➡ 🛜🚻
- ➡ ⊖Blackfriars, Southwark, London Bridge

Shibboleth fissure in the floor; and Robert Morris' climbable geometric sculpture), but others insist this makes art more accessible. Originally visitors were invited to trample over Ai Weiwei's thoughtful and compelling *Sunflower Seeds* – a huge carpet of hand-painted ceramic seeds – until it was discovered people were making off with them in their shoes and turn-ups (to later appear on eBay) and the dust emitted by the 'seeds' was diagnosed a health risk.

Permanent Collection

Tate Modern's permanent collection is arranged by both theme and chronology on levels 2, 3 and 4. More than 60,000 works are on constant rotation, which can be frustrating if you'd like to see one particular piece, but is thrilling for repeat visitors. Helpfully, you can check the excellent website to see whether a specific work is on display – and where.

The curators have at their disposal paintings by Georges Braque, Henri Matisse, Piet Mondrian, Andy Warhol, Mark Rothko and Jackson Pollock, as well as pieces by Joseph Beuys, Damien Hirst, Rebecca Horn, Claes Oldenburg and Auguste Rodin.

Level 2: Poetry & Dream; Making Trace

This collection submerges the viewer in the world of surrealism and the dreamlike mindscapes of Yves Tanguy, Max Ernst, Salvador Dalí and other artists. It seeks to show visitors how contemporary art has grown from the past and can, in turn, provide new insights. In Making Traces, visitors will get a sense of the artist in action, with pieces illustrating the process of creating. The display is centred around Mark Rothko's Seagram murals.

Level 4: Evolution of Abstraction & Radical Art

Focussing on the evolution of abstract art since the beginning of the 20th century, including cubism, geometric abstraction and minimalism, **Structure & Clarity** includes work by early adopters such as Matisse, Braque and Picasso *(Seated Nude)*. **Energy & Process** highlights Arte Povera, a revolutionary Italian art movement from the 1960s, as its main focus.

Special Exhibitions

Special exhibitions (levels 2 and 3, subject to admission charge) have included retrospectives on Henri Matisse, Edward Hopper, Frida Kahlo, Roy Lichtenstein, August Strindberg, Nazism and 'Degenerate' Art, and Joan Miró.

FURTHER INFORMATION

Audioguides (in five languages) are available for £4 – they contain explanations about 50 artworks across the galleries and offer suggested tours for adults or children. Free guided highlights tours depart at 11am, noon, 2pm and 3pm daily.

Swiss architects Herzog & de Meuron scooped the prestigious Pritzker Prize for their transformation of empty Bankside Power Station, which closed in 1981. Leaving the building's single central 99m-high chimney, adding a two-storey glass box onto the roof and employing the cavernous Turbine Hall as a dramatic entrance space were three strokes of genius. They also designed the new Tate extension, opening in 2016.

TATE TO TATE BOAT

For the most scenic of culture trips, take the **Tate Boat** (Map p420; www.tate.org.uk/visit/tate-boat; one way adult/child £6.50/3.25) between the Bankside Pier at Tate Modern and the Millbank Pier at its sister-museum, Tate Britain (p92).

THE SOUTH BANK TATE MODERN

TOP SIGHT
SHAKESPEARE'S GLOBE

Unlike other venues for Shakespearean plays, the new Globe was designed to resemble the original as closely as possible, painstakingly constructed with 600 oak pegs (not a nail or a screw in the house), specially fired Tudor bricks and thatching reeds from Norfolk that pigeons supposedly don't like. Even the plaster contains goat hair, lime and sand, as it did in Shakespeare's time. It even means having the arena open to the fickle London skies and roar of passing aircraft, leaving the 700 'groundlings' to stand in London's notorious downpours.

Despite the worldwide popularity of Shakespeare over the centuries, the Globe was almost a distant memory when American actor (and, later, film director) Sam Wanamaker came searching for it in 1949. Undeterred by the fact that the theatre's foundations had vanished beneath a row of heritage-listed Georgian houses, Wanamaker set up the Globe Playhouse Trust in 1970 and began fundraising for a memorial theatre. Work started only 200m from the original Globe site in 1987, but Wanamaker died four years before it opened in 1997.

The Globe also opened the **Sam Wanamaker Playhouse** in 2014, an indoor Jacobean theatre. Shakespeare wrote for both outdoor and indoor theatre and the playhouse had always been part of the Globe's ambitions.

Visits include tours of the Globe (which depart half-hourly, generally in the morning so as not to clash with performances) and sometimes the Playhouse, as well as access to the exhibition space beneath the theatre, which has fascinating exhibits about Shakespeare and theatre in the 17th century (including costumes and props), and fun live talks and demonstrations. Or you can of course take in a play (p171).

DON'T MISS...

➡ Exhibition Hall and Tour
➡ Interior of the Globe Theatre
➡ Sam Wanamaker Playhouse

PRACTICALITIES

➡ Map p420, D3
➡ www.shakespeares-globe.com
➡ 21 New Globe Walk, SE1
➡ adult/child £13.50/8
➡ ⊙9am-5.30pm
➡ 🚻
➡ ⊖Blackfriars, Southwark or London Bridge

TOP SIGHT
LONDON EYE

It's hard to remember what London looked like before the landmark London Eye (officially the Coca-Cola London Eye) began twirling at the southwestern end of Jubilee Gardens in 2000. Not only has it fundamentally altered the South Bank skyline but, standing 135m tall in a fairly flat city, it is visible from numerous locations.

A ride – or 'flight', as it is called here – in one of the wheel's 32 glass-enclosed eye pods takes a gracefully slow 30 minutes and, weather permitting, you can see 25 miles in every direction from the top of the eye. Don't let poor weather put you off however: the close-up views of Westminster, just across the river, are probably the highlight of the ride. Interactive tablets provide great information (in six languages) about landmarks as they come up in the skyline.

At peak times (July, August and school holidays) it may feel like you'll spend more time in the queue than in the pod. Save money and time by buying tickets online, or cough up an extra £10 to showcase your fast-track swagger. Alternatively, visit before 11am or after 3pm to avoid peak density.

DID YOU KNOW?

The London Eye has been the focal point of the capital's celebrated New Year's Eve fireworks, which begin after Big Ben, across the river, has rung the 12 gong. In 2014, 12,000 fireworks were launched from the wheel.

PRACTICALITIES

➤ Map p420, A4
➤ ☑0871 781 3000
➤ www.londoneye.com
➤ adult/child £21.50/15.50
➤ ⊙10am-8pm
➤ ⊖Waterloo

loves veg

TOP SIGHT
BOROUGH MARKET

Located here in some form or another since the 13th century, 'London's Larder' has enjoyed an astonishing renaissance in the past 15 years. Always overflowing with food lovers, inveterate gastronomes, wide-eyed visitors and Londoners in search of inspiration for their next dinner party, this fantastic market has become firmly established as a sight in its own right.

The market specialises in high-end fresh products so you'll find the usual assortment of fruit and vegetable stalls, cheesemongers, butchers, fishmongers, bakeries as well as delis and gourmet stalls selling spices, nuts, preserves and condiments. Prices tend to be high but many traders offer free samples, a great perk for visitors and locals alike.

Food window-shopping (and sampling) over, you'll be able to grab lunch in one of the myriad of takeaway stalls – anything from sizzling gourmet sausages, chorizo sandwiches, falafel wraps and raclette portions (cheese melted over cured meats and potatoes). There also seems to be an unreasonable number of cake stalls – walking out without a treat will be a challenge! Many of the lunch stalls cluster in Green Market (the area closest to Southwark Cathedral). If you'd rather eat indoors, there are some fantastic cafes and restaurants too – try **Monmouth Coffee** (Map p420; www. monmouthcoffee.co.uk; 2 Park St, SE1; flat white £2.50; ⊙7.30am-6pm; ⊖London Bridge) or Arabica Bar & Kitchen (p167).

The market simply heaves on Saturdays, so get here early for the best pickings or enjoy the craze at lunch time: if you'd like some elbow space to enjoy your takeaway, head to Southwark Cathedral (p165) gardens or walk five minutes in either direction along the Thames for river views.

Note that although the full market runs from Wednesday to Saturday, some traders and takeaway stalls do open Mondays and Tuesdays.

DON'T MISS...

➡ Free samples
➡ Eating takeaway in Southwark Cathedral gardens
➡ Foodscapes (really!)

PRACTICALITIES

➡ Map p420, E4
➡ www.boroughmarket. org.uk
➡ 8 Southwark St, SE1
➡ ⊙10am-5pm Wed & Thu, to 6pm Fri, 8am-5pm Sat
➡ ⊖London Bridge

◉ SIGHTS

◉ Waterloo

ROUPELL ST
STREET

Map p420 (Roupell St, SE1; ⊜Waterloo) Waterloo station isn't exactly scenic, but wander around the back steets of this transport hub and you'll find some amazing architecture. Roupell St is an astonishingly pretty row of workers' cottages, all dark bricks and coloured doors, dating back to the 1820s. The street is so uniform it looks like a film set.

The same architecture extends to Theed and Whittlesey Sts (which run parallel to Roupell St to the north). The terraced houses were developed for artisan workers by John Palmer Roupell, a gold refiner, between the 1820s and the 1840s. They have survived WWII damage and the many developments of the area intact.

SOUTHBANK CENTRE
CONCERT HALL

Map p420 (✆020-7960 4200; www.southbankcentre.co.uk; Belvedere Rd, SE1; 🛜👪; ⊜Waterloo) The flagship venue of the Southbank Centre, Europe's largest centre for performing and visual arts, is the **Royal Festival Hall**. Its gently curved facade of glass and Portland stone is more humane than its 1970s Brutalist neighbours. It is one of London's leading music venues and the epicentre of life on this part of the South Bank, hosting cafes, restaurants, shops and bars.

Just north, the austere **Queen Elizabeth Hall** is a Brutalist icon, the second-largest concert venue in the centre, hosting chamber orchestras, quartets, dance performances, choirs and sometimes opera. Underneath its elevated floor is a graffiti-decorated **skateboarders' hang-out**.

The opinion-dividing 1968 **Hayward Gallery**, another Brutalist beauty, is a leading contemporary-art exhibition space.

The QEH and Hayward Gallery closed in September 2015 for two years to receive a 21st century facelift.

NATIONAL THEATRE
THEATRE

Map p420 (✆020-7452 3000; www.nationaltheatre.org.uk; South Bank, SE1; ⊜Waterloo) The nation's flagship theatre complex comprises three auditoriums for performances (p171). Fantastic **backstage tours** (adult/child £9/8), lasting 1¼ hours, are available. Every tour is different but you're likely to see rehearsals,

---

◉ TOP SIGHT
LONDON DUNGEON

This attraction has been milking it since 1974, spawning six other 'dungeons' in the UK and Europe. It's a highly entertaining whirlwind through London's most famous historical anecdotes – the Gunpowder plot, the Great Plague, Jack the Ripper, Sweeney Todd and his cronies – narrated through a combination of rides, actors and special effects. There is great audience participation, so prepare for a few startled screams (yours or other people's)!

The best bits are the vaudevillian delights of being sentenced by a mad, bewigged judge on trumped-up charges, the utterly disorientating Whitechapel labyrinth, the unnervingly sweet Mrs Lovett, and the Drop Dead Drop Ride that has you 'plummeting' to your death by hanging from the gallows.

It takes about 90 minutes to work your way through the gory dungeon. Buy tickets online to avoid the mammoth queues and save a few pounds too. Note that children younger than eight might find some of the attractions too scary.

DON'T MISS...

➡ Jack the Ripper

➡ Sweeney Todd

➡ The Judge

➡ Drop Dead Drop Ride

PRACTICALITIES

➡ Map p420, A5

➡ www.thedungeons.com/london

➡ County Hall, Westminster Bridge Rd, SE1

➡ adult/child £25.95/20.95

➡ ⊙10am-5pm, to 6pm Sat & Sun

➡ ⊜Waterloo, Westminster

changes of sets or bump into actors in the corridors. There is generally one tour a day, sometimes more. Consult the website for exact times and make sure you book.

LONDON SEA LIFE AQUARIUM   AQUARIUM

Map p420 (www.visitsealife.com; County Hall, Westminster Bridge Rd, SE1; adult/child £23.50/16.95; ⊙10am-7pm; ⊜Waterloo, Westminster) Displays look somewhat dated, but there are a couple of stand-out sights, including the shark tunnel, ray lagoon and the Gentoo penguin enclosures (penguins jump and dive at mesmerising speed). Feeds and talks are scheduled throughout the day so your chances of catching one during your visit are high.

LEAKE STREET GRAFFITI TUNNEL   PUBLIC ART

Map p420 (Leake St; ⊜Waterloo) FREE A dingy road under the disused Eurostar platforms at Waterloo station (enter from Lower Marsh or York Rd) seems an unlikely place to find art, but the walls of the 200-metre long Leake Street Tunnel are covered with some seriously impressive spray-painted works. Opened by famous street artist Banksy in 2008, the tunnel still sees new taggers and artists turn up daily. Banksy's work is long gone, but you can watch the artists in action as they paint over what was put up yesterday.

COUNTY HALL   HISTORIC BUILDING

Map p420 (Westminster Bridge Rd, SE1; ⊜Westminster, Waterloo) Begun in 1909 but not completed until 1922, this grand building with its curved, colonnaded facade was the home of the London County Council, subsequently the Greater London Council, until 1986. It now houses a number of attractions.

⊙ Bankside & Southwark

TATE MODERN   MUSEUM
See p158.

SHAKESPEARE'S GLOBE   HISTORIC BUILDING
See p160.

MILLENNIUM BRIDGE

The Millennium Bridge got off on the wrong footing when it was closed just three days after opening in June 2000 due to an alarming swing; a costly 18-month refit put things right.

MILLENNIUM BRIDGE   BRIDGE

Map p420 (⊜St Paul's, Blackfriars) The elegant Millennium Bridge staples the south bank of the Thames, in front of Tate Modern, with the north bank, at the steps of Peter's Hill below St Paul's Cathedral. The low-slung frame designed by Sir Norman Foster and Antony Caro looks spectacular, particularly lit up at night with fibre optics.

The view of St Paul's from the South Bank is one of London's iconic images.

GOLDEN HINDE   HISTORIC SHIP

Map p420 (☎020-7403 0123; www.goldenhinde. com; St Mary Overie Dock, Cathedral St, SE1; self-guided tours adult/child £6/4.50, events adult/child £7/5; ⊙10am-5.30pm; 🚹; ⊜London Bridge) Stepping aboard this replica of Sir Francis Drake's famous Tudor ship will inspire genuine admiration for the admiral and his rather short (average height: 1.6m) crew, which counted between 40 and 60. It was in a tiny five-deck galleon just like this that Drake and his crew circumnavigated the globe from 1577 to 1580. Visitors can explore the ship by themselves or join a guided tour led by a costumed actor – children love these.

As well as guided tours, Golden Hinde runs a number of events designed for children where they can go on a treasure hunt, fire the cannons, raise the anchor, take part in games and listen to riveting stories. Check the website for schedule and bookings.

⊙ London Bridge

SHARD   NOTABLE BUILDING

Map p420 (www.theviewfromtheshard.com; 32 London Bridge St, SE1; adult/child £29.95/23.95; ⊙10am-10pm; ⊜London Bridge) Puncturing the skies above London, the dramatic splinter-like form of the Shard has rapidly become an icon of London. The viewing platforms on floors 68, 69 and 72 are open to the public and the views are, as you'd expect from a 244m vantage point, sweeping, but they come at a hefty price – book online at least a day in advance to save £5.

To take in the view for less, visit one of the building's restaurants or bars; you'll pay less than half the viewing platform ticket price for breakfast or a cocktail at **Aqua Shard** (Map p420; www.aquashard.co.uk; 31st fl, 31 St Thomas St, SE1; ⊙bar noon-1am, restaurant 7am-11pm Mon-Sat, 9am-11pm Sun; ⊜London Bridge) or Oblix (p170) where the views are still spectacular.

TOP SIGHT
SOUTHWARK CATHEDRAL

The earliest surviving parts of this relatively small cathedral are the **retrochoir** at the eastern end, which contains four chapels and was part of the 13th-century Priory of St Mary Overie, some ancient arcading by the southwest door, 12th-century wall cores in the north transept, and an arch that dates to the original Norman church. But most of the cathedral is Victorian.

Enter via the southwest door and immediately to the left is a length of arcading dating to the 13th century; nearby is a selection of intriguing **medieval roof bosses** from the 15th century. Walk up the north aisle of the nave and on the left you'll see the **tomb of John Gower**, the 14th-century poet who was the first to write in English. Cross into the choir to admire the 16th-century **Great Screen** separating the choir from the retrochoir.

In the south aisle of the nave have a look at the green alabaster **monument to William Shakespeare**. Beside the monument is a **plaque to Sam Wanamaker** (1919–93), American playwright and founder of Shakespeare's Globe (p160) theatre; nearby hangs a splendid **icon** of Jesus Christ illuminated by devotional candles. Do hunt down the exceedingly fine **Elizabethan sideboard** in the north transept.

DON'T MISS...
→ Retrochoir
→ Ancient arcading
→ Great Screen

PRACTICALITIES
→ Map p420, E3
→ 020-7367 6700
→ cathedral.southwark.anglican.org
→ Montague Close, SE1
→ 8am-6pm Mon-Fri, 9am-6pm Sat & Sun; evensong 5.30pm Tue, Thur & Fri, 4pm Sat, 3pm Sun
→ London Bridge

THE SOUTH BANK SIGHTS

HMS BELFAST
SHIP

Map p420 (www.iwm.org.uk/visits/hms-belfast; Queen's Walk, SE1; adult/child £14.50/7.25; 10am-6pm Mar-Oct, to 5pm Nov-Feb; London Bridge) HMS *Belfast* is a magnet for naval-gazing kids of all ages. This large, light cruiser – launched in 1938 – served in WWII, helping to sink the German battleship *Scharnhorst*, shelling the Normandy coast on D-Day and later participated in the Korean War. Her 6in guns could bombard a target 14 land miles distant. Displays offer a great insight into what life on board was like, in peace times and during military engagements.

There are excellent audioguides (included in your admission fee) featuring anecdotes from former crew members.

LONDON BRIDGE EXPERIENCE & LONDON TOMBS
HISTORIC ATTRACTION

Map p420 (www.thelondonbridgeexperience.com; 2-4 Tooley St, SE1; adult/child £24/18; 10am-5pm Mon-Fri, to 6pm Sat & Sun; London Bridge) Stuffed away in the vaults beneath so-called New London Bridge (dating back to 1831), this historical attraction takes you on a whistle-stop tour of London's most famous span – from the Romans to Peter de Colechurch's 'Old London Bridge' (1209) lined with shops, to the American Robert McCulloch, who bought the bridge in 1967 for US$2.50 and transported it to Arizona.

Things ratchet up as you descend into a series of tombs and plague pits dating as far back as the 14th century, where darkness, rodents (animatronics) and claustrophobia meet zombies-from-nowhere (actors). It's all great, occasionally heart-in-the-mouth entertainment. Save up to 20% (and the queues) by buying tickets online.

OLD OPERATING THEATRE MUSEUM & HERB GARRET
MUSEUM

Map p420 (www.thegarret.org.uk; 9a St Thomas St, SE1; adult/child £6.50/3.50; 10.30am-5pm; London Bridge) This unique museum, 32 steps up a spiral stairway in the tower of **St Thomas Church** (1703), is the unlikely home of Britain's oldest operating theatre. Rediscovered in 1956, the garret was used by the apothecary of St Thomas's Hospital to store medicinal herbs. The museum looks back at the horror of 19th-century medicine – all pre-ether, pre-chloroform and pre-antiseptic.

⊙ Bermondsey

CITY HALL NOTABLE BUILDING

Map p420 (www.london.gov.uk/city-hall; Queen's Walk, SE1; ☉8.30am-5.30pm Mon-Fri; ⊜London Bridge) Home to the Mayor of London, bulbous City Hall was designed by Foster and Partners and opened in 2002. The 45m, glass-clad building has been compared to a host of objects – from an onion, to Darth Vader's helmet, a woodlouse and a 'glass gonad'. The scoop amphitheatre outside the building is the venue for a variety of free entertainment in warmer weather, from music to theatre. Free exhibitions relating to London are also periodically held at City Hall.

FASHION & TEXTILE MUSEUM MUSEUM

Map p420 (☏020-7407 8664; www.ftmlondon. org; 83 Bermondsey St, SE1; adult/child £8.80/ free; ☉11am-6pm Tue, Wed & Fri, to 8pm Thu, to 5pm Sat; ⊜London Bridge) This brainchild of designer Zandra Rhodes has no permanent collection, just quarterly temporary exhibitions, which have included retrospectives on Swedish fashion, the evolution of underwear and 20th century art in textiles.

WHITE CUBE BERMONDSEY GALLERY

Map p420 (www.whitecube.com; 144-152 Bermondsey St, SE1; ☉10am-6pm Tue-Sat, noon-6pm Sun; ⊜London Bridge) **FREE** The newest and largest of the White Cube galleries – the brainchild of Jay Jopling, dealer to the stars of the Brit Art movement who made his reputation in the 1990s by exhibiting then-unknown artists such as Damien Hirst and Antony Gormley – this gallery impresses by its large exhibition spaces, which lend themselves to monumental pieces or expansive installations using several mediums.

DESIGN MUSEUM MUSEUM

Map p420 (www.designmuseum.org; 28 Shad Thames, SE1; adult/child £13/6.60; ☉10am-5.45pm; ⊜London Bridge) Dedicated to popularising the importance of good design in everyday life, the Design Museum has a revolving programme of special exhibitions. Past shows have ranged from Manolo Blahnik shoes to Formula One racing cars. The annual 'Design of the Year' exhibition showcases the best and latest design innovations – as the museum's tagline has it, 'someday, the other museums will be showing this stuff'.

The museum has a fantastic permanent collection that it has struggled to showcase in its Thames location; it will therefore be moving to new premises in Kensington in late 2016. And of course it picked a design jewel: the former Commonwealth Institute building, a listed 1960s beauty, which has been given a 21st century facelift for the occasion.

⊙ Rotherhithe

Nestled in a bend of the River Thames east of Bermondsey, the neighbourhood of Rotherhithe makes for a fascinating detour. The area was an important port along the river and had working docks until the 1970s, an architectural heritage that is still in evidence today in the shape of converted warehouses and preserved wharves.

BRUNEL MUSEUM MUSEUM

(www.brunel-museum.org.uk; Railway Ave, SE16; adult/child £3/free; ☉10am-5pm; ⊜Rotherhithe) This small museum celebrates the world's first underwater tunnel, built here in 1843. The tunnel was the brainchild of engineer Marc Isambard Brunel (father of Isambard Kingdom Brunel, another famous structural engineer), who had thought of a tunnel as an alternative to a bridge to allay congestion on the Thames. The museum has fascinating exhibits retracing the project's (mis)fortunes and the pioneering technology used to dig the tunnel.

Works started in 1825 and the tunnel, initially designed for pedestrians (it is now used by trains), opened to great fanfare in 1843. **Guided tours** (adult/child £10/free) that include access to the tunnel shaft, the former Grand Entrance, meet at Bermondsey tube station Mondays at 11am, Tuesdays at 4.30pm and Sundays at 10.45am.

✕ EATING

✕ Waterloo

The area around the Southbank Centre is full of chains – head 'inland' to discover authentic gastronomic gems.

KONDITOR & COOK BAKERY £

Map p420 (www.konditorandcook.com; 22 Cornwall Rd, SE1; cakes £2-3, hot food £3.25-6.15; ☉7.30am-7pm Mon-Fri, 8.30am-6pm Sat, 11am-5pm Sun; ✎;

Waterloo) This elegant cake shop and bakery produces wonderful cakes – lavender and orange, lemon and almond – massive raspberry meringues, cookies and loaves of warm bread with olives, nuts and spices. It also serves hot takeaway food such as quiches or risottos, popular with local office workers (daily menu posted on the website).

★ **SKYLON** MODERN EUROPEAN ££
Map p420 (020-7654 7800; www.skylon-restaurant.co.uk; 3rd fl, Royal Festival Hall, Southbank Centre, Belvedere Rd, SE1; grill 2-/3-course menu £18/21, restaurant 2-/3-course menu £42/48; grill noon-11pm Mon-Sat & noon-10.30pm Sun, restaurant noon-2.30pm & 5.30-10.30pm Mon-Sat & noon-4pm Sun; Waterloo) This excellent restaurant inside the Royal Festival Hall is divided into grill and fine-dining sections by a large bar (p169). The decor is cutting-edge 1950s: muted colours and period chairs (trendy then, trendier now) while floor-to-ceiling windows bathe you in magnificent views of the Thames and the City. Booking is advised.

✕ Bankside & Southwark

★ **BALTIC** EASTERN EUROPEAN ££
Map p420 (020-7928 1111; www.balticrestaurant.co.uk; 74 Blackfriars Rd, SE1; mains £10.50-19; noon-3pm & 5.30-11.15pm Tue-Sun, 5.30-11.15pm Mon; Southwark) In a bright and airy, high-ceilinged dining room with glass roof and wooden beams, Baltic is travel on a plate: dill and beetroot, dumplings and blini, pickle and smoke, rich stews and braised meat. From Poland to Georgia, the flavours are authentic and the dishes beautifully presented. The wine and vodka lists are equally diverse.

ANCHOR & HOPE GASTROPUB ££
Map p420 (www.anchorandhopepub.co.uk; 36 The Cut, SE1; mains £12-20; noon-2.30pm Tue-Sat, 6-10.30pm Mon-Sat, 12.30-3pm Sun; Southwark) A stalwart of the South Bank food scene, the Anchor & Hope is a quintessential gastropub: elegant but not formal, and utterly delicious (European fare with a British twist). Think salt marsh lamb shoulder cooked for seven hours, wild rabbit with anchovies, almonds and rocket, and panna cotta with rhubarb compote.

★ **UNION STREET CAFE** ITALIAN £££
Map p420 (020-7592 7977; www.gordonramsay.com/union-street-cafe; 47-51 Great Suffolk St, SE1;

mains £11-25, 1-/2-course lunch menu £12/19; noon-3pm & 6-11pm Mon-Fri, noon-4pm & 6-10.30pm Sat, noon-5pm Sun; Southwark) There's not a scrap of snootiness about this canteen-style Gordon Ramsay bistro. The dining room works the industrial chic look and staff are positively lovely. On the plate, it's a yummy mix of classic antipasti, pasta, meats and more unusual Italian dishes. Sunday brunch deserves a special mention: kids go free and, for £12, it's free-flowing prosecco. Hurrah!

✕ London Bridge

★ **ARABICA BAR & KITCHEN** MIDDLE EASTERN £££
Map p420 (020-3011 5151; www.arabicabarandkitchen.com; 3 Rochester Walk, Borough Market, SE1; dishes £4-14; 11am-11pm Mon-Wed, 8.30am-11pm Thu-Sat; London Bridge) Pan–Middle Eastern cuisine is a well rehearsed classic these days, but Arabica Bar & Kitchen have managed to bring something fresh to their table: the decor is contemporary and bright, the food delicate and light, with an emphasis on sharing (two to three small dishes per person). The downside of this tapas approach is that the bill adds up quickly.

✕ Bermondsey

★ **WATCH HOUSE** CAFE £
Map p420 (www.watchhousecoffee.com; 193 Bermondsey St, SE1; mains from £4.95; 7am-6pm Mon-Fri, 8am-6pm Sat, 9am-5pm Sun; Borough) Saying that the Watch House nails the sandwich wouldn't really do justice to this tip-top cafe: the sandwiches really are delicious (with artisan breads from a local baker). But there is also great coffee, treats for the sweet-toothed, and the small but lovely setting: a renovated 19th-century watch house where guards looked out for grave robbers in the next-door cemetery.

M MANZE BRITISH £
Map p420 (www.manze.co.uk; 87 Tower Bridge Rd, SE1; mains £2.95-6.65; 11am-2pm Mon-Thu, 10am-2.30pm Fri & Sat; Borough) Dating to 1902, M Manze started off as an ice-cream seller before moving on to selling its legendary staples: pies (minced beef). It's a classic operation, from the ageing tile work to the traditional working-man's menu: pie an...

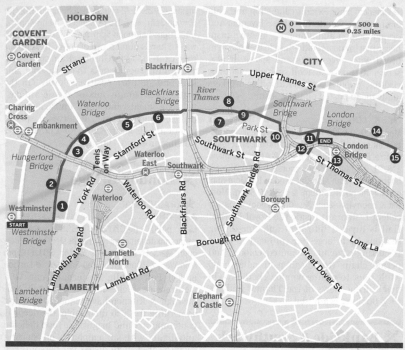

Neighbourhood Walk
South Bank Stroll

START WESTMINSTER TUBE STATION
END LONDON BRIDGE TUBE STATION
LENGTH 2.8 MILES; 3½ HOURS

From Westminster tube station, cross the river on Westminster Bridge and admire the views of Big Ben. As you reach the South Bank, the first building you'll walk past is the sombre ❶ **County Hall** (p164), the seat of London's local government from 1922 until Margaret Thatcher dissolved the Greater London Council in 1986.

The ❷ **London Eye** (p161) gracefully rotates next to it and the atmosphere on this stretch of the river is always party-like, with ice-cream vans, street performers, dozens of visitors and Londoners on their lunch-time run. Push on east past the ❸ **Southbank Centre** (p163) and pause to admire the acrobatics of local teenagers at the graffitied skatepark underneath ❹ **Queen Elizabeth Hall** (p163).

Carry on strolling along the river, past the boutiques of ❺ **Gabriel's Wharf** and

the ❻ **Oxo Tower**. After 20 to 30 minutes you'll emerge in front of the imposing ❼ **Tate Modern** (p158). Opposite is the ❽ **Millennium Bridge** (p164), Sir Norman Foster's 'blade of light'.

Just 100m past the Tate is the magnificently rebuilt ❾ **Shakespeare's Globe** (p160). Walk under Southwark Bridge, which is beautifully lit at night, past the perennially busy ❿ **Anchor pub**, and down the maze of streets leading to ⓫ **Southwark Cathedral** (p165).

Spreading around the railway arches is ⓬ **Borough Market** (p162), London's premier gourmet products market (and one of its oldest), at its busiest on Fridays and Saturdays. Lording over this area is the ⓭ **Shard** (p164), the EU's tallest building. Pass London Bridge, and the intimidating ⓮ **HMS Belfast** (p165), for glorious views of Tower Bridge. You'll also see ⓯ **City Hall** (p166) on your right, nicknamed 'the egg' (or, more cheekily, 'the testicle'). Then retrace your steps to the London Bridge tube station.

mash (£3.70), pie and liquor (£2.95), and you can take your eels jellied or stewed (£4.65).

ZUCCA
ITALIAN ££

Map p420 (☑020-7378 6809; www.zuccalondon.com; 184 Bermondsey St, SE1; mains £12-19; ☺noon-3pm Tue-Sun, 6-10pm Tue-Sat; ⊘; ⊖London Bridge) In a crisp, minimalist dining room with wrap-around bay windows and an open kitchen, an (almost) all-Italian staff serves contemporary Italian fare. The pasta is made daily on the premises and the menu is kept deliberately short to promote freshness.

CASSE-CROÛTE
FRENCH ££

Map p420 (☑020-7407 2140; www.cassecroute.co.uk; 109 Bermondsey St, SE1; mains £15; ☺noon-10pm Mon-Sat, noon-4pm Sun; ⊖Borough, London Bridge) You'll have to keep reminding yourself that you are in London and not in France, so typical is the interior of French brasseries and bistros. The fare too is quintessentially French, from *lapin à la moutarde* (rabbit in mustard sauce), to *île flottante* (a soft-set meringue in vanilla custard) and the all-French wine list. The all-day service however is definitely a London touch!

JOSE
SPANISH ££

Map p420 (www.josepizarro.com; 104 Bermondsey St, SE1; tapas £4-12; ☺noon-10.30pm Mon-Sat, to 5.30pm Sun; ⊖London Bridge) From the tiled bar counter to the barrel table, the leg of ham on its stand and the espresso machine behind the bar, Jose looks straight out of the streets of Madrid or Valencia. The food too is authentic: exquisitely tender *pluma ibérica* (grilled pork), garlic-rubbed *pan con tomate* (toasted bread with puréed tomatoes) and of course, *jamón* (ham) and chorizo.

The wine (and sherry) list is exclusively Spanish, with every wine available by the glass or bottle (a rare thing in London).

🍷 DRINKING & NIGHTLIFE

The South Bank is a strange combination of good, down-to-earth boozers, which just happen to have been here for hundreds of years, and modern bars – all neon and alcopops – patronised by a younger, trendier crowd.

📍 Waterloo

⭐ SCOOTERCAFFE
CAFE, BAR

Map p420 (132 Lower Marsh, SE1; ☺8.30am-11pm Mon-Fri, 10am-midnight Sat, 10am-11pm Sun; 🤶; ⊖Waterloo) A well-established fixture on the up-and-coming Lower Marsh road, this funky cafe-bar and former scooter repair shop with a Piatti scooter in the window serves killer hot chocolates, coffee and decadent cocktails. Unusually, you're allowed to bring takeaway food. The tiny patio at the back is perfect to soak up the sun.

SKYLON
BAR

Map p420 (www.skylon-restaurant.co.uk; Royal Festival Hall, Southbank Centre, Belvedere Rd, SE1; ☺noon-1am Mon-Sat, to 10.30pm Sun; ⊖Waterloo) With its ravishing 1950s decor and show-stopping views, Skylon is a memorable place to come for a drink or meal (p167). You'll have to come early to bag the tables at the front with plunging views of the river however. Drinks-wise, just ask: from superb seasonal cocktails to infusions and a staggering choice of whiskys (and whiskeys!).

FOUR CORNERS CAFE
CAFE

Map p420 (www.four-corners-cafe.com; 12 Lower Marsh, SE1; ☺7.30am-6.30pm Mon-Fri, 9am-5pm Sat; 🤶 ⊖Waterloo) With its excellent coffee and unusually large selection of teas, Four Corners Cafe attracts a loyal following, but occasional visitors will feel at home with the travel theme: from the map-lined coffee counter to the old guidebook collection (some Lonely Planet numbers!), the place has a buzz. You can even trade your old guidebooks (if they don't have it already) for free coffee!

KING'S ARMS
PUB

Map p420 (☑020-7207 0784; www.thekingsarmslondon.co.uk; 25 Roupell St, SE1; ☺11am-11pm Mon-Fri, noon-11pm Sat, noon-10.30pm Sun; ⊖Waterloo, Southwark) Relaxed and charming when not crowded, this neighbourhood boozer at the corner of a terraced Waterloo backstreet was a funeral parlour in a previous life. The large traditional bar area, serving up a good selection of ales and bitters, gives way to a fantastically odd conservatory bedecked with junk-store eclectica of local interest and serving decent Thai food.

🍷 Bankside & Southwark

DANDELYAN & RUMPUS ROOM   COCKTAIL BAR

Map p420 (www.mondrianlondon.com; Mondrian London, 20 Upper Ground, SE1; ⊘4pm-1am Mon-Wed, noon-1.30am Thu-Sat, noon-12.30am Sun; ⊜Southwark) These two swanky hotel bars are perfect for a special night out. Riverside Dandelyan offers cocktails with unexpected ingredients such as douglas fir, chalk bitters and dandelion capillaire, but the real show-stopper is Rumpus Room (5pm to 1am Wednesday to Saturday) on the 12th floor, with knock-out views and an emphasis on bubblies. Dress to impress. Reservations essential.

🍷 London Bridge

★WINE PANTRY   WINE BAR

Map p420 (www.winepantry.co.uk; 1 Stoney St, SE1; tasting session £5; ⊘noon-8pm Thu-Fri, 11am-7pm Sat; ⊜London Bridge) British and proud, the Wine Pantry supports domestic winemakers with an exciting range of vintages including Nyetimber, Bolney and Ridgeview. You can buy by the glass (£5 to £7) and sit at one of the handful of tables on the edge of Borough Market (p162). You're welcome to provide your own nibbles or grab a bottle to take away.

You can taste five wines for £5 if it's quiet (best time to try is 3pm to 5pm). In winter, there's a bubbling cauldron of mulled wine for marketside quaffing. Tip: for an extra £0.50, they'll spike your mulled wine with a shot of something stronger from a tempting top shelf.

★OBLIX   BAR

Map p420 (www.oblixrestaurant.com; Level 32, The Shard, 31 St Thomas St, SE1; ⊘noon-11pm; ⊜London Bridge) On the 32nd floor of the Shard, Oblix offers mesmerising vistas of London. You can come for anything from a coffee (£3.50) to a couple of cocktails (from £10) and enjoy virtually the same views as the official viewing galleries of the Shard (but at a reduced cost and with the added bonus of a drink!). Live music every night from 7pm.

RAKE   PUB

Map p420 (☎020-7407 0557; www.utobeer.co.uk; 1 Winchester Walk, SE1; ⊘noon-11pm Mon-Sat, to 1pm Sun; ⊜London Bridge) The Rake offers more than 130 beers – many of them international craft brews – at any one time. There are 10 taps and the selection of craft beers, real ales, lagers and ciders (with one-third pint measures) changes constantly. It's a tiny place yet always busy; the bamboo-decorated decking outside is especially popular.

GEORGE INN   PUB

Map p420 (☎020-7407 2056; www.nationaltrust.org.uk/george-inn; 77 Borough High St, SE1; ⊘11am-11pm; ⊜London Bridge) This magnificent old boozer is London's last surviving galleried coaching inn, dating from 1677 (after a fire destroyed it the year before) and mentioned in Dickens' *Little Dorrit*. It is on the site of the Tabard Inn, where the pilgrims in Chaucer's *Canterbury Tales* gathered before setting out (well lubricated, we suspect) on the road to Canterbury, Kent.

The huge courtyard full of picnic tables fills up on balmy evenings.

🍺 Bermondsey

★40 MALTBY STREET   WINE BAR

Map p420 (www.40maltbystreet.com; 40 Maltby St, SE1; ⊘5.30-10pm Wed & Thu, 12.30-2pm & 5.30-10pm Fri, 11am-10pm Sat) This tunnel-like wine-bar-cum-kitchen sits under the railway arches taking trains in and out of London Bridge. It is first and foremost a wine importer focusing on organic vintages but its hospitality venture has become incredibly popular. The wine recommendations are obviously top-notch (most of them by the glass) and the food – simple, gourmet bistro fare – is spot on.

WOOLPACK   PUB

Map p420 (www.woolpackbar.com; 98 Bermondsey St, SE1; ⊘11am-11pm Mon-Fri, 9.30am-11.30pm Sat, 9.30am-10.30pm Sun; ⊜London Bridge) This lovely free house (a pub that doesn't belong to a brewery) is a crowdpleaser: the British food is good, the decor lovely – dark-wood panels downstairs, sumptuous Victorian wallpaper upstairs – the garden spacious, and it shows football and rugby games.

🍺 Rotherhithe

★MAYFLOWER   PUB

(www.mayflowerpub.com; 117 Rotherhithe St, SE16; ⊘11am-11pm Mon-Sat, noon-10.30pm Sun; ⊜Rotherhithe) This 15th-century pub

BERMONDSEY'S BEER MILE

Craft beer is having its moment in London and Bermondsey is at the epicentre of this revival. There are seven microbreweries within a mile. They all produce a full range of beers – pale ales, porters, stouts, IPAs etc – and welcome discerning drinkers on Saturdays, generally from 11am to 4pm or 5pm.

Try **Southwark Brewing Company** (Map p420; www.southwarkbrewing.co.uk; 46 Druid St, SE1; ⊙11am-5pm Sat; ⊖London Bridge), the newest kid on the block, located in a hangar-like space kitted out with big tables and sofas (you're welcome to bring goodies from nearby **Borough** (p162) or **Maltby Street** (p173) markets to accompany your beer). The London Pale Ale has a nice zing. Also good is **Anspach & Hobday** (Map p420; www.anspachandhobday.com; 118 Druid St, SE1; ⊙5-9.30pm Fri, 11am-6pm Sat, noon-5pm Sun; ⊖London Bridge). Porter (a dark, roasted beer) is the name of the game here. There is a nice outdoor seating area.

is named after the vessel that took the pilgrims to America in 1620. The ship set sail from Rotherhithe, and Captain Christopher Jones supposedly charted out its course here while supping schooners. There's seating on a small back terrace, from which you can view the Thames.

☆ ENTERTAINMENT

The South Bank of London is home to some heavy hitters when it comes to London's theatre scene. Music and performing arts are big generally at the Southbank Centre.

NATIONAL THEATRE   THEATRE

Map p420 (☏020-7452 3000; www.nationaltheatre.org.uk; South Bank, SE1; ⊖Waterloo) England's flagship theatre showcases a mix of classic and contemporary plays performed by excellent casts in three theatres (Olivier, Lyttelton and Dorfman). Outstanding artistic director Nicholas Hytner oversaw a golden decade at the theatre, with landmark productions such as *War Horse*. His replacement, Rufus Norris, started in April 2015.

Travelex tickets costing just £15 are available to certain performances during the peak period; same day tickets also cost £15. Under-18s pay half price.

SOUTHBANK CENTRE   CONCERT VENUE

Map p420 (☏0844 875 0073; www.southbankcentre.co.uk; Belvedere Rd, SE1; ⊖Waterloo) The Southbank Centre's **Royal Festival Hall** (Map p420; ☏0844 875 0073; www.southbankcentre.co.uk; Southbank Centre, Belvedere Rd, SE1; admission £6-60; ☏; ⊖Waterloo) seats

3000 in its amphitheatre and is one of the best places for catching world and classical music artists. The sound is fantastic, the programming impeccable and there are frequent free gigs in the wonderfully expansive foyer.

The centre organises fantastic festivals, including **London Wonderground** (dedicated to circus and cabaret), **Udderbelly** (a festival of comedy in all its guises – stand up, music, mime etc) and **Meltdown** (a music event curated by the best and most eclectic names in music – Yoko Ono in 2013, Massive Attack in 2008, etc).

SHAKESPEARE'S GLOBE   THEATRE

Map p420 (☏020-7401 9919; www.shakespearesglobe.com; 21 New Globe Walk, SE1; seats £10-43, standing £5; ⊖Blackfriars, London Bridge) If you love Shakespeare and the theatre, the Globe (p160) will knock you off your feet. This authentic Shakespearean theatre is a wooden O without a roof over the central stage area, and although there are covered wooden bench seats in tiers around the stage, many people (there's room for 700) do as 17th-century 'groundlings' did, standing in front of the stage.

The theatre season runs from late April to mid-October and includes works by Shakespeare and his contemporaries such as Christopher Marlowe.

Because the building is quite open to the elements, you may have to wrap up. No umbrellas are allowed, but cheap raincoats are on sale. A warning: two pillars holding up the stage canopy (the so-called Heavens) obscure much of the view in section D; you'd almost do better to stand.

If you don't like the idea of standing in the rain or sitting in the cold, opt for an indo

LOCAL KNOWLEDGE

ALL LONDON'S A STAGE

Tom Bird is executive producer at **Shakespeare's Globe** (p160) theatre. As well as working on productions in London (including international plays), his main responsibility is to take the Globe to the world, on tours, festivals and off-beat locations.

Seating or Standing at the Globe?
Standing! I absolutely love it. You can sit down in every other theatre but there is nowhere in the world where standing offers the best seats in the house. And for just £5.

North or South of the river?
I lived in Hackney (North London) for years and moved to New Cross (South London) a couple of years ago. There are a lot of people who seem to be making that journey and I think southeast London is becoming very exciting.

Weekend plans?
I love swimming in the **ponds** (p254) in Hampstead Heath. It is so unique – there is nowhere else in the world like this and it's a totally new way to discover the city.

Top tip for visitors?
My advice would be to get out of Zone 1 (the West End and the South Bank) and to explore areas on the edge of the centre, like Hackney, Hampstead or East London: that's the London that tourists don't always see.

candle-lit play in the **Sam Wanamaker Playhouse**, a Jacobean theatre similar to the one Shakespeare would have used in winter. The programming also includes opera.

BFI SOUTHBANK CINEMA
Map p420 (☑020-7928 3232; www.bfi.org.uk; Belvedere Rd, SE1; tickets £8-12; ☉11am-11pm; ☻Waterloo) Tucked almost out of sight under the arches of Waterloo Bridge is the British Film Institute, containing four cinemas that screen thousands of films each year (mostly arthouse), a gallery devoted to the moving image and the mediatheque, where you watch film and TV highlights from the BFI National Archive.

There's also a film store for books and DVDs, a restaurant and a gorgeous cafe. Largely a repertory or art-house theatre, the BFI runs regular retrospectives and is the major venue for the **BFI London Film Festival**, which screens some 300 films from around the world in October every year.

OLD VIC THEATRE
Map p420 (☑0844 871 7628; www.oldvictheatre.com; The Cut, SE1; ☻Waterloo) American actor Kevin Spacey took the theatrical helm of this stalwart of the London theatre scene in 2003 and gave it a new lease of life. He

stood down in April 2015 and was succeeded by Matthew Warchus (who directed *Matilda the Musical* and the film *Pride*). His aim is to bring an eclectic – and busier – programme to the theatre.

YOUNG VIC THEATRE
Map p420 (☑020-7922 2922; www.youngvic.org; 66 The Cut, SE1; ☻Southwark, Waterloo) This ground-breaking theatre is as much about showcasing and discovering new talent as it is about people discovering theatre. The Young Vic features actors, directors and plays from across the world, many of whom tackle contemporary political or cultural issues such as the death penalty, racism or corruption, often blending dance and music with acting.

Discounts are available for children, students and over 60s.

BFI IMAX CINEMA CINEMA
Map p420 (www.odeon.co.uk/cinemas/bfi_imax; 1 Charlie Chaplin Walk, SE1; adult/child from £16.60/11.20; ☻Waterloo) The British Film Institute's IMAX Cinema screens 2D and 3D documentaries about travel, space and wildlife, lasting anywhere from 40 minutes to 1½ hours, as well as recently released blockbusters.

🛍 SHOPPING

Along with the following, check out the cute boutiques at Gabriel's Wharf and the Oxo Tower.

LOVELY & BRITISH   GIFTS

Map p420 (📞020-7378 6570; www.facebook. com/LovelyandBritish; 132a Bermondsey St, SE1; ⊙10am-3pm Mon, 11.30am-6pm Tue, 10am-6pm Wed-Fri, 10am-5.30pm Sat, 11am-4pm Sun; ⊜London Bridge) As the name suggests, this gorgeous Bermondsey boutique prides itself on stocking prints, jewellery and home furnishings from British designers. It's an eclectic mix of vintage and new, with very reasonable prices.

SOUTHBANK CENTRE SHOP   HOMEWARES

Map p420 (www.southbankcentre.co.uk; Festival Tce, SE1; ⊙10am-9pm Mon-Fri, to 8pm Sat, noon-8pm Sun; ⊜Waterloo) This is the place to come for quirky London books, '50s-inspired homewares, original prints and creative gifts for children. The shop is rather eclectic but you're sure to find unique gifts or souvenirs to take home.

NATIONAL THEATRE GIFT SHOP   BOOKS

Map p420 (📞020-7452 3456; www.nationaltheatre.org.uk; South Bank, SE1; ⊙9.30am-10.45pm Mon-Sat, 12-6pm Sun; ⊜Waterloo) You'll find an extensive selection of books covering literature, history, art and more, as well as NT merchandise and unusual gifts. Jewellery and children's gifts are lined up next to fold-out craft beer maps and skull-shaped erasers.

MALTBY STREET MARKET   MARKET

Map p420 (www.maltby.st; Maltby St, SE1; ⊙9am-4pm Sat, 11am-4pm Sun; ⊜London Bridge) Started as an alternative to the juggernaut that is Borough Market, Maltby Street Market is becoming victim of its own success, with brick and mortar shops and restaurants replacing the old workshops, and with throngs of visitors. That said, it is still much smaller than other popular London weekend markets and boasts some original – and all top notch – food stalls (smoked salmon from east London, African burgers, seafood counters and lots of pastries).

For drinks, look no further than **Little Bird Gin's bar** (Map p420; www.littlebirdgin. com; Maltby St, SE1; ⊙10am-4pm Sat, from 11am Sunday; ⊜London Bridge), which uses its eponymous gin (a small batch, citrusy gin distilled in London) to make eye-poppingly good cocktails (£5 to £7) served in jam jars or apothecary's glass bottles. Equally fantastic is **Jensen** (Map p420; www.jensengin. com; 55 Stanworth St, SE1; ⊙10am-4pm Sat; ⊜London Bridge), another gin specialist, this time with a distillery on the premises (bottles £20 to £25, cocktails £4.95). Both allow you to bring in your takeaway goodies whilst you enjoy their cocktails.

SOUTH BANK BOOK MARKET   MARKET

Map p420 (Riverside Walk, SE1; ⊙11am-7pm, shorter hours in winter; ⊜Waterloo) The South Bank Book Market, with prints and second-hand books, takes place daily under the arches of Waterloo Bridge. You'll find anything from fiction to children's books, comics and classics.

BERMONDSEY MARKET   MARKET

Map p420 (Bermondsey Sq; ⊙5am-3pm Fri; ⊜Borough, Bermondsey) Reputedly it's legal to sell stolen goods here before dawn, but late risers will find this market altogether upright and sedate, with cutlery and other old-fashioned silverware, antique porcelain, paintings and some costume jewellery.

Kensington & Hyde Park

KNIGHTSBRIDGE | SOUTH KENSINGTON | HYDE PARK | KENSINGTON GARDENS | CHELSEA & BELGRAVIA | VICTORIA | PIMLICO

Neighbourhood Top Five

1 Thumbing through an encyclopaedic A–Z of decorative and design works from across the globe in the **Victoria & Albert Museum** (p176).

2 Becoming hypnotised by the awe-inspiring stonework and inexhaustible collection of the world-leading

Natural History Museum (p180).

3 Enjoying a picnic in London's green lung, **Hyde Park** (p182).

4 Nurturing a wide-eyed fascination for the perplexities of the world and the cosmos in the electrifying **Science Museum** (p184).

5 Shopping – or just window-shopping! – at the extravagant **Harrods** (p194).

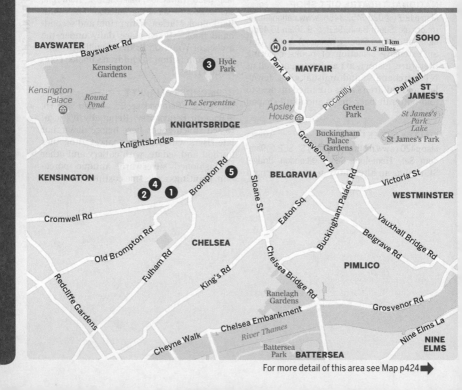

For more detail of this area see Map p424 ➡

Explore: Kensington & Hyde Park

You can navigate a serious learning-curve or at least catch up on all you forgot since high school at South Kensington's magnificent museums of the arts and sciences. You'll need several days – and considerable calorific reserves – to do them all justice. Museums open at 10am, so you don't have to set your alarm too early, but being near the front of the queue when the doors open gives useful elbow room.

Shoppers will make an eager beeline for Knightsbridge, Harrods and Harvey Nichols, but there are tranquil shopping escapes – such as John Sandoe Books – to sidestep the maddening crowds.

Earmark a sight-packed day for a visit to Hyde Park and conjoined Kensington Gardens – crucial to see why Londoners love their green spaces. Begin by exploring the opulence of Apsley House before walking across the park, via the Serpentine, to the Albert Memorial, Royal Albert Hall and Kensington Palace.

Outstanding restaurants will be with you every step of the way: Kensington, Knightsbridge and Chelsea take their dining particularly seriously, so some of your fondest memories could well be gastronomic, whether you're grazing, snacking or plain feasting.

Local Life

➡**Hang-outs** Join Londoners swooning before the lawn of Fulham Palace (p188), linger over coffee and cake at Tomtom Coffee House (p193) or snap your fingers with local jazz hounds at the swinging 606 Club (p194).

➡**Museums** Late-night Fridays at the Victoria & Albert (p176) mean fewer crowds (especially children) and locals can get a look-in.

➡**Parks** When the sun's out, Londoners dust off their shades, get outdoors to expanses of green like Hyde Park (p182) and lie on the grass reading chunky novels.

Getting There & Away

➡**Underground** Kensington and Hyde Park are well connected to the rest of London via stations at South Kensington, Sloane Sq, Victoria, Knightsbridge and Hyde Park Corner. The main lines are Circle, District, Piccadilly and Victoria.

➡**Bus** Handy routes include 74 from South Kensington to Knightsbridge and Hyde Park Corner; 52 from Victoria to High St Kensington; 360 from South Kensington to Sloane Sq and Pimlico; and 11 from Fulham Broadway to King's Road, Sloane Sq and Victoria.

➡**Bicycle** Santander Cycles (p67) are very handy for pedal-powering your way in, out and around the neighbourhood.

Lonely Planet's Top Tip

Catch the Queen's Life Guard (Household Cavalry) departing for Horse Guards Parade at 10.28am (9.28am Sundays) from Hyde Park Barracks for the daily Changing of the Guard, performing a ritual that dates to 1660. They troop via Hyde Park Corner, Constitution Hill and the Mall. It's not as busy as the Changing of the Guard at Buckingham Palace and you can get closer to the action.

✕ Best Places to Eat

➡ Tom's Kitchen (p189)

➡ Rabbit (p192)

➡ Dinner by Heston Blumenthal (p191)

➡ Launceston Place (p191)

➡ Pimlico Fresh (p192)

For reviews, see p189 ➡

🍷 Best Places to Drink

➡ Tomtom Coffee House (p193)

➡ Phene (p193)

➡ Queen's Arms (p193)

➡ Buddha Bar (p193)

➡ Anglesea Arms (p193)

For reviews, see p193 ➡

🔒 Best Shopping

➡ Harrods (p194)

➡ Conran Shop (p194)

➡ Slightly Foxed on Gloucester Road (p195)

➡ British Red Cross (p194)

➡ Pickett (p195)

For reviews, see p194 ➡

KENSINGTON & HYDE PARK

TOP SIGHT
VICTORIA & ALBERT MUSEUM

The Museum of Manufactures, as the V&A was known when it opened in 1852, was part of Prince Albert's legacy to the nation in the aftermath of the successful Great Exhibition of 1851. Its original aims – which still hold today – were the 'improvement of public taste in design' and 'applications of fine art to objects of utility'. It's done a fine job so far.

Collection

Through 146 galleries, the museum houses the world's greatest collection of decorative arts, from ancient Chinese ceramics to modernist architectural drawings, Korean bronze and Japanese swords, cartoons by Raphael, gowns from the Elizabethan era, ancient jewellery, a Sony Walkman – and much, much more.

Entrance

Entering under the stunning blue-and-yellow blown glass **chandelier** by Dale Chihuly, you can grab a museum map (£1 donation requested) at the information desk. (If the 'Grand Entrance' on Cromwell Rd is too busy, there's another around the corner on Exhibition Rd, or you can enter from the tunnel in the basement, if arriving by tube.)

Level 1

The street level is mostly devoted to art and design from India, China, Japan, Korea and Southeast Asia, as well as European art. One of the museum's highlights is the **Cast Courts** in rooms 46a and 46b, containing staggering plaster casts collected in the Victorian era, such as Michelangelo's *David*, acquired in 1858.

DON'T MISS...
➡ Jewellery Gallery
➡ Raphael cartoons
➡ Ardabil Carpet

PRACTICALITIES
➡ V&A
➡ Map p424, C4
➡ www.vam.ac.uk
➡ Cromwell Rd, SW7
➡ admission free
➡ ⊙10am-5.45pm Sat-Thu, to 10pm Fri
➡ ⊖South Kensington

The **TT Tsui Gallery** (rooms 44 and 47e) displays lovely pieces, including a beautifully lithe wooden statue of Guanyin seated in *lalitasana* pose from AD 1200; also check out a leaf from the 'Twenty views of the Yuanmingyuan Summer Palace' (1781–86), revealing the Haiyantang and the 12 animal heads of the fountain (now ruins) in Beijing. Within the subdued lighting of the **Japan Gallery** (room 45) stands a fearsome suit of armour in the Domaru style. More than 400 objects are within the **Islamic Middle East Gallery** (room 42), including ceramics, textiles, carpets, glass and woodwork from the 8th-century up to the years before WWI. The exhibition's highlight is the gorgeous mid-16th-century **Ardabil Carpet**.

For fresh air, the landscaped **John Madejski Garden** is a lovely shaded inner courtyard. Cross it to reach the original **Refreshment Rooms** (Morris, Gamble and Poynter Rooms), dating from the 1860s and redesigned by McInnes Usher McKnight Architects (MUMA), who also renovated the **Medieval and Renaissance galleries** (1350–1600) to the right of the Grand Entrance.

Levels 2 & 4

The **British Galleries**, featuring every aspect of British design from 1500 to 1900, are divided between levels 2 (1500–1760) and 4 (1760–1900). Level 4 also boasts the **Architecture Gallery** (rooms 127 to 128a), which vividly describes architectural styles via models and videos, and the spectacular brightly illuminated **Contemporary Glass Gallery** (room 129).

Level 3

The **Jewellery Gallery** (rooms 91 to 93) is outstanding; the mezzanine level – accessed via the glass-and-perspex spiral staircase – glitters with jewel-encrusted swords, watches and gold boxes. The **Photographs Gallery** (room 100) is one of the nation's best, with access to more than 500,000 images collected since the mid-19th century. **Design Since 1946** (room 76) celebrates design classics from a 1985 Sony credit-card radio to a 1992 Nike 'Air Max' shoe, Peter Ghyczy's Garden Egg Chair from 1968 and the now ubiquitous selfie stick.

Level 6

Among the pieces in the **Ceramics Gallery** (rooms 136 to 146) – the world's largest – are standout items from the Middle East and Asia. The **Dr Susan Weber Gallery** (rooms 133 to 135) celebrates furniture design over the past six centuries.

V&A ARCHITECTURE

Look around you at the fabric of the Victoria & Albert Museum – tiled staircases and floors, painted, vaulted ceilings and the astonishing frescoes in the Leighton Corridor – the museum is a work of art in itself.

When militant suffragettes threatened to damage exhibits at public museums in 1913, the V&A considered denying women entry to the museum, but instead opted for scrapping admission charges to the museum to boost visitor numbers and so help protect the V&A's collection.

V&A TOURS

Several free one-hour guided tours leave the main reception area every day. Times are prominently displayed; alternatively, check the website for details.

The V&A's temporary exhibitions are compelling and fun (note that admission fees apply). There are also talks, workshops, events and one of the best museum shops around.

Victoria & Albert Museum

HALF-DAY HIGHLIGHTS TOUR

The art- and design-packed V&A is vast: we have devised an easy-to-follow tour of the museum highlights to help cover some signature pieces while also allowing you to appreciate some of the grandeur of the museum architecture.

Enter the V&A by the Grand Entrance off Cromwell Rd and immediately turn left to explore the Islamic Middle East Gallery and to discover the sumptuous silk-and-wool **Ardabil Carpet ❶**. Among the pieces from South Asia in the adjacent gallery is the terrifying automated **Tipu's Tiger ❷**. Continue to the outstanding **Fashion Gallery ❸** with its displays of clothing styles through the ages. The magnificent gallery opposite houses the **Raphael Cartoons ❹**, large paintings by Raphael used to weave tapestries for the Vatican. Take the stairs to Level 2 and the Britain 1500–1760

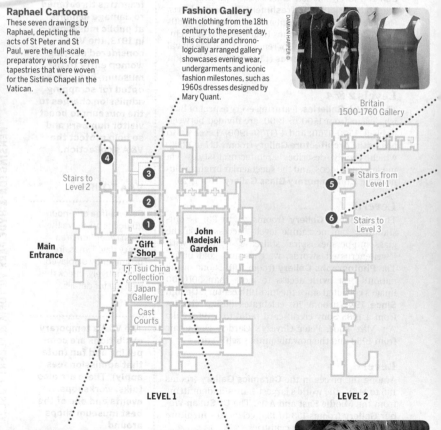

Raphael Cartoons
These seven drawings by Raphael, depicting the acts of St Peter and St Paul, were the full-scale preparatory works for seven tapestries that were woven for the Sistine Chapel in the Vatican.

Fashion Gallery
With clothing from the 18th century to the present day, this circular and chronologically arranged gallery showcases evening wear, undergarments and iconic fashion milestones, such as 1960s dresses designed by Mary Quant.

DAMIAN HARPER ©

Britain 1500-1760 Gallery

Stairs from Level 1

Stairs to Level 2

Stairs to Level 3

Main Entrance

Gift Shop

John Madejski Garden

Tsui China collection

Japan Gallery

Cast Courts

LEVEL 1

LEVEL 2

The Ardabil Carpet
One of the world's most beautiful carpets, the Ardabil was completed in 1540, one of a pair commissioned by Shah Tahmasp, ruler of Iran. The piece is most astonishing for the artistry of the detailing and the subtlety of design.

Tipu's Tiger
This disquieting 18th-century wood-and-metal mechanical automaton depicts a European being savaged by a tiger. When a handle is turned, an organ hidden within the feline mimics the cries of the dying man, whose arm also rises.

GREG BALFOUR EVANS / ALAMY ©

Gallery; turn left in the gallery to find the **Great Bed of Ware** ❺, beyond which rests the exquisitely crafted artistry of **Henry VIII's Writing Box** ❻. Head up the stairs into the Metalware Gallery on Level 3 for the **Hereford Screen** ❼. Continue through the Ironwork and Sculpture Galleries and through the Leighton Corridor to the glittering **Jewellery Gallery** ❽. Exit through the Stained Glass gallery, at the end of which you'll find stairs back down to level 1.

TOP TIPS

» **More Info** Museum attendants are always at hand along the route.

» **Photography** Allowed in most galleries, except the Jewellery Gallery, the Raphael Cartoons and in exhibitions.

» **Evening Exploration** Avoid daytime crowds: visit the V&A till 10pm on Friday.

The Great Bed of Ware
Created during the reign of Queen Elizabeth I, its headboard and bedposts are etched with ancient graffiti; the 16th-century oak Great Bed of Ware is famously name-dropped in Shakespeare's *Twelfth Night*.

Henry VIII's Writing Box
This exquisitely ornate walnut and oak 16th-century writing box has been added to over the centuries, but the original decorative motifs are superb, including Henry's coat of arms, flanked by Venus (holding Cupid) and Mars.

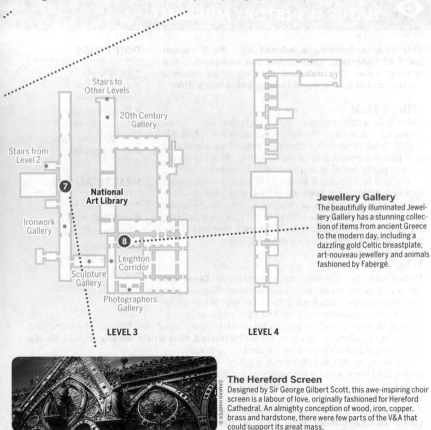

Stairs to Other Levels

20th Century Gallery

Stairs from Level 2

National Art Library

❼

Ironwork Gallery

❽

Leighton Corridor

Sculpture Gallery

Photographers Gallery

LEVEL 3

LEVEL 4

Jewellery Gallery
The beautifully illuminated Jewellery Gallery has a stunning collection of items from ancient Greece to the modern day, including a dazzling gold Celtic breastplate, art-nouveau jewellery and animals fashioned by Fabergé.

The Hereford Screen
Designed by Sir George Gilbert Scott, this awe-inspiring choir screen is a labour of love, originally fashioned for Hereford Cathedral. An almighty conception of wood, iron, copper, brass and hardstone, there were few parts of the V&A that could support its great mass.

DAMIAN HARPER ©

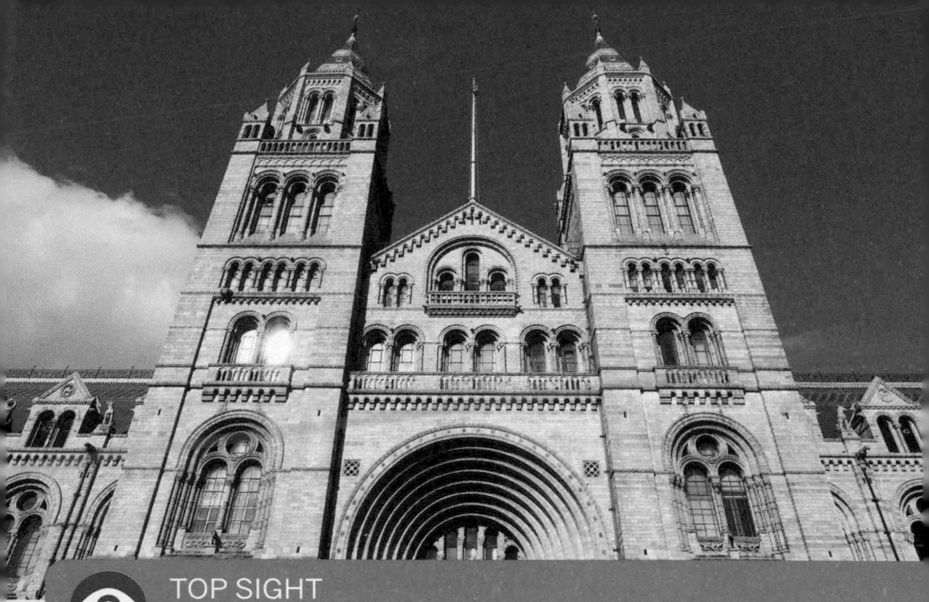

TOP SIGHT
NATURAL HISTORY MUSEUM

This colossal building is infused with the Victorian spirit of collecting, cataloguing and interpreting the natural world. The museum building is as much a reason to visit as the world-famous collection within.

Hintze Hall

This grand central hall resembles a cathedral nave – quite fitting for a time when the natural sciences were challenging the biblical tenets of Christian orthodoxy. Naturalist and first superintendent of the museum, Richard Owen, celebrated the building as a 'cathedral to nature'.

The hall is dominated by the dramatically overarching cast of a **diplodocus skeleton** (nicknamed Dippy), which has inspired generations of children to drag their parents to the fantastic Dinosaurs Gallery in the Blue Zone. In 2017, Dippy will be replaced by the skeleton of a blue whale, displayed in a diving position for dramatic effect.

Blue Zone

Undoubtedly the museum's star attraction, the **Dinosaurs Gallery** takes you on an impressive overhead walkway, past a dromaeosaurus (a small and agile meat eater) before reaching a roaring animatronic T-rex and then winding its way through skeletons, fossils, casts and fascinating displays about how dinosaurs lived and died.

Another highlight of this zone is the **Mammals & Blue Whale Gallery**, with its life-size blue whale model and extensive displays on cetaceans.

The museum has also dedicated a gallery to **Human Biology**, where you'll be able to understand more about what makes us tick (senses, hormones, our brain and so on).

Green Zone

While children love the Blue Zone, adults may prefer the Green Zone, especially the **Treasures in Cadogan Gallery**, on the first floor, which houses the museum's most prized posses-

DON'T MISS...

➡ Hintze Hall
➡ Treasures at Cadogan Gallery
➡ Dinosaurs Gallery
➡ Darwin Centre
➡ Wildlife Photographer of the Year

PRACTICALITIES

➡ Map p424, C4
➡ www.nhm.ac.uk
➡ Cromwell Rd, SW7
➡ admission free
➡ ⊙10am-5.50pm
➡ 🛜
➡ ⊖South Kensington

sions, each with a unique history. Exhibits include a chunk of moon rock, an Emperor Penguin egg collected by Captain Scott's expedition and a first edition of Charles Darwin's *On the Origin of Species*.

Equally rare and exceptional are the gems and rocks held in the **Vault**, including a Martian meteorite and the largest emerald ever found.

Take a moment to marvel at the trunk section of a 1300 year-old **giant sequoia tree** on the second floor: its size is mind-boggling.

Red Zone

This zone explores the ever-changing nature of our planet and the forces shaping it. The **earthquake simulator** (in the **Volcanoes and Earthquakes Gallery**), which re-creates the 1995 Kobe earthquake in a grocery store, is a favourite, as is the **From the Beginning Gallery**, which retraces Earth's history.

In **Earth's Treasury**, you can find out more about our planet's mineral riches and how they are being used in our every day lives – from jewellery to construction and electronics.

Access to most of the galleries in the Red Zone is via **Earth Hall** and a very tall escalator that disappears into a large earth-metal sculpture. The most intact **stegosaurus fossil skeleton** ever found is displayed at the base.

Orange Zone

The **Darwin Centre** is the beating heart of the museum: this is where the museum's millions of specimens are kept and where its scientists work. The top two floors of the amazing '**cocoon**' building are dedicated to explaining the kind of research the museum does – windows allow you to see the researchers at work.

If you'd like to find out more, pop into the **Attenborough Studio** (named after famous naturalist and broadcaster David Attenborough) for one of the daily talks with the museum's scientists. The studio also shows films throughout the day.

Exhibitions

The museum hosts regular exhibitions (admission fees apply), some of them on a recurrent basis. **Wildlife Photographer of the Year** (adult/child £12.60/6.30; ⊙Nov-Aug), has show-stopping images, while **Sensational Butterflies** (Map p424; adult/family £4.90/19.80; ⊙Apr–mid-Sep), a tunnel tent on the East Lawn that swarms with what must originally have been called 'flutter-bys', has become a firm summer favourite.

Wildlife Gardens

A slice of English countryside in SW7, these beautiful gardens encompass a range of British lowland habitats, including a meadow with farm gates and a bee tree where a colony of honey bees fills the air.

SKATING AT THE MUSEUM

From Halloween to January, a section by the East Lawn of the museum is transformed into a glittering and highly popular ice rink, complete with a hot-drinks stall. Our advice: book your slot well ahead, browse the museum and skate later.

Children love the Natural History Museum and there are great resources for them: borrow an Explorer backpack (for under 7s, complete with activity booklet, explorer hat and binoculars!) or buy a discover guide (£1): themes include dinosaurs, mammals, and rocks and soils (available for ages five to seven or eight to 11).

CLEVER SHOP

As well as the obligatory dinosaur figurines and animal soft toys, the museum's shop has a huge and brilliant collection of children's books about nature, animals and, of course, dinosaurs. On the adult side, beautiful jewellery and lovely stationery are treats to look out for.

KENSINGTON & HYDE PARK NATURAL HISTORY MUSEUM

TOP SIGHT
HYDE PARK

London's largest royal park spreads itself over 142 hectares of neat gardens, wild expanses of overgrown grass and glorious trees. As well as being a fantastic green space in the middle of London, it is home to a handful of fascinating sights.

Green Spaces

The eastern half of the park is covered with expansive lawns, which become one vast picnic-and-frolic area on sunny days. The western half is more untamed, with plenty of trees and areas of wild grass.

If you're after somewhere more colourful (and some shade), head to the **Rose Garden** (Map p424; ⊖Hyde Park Corner, Knightsbridge), a beautifully landscaped garden with flowers year-round, ideal to sit and contemplate for a while.

A little further west, you'll find the **Holocaust Memorial Garden** (Map p424; ⊖Hyde Park Corner, Knightsbridge), a simple stone marker in a grove of trees.

Speakers' Corner

Frequented by Karl Marx, Vladimir Lenin, George Orwell and William Morris, **Speakers' Corner** (Map p424; Park Lane; ⊖Marble Arch) in the northeastern corner is traditionally the spot for oratorical acrobatics and soapbox ranting. If you have something to get off your chest, do so on Sunday, although you'll mainly have religious fanatics and hecklers for company.

It's the only place in Britain where demonstrators can assemble without police permission. This concession was granted in 1872 after serious riots 17 years earlier had 150,000 people gathered to demonstrate against the Sunday Trading Bill before Parliament, only to be unexpectedly ambushed by police concealed within Marble Arch.

The Serpentine Galleries

Straddling the Serpentine lake, the **Serpentine Galleries** (Map p424; www.serpentinegalleries. org; Kensington Gardens, W2; ⊗10am-6pm Tue-Sun; ☜; ⊖Lancaster Gate, Knightsbridge) **FREE** may

DON'T MISS...

➡ The Serpentine Galleries
➡ Speakers' Corner
➡ Diana, Princess of Wales Memorial Fountain

PRACTICALITIES

➡ Map p424, D2
➡ www.royalparks.org. uk/parks/hyde-park
➡ ⊗5am-midnight
➡ ⊖Marble Arch, Hyde Park Corner, Queensway

look like quaint historical buildings but they are one of London's most important contemporary art galleries. Damien Hirst, Andreas Gursky, Louise Bourgeois, Gabriel Orozco, Tomoko Takahashi and Jeff Koons have all exhibited here.

The original exhibition space is the 1930s former tea pavilion located in Kensington Gardens. In 2013, the gallery opened the **Serpentine Sackler Gallery** (Map p424; www.serpentinegalleries.org; West Carriage Drive, W2; ⊘10am-6pm Tue-Sun; ⊖Lancaster Gate) FREE within **the Magazine**, a former gunpowder depot, across the Serpentine Bridge in Hyde Park. Built in 1805, it has been augmented with a daring, undulating extension designed by Pritzker Prize–winning architect Zaha Hadid.

The galleries run a full programme of exhibitions, readings, talks and open-air cinema screenings. A leading architect who has never previously built in the UK is annually commissioned to build a new 'Summer Pavilion' nearby, open from June to October.

The Serpentine

Hyde Park is separated from Kensington Gardens by the L-shaped Serpentine, a small lake once fed with waters from the River Westbourne; the lake hosted the Olympic triathlon and marathon swimming events in 2012.

You can have a swim too – between May and September – at the **Serpentine Lido** (Map p424; ☑020-7706 3422; Hyde Park, W2; adult/child £4.60/1.60; ⊘10am-6pm daily Jun-Aug, Sat & Sun May; ⊖Hyde Park Corner, Knightsbridge), where a swimming area within the lake is ring-fenced. There is also a paddling pool for children.

If you'd rather stay dry, rent a paddle boat from the **Serpentine boathouse** (Map p424; ☑020-7262 1330; adult/child per 30min £10/4, per 1hr £12/5; ⊖Hyde Park Corner, Kinghtsbridge).

Diana, Princess of Wales Memorial Fountain

This **memorial fountain** (Map p424; ⊖Knightsbridge) is dedicated to the late Princess of Wales. Envisaged by the designer Kathryn Gustafson as a 'moat without a castle' and draped 'like a necklace' around the southwestern edge of Hyde Park near the Serpentine Bridge, the circular double stream is composed of 545 pieces of Cornish granite, its waters drawn from a chalk aquifer more than 100m below ground. Unusually, visitors are actively encouraged to splash about, to the delight of children.

A **solar shuttle** (Map p424; ☑020-7262 1330; www.solarshuttle.co.uk; adult/child £5/3) ferries passengers from the Serpentine Boathouse to the fountain at weekends from March to September (every day from mid-July to late August).

HISTORY

Henry VIII expropriated the park from the church in 1536, after which it emerged as a hunting ground for kings and aristocrats; later it became a popular venue for duels, executions and horse racing. It was the first royal park to open to the public in the early 17th century, the famous venue of the Great Exhibition in 1851, and during WWII it became a vast potato bed. These days, it's an occasional concert and music-festival venue (Bruce Springsteen, The Rolling Stones, Madonna).

Found the perfect spot? Hire a deck chair (1/4 hours £1.60/4.60). They are available throughout the park from March to October, weather permitting.

ROYAL GUN SALUTES

Royal Gun Salutes are fired in Hyde Park on 10 June for the Duke of Edinburgh's birthday and on 14 November for the Prince of Wales's birthday. The salutes are fired at midday and include 41 rounds (21 is standard but being a royal park, Hyde Park gets a bonus 20 rounds).

TOP SIGHT
SCIENCE MUSEUM

With seven floors of interactive and educational exhibits, this scientifically spellbinding museum will mesmerise adults and children alike.

The most popular galleries are on the ground floor, starting with **Exploring Space**, featuring genuine **rockets** and **satellites** and a full size replica of **'Eagle'**, the lander that took Neil Armstrong and Buzz Aldrin to the moon in 1969.

Next is the **Making the Modern World Gallery**, a visual feast of locomotives, planes, cars, engines and other revolutionary inventions (penicillin, cameras etc).

The fantastic **Information Age Gallery** on level 2 showcases how information and communication technologies – from the telegraph to smartphones – have transformed our lives since the 19th century. Standout displays include wireless sent by a sinking Titanic, the first BBC radio broadcast and a Soviet BESM 1965 supercomputer. Also on level 2 is **Media Space**, a gallery dedicated to excellent photographic exhibitions from the National Photography Collection (adult/child £8/free).

The 3rd-floor **Flight Gallery** (free tours 1pm most days) is a favourite place for children, with its gliders, hot-air balloons and aircraft, including the *Gipsy Moth*, which Amy Johnson flew to Australia in 1930. This floor also features a **Red Arrows 3D flight simulation theatre** (adult/children £6/5) and a **Fly 360-degree flight-simulator capsules** (£12 per capsule). **Launchpad**, on the same floor, is stuffed with (free) hands-on gadgets exploring physics and the properties of liquids.

Glimpses of Medical History on level 4 isn't as high-tech as the rest of the museum but is highly evocative with models and life-size reconstructions showing how medicine – from dentistry to childbirth – was practised through the ages.

If you've kids under the age of five, pop down to the basement and the **Garden**, where there's a fun-filled play zone, including a water-play area, besieged by tots in orange waterproof smocks.

DON'T MISS...

➡ Exploring Space Gallery

➡ Information Age Gallery

➡ Making the Modern World Gallery

➡ Flight simulators

PRACTICALITIES

➡ Map p424, C4

➡ www.sciencemuseum.org.uk

➡ Exhibition Rd, SW7

➡ admission free

➡ ⊙10am-6pm

➡ 🛜

➡ ⊖South Kensington

◉ SIGHTS

◉ Knightsbridge & South Kensington

VICTORIA & ALBERT MUSEUM   MUSEUM
See p176.

NATURAL HISTORY MUSEUM   MUSEUM
See p180.

SCIENCE MUSEUM   MUSEUM
See p184.

WELLINGTON ARCH   MUSEUM
Map p424 (www.english-heritage.org.uk/visit/places/wellington-arch/; Hyde Park Corner, W1; adult/child £4.30/2.60, with Apsley House £10/6; ⊙10am-6pm Apr-Sep, to 4pm Nov-Mar; ⊜Hyde Park Corner) Dominating the green space throttled by the Hyde Park Corner roundabout, this imposing neoclassical 1826 arch originally faced the Hyde Park Screen, but was shunted here in 1882 for road widening. Once a police station, it is now a gallery with temporary exhibitions and a permanent display about the history of the arch. The open-air balconies (accessible by lift) afford unforgettable views of Hyde Park, Buckingham Palace and the Mall.

Originally crowned by a disproportionately large equestrian statue of the Duke of Wellington, it was replaced by the current *Peace Descending on the Quadriga of War* in 1912, Europe's largest bronze sculpture.

ROYAL ALBERT HALL   HISTORIC BUILDING
Map p424 (☑box office 0845 401 5034; www.royalalberthall.com; Kensington Gore, SW7; ⊜South Kensington) Built in 1871 thanks in part to the proceeds of the 1851 Great Exhibition organised by Prince Albert (Queen Victoria's husband), this huge, domed, red-brick amphitheatre, adorned with a frieze of Minton tiles, is Britain's most famous concert venue and home to the BBC's Promenade Concerts (the Proms) every summer. Book an informative one-hour front-of-house **guided tour** (☑0845 401 5045; adult/concession £12.25/5.25; ⊙hourly 10am-4.30pm), operating most days, to find out about the hall's intriguing history and royal connections.

The hall was never intended as a concert venue but as a 'Hall of Arts and Sciences', so it spent the first 133 years of its existence tormenting everyone with shocking acoustics. The huge mushroom-like acoustic reflectors first dangled from the ceiling in 1969, and a further massive refurbishment was completed in 2004.

ROYAL COLLEGE OF MUSIC MUSEUM   MUSEUM
Map p424 (☑020-7591 4842; www.rcm.ac.uk/museum; Prince Consort Rd, SW7; ⊙11.30am-4.30pm Tue-Fri term time & summer; ⊜South Kensington) **FREE** If you've a musical ear and the vast museums of South Kensington have left your head spinning, a far smaller and more manageable collection can be discovered downstairs at the illustrious Royal College of Music. There are some fascinating instruments on display, including a clavicytherium dated c 1480, one of the world's earliest guitars, a world-renowned portrait of Joseph Haydn, a host of Eastern European plucked instruments and trombones owned by Elgar and Holst.

There is a small but comfortable Children's Corner with activities and special displays. **Guided tours** of the museum cost £5 for an adult and must be booked in advance. If you find this interesting, consider a trip to the outstanding Horniman Museum (p277) in Forest Hill, which has a superlative collection of instruments from around the world.

BROMPTON ORATORY   CHURCH
Map p424 (☑020-7808 0900; www.brompton-oratory.com; 215 Brompton Rd, SW7; ⊙7am-8pm; ⊜South Kensington) Also known as the London Oratory and the Oratory of St Philip Neri, this Roman Catholic church is second in size only to the incomplete Westminster Cathedral. Built in Italian baroque style in 1884, the impressive interior is swathed in marble and statuary; much of the decorative work predates the church and was imported from Italian churches. Intriguingly, the church was employed by the KGB during the Cold War as a dead-letter box.

KENSINGTON & HYDE PARK SIGHTS

RIVER WESTBOURNE

One of London's many underground rivers, the River Westbourne flows secretly through a highly visible steel conduit above the platform of Sloane Sq tube station, on its underground journey to the Thames. The watercourse is also the source of the name Knightsbridge, a former crossing point of the river.

There is a busy schedule of services (five on weekdays, more at the weekend), including a Solemn Mass in Latin on Sundays (11am).

MICHELIN HOUSE
HISTORIC BUILDING

Map p424 (81 Fulham Rd, SW3; ⊖South Kensington) Built for Michelin between 1905 and 1911 by François Espinasse, and completely restored in 1985, the building blurs the stylish line between art nouveau and art deco. The iconic roly-poly Michelin Man (Bibendum) appears in the exquisite modern stained glass (the originals were removed at the outbreak of WWII and subsequently vanished), while the lobby is decorated with tiles showing early-20th-century cars.

◉ Hyde Park & Kensington Gardens

HYDE PARK
PARK

See p182.

KENSINGTON GARDENS
PARK

Map p424 (www.royalparks.org.uk/parks/kensington-gardens; ⊙6am-dusk; ⊖Queensway, Lancaster Gate) Immediately west of Hyde Park and across the Serpentine lake, these picturesque 275-acre gardens are technically part of Kensington Palace. The park is a gorgeous collection of manicured lawns, tree-shaded avenues and basins. The largest is the **Round Pond**, close to the palace. Also worth a look are the lovely fountains in the **Italian Gardens** (Map p424), believed to be a gift from Albert to Queen Victoria.

The **Diana, Princess of Wales Memorial Playground** (Map p424; ⊖Queensway), in the northwest corner of the gardens, has some pretty ambitious attractions for children. Next to the playground stands the delightful **Elfin Oak**, a 900-year-old tree stump carved with elves, gnomes, witches and small creatures. George Frampton's celebrated **Peter Pan statue** (Map p424; ⊖Lancaster Gate) is close to the lake.

ALBERT MEMORIAL
MONUMENT

Map p424 (Kensington Gardens; tours adult/concession £8/7; ⊙tours 2pm & 3pm 1st Sun of month Mar-Dec; ⊖Knightsbridge, Gloucester Rd) This splendid Victorian confection on the southern edge of Kensington Gardens is as ostentatious as the subject. Queen Victoria's German husband Albert (1819–61), was purportedly humble. Albert explicitly insisted he did not want a monument; ignoring the

◉ TOP SIGHT
APSLEY HOUSE

This stunning house, containing exhibits about the Duke of Wellington, victor of Waterloo against Napoleon Bonaparte, was once the first building to appear when entering London from the west and was therefore known as 'No 1 London'. Still one of London's finest, Apsley House was designed by Robert Adam for Baron Apsley in the late 18th century, but later sold to the first Duke of Wellington, who lived here until he died in 1852.

In 1947, the house was given to the nation (although the duke's descendants still live in a flat here); 10 of its rooms are open to the public. Wellington memorabilia, including his **death mask**, fills the basement gallery, while there's an astonishing **collection of china and silver,** including a dazzling **Egyptian service**, a divorce gift (call it a golden handshake) from Napoleon to Josephine, which she declined.

The stairwell is dominated by Antonio Canova's staggering 3.4m-high **statue** of a fig-leafed Napoleon with titanic shoulders, adjudged by the subject as 'too athletic'. The 1st-floor **Waterloo Gallery** contains paintings by Velasquez, Rubens, Van Dyck, Brueghel, Murillo and Goya. A highlight is the Portuguese silver service, presented to Wellington in honour of his triumph over 'Le Petit Caporal'.

DON'T MISS...

➡ Egyptian service
➡ Canova's statue of Napoleon
➡ Waterloo Gallery paintings

PRACTICALITIES

➡ Map p424, F3
➡ www.english-heritage.org.uk/visit/places/apsley-house/
➡ 149 Piccadilly, Hyde Park Corner, W1
➡ adult/child £8.30/5, with Wellington Arch £10/6
➡ ⊙11am-5pm Wed-Sun Apr-Oct, 10am-4pm Sat & Sun Nov-Mar
➡ ⊖Hyde Park Corner

TOP SIGHT
KENSINGTON PALACE

Built in 1605, the palace became the favourite royal residence under William and Mary of Orange in 1689, and remained so until George III became king and relocated to Buckingham Palace. Today, it is still a royal residence, with the likes of the Duke and Duchess of Cambridge (Prince William and his wife Catherine) and Prince Harry living here.

A large part of the palace is open to the public, including the King's and Queen's State Apartments. The **King's State Apartments** are the most lavish, starting with the **Grand Staircase**, a dizzying feast of trompe l'oeil. The beautiful **Cupola Room** is arranged with gilded statues and a gorgeous painted ceiling. The **Drawing Room** is beyond, where the king and courtiers would entertain themselves with cards.

Visitors can also access **Victoria's Apartments** where Queen Victoria (1819–1901) was born and lived until she became Queen. An informative narrative about her life is told through a few personal effects, extracts from her journals and plenty of visual props.

A long-running exhibition about royal dress, **Fashion Rules**, is also on show, with dresses from Queen Elizabeth in the 1950s, her sister Princess Margaret in the 1960s and 1970s and Diana, Princess of Wales, in the 1980s.

DON'T MISS...

➡ Cupola Room
➡ King's Grand Staircase
➡ Victoria's Apartments

PRACTICALITIES

➡ Map p424, A2
➡ www.hrp.org.uk/kensingtonpalace
➡ Kensington Gardens, W8
➡ adult/child £17.50/free
➡ ⏰10am-6pm Mar-Oct, to 5pm Nov-Feb
➡ ⊖High St Kensington

good prince's wishes, the Lord Mayor instructed George Gilbert Scott to build the 53m-high, gaudy Gothic memorial in 1872.

An eye-opening blend of mosaic, gold leaf, marble and Victorian bombast, the renovated monument is topped with a crucifix. The 4.25m-tall gilded statue of the prince, surrounded by 187 figures representing the continents (Asia, Europe, Africa and America), the arts, industry and science, was erected in 1876. The statue was painted black for 80 years, originally – some say – to disguise it from WWI Zeppelins (nonetheless, the memorial was selected by German bombers during WWII as a landmark). To step beyond the railings for a close-up of the 64m-long *Frieze of Parnassus* along the base, join one of the 45-minute tours.

MARBLE ARCH   MONUMENT

Map p414 (⊖Marble Arch) Designed by John Nash in 1828, this huge white arch was moved here from its original spot in front of Buckingham Palace in 1851, when adjudged too unimposing an entrance to the royal manor. If you're feeling anarchic, walk through the central portal, a privilege reserved by (unenforced) law for the Royal Family and the ceremonial King's Troop Royal Horse Artillery.

Lending its name to the entire area, the arch contains three rooms (inaccessible to the public) and was a police station from 1851 to 1968 (two doors access the interior).

A ground **plaque** (Map p414) on the traffic island between Bayswater Rd and Edgware Rd indicates the spot where the infamous Tyburn Tree, a three-legged gallows, once stood. An estimated 50,000 people were executed here between 1571 and 1783, many having been dragged from the Tower of London. During the 16th century many Catholics were executed for their faith and it later became a place of Catholic pilgrimage.

To the west of the arch stands a magnificent outsize bronze sculpture of a horse's head called *Still Water*, created by Nic Fiddian-Green.

TYBURN CONVENT   CONVENT

Map p424 (⌀020-7723 7262; www.tyburnconvent.org.uk; 8 Hyde Park Pl, W2; ⏰6.30am-8.30pm; ⊖Marble Arch) FREE A convent was established here in 1903, close to the site of the Tyburn Tree gallows. The crypt contains the relics of 105 martyrs, along with

WORTH A DETOUR

FULHAM PALACE

Within stumbling distance of the Thames, **Fulham Palace** (www.fulhampalace.org; Bishop's Ave, SW6; ⊘palace 12.30-4.30pm Mon-Thu, noon-5pm Sun, gardens dawn-dusk daily; ⊜Putney Bridge) FREE was the summer home of the bishops of London from 704 to 1975. The building is an appealing blend of architectural styles immersed in beautiful gardens and, until 1924, when filled with rubble, enclosed by the longest moat in England. The oldest surviving palace chunk is the little red-brick Tudor gateway, while the main building dates from the mid-17th century, remodelled in the 19th century.

The lovely courtyard draws watercolourists on sunny days and the genteel **Drawing Room Café** (www.fulhampalace.org; Fulham Palace; mains £5-12; ⊘9.30am-5pm Apr-Oct, to 4pm Nov-Mar; ⊜Putney Bridge) at the rear, looking out onto the gorgeous lawn, is a superlative spot for some carrot cake and a coffee. There's also a pretty **walled garden** and, detached from the main house, a **Tudor Revival chapel** designed by Butterfield in 1866.

There are two permanent displays inside the palace relating its history and that of its inhabitants. **Guided tours** (£5, 1½ hours, four to five tours per month) usually take in the Great Hall, the Victorian chapel, Bishop Sherlock's Room and the Dining Room. There are also **garden walks** (£5, 1¼ hours); check the website for dates and times.

The surrounding land, once totalling almost 15 hectares but now reduced to just over five, forms **Bishop's Park**, a beautiful park with a lovely promenade along the river and the usual assortment of playgrounds, fountains and cafes.

paintings commemorating their lives and recording their deaths. Crypt tours run at 10.30am, 3.30pm and 5.30pm daily. A closed order of Benedictine sisters still forms a community here.

The brick building at No 10, next door, is considered by some to be the smallest house in London, with a width of a mere three foot six inches.

⊙ Chelsea & Belgravia

SAATCHI GALLERY   GALLERY
Map p424 (www.saatchigallery.com; Duke of York's HQ, King's Rd, SW3; ⊘10am-6pm; ⊜Sloane Sq) FREE This enticing gallery hosts temporary exhibitions of experimental and thought-provoking work across a variety of media. The white and sanded bare-floorboard galleries are magnificently presented, but save some wonder for Gallery 15, where Richard Wilson's *20:50* is on permanent display. Mesmerising, impassive and ineffable, it's a riveting tour de force. A cool shop chips in on the first floor.

KING'S ROAD   STREET
Map p424 (⊜Sloane Sq) At the counter-cultural forefront of London fashion during the technicolour '60s and anarchic '70s, King's Road today is more a stamping ground for the leisure-class shopping set.

The last green-haired Mohawk punks – once tourist sights in themselves – shuffled off sometime in the 1990s. Today it's all Bang & Olufsen, Kurt Geiger and a sprinkling of specialist shops; even pet canines are slim and snappily dressed.

In the 17th century, Charles II fashioned a love nest here for himself and his mistress Nell Gwyn, an orange-seller turned actress at the Drury Lane Theatre. Heading back to Hampton Court Palace at eventide, Charles would employ a farmer's track that inevitably came to be known as the King's Road.

ROYAL HOSPITAL
CHELSEA   HISTORIC BUILDINGS
Map p424 (www.chelsea-pensioners.co.uk; Royal Hospital Rd, SW3; ⊘grounds 10am-noon & 2-4pm Mon-Sat, museum 10am-noon & 2-4pm Mon-Fri; ⊜Sloane Sq) FREE Designed by Christopher Wren, this superb structure was built in 1692 to provide shelter for ex-servicemen. Since the reign of Charles II it has housed hundreds of war veterans, known as Chelsea Pensioners. They're fondly regarded as national treasures, and cut striking figures in the dark-blue greatcoats (in winter) or scarlet frock coats (in summer) that they wear on ceremonial occasions.

The **museum** contains a huge collection of war medals bequeathed by former residents and plenty of information about the institution's history and its residents. Visitors can also peek at the hospital's Great Hall refectory, Octagon Porch, chapel and courtyards.

Former Prime Minister Margaret Thatcher is buried here, in the old **cemetery**. The extensive grounds are home to the Chelsea Flower Show, the annual jamboree of the gardening world, held in May.

CHELSEA PHYSIC GARDEN   GARDENS
Map p424 (www.chelseaphysicgarden.co.uk; 66 Royal Hospital Rd, SW3; adult/child £9.90/6.60; ☺11am-6pm Tue-Fri & Sun Apr-Oct, 9.30am-4pm Mon-Fri Nov-Mar; ⊜Sloane Sq) This walled pocket of botanical enchantment was established by the Apothecaries' Society in 1676 for students working on medicinal plants and healing. One of Europe's oldest of its kind, the small grounds are a compendium of botany, from carnivorous pitcher plants to rich yellow flag irises, a cork oak from Portugal, delightful ferns, and rare trees and shrubs.

The fascinating pharmaceutical garden grows plants used in contemporary Western medicine; the world medicine garden has a selection of plants used by indigenous peoples in Australia, China, India, New Zealand and North America; and there's a heady perfume and aromatherapy garden. Enter from Swan Walk. Free tours are held three times daily and a host of courses and lectures detail plant remedies.

CARLYLE'S HOUSE   HISTORIC BUILDING
Map p424 (✆020-7352 7087; www.nationaltrust.org.uk/carlyles-house; 24 Cheyne Row, SW3; adult/child £5.10/2.60; ☺11am-5pm Wed-Sun Mar-Oct; ⊜Sloane Sq) From 1834 until his death in 1881, the eminent Victorian essayist and historian Thomas Carlyle dwelt in this three-storey terrace house, bought by his parents when it was surrounded by open fields in what was then a deeply unfashionable part of town. The lovely Queen Ann house – built in 1708 – is magnificently preserved as it looked in 1895, when it became London's first literary shrine. It's not big but has been left much as it was when Carlyle was living here and Chopin, Tennyson and Dickens came to call.

CHELSEA OLD CHURCH   CHURCH
Map p424 (✆020-7795 1019; www.chelseaoldchurch.org.uk; cnr Old Church St & Embankment, SW3; ☺2-4pm Tue-Thu; ⊜South Kensington, Sloane Sq) This beautiful and original church stands behind a bronze monument to Thomas More (1477–1535), who had a close association with it. Original features of the largely rebuilt church (it was badly bombed in 1941) include more than one hundred monuments dating from 1433 to 1957, including Thomas More (1532) and Henry James (1916). Don't miss the chained books at the western end of the southern aisle, the only ones of their kind in a London church.

The central tome is a 'Vinegar Bible' from 1717 (so-named after an erratum in Luke, chapter 20), alongside a 'Book of Common Prayer' from 1723 and a 1683 copy of 'Homilies'. Also look out for fragments of 17th-century Flemish stained glass, of exceptional clarity and artistry.

NATIONAL ARMY MUSEUM   MUSEUM
Map p424 (✆020-7730 0717; www.nam.ac.uk; Royal Hospital Rd, SW3; ⊜Sloane Sq) This museum tells the history of the British army, and its role in past and modern history, from the perspective of its servicemen and servicewomen. The museum was closed at the time of writing for major renovations and planned to reopen with a bang in 2016.

✕ EATING

Quality and cashola being such easy bedfellows, you'll find some of London's finest establishments in the smart hotels and ritzy mews of Chelsea, Belgravia and Knightsbridge, but there's choice in all budget ranges. Chic and cosmopolitan South Kensington has always been reliable for pan-European options.

✕ Knightsbridge & South Kensington

V&A CAFÉ   CAFE £
Map p424 (Victoria & Albert Museum, Cromwell Rd, SW7; mains £6.95-11.50; ☺10am-5.15pm Sat-Thu, to 9.30pm Fri; 🛜; ⊜South Kensington) There is plenty of hot and cold food to choose from at the V&A Café and although the quality is nothing to rave about, the setting most definitely is: the extraordinarily decorated Morris, Gamble & Poynter Rooms (1860) show Victorian Gothic style at its best.

★TOM'S KITCHEN   MODERN EUROPEAN ££
Map p424 (✆020-7349 0202; www.tomskitchen.co.uk/chelsea; 27 Cale St, SW3; mains £10.50-28, 2-/3-course lunch menu £16.50/19.50; ☺8am-2.30pm & 6-10.30pm Mon-Fri, 10am-3.30pm & 6-10.30pm Sat & Sun; 🛜✐; ⊜South Kensington)

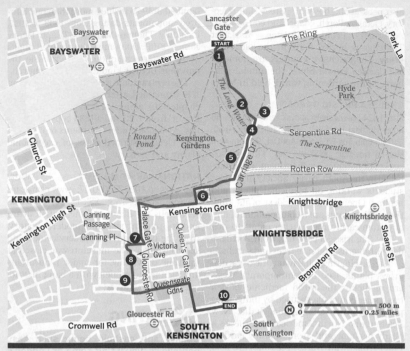

Neighbourhood Walk
Gardens and Mews

START LANCASTER GATE TUBE STATION
END NATURAL HISTORY MUSEUM
LENGTH 3.5KM; 1½ HOURS

Begin outside Lancaster Gate tube station and head to the park. Bear left at the ❶ **Italian Gardens** (p186) (thought to be a gift from Prince Albert to Queen Victoria) and follow the path along Long Water until you reach ❷ **The Arch**, a large marble statue by Henry Moore. There are fantastic views of Kensington Palace, the Tudors' favourite palace and current residence of Princes William and Harry. As you reach the road, look left at the ❸ **Serpentine Sackler Gallery** (p183), a former gun depot with a modern extension designed by prize-winning architect Zaha Hadid.

Cross the ❹ **Bridge** over the Serpentine – the lake separates Hyde Park from Kensington Gardens – and take in the views. Turn right into Kensington Gardens, walk past the ❺ **Serpentine Gallery** (p182), a famous contemporary art gallery, and make your way south to the ❻ **Albert Memo-**rial (p186), a Victorian Gothic confection commemorating the Prince Consort. Carry on west through the park and exit at Palace Gate. Walk down and turn right onto Canning Place. Take a moment to admire the gorgeous ❼ **Canning Mews** to your right: you can just picture the horses and carriages.

Turn left onto Canning Passage and then left again onto Victoria Grove. The boutiques and wisteria-clad houses on this little square look straight out of a Cotswold village. Bear right along ❽ **Launceston Place** and walk on past ivy-covered walls and exquisite houses: this is some of the most coveted real estate in London. Take a small detour down ❾ **Kynance Mews** on the right (there is a public right of way until about halfway down the mews) to see the storybook cottages.

Take a left at Cornwall Gardens; cross to Queen's Gate Gardens, then turn right at Queen's Gate (all these streets are lined with white stuccoed buildings typical of the area): the ❿ **Natural History Museum** is just ahead of you. The main entrance is a little further on Cromwell Rd.

✒ Recipe for success: mix one part relaxed and smiling staff, one part light and airy decor to two parts divine food and voila, you have Tom's Kitchen. Classics such as grilled steaks, burgers, slow-cooked lamb and chicken schnitzel are cooked to perfection, while seasonal fares such as the home-made ricotta or baked scallops with sea herbs are sublime.

The restaurant goes to great lengths to support British farmers, growers and fishers. You can read about its suppliers online, or in little cards in the restaurant.

OGNISKO   POLISH ££
Map p424 (☑020-7589 0101; www.ognisko-restaurant.co.uk; 55 Prince's Gate, Exhibition Rd, SW7; mains £11-17; ◷12.30-3pm & 5.30-11.15pm; ◉South Kensington) Ognisko has been a stalwart of the Polish community in London since 1940 (it's part of the Polish Hearth Club). The grand dining room is stunning, bathed in light from tall windows and adorned with modern art and chandeliers, and the food couldn't be more authentic: try the delicious *pierogi* (dumplings stuffed with cheese and potatoes) or the blinis.

L'ETO   CAFE ££
Map p424 (www.letocaffe.co.uk; 243 Brompton Rd, SW3; mains £11.50-19.95; ◷9am-10pm Sun-Wed, to 11pm Thu-Sat; ☎🗐; ◉South Kensington, Knightsbridge) With its all-day service, this upmarket cafe has found an excellent niche between the museum district of South Kensington and the shopping vortex of Knightsbridge. The salad bar and eye-popping sweets counter are great, although the à la carte menu is good too, if a little overpriced.

★DINNER BY HESTON BLUMENTHAL   MODERN BRITISH £££
Map p424 (☑020-7201 3833; www.dinnerby-heston.com; Mandarin Oriental Hyde Park, 66 Knightsbridge, SW1; 3-course set lunch £38, mains £28-42; ◷noon-2.30pm & 6.30-10.30pm; ☎; ◉Knightsbridge) Sumptuously presented Dinner is a gastronomic tour de force, taking diners on a journey through British culinary history (with inventive modern inflections). Dishes carry historical dates to convey context, while the restaurant interior is a design triumph, from the glass-walled kitchen and its overhead clock mechanism to the large windows looking onto the park. Book ahead.

ZUMA   JAPANESE £££
Map p424 (☑020-7584 1010; www.zumarestaurant.com; 5 Raphael St, SW7; mains £15-75; ◷noon-3pm & 6-11pm; ☎; ◉Knightsbridge) A modern-day take on the traditional Japanese *izakaya* ('a place to stay and drink sake'), where drinking and eating harmonise, Zuma oozes style. The *robata* (chargrilled) dishes are the star of the show; wash them down with one of the 40 types of sake on offer. Booking is advised, although there are walk-in spaces at the *robata* and sushi counters.

LAUNCESTON PLACE   MODERN BRITISH £££
Map p424 (☑020-7937 6912; www.launceston-place-restaurant.co.uk; 1a Launceston Pl, W8; 3-course lunch/Sun lunch/dinner £28.50/40/55; ◷6-11pm Tue, noon-4pm & 6-11pm Wed-Sun; 🗐; ◉Gloucester Rd, High St Kensington) This exceptionally handsome, superchic Michelin-starred restaurant is hidden away on a picture-postcard Kensington street of Edwardian houses. Prepared by Yorkshire chef Tim Allen, the food belongs within the acme of gastronomic pleasures, and is accompanied by an award-winning wine list. The adventurous will aim for the six-course tasting menu (£70; vegetarian version available).

BAR BOULUD   INTERNATIONAL £££
Map p424 (www.barboulud.com/london; Mandarin Oriental Hyde Park, 66 Knightbridge, SW1; mains £15-34, 2-/3-course lunch menu £17/19; ◷noon-11pm; ☎🗐; ◉Knightsbridge) Combining French gastronomy with American influences must have raised a few chef's hats in Daniel Boulud's native France, but diners vote with their forks and the *coq au vin* is as popular (and delicious) as the burgers (the Frenchie, with pork belly and morbier cheese, is excellent).

The drinks list is just as trans-Atlantic with a spectacular cellar (the wine list is 27 pages long) and equally great cocktails (the white cosmopolitan, with vodka, elderflower liqueur and white cranberry, is to die for).

RIB ROOM   BRITISH £££
Map p424 (☑020-7858 7250; www.theribroom.co.uk; Jumeirah Carlton Tower, Cadogan Place, SW1; mains from £26, 2-/3-course set lunch £28/34; ◷7-11am, noon-2.45pm & 6.30-10pm; ☎; ◉Knightsbridge) Head chef Ian Rudge's faultless preparation is the cornerstone of the much-lauded carnivorous menu at the re-styled Rib Room, busy satiating Knightsbridge diners on steaks, cutlets, roast rib of beef and oysters since the swinging '60s. Prices may give pause for thought, but the food is superlative (set lunches soften the assault on your wallet) and service is outstanding.

✘ Hyde Park & Kensington Gardens

MAGAZINE   INTERNATIONAL ££

Map p424 (☑020-7298 7552; www.magazine-restaurant.co.uk; Serpentine Sackler Gallery, West Carriage Dr, W2; mains £13-24, 2-/3-course lunch menu £17.50/21.50; ☺8am-6pm Tue-Sat, from 9am Sun; ⊖Lancaster Gate, Knightsbridge) Located in the ethereally beautiful extension of the Serpentine Sackler Gallery (p183), Magazine is no ordinary museum cafe. The food is as contemporary and elegant as the building, and artworks from current exhibitions add yet another dimension. The afternoon tea (£17.50) is particularly original: out with cucumber sandwiches, in with beef tartare and goat's curd.

Magazine opens for dinner on Fridays and Saturdays from April to September, with the added bonus of live music.

ORANGERY   CAFE ££

Map p424 (☑020-3166 6113; www.orangerykensingtonpalace.co.uk; Kensington Palace, Kensington Gardens, W8; mains £12.50-16, afternoon tea £26; ☺10am-6pm; ☑; ⊖Queensway, High St Kensington) The Orangery, housed in an 18th-century conservatory on the grounds of Kensington Palace, is lovely for a late breakfast or lunch, but the standout experience here is afternoon tea. Book ahead to bag a table on the beautiful terrace.

MIN JIANG   CHINESE £££

Map p424 (☑020-7361 1988; www.minjiang.co.uk; Royal Garden Hotel, 10th fl, 2-24 Kensington High St, W8; mains £12-68; ☺noon-3pm & 6-10.30pm; ☑; ⊖High St Kensington) Min Jiang serves up seafood, excellent wood-fired Peking duck (half/whole £32/58) and sumptuously regal views over Kensington Palace and Gardens. The menu is diverse, with a sporadic accent on spice (the Min Jiang is a river in Sichuan).

> ### ❶ FINE BUT AFFORDABLE DINING
> ....
> Chelsea and Kensington have some of the finest – and most expensive – restaurants in London. One way of enjoying them without breaking the bank is to go for the set lunch menus, which offer great value (two to three courses for less than £30).

✘ Chelsea & Belgravia

★RABBIT   MODERN BRITISH ££

Map p424 (www.rabbit-restaurant.com; 172 King's Rd, SW3; mains £6-24; ☺noon-midnight Tue-Sat, 6-11pm Mon, noon-4pm Sun; ☑; ⊖Sloane Sq) Three brothers grew up on a farm. One became a farmer, another a butcher, while the third worked in hospitality. Noticing how complementary their trades were, they teamed up and founded Rabbit. Genius! Rabbit is a breath of fresh air in upmarket Chelsea: the restaurant rocks the agri-chic (yes) look and the creative, seasonal modern British cuisine is fabulous.

The drinks list is just as good, with a great selection of wines from the family vineyard in Sussex, and local beers and ciders.

PAINTED HERON   INDIAN ££

Map p424 (☑020-7351 5232; www.thepaintedheron.com; 112 Cheyne Walk, SW10; mains £13.50-20, 2-course lunch menu £15.94; ☺11.30am-3.30pm & 6-11pm; ☑; ⊖Sloane Sq) The rather formal setting – starched white tablecloths, cubby holes and leather banquettes – is softened by intimate lighting in the evenings and affable service on all occasions. As for the food, it's a delight, from classics such as biryani and tikka masala to Modern Indian innovations such as venison curry with red wine and chocolate samosas for dessert.

MEDLAR   MODERN EUROPEAN £££

Map p424 (☑020-7349 1900; www.medlarrestaurant.co.uk; 438 King's Rd, SW10; 3-course lunch £28-30, dinner £35-45; ☺noon-3pm & 6.30-10.30pm; ⊖Fulham Broadway, Sloane Sq) With its uncontrived yet crisply modern green-on-grey design, Medlar has quickly become a King's Rd sensation. With no à la carte menu and scant pretentiousness, the prix fixe modern European cuisine is delightfully assured: the menu changes with the season but tries hard to promote British ingredients as well as underrated meats such as pigeon and guinea fowl.

✘ Victoria & Pimlico

★PIMLICO FRESH   CAFE £

Map p424 (86 Wilton Rd, SW1; mains from £4.50; ☺7.30am-7.30pm Mon-Fri, 9am-6pm Sat & Sun; ⊖Victoria) This friendly two-room cafe will see you right whether you need breakfast (French toast, bowls of porridge laced with honey or maple syrup), lunch (home-made quiches and soups, 'things' on toast) or just a good old latte and cake.

DAYLESFORD ORGANIC
DELI ££

Map p424 (☑020-7881 8060; www.daylesford-organic.com; 44b Pimlico Rd, SW1; mains £8-17; ☺8am-8pm Mon-Sat, 10am-4pm Sun; ☑; ☻Sloane Sq) A chomping ground for the Chelsea and Pimlico set, with a deli counter, a farmhouse shop and a modernist cafe serving delicious breakfasts, light lunches and afternoon teas.

HUNAN
CHINESE £££

Map p424 (☑020-7730 5712; www.hunanlondon.com; 51 Pimlico Rd, SW1; set lunch/dinner from £34.80/55.80; ☺12.30-2pm & 6.30-11pm Mon-Sat; ☑; ☻Sloane Sq) In business for more than three decades, this understated Chinese restaurant imaginatively exercises a no-menu policy, so just present your preferences and let the *dachu* (chef) get cracking. A meal will comprise 12 to 18 small, tapas-style dishes – many with a pronounced Taiwan accent – to encourage a spectrum of flavour and colour. Vegetarian options available.

🍷 DRINKING & NIGHTLIFE

★TOMTOM COFFEE HOUSE
CAFE

Map p424 (www.tomtom.co.uk; 114 Ebury St, SW1; ☺8am-6pm Sun-Tue, to 9pm Wed-Sat, shorter hours in winter; ☻Victoria) Tomtom has built its reputation on its amazing coffee: not only are the drinks fabulously presented (forget ferns and hearts in your latte, here it's peacocks fanning their tails), the selection is dizzying, from the usual espresso-based suspects to filter, and a full choice of beans. You can even spice things up with a bonus tot of cognac or scotch (£3).

The cafe also serves lovely food throughout the day, from toasties on sourdough bread to home-made pies (mains £5 to £10).

PHENE
BAR

Map p424 (www.thephene.com; 9 Phene St, SW3; ☺noon-11pm Mon-Fri, from 11am Sat & Sun; ☎; ☻Sloane Sq) This beautiful bar/pub in the heart of Chelsea is a hit – from the red banquette in the stylish dining room to the elegant terrace for summer evenings, the range of beers brewed by the capital's many small breweries and the original G&Ts (lots of different gins and flavoured tonics).

QUEEN'S ARMS
PUB

Map p424 (www.thequeensarmskensington.co.uk; 30 Queen's Gate Mews, SW7; ☺noon-11pm; ☻Gloucester Rd) Just around the corner from the Royal Albert Hall, this godsend of a blue-grey painted pub in an adorable cobbled mews setting off bustling Queen's Gate beckons with a cosy interior and a right royal selection of ales and ciders on tap.

BUDDHA BAR
BAR

Map p424 (☑020-3667 5222; www.buddhabar-london.com; 145 Knightsbridge, SW1; cocktails from £11; ☺5-11.30pm Mon-Sat, 11am-11.30pm Sun; ☻Knightsbridge) When you've shopped your legs off in Knightsbridge, this serene Pan-Asian zone welcomes you into a world of Chinese birdcage lanterns, subdued lighting, tucked-away corners and booths, perfect for sipping on a raspberry saketini and chilling out.

ANGLESEA ARMS
PUB

Map p424 (www.metropolitanpubcompany.com/our-pubs/the-anglesea-arms/; 15 Selwood Tce, SW7; ☺11am-11pm Mon-Sat, noon-10.30pm Sun; ☻South Kensington) Seasoned with age and decades of ale-quaffing patrons (including Charles Dickens, who lived on the same road, and DH Lawrence), this old-school pub boasts a haunted cellar and a strong showing of beers, while the terrace out front swarms with punters in warmer months.

ZUMA
BAR

Map p424 (www.zumarestaurant.com; 5 Raphael St, SW7; ☺6-11.30pm; ☎; ☻Knightsbridge) After the hectic shopping swirl of Knightsbridge, the stylish simplicity and muted elegance of Zuma is refreshingly soothing. As are the ambitious 40-plus varieties of sake and exquisitely presented cocktails (many blended with Japanese spirits) served to the assorted high-rollers at the bar.

DRAYTON ARMS
PUB

Map p424 (☑020-7835 2301; www.thedrayton-armssw5.co.uk; 153 Old Brompton Rd, SW5; ☺noon-midnight Mon-Fri, from 10am Sat & Sun; ☻Gloucester Rd) This vast, comely Victorian corner boozer is delightful inside and out, with some bijou art-nouveau features (sinuous tendrils and curlicues above the windows and the doors), contemporary art on the walls, a fabulous coffered ceiling and a heated beer garden. The crowd is both hip and down-to-earth; great beer and wine selection.

☆ ENTERTAINMENT

ROYAL ALBERT HALL
CONCERT VENUE

Map p424 (☎0845 401 5034; www.royalalberthall. com; Kensington Gore, SW7; ⊖South Kensington) This splendid Victorian concert hall hosts classical music, rock and other performances, but is most famously the venue for the BBC-sponsored Proms. Booking is possible, but from mid-July to mid-September Proms punters also queue for £5 standing (or 'prom-enading') tickets that go on sale one hour before curtain-up. Otherwise, the box office and prepaid ticket collection counter are both through door 12 (south side of the hall).

606 CLUB
BLUES, JAZZ

(☎020-7352 5953; www.606club.co.uk; 90 Lots Rd, SW10; ⊗7-11.15pm Sun-Thu, 8pm-12.30am Fri & Sat; 🚇Imperial Wharf) Named after its old address on King's Rd which cast a spell over jazz lovers London-wide back in the '80s, this fantastic, tucked-away basement jazz club and restaurant gives centre stage to contemporary British-based jazz musicians nightly. The club can only serve alcohol to people who are dining and it is highly advisable to book to get a table.

There is no entry charge, but a music fee (£10 Sunday to Thursday and £12 Friday and Saturday) will be added to your food/drink bill at the end of the evening; it's open for occasional Sunday lunches.

ROYAL COURT THEATRE
THEATRE

Map p424 (☎020-7565 5000; www.royalcourt-theatre.com; Sloane Sq, SW1; tickets £12-35; ⊖Sloane Sq) Equally renowned for staging innovative new plays and old classics, the Royal Court is among London's most progressive theatres and has continued to foster major writing talent across the UK. There are two auditoriums, the main Jerwood Theatre Downstairs, and the much smaller studio Jerwood Theatre Upstairs. Tickets for Monday performances are all £10.

CADOGAN HALL
CONCERT VENUE

Map p424 (☎020-7730 4500; www.cadoganhall. com; 5 Sloane Tce, SW1; tickets £15-40; ⊖Sloane Sq) Home of the Royal Philharmonic Orchestra, Cadogan Hall is a major venue for opera, classical music and choral music, with occasional dance, rock, jazz and family concerts.

CINÉ LUMIÈRE
CINEMA

Map p424 (☎020-7871 3515; www.institut-fran-cais.org.uk; 17 Queensberry Pl, SW7; ⊖South Kens-ington) Ciné Lumière is attached to South Kensington's French Institute, and its large art-deco 300-seat *salle* (cinema) screens great international seasons (including the London Spanish Film Festival) and French and other foreign films subtitled in English.

🛍 SHOPPING

Frequented by models, celebrities and Russian oligarchs, and awash with new money (much from abroad), this well-heeled part of town is all about high fashion, glam shops, groomed shoppers and iconic top-end department stores. Even the charity shops along the chic King's Rd resemble fashion boutiques.

HARRODS
DEPARTMENT STORE

Map p424 (www.harrods.com; 87-135 Brompton Rd, SW1; ⊗10am-9pm Mon-Sat, 11.30am-6pm Sun; ⊖Knightsbridge) Garish and stylish in equal measures, perennially crowded Harrods is an obligatory stop for visitors, from the cash-strapped to the big, big spenders. The stock is astonishing, as are many of the price tags. High on kitsch, the 'Egyptian Elevator' resembles something out of an Indiana Jones epic, while the memorial fountain to Dodi and Di (lower ground floor) merely adds surrealism.

Many visitors don't make it past the ground floor where designer bags, the myriad scents from the perfume hall and the mouth-watering food hall provide plenty of entertainment. The latter actually makes for an excellent, and surprisingly affordable, option for a picnic in nearby Hyde Park.

CONRAN SHOP
DESIGN

Map p424 (www.conranshop.co.uk; Michelin House, 81 Fulham Rd, SW3; ⊗10am-6pm Mon, Tue, Fri & Sat, to 7pm Wed & Thu, noon-6pm Sun; ⊖South Kensington) The original design store (going strong since 1987), the Conran Shop is a treasure trove of beautiful things – from radios to sunglasses, kitchenware to children's toys and books, bathroom accessories to greeting cards.

BRITISH RED CROSS
VINTAGE

Map p424 (69-71 Old Church St, SW3; ⊗10am-6pm Mon-Sat; ⊖Sloane Sq) The motto 'One man's rubbish is another man's treasure' couldn't be truer in this part of London, where the 'rubbish' is made up of designer gowns and cashmere jumpers. Obviously the price tags are a little higher than in your run-of-the-mill charity shop (£40 rather than £5 for a jumper or jacket) but it's still a bargain for the quality.

SLIGHTLY FOXED ON
GLOUCESTER ROAD
BOOKS

Map p424 (☑020-7370 3503; www.foxedbooks.com; 123 Gloucester Rd, SW7; ☺10am-7pm Mon-Sat, 11am-5pm Sun; ⊜Gloucester Rd) Once owned by a nephew of Graham Greene and run by the namesake literary quarterly, this delightfully calming two-floor oasis of literature has a strong lean towards second-hand titles (in good condition). There's also a selection of new books, many with handwritten reviews from the staff, children's books and a slab or two of Slightly Foxed's own publications.

PICKETT
GIFTS

Map p424 (www.pickett.co.uk; cnr Sloane St & Sloane Tce, SW1; ☺9.30am-6.30pm Mon-Fri, 10am-6pm Sat; ⊜Sloane Sq) ⏹ Walking into Pickett as an adult is a bit like walking into a sweet shop as a child: the exquisite leather goods are all so colourful and beautiful, you don't really know where to start. Choice items include the perfectly finished handbags, the exquisite roll-up backgammon sets and the men's grooming sets. All leather goods are made in Britain.

T2
FOOD & DRINK

Map p424 (www.t2tea.com; 96 Kings Rd, SW3; ☺10am-7pm Mon-Sat, noon-6pm Sun; ⊜Sloane Sq) This Australian brand is the tea lovers' answer to the coffee craze of the last few years. There are dozens of blends from around the world to choose from, which all come packaged in funky, bright orange cardboard boxes. The original teaware is another draw.

JO LOVES
BEAUTY

Map p424 (www.joloves.com; 42 Elizabeth St, SW1; ☺10am-6pm Mon-Sat, noon-5pm Sun; ⊜Victoria) The latest venture of famed British scentmaker Jo Malone, Jo Loves features the entrepreneur's signature candles, fragrances and bath products in a range of delicate scents – Arabian amber, white rose and lemon leaves, oud and mango. All products come exquisitely wrapped in red boxes with black bows.

RIPPON CHEESE
FOOD

Map p424 (☑020-7931 0628; www.ripponcheeselondon.com; 26 Upper Tachbrook St, SW1; ☺8am-5.30pm Mon-Fri, 8.30am-5pm Sat; ⊜Victoria or Pimlico) A potently inviting pong greets you as you near this cheesemonger with its 500 varieties of mostly English and French cheeses. Ask the knowledgable staff for recommendations (and taste as you go!) and stock up for a picnic in a London park.

LIMELIGHT MOVIE ART
VINTAGE

Map p424 (☑020-7751 5584; www.limelightmovieart.com; 313 King's Rd, SW3; ☺11.30am-6pm Mon-Sat; ⊜Sloane Sq, South Kensington) This spiffing poster shop is a necessary stop for collectors of vintage celluloid memorabilia, nostalgic browsers or film buffs. Prints are all original and prices start at around £70 for the smaller formats (such as lobby cards) but can go into four figures for larger, rarer posters.

JOHN SANDOE BOOKS
BOOKS

Map p424 (www.johnsandoe.com; 10 Blacklands Tce, SW3; ☺9.30am-6.30pm Mon-Sat, 11am-5pm Sun; ⊜Sloane Sq) The perfect antidote to impersonal book superstores, this atmospheric little bookshop is a treasure trove of literary gems and hidden surprises. In business for decades, loyal customers swear by it and the knowledgable booksellers spill forth with well-read pointers.

LULU GUINNESS
FASHION

Map p424 (☑020-7823 4828; www.luluguinness.com; 3 Ellis St, SW1; ☺10am-6pm Mon-Sat; ⊜Sloane Sq) Quirky, whimsical and eye-catching British designs, from small evening bags resembling bright lips to fun umbrellas and cosmetic bags.

SHANGHAI TANG
CLOTHING

Map p424 (www.shanghaitang.com; 6a/b Sloane St; ☺10am-6.30pm Mon-Sat, noon-6pm Sun; ⊜Knightsbridge) Traditionally Chinese inspired and superswish silk scarves, *qipao* (*cheongsam*), elegant Chinese jackets, delicious tops, exquisite cardigans, gorgeous handbags and clutches, many served up in trademark vibrant colours.

HARVEY NICHOLS
DEPARTMENT STORE

Map p424 (www.harveynichols.com; 109-125 Knightsbridge, SW1; ☺10am-8pm Mon-Sat, 11.30am-6pm Sun; ⊜Knightsbridge) At London's temple of high fashion, you'll find Chloé and Balenciaga bags, the city's best denim range, a massive make-up hall with exclusive lines and great jewellery. The food hall and in-house restaurant, **Fifth Floor**, are, you guessed it, on the 5th floor.

Clerkenwell, Shoreditch & Spitalfields

CLERKENWELL | FINSBURY & ST LUKE'S | SPITALFIELDS | HOXTON | SHOREDITCH

Neighbourhood Top Five

1 Capping off a day wandering through wonderfully preserved Georgian Spitalfields with a candlelit visit to **Dennis Severs' House** (p200).

2 Donning your craziest outfit, grooming your beard and heading to **Shoreditch** (p208) for cocktails and carousing.

3 Market crawling with the multicultural masses on a sunny Sunday in **Spitalfields** (p210).

4 Stepping back through the living rooms of time at the **Geffrye Museum** (p198).

5 Learning about the surprisingly tangled origins of everyone's favourite knights in shiny ambulances with a tour of **St John's Gate** (p198).

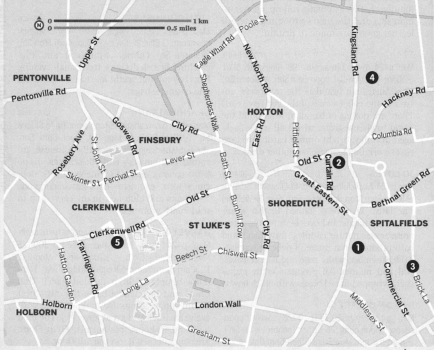

For more detail of this area see Map p426 ➡

Explore: Clerkenwell, Shoreditch & Spitalfields

These historic city-fringe neighbourhoods contain a few significant sights, mainly around Clerkenwell and Spitalfields, but the area is best known for its nightlife. Shoreditch and Hoxton long ago replaced Soho and Camden as the hippest, most alternative parts of London, and although some of the action has moved further east, they're still holding their own.

Swing by during the day to explore the boutiques, vintage shops, markets and cafes. But make sure you come back after dark for a meal at one of the excellent eateries followed by an evening flitting between kooky cocktail bars and subterranean nightspots.

Sunday is a great day to join the crowds shrugging off their hangovers with a stroll through Spitalfields' many markets.

Local Life

➡**Nights Out with a Difference** Mingle with London's hiperati at DreamBagsJaguarShoes (p209), learn to life draw or play ping pong at the Book Club (p209), or take in a moonlit flick on the roof of the Queen of Hoxton (p209).

➡**Coffee Crawl** The area has so many excellent cafes that a mild caffeine tremor is de rigueur. Sink a silky flat white or a shotgun espresso at Prufrock Coffee (p201), Shoreditch Grind (p204), Ozone Coffee Roasters (p205) or Allpress Espresso (p205).

➡**The Pho Mile** Spend some time working out which is your favourite Vietnamese restaurant on Kingsland Rd/Old St strip.

Getting There & Away

➡**Underground** Farringdon and Barbican, on the Circle, Hammersmith & City and Metropolitan lines, are the stopping-off points for Clerkenwell. These and the Central Line also head through Liverpool St, the closest tube stop to Spitalfields. Old St, on the Bank branch of the Northern Line, is the best stop for the western edge of Hoxton and Shoreditch.

➡**Overground** Shoreditch High St and Hoxton are the closest stations to Spitalfields and the eastern parts of Shoreditch and Hoxton.

➡**Bus** Clerkenwell and Old St are connected with Oxford St by the 55 and with Waterloo by the 243. The 38 runs up Rosebery Ave and edges past Exmouth Market on its way from Victoria to Islington. The 8 and 242 zip through the city and up Shoreditch High St.

Lonely Planet's Top Tip

Fancy a late one? Nightjar, 333 Mother, XOYO, Cargo and the Horse & Groom all stay open until at least 3am on weekends, while Fabric can see you through to dawn. Brick Lane Beigel Bake will serve you munchies throughout the night, and for breakfast with a pint, the Fox & Anchor throws back its doors at 7am (8.30am on weekends).

✗ Best Places to Eat

➡ Clove Club (p206)
➡ Morito (p202)
➡ St John (p202)
➡ Polpo (p201)
➡ Prufrock Coffee (p201)

For reviews, see p201 ➡

☕ Best Places to Drink

➡ Worship St Whistling Shop (p208)
➡ Jerusalem Tavern (p207)
➡ Ye Olde Mitre (p207)
➡ Zetter Townhouse Cocktail Lounge (p207)
➡ Old Blue Last (p209)

For reviews, see p207 ➡

☆ Best Places to Dance

➡ Fabric (p207)
➡ XOYO (p209)
➡ Cargo (p209)

For reviews, see p207 ➡

 **SIGHTS**

◉ Clerkenwell

Immediately north of the ancient city, this venerable part of London was once home to medieval monks, political revolutionaries and *Oliver Twist*. The well from which it takes its name was first mentioned in 12th-century texts, but was only rediscovered during construction work in 1924. You can peer at it through a window of a 1980s building at **14 Farringdon Lane**.

Oliver Cromwell once had a house here, and Vladimir Lenin is said to have met Josef Stalin at a pub on Clerkenwell Green. Charles Dickens set his famous book in Clerkenwell's notorious Victorian-era 'rookeries' (slums), placing Fagin's lair on Saffron Hill (a lane running parallel to Farringdon Rd) and the Green as the site of Oliver's first pickpocketing lesson. The authorities eventual answer to the slum problem was to smash Clerkenwell Rd right through the middle of the worst of them.

Clerkenwell's a much more salubrious area now, perhaps even a little posh in parts. The liveliest area is **Exmouth Market**, home to a great little stretch of restaurants and bars.

★**ST JOHN'S GATE**   HISTORIC BUILDING
Map p426 (www.museumstjohn.org.uk; St John's Lane, EC1M; tour suggested donation £5; ⊙10am-5pm Mon-Sat, tours 11am & 2.30pm Tue, Fri & Sat; ⊖Farringdon) **FREE** This surprisingly out-of-place Tudor gate is no Victorian folly but the real deal. During the 12th century, the Knights Hospitaller (a religious and military order with a focus on providing care to the sick) established a priory here. Inside is a small museum that covers the history of the order (including rare examples of the knights' armour), as well as its 19th-century revival in Britain as the secular Order of St John and the foundation of St John Ambulance.

The gate was built in 1504 as a grand entrance to the priory and although most of the buildings were destroyed when Henry VIII dissolved every monastery in the country between 1536 and 1540, the gate survived. It had a varied afterlife, not least as a Latin-speaking coffee house run, without much success, by William Hogarth's father during Queen Anne's reign. Restored in the

---

◉ **TOP SIGHT**
GEFFRYE MUSEUM

If you like nosing around other people's homes, you'll love this museum, devoted entirely to middle-class domestic interiors.

Built in 1714 as a home for poor pensioners, these beautiful ivy-clad almshouses have been converted into a series of living rooms, dating from 1630 to the Victorian era. An extension completed in 1998 contains several 20th-century rooms (a flat from the 1930s, a 1960s suburban lounge and an all-too-familiar 1990s loft-style apartment) as well as a gallery for temporary exhibits, a shop and a cafe.

The rear **garden** is also organised by era, mirroring the museum's exploration of domesticity through the centuries. There's also a very impressive walled **herb garden**, featuring 170 different plants. The lawns at the front are a popular spot for lazing about.

One of the original almshouses has been completely restored and furnished to show the living conditions of the original pensioners in the 18th and 19th centuries. It's the absolute attention to detail that impresses, right down to the vintage newspaper left open on the breakfast table. The setting is so fragile, however, that **tours** (adult/child £3/free) are only held a few times a month; check the website for up-to-date tour dates.

DON'T MISS...

→ Herb garden (Apr-Oct)
→ Almshouse interior

PRACTICALITIES

→ Map p426, G2
→ www.geffrye-museum.org.uk
→ 136 Kingsland Rd, E2
→ admission free
→ ⊙10am-5pm Tue-Sun
→ ⊖Hoxton

19th century, it also housed the Old Jerusalem Tavern, where writers and artists, including Charles Dickens, met.

Try to time your visit with one of the comprehensive **guided tours** of the gate and the priory church. You'll also be shown upstairs to the sumptuous 1902 chapter hall and council chamber, which are still used by the order to this day.

ST JOHN'S PRIORY

CHURCH
CHURCH, GARDENS

Map p426 (www.museumstjohn.org.uk; St John's Sq, EC1M; ⊙11am-4pm Mon-Sat; ⊜Farringdon) Clerkenwell has plenty of secrets and two of them are hidden in plain sight on St John's Sq: one of London's oldest churches and one of its prettiest little gardens. This whole area was originally part of the medieval St John's Priory and is now associated with the revived Order of St John. The walled garden, planted with medicinal herbs and flowers, was built as a memorial to St John's workers who died during the world wars.

If the somewhat boxy street-level church doesn't seem like it ever belonged to a medieval priory, that's because it didn't. The real treasure lies beneath, where the nave of the original church has been preserved as a darkened crypt. Built in the 1380s in the Norman Romanesque style, it's one of the oldest buildings in London. Inside there's a sturdy alabaster effigy of a Castilian knight (1575) and a battered monument portraying the last prior, Sir William Weston, as a decaying body in a shroud (a memento mori designed to remind viewers of their own mortality).

The nave once abutted a large circular chancel that was demolished following the dissolution of the priory. Outside, the outline of the original church has been traced onto the square.

CHARTERHOUSE
HISTORIC BUILDING

Map p426 (☎020-7253 9503; www.thecharterhouse.org; Charterhouse Sq, EC1M; tours £10; ⊙tours 2.15pm Tue-Thu & every 2nd Sat; ⊜Barbican) From a monastery, to a Tudor mansion, to the charitable foundation that's operated here since 1611, Charterhouse has played a discreet but important part in London's history. The history-steeped buildings can only be visited on fascinating 1½-hour guided tours (book online), or by attending the morning or evening services in the chapel. Tours commence at the 14th-century gatehouse on Charterhouse Sq and explore the complex's many grand halls, courts and gardens.

Charterhouse was founded in 1371 as a Carthusian monastery (the name derives from Chartreuse in France, where the order is based). The strictest of all Catholic monastic orders, the monks live mainly in isolation in their cells and take vows of silence, broken only for three hours on Sundays.

In 1537 the monastery was dissolved and the property transferred to King Henry VIII. The prior and 15 of the monks were executed – some were hung, drawn and quartered at Tyburn (near Marble Arch) and the rest sent to Newgate Gaol, where they were chained upright and died of starvation. They were the first of England's Catholic martyrs of the Reformation and three of them were subsequently canonised.

The king sold the property in 1545 to Sir Edward North, who converted it into his London mansion, knocking down the original church and much of the cloister in the process. In 1611 it was purchased by Thomas Sutton, known at the time as the 'richest commoner in England'. In his will, Sutton directed that it should become a school for boys and an almshouse for 'destitute gentlemen'. Around 40 pensioners (known as 'brothers') still live here today and one of their number leads the tours. Charterhouse School moved to Surrey in 1872 and is still going strong.

Famous people associated with Charterhouse include Elizabeth I and James I, both of whom came here prior to their coronations. William Makepeace Thackeray (writer), John Wesley (the founder of the Methodist church) and Robert Baden-Powell (the founder of the Scouts) all attended the school, while Purcell and Handel have played the chapel organ.

MARX MEMORIAL LIBRARY
LIBRARY

Map p426 (☎020-7253 1485; www.marx-memorial-library.org; 37a Clerkenwell Green, EC1R; tours £5; ⊙tours 1pm Tue & Thu; ⊜Farringdon) Built in 1738 to house a Welsh charity school, this unassuming building is an interesting reminder of Clerkenwell's radical history. In 1902 and 1903, during his European exile, Lenin edited 17 editions of the Russian-language Bolshevik newspaper *Iskra* (Spark) from here. Then in 1933, 50 years after the death of Karl Marx and around the time of the Nazi book burnings, it was decided that the building would be converted into a library to honour the founder of communism.

TOP SIGHT
DENNIS SEVERS' HOUSE

This quirky hotchpotch of a cluttered house (built c 1724) is named after the late American eccentric who restored and turned it into what he called a 'still-life drama'. Severs was an artist who lived in the house (in a similar way to the original inhabitants) until his death in 1999.

Visitors today find they've entered the home of a family of Huguenot silk weavers, who were common to the Spitalfields area in the 18th century. However, while they see the Georgian interiors, with meals and drinks half-abandoned and rumpled sheets, and while they smell cooking and hear creaking floorboards, their 'hosts' always remain tantalisingly just out of reach.

From the cellar to the bedrooms, the interiors demonstrate both the original function and design of the rooms, as well as the highs and lows of the area's history. The family's fortunes fade as you progress upstairs, ending in a state of near-destitution on the upper level.

It's a unique and intriguing proposition by day, but 'Silent Night' tours by candlelight every Monday and Wednesday evening (£15, bookings essential) are even more memorable.

DON'T MISS...
- ➜ Silent Night tours
- ➜ The house cat
- ➜ Hogarth tableau

PRACTICALITIES
- ➜ Map p426, G6
- ➜ ☏020-7247 4013
- ➜ www.dennissevers-house.co.uk
- ➜ 18 Folgate St, E1
- ➜ day/night £10/15
- ➜ ☻noon-4pm Sun, noon-2pm & 5-9pm Mon, 5-9pm Wed
- ➜ ⊖Shoreditch High St

Copies of *Iskra* have been preserved in the library, along with other socialist literature, Spanish Civil War banners and relics from various industrial disputes. Tours visit the room where Lenin worked and the building's 15th-century cellar.

If you think it's odd that Clerkenwell should have a memorial to Marx, you might be surprised to learn that from 1942 to 1951 a bust of Lenin stood in Holford Sq in neighbouring Finsbury, gazing towards his former residence. After being repeatedly vandalised it was moved to Islington Town Hall, where it remained on display until 1996, when it was consigned to a museum.

☉ Finsbury & St Luke's

BUNHILL FIELDS   CEMETERY
Map p426 (Bunhill Row, EC1; ☻8am-7pm Mon-Fri, 9.30am-7pm Sat & Sun Apr-Sep, to 4pm Oct-Mar; ⊖Old St) ✿ This cemetery just outside the city walls has been a burial ground for more than 1000 years ('Bunhill' probably derives from the area's macabre historical name – 'Bone Hill'). Famous burials include such literary giants as Daniel Defoe, John Bun-

yan and William Blake. It's a lovely place for a stroll, and a rare green space in this built-up area.

WESLEY'S CHAPEL   CHURCH
Map p426 (www.wesleyschapel.org.uk; 49 City Rd, EC1Y; ☻10am-4pm Mon-Sat, 12.30-1.45pm Sun; ⊖Old St) Built in 1778 this warm and welcoming church was the place of work and worship for John Wesley, the founder of the Methodist Church. You can learn more about him in the **Museum of Methodism** downstairs, and visit his house (at the front) and his grave (behind the church).

☉ Spitalfields

Crowded around its famous market and grand parish church, Spitalfields has long been one of the capital's most multicultural areas. Waves of Huguenot (French Protestant), Jewish, Irish and, more recently, Indian and Bangladeshi immigrants have made Spitalfields home.

A walk along **Brick Lane** is the best way to experience the sights, sounds and smells of Bangladeshi London, but to get a sense of what Georgian Spitalfields was like, branch off to Princelet, Fournier, Elder and Wilkes Streets. Having fled persecution in France, the Huguenots set up shop here from the late 17th century, practising their trade of silk weaving. The attics of these grand town houses were once filled with clattering looms and the area became famous for the quality of its silk, even providing the material for Queen Victoria's coronation gown.

CHRIST CHURCH SPITALFIELDS   CHURCH

Map p426 (🖉020-7377 2440; www.ccspitalfields. org; Commercial St, E1; ⊘10am-4pm Mon-Fri; ⊜Shoreditch High St) This imposing English baroque structure, with a tall spire sitting on a portico of four great Tuscan columns, was designed by Nicholas Hawksmoor and completed in 1729. The heaviness of the exterior gives way to a brilliantly white and lofty interior, with Corinthian columns and large brass chandeliers.

BRICK LANE GREAT MOSQUE   MOSQUE

Map p426 (Brick Lane Jamme Masjid; www. bricklanejammemasjid.co.uk; 59 Brick Lane, E1; ⊜Shoreditch High St, Liverpool St) No building symbolises the different waves of immigration to Spitalfields quite as well as this one. Built in 1743 as the New French Church for the Huguenots, it was a Methodist chapel from 1819 until it was transformed into the Great Synagogue for Jewish refugees from Russia and central Europe in 1898. In 1976 it changed faiths yet again, becoming the Great Mosque. Look for the sundial, high up on the Fournier St frontage.

OLD TRUMAN BREWERY   HISTORIC BUILDING

Map p426 (www.trumanbrewery.com; 91 Brick Lane, E1; ⊜Shoreditch High St) Founded here in the 17th century, Truman's Black Eagle Brewery was, by the 1850s, the largest brewery in the world. Spread over a series of brick buildings and yards straddling both sides of Brick Lane, the complex is now completely given over to edgy markets, pop-up fashion stores, vintage clothes shops, indie record hunters, cafes, bars and live-music venues. Beer may not be brewed here any more, but it certainly is consumed.

After decades of decline, Truman's Brewery finally shut up shop in 1989 – temporarily as it turned out, with the brand subsequently resurrected in 2010 in new premises in Hackney Wick. In the 1990s the abandoned brewery premises found new purpose as a deadly cool hub for boozy Brit-

poppers and while it may not have quite the same caché today, it's still plenty popular.

Several of the buildings are heritage listed, including the Director's House at 91 Brick Lane (built in the 1740s); the old Vat House directly opposite, with its hexagonal bell tower (c 1800); and the Engineer's House right next to it (at 150 Brick Lane), dating from the 1830s.

✗ EATING

As well as a wealth of fantastic cafes and restaurants, this area also has popular food markets with stalls devoted to a wide variety of cuisines. Check out Exmouth Market and Whitecross St Market for weekday lunches, and Brick Lane and the surrounding streets on Sundays. Hoxton's Kingsland Rd and Old St are well known for their reasonably priced Vietnamese eateries.

✗ Clerkenwell

★POLPO   ITALIAN £

Map p426 (🖉020-7250 0034; www.polpo.co.uk; 3 Cowcross St, EC1M; dishes £6-10; ⊘noon-11pm Mon-Sat, to 4pm Sun; ⊜Farringdon) Occupying a sunny spot on semipedestrianised Cowcross St, this sweet little place serves rustic Venetian-style meatballs, *pizzette*, grilled meat and fish dishes. Portions are larger than your average tapas but a tad smaller than a regular main – perfect for a light meal for one, or as part of a feast split between friends.

★PRUFROCK COFFEE   CAFE £

Map p426 (www.prufrockcoffee.com; 23-25 Leather Lane, EC1N; mains £4-7; ⊘8am-6pm Mon-Fri, 10am-5pm Sat & Sun; 🤖📶; ⊜Farringdon) Not content with being one of the kings of London's coffee-bean scene (it offers barista training and workshops in 'latte art'), Prufrock also dishes up delicious breakfasts, lunches and cuppa-friendly pastries and snacks. Judging by the number of laptops, plenty of customers treat it as their office.

COACH & HORSES   GASTROPUB £

Map p426 (www.thecoachandhorses.com; 26-28 Ray St, EC1R; mains £6-13; ⊘noon-3pm & 5-10pm Mon-Fri; 🤖; ⊜Farringdon) One of Clerkenwell's better gastropubs, sacrificing none of its old-world pub charm in attracting a well-heeled crowd for its range of dishes, which change daily.

★ MORITO
TAPAS ££

Map p426 (☎020-7278 7007; www.morito.co.uk; 32 Exmouth Market, EC1R; tapas £4.50-9.50; ⊙noon-11pm Mon-Sat, to 4pm Sun; 🕏; ⊖Farringdon) This diminutive eatery is a wonderfully authentic take on a Spanish tapas bar. Seats are at the bar, along the window, or at one of the small tables inside or out. It's relaxed, convivial and often completely crammed. The food is excellent.

★ ST JOHN
BRITISH ££

Map p426 (☎020-7251 0848; www.stjohnrestaurant.com; 26 St John St, EC1M; mains £17-20; ⊙noon-3pm & 6-11pm Mon-Fri, 6-11pm Sat, 1-3pm Sun; ⊖Farringdon) Whitewashed brick walls, high ceilings and simple wooden furniture keep diners free to concentrate on St John's famous nose-to-tail dishes. Serves are big, hearty and a celebration of England's culinary past. Don't miss the signature roast bone marrow and parsley salad.

MEDCALF
BRITISH ££

Map p426 (☎020-7833 3533; www.medcalfbar.co.uk; 40 Exmouth Market, EC1R; mains £13-18; ⊙noon-3pm & 5.30pm-midnight Mon-Sat, to 5pm Sun; ⊖Farringdon) Housed in a beautifully converted butcher shop dating back to 1912, Medcalf serves up tasty and well-realised British fare, such as hand-picked Dorset crab and Welsh rarebit. In summer, tables spill out onto the pavement.

COMPTOIR GASCON
FRENCH, DELI ££

Map p426 (☎020-7608 0851; www.comptoirgascon.com; 63 Charterhouse St, EC1M; mains £14-21; ⊙noon-2.30pm & 6.30-10pm Tue-Sat; 🕏; ⊠Farringdon) The menu is divided into 'duck' and 'surf and turf' sections at this oddly angular bistro/deli, specialising in the food and wine of southwest France. It may not sound very French, but we find it hard to go past the juicy duck burger (£9.50) – sans foie gras, naturally.

ST JOHN BREAD & WINE
BRITISH ££

Map p426 (☎020-7251 0848; www.stjohngroup.uk.com; 94-96 Commercial St, E1; mains £16-18; ⊙9am-3pm & 6-11pm Tue-Sun, to 9pm Mon; ⊖Shoreditch High St) Offers nose-to-tail traditional British fare (potted pork, devilled kidneys, meaty pies) in a simple, clean and bright space. It also has an excellent selection of British cheeses and puddings.

🏃 Neighbourhood Walk
The Spitalfields-Shoreditch Shuffle

START LIVERPOOL ST STATION
END OLD ST STATION
LENGTH 1.8 MILES, 1½ HOURS

This route leads straight through the heart of historic, multicultural Spitalfields and on to hipper-than-thou Shoreditch. You'll find it at its liveliest on a Sunday, when the various markets are effervescing – but be prepared for a much slower stroll. During the rest of the week, there are still plenty of diverting shops and bars to break your stride.

Leaving the tube station, cross busy Bishopsgate, turn left and then right when you come to ❶ **Middlesex St**. This used to be known as Petticoat Lane after the lacy women's undergarments that were sold here, but that proved too saucy for the authorities and the name was changed in 1830 (to Middlesex!). The East End locals weren't nearly so prudish and the ragtag Sunday market that's been based here for more than 400 years is still known by its former name.

Veer left into Widegate St and continue into narrow ❷ **Artillery Passage**, one of Spitalfields's most atmospheric lanes, lined with historic shopfronts and drinking dens. From here, a left then a right will bring you onto Gun St and, at its far end, ❸ **Old Spitalfields Market** (p211).

Enter the market and turn right into the covered lane lined with fancy gift stores and eateries – a far cry from the fruit-and-veggie stands that the market was famous for until 1991 when 'New Spitalfields' opened in Leyton. Continue on through the artisan craft and fashion stalls of the market proper and then step out onto Commercial St.

Just over the road is the ❹ **Ten Bells** (p210) pub – famous as one of Jack the Ripper's possible pickup joints – and the hulking presence of ❺ **Christ Church** (p201). Running between the two, Fournier St is one of Spitalfield's most intact Georgian streetscapes. As you wander along, note the oddball, Harry Potterish numbering (11½ Fournier St) and keep an eye out for famous artsy residents Tracey Emin and Gilbert & George. The

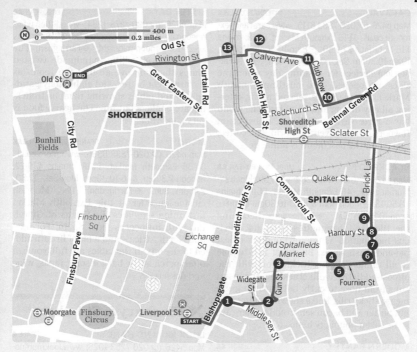

last building on the left of Fournier St is **6 Brick Lane Great Mosque** (p201).

Turn left onto crazy, colourful **7 Brick Lane** itself. Today this narrow but famous thoroughfare is the centrepiece of a thriving Bengali community in an area nicknamed Banglatown. Expect to be cajoled by eager touts as you pass the long procession of curry houses. For the most part the standard is pretty average, despite extravagant claims to the contrary.

Stop at the corner of **8 Hanbury St** to admire the graffiti and then continue on to **9 Old Truman Brewery** (p201). North of here Brick Lane is a different place, stuffed with eclectic clothing stores, old-time Jewish bagel bakeries and a surfeit of cafes and bars.

At the traffic lights cross Bethnal Green Rd, turn left and then veer right onto Redchurch St, where there are more interesting independent shops to peruse. As you turn right into Club Row keep an eye out for an elaborate black-and-red piece of street sculpture called **10 Portal**, dedicated to the artist CityZenKane's late son.

Leafy Club Row terminates in **11 Arnold Circus**, a circular intersection topped with a wooded mound and a bandstand. Until 1891

this was the very heart of London's worst slum, the Old Nichol rookery. Nearly 6000 people lost their homes when the slum was cleared, with most having no choice but to rent similarly impoverished rooms further east. The rubble from the 730 demolished houses lies under the bandstand.

Take the third road on the left (Calvert Ave) and walk past **12 St Leonard's Church** (built in the Palladian style in around 1740) to Shoreditch High St. Turn left and cross over to Rivington St.

Just past the railway bridge, look out for a wrought-iron gate on the right leading into **13 Cargo** (p209). Just inside the gate, protected under perspex, there's a piece by famous graffiti artist Banksy picturing a security guard holding a poodle on a leash. Banksy's just one of many accomplished street artists to have left their mark on Shoreditch's streets – you'll spot plenty more as you continue along Rivington St.

At the end, turn right onto Great Eastern St and then veer left onto traffic-clogged Old St. Believed to have had its origins as a Roman road, it remains a major route. Soon the distinctive arcs straddling the Old St tube station will come into view.

CARAVAN
INTERNATIONAL ££

Map p426 (☎020-7833 8115; www.caravanonexmouth.co.uk; 11-13 Exmouth Market, EC1R; mains £16-17, brunch £7-9.50; ⊗8am-10.30pm Mon-Fri, 10am-10.30pm Sat, 10am-4pm Sun; ☎; ⊖Farringdon) Perfect for a sunny day when the sides are opened onto bustling Exmouth Market, this place is a relaxed affair, offering all-day dining and drinking. The menu has a huge variety of dishes, drawing on flavours from all over the world. The coffee, roasted in the basement, is fantastic.

BLACKFOOT
MODERN EUROPEAN ££

Map p426 (☎020-7837 4384; www.blackfootrestaurant.co.uk; 46 Exmouth Market, EC1R; mains £8.50-13; ⊗noon-3pm & 5.30-10.30pm Mon-Fri, noon-10.30pm Sat; ⊖Farringdon) Retaining the tiles and banquettes from its previous incarnation as one of London's oldest pie-and-mash shops, Blackfoot is a temple to all things porcine. Kicking off with the almost-addictive chilli crackling, the menu runs from nose to curly tail, including immense sticky ribs, and a show-stopping peanut butter and bacon semifreddo. There are some token nonpiggy items, too.

MODERN PANTRY
FUSION ££

Map p426 (☎020-7553 9210; www.themodernpantry.co.uk; 47-48 St John's Sq, EC1V; mains £17-20, breakfast £5.50-9.80, 2/3-course lunch £23/26; ⊗8am-10.30pm Mon-Fri, 10am-4pm & 6-10.30pm Sat & Sun; ☎; ⊖Farringdon) This three-floor Georgian town house in the heart of Clerkenwell has a cracking all-day menu that gives almost as much pleasure to read as to eat from. Ingredients are combined sublimely into unusual dishes such as miso-marinated onglet steak or panko-crusted turkey escalope. The breakfasts are great, too, though portions can be on the small side.

EAGLE
GASTROPUB ££

Map p426 (☎020-7837 1353; www.theeaglefarringdon.co.uk; 159 Farringdon Rd, EC1R; mains £8.50-15; ⊗12.30-3pm & 6.30-10.30pm Mon-Sat, 12.30-4pm Sun; ⊖Farringdon) London's first gastropub may have seen its original owners move on, but it's still a great place for a bite and a pint, especially at lunchtime, when it's relatively quiet. The menu fuses British and Mediterranean elements, and the atmosphere is lively. Watch the chefs work their magic right behind the bar, above which is chalked the menu.

LITTLE BAY
EUROPEAN ££

Map p426 (☎020-7278 1234; www.littlebayfarringdon.co.uk; 171 Farringdon Rd, EC1R; mains £6.25-13; ⊗noon-midnight; ⊖Farringdon) The crushed-velvet ceiling, handmade twisted lamps that improve around the room (as the artist got better) and elaborately painted bar and tables showing nymphs frolicking are bonkers but fun. The hearty food is very good value.

MORO
SPANISH, MOROCCAN £££

Map p426 (☎020-7833 8336; www.moro.co.uk; 34-36 Exmouth Market, EC1R; mains £19-22; ⊗noon-2.30pm & 6-10.30pm Mon-Sat, 12.30-2.45pm Sun; ⊖Farringdon) The Moorish cuisine on offer at this Exmouth Market institution straddles the Straits of Gibraltar, with influences from Spain, Portugal and North Africa – and a bit of Britain added to the mix. If the tables are full, you can often perch at the bar for some tapas, wine and dessert.

✖ Finsbury & St Luke's

LOOK MUM NO HANDS!
CAFE £

Map p426 (☎020-7253 1025; www.lookmumnohands.com; 49 Old St, EC1V; dishes £4.25-8.80; ⊗7.30am-10pm Mon-Fri, 9am-10pm Sat & Sun; ☎; ⊖Barbican) Cyclists and noncyclists alike adore this cafe/workshop, set in a light-filled space looking out onto Old St. Excellent home-made pies and wholesome salads are accompanied by daily specials, baguettes, cakes, pastries and good coffee. There are also a few outdoor tables and it'll loan you a lock if you need to park your wheels.

SHOREDITCH GRIND
CAFE £

Map p426 (www.shoreditchgrind.com; 213 Old St, EC1V; items £2-5; ⊗7am-11pm Mon-Thu, 8am-1am Fri & Sat, 9am-7pm Sun; ☎; ⊖Old St) Housed in a striking little round building, this hip cafe serves top coffee, cooked breakfasts, light lunches and then rustic dinners and cocktails after dusk. Sit at a window and watch the hipsters go by.

✖ Hoxton

SÔNG QUÊ
VIETNAMESE £

Map p426 (www.songque.co.uk; 134 Kingsland Rd, E2; mains £7.20-9.10; ⊗noon-3pm & 5.30-11pm

Mon-Fri, noon-11pm Sat & Sun; ⊜Hoxton) With the kind of demand for seats that most London restaurants can only dream of, this no-frills, hospital-green Vietnamese joint often has a line of people waiting. Service is abrupt, but the food is great, with two dozen types of pho to choose from.

KÊU! VIETNAMESE £

Map p426 (www.vietnamesekitchen.co.uk; 332 Old St, EC1V; items £6-8; ⊙9am-9pm Mon-Sat; ⊜Old St) This deli/cafe assembles lip-smacking *banh mi* (filled baguettes) to eat in or takeaway, as well as soups, salads and rice dishes.

CÂY TRE VIETNAMESE ££

Map p426 (☑020-7729 8662; www.caytre.co.uk; 301 Old St, EC1V; mains £9-13; ⊙noon-11pm Mon-Thu, to 11.30pm Fri & Sat, to 10.30pm Sun; ⊜Old St) Cây Tre serves up all the fresh and fragrant classics to a mix of Vietnamese diners and Hoxton scenesters in a simple but nicely decorated and tightly packed space. It's worth stopping in for the pho – the broth takes 18 hours to make.

FIFTEEN MODERN BRITISH £££

Map p426 (☑020-3375 1515; www.fifteen.net; 15 Westland Pl, N1; mains £22-24, 2/3-course lunch £19/24, Sun £15-19; ⊙noon-3pm & 6-11pm Mon-Sat, noon-9pm Sun; ☎; ⊜Old St) It would be easy to dismiss Jamie Oliver's nonprofit restaurant as a gimmick if it weren't so good. Here, young chefs from disadvantaged backgrounds train with experienced professionals, creating ambitious and interesting dishes. On Sundays it offers a cheaper but limited all-day menu.

✕ Shoreditch

ALLPRESS ESPRESSO CAFE £

Map p426 (www.allpressespresso.com; 58 Redchurch St, E2; dishes £4-6; ⊙8am-5pm; ⊜Shoreditch High St) Part of the great Antipodean takeover of London cafes, this distant outpost of a New Zealand brand serves perfectly crafted coffee from its neat-as-a-pin roastery. Also on the menu are pastries, cakes, sandwiches and a particularly good breakfast platter.

OZONE COFFEE ROASTERS CAFE £

Map p426 (www.ozonecoffee.co.uk; 11 Leonard St, EC2A; mains £5-13; ⊙7.30am-10pm Mon-

SHOREDITCH DISTINCTIONS

Hoxditch? Shoho? Often (confusingly) used interchangeably by Londoners, Hoxton and Shoreditch signify the area stretching north and east from the roundabout at Old St tube station. The name Shoreditch relates to a settlement that grew up immediately north of the old city, around the junction of two important Roman thoroughfares: Kingsland Rd and Old St. Shoreditch was the name of the parish, within which was the village of Hoxton. These days Hoxton is generally known as the area to the north of Old St, up to Kingsland Rd, with Shoreditch being the roads to the south, stretching to the east as far as Brick Lane. But switch them around, or get them confused, and no one will bat an eyelid.

Fri, 9am-5pm Sat & Sun; ⊜Old St) During the day this Kiwi-run cafe is full of artsy types hunched over their computers and new-media mavens appropriating booth seats for impromptu meetings. Coffee is Ozone's raison d'être, but you could instead opt for a New Zealand wine to accompany your risotto or fish of the day. In the evening the menu shifts towards shared plates.

PRINCESS OF SHOREDITCH MODERN BRITISH ££

Map p426 (☑020-7729 9270; www.theprincessofshoreditch.com; 76 Paul St, EC2A; mains £17-20; ⊙noon-3pm & 6.30-10pm Mon-Sat, noon-9pm Sun; ☎; ⊜Old St) The handsome pub downstairs is a buzzy place for a drink, but swirl up the tight spiral staircase and an entirely different Princess presents itself. Polished stemware glistens on wooden Edwardian tables, while the waitstaff buzz around delivering plates of inventive contemporary fare crafted from top-notch British ingredients.

ANDINA SOUTH AMERICAN ££

Map p426 (☑020-7920 6499; www.andinalondon.com; 1 Redchurch St, E2; dishes £5.50-13; ⊙8am-11pm Mon-Fri, 10am-11pm Sat & Sun; ☎; ⊜Shoreditch High St) Cheerful Andina sits on the corner of trendy Redchurch St and serves high-quality Peruvian street food. The lively restaurant, set over two floors, is a great place to try creamy *aji de gallina* (chicken casserole), piquant ceviche and succulent grilled meat skewers. Unsurprisingly, it knocks out a mean pisco sour.

EYRE BROTHERS
SPANISH, PORTUGUESE ££

Map p426 (020-7613 5346; www.eyrebrothers.co.uk; 70 Leonard St, EC2A; mains £16-24; noon-3pm & 6.30-10.45pm Mon-Fri, 7-11pm Sat; ; Old St) The cuisine at this elegant Shoreditch restaurant is Iberian with a touch of African flair, courtesy of the eponymous brothers' upbringing in Mozambique, and it's every bit as exciting as it sounds. The rare acorn-fed Ibérico pork, in particular, is top-notch. It's all accompanied by an extensive list of Portuguese and Spanish wines.

ALBION
BRITISH ££

Map p426 (020-7729 1051; www.albioncaff.co.uk; 2-4 Boundary St, E2; mains £7.50-14; 8am-11pm; ; Shoreditch High St) For those wanting to be taken back to Dear Old Blighty's cuisine, but with rather less grease and stodge, this self-consciously retro 'caff' serves up top-quality bangers and mash along with game-meat pies, devilled kidneys and, of course, fish and chips.

★CLOVE CLUB
MODERN BRITISH £££

Map p426 (020-7729 6496; www.thecloveclub.com; 380 Old St, EC1V; 3-course lunch £35, 5-course dinner £65; noon-2pm Tue-Sat, 6-9.30pm Mon-Sat; ; Old St) From humble origins as a supper club in a Dalston flat, the Clove Club has transformed into this incredibly impressive Michelin-starred restaurant in Shoreditch Town Hall. Hold onto your hats as you're taken on a culinary canter through multiple courses of intricately arranged, well-thought-out, flavoursome food – including numerous unbidden amuse-bouches and palate cleansers. Sensational.

HKK
CHINESE £££

Map p426 (020-3535 1888; www.hkklondon.com; 88 Worship St, EC2A; mains £13-29, 4-course lunch £29; noon-2.30pm & 6-9.45pm; ; Liverpool St) If the surrounds are a tad corporate (especially compared with glitzy sister restaurant Hakkasan), HKK compensates with the high theatre of chefs slicing and dicing in the centre of the dining room. Duck is a speciality, along with exquisitely constructed dumplings and plenty of other Cantonese delights.

✖ Spitalfields

NUDE ESPRESSO
CAFE £

Map p426 (www.nudeespresso.com; 26 Hanbury St, E1; dishes £4.50-12; 7am-6pm Mon-Fri, 9.30am-5pm Sat & Sun; Shoreditch High St) A simply styled, cosy cafe serving top-notch coffee along with cooked breakfasts, light lunches and sweet treats. If it's just coffee you're after, head to its giant-sized roastery directly across the road.

BRICK LANE BEIGEL BAKE
BAKERY £

Map p426 (159 Brick Lane, E2; bagels £1-4.20; 24hr; Shoreditch High St) This relic of the Jewish East End still makes a brisk trade serving dirt-cheap home-made bagels (filled with salmon, cream cheese and/or salt beef) to hungry shoppers and late-night boozers.

POPPIES
FISH & CHIPS ££

Map p426 (www.poppiesfishandchips.co.uk; 6-8 Hanbury St, E1; mains £5.90-16; 11am-11pm Mon-Thu, to 11.30pm Fri & Sat, to 10.30pm Sun; ; Shoreditch High St) This glorious re-creation of a 1950s East End chippy comes complete with waitresses in pinnies and hairnets, and Blitz memorabilia. As well as the usual fishy suspects, it does those old-time London staples – jellied eels and mushy peas.

GALVIN CAFÉ À VIN
FRENCH ££

Map p426 (020-7299 0404; www.galvinrestaurants.com; 35 Spital Sq, E1; mains £15-18; 11.30am-10.30pm; Shoreditch High St) It may be the little sister of glamorous La Chapelle next door, but this informal cafe still manages a high glitz quotient all of its own. Expect traditional but well-executed bistro fare. In summer, grab a table on the square.

ROSA'S
THAI ££

Map p426 (020-7247 1093; www.rosaslondon.com; 12 Hanbury St, E1; mains £8-13; 11am-10.30pm; ; Shoreditch High St) Simply kitted out with low benches and stools, red-fronted Rosa's serves tasty Thai food and surprisingly good coffee (courtesy of Monmouth roasters). Go for its signature pumpkin curry, one of the zingy salads, or a delicious chargrill.

GALVIN LA CHAPELLE
FRENCH £££

Map p426 (020-7299 0400; www.galvinrestaurants.com; 35 Spital Sq, E1; mains £27-35,

2/3-course lunch or early dinner £24/29; ⊙noon-2.30pm & 6-10.30pm Mon-Sat, noon-3pm & 6-8.30pm Sun; ⊜Shoreditch High St) For lashings of la-di-da with an extra serve of ooh la la, you can't beat the incredibly grand surrounds of this soaring Victorian hall, inhabited by bow-tied and waistcoated waitstaff and very-well-heeled guests. The Michelin-starred menu rises to the challenge, delivering traditional French cuisine with lots of contemporary embellishments. Early diners can take advantage of a good-value set menu.

WRIGHT BROTHERS SEAFOOD £££
Map p426 (☑020-7377 8706; www.thewright-brothers.co.uk; 8a Lamb St, E1; mains £17-26; ⊙noon-10.30pm Mon-Sat, 11am-9pm Sun; ⊜Shoreditch High St) For these Wright Brothers, the oyster's their world: they operate the Duchy of Cornwall oyster farm on Prince Charle's estate. This chic dining bar serves up freshly shucked shellfish, delicately constructed fish dishes and exquisite cocktails, all on the edge of Spitalfields market.

HAWKSMOOR STEAK £££
Map p426 (☑020-7426 4850; www.thehawks-moor.com; 157 Commercial St, E1; mains £13-30; ⊙noon-2.30pm & 5-10.30pm Mon-Sat, noon-4.30pm Sun; 🕿; ⊜Shoreditch High St) You could easily miss discreetly signed Hawksmoor, but confirmed carnivores will find it worth seeking out. The dark wood, bare bricks and velvet curtains make for a handsome setting in which to gorge yourself on the best of British meat. The Sunday roasts (£20) are legendary.

🍷 DRINKING & NIGHTLIFE

🍸 Clerkenwell

★FABRIC CLUB
Map p426 (www.fabriclondon.com; 77a Charterhouse St, EC1M; admission £14-26; ⊙from 11pm Fri-Sun; ⊜Farringdon) London's second most famous club (after Ministry of Sound), Fabric is comprised of three separate dance floors in a huge converted cold store opposite Smithfield meat market. Friday's FabricLive rumbles with drum and bass and dubstep, while Saturday's Fabric at Fabric

and Sunday's WetYourSelf! deliver house, techno and electronica.

★JERUSALEM TAVERN PUB
Map p426 (www.stpetersbrewery.co.uk; 55 Britton St, EC1M; ⊙11am-11pm Mon-Fri; 🕿; ⊜Farringdon) Pick a wood-panelled cubicle to park yourself in at this tiny and highly atmospheric 1720 pub, and select from the fantastic beverages brewed by St Peter's Brewery in North Suffolk. Be warned, it's hugely popular and often very crowded.

★YE OLDE MITRE PUB
Map p426 (www.yeoldemitreholborn.co.uk; 1 Ely Ct, EC1N; ⊙11am-11pm Mon-Fri; 🕿; ⊜Farringdon) A delightfully cosy historic pub with an extensive beer selection, tucked away in a backstreet off Hatton Garden (look for a Fuller's sign above a low archway on the left), Ye Olde Mitre was built in 1546 for the servants of Ely Palace. There's no music, so the rooms only echo with the sound of amiable chit-chat.

★ZETTER TOWNHOUSE COCKTAIL LOUNGE COCKTAIL BAR
Map p426 (☑020-7324 4545; www.thezet-tertownhouse.com; 49-50 St John's Sq, EC1V; ⊙7.30am-12.45am; ⊜Farringdon) Tucked away behind an unassuming door on St John's Sq, this ground-floor bar is quirkily decorated with plush armchairs, stuffed animal heads and a legion of lamps. The cocktail list takes its theme from the area's distilling history – recipes of yesteryear and homemade tinctures and cordials are used to create interesting and unusual tipples.

FOX & ANCHOR PUB
Map p426 (www.foxandanchor.com; 115 Charterhouse St, EC1M; ⊙7am-11pm Mon-Fri, 8.30am-11pm Sat, 8.30am-9pm Sun; 🕿; ⊜Barbican) Behind the Fox & Anchor's wonderful art-nouveau facade is a traditional Victorian pub that has retained its three beautiful snugs at the back of the bar. Fully celebrating its proximity to Smithfield Market, food here is gloriously meaty – only the most voracious of carnivores should opt for the City Boy Breakfast (£17).

THREE KINGS PUB
Map p426 (7 Clerkenwell Cl, EC1R; ⊙noon-11pm Mon-Fri, 5.30-11pm Sat; 🕿; ⊜Farringdon) This down-to-earth and welcoming backstreet pub attracts a friendly bunch of relaxed

locals for its quirky decor, great music and good times.

5CC
COCKTAIL BAR

Map p426 (www.5cc-london.com; 23 Exmouth Market, EC1R; ⊘6-11.30pm Tue-Sat; 🛜; ⊜Farringdon) Seek out the entrance to this wonderfully covert cocktail bar at the back of the Exmouth Arms pub. The L-shaped space is finely dressed in dark wood and green leather, with copper tabletops and antlers adorning the walls. Bartenders adeptly craft beautifully presented drinks from fresh ingredients and an extensive spirit list, which specialises in tequila and mescal.

VINOTECA
WINE BAR

Map p426 (www.vinoteca.co.uk; 7 St John St, EC1M; ⊘noon-11pm Mon-Sat; 🛜; ⊜Farringdon) Simple yet elegant oak decor, an astonishingly comprehensive wine list and amiable service make this a popular choice with suited City workers and local creatives. At the on-site shop you can also buy bottles of all of the wines available in the bar – and the food is good too.

🍸 Hoxton

HAPPINESS FORGETS
COCKTAIL BAR

Map p426 (www.happinessforgets.com; 8-9 Hoxton Sq, N1; ⊘5-11pm; ⊜Old St) The menu promises 'mixed drinks and mischief' at this low-lit, basement bar with good-value cocktails in a relaxed and intimate setting. Look for the signs for Ruby cafe and take the stairs heading down.

NIGHTJAR
COCKTAIL BAR

Map p426 (📞020-7253 4101; www.barnightjar. com; 129 City Rd, EC1V; ⊘6pm-1am Sun-Thu, to 3am Fri & Sat; ⊜Old St) There's live music most nights at this slick, low-lit speakeasy. The well-executed cocktails are divided into four eras: before and during US prohibition, postwar and Nightjar signatures.

WHITE LYAN
COCKTAIL BAR

Map p426 (www.whitelyan.com; 153-155 Hoxton St, N1; ⊘6pm-midnight; ⊜Hoxton) Located away from all the hype and hoopla of the main strip, White Lyan can concentrate on the serious business of rebooting the art of the cocktail. It prides itself on eschewing 'ice, perishables or brands', meaning that all of its spirits, cordials and infusions are created in-house.

BRIDGE
BAR, CAFE

Map p426 (15 Kingsland Rd, E2; ⊘noon-2.30am; 🛜; ⊜Hoxton) It doesn't look like much from the outside, but shuffle into this Eastern Mediterranean–style cafe-bar and an Aladdin's cave reveals itself. Upstairs is particularly over the top: it's been described as the 'bastard love child of Louis XIV and your eccentric auntie with all the cats'. Hold court with a strong drink (coffee or spirits) and a slice of baklava.

RED LION
PUB

Map p426 (www.redlionhoxtonst.com; 41 Hoxton St, N1; ⊘noon-11pm; 🛜; ⊜Old St) Just far enough from Hoxton Sq to avoid being overrun by weekend blow-ins, the Red Lion has a local-pub vibe – but given this is Hoxton, the locals are anything but typical. It's spread over four floors, but the roof terrace is the major drawcard.

MACBETH
PUB

Map p426 (www.themacbeth.co.uk; 70 Hoxton St, N1; ⊘5pm-1am; 🛜; ⊜Hoxton) This enormous old boozer on a still-to-be-yuppified stretch, just a short walk north of Hoxton Sq, is an established stop on the ever-changing Hoxton scene. It provides a great platform for up-and-coming talent, as well as the occasional big name on its downstairs stage. There's also a cocktail bar and a large roof terrace.

333 MOTHER
BAR, CLUB

Map p426 (www.333mother.com; 333 Old St, EC1V; ⊘4pm-2.30am Mon-Thu, to 4.30am Fri, noon-3.30am Sat & Sun; ⊜Old St) Hoxton's true old-timer, this Mother just keeps going, despite its hipness halo slipping slightly. Upstairs, Mother Bar still hosts some great nights that are simultaneously scruffy and innovative, covering indie, electro, dubstep and hip hop. Downstairs there's the pubby London Apprentice and the glitzy Mother Superior, where you can hire a private booth for your own cocktail party.

🍸 Shoreditch

★WORSHIP ST WHISTLING SHOP
COCKTAIL BAR

Map p426 (📞020-7247 0015; www.whistling-shop.com; 63 Worship St, EC2A; ⊘5pm-midnight Mon-Thu, to 2am Fri & Sat; ⊜Old St) While the name is Victorian slang for a place selling illicit booze, this subterranean drinking den's master mixologists explore the futuristic outer limits of cocktail chemistry and aromatic science. Many ingredients are made with the rotary evaporators in the on-site lab.

★ **XOYO** CLUB

Map p426 (www.xoyo.co.uk; 32-37 Cowper St, EC2A; ⊗hours vary; ⊖Old St) This excellent Shoreditch warehouse club throws together a pulsingly popular mix of gigs, club nights and art events. The varied line-up – expect indie bands, hip hop, electro, dubstep and much in between – attracts a mix of clubbers, from skinny-jeaned hipsters to more mature hedonists.

OLD BLUE LAST PUB

Map p426 (www.theoldbluelast.com; 38 Great Eastern St, EC2A; ⊗9am-12.30am Mon-Fri, 12.30pm-12.30am Sat & Sun; ⊛; ⊖Old St) Frequently crammed with a hip teenage-and-up crowd, this scuffed corner pub's edgy credentials are courtesy of *Vice* magazine, the bad-boy rag that owns the place. It hosts some of the best Shoreditch parties and lots of live music.

CALLOOH CALLAY COCKTAIL BAR

Map p426 (☑020-7739 4781; www.calloohcallaybar.com; 65 Rivington St, EC2A; ⊗6pm-1am; ⊖Old St) Given it's inspired by *Jabberwocky*, Lewis Carroll's nonsense poem, this bar's eccentric decor is to be expected. The cocktails are top-notch.

BOOK CLUB BAR

Map p426 (☑020-7684 8618; www.wearetbc.com; 100 Leonard St, EC2A; ⊗8am-midnight Mon-Wed, to 2am Thu & Fri, 10am-2am Sat, 10am-midnight Sun; ⊛; ⊖Old St) A creative vibe animates this fantastic one-time Victorian warehouse, which hosts DJs and oddball events (life drawing, workshops, twerking lessons, the Crap Film Club) to complement the drinking and enthusiastic ping pong and pool playing. Food is served throughout the day and there's a scruffy basement bar below.

DREAMBAGSJAGUARSHOES BAR

Map p426 (www.jaguarshoes.com; 32-36 Kingsland Rd, E2; ⊗noon-1am; ⊖Hoxton) The bar is named after the preexisting signs on the two shops whose space it now occupies, and this nonchalance is a typical example of the we-couldn't-care-less Shoreditch chic. The street-level interior is filled with Formica-topped tables and hung with art. Down-

SHOREDITCH COOL

The Shoreditch phenomenon began in the late 1990s, when creative types chased out of the West End by prohibitive rents began taking over warehouses in this then-urban wasteland, abandoned after the collapse of the fabrics industry. Within a few years the area was seriously cool, boasting oddball bars, clubs, galleries and restaurants that catered to the new-media/creative/freelance squad.

Despite the general expectation that the Shoreditch scene would collapse under the weight of its own beards, the regenerated area is still flourishing, with new developments bringing life to some of London's poorest corners, spilling over into nearby Hackney and Bethnal Green.

stairs there's a larger space where DJs hit the decks on weekends.

BREWDOG BAR

Map p426 (www.brewdog.com; 51-55 Bethnal Green Rd, E1; ⊗noon-midnight; ⊛; ⊖Shoreditch High St) BrewDog is an ale aficionado's paradise, with about 20 different brews on tap, hundreds by the bottle and Dirty Burgers to soak it all up with. Its own crowd-funded eco-brewery sits up in Scotland, near Aberdeen, but it stocks plenty of other microbrewery beers, too.

QUEEN OF HOXTON BAR

Map p426 (www.queenofhoxton.com; 1 Curtain Rd, EC2A; ⊗5pm-midnight Mon-Wed, to 2am Thu-Sat; ⊛; ⊖Liverpool St) This industrial-chic bar has a games room, basement and varied music nights, though the real drawcard is the vast rooftop bar, decked out with flowers, fairy lights and even a wigwam. It has fantastic views across the city and a popular outdoor film club (www.rooftopfilmclub.com).

CARGO BAR, CLUB

Map p426 (www.cargo-london.com; 83 Rivington St, EC2A; ⊗noon-1am Sun-Thu, to 3am Fri & Sat; ⊖Shoreditch High St) Cargo is one of London's most eclectic clubs. Under its brick railway arches you'll find a dance floor, bar and outside terrace adorned with two original Banksy images. The music policy is varied, with plenty of up-and-coming bands also on the menu. Food is available throughout the day.

HORSE & GROOM
PUB, CLUB

Map p426 (www.thehorseandgroom.net; 28 Curtain Rd, EC2A; ☺11.30am-11pm Mon-Wed, to 2am Thu, to 4pm Fri, 6pm-4am Sat; ⊜Shoreditch High St) Nicknamed the 'disco pub', this relaxed venue has two intimate spaces serving up hedonistic nights where you're most likely to hear house, funk, soul and, of course, disco. The site's had a long history in entertainment – under the women's toilets, archaeologists have found the remains of the theatre where Shakespeare premiered *Romeo & Juliet* and *Henry V*.

📍 Spitalfields

HAWKSMOOR
COCKTAIL BAR

Map p426 (📞020-7247 7392; www.thehawksmoor.com; 157b Commercial St, E1; ☺5.30-11pm Mon-Fri, noon-11pm Sat & Sun; ⊜Shoreditch High St) Candlelight glisters on black leather, bevelled mirror tiles and a copper wall in this darkly glamorous basement bar below a popular steak restaurant. The adventurous cocktail list is matched with a good selection of beer, cider and wine, and tempting takes on classic American bar food (burgers, hot dogs, wings).

GOLDEN HEART
PUB

Map p426 (110 Commercial St, E1; ☺11am-midnight Sun-Wed, to 1.30am Thu-Sat; ⊜Shoreditch High St) It's a distinctly bohemian crowd that mixes in the cosy, traditional interior of this brilliant Spitalfields boozer. While it's famous as the watering hole for the cream of London's art crowd, our favourite part of any visit is a chat with Sandra, the landlady-celebrity who talks to all comers and ensures the bullshit never outstrips the fun.

TEN BELLS
PUB

Map p426 (www.tenbells.com; 84 Commercial St, E1; ☺noon-midnight; ⊜Shoreditch High St) With its large windows and beautiful tiles, this landmark Victorian pub is perfectly positioned for a pint after a wander around Spitalfields Market. The most famous Jack the Ripper pub, it was patronised by his last victim before her grisly end – and possibly by the serial killer himself.

93 FEET EAST
BAR, CLUB

Map p426 (www.93feeteast.co.uk; 150 Brick Lane, E1; ☺5-11pm Thu, to 1am Fri & Sat, 2-10.30pm Sun; ⊜Shoreditch High St) Part of the Old Truman Brewery complex, this venue has a courtyard, three big rooms and an outdoor terrace that gets crowded with a cool East End crowd on sunny afternoons. As well as DJs, there's plenty of live music on offer.

☆ ENTERTAINMENT

SADLER'S WELLS
DANCE

Map p426 (📞0844 412 4300; www.sadlerswells.com; Rosebery Ave, EC1R; ⊜Angel) A glittering modern venue that was, in fact, first estab-

---

SUPER MARKET SUNDAY

Head to the East End on a Sunday and it can feel as though you can't move for markets. Starting at **Columbia Road Flower Market** (p216) and working your way south via Brick Lane to **Old Spitalfields Market** makes for a colourful consumerist crawl.

Brick Lane Market (Map p430; www.visitbricklane.org; Brick Lane, E1; ☺9am-5pm Sun; ⊜Shoreditch High St) Spilling out into its surrounding streets, this irrepressibly vibrant market fills a vast area with household goods, bric-a-brac, secondhand clothes, cheap fashion and ethnic food.

Backyard Market (Map p426; www.backyardmarket.co.uk; 146 Brick Lane, E1; ☺11am-5pm Sat & Sun; ⊜Shoreditch High St) Just off Brick Lane, the Backyard Market fills a large brick warehouse (part of the Old Truman Brewery complex) with vintage clothing, ceramics and furniture stalls.

Sunday UpMarket (Map p426; www.sundayupmarket.co.uk; Old Truman Brewery, 91 Brick Lane, E1; ☺10am-5pm Sun; ⊜Shoreditch High St) The best of all the Sunday markets, this workaday covered car park fills up with young designers selling their wares, quirky crafts and a drool-inducing array of food stalls.

lished in 1683, Sadler's Wells is the most eclectic modern-dance and ballet venue in town, with experimental dance shows of all genres and from all corners of the globe. The Lilian Baylis Studio stages smaller productions.

ELECTRIC CINEMA   CINEMA
Map p426 (☑020-3350 3490; www.electriccinema.co.uk; 64-66 Redchurch St, E2; tickets £8-18; ⊜Shoreditch High St) Run by Shoreditch House, an uber-fashionable private member's club, this is cinema-going to impress a date, with space for an intimate 48 on the comfy armchairs. There's a full bar and restaurant in the complex, not to mention a barber, beautician and a shop selling homeware and clothes. Tickets go like crazy, so book ahead.

COMEDY CAFE THEATRE   COMEDY
Map p426 (☑020-7739 5706; www.comedycafetheatre.co.uk; 68 Rivington St, EC2A; admission free-£12; ⊜Shoreditch High St) This purpose-built comedy venue offers comedy and dinner, with two-hour shows starting at 8pm most Friday and Saturday nights. The free New Act Night on Wednesdays is a good option for some wincing entertainment. The attached **Bedroom Bar** (www.bedroom-bar.co.uk) has live music most nights.

🛍 SHOPPING

This is a top area for discovering cool boutiques and market stalls showcasing up-and-coming designers, not to mention endless vintage stores. There are tonnes of shops on and around Brick Lane, especially in burgeoning Cheshire St, Hanbury St and the Old Truman Brewery. Each December the East London Design Show (www.eastlondondesignshow.co.uk) takes place at the brewery, showcasing the latest products, clothes, jewellery and art. Clerkenwell is mostly known for its jewellery and the work of its artisan craftspeople.

★OLD SPITALFIELDS MARKET   MARKET
Map p426 (www.oldspitalfieldsmarket.com; Commercial St, E1; ⊙10am-5pm; ⊜Shoreditch High St) Traders have been hawking their wares here since 1638 and it's still one of Lon-

don's best markets. Today's covered market was built in the late 19th century, with the more modern development added in 2006. Sundays are the biggest and best days, but Thursdays are good for antiques and Fridays for independent fashion. There are plenty of food stalls, too.

★ROUGH TRADE EAST   MUSIC
Map p426 (www.roughtrade.com; Old Truman Brewery, 91 Brick Lane, E1; ⊙8am-9pm Mon-Fri, 11am-7pm Sat & Sun; ⊜Shoreditch High St) Although it's no longer directly associated with the legendary record label (home to The Smiths and The Libertines, among many others), this large record store is still the best place to come for music of an indie or alternative bent. Apart from the impressive selection of CDs and vinyl, it also dispenses coffee and stages promotional gigs.

BOXPARK   SHOPPING CENTRE
Map p426 (www.boxpark.co.uk; 2-10 Bethnal Green Rd, E1; ⊙11am-7pm; ⊜Shoreditch High St) A great place to find both up-and-coming and established brands, Boxpark is a quirky pop-up shopping mall created from shipping containers. Each of the series of tiny shops inhabits its own container, selling a wide variety of things: fashion, design, gifts, art and wine. Head to the upper level for restaurants, bars and a terrace.

HOUSE OF HACKNEY   HOMEWARES
Map p426 (www.houseofhackney.com; 131 Shoreditch High St, E1; ⊙10am-7pm Mon-Sat, 11am-5pm Sun; ⊜Shoreditch High St) Selling everything from furniture to china and clothing, all in the craziest prints you ever did see, this store is well worth a gander. If you ever wanted to have your coffee mug match the jungle print on your wallpaper and lampshade, it's the store for you.

BLITZ LONDON   VINTAGE
Map p426 (www.blitzlondon.co.uk; 55-59 Hanbury St, E1; ⊙11am-7pm; ⊜Shoreditch High St) One of the capital's best secondhand-clothes stores, with more than 20,000 hand-selected items of men's and women's clothing, shoes and accessories.

PRESENT   CLOTHING
Map p426 (www.present-london.com; 140 Shoreditch High St, E1; ⊙10.30am-7pm Mon-Sat, 11am-5pm Sun; ⊜Shoreditch High St) Everything for the hip and financially endowed gentleman, including designer gear, shoes and chutney.

START
CLOTHING

Map p426 (www.start-london.com; 42-44 Rivington St, EC2A; ◐10.30am-6.30pm Mon-Sat, 11am-5pm Sun; ◉Old St) This clump of three boutiques is brought to you by Philip Start and his wife, former Fall guitarist Brix Smith Start, a cult rocker who loves girly clothes. Designer labels dominate, and Brix prides herself on her selection of flattering jeans, for which the store offers a fitting service.

Start Menswear (Map p426; 59 Rivington St, EC2A; ◐10.30am-6.30pm Mon-Sat, 11am-5pm Sun; ◉Old St) and **Mr Start** (Map p426; 40 Rivington St, EC2A; ◐10.30am-6.30pm Mon-Sat, 11am-5pm Sun; ◉Old St), a men's tailoring shop, complete the set.

LABOUR & WAIT
HOMEWARES

Map p426 (www.labourandwait.co.uk; 85 Redchurch St, E2; ◐11am-6pm Tue-Sun; ◉Shoreditch High St) Dedicated to simple and functional, yet scrumptiously stylish, traditional British and European homewares, Labour & Wait specialises in items by independent manufacturers who make their products the old-fashioned way. There are shaving soaps, enamel coffee pots, luxurious lambs-wool blankets, elegant ostrich-feather dusters and even kitchen sinks.

TATTY DEVINE
JEWELLERY

Map p426 (☎020-7739 9191; www.tattydevine.com; 236 Brick Lane, E2; ◐10am-6.30pm Mon-Sat, 10am-5pm Sun; ◉Shoreditch High St) Harriet Vine and Rosie Wolfenden make hip and witty jewellery that's become the favourite of many young Londoners. Their original designs feature all manner of flora- and fauna-inspired necklaces, as well as creations sporting moustaches, dinosaurs and bunting. Perspex name necklaces (made to order; from £28) are also a treat.

ABSOLUTE VINTAGE
VINTAGE

Map p426 (☎020-7247 3883; www.absolute-vintage.co.uk; 15 Hanbury St, E1; ◐11am-7pm; ◉Shoreditch High St) As well as secondhand clothes for men and women, check out the mammoth vintage shoe collection here. There are colours and sizes for all, with footwear ranging from designer vintage to something out of your grandma's storage.

MAGMA
BOOKS, GIFTS

Map p426 (www.magmabooks.com; 117-119 Clerkenwell Rd, EC1R; ◐10am-7pm Mon-Sat; ◉Chancery Lane) This much-loved shop sells coffee-table books, magazines and almost anything on the design cutting edge. Great for present shopping.

HATTON GARDEN
JEWELLERY

Map p426 (www.hatton-garden.net; EC1N; ◉Farringdon) If you're in the market for classic settings or unmounted stones, stroll along Hatton Garden – it's chock-a-block with gold, diamond and jewellery shops, especially at the southern end.

Over the quiet Easter weekend of 2015, in a heist worthy of a Hollywood film, thieves using a stolen industrial-sized diamond-tipped drill cut through a 50cm reinforced-concrete wall to break into the basement vault of a safe-deposit company here. They escaped with an estimated £60 million of loot.

E.C.ONE
JEWELLERY

Map p426 (☎020-7713 6185; www.econe.co.uk; 41 Exmouth Market, EC1R; ◐10am-6pm Mon-Sat; ◉Farringdon) Husband-and-wife team Jos and Alison Skeates sell gorgeous contemporary collections by British and international jewellery designers. Watch the jewellers at work at the rear of the store.

CRAFT CENTRAL
CRAFT

Map p426 (www.craftcentral.org.uk; 33-35 St John's Sq, EC1M; ◉Farringdon) Headquarters for a not-for-profit organisation supporting local craftspeople and designers, Craft Central has a small shop showcasing work from a different artisan every week. The real trick is to time your visit with one of the biannual Made In Clerkenwell open days (admission £3), when more than 100 designers open up their workshops and sell their wares.

East London

WAPPING | WHITECHAPEL | BETHNAL GREEN | DALSTON | HACKNEY | BOW & MILE END | LIMEHOUSE | ISLE OF DOGS | ROYAL VICTORIA DOCKS | LOWER LEA VALLEY

Neighbourhood Top Five

1 Stopping to smell the roses at London's most fragrant market, **Columbia Road** (p216).

2 Admiring the ever-changing exhibitions at the edgy **Whitechapel Gallery** (p215).

3 Reliving Games memories among the extensive parklands and interesting architecture of **Queen Elizabeth Olympic Park** (p221).

4 Strolling along the Regent's Canal to **Broadway Market** (p228), feasting from a market stall, then staking a place at one of the pubs.

5 Heading to **Whitechapel** (p215) for a burst of multicultural London and authentic subcontinental cuisine.

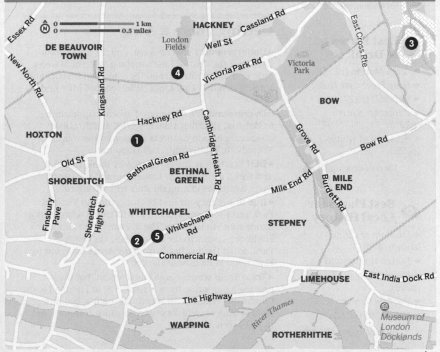

For more detail of this area see Map p430 and p432 ➡

Lonely Planet's Top Tip

The most relaxed way to explore East London is along the water. Cyclists and pedestrians can drop to Regent's Canal at the bottom of Broadway Market and follow the waterway to Limehouse. Branching east at Victoria Park, the Hertford Union Canal delivers you to Hackney Wick and Olympic Park. From Limehouse Basin you can also pick up the Thames Path and follow it to St Katharine Docks.

✕ Best Places to Eat

➡ Corner Room (p222)
➡ Brawn (p222)
➡ Counter Cafe (p224)
➡ Empress (p224)
➡ Rotorino (p223)

For reviews, see p222 ➡

🍷 Best Places to Drink

➡ Cat & Mutton (p227)
➡ Dove Freehouse (p227)
➡ Netil360 (p227)
➡ Carpenter's Arms (p225)
➡ Prospect of Whitby (p225)

For reviews, see p225 ➡

☉ Best Places for Local History

➡ Museum of London Docklands (p220)
➡ Sutton House (p217)
➡ Ragged School Museum (p219)
➡ Hackney Museum (p217)
➡ House Mill (p221)

For reviews, see p216 ➡

Explore: East London

A vast area, East London has a few standout sights but will really repay those happy to wander through and soak up the unique character of each of its neighbourhoods. It includes the heart of the old East End (Whitechapel, Bethnal Green, Bow, Mile End) and most of London's historic Docklands (Wapping, Limehouse, the Isle of Dogs, Royal Victoria Docks), along with Hackney and Dalston to the north, and the Lea Valley further east. Each of these areas has a few don't-miss attractions, but also plenty of places to linger over a coffee, a lazy lunch or a few pints of ale.

Local Life

➡**Picnics** On sunny Saturdays, East Londoners of all stripes grab goodies from Broadway Market (p228) and head to London Fields (p217) for a picnic and a dip in the lido.

➡**Gallery** With free admission and no permanent collection, there's always something new to check out at Whitechapel Gallery (p215).

➡**Old-style caffs** The spirit of the prewar East End survives in ungentrified eateries such as E Pellicci (p222) and F Cooke (p224).

Getting There & Away

➡**Underground** Three lines cut straight through the East End: the Central Line (stopping at Bethnal Green, Mile End and Stratford) and the conjoined District and Hammersmith & City Lines (Whitechapel, Mile End, Bow).

➡**Overground** The overground affords a quick link to Dalston, Hackney, Hackney Wick and Stratford. A separate branch connects Dalston to Hoxton, Shoreditch, Whitechapel and Wapping.

➡**DLR** Starting at Tower Gateway or Bank, the DLR provides a scenic link to Limehouse and the Isle of Dogs, as well as joining the dots with Stratford.

➡**Bus** Buses are your best bet for getting to Victoria Park and Broadway Market. The 55 from Oxford St is a handy route to Hackney. The 277 runs from Islington's Highbury Corner to the Isle of Dogs, via Victoria Park, while the 394 heads from the Angel Islington to Hackney, via Broadway Market.

➡**Train** Train services aren't as frequent, but they provide a quick ride from Liverpool St to London Fields, Cambridge Heath or Stratford. The high-speed link from St Pancras whisks you to Stratford International in just seven minutes.

⊙ SIGHTS

⊙ Wapping

Once notorious for slave traders, drunk sailors and prostitutes, the towering early 19th-century warehouses of Wapping (pronounced 'whopping') still give an atmospheric picture of the area's previous existence.

Although there's nothing to actually mark it, down on the riverside below Wapping New Stairs (near the marine police station) was Execution Dock, where convicted pirates were hanged and their bodies chained in a gibbet at low tide, to be left until three tides had washed over their heads. Among the more famous people who died this way was Captain William Kidd, hanged here in 1701, and whose grisly tale you can read about in the nearby Captain Kidd (p225) pub.

ST KATHARINE DOCKS   HARBOUR
Map p430 (www.skdocks.co.uk; St Katharine's Way, E1W; ⊖Tower Hill) Sitting in the shadow of Tower Bridge, this once-booming part of London's Docklands was built in 1828 by engineer-extraordinaire Thomas Telford. To make way for it, 1250 'insanitary' houses were razed and 11,300 people made homeless. The dock was badly bombed during WWII and was finally abandoned altogether in 1968. Its current incarnation, as a marina for luxury yachts surrounded by cafes, restaurants and twee shops, dates from the 1980s.

It's the perfect starting point for a stroll along the Thames Path to Wapping and Limehouse.

⊙ Whitechapel

★**WHITECHAPEL ROAD**   STREET
Map p430 (⊖Whitechapel) The East End's main thoroughfare hums with a constant cacophony of Asian, African, European and Middle Eastern languages, its busy shops and market stalls selling everything from Indian snacks to Nigerian fabrics and Turkish jewellery, as the area's multitudinous ethnic groupings rub up against each other more or less comfortably. It's a chaotic and poor place, but it's full of life.

Within a few minutes' walk of Whitechapel tube station you'll pass the enormous **East London Mosque** (Map p430; www.eastlondonmosque.org.uk; 46-92 Whitechapel Rd, E1) and,

EAST LONDON SIGHTS

⊙ TOP SIGHT
WHITECHAPEL GALLERY

A firm favourite of art students and the avant-garde cognoscenti, this groundbreaking gallery doesn't have a permanent collection but instead is devoted to hosting edgy exhibitions of contemporary art. It first opened the doors of its main art-nouveau building in 1901 and in 2009 it extended into the library next door, doubling its exhibition space to 10 galleries.

Founded by Victorian philanthropist Canon Samuel Barnett to bring art to the East End, the gallery made its name staging exhibitions by both established and emerging artists, including the first UK shows by Pablo Picasso (whose *Guernica* was exhibited here in 1939), Jackson Pollock, Mark Rothko and Frida Khalo. British artists David Hockney and Gilbert & George debuted here.

The gallery's ambitiously themed shows change every couple of months and there's often live music, poetry readings, talks and films on Thursday evenings. Don't miss the 'social sculptures' in various (and ephemeral) spaces throughout – even on the roof of the building. Other features are an excellent bookshop and a cafe.

DON'T MISS...
➡ Rachel Whiteread's frieze of gilded leaves on the art-nouveau facade
➡ Social sculptures
➡ Bookshop

PRACTICALITIES
➡ Map p430, B5
➡ ☎020-7522 7888
➡ www.whitechapelgallery.org
➡ 77-82 Whitechapel High St, E1
➡ admission free
➡ ◷11am-6pm Tue, Wed & Fri-Sun, to 9pm Thu
➡ ⊖Aldgate East

directly behind it, the now defunct **Fieldgate St Great Synagogue** (Map p430; 41 Fieldgate St, E1), built in 1899. Further down the road, oversized **Tower House** (Map p430; 81 Fieldgate St, E1) was once a hostel and then a dosshouse, but is now a redeveloped apartment block. Past residents include Joseph Stalin and authors Jack London and George Orwell. The latter described it in detail in *Down and Out in Paris and London* (1933).

Whitechapel Rd morphs into Mile End Rd at the intersection with Cambridge Heath Rd, but just before it does you'll find the **Blind Beggar** (Map p430; www.theblindbeggar.com; 337 Whitechapel Rd, E1; ⊖Whitechapel). William Booth, the founder of the Salvation Army, preached his first sermon outside this pub in 1865; there's a **statue** (Map p430) to his memory near the beginning of Mile End Rd. The pub is also famous as the place where notorious gangster Ronnie Kray shot and killed George Cornell in 1966 during a turf war over control of the East End's organised crime. He was jailed for life and died in 1995.

It's worth strolling 150m along Mile End Rd to take a look at the **Trinity Green Almshouses** (Map p430). Built for injured or retired sailors in 1695, the two rows of almshouses run at right angles away from the street, facing a lawn and a central chapel with a clock tower.

WHITECHAPEL BELL
FOUNDRY   HISTORIC SITE
Map p430 (☎020-7247 2599; www.whitechapelbellfoundry.co.uk; 32-34 Whitechapel Rd, E1; tours per person £14; ⊙shop 9.30am-4.15pm Mon-Fri, tours 10am, 1.15pm & 4pm selected Sat; ⊖Whitechapel) Both Big Ben (1858) and Philadelphia's Liberty Bell (1752) were cast at the Whitechapel Bell Foundry. It also cast a new bell for New York City's Trinity Church, damaged in the terrorist attacks of 11 September 2001. Guided 1½-hour tours (maximum 25 people) are conducted on particular Saturdays (check the website) but are often booked out well in advance. On weekdays you can view a few small but informative exhibits in the foyer and buy bell-related items from the shop.

The foundry has been standing on this site since 1738, although an earlier foundry nearby is known to have been in business in 1570.

◉ Bethnal Green

★COLUMBIA ROAD
FLOWER MARKET   MARKET
Map p430 (www.columbiaroad.info; Columbia Rd, E2; ⊙8am-3pm Sun; ⊖Hoxton) A wonderful explosion of colour and life, this weekly market sells a beautiful array of flowers, pot plants, bulbs, seeds and everything you might need for the garden. It's a lot of fun and the best place to hear proper Cockney barrow-boy banter ('We got flowers cheap enough for ya muvver-in-law's grave' etc). It gets really packed, so go as early as you can, or later on, when the vendors sell off the cut flowers cheaply.

V&A MUSEUM OF CHILDHOOD   MUSEUM
Map p430 (☎020-8983 5200; www.museumofchildhood.org.uk; Cambridge Heath Rd, E2; ⊙10am-5.45pm; ▮; ⊖Bethnal Green) FREE Housed in a purpose-built Victorian-era building, this branch of the Victoria & Albert Museum is aimed at both kids (with play areas, interactive exhibits and dressing-up boxes) and nostalgic grown-ups who come to admire the antique toys. From teddies, doll's houses and dolls to Meccano, Lego and computer games, it's a wonderful toy-cupboard trip down memory lane. There's a cafe on the ground floor, too.

HACKNEY CITY FARM   FARM
Map p430 (www.hackneycityfarm.co.uk; 1a Goldsmiths Row, E2; ⊙10am-4.30pm Tue-Sat; ⊖Hoxton) FREE If there's a less bucolic landscape than Hackney Rd, we can't imagine it. All the more reason to bring a slice of the country to kids who have only ever known eggs to have come from a supermarket. There are plenty of animals to pat and, after appropriate hand washing, a cafe serving home-made gelato.

◉ Dalston

RIDLEY ROAD MARKET   MARKET
Map p430 (Ridley Rd, E8; ⊙6am-6pm Mon-Sat; ⊖Dalston Kingsland) Massively popular with the ethnically diverse community it serves, this market is best for its exotic fruit and vegetables, specialist cuts of meat and colourful fabrics. You'll also find the usual assortment of plastic tat, cheap clothing and mobile-phone accessories.

WORTH A DETOUR

CABLE STREET

Cutting a line between Wapping and Whitechapel, Cable St takes its name from the use of the length of the thoroughfare to twist hemp rope into ships' cables (similarly named, the shorter and narrower Twine Ct runs south from here). It's most famous for the Battle of Cable St (1936), in which the British fascist Oswald Mosley planned to march a bunch of his blackshirts into the area, supposedly as a celebration of the fourth anniversary of the British Union of Fascists. Although pockets of fascist supporters existed in the East End, the march was successfully repelled by local people – over 100,000 Jews, communists, dockers, trade unionists and other ordinary East Enders turned out in solidarity against them. At No 236 you'll find **St George's Town Hall** (Map p430; 236 Cable St, E1; Shadwell DLR), its west wall completely covered in a large, vibrant mural commemorating the riots.

The church just behind this building is **St George-in-the-East** (Map p430; www.stgite.org.uk; 16 Cannon St Rd, E1; Shadwell DLR), erected by Nicholas Hawksmoor in 1729 and badly damaged in the Blitz. All that now remains is the tower and exterior walls, enclosing a smaller modern core.

DALSTON EASTERN CURVE GARDENS
GARDENS

Map p430 (www.dalstongarden.org; 13 Dalston Lane, E8; 11am-7pm Sun-Thu, to 11pm Fri & Sat; Dalston Junction) **FREE** This garden is typical of the kind of grassroots regeneration happening around Dalston: a project led by the community, for the community, and a roaring success. There's a simple cafe and regular workshops and events, from gardening sessions to acoustic music. It's a nice place to rest your legs, or to meet friendly locals.

The site used to be a derelict railway line and old sleepers have been used to make a boardwalk and raised beds for the veggie patch. Sadly, a question mark hangs over the garden's future as there are plans to redevelop the neighbouring shopping centre.

Hackney

SUTTON HOUSE
HISTORIC BUILDING

Map p430 (NT; 020-8986 2264; www.nationaltrust.org.uk/sutton-house; 2-4 Homerton High St, E9; adult/child £3.50/1; noon-5pm Wed-Sun, daily Aug, closed Jan; Hackney Central) On a moderately busy road, it would be easy to walk straight past this relatively inconspicuous brick house without noticing its great age. Originally known as Bryk Place, it was built in 1535 by Sir Ralph Sadleir, a prominent courtier of Henry VIII, when Hackney was still a village. Highlights include the Linenfold Parlour, where the Tudor oak panelling on the walls has been carved to resemble draped cloth; the panelled Great Chamber; the Victorian study; and the Georgian parlour.

Abandoned and taken over by squatters in the 1980s, Sutton House could have been lost to history. Enter the National Trust, which has set about conserving and preserving it.

ST AUGUSTINE'S TOWER
CHURCH

Map p430 (www.hhbt.org.uk; Mare St, E8; Hackney Central) Set at the edge of the beautiful St John's Churchyard Gardens, this 13th-century tower is the oldest building in Hackney and the only remains of a church that was demolished in 1798. The tower's 135 steps can be climbed on special open days; see the website for details.

HACKNEY MUSEUM
MUSEUM

Map p430 (020-8356 3500; www.hackney.gov.uk/museum; 1 Reading Lane, E8; 9.30am-5.30pm Tue, Wed, Fri & Sat, to 8pm Thu; Hackney Central) **FREE** Devoted to items relating to Hackneyites past and present, this interesting little museum is as diverse as the ethnically mixed community it serves. Most exhibits are everyday things used by everyday people, but more unusual items include a 1000-year-old Saxon log boat and a coin from the 'Hackney hoard'. This was one of 160 gold coins discovered in 2007 after being hidden by a Jewish family who moved to Hackney to escape the Nazis, only to die in the Blitz.

LONDON FIELDS
PARK

Map p430 (Richmond Rd, E8; Hackney Central) A strip of green in an increasingly hip part of Hackney, London Fields is where locals hang out after a meander up Broadway Market. The park also has two children's play areas, a decent pub and the London Fields Lido (p229).

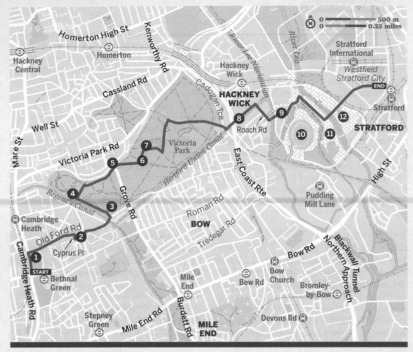

Neighbourhood Walk
East End Eras

START BETHNAL GREEN STATION
END STRATFORD STATION
LENGTH 3.6 MILES, 2½ HOURS

This route offers an insight into the old and new of East London. Exit the tube station towards the **1** **Museum of Childhood** (p216). Just past the museum, turn right into Old Ford Rd, then continue on to Cyprus Pl and turn right. The surrounding area was heavily bombed during WWII and the many tower blocks were subsequently erected on the bomb sites. As you turn left into beautifully preserved **2** **Cyprus St** you'll get a taste of what Victorian Bethnal Green would have looked like. At the end of the street, turn left then right to get back onto Old Ford Rd.

Just over Regent's Canal lies **3** **Victoria Park**. Take the path on the left along the lake until you reach the **4** **Dogs of Alciabiades** howling on plinths. Turn right here and then again at the end of the road. Head through the ornate wrought-iron gates, cross the road and enter the eastern section of the park near the **5** **Royal Inn** (p227).

Veer right for a look at the **6** **Burdett-Coutts Memorial** (1862), a gift of Angela Burdett-Coutts, once the richest woman in England and a prominent philanthropist. From here, ramble on to **7** **East Lake** and exit at the park's southeastern tip.

Cross Cadogan Tce and pick up the much-graffitied **8** **canal path**. This area is Hackney Wick, home to a warren of warehouses and a community of artists. Cross the canal at the metal footbridge with the big hoop, continue onto Roach Rd and then turn left to cross the bridge and enter **9** **Queen Elizabeth Olympic Park** (p221).

Keeping the main **10** **stadium** on your right, cross the River Lea and walk through the playground towards the tangled tentacles of the **11** **ArcelorMittal Orbit** (p221). Turn left, cross the bridge and examine the elegant curves of the **12** **London Aquatics Centre** (p229). From here you can either head straight on to Stratford Station or continue following the river north to explore the park's wetlands and the Lee Valley VeloPark.

VIKTOR WYND MUSEUM OF CURIOSITIES, FINE ART & NATURAL HISTORY MUSEUM

Map p430 (www.thelasttuesdaysociety.org; 11 Mare St, E8; admission £3; ⊘11am-10pm Wed-Sun; ⊜Bethnal Green) Museum? Art project? Bar? This is not a venue that's easily classifiable. Taking its lead from Victorian-era cabinets of curiosities, Wynd's wilfully eccentric collection includes stuffed birds, pickled genitals, shrunken heads, skeletons, celebrity excrement, ancient Chinese dildos and toys from McDonald's Happy Meals. Make of it what you will. Or just call in for a cocktail.

◉ Bow & Mile End

VICTORIA PARK PARK

Map p430 (www.towerhamlets.gov.uk/victoria-park; Grove Rd, E3; ⊘7am-dusk; ⊜Hackney Wick) The 'Regent's Park of the East End', Victoria Park is an 86-hectare leafy expanse of ornamental lakes, monuments, tennis courts, flower beds and large lawns. When it opened in 1845 it was the first public park in the East End, given the go-ahead after a local MP presented Queen Victoria with a petition of 30,000 signatures. It quickly gained a reputation as the 'People's Park' when many large political rallies were held here.

During WWII the park was largely closed to the public and was used as a base for anti-aircraft guns and as an internment camp for Italian and then German prisoners of war.

MILE END PARK PARK

Map p430 (www.towerhamlets.gov.uk/mileend-park; ⊜Mile End) The 36-hectare Mile End Park is a long, narrow series of interconnected green spaces wedged between Burdett and Grove Rds and Regent's Canal. Landscaped to great effect during the millennium year, it incorporates a go-kart track, a skate park, an ecology area, a climbing wall and a sports stadium. The centrepiece, though, is architect Piers Gough's plant-covered Green Bridge linking the northern and southern sections of the park over busy Mile End Rd.

TOWER HAMLETS CEMETERY PARK CEMETERY

Map p430 (www.fothcp.org; Southern Grove, E3; ⊘8am-dusk; ⊜Mile End) Opened in 1841 this 13-hectare cemetery was the last of the 'Magnificent Seven': suburban cemeteries (including Highgate and Abney Park) created by an act of Parliament in response to

London's rapid population growth. Some 270,000 souls were laid to rest here until the cemetery was closed for burials in 1966 and turned into a park and local nature reserve in 2001. Today it's an eerily beautiful site, its crumbling Victorian monuments draped in ever-encroaching greenery.

RAGGED SCHOOL MUSEUM MUSEUM

Map p430 (✆020-8980 6405; www.ragged-schoolmuseum.org.uk; 46-50 Copperfield Rd, E3; ⊘10am-5pm Wed & Thu, 2-5pm 1st Sun of month; ⊜Mile End) FREE Both adults and children are inevitably charmed by this combination of mock Victorian schoolroom (with hard wooden benches and desks, slates, chalk, inkwells and abacuses), re-created East End kitchen and social-history museum. The school closed in 1908, but you can experience what it would have been like during its Sunday openings, when you can take part in a lesson. As a pupil you'll be taught reading, writing and 'rithmetic by a strict school ma'am in full Victorian regalia.

The museum celebrates the legacy of Dr Thomas Barnardo, who founded this school for destitute East End children in the 1870s. 'Ragged' refers to the pupils' usually torn, dirty and dishevelled clothes. Sunday lessons take place at 2.15pm and 3.30pm (suggested donation £2).

◉ Limehouse

There isn't much to Limehouse, although it became the centre of London's Chinese community – its first Chinatown – after 300 sailors settled here in 1890. It gets a mention in Oscar Wilde's *The Picture of Dorian Gray* (1891), when the protagonist passes by this way in search of opium.

ST ANNE'S LIMEHOUSE CHURCH

Map p430 (www.stanneslimehouse.org; Three Colt St, E14; ⊜DLR Westferry) Nicholas Hawksmoor's earliest church (built 1714–27) still boasts the highest church clock in the city. In fact, the 60m-high tower was until recently a 'Trinity House mark' for navigation on the Thames, which is why it often flies the Royal Navy's white ensign.

◉ Isle of Dogs

This odd protuberance on a loop in the Thames, made an island by various dock basins and canals, is completely dominated by the cluster of tower blocks at Canary Wharf. Londoners are divided on their opinion of this area – despite its perceived soullessness, its radical redevelopment is certainly impressive.

The centrepiece is Cesar Pelli's 235m-high, pyramid-topped **One Canada Square** (Map p432; 1 Canada Sq, E14; ⓢCanary Wharf) building, which was the UK's tallest building when it opened in 1991 – a title it held until 2010 when the Shard knocked it off its perch. It's surrounded by more recent towers housing a wealth of financial giants.

Etymologists are still out to lunch over the origin of the island's name. Some believe it relates to the royal kennels, which were located here during the reign of Henry VIII. Others maintain it's a corruption of the Flemish word *dijk* (dyke), recalling the Flemish engineers who shored up the area's muddy banks.

MUDCHUTE   PARK, FARM

Map p432 (www.mudchute.org; Pier St, E14; ⊙farm 9am-5pm; ⛭; ⓓDLR Mudchute) 🎟FREE Entering Mudchute Park from East Ferry Rd through the canopy of trees, you're greeted by the delightfully surprising sight of cows and sheep roaming freely in 13 grassy hectares of parkland. There are also pigs, goats, llamas, alpacas, donkeys, ducks, turkeys, chickens... junior city slickers love this place! Looking back to the skyscrapers of Canary Wharf gives you a clear sense of the contrasts of this part of London. There's also a good cafe.

◉ Royal Victoria Docks

THE CRYSTAL   MUSEUM

Map p430 (www.thecrystal.org; One Siemens Brothers Way, E16; adult/child £8/free; ⊙10am-5pm Tue-Fri, to 7pm Sat & Sun; ⓓDLR Royal Victoria) Housed in a dramatically modern structure, this creative, highly interactive and thoroughly engaging exhibition focuses on urban sustainability and the pressures facing the modern city, from water to energy consumption, transport needs and beyond. Engaging for both adults and youngsters, you can tie it in with a cable-car journey across the river from North Greenwich.

EMIRATES AIR LINE   CABLE CAR

Map p430 (www.emiratesairline.co.uk; 27 Western Gateway, E16; one way adult/child £4.50/2.30, with Oyster Card or Travelcard £3.40/1.70; ⊙7am-9pm Mon-Fri, 9am-9pm Sat & Sun, closes 8pm Oct-Mar; ⓓDLR Royal Victoria, ⓢNorth Greenwich) Capable of ferrying 2400 people per hour

---

◉ TOP SIGHT
MUSEUM OF LONDON DOCKLANDS

Housed in an 1802 warehouse, this museum combines artefacts and multimedia displays to chart the city's history through its river and docks. The best strategy is to begin on the 3rd floor, where displays cover the Roman settlement of Londinium, and work your way down through the ages. Highlights include a scale model of old London Bridge, back when it was lined with buildings, and Sailortown, a re-creation of the cobbled streets, bars and lodging houses of a mid-19th-century dockside community.

The most illuminating and disturbing gallery is London, Sugar & Slavery, which examines the city's role in the transatlantic slave trade. There are also fascinating displays about the docks during the world wars and their controversial transformation into the Docklands during the 1980s.

There's lots for kids, including the hands-on Mudlarks gallery, where children can explore the Thames' history, tip the clipper, try on old-fashioned diving helmets and even construct a simple model of Canary Wharf. There are special exhibitions every few months, for which there is usually a charge.

DON'T MISS...

→ Sailortown
→ London, Sugar & Slavery
→ Docklands at War
→ New Port New City
→ Scale model of London Bridge

PRACTICALITIES

→ Map p432, A1
→ www.museumoflondon.org.uk/docklands
→ West India Quay, E14
→ admission free
→ ⊙10am-6pm
→ ⓓDLR West India Quay

across the Thames in either direction, this cable car makes quick work of the journey from the Greenwich Peninsula to the Royal Docks. Although it's mostly patronised by tourists for the views over the river, it's also listed on the London Underground map as part of the transport network. Oyster Card and Travelcard holders nab discounts for journeys, which are bike friendly, too.

◉ Lower Lea Valley

From the mills of Cistercian monks in the 1st century to the Stratford railway hub of the 1880s (from which goods from the Thames were transported all over Britain), the tidal Lower Lea Valley had long been the source of what Londoners required to fuel their industries. But until building work on the Olympic Park began in 2008, this vast area of East London had become derelict, polluted and largely ignored.

Creating world-class sporting facilities for the 2012 Olympic Games was at the forefront of this area's redevelopment, but this was well balanced with the aim of regenerating the area for generations to come. More than 30 new bridges were built to criss-cross the park. Waterways in and around the park were upgraded, with waste cleared and contaminated soil cleaned on a massive scale.

★ QUEEN ELIZABETH OLYMPIC PARK

PARK

Map p430 (www.queenelizabetholympicpark. co.uk; E20; ⊜Stratford) The glittering centrepiece of London's 2012 Olympic Games, this vast 227-hectare expanse includes the main Olympic venues as well as playgrounds, walking and cycling trails, gardens and a diverse mix of wetland, woodland, meadow and other wildlife habitats as an environmentally fertile legacy for the future. The main focal point is the **stadium** (Map p430), with a Games capacity of 80,000, scaled back to 54,000 seats for its new role as the home ground for West Ham United FC.

Other signature buildings include the London Aquatics Centre (p229), Lee Valley VeloPark (p229), ArcelorMittal Orbit and the **Copper Box Arena** (Map p430; www.better. org.uk/leisure/copper-box-arena), a 6000-seat indoor venue for sports and concerts. Then there's **Here East**, a vast 'digital campus' covering an area equivalent to 16 football fields.

For a different perspective on the park, or if you're feeling lazy, take a tour through its waterways with Lee & Stort Boats (p229).

ARCELORMITTAL ORBIT

TOWER

Map p430 (☎0333 800 8099; www.arcelormittalorbit.com; Queen Elizabeth Olympic Park, E20; adult/child £15/7; ⊙10am-6pm Apr-Sep, to 4pm Oct-Mar; ⊜Stratford) Love it or loathe it, Turner Prize–winner Anish Kapoor's 115m-high, twisted-steel sculpture towers strikingly over the southern end of Olympic Park. In essence it's an artwork, but at the 80m mark it also offers a fantastic panorama from its mirrored viewing platform, which is accessed by a lift from the base of the sculpture. A slide running down the tower is due to open in spring 2016.

Descend 4m (via a caged external staircase) from the platform for more vistas, interpretative screens and an outside section. From here, you can opt to skip down 431 steps to the ground (accompanied by soundscapes of London), or hop back in the lift.

For a truly unique night out, attend an **Orbit Late**, when live music and DJs are hosted in the viewing platforms. For an added thrill, you can take a **freefall abseil** off the tower (£85, book ahead).

The tower has had its share of critics, with the *Daily Mail* likening it to a collision between two cranes. Trust London's loquacious mayor Boris Johnson to come up with its most enduring nickname – he famously described it as a giant hubble-bubble pipe (we think he means a shisha water pipe) and so the 'hubble-bubble tower' it is.

VIEW TUBE

VIEWPOINT

Map p430 (www.theviewtube.co.uk; The Greenway, E20; ⊙9am-5pm; ⬜DLR Pudding Mill Lane) FREE Built to give the general public a chance to have a nosy at Olympic Park during construction, this raised platform provides good views towards the stadium, tower and aquatics centre. There's also a cafe and information panels, although some of those are now a little out of date.

HOUSE MILL

HISTORIC BUILDING

Map p430 (www.housemill.org.uk; Three Mill Lane, E3; adult/child £3/free; ⊙11am-4pm Sun May-Oct, 1st Sun only Mar, Apr & Dec; ⊜Bromley-by-Bow) One of two remaining mills from a trio that once stood on this small island in the River Lea, House Mill (1776) operated as a sluice tidal mill, grinding grain for a nearby distillery until 1941. Tours, which run according to demand and last about 45 minutes, take visitors to all four floors of the mill and offer a fascinating look at traditional East End industry.

◉ EATING

East London's multiculturalism has ensured that its ethnic cuisine stretches far and wide, with some fantastic low-key eateries serving authentic and value-for-money fare. But the area's gentrification has introduced a slew of gastropubs and some more upmarket restaurants, too. Excellent coffee shops have sprouted up all over the East End, though you can still – if you must – find plenty of greasy-spoon cafes, or a traditional pie with mash and liquor. Places to head to if you want to sniff out your own favourites include Columbia Rd, Broadway Market and the streets just to the north of Victoria Park.

✗ Whitechapel

KOLAPATA   BANGLADESHI **£**
Map p430 (☑020-7377 1200; www.kolapata. co.uk; 222 Whitechapel Rd, E1; mains £4.50-7.95; ◷noon-11.30pm; ◉Whitechapel) This modest restaurant serves up excellent Bangladeshi cuisine. Try the *shoirsha elish* (Bangladesh's national fish, served with mustard sauce), the *bhaji* (vegetable sides) and the *borhani* (a spiced yoghurt drink, like a lassi).

CAFE SPICE NAMASTÉ   INDIAN **££**
Map p430 (☑020-7488 9242; www.cafespice. co.uk; 16 Prescot St, E1; mains £7-20; ◷noon-midnight Mon-Fri, 6.30pm-midnight Sat; ☒; ◉Tower Hill) TV chef Cyrus Todiwala has taken an old magistrates court just a 10-minute walk from Tower Hill, decorated it in carnival colours and filled it with fragrant aromas. The Parsi and Goan menu is famous for its superlative *dhansaak* (lamb stew with rice and lentils) but the tandoori dishes are just as good.

TAYYABS   PAKISTANI **££**
Map p430 (☑020-7247 9543; www.tayyabs. co.uk; 83-89 Fieldgate St, E1; mains £5.60-16; ◷noon-11.30pm; ☒; ◉Whitechapel) This buzzing (OK, crowded) Punjabi restaurant is in another league to its Brick Lane equivalents. *Seekh* kebabs, masala fish and other starters served on sizzling-hot plates are delicious, as are accompaniments such as dhal, naan and raita. On the downside, it can be noisy, service can be haphazard and queues often snake out the door.

✗ Bethnal Green

E PELLICCI   CAFE **£**
Map p430 (332 Bethnal Green Rd, E2; dishes £1.60-8; ◷7am-4pm Mon-Sat; ◉Bethnal Green) Opened in 1900, this diminutive Anglo-Italian caff captures the distilled essence of the old East End. Portions are generous and although the food's nothing special (fry-ups, pasta, sandwiches), the warm welcome and the banter from the ragtag collection of local characters crammed around tightly packed tables make it well worth a visit.

GALLERY CAFE   VEGETARIAN, CAFE **£**
Map p430 (www.stmargaretshouse.org.uk; 21 Old Ford Rd, E2; mains £4.50-8; ◷8am-9pm; ☒☒; ◉Bethnal Green) Set in the basement of a lovely Georgian building, this pretty cafe serves simple but delicious vegan and vegetarian fare to relaxed locals. There's a cute courtyard at the front for sunny days. Check the website for sporadic evening events such as live music, comedy and film nights.

★CORNER ROOM   MODERN BRITISH **££**
Map p430 (☑020-7871 0460; www.townhallhotel. com/cornerroom; Patriot Sq, E2; mains £10-15, 2/3-course lunch £19/23; ◷7.30-10am, noon-3pm & 6-10pm; ◉Bethnal Green) Someone put this baby in the corner, but we're certainly not complaining. Tucked away on the 1st floor of the Town Hall Hotel, this relaxed restaurant serves expertly crafted dishes with complex yet delicate flavours, highlighting the best of British seasonal produce.

★BRAWN   BRITISH, FRENCH **££**
Map p430 (☑020-7729 5692; www.brawn.co; 49 Columbia Rd, E2; mains £14-18; ◷noon-3pm Tue-Sun, 6-10.30pm Mon-Sat; ◉Hoxton) There's a Parisian bistro feel to this relaxed corner restaurant, yet the menu walks a fine line between British and French traditions. Hence oxtail and veal kidney pie sits alongside plaice Grenobloise, and souffles are filled with Westcombe cheddar. Try its legendary spicy Scotch egg starter – a Brit classic delivered with French finesse.

LAXEIRO   TAPAS **££**
Map p430 (☑020-7729 1147; www.laxeiro.co.uk; 93 Columbia Rd, E2; tapas £4.50-9; ◷noon-4pm & 7-11pm Tue-Sat, 9am-4.30pm Sun; ◉Hoxton) Regulars return to this homely yet stylish restaurant for the friendly service and authentic tapas – the barbecue lamb is a sure-

COCKNEY RHYMING SLANG

Traditionally cockneys were people born within earshot of the Bow Bells – the church bells of **St Mary-le-Bow** (p148) on Cheapside. Since few people actually live in the City, this definition has broadened to take in those living further east. The term cockney is often used to describe anyone speaking what is also called estuarine English (in which 't' and 'h' are routinely dropped and glottal stops – what the two 't's sound like in 'bottle' – abound).

In fact, the true cockney language also uses something called rhyming slang, which may have developed among London's costermongers (street traders) as a code to avoid police attention. This code replaced common nouns and verbs with rhyming phrases. So 'going up the apples and pears' meant going up the stairs, the 'trouble and strife' was the wife, 'telling porky pies' was telling lies and 'would you Adam and Eve it?' was would you believe it? Over time the second of the two words tended to be dropped so the rhyme vanished.

Few, if any, people still use pure cockney but a good many still understand it. You're more likely to come across it in residual phrases such as 'telling porkies' (lying), 'use your loaf' ('loaf of bread' for head), 'ooh, me plates of meat' (feet) or 'e's me best china' ('china plate' for mate).

fire winner. The handful of more ambitious dishes includes large serves of paella to be shared. In summer there are tables outside on the picturesque street.

✖ De Beauvoir Town

TOWPATH
CAFE £

Map p430 (rear 42-44 De Beauvoir Cres, N1; mains £6.50-9; ⊗9am-5.30pm Tue-Sun; ⊜Haggerston) Occupying four small units on the Regent's Canal towpath, this simple cafe is a super place to sip a cuppa and watch the ducks and narrowboats glide by. The food's excellent too, with delicious frittatas and brownies on the counter and cooked dishes chalked up on the blackboard daily.

DUKE'S BREW & QUE
AMERICAN ££

Map p430 (☑020-3006 0795; www.dukesbrewandque.com; 33 Downham Rd, N1; mains £12-27; ⊗6-10pm Mon-Fri, 11am-3pm & 5-9.30pm Sat & Sun; ⊜Haggerston) The house speciality at this attractive 18th-century pub is ribs – pork or beef – smoked over hickory and lovingly barbecued until the meat falls off the bone. Washed down with a beer from the nearby Beavertown Brewery, it is lip-smackin' food par excellence. The weekend brunch is similarly delicious with pancakes and whopper omelettes filled with BBQ cuts.

✖ Dalston

L'ATELIER
CAFE £

Map p430 (31 Stoke Newington Rd, N16; mains £4.50-9; ⊗8am-10.30pm Mon-Fri, 10am-10pm Sat & Sun; ⊘; ⊜Dalston Kingsland) L'Atelier sports the kitsch/vintage decor that is standard in N16 – mismatched furniture, retro posters, fresh flowers at every table – with French music and the smell of espresso coffee for ambience. It's a lovely spot to grab a salad or an open sandwich and a cup of something.

★ROTORINO
ITALIAN ££

Map p430 (☑020-7249 9081; www.rotorino.com; 434 Kingsland Rd, E8; mains £9.50-17; ⊗6-11pm Mon-Fri, noon-3pm & 6-11pm Sat, noon-9pm Sun; ⊜Dalston Junction) Decked out with blue tiles, 1950s lino and exposed brick, Rotorino's chic interior comes as a welcome surprise, especially after stepping off such a shabby section of Kingsland Rd. The menu is full of delicious, robust Italian dishes, divided into antipasto-style 'starters', 'pasta', 'wood grill' and 'stove'.

MANGAL OCAKBASI
TURKISH ££

Map p430 (www.mangal1.com; 10 Arcola St, E8; mains £8-15; ⊗noon-midnight; ⊜Dalston Kingsland) Mangal is the quintessential Turkish *ocakbasi* (open-hooded charcoal grill, the mother of all BBQs): cramped, smoky and serving superb mezze, grilled lamb chops, quail and a lip-smacking assortment of kebabs. BYO alcohol.

A LITTLE OF WHAT YOU FANCY
BRITISH ££

Map p430 (☑020-7275 0060; www.alittleofwhatyoufancy.info; 464 Kingsland Rd, E8; mains £16-17; brunch £14-16; ⊗6.30-10pm Tue & Wed, 10.30am-10.30pm Thu-Sat, 11am-5pm Sun; ⊜Dalston Junction) A taste of Britain in an area more known for its ethnic cuisine, the food in this simple bistro follows a philosophy of 'less is more' (actually the portions are on the 'more' side). Expect soups, tarts, mussels and chips and roast chicken – all simple but divine.

✖ Hackney

GREEN PAPAYA
VIETNAMESE £

Map p430 (☑020-8985 5486; www.green-papaya. com; 191 Mare St, E8; mains £7-12; ☉5-11pm Tue-Sun; ⊜Hackney Central) This neighbourhood restaurant differentiates itself from the great mass of East London Vietnamese joints by having a much more appealing ambience than most and by specialising in food from North Vietnam. The menu is particularly strong on seafood dishes and it also makes a delicious green-tea ice cream.

CLIMPSON & SONS
CAFE £

Map p430 (www.climpsonandsons.com; 67 Broadway Market, E8; dishes £2.50-5.50; ☉7.30am-5pm Mon-Sat, 9am-5pm Sun; 🚇394) Small and sparsely furnished, this deservedly popular cafe has assumed the name of the butcher that once stood here. The coffee is superb – it roasts its own just around the corner – and it also does a fine line in breakfasts, sandwiches, salads and pastries.

F COOKE
BRITISH £

Map p430 (9 Broadway Market, E8; mains £2.70-4; ☉10am-6pm; 🚇394) If you want a glimpse of pregentrification Broadway Market, head to F Cooke pie-and-mash shop. This family business has been going strong since 1900, and the shop has its original signage and tiles, along with plenty of family photographs around the walls and sawdust on the floor. It still serves warm jellied eels, too!

LOAFING
CAFE £

Map p430 (www.loafing.co.uk; 79 Lauriston Rd, E9; dishes £4-6.50; ☉7.30am-6pm Mon-Sat, 9am-6pm Sun; 🚇277) We dare you to resist the lovingly displayed cake selection at this cute corner cafe. It also offers sandwiches, pastries, Monmouth coffee and a great range of teas, served in mismatched fine bone china. The outdoor tables and large windows make it perfect for people-watching and there's also a tiny garden at the back.

★EMPRESS
MODERN BRITISH ££

Map p430 (☑020-8533 5123; www.empresse9. co.uk; 130 Lauriston Rd, E9; mains £15-16; ☉10am-9.30pm Sun, 6-10.15pm Mon, noon-3.30pm & 6-10.15pm Tue-Fri, 10am-3.30pm & 6-10.15pm Sat; 🚇277) This upmarket pub conversion belts out excellent modern British cuisine under the watchful eye of chef Elliott Lidstone. On Mondays there's a £10 main-plus-drink deal and on weekends it serves an excellent brunch.

LARDO
ITALIAN ££

Map p430 (☑020-8985 2683; www.lardo.co.uk; 197-201 Richmond Rd, E8; mains £11-17; ☉11am-11.30pm Mon-Fri, noon-10.30pm Sat, noon-9.30pm Sun; ⊜Hackney Central) A simple, one-room affair that celebrates *lardo* – the cured back fat of rare-breed pigs scented with aromatic herbs. You'll find it on one of the excellent pizzas and among the antipasti. A couple of pasta and main dishes round out the menu.

BISTROTHEQUE
MODERN BRITISH ££

Map p430 (☑020-8983 7900; www.bistrotheque.com; 23-27 Wadeson St, E2; mains £15-18, 3-course early dinner £20; ☉6-10.30pm Mon-Fri, 11am-4pm & 6-10pm Sat & Sun; ⊜Bethnal Green) Aside from being too cool to have a sign, this warehouse conversion ticks all the boxes of a contemporary upmarket London bistro (the name made more sense when there was a club-like cabaret space downstairs). The food and service are uniformly excellent.

LITTLE GEORGIA
GEORGIAN ££

Map p430 (☑020-7739 8154; www.littlegeorgia. co.uk; 87 Goldsmith's Row, E2; lunch £5-10, dinner £10-13; ☉9am-5pm Mon, to 11pm Tue-Sun; 🚇Hoxton) A charming slice of the Caucasus in East London, this cosy eatery is a good introduction to the cuisine of Georgia. During the day it serves cooked breakfasts and a delicious range of salads and sandwiches.

FISH HOUSE
SEAFOOD ££

Map p430 (☑020-8533 3327; www.fishhouse. co.uk; 126-128 Lauriston Rd, E9; mains £9.50-14; ☉noon-10pm; 🚇277) The freshest of fresh fish and crustaceans are dispensed from both a busy takeaway section and a cheerful sit-down restaurant. The Colchester oysters are always good, while the generous fish pie, bursting with goodies from the briny deep, is exceptional.

✖ Hackney Wick

★COUNTER CAFE
CAFE £

Map p430 (www.counterproductive.co.uk; 7 Roach Rd, E3; dishes £4-8.50; ☉8am-5pm; 🚇) ⊜Hackney Wick) Housed within the Stour Space gallery and directly overlooking the Olympic stadium, this friendly canal-side cafe serves fantastic coffee, breakfasts, sandwiches and pies. The mismatched, thrift-store furniture, art-clad walls and relaxed atmosphere make it a favourite with the local artistic community.

FORMANS
MODERN BRITISH ££

Map p430 (☑020-8525 2365; www.formans. co.uk; Stour Rd, E3; mains £15-20, brunch £6-10; ☺7-11pm Thu & Fri, 10am-2pm & 7-11pm Sat, noon-5pm Sun; ☍; ☺Hackney Wick) Curing fish since 1905, riverside Formans boasts prime views over the Olympic stadium and has a gallery overlooking its smokery. The menu includes a delectable choice of smoked salmon (including its signature 'London cure'), plenty of other seafood and a few nonfishy things. There's a great selection of British wines and spirits, too.

HACKNEY PEARL
CAFE ££

Map p430 (☑020-8510 3605; www.thehackney-pearl.com; 11 Prince Edward Rd, E9; mains £12-17; ☺10am-11pm; ☍; ☺Hackney Wick) With large windows, outdoor tables and the obligatory salvaged furniture, this is a relaxed spot for brunch or an £8 weekday lunch special. It's also open into the evening with a frequently changing bistro-style menu.

✕ Isle of Dogs

THE GUN
MODERN BRITISH £££

Map p432 (☑020-7515 5222; www.thegundock-lands.com; 27 Coldharbour, E14; mains £15-29; ☺11am-midnight Mon-Sat, to 11pm Sun; ☍; ☺Canary Wharf) Set at the end of a residential street that somehow survived the Blitz, this early 18th-century riverside pub has been seriously dolled up, but still manages to ooze history. It's claimed that Lord Nelson had secret assignations with Lady Emma Hamilton here (hence the names on the toilet doors). The menu's excellent, focusing on British meats, especially game.

☕ DRINKING & NIGHTLIFE

☕ Wapping

★PROSPECT OF WHITBY
PUB

Map p430 (57 Wapping Wall, E1; ☺noon-11pm; ☍; ☺Wapping) Once known as the Devil's Tavern, the Whitby is said to date from 1520,

making it the oldest riverside pub in London. Famous patrons have included Charles Dickens and Samuel Pepys. It's firmly on the tourist trail, but there's a smallish terrace overlooking the Thames, a restaurant upstairs and open fires in winter.

CAPTAIN KIDD
PUB

Map p430 (108 Wapping High St, E1; ☺noon-11pm Mon-Sat, 12.30-9.30pm Sun; ☍; ☺Wapping) With its large windows, fine beer garden and displays recalling the hanging nearby of the eponymous pirate in 1701, this is a favourite riverside pub. Although it inhabits a 17th-century building, the pub itself only dates to the 1980s. It stocks a good range of Samuel Smith craft beer from Yorkshire.

☕ Whitechapel

INDO
PUB

Map p430 (133 Whitechapel Rd, E1; ☺noon-1am Sun-Thu, to 3am Fri & Sat; ☍; ☺Whitechapel) Bang opposite the East London Mosque, this tiny pub has battered old tables, pews and a couple of knackered Chesterfields under the only window. Friendly staff work the beautifully tat-cluttered bar and serve decent pizzas to drinkers with the munchies. There's art for sale on the walls, DJs on weekend nights and interesting bands on an irregular schedule.

RHYTHM FACTORY
BAR, CLUB

Map p430 (www.rhythmfactory.co.uk; 16-18 Whitechapel Rd, E1; ☺11am-late; ☺Aldgate East) Perennially popular, the Rhythm Factory is a club and venue hosting a variety of bands, comedians and DJs of all genres who keep the up-for-it crowd happy until late.

☕ Bethnal Green

★CARPENTER'S ARMS
PUB

Map p430 (www.carpentersarmsfreehouse. com; 73 Cheshire St, E2; ☺4-11.30pm Mon-Wed, noon-11.30pm Thu-Sun; ☍; ☺Shoreditch High St) Once owned by infamous gangsters the Kray brothers (who bought it for their old ma to run), this chic yet cosy pub has been beautifully restored and its many wooden surfaces positively gleam. A back room and small yard provide a little more space for the convivial drinkers. There's a great range of beers and ciders.

ROYAL OAK
PUB

Map p430 (www.royaloaklondon.com; 73 Columbia Rd, E2; ⊖4-11pm Mon-Fri, noon-11pm Sat & Sun; ⊖Hoxton) This lovely wood-panelled pub really hits its stride on Sundays when London's famous flower market (p216) is just outside the door. There's a handsome central bar with a good selection of bitter and a better-than-average wine list, plus a little garden at the back.

SATAN'S WHISKERS
COCKTAIL BAR

Map p430 (343 Cambridge Heath Rd, E2; ⊖5pm-midnight; ⊖Bethnal Green) Friendly bar staff, great cocktails, crazy taxidermy and hip hop on the sound system make this a memorable stop on a Bethnal Green crawl.

BETHNAL GREEN WORKING MEN'S CLUB
CLUB

Map p430 (www.workersplaytime.net; 42-44 Pollard Row, E2; ⊖vary; ⊖Bethnal Green) As it says on the tin, this is a true working men's club. Except that this one has opened its doors and let in all kinds of off-the-wall club nights, including trashy burlesque, gay and lesbian shindigs, retro nights, beach parties and bake-offs. Expect sticky carpets, a shimmery stage set and a space akin to a school-hall disco.

SAGER + WILDE
WINE BAR

Map p430 (www.sagerandwilde.com; 193 Hackney Rd, E2; ⊖5pm-midnight Mon-Fri, noon-midnight Sat & Sun; 🛜; ⊖Hoxton) A good-looking addition to the East End drinking scene, this quietly stylish wine bar offers a modish bar-bites menu, an eye-catching glass-brick bar counter and excellent wines by the bottle and glass. There are a few outdoor tables for streetside supping.

🍸 Dalston

DALSTON SUPERSTORE
GAY

Map p430 (www.dalstonsuperstore.com; 117 Kingsland High St, E8; ⊖10am-12.30am Sun-Tue, to 2am Wed-Fri, to 4am Sat; ⊖Dalston Kingsland) Bar, club or diner? Gay or straight? Dalston Superstore is hard to pigeonhole, which we suspect is the point. This two-level industrial space is open all day but really comes into its own after dark when there are club nights in the basement. Lesbians should check out Clam Jam on Thursday.

FARR'S SCHOOL OF DANCING
BAR

Map p430 (www.farrsschoolofdancing.com; 17-19 Dalston Lane, E8; ⊖4pm-midnight Mon-Fri, noon-1am Sat, noon-11pm Sun; ⊖Dalston Junction) There was actually a dance school here in the 1930s, but rest assured, nobody's going to expect you to tackle a tango in this big, knowingly grungy boozer nowadays. You could, however, conceivably bust a move to '80s tunes as the evening progresses. Expect a big central bar, mismatched tables topped with candles and flowers, and a relaxed, good-time crowd.

POND DALSTON
COCKTAIL BAR

Map p430 (www.pond-dalston.com; Stamford Works, 3 Gillett St, N16; ⊖5-11pm Mon-Sat; ⊖Dalston Kingsland) A Victorian-era warehouse down a dodgy lane may be an odd setting for a Hawaiian-themed restaurant and cocktail bar, but this is Dalston after all and Pond nails the chic/industrial/kitsch balance perfectly. Pineapples, toucans and sharks dangle among the exposed ducting, while experienced bar staff shake up adventurous cocktail concoctions below.

THE NEST
CLUB

Map p430 (www.ilovethenest.com; 36 Stoke Newington Rd, N16; ⊖from 10pm Fri & Sat; ⊖Dalston Kingsland) The occasional big-name DJ joins the up-and-comers at this low-ceilinged Dalston dance club.

VIVA
COCKTAIL BAR

Map p430 (www.vivadalston.co.uk; 2 Stoke Newington Rd, N16; ⊖6-11pm Sun-Thu, 4pm-midnight Fri & Sat; ⊖Dalston Kingsland) It may be a Mexican-themed tapas bar but this being Dalston, there's vintage furniture rather than sombreros and fake cacti. The sound is positively loungey too, with not a mariachi band in earshot. The nibbles and cocktails are bang on trend, however, with plenty of tequila and rum. *Ay caramba* indeed.

DALSTON ROOF PARK
BAR

Map p430 (www.bootstrapcompany.co.uk; Print House, 18 Ashwin St, E8; ⊖5-11pm Tue-Fri, 3pm-midnight Sat, 3-10pm Sun May-Sep; ⊖Dalston Junction) It's spaces like this that make you regret the fact that London isn't sunny year-round. Because when you sit in the colourful chairs on the bright-green AstroTurf looking over the Dalston skyline with a drink in your hand, it really is something. Purchase a £5 annual membership and head on up.

📍 Hackney

⭐CAT & MUTTON   PUB
Map p430 (www.catandmutton.com; 76 Broadway Market, E8; ⏱noon-midnight; 🚌394) At this fabulous Georgian pub, Hackney hipsters sup pints under the watchful eyes of hunting trophies, black-and-white photos of old-time boxers and a large portrait of Karl Marx. If it's crammed downstairs, as it often is, head up the spiral staircase to the comfy couches. DJs spin funk, disco and soul on the weekends.

⭐DOVE FREEHOUSE   PUB
Map p430 (📞020-7275 7617; www.dovepubs.com; 24-28 Broadway Market, E8; ⏱noon-11pm; 📶; 🚌394) Alluring at any time, the Dove has a rambling series of rooms and a wide range of Belgian Trappist, wheat and fruit-flavoured beers. Drinkers spill onto the street in warmer weather, or hunker down in the low-lit back room with board games when it's chilly.

⭐NETIL360   BAR
Map p430 (www.netil360.com; 1 Westgate St, E8; ⏱10am-10pm Mon-Fri, noon-11pm Sat & Sun; 📶; 🚌55) Perched atop Netil House, this uber-hip rooftop cafe/bar offers incredible views over London, with brass telescopes enabling you to get better acquainted with workers in the Gherkin. In between drinks you can knock out a game of croquet on the AstroTurf, or perhaps book a hot tub for you and your mates to stew in.

ROYAL INN ON THE PARK   PUB
Map p430 (www.royalinnonthepark.com; 111 Lauriston Rd, E9; ⏱noon-11pm; 📶; 🚌277) On the northern border of Victoria Park, this excellent establishment – once a poster pub for Transport for London – has a half-dozen real ales and Czech lagers on tap, outside seating to the front and a large courtyard at the back. It's always lively and attracts a mixed crowd.

PEOPLE'S PARK TAVERN   PUB
Map p430 (www.peoplesparktavern.pub; 360 Victoria Park Rd, E9; ⏱noon-midnight Sun-Fri, to 2am Sat; 📶; 🚇Homerton) If you're wandering through Victoria Park and wonder where that barbecue smell is emanating from, chances are the culprit will be this large, rambling old pub. There's a fabulous beer garden, right on the park, and it also has its own in-house microbrewery.

📍 Bow & Mile End

PALM TREE   PUB
Map p430 (127 Grove Rd, E3; ⏱noon-midnight Sun-Thu, to 2am Fri & Sat; 🚇Mile End) All by itself, right on Regent's Canal, the Palm Tree is an old-time East End pub with gold flocked wallpaper, photos of also-ran local celebrities, regular live music and plenty of Cockney accents. It can get a bit edgy at times, but it's a quiet spot during the day, with many drinkers relocating to the park when the sun shines.

📍 Limehouse

THE GRAPES   PUB
Map p430 (www.thegrapes.co.uk; 76 Narrow St, E14; ⏱noon-11pm; 🚇DLR Limehouse) One of Limehouse's renowned historic pubs, the Grapes dates to 1583 and has insinuated its way into the writing of Pepys, Dickens, Wilde, Arthur Conan Doyle and Peter Ackroyd. It really is tiny, especially the riverside terrace, which can only really comfortably fit about a half-dozen close friends, but it's cosy inside and exudes plenty of old-world charm.

WHITE SWAN   GAY, PUB
Map p430 (www.bjswhiteswan.com; 556 Commercial Rd, E14; ⏱9pm-2am Tue-Thu, 4pm-4am Fri & Sat; 🚇DLR Limehouse) The White Swan is a fun East End kind of place, with a large dance floor as well as a more relaxed pub area. Its legendary amateur strip night takes place every Wednesday and there are also cabaret and karaoke nights. Club classics and cheesy pop predominate.

OLD SHIP   GAY, PUB
Map p430 (www.oldship.net; 17 Barnes St, E14; ⏱noon-midnight; 🚇DLR Limehouse) In every respect this is your typical little East End corner pub...except, that is, for the drag-queen cabaret shows on Sundays and Saucy Sophie's quiz on Wednesdays.

☆ ENTERTAINMENT

⭐WILTON'S   THEATRE
Map p430 (📞020-7702 2789; www.wiltons.org.uk; 1 Graces Alley, E1; tour £6; ⏱tours 6pm most Mon, bar 5-11pm Mon-Sat; 🚇Tower Hill) A gloriously atmospheric example of one of London's Victorian public-house music halls,

Wilton's hosts a variety of shows, from comedy and classical music to theatre and opera. One-hour guided tours offer an insight into its fascinating history. The Mahogany Bar is a great way to get a taste of the place if you're not attending a performance.

HACKNEY EMPIRE   THEATRE
Map p430 (✆020-8985 2424; www.hackneyempire.co.uk; 291 Mare St, E8; ◉Hackney Central) One of London's most beautiful theatres, this renovated Edwardian music hall (1901) offers an extremely diverse range of performances – from hard-edged political theatre to musicals, opera and comedy. It's one of the very best places to catch a pantomime at Christmas.

PASSING CLOUDS   CLUB
Map p430 (www.passingclouds.org; 1 Richmond Rd, E8; ◔7pm-12.30am Mon-Thu, to 3.30am Fri & Sat, 2pm-12.30am Sun; ◉Dalston Junction) Decked out with colourful lanterns and tropical titbits, Passing Clouds throws legendary parties that go until the early hours of the morning, with DJs, live music and a multicultural crowd that makes you feel you're really in London. The music is predominantly world oriented, with regular Afrobeat bands and a reputable Sunday-night jam session (from 8.30pm).

VORTEX JAZZ CLUB   JAZZ
Map p430 (www.vortexjazz.co.uk; 11 Gillet Sq, N16; ◉Dalston Kingsland) The Vortex hosts an outstanding line-up of jazz musicians, singers and songwriters from the UK, US, Europe, Africa and beyond. It's a small venue so make sure you book if there's an act you particularly fancy.

ARCOLA THEATRE   THEATRE
Map p430 (✆020-7503 1646; www.arcolatheatre.com; 24 Ashwin St, E8; ◉Dalston Junction) Dalston's a fair schlep from the West End, but drama buffs still flock to this innovative theatre for its adventurous and eclec-

---

AN EAST LONDON PLAYLIST

→ The Rolling Stones – *Play With Fire* (1965)

→ Pulp – *Mile End* (1995)

→ Morrissey – *Dagenham Dave* (1995)

→ Razorlight – *Dalston* (2004)

→ Plan B – *Ill Manors* (2012)

---

tic productions. A unique annual feature is Grimeborn, an opera festival focusing on lesser-known or new works – it's Dalston's answer to the world-famous Glyndebourne opera festival taking place around the same time (August).

RIO CINEMA   CINEMA
Map p430 (www.riocinema.org.uk; 107 Kingsland High St, E8; ◉Dalston Kingsland) The Rio is Dalston's neighbourhood art-house, classic and new-release cinema, and a venue for non-mainstream festivals such as the East End Film Festival, the London Turkish Film Festival, the UK Green Film Festival and the Fringe! Queer Film & Arts Fest. It also holds regular Q&A sessions with film directors.

GENESIS   CINEMA
Map p430 (✆020-7780 2000; www.genesis-cinema.co.uk; 93-95 Mile End Rd, E1; ◉Stepney Green) Snuggle up under a blanket on a couch to watch a flick at this wonderful little five-screen cinema.

CAFE OTO   LIVE MUSIC
Map p430 (www.cafeoto.co.uk; 18-22 Ashwin St, E8; ◔8pm-12.30am; ☎; ◉Dalston Junction) Dedicated to promoting experimental and alternative international musicians, this is Dalston's premier venue for hipsters to stroke their beards in while listening to electronic bleeps, Japanese psychedelica or avant folk. Set in a converted print warehouse, it's one of London's most idiosyncratic live-music venues. When there are no gigs on, it's open as a cafe/bar.

🔒 SHOPPING

The boutiques and galleries lining Columbia Rd (many of which are only open at the weekend when the flower market (p216) is in full bloom) and the shops along Broadway Market and Cheshire St are part of London's up-and-coming independent retail scene. If you're after something a little more mainstream, Westfield Stratford City can't fail to satisfy. There's also a shopping mall beneath the Canary Wharf skyscrapers, with similar shops, bars and restaurants.

★BROADWAY MARKET   MARKET
Map p430 (www.broadwaymarket.co.uk; Broadway Market, E8; ◔9am-5pm Sat; ▢394) There's been a market down this pretty street since the late 19th century. The focus these days

is artisan food, arty knick-knacks, books, records and vintage clothing. Stock up on edible treats then head to London Fields (p217) for a picnic.

BEYOND RETRO   VINTAGE

Map p430 (☎020-7923 2277; www.beyondretro. com; 92-100 Stoke Newington Rd, N16; ⏰10am-7pm Mon-Sat, 11.30am-6pm Sun; ⓢDalston Kingsland) A riot of colour, furbelow, frill, feathers and flares, this vast store has every imaginable type of vintage clothing for sale, from hats to shoes. When it all gets too overwhelming, retreat to the licensed cafe. There's a smaller but even cheaper outlet branch in **Bethnal Green** (Map p430; 110-112 Cheshire St, E2; ⏰10am-7pm Mon-Sat, 11.30am-6pm Sun; ⓢShoreditch High St).

TRAID   CLOTHING

Map p430 (www.traid.org.uk; 106-108 Kingsland High St, E8; ⏰10am-6pm; ⓢDalston Kingsland) Banish every preconception you have about charity shops, for Traid is nothing like the ones you've seen before: big and bright, with not a whiff of mothball. The offerings aren't necessarily vintage but rather quality, contemporary secondhand clothes for a fraction of the usual prices. It also sells its own creations made from offcuts.

PRINGLE OF SCOTLAND OUTLET STORE   CLOTHING

Map p430 (www.pringlescotland.com; 90 Morning Lane; ⏰10am-6.30pm Mon-Sat, 11am-5pm Sun; ⓢHackney Central) There are proper bargains to be had at this excellent outlet store that stocks seconds and end-of-line items from the Pringle range. Expect high-quality merino, cashmere and lambswool knitwear for both men and women.

BURBERRY OUTLET STORE   CLOTHING

Map p430 (www.burberry.com; 29-31 Chatham Pl, E9; ⏰10am-5pm; ⓢHackney Central) This outlet shop has excess international stock from the reborn-as-trendy Brit brand's current and last-season collections. Prices are around 30% lower than those in the main shopping centres – but still properly pricey.

WESTFIELD STRATFORD CITY   MALL

(http://uk.westfield.com; Westfield Ave, E20; ⏰10am-9pm Mon-Sat, noon-6pm Sun; ⓢStratford) Right by Queen Elizabeth Olympic Park, this is Britain's third-largest mall – a behemoth containing more than 250 shops, 70 places to eat and drink, a 17-screen cinema, a bowling alley and a casino.

🏃 SPORTS & ACTIVITIES

LONDON AQUATICS CENTRE   SWIMMING

(www.londonaquaticscentre.org; Queen Elizabeth Olympic Park, E20; adult/child £4.50/2.50; ⏰6am-10.30pm; ⓢStratford) The sweeping lines and wave-like movement of Zaha Hadid's award-winning Aquatics Centre make it the architectural highlight of Olympic Park. Bathed in natural light, the 50m competition pool beneath the huge undulating roof (which sits on just three supports) is an extraordinary place to swim. There's also a second 50m pool, a diving area, gym, creche and cafe.

LEE VALLEY VELOPARK   CYCLING

Map p430 (☎0845 6770 603; www.visitleevalley. org.uk/velopark; Abercrombie Rd, E20; 1hr taster session adult/child £35/25, pay-and-ride £5/3, bike hire from £10/6; ⏰9am-10pm; ⓢHackney Wick) Another architectural highlight of Olympic Park, the velodrome is now open to the public – either to wander through and watch the pros tear around the steep-sloped circuit, or to have a go yourself. Both the velodrome and the attached BMX park offer taster sessions. Mountain bikers and road cyclists can attack the tracks on a pay-and-ride basis.

LEE & STORT BOATS   BOAT TOUR

Map p430 (www.leeandstortboats.co.uk; Stratford Waterfront Pontoon, E20; adult/child £8/4; ⏰Sat & Sun Mar, daily Apr-Sep, selected days Oct-Feb; ⓢStratford) Offers 45-minute tours on the waterways through Queen Elizabeth Olympic Park. Check the display boards in the park for departure times, which are usually on the hour from midday onwards.

LONDON FIELDS LIDO   SWIMMING

Map p430 (www.better.org.uk/leisure/london-fields-lido; London Fields Westside, E8; adult/child £4.80/2.85; ⏰6.30am-9pm; ⓢHackney Central) Built in the 1930s but abandoned by the '80s, this heated outdoor pool reopened to local delight in 2006. It gets packed with swimmers and sunbathers during summer.

Camden & North London

KING'S CROSS | EUSTON | REGENT'S PARK | PRIMROSE HILL | CAMDEN TOWN | HAMPSTEAD | HIGHGATE | HIGHBURY | ISLINGTON

Neighbourhood Top Five

1 Walking in gorgeous **Hampstead Heath** (p242): enjoying the sweeping views of London from Parliament Hill, getting a culture fix at beautiful Kenwood House and slumping in a couch at the Garden Gate pub to recover.

2 Soaking up the sights, sounds, smells and frantic energy of **Camden Market** (p240).

3 Discovering the treasures of the **British Library** (p232) and marvelling at the sheer volume of knowledge stored within its walls.

4 Enjoying a thought-provoking afternoon exploring questions of life, death and art at the **Wellcome Collection** (p236).

5 Taking a walk on the creepy side in **Highgate Cemetery** (p243).

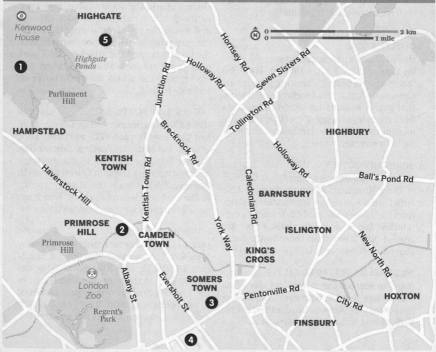

For more detail of this area see Map p433, p434 and p436 ➡

Explore: Camden & North London

North London is a big place – you could spend a week exploring its parks, checking the sights, lounging in gastropubs and sampling the nightlife. So if you're short on time, you'll have to pick and choose carefully.

Hampstead Heath and Camden Market should be on top of your list; Camden Town has an intoxicating energy, while Hampstead Heath offers glorious walks, city views, wonderful art and an insight into how North Londoners spend their weekends. The Wellcome Collection and the British Library are highly recommended and easily accessible. Because this part of London is predominantly residential, it's at its busiest at the weekend, leaving most sights relatively quiet midweek.

King's Cross, Islington and Camden Town offer a variety of excellent eateries, and it's also worth seeking out some of the great places off the beaten track in neighbourhoods such as Barnsbury. Nightlife hotspots are Camden Town and King's Cross, and there are also some wonderful pubs in Hampstead, Highgate and Islington.

Local Life

➡ **Live music** North London is well known for being the home of indie rock. Music fans flock to numerous bars and theatres around Camden Town to watch bands aiming for the big time.

➡ **Sunday pub lunch** Hampstead is a particularly good place to experience this institution of English life, although there are plenty of suitable venues all over North London.

➡ **Swimming** Hampstead Heath's ponds (p254) are open year-round and a small group of hard-core aficionados swim every day, rain or shine.

Getting There & Away

➡ **Underground** North London is served by the Northern, Piccadilly, Victoria, Jubilee and Bakerloo lines. Additionally the Circle, Hammersmith & City and Metropolitan lines call into King's Cross St Pancras, Euston Sq and Baker St.

➡ **Overground** The Overground crosses North London from east to west, with useful stops at Highbury & Islington, Caledonian Rd & Barnsbury, Camden Rd and Hampstead Heath.

➡ **Bus** There is a good network of buses in North London connecting various neighbourhoods to each other and the centre of the city. Buses are particularly useful for getting to the zoo (route 274) and the northern part of Hampstead Heath (210).

Lonely Planet's Top Tip

If the sun's shining, drop any plans you might have made and head straight to a park. North London has some of the capital's biggest and best green spaces, so pack a picnic and do as Londoners do: head to the pub afterwards!

Best Places to Eat

➡ Roots at N1 (p246)
➡ Grain Store (p244)
➡ Market (p245)
➡ Ottolenghi (p247)
➡ Chin Chin Labs (p245)

For reviews, see p244 ➡

Best Places to Drink

➡ Holly Bush (p250)
➡ Drink, Shop & Do (p248)
➡ Edinboro Castle (p250)
➡ Bar Pepito (p249)
➡ Euston Tap (p248)

For reviews, see p248 ➡

Best Places for Live Music

➡ Proud Camden (p249)
➡ Dublin Castle (p249)
➡ Scala (p251)
➡ KOKO (p251)
➡ Jazz Cafe (p251)

For reviews, see p248 ➡

TOP SIGHT
BRITISH LIBRARY

Consisting of low-slung red-brick terraces and fronted by a large plaza featuring an oversized statue of Sir Isaac Newton, Colin St John Wilson's British Library building is a love-it-or-hate-it affair (Prince Charles once famously likened it to a secret-police academy). Completed in 1998 it's home to some of the greatest treasures of the written word.

The Collection

The British Library is the nation's principal copyright library, which means that it automatically receives a copy of everything published in Britain and Ireland. Among its more than 150 million items are historic manuscripts, books and maps from the British Museum.

What you can see is the tip of the iceberg. Under your feet, on five basement levels, run 625km of shelving (growing by 12km every year). The library currently contains 14 million books, 920,000 journal and newspaper titles, 60 million patents, eight million stamps and three million sound recordings.

King's Library

At the centre of the building is the wonderful King's Library, the 85,000-volume collection of King George III, displayed in a beautiful six-storey, 17m-high **glass-walled tower**.

The collection is considered to be one of the most significant of the Enlightenment period. After being bequeathed to the nation by George IV in 1823, it was kept at the British Museum, in the specially built King's Library Gallery. After a bomb fell on the collection during WWII, it was moved to the Bodleian Library in Oxford and finally moved back to London in 1998 when the new British Library opened.

DON'T MISS...

➜ Sir John Ritblat Gallery
➜ King's Library
➜ Philatelic Exhibition

PRACTICALITIES

➜ Map p434, A6
➜ www.bl.uk
➜ 96 Euston Rd, NW1
➜ admission free
➜ ⊘galleries 9.30am-6pm Mon, Fri & Sat, to 8pm Tue-Thu, 11am-5pm Sun
➜ 🛜
➜ Ⓔ King's Cross St Pancras

Sir John Ritblat Gallery

Housing the Treasures of the British Library, the library's most precious and high-profile documents, this darkened gallery is the highlight of any visit. The collection spans almost three millennia and contains manuscripts, religious texts, maps, music scores, autographs, diaries and more.

Rare texts from all the main religions include the **Codex Sinaiticus**, the first complete text of the New Testament, written in Greek in the 4th century; a **Gutenberg Bible** (1455), the first Western book printed using movable type; and the spectacularly illustrated **Jain sacred texts**.

There are also historical documents, including one of four remaining copies of the **Magna Carta** (1215), the charter credited with setting out the basis of human rights in English law. Not so important, but extremely poignant, is **Captain Scott's final diary**, including an account of fellow explorer Lawrence Oates' death.

Literature is also well represented, with **Shakespeare's First Folio** (1623) and manuscripts by some of Britain's best-known authors (such as Lewis Carroll, Jane Austen, George Eliot and Thomas Hardy). Music fans will love **The Beatles' handwritten lyrics** (including *A Hard Day's Night* scribbled on the back of one of Julian Lennon's birthday cards) and original scores by Bach, Handel, Mozart and Beethoven.

Other Exhibitions

The library runs regular high-profile exhibitions in the PACCAR gallery, all connected to its records (admission charges vary). Smaller free exhibitions also take place around the library, focusing on particular authors, genres or themes (science fiction, the census, crime fiction etc). One permanent display is the **Philatelic Exhibition**, which consists of more than 80,000 items, including postage stamps from almost every country. They're housed in sliding racks mounted to the wall near the Sir John Ritblat Gallery, designed to reduce the stamps' exposure to light.

LIBRARY CAFES

All the catering at the British Library comes courtesy of **Peyton & Byrne**, the progeny of Irish chef Oliver Peyton. There are four main outfits: the 1st-floor **restaurant**, with views of the King's Library tower, the ground-floor **cafe**, the **Last Word** cafe on the plaza and the **Short & Sweet** espresso bar facing Euston Rd.

The British Library has wi-fi throughout the building. You need to register to use it, but it is free of charge.

READER PASSES

To access the reading rooms and the bulk of the library collection, you'll need to apply for a Reader Pass. Anyone can apply but passes are only issued if you can demonstrate a need to see specific items in the collection – usually for an academic or specific research purpose. Passes are issued for a period of one month to three years.

TOP SIGHT
LONDON ZOO

Established in 1828, these zoological gardens are among the oldest in the world – they're actually where the word 'zoo' originated. The emphasis nowadays is firmly placed on conservation, education and breeding (the zoo is involved in some 130 breeding programs), with fewer species and more spacious conditions.

Enclosures

The zoo's latest development is **Land of the Lions**, a new enclosure to house its Asiatic lions, which was still being completed when we visited. **Tiger Territory** is a little slice of Indonesian forest and the new home of the zoo's four endangered Sumatran tigers. The enclosure allows the animals to climb and bathe as well as wander around more freely.

Penguin Beach, with its underwater viewing area, is another popular attraction and is a key element of the zoo's breeding program of Humboldt, macaroni and rockhopper penguins. London Zoo is also active in gorilla conservation in central Africa. The park has four gorillas who live on their own island, **Gorilla Kingdom**.

Clore Rainforest Life – a slice of the humid South American rainforest complete with sloths, monkeys and birds – is one of several immersive exhibits where the animals wander freely among the visitors. Others include the **spider monkey** and **lemur** enclosures, and **Butterfly Paradise**, where myriad butterflies and moths flutter from flower to flower.

There is also plenty to see indoors, with an **aquarium**, a **reptile house** and a building called **Bugs** full of creepy-crawlies.

DON'T MISS...

➡ Tiger Territory
➡ Penguin Beach
➡ Gorilla Kingdom
➡ Clore Rainforest Life
➡ Butterfly Paradise

PRACTICALITIES

➡ Map p436, B4
➡ www.londonzoo.co.uk
➡ Outer Circle, Regent's Park, NW1
➡ adult/child £26/18
➡ ⊙10am-5.30pm Mar-Oct, to 4pm Nov-Feb
➡ 🚌274

⊙ SIGHTS

⊙ King's Cross & Euston

King's Cross used to be something of a blind spot on London's map, somewhere you only ever went through rather than to. The surrounding streets were the capital's red-light district, and when the British Library first opened here in 1998, drug addicts could regularly be found in the toilets. In fact, it was the area's reputation that poured cold water on plans to renovate the hotel at St Pancras Station in the 1980s and 1990s.

Fast forward a couple of decades and King's Cross' transformation isn't far removed from the metamorphosis of Stratford following the 2012 Olympic Games. Not only do friends now gather and chat on the plaza in front of King's Cross Station, families also stroll through the former railyards behind the station along broad avenues lined with trees. This one-time industrial wasteland is now home to hip new eateries, glitzy corporate headquarters (Google is planning to build a £650-million campus here) and, perhaps most surprising of all, an outdoor freshwater bathing pond cleaned entirely by plants.

King's Cross was once known as Battle Bridge and was traditionally believed to be the site of the major battle around AD 61 between the Romans and the native Iceni tribe, led by the famous Queen Boudica (Boudicea). Folk legend places the queen's final resting place beneath platform nine. The name 'King's Cross' derives from a monstrously tall statue of King George IV erected in 1840. The king wasn't particularly popular and the monument only survived until 1845.

The surrounding St Pancras parish takes the name of a 14-year-old Roman boy martyred under the Emperor Diocletian. It's thought that some of his remains were brought here in the 6th century and installed in a church where St Pancras Old Church now stands. Some historians think there may have been a church on this site since the early 4th century, which would make it one of the earliest places of Christian worship in Britain.

BRITISH LIBRARY   LIBRARY
See p232.

ST PANCRAS STATION & HOTEL   HISTORIC BUILDING

Map p434 (⌕020-8241 6921; Euston Rd, NW1; tour per person £20; ⊙tours 10.30am, noon, 2pm & 3.30pm Sat & Sun; ⊖King's Cross St Pancras) Looking at the jaw-dropping Gothic splendour of St Pancras, it's hard to believe that the 1873 Midland Grand Hotel languished empty for years and even faced demolition in the 1960s. Now home to a five-star hotel, 67 luxury apartments and the Eurostar terminal, the entire complex has been returned to its former glory. Tours take you on a fascinating journey through the building's history, from its inception as the southern terminus for the Midlands Railway line.

Designed by George Gilbert Scott (who also built the Albert Memorial in Hyde Park), the Midland Grand Hotel was the most luxurious hotel in London when it first opened. All of the materials (including the stone, iron and 60 million red bricks) were brought down from the Midlands as a showcase for the kind of products the railway link could provide. The whole thing cost an astounding £438,000 – somewhere between £500 and £600 million in today's money.

You can get an idea of the original over-the-top decor in the **Gilbert Scott Bar**, which was originally the hotel's reception. The neighbouring dining room (now a fine-dining restaurant run by acclaimed chef Marcus Wareing) showcases the more restrained style of a 1901 refurbishment. The building was incredibly modern for its time, with England's first hydraulic lift, London's first revolving door and a thick layer of concrete between the floors to act as a firebreak. Ironically, this contributed to its undoing, as it made it extremely difficult to adapt the rooms to new trends such as private bathrooms.

The hotel closed in 1935 and was used for railway offices and finally abandoned in 1988. It was only when plans to use St Pancras as the Eurostar terminal came up in the 1990s that local authorities decided to renovate the building and open a hotel. The Eurostar first arrived at **St Pancras International** in 2007 and **St Pancras Renaissance London Hotel** opened its doors in 2011.

Tours take you up the glorious grand staircase (the real star of the Spice Girls' *Wannabe* video) and along the exquisitely decorated corridors into one of the 37 remaining original Victorian rooms. They then head into the station proper, where sky-blue iron girders arc over what was, at the time, the largest unsupported space ever built. A modern addition to the concourse is **Meeting Place**, a giant statue of two lovers embracing by sculptor Paul Day – be sure to examine the wonderful railway-themed frieze winding around its base. Also worth a look is the the fabulously ornate Booking Office Bar & Restaurant (p249), housed in the station's original ticket office.

KING'S CROSS STATION   HISTORIC BUILDING

Map p434 (Euston Rd; ⊖King's Cross St Pancras) With its clean lines and the simple arches of its twin train sheds, you might be forgiven for thinking that King's Cross is a more modern building than its show-offy neighbour St Pancras, but it actually opened its doors over a decade earlier. Built in 1852 in the classic muddy-yellow London stock brick, it stands apart from the prevailing Victorian sensibility of more is more.

In 2012 a major refurbishment was completed with the opening of a new departures terminal under an exceedingly beautiful, curving, canopy-like roof formed from a lattice-like web of steel. Shabby extensions have been removed from the front of the building, showcasing the facade and opening up an expansive plaza crowned with a **Henry Moore sculpture**.

Of course, for many people – especially of the more junior persuasion – King's Cross Station means just one thing: the departure point for Hogwarts School of Witchcraft and Wizardry. You'll need to be embarking on an actual train journey to visit the platforms, so the kind people at Network Rail have moved the magical portal leading to **platform 9¾** to a more convenient location in the new departures terminal. A sign has been permanently erected, along with a trolley half disappearing into the wall carrying a trunk and an owl cage. You can have your picture taken by wizards from the Harry Potter Shop (p253) located next door.

GRANARY SQUARE   SQUARE

Map p434 (www.kingscross.co.uk; Stable St, N1; ⊖King's Cross St Pancras) Positioned by a sharp bend in the Regent's Canal north of King's Cross Station, Granary Sq is at the heart of a major redevelopment of a 27-hectare expanse once full of abandoned freight warehouses. Its most striking feature is a fountain made of 1080 individually lit water jets, which pulse and dance in sequence. You can even download an app (www.kingscross.

⊙ TOP SIGHT
WELLCOME COLLECTION

The Wellcome Collection styles itself as a 'free destination for the incurably curious', a pretty accurate tag for an institution that seeks to explore the links between medicine, science, life and art. It's a serious topic, but the genius of the museum is that it presents it in an accessible way. The building is light and modern, with varied and interactive displays ranging from interviews with researchers, doctors and patients, to art depicting medicine and models of human organs.

The heart of the permanent collection is Sir Henry Wellcome's eccentric array of objects from around the world. Wellcome (1853–1936), a pharmacist, entrepreneur and collector, was fascinated with medicine and amassed more than one million objects from different civilisations associated with life, birth, death and sickness.

To ease your way through the large collection there's a range of free themed 'trail' brochures – choose between *Deeper*, *Braver*, *Bloodier* and *Spicier*. The museum also runs outstanding (and free) temporary exhibitions on topics exploring the frontiers of modern medicine, its place in society and its history.

DON'T MISS...

➡ Temporary exhibitions

➡ Medicine Now permanent exhibition

➡ Medicine Man, featuring objects from Henry Wellcome's personal collection

PRACTICALITIES

➡ Map p436, F6

➡ www.wellcomecollection.org

➡ 183 Euston Rd, NW1

➡ admission free

➡ ⊙10am-6pm Tue, Wed & Fri-Sun, to 10pm Thu

➡ ⊖Euston Sq

ALL ABOARD THE HOGWARTS EXPRESS

Warner Bros Studio Tour: the Making of Harry Potter (www.wbstudiotour.co.uk; Studio Tour Dr, Leavesden, WD25; adult/child £33/26; ⊘9am-10pm; ⊠Watford Junction, then shuttle bus) Whether you're a fair-weather fan or a full-on Pothead, this studio tour is well worth the admittedly hefty admission price. You'll need to pre-book your visit for an allocated time slot and then allow two to three hours to do the complex justice. It starts with a short film before you're ushered through giant doors into the actual set of Hogwarts' Great Hall – the first of many 'wow' moments.

From here, you're left to explore the rest of the complex on your own, including a large hangar featuring all of the most familiar interior sets (Dumbledore's office, the Gryffindor common room, Hagrid's hut), another featuring Platform 9¾ and the Hogwarts Express, and an outdoor section with the exterior of Privet Dr, the purple triple-decker Knight Bus and a shop selling snacks and butterbeer (super sweet, but worth trying). Along the way, video screens burst into life to discuss elements of the production. The attention to detail is fascinating: there's even a section devoted to the graphic design of elements such as the cereal boxes in the Weasley kitchen!

Other highlights include the animatronic workshop (say hi to the Hippogriff) and a stroll along Diagon Alley. But the most magical treat is kept until last – a giant, gasp-inducing scale model of Hogwarts that was used for the exterior shots. Then comes the biggest challenge for true fans and parents: a quite extraordinary gift shop stocked with all your wizardry accessories, including uniforms for each of the Hogwarts houses and replicas of the individually designed wands used by pretty much any character you can think of.

If you're driving, there's a large free car park and extensive directions on the website. Otherwise, catch a train to Watford Junction from Euston station (£9.70, 20 minutes) and then catch the shuttle bus (return £2, 10 minutes).

co.uk/granarysquirt) that enables you to take control of the fountain in the evening and use it to play computer games.

The vast brick 1851 warehouse fronting the square is now home to some excellent eateries and the main campus of the Central St Martins University of the Arts, including its **Platform Theatre** (www.platform-theatre.com). Also worth noting is the wavy glass frontage of the nearby **Kings Place** building. Completed in 2008, it's home to a concert hall, restaurants, commercial galleries and the offices of the *Guardian* and *Observer* newspapers.

HOUSE OF ILLUSTRATION   GALLERY

Map p434 (www.houseofillustration.org.uk; 2 Granary Sq, N1C; adult/child £7/5; ⊘10am-6pm Tue-Sun; ⊜King's Cross St Pancras) This new charity-run gallery in the Granary Sq complex stages ever-changing exhibitions of illustrations – everything from cartoons and book illustrations to advertisements and scientific drawings.

LONDON CANAL MUSEUM   MUSEUM

Map p434 (☑020-7713 0836; www.canalmuseum.org.uk; 12-13 New Wharf Rd, N1; adult/child £4/2; ⊘10am-4.30pm Tue-Sun & bank holidays; ⊜King's Cross St Pancras) This little museum traces the history of the Regent's Canal and explores what life was like for families living and working on Britain's canal system. The exhibits in the stables upstairs are dedicated to the history of canal transport in Britain, with a fascinating 1925 film of a journey along the Regent's Canal.

The museum is housed in a warehouse dating from 1858, where ice was once stored in two deep wells. The ice trade was huge in Victorian London, with 35,000 tonnes imported from Norway in 1899 alone. You can access the wharf at the back of the museum where narrow boats are moored.

⊙ Regent's Park

LONDON ZOO   ZOO

See p234.

REGENT'S PARK   PARK

Map p436 (www.royalparks.org.uk; ⊘5am-9.30pm; ⊜Regent's Park) The most elaborate and formal of London's many parks, Regent's Park is one of the capital's loveliest

WORTH A DETOUR

WITH THE BEATLES

Abbey Road Studios (www.abbeyroad.
com; 3 Abbey Rd, NW8; ◉St John's Wood)
Beatles aficionados can't possibly visit
London without making a pilgrimage
to this famous recording studio in St
John's Wood. The studios themselves
are off limits, so you'll have to content
yourself with examing the decades of
fans' graffiti on the fence outside. Stop-
start local traffic is long accustomed
to groups of tourists lining up on the
zebra crossing to re-enact the cover of
the fab four's 1969 masterpiece *Abbey
Road*. In 2010 the crossing was rewarded with Grade II heritage status.

For a strangely engrossing live view
of the crossing, check out the webcam
on the studio's website. To get here,
take the tube to St John's Wood, cross
the road, follow Grove End Rd to its end
and turn right.

green spaces. Among its many attractions
are London Zoo (p234), Regent's Canal, an
ornamental lake and sports pitches where
locals meet to play football, rugby and vol-
leyball. **Queen Mary's Gardens**, towards
the south of the park, are particularly pretty, especially in June when the roses are in
bloom. Performances take place here in an
open-air theatre (p252) during summer.

The Prince Regent, the future George IV,
commissioned star architect John Nash (the
man behind Buckingham Palace, Marble
Arch and Brighton's Royal Pavilion) to design the park in what was once a royal hunting ground. The original design included a
royal palace and houses for the aristocracy.
Although only a fraction of the grand scheme
ever came to fruition, you can get some idea
of what Nash might have achieved by the
look of the buildings along the Outer Circle.

LORD'S STADIUM
(☏tour info 020-7616 8595; www.lords.org; St
John's Wood Rd, NW8; tours adult/child £18/12;
⏲tours hourly 11am-2pm; ◉St John's Wood) The
'home of cricket' is a must for any devotee
of this particularly English game. Book early
for the Test matches here, but cricket buffs
should also take the absorbing and anec-
dote-filled 100-minute tour of the ground
and facilities.

Tours take in the famous Long Room,
where members watch the games surrounded by portraits of cricket's great and good,
and a museum featuring evocative memorabilia that will appeal to fans old and new.
The famous little urn containing the Ashes,
the prize of the most fiercely contested
competition in cricket, resides here when in
English hands.

LONDON CENTRAL MOSQUE MOSQUE
Map p436 (www.iccuk.org; 146 Park Rd, NW8;
◉St John's Wood) Completed in 1978 this
striking large white mosque is topped with
a glistening golden dome and a minaret,
and can hold more than 5000 worshippers.
Provided you take your shoes off and dress
modestly, you're welcome to go inside but,
as is the way with mosques, the interior is
intentionally simple.

◉ Primrose Hill

Wedged between well-heeled Regent's Park
and grungy Camden, the little neighbourhood of Primrose Hill is high on the property wish list of many Londoners – but
utterly unaffordable for most. With its independent boutiques, good restaurants and
appealing pubs, it has a rare village feel. Famous residents include celebrity chef Jamie
Oliver, comedian David Walliams and fashion designer Stefano Gabbana.

PRIMROSE HILL PARK
Map p436 (◉Chalk Farm) On summer weekends, Primrose Hill park is absolutely packed
with locals enjoying a picnic and the extraordinary views over the city skyline. Come
weekdays, however, and there's mostly just
dog walkers and nannies. It's a lovely place to
enjoy a quiet stroll or an al fresco sandwich.

◉ Camden Town

JEWISH MUSEUM LONDON MUSEUM
Map p436 (www.jewishmuseum.org.uk; 129-131
Albert St, NW1; adult/child £7.50/3.50; ⏲10am-
5pm Sun-Fri; ◉Camden Town) This interesting
little museum has permanent displays per-
taining to the Jewish faith, the history of
Jewish people in Britain and the Holocaust.
One of its more important artefacts is a
mikveh (sunken ritual bath), which was uncovered from Milk St in the City of London
in 2001. It dates from the mid-12th century,

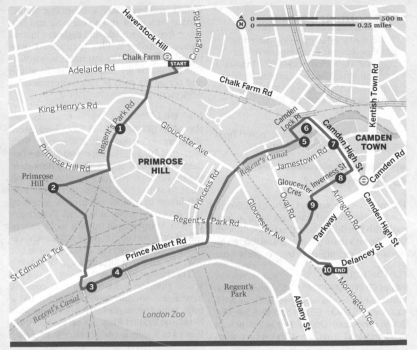

Neighbourhood Walk
A Northern Point of View

START CHALK FARM TUBE STATION
FINISH EDINBORO CASTLE
LENGTH 4KM; 2 HOURS

This walk takes in North London's most interesting locales, including celebrity-infested Primrose Hill and chaotic Camden Town, home to loud guitar bands and the last of London's cartoon punks. When you come out of Chalk Farm station, cross the road and walk up Regent's Park Rd. Turn left on the railway bridge and continue up the southern, boutique-lined stretch of **1 Regent's Park Rd**. This is one of London's most affluent neighbourhoods, home to many darlings of the women's mags, so keep your eyes open for famous faces.

When you reach **2 Primrose Hill** (p238), walk to the top of the park where you'll find a classic view of central London's skyline. On sunny days the park is full of revellers sunbathing, enjoying a picnic or a kick-about.

Walk down the hill through the park, bearing right towards Primrose Hill Lodge.

Cross the road and join the towpath along **3 Regent's Canal**, turning left. You'll walk past the large aviary at **4 London Zoo** (p234), quaint narrow boats, superb mansions and converted industrial buildings.

At **5 Camden Lock**, turn left and head into the **6 Lock Market** (p253). With its original fashion, ethnic art and dozens of food stalls, it's a fun, buzzing place, particularly at weekends. Exit onto **7 Camden High St**, taking note of the giant Doc Martin boots, angels and dragons projecting from the upper levels of the shops. Turn right onto **8 Inverness St**, which hosts its own little market and is lined with bars.

At **9 Gloucester Cres** turn left and walk past the glorious Georgian townhouses. At the end of the road, turn left onto Oval Rd, then cross Parkway onto Delancey St and make a beeline for the **10 Edinboro Castle** (p250), where this walk ends with a well-deserved drink! Warning: if it's a balmy spring or summer day, you may be there a while. And when you're ready to go home, Camden Town tube station is a five-minute walk away.

ℹ COMBINED TICKET

Visitors interested in seeing both No 2 Willow Rd and Fenton House should consider a combined ticket (£9) to save a few pounds. The two sights are only about 15 minutes' walk from each other across leafy Hampstead.

shortly before the Jews were expelled from England for nearly four centuries.

⊙ Hampstead

The most well-heeled and leafy part of North London, Hampstead has long been associated with intellectuals and artists, although these days it's mainly bankers and foreign oligarchs who can afford to buy property here.

FENTON HOUSE   HISTORIC BUILDING

Map p433 (NT; ☎020-7435 3471; www.national-trust.org.uk/fenton-house; Hampstead Grove, NW3; adult/child £6.50/3; ⊙11am-5pm Wed-Sun Mar-Oct; ⊖Hampstead) One of the oldest houses in Hampstead, this late-17th-century mer-

chant's residence has a charming walled garden with roses and an orchard, and fine collections of porcelain and keyboard instruments, including a 1612 harpsichord once played by Handel. The interior is very evocative thanks to original Georgian furniture and period art such as 17th-century needlework pictures.

NO 2 WILLOW ROAD   NOTABLE BUILDING

Map p433 (NT; ☎020-7435 6166; www.nationaltrust.org.uk/2-willow-road; 2 Willow Rd, NW3; adult/child £6/3; ⊙11am-5pm Wed-Sun Mar-Oct, tours 11am, noon, 1pm & 2pm; ⊖Hampstead Heath) Fans of modern architecture will want to swing past this property, the central house in a block of three designed by the 'structural rationalist' Ernö Goldfinger in 1939. Many people think it looks uncannily like the sort of mundane 1950s architecture you see everywhere. It may do now, but 2 Willow Rd was a forerunner in this style.

The interior has cleverly designed storage space, amazing light (rooms that couldn't have a side window have a skylight) and a collection of artworks by Henry Moore, Max Ernst and Bridget Riley. It's accessible to all, thanks to hugely knowledgeable staff. Entry

◉ TOP SIGHT
CAMDEN MARKET

Although – or perhaps because – it stopped being cutting edge several thousand cheap leather jackets ago, Camden Market gets a whopping 10 million visitors each year and is one of London's most popular attractions.

What started out as a collection of attractive craft stalls by Camden Lock on the Regent's Canal now extends in various shape or form most of the way from Camden Town tube station to Chalk Farm tube station. There are four main market areas – the **Stables Market** (p253), **Camden Lock Market** (p253), **Camden Lock Village** (p253) and the **Buck Street Market** (p253) – although they seem to blend into one with the crowds snaking along and the 'normal' shops lining the streets. You'll find a bit of everything: clothes (of variable quality) in profusion, bags, jewellery, arts and crafts, candles, incense and myriad decorative titbits.

There are dozens of food stalls at the Lock Market and the Stables Market. Virtually every type of cuisine is offered, from French to Argentinian, Japanese and Caribbean. Quality varies but is generally pretty good and affordable, and you can eat on the big communal tables or by the canal.

DON'T MISS...

➡ Stables Market
➡ Camden Lock Market
➡ Lunch at the food stalls

PRACTICALITIES

➡ Map p436, D2
➡ www.camdenmarket.com
➡ Camden High St, NW1
➡ ⊙10am-6pm
➡ ⊖Camden Town

TOP SIGHT
KENWOOD HOUSE

This magnificent neoclassical mansion stands at the northern end of Hampstead Heath in a glorious sweep of landscaped gardens leading down to a picturesque lake.

The 17th-century house was substantially remodelled by Robert Adam in the 1760s and rescued from developers by Lord Iveagh Guinness, one of the famous brewing family, who donated it and the wonderful collection of art it contains to the nation in 1927. The Iveagh Bequest, as it is known, contains paintings by such greats as Rembrandt (one of his many self-portraits), Constable, Gainsborough, Reynolds, Hals, Vermeer and Van Dyck and is one of the finest small collections in Britain. Head up the great stairs for the Suffolk Collection, consisting of Jacobean portraits by William Larkin and a set of royal Stuart portraits.

Junior artistocrats will enjoy the Orangery, where there's a collection of toys and a large doll's house.

In spring the gardens erupt in a blaze of rhododendrons and camelias. It's also worth seeking out the sculptures by Henry Moore and Barbara Hepworth on the lawn. The old servant's wing now houses a sit-down cafe and a snack bar with an ice-cream counter.

DON'T MISS...

➡ Rembrandt self-portrait

➡ The pink and blue library

➡ Strolling in the landscaped gardens

PRACTICALITIES

➡ EH

➡ Map p433, B2

➡ www.english-heritage.org.uk

➡ Hampstead Lane, NW3

➡ admission free

➡ ⊙10am-5pm

➡ 🚌210

---

is by guided tour only until 3pm, after which unguided visits are allowed.

KEATS HOUSE
HISTORIC BUILDING

Map p433 (www.cityoflondon.gov.uk/keats; 10 Keats Grove, NW3; adult/child £5.50/free; ⊙1-5pm Tue-Sun Mar-Oct, Fri-Sun Nov-Feb; ☐Hampstead Heath) This elegant Regency house was home to the golden boy of the Romantic poets from 1818 to 1820. The house is sparsely furnished but does a good job of conveying what daily life would have been like in Keats' day.

Never short of generous mates, Keats was persuaded to take refuge in this house by Charles Armitage Brown, and it was here that he met his fiancée Fanny Brawne, literally the girl next door. He wrote his most celebrated poem, 'Ode to a Nightingale', while sitting under a long-gone plum tree in the garden in 1819.

FREUD MUSEUM
MUSEUM

(www.freud.org.uk; 20 Maresfield Gardens, NW3; adult/child £7/4; ⊙noon-5pm Wed-Sun; ☐Finchley Rd) After fleeing Nazi-occupied Vienna in 1938, Sigmund Freud lived the last year of his life here. The fascinating Freud Museum maintains his study and library much as he left it, with his couch, books and collection of small Egyptian figures and other antiquities. Excerpts of dream analyses are scattered around the house, and there's a video presentation upstairs.

⊙ Highgate

HIGHGATE WOOD
PARK

Map p433 (www.cityoflondon.gov.uk; Archway Rd; ⊙7.30am-sunset; ☐Highgate) 🌿 With more than 28 hectares of ancient woodland, this park is a wonderful spot for a walk any time of the year. It's also teeming with life: 70 different bird species have been recorded here, along with seven types of bats, 12 types of butterflies and 80 different kinds of spiders. There's a huge clearing in the centre for sports and it also has a popular playground.

⊙ Highbury

ARSENAL EMIRATES STADIUM
STADIUM

Map p434 (☎020-7619 5000; www.arsenal.com/tours; Hornsey Rd, N5; self-guided tour adult/child

TOP SIGHT
HAMPSTEAD HEATH

Sprawling Hampstead Heath, with its rolling woodlands and meadows, feels a million miles away – despite being approximately four – from the City of London. It covers 320 hectares, most of it woods, hills and meadows, and is home to about 180 bird species, 23 species of butterflies, grass snakes, bats and a rich array of flora.

It's a wonderful place for a ramble, especially to the top of **Parliament Hill**, which offers expansive views across the city and is one of the most popular places in London to fly a kite. Alternatively head up the hill to Ken Wood or lose yourself in the West Heath. Signage is limited, but getting a little lost is part of the experience.

If walking is too pedestrian for you, another major attraction is the bathing ponds (separate ones for men and women and a slightly less pleasant **mixed pond** (p254)). Those of a more artistic bent should make a beeline for **Kenwood** (p241).

Once you've had your fill of fresh air and/or culture, do as Londoners do and head to one of the wonderful nearby pubs for a restorative pint.

DON'T MISS...

➜ Views from Parliament Hill

➜ Strolling in the woodlands

➜ Kenwood

PRACTICALITIES

➜ Map p433, B3

➜ ⊜ Hampstead Heath

£20/10, guided tour £40; ⊙10am-6pm Mon-Sat, to 4pm Sun; ⊜Holloway Rd) When Arsenal's new stadium opened in 2006, fans claimed it would never be the same again. It's true that the 64,000-seat stadium lacks some of the bonhomie of the old Highbury ground, but it's still a sell-out at every game. Match tickets are tricky to come by, even if you have a first-born to sacrifice, so if you're a fan, consider taking a stadium tour instead.

Self-guided audio tours (available in nine languages) are very entertaining, or you could shell out for a guided tour with a former Arsenal player. Both take you everywhere, from the back entrance used by the players to the entertainment suites where corporate bigwigs watch the game. You'll get to walk to the pitch through 'the tunnel', sit on the team's pitch-side benches and even check out the changing rooms (complete with a spa and physio suite on Arsenal's side). Tours also include entry to a museum that focuses on the history of the club and its fans, and is therefore likely to only interest the most ardent Arsenal supporters. Visits finish in the stadium's enormous shop where Arsenal merchandise of every guise is available.

⊙ Islington

Gathered around attractive Upper St, Islington is generally portrayed in the press as a hotbed of champagne socialism, due in part to its association with New Labour in the 1990s (the Blairs famously lived here, along with other key figures). The area's gentrification is reflected in design stores, excellent eateries and a thriving theatre scene, but there are still enough raucous pubs and live-music venues to add some edge.

Less than 200 years ago, Islington was still a quiet village surrounded by farmland, set on the banks of the pleasantly languid New River (most of which is now below street level). Two medieval roads out of London met at what is now Islington High St: one led directly from the City and the other from the Smithfield meat market. Subsequently, Islington became an important rest stop, both for visitors to the City and for livestock. Inns sprung up in the area from the 10th century, the most famous of which was the Angel, which became particularly fashionable in the 18th century when it doubled as a theatre, starting a theatrical tradition that continues in Islington to this day.

Before 1855, Upper St was a veritable livestock highway, with an annual traffic flow that included 50,000 cattle and half a million sheep. By the end of that century, Islington had completely lost its rural feel under the weight of a soaring population. During WWII, 78,000 homes were damaged in the borough and 958 Islingtonians died in air raids.

ST MARY'S CHURCH
CHURCH

Map p434 (www.stmaryislington.org; Upper St, N1; ⊖Highbury & Islington) Although there has been a church on this site since the 12th century, the oldest part of the present-day St Mary's is the tower with its distinctive spire, dating from 1754. The rest of this elegant Georgian church was rebuilt after being destroyed during the Blitz. The surrounding churchyard is now a leafy little park.

CANONBURY SQUARE
SQUARE

Map p434 (Canonbury Rd, N1; ⊙8am-dusk; ⊖Highbury & Islington) A short walk from bustling Upper St, this pretty, park-like square was once home to authors Evelyn Waugh and George Orwell. The latter moved here with his family after his flat in St John's Wood was destroyed during the Blitz. His house at number 27b is marked by a blue plaque, while Waugh's residence at number 17 is unmarked. It's worth pausing in the park to soak up the atmosphere and peruse the dedications on the benches.

Just around the corner, on Canonbury Pl, is privately owned **Canonbury Tower**, a relic of the area's original manor house. Dating from 1509, it's known to have hosted such famous figures as Sir Francis Bacon and Queen Elizabeth I.

ESTORICK COLLECTION OF MODERN ITALIAN ART
GALLERY

Map p434 (www.estorickcollection.com; 39A Canonbury Sq, N1; adult/child £5/free; ⊙11am-6pm Wed-Sat, noon-5pm Sun; ⊖Highbury & Islington) Housed in a listed Georgian building, the Estorick is the only gallery in Britain devoted to Italian art, and one of the leading collections of Futurist painting in the world. The collection of paintings, drawings, etchings and sculpture was amassed by American writer and art dealer Eric Estorick and his wife, Salome. It includes works by such greats as Giacomo Balla, Umberto Boccioni, Gino Severini and Amedeo Modigliani.

TOP SIGHT
HIGHGATE CEMETERY

A Gothic wonderland of shrouded urns, obelisks, broken columns, sleeping angels, Egyptian-style tombs and overgrown graves, Highgate is a Victorian Valhalla spread over 20 wonderfully wild and atmospheric hectares. On the eastern side you can pay your respect to the graves of Karl Marx and Mary Ann Evans (better known as novelist George Eliot). The real highlight, however, is the overgrown **West Cemetery**, where a maze of winding paths leads to the Circle of Lebanon – rings of tombs flanking a circular path and topped with a majestic cedar of Lebanon.

Admission to the West Cemetery is by **guided tour** (adult/child £12/6; ⊙1.45pm Mon-Fri, every 30min 11am-3pm Sat & Sun Nov-Mar, to 4pm Apr-Oct) only; bookings are essential for weekday tours. Guides will explain the various symbols and point out the tombs of the eminent dead. Tours of the **East Cemetery** (adult/child £8/4) take place at 2pm on Saturdays.

Highgate remains a working cemetery – the most well-known recent internment was that of Russian dissident Alexander Litvinenko, who died under sinister circumstances in 2006 when the radioactive isotope Polonium 210 somehow made it into his tea in a Mayfair hotel.

DON'T MISS...

➔ Karl Marx's grave
➔ Tour of the West Cemetery
➔ Circle of Lebanon

PRACTICALITIES

➔ Map p433, D2
➔ www.highgatecemetery.org
➔ Swain's Lane, N6
➔ East Cemetery adult/child £4/free
➔ ⊙11am-5pm
➔ ⊖Archway

WORTH A DETOUR

MORE THAN JUST WALLPAPER

William Morris Gallery (☎020-8496 4390; www.wmgallery.org.uk; Lloyd Park, Forest Rd, E17; ⊙10am-5pm Wed-Sun; ⊜Walthamstow Central) Fans of Victoriana and the Arts and Crafts Movement should make time for this sensational little gallery. The beautiful Georgian mansion, located in Walthamstow in northeast London, was the family home of William Morris (1834–96), founder of interior-design company Morris & Co, famous far and wide for its patterned wallpaper. The gallery gives pride of place to his wide-ranging artistic endeavours, with a workshop explaining his production processes and an evocative re-creation of his shop.

The museum also covers Morris' activism and writing (for which he was more famous than his designs in his lifetime), providing a fully rounded portrait of the man. He was appalled by the consequences of industrialisation – on manufacturing processes, quality, people's living conditions and the environment – and he became a socialist in the 1880s, campaigning tirelessly against capitalism.

The gallery's shop sells beautiful, Morris-inspired design objects and the Tea Room in the glasshouse is the perfect place for a break or a light lunch. Children will love the interactive displays, as well as the play area in the lovely park at the back.

To get here from the tube station, turn right and then first left into Hoe St. Continue on this road for 600m and then turn left into Gaywood Rd. The gallery is across the road, at the end of the street.

Well-conceived special exhibitions have included many 20th-century art movements and lesser-known artists from Italy and beyond. There's also a garden cafe, a small shop and an extensive library.

✖ EATING

North London is full of eating gems, with historic pubs, smart cafes, market stalls and ethnically diverse restaurants. It's particularly good for vegetarians, with some excellent exclusively vegetarian and vegan establishments and plenty of others offering a good meat-free selection.

✖ King's Cross & Euston

FOODILIC   CAFE £
Map p434 (www.foodilic.com; 260 Pentonville Rd, N1; mains £3.50-7.50; ⊙7am-9pm Mon-Sat; ✐; ⊠King's Cross St Pancras) An enticing display of salads, quiches and *feuilletés* (savoury pastries) covers the counter, presenting plenty of difficult choices – but at these prices you can afford to pile your plate high. Seating is limited to half-a-dozen mushroom-shaped chunky wooden tables at the rear. Gnome chic, perhaps?

DIWANA BHEL POORI HOUSE   INDIAN, VEGETARIAN £
Map p436 (☎020-7387 5556; www.diwanabph. com; 121-123 Drummond St, NW1; mains £6.10-7.05; ⊙noon-11.30pm; ✐; ⊜Euston) One of the best Indian vegetarian restaurants in London, Diwana specialises in Bombay-style *bhel poori* (a tangy, soft and crunchy 'party mix' dish) and *dosas* (filled crispy pancakes made from rice flour). Solo diners should consider a *thali* (a complete meal consisting of lots of small dishes). The all-you-can-eat lunchtime buffet (£7) is legendary.

★GRAIN STORE   INTERNATIONAL ££
Map p434 (☎020-7324 4466; www.grainstore. com; 1-3 Stable St, N1C; weekend brunch £6-17, lunch £11-17, dinner £15-17; ⊙noon-2.30pm & 6-10.30pm Mon-Sat, 11am-3.45pm Sun; ✐; ⊜King's Cross St Pancras) Fresh seasonal vegetables take top billing at Bruno Loubet's bright and breezy Granary Sq restaurant. Meat does appear but it lurks coyly beneath leaves, or adds crunch to mashes. The creative menu gainfully plunders from numerous cuisines to produce dishes that are simultaneously healthy and delicious.

CARAVAN   INTERNATIONAL ££
Map p434 (☎020-7101 7661; www.caravankingscross.co.uk; 1 Granary Sq, N1C; mains £10-17; ⊙8am-10.30pm Mon-Fri, 10am-11.30pm Sat, 10am-4pm Sun; ⊛✐; ⊜King's Cross St Pancras)

Housed in the lofty Granary Building, Caravan is a vast, industrial-chic destination for tasty bites from around the world. You can opt for several small plates to share meze/tapas style, or stick to main-sized plates.

KARPO
EUROPEAN ££

Map p434 (⌨020-7843 2221; www.karpo.co.uk; 23-27 Euston Rd, NW1; mains £14-24, breakfast £7-15; ⊘7am or 8am-10pm; ⊜King's Cross St Pancras) There is something utterly refreshing about Karpo, with its bright, modern space, its 'living wall', gracious service and delicious, seasonal brasserie-style menu served round the clock. It all looks effortless. Breakfasts include all the usual eggy suspects, as well as smoothies and pancakes. On weekdays it offers a good-value set lunch (two courses and a drink for £19).

ADDIS
AFRICAN ££

Map p434 (www.addisrestaurant.co.uk; 40-42 Caledonian Rd, N1; mains £9-12; ⊘noon-midnight; ⬦; ⊜King's Cross St Pancras) Cheery Addis serves pungent Ethiopian dishes such as *ayeb be gomen* (cottage cheese with spinach and spices) and *fuul musalah* (crushed fava beans topped with feta cheese, falafel and sautéed in ghee), which are eaten on a platter-sized piece of soft but slightly elastic injera bread. The restaurant is normally full of African diners, which is always a good sign.

✖ Primrose Hill

MANNA
VEGAN ££

Map p436 (⌨020-7722 8028; www.mannav.com; 4 Erskine Rd, NW3; mains £12-14; ⊘noon-3pm & 6.30-10pm Tue-Sat, noon-8.30pm Sun; ⬦; ⊜Chalk Farm) Tucked away on a side street, this upmarket little place does a brisk trade in inventive vegan cooking. The menu features mouth-watering, beautifully presented dishes incorporating elements of Californian, Mexican and Asian cuisine with nods to the raw-food trend.

✖ Camden Town

★CHIN CHIN LABS
ICE CREAM £

Map p436 (www.chinchinlabs.com; 49-50 Camden Lock Pl, NW1; ice cream £4-5; ⊘noon-7pm Tue-Sun; ⊜Camden Town) This is food chemistry at its absolute best. Chefs prepare the ice-cream mixture and freeze it on the spot by adding liquid nitrogen. Flavours change

regularly and match the seasons (spiced hot cross bun, passionfruit and coconut etc). Sauces and toppings are equally creative. It's directly opposite the giant Gilgamesh statue inside Camden Lock Market.

★MARKET
MODERN BRITISH ££

Map p436 (⌨020-7267 9700; www.marketrestaurant.co.uk; 43 Parkway, NW1; 2-course lunch £10, mains £15-19; ⊘noon-2.30pm & 6-10.30pm Mon-Sat, 11am-3pm Sun; ⊜Camden Town) This fabulous restaurant is an ode to great, simple British food, with a measure of French sophistication thrown in. The light and airy space (bare brick walls, steel tables and basic wooden chairs) reflects this stripped-back approach.

NAMAASTE KITCHEN
INDIAN ££

Map p436 (⌨020-7485 5977; www.namaastekitchen.co.uk; 64 Parkway, NW1; mains £7.50-19; ⊘noon-3pm & 5.30-11pm Mon-Fri, noon-11pm Sat & Sun; ⬦; ⊜Camden Town) Although everything's of a high standard, if there's one thing you should try at Namaaste, it's the kebab platter: the meat and fish coming out of the kitchen grill are beautifully tender and incredibly flavoursome. The bread basket is another hit, with specialities such as the spiced *missi roti* making a nice change from the usual naans.

YORK & ALBANY
MODERN BRITISH ££

Map p436 (⌨020-7388 3344; www.gordonramsay.com/yorkandalbany; 127-129 Parkway, NW1; mains £14-24, breakfast £5-9.50, 2-/3-course lunch & early dinner £21/24; ⊘7am-3pm & 6-11pm Mon-Sat, 7am-9pm Sun; ⬦; ⊜Camden Town) Part of chef Gordon Ramsay's culinary empire, this chic hotel brasserie serves British classics in its light-filled dining room. You can also grab a wood-fired pizza at the bar (£11.50).

✖ Kentish Town

DIRTY BURGER
BURGERS £

Map p433 (www.eatdirtyburger.com; 79 Highgate Rd, NW5; burgers £5-8; ⊘noon-midnight Mon-Fri, 9am-1am Sat, 9am-11pm Sun; ⊜Kentish Town) Apart from eggs with sausages or bacon until 11am, this chic shack serves nothing but burgers, fries and milkshakes. And what burgers: thick, juicy and horribly messy with mustard, gherkin and cheese. It's a little hard to find, hidden around the corner from Pizza East at the entrance to Highgate Studios.

✖ Hampstead

WOODLANDS   INDIAN, VEGETARIAN £
Map p433 (☑020-7794 3080; www.woodland-srestaurant.co.uk; 102 Heath St, NW3; dishes £5-8, thali £19; ⊘noon-2.45pm Fri-Sun, 6-10.45pm Tue-Sun; ✈; ⊖Hampstead) Don't expect cutting-edge cuisine or faultless service, but this south Indian restaurant is your best bet for an affordable vegetarian meal in Hampstead. Its rallying cry is 'Let Vegetation Feed the Nation'.

WELLS TAVERN   GASTROPUB ££
Map p433 (☑020-7794 3785; www.thewellshampstead.co.uk; 30 Well Walk, NW3; mains £12-21; ⊘noon-3pm & 7-10pm; ⊖Hampstead) This popular gastropub has a surprisingly modern interior, given its traditional exterior. The menu is proper posh English pub grub – Cumberland sausages, mash and onion gravy, or just a full roast with all the trimmings. At the weekend you'll need to fight to get a table or, more wisely, book ahead.

STAG   GASTROPUB ££
Map p433 (☑020-7722 2646; www.thestaghampstead.com; 67 Fleet Rd, NW3; mains £9.50-18; ⊘noon-11pm; ⊖Hampstead Heath) Although the Stag is a fantastic pub for craft beer, it's known in North London for its outstanding food – the Sunday roast and beef-and-ale pie in particular. The summer BBQ in the garden is another delight. The only bum note is that service can be slow.

GAUCHO   SOUTH AMERICAN £££
Map p433 (☑020-7431 8222; www.gauchorestaurants.co.uk; 64 Heath St, NW3; mains £15-60, 2-/3-course lunch £23-26; ⊘noon-11pm Mon-Sat, 10am-11.30pm Sun; ⊖Hampstead) Carnivores, rejoice; this is one of the finest places for steak in London. There are several branches of this Argentinian grill across the capital, but this one has the advantage of being less busy than its counterparts. We love the glitzy decor, too: shiny black walls and cowhide.

✖ Barnsbury

★**ROOTS AT N1**   INDIAN ££
Map p434 (☑020-7697 4488; www.rootsatn1.com; 115 Hemingford Rd, N1; mains £16-21; ⊘6-10pm Tue-Sun; ⊖Caledonian Rd & Barnsbury) Hailing from Uttarakhand in northern India, and having done time in the top hotel restaurants in India and London, the chefs behind Roots have transformed this former pub into one of London's best modern Indian restaurants. Despite the name, it's not shackled by tradition, with some Mediterranean and Chinese flavours creeping into the mix.

IBERIA   GEORGIAN ££
Map p434 (☑020-7700 7750; www.iberiarestaurant.co.uk; 294-296 Caledonian Rd, N1; mains £8.90-17; ⊘5-11pm Tue-Fri, 1-11pm Sat, 1-9pm Sun; ⊖Caledonian Rd & Barnsbury) In an insalubrious strip of affordable ethnic eateries,

CAMDEN & NORTH LONDON EATING

LOCAL KNOWLEDGE

WALKING ALONG REGENT'S CANAL

Regent's Canal (Map p436) To escape the crowded streets and enjoy a picturesque, waterside angle on North London, take to the canals that once played such a vital role in the transport of goods across the capital. The towpath of the Regent's Canal also makes an excellent shortcut across North London, either on foot or by bike.

In full, the ribbon of water runs nine miles from Little Venice (where it connects with the Grand Union Canal) to the Thames at Limehouse, but you can make do with walking from Little Venice to Camden Town in less than an hour, passing Regent's Park and London Zoo, as well as beautiful villas designed by architect John Nash and redevelopments of old industrial buildings. Allow 25 to 30 minutes between Little Venice and Regent's Park, and 15 to 20 minutes between Regent's Park and Camden Town. There are plenty of well-signed exits along the way.

If you decide to continue on, it's worth stopping at the **London Canal Museum** (p237) in King's Cross to learn more about the canal's history. Shortly afterwards you'll hit the 878m-long Islington Tunnel and have to take to the roads for a spell. After joining it again near Colebrooke Row, you can follow the water all the way to the Thames at Limehouse Basin, or divert onto the Hertford Union Canal at **Victoria Park** (p219) and head to **Queen Elizabeth Olympic Park** (p221).

WORTH A DETOUR

THREE GOOD REASONS TO GET STOKED

East of Holloway and north of Dalston, **Stoke Newington** is a step too far off the beaten track for most visitors to London, which is a shame, as there are a few excellent reasons to seek it out. Set on the old Roman road heading north from the City of London, Stokey (as the locals call it) was a small village on the edge of the woods where travellers might stop to water their horses right up until Tudor times. Despite being gobbled up by London in the intervening centuries, it still retains traces of a village feel.

The best way to get here is to catch any bus heading north on Kingsland High St from Dalston, or to get a tube on the Piccadilly Line to Manor House and then switch to the 73 bus.

Abney Park Cemetery (www.abneypark.org; Stoke Newington Church St, N16; ⊗8am-dusk; ⬛73) This enchanting place was bought and developed by a private firm in 1840 as a burial ground and arboretum catering for central London's overflow. It was a dissenters (ie non–Church of England) cemetery and many of the most influential Presbyterians, Quakers and Baptists are buried here, including the Salvation Army founder, William Booth. The derelict chapel at its centre could be right out of a horror film, and the atmosphere of the whole place is nothing short of magical.

After being neglected for several decades, during which time it turned into a delightfully overgrown ruin and developed a reputation as a gay cruising ground, it's care was taken over by a charitable trust in 1991. It's now a managed wilderness, providing an important urban habitat for birds, butterflies and bugs – if you're very lucky you might spot tawny owls or sparrowhawks.

The trust, based in the wonderful Egyptian-style entrance on Stoke Newington High St, hosts events in the cemetery and offers free guided tours (donations welcome) at 2pm on the first Sunday of the month. In summer there are also themed tours visiting the graves of the Victorian era's biggest music-hall stars (check the website for details).

Rasa (⌕020-7249 0344; www.rasarestaurants.com; 55 Stoke Newington Church St, N16; mains £4.50-6.50; ⊗6-10.45pm Mon-Fri, noon-3pm & 6-11pm Sat & Sun; ⯒; ⬛73) The flagship restaurant of the Rasa chain, this south Indian vegetarian eatery is Stoke Newington's best-known restaurant. Friendly service, a calm atmosphere, reasonable prices and outstanding food from the Indian state of Kerala are its distinctive features. The multi-course Keralan Feast (£16) is for ravenous tummies only.

Auld Shillelagh (www.theauldshillelagh.co.uk; 105 Stoke Newington Church St, N16; ⊗11am-midnight; ⬛73) We're going out on a limb and calling this London's best Irish pub. The staff are sharp, the Guinness is good and the live entertainment is frequent and varied (from trad bands to rappers, sometimes even both at once). It's a great spot to watch the rugby or football and there's a beer garden out the back.

Iberia stands out for its pleasant surrounds, friendly service and excellent, traditional Georgian fare. If you're not familiar with the cuisine, expect a meaty morph of Russian and Middle Eastern flavours.

✕ Islington

CHILANGO MEXICAN £

Map p434 (www.chilango.co.uk; 27 Upper St, N1; burritos & tacos £6-7; ⊗11.30am-10pm; ⯒; ⊖Angel) The good value and tastiness of Chilango's Mexican fare is no secret among Islingtonians on a budget. Burritos come bursting to the seams with your choice of meat (chicken, prawns, pork or beef), beans, salad, rice and sauces. Vegetarians are well catered for, too. Eat in the bright, colourful interior or take it away.

★OTTOLENGHI BAKERY, MEDITERRANEAN ££

Map p434 (⌕020-7288 1454; www.ottolenghi. co.uk; 287 Upper St, N1; breakfast £6-9.50, lunch £12-17, dinner £9-13; ⊗8am-10.30pm Mon-Sat, 9am-7pm Sun; ⯒; ⊖Highbury & Islington) Mountains of meringues tempt you through the door, where a sumptuous array

A NORTH LONDON PLAYLIST

➡ Madness – *Driving In My Car* (1982), *NW5* (2009)

➡ The Smiths – *London* (1987)

➡ Pet Shop Boys – *King's Cross* (1987)

➡ Blur – *For Tomorrow (Visit To Primrose Hill Extended)* (1993)

➡ Morrissey – *Come Back to Camden* (2004)

➡ Babyshambles – *Pentonville* (2005)

of baked goods and fresh salads greets you. Meals are as light and bright as the brilliantly white interior design, with a strong influence from the eastern Mediterranean.

YIPIN CHINA
CHINESE ££

Map p434 (☑020-7354 3388; www.yipinchina. co.uk; 72 Liverpool Rd, N1; mains £8-22; ☻noon-11pm; ☑; ☻Angel) The kind of Chinese restaurant that's usually full of Chinese people (ie the good kind), Yipin specialises in the spicy, fragrant, colourful cuisine of Hunan, but there are plenty of fiery Sichuanese and familiar Cantonese dishes to choose from, too. The lengthy picture menu makes the choosing (slightly) easier.

TRULLO
ITALIAN ££

Map p434 (☑020-7226 2733; www.trullorestaurant.com; 300-302 St Paul's Rd, N1; mains £16-22; ☻12.30-3pm daily, 6-10.30pm Mon-Sat; ☻Highbury & Islington) Trullo's homemade pasta is delicious, but the main attraction here is the charcoal grill, which churns out the likes of succulent Italian-style pork chops, steaks and fish. The service is excellent, too.

SMOKEHOUSE
BARBECUE ££

Map p434 (☑020-7354 1144; www.smokehouseislington.co.uk; 63-69 Canonbury Rd, N1; mains £16-18; ☻6-11pm Mon-Fri, 11am-midnight Sat, noon-10.30pm Sun; ☜; ☻Highbury & Islington) In this lovely, light-filled boozer, elegantly turned out in dark wood and whitewashed walls, you'll find a meaty menu of international dishes, all imbued – as the name suggests – with a smoky flavour. Ingredients are carefully sourced and skilfully combined, and there is a particularly extensive beer list. The little leafy garden is a boon in the warmer months.

KIPFERL
AUSTRIAN ££

Map p434 (www.kipferl.co.uk; 20 Camden Passage, N1; mains £10-14; ☻10am-6pm Mon, 9am-10pm Tue-Sun; ☻Angel) Part cafe, part restaurant and totally Austrian, Kipferl serves classic comfort food such as Weiner schnitzel, *kasespatzle* (egg noodles with cheese) and spinach dumplings. Otherwise just sidle in and choose a coffee from the 'colour palette' menu typical of Viennese cafes, and pick from the mouth-watering selection of cakes (Sacher torte, *apfelstrudel* etc).

🍷 DRINKING & NIGHTLIFE

Camden Town is one of North London's favoured drinking areas, with more bars and pubs pumping out music than you could ever manage to crawl between. The hills of Hampstead are a real treat for old-time-pub aficionados, while Islington is known for theatre pubs and tucked-away wine and cocktail bars. As for King's Cross, there are new places opening all the time, many in converted Victorian buildings.

🍷 King's Cross & Euston

⭐DRINK, SHOP & DO
BAR

Map p434 (☑020-7278 4335; www.drinkshopdo. com; 9 Caledonian Rd, N1; ☻10.30am-midnight Mon-Thu, to 2am Fri, 9am-2am Sat, 10.30am-10pm Sun; ☜; ☻King's Cross St Pancras) This kooky little outlet will not be pigeonholed. As its name suggests, it is many things to many people: a bar, a cafe, an activities centre, a gift store, a disco even. But the idea is that there will always be drinking (be it tea or gin), music and activities – anything from dancing to building Lego robots.

⭐EUSTON TAP
BAR

Map p434 (☑020-3137 8837; www.eustontap. com; 190 Euston Rd, NW1; ☻noon-11pm; ☻Euston) Part of a twinset with the **Cider Tap**, this specialist boozery inhabits a monumental stone structure on the approach to Euston Station. Craft beer devotees can choose between eight cask ales, 20 keg beers and 150 by the bottle. Cider rules over the road. Grab a seat on the pavement, or take the tight spiral staircase upstairs.

★ BAR PEPITO — WINE BAR

Map p434 (www.barpepito.co.uk; 3 Varnishers Yard, The Regent's Quarter, N1; ⊙5pm-midnight Mon-Sat; ⊖King's Cross St Pancras) This tiny, intimate Andalusian bodega specialises in sherry and tapas. Novices fear not: the staff are on hand to advise. They're also experts at food pairings (top-notch ham and cheese selections). To go the whole hog, try a tasting flight of three selected sherries with snacks to match.

CAMINO — BAR

Map p434 (www.camino.uk.com; 3 Varnishers Yard, The Regent's Quarter, N1; ⊙noon-midnight; ⊛; ⊖King's Cross St Pancras) Festive Camino is popular with London's Spanish community and therefore feels quite authentic. Drinks, too, are representative of what you'd find in Spain: cava, Estrella on tap and a long, all-Spanish wine list. It's a brilliant place to watch football – international games in particular – and DJs hit the turntables on weekends. In summer, the courtyard gets absolutely crammed.

BIG CHILL HOUSE — PUB, CLUB

Map p434 (www.wearebigchill.com; 257-259 Pentonville Rd, N1; ⊙9am-midnight Mon-Thu, to 3am Fri, 11am-3am Sat, 11am-midnight Sun; ⊛; ⊖King's Cross St Pancras) Come the weekend, the only remotely chilled-out space in this large, buzzy Victorian pub is its first-rate and generously proportioned rooftop terrace. It's run by the people behind the Big Chill record label, so it can be counted on for a varied roster of live music and DJs. The sound system is fantastic and entry is free most nights.

BOOKING OFFICE BAR & RESTAURANT — BAR

Map p434 (www.bookingofficebar.com; St Pancras Renaissance London Hotel, Euston Rd, NW1; ⊙6.30am-10pm Mon-Thu, to 3am Fri, 11am-midnight Sat & Sun; ⊖King's Cross St Pancras) As the name suggests this was, in a former life, the booking office of St Pancras train station. The space has been transformed into a showstopping bar, with dizzyingly high ceilings and prices to match. The cocktail list takes inspiration from the architecture, featuring plenty of popular Victorian ingredients such as tea, orange peel, elderflower cordial and gin.

6 ST CHAD'S PLACE — BAR

Map p434 (www.6stchadsplace.com; 6 St Chad's Pl, WC1X; ⊙8am-11pm Mon-Fri; ⊛; ⊖King's Cross

St Pancras) Once a mechanic's workshop, this Victorian warehouse has scrubbed up very well indeed. It tends to be favoured by local businesspeople for informal meetings during the day, but the same customers let their hair down here in the evening. DJs rev things up on Friday nights.

EGG LDN — CLUB

Map p434 (www.egglondon.co.uk; 200 York Way, N7; ⊙10pm-6am Tue, 11pm-8am Fri, 11pm-10am Sat; ⊖Caledonian Rd & Barnsbury) Egg has a superb layout with two vast exposed-concrete rooms, a wooden loft space, a garden and a roof terrace. It specialises in house and techno and attracts some heavyweight DJs, particularly on Saturday nights. At weekends, it runs a free shuttle bus from 11pm onwards from outside 68 York Way.

⚑ Primrose Hill

QUEEN'S — PUB

Map p436 (www.thequeensprimrosehill.co.uk; 49 Regent's Park Rd, NW1; ⊙11am-11pm; ⊛⊡; ⊖Chalk Farm) Perhaps because this is Primrose Hill, the Queen's is a bit more cafe-like than your average pub. Still, it's a good one, with a creditable wine and beer selection and, more importantly, plenty of people-watching to do while sipping your pint – Jude Law has been known to come here for a tipple.

⚑ Camden Town

★ PROUD CAMDEN — BAR

Map p436 (www.proudcamden.com; Stables Market, Chalk Farm Rd, NW1; free-£15; ⊙10.30am-1.30am Mon-Sat, noon-midnight Sun; ⊖Chalk Farm) Proud occupies a former horse hospital within Stables Market, with private booths in the stalls, ice-cool rock photography on the walls and a kooky garden terrace complete with a hot tub. It's also one of Camden's best music venues, with live bands and DJs most nights.

★ DUBLIN CASTLE — PUB

Map p436 (www.thedublincastle.com; 94 Parkway, NW1; ⊙1pm-2am; ⊖Camden Town) There's live punk or alternative bands most nights in this comfortingly grungy pub's back room (cover charges are usually between £4.50 and £7). DJs take over after the bands on Friday, Saturday and Sunday nights.

★EDINBORO CASTLE   PUB

Map p436 (www.edinborocastlepub.co.uk; 57 Mornington Tce, NW1; ⊘noon-11pm; 🕾; ⊖Camden Town) The large and relaxed Edinboro has a refined atmosphere, gorgeous furniture designed for slumping, a fine bar and a full menu. The highlight, however, is the huge beer garden, complete with a BBQ and foosball table and adorned with coloured lights on long summer evenings.

LOCK TAVERN   PUB

Map p436 (www.lock-tavern.com; 35 Chalk Farm Rd, NW1; ⊘noon-midnight; ⊖Chalk Farm) An institution in Camden, the black-clad Lock Tavern rocks for several reasons: it's cosy inside; there's an ace roof terrace from where you can watch the market throngs as well as a rear beer garden; the beer is plentiful; and it also has a roll call of guest bands and DJs at the weekend to rev things up.

BLUES KITCHEN   PUB

Map p436 (☑020-7387 5277; www.theblueskitchen.com; 111-113 Camden High St, NW1; ⊘noon-midnight Mon-Thu, to 3am Fri, 10am-3.30am Sat, 10am-1am Sun; ⊖Camden Town) The Blues Kitchen's recipe for success is simple: select brilliant blues bands, host them in a fabulous bar, make it (mostly) free and offer some fabulous food and drink. Which means that the crowds keep on comin'. There's live music every night – anything from folk to rock 'n' roll – and blues jams from 7pm on Sundays.

BREWDOG CAMDEN   BAR

Map p436 (www.brewdog.com; 113 Bayham St, NW1; ⊘noon-11.30pm; ⊖Camden Town) The hair of this particular dog is craft beer, with around 20 different brews on tap. BrewDog's own brewery is up in Scotland, but more than half of the bar's stock is comprised of guest beers sourced from boutique breweries the world over.

♀ Hampstead

Hampstead is *the* place to go for historic, charming old pubs where Sunday lunch always seems to turn into an afternoon.

★HOLLY BUSH   PUB

Map p433 (www.hollybushhampstead.co.uk; 22 Holly Mount, NW3; ⊘noon-11pm; 🕾🍴; ⊖Hampstead) This beautiful Georgian pub has an antique interior, a secluded hilltop location, open fires in winter and a knack for making you stay longer than you had intended. Set above Heath St, it's reached via the Holly Bush Steps.

SPANIARD'S INN   PUB

Map p433 (www.thespaniardshampstead.co.uk; Spaniards Rd, NW3; ⊘noon-11pm; 🚍210) Dating from 1585, this historic tavern has more character than a West End musical. It was highwayman Dick Turpin's hang-out between robbery escapades, but it's also served as a watering hole for more savoury characters such as Dickens, Shelley, Keats and Byron. It even gets a mention in *Dracula*. There's a big, blissful garden that gets crammed at weekends.

GARDEN GATE   PUB

Map p433 (www.thegardengatehampstead.co.uk; 14 South End Rd, NW3; ⊘noon-11pm Mon-Fri, 10.30am-midnight Sat, 10.30am-10.30pm Sun; 🕾; ⊖Hampstead Heath) At the bottom of the heath hides this gem of a pub, a 19th-century cottage with a gorgeous beer garden. The interior is wonderfully cosy, with dark-wood tables, upholstered chairs and an assortment of distressed sofas. It serves Pimms and lemonade in summer and mulled wine in winter, both ideal after a long walk. The food's good, too.

♀ Highgate

FLASK TAVERN   PUB

Map p433 (www.theflaskhighgate.com; 77 Highgate West Hill, N6; ⊘noon-11pm; 🕾; ⊖Highgate) Charming nooks and crannies, an old circular bar and an enticing beer garden make this 1663 pub the perfect place for a pint en route between Hampstead Heath and Highgate Cemetery. In the winter, huddle down in the cosy interior and enjoy the Sunday roast and open fires. It's like a village pub in the city.

♀ Islington

THE BULL   PUB

Map p434 (www.thebullislington.co.uk; 100 Upper St, N1; ⊘noon-midnight; 🕾; ⊖Angel) One of Islington's liveliest pubs, the Bull serves a large range of draught lager, real ales, fruit beers, ciders and wheat beer, plus a good wine selection. The mezzanine is generally a little quieter than downstairs, although on weekend nights you'll generally struggle to find a seat.

PUBLIC HOUSE BAR

Map p434 (www.boutiquepubs.com; 54 Islington Park St, N1; ◷5pm-midnight; ⊜Highbury & Islington) This handsome bar adds a splash of boudoir/burlesque glam to Islington's drinking scene. Everything is pretty fabulous, from the carefully prepared cocktails (all seasonal) to the gastropub menu and the long list of after-dinner drinks (brandies, whiskies, dessert wines).

THE CASTLE PUB

Map p434 (www.geronimo-inns.co.uk/thecastle; 54 Pentonville Rd, N1; ◷11am-11pm; 🛜; ⊜Angel) A gorgeous, boutique pub with a winning formula of snazzy decor (wooden floors, designer wallpaper, soft furnishings, large maps on the walls), good gastropub food, a rotating selection of craft beers and, to top it all off, a wonderful roof terrace.

BARRIO NORTH BAR

Map p434 (www.barrionorth.com; 45 Essex Rd, N1; ◷5pm-midnight Sun-Thu, to 3am Fri & Sat; ⊜Angel) A good bet for a fun night out, this cocktail/DJ bar's atmosphere, decor and music are a celebration of all things Latino, with a hint of London and New York thrown in. If you can, grab a seat in the fairy-lit cut-out caravan. 'Amigo hour' is between 5pm and 8pm.

69 COLEBROOKE ROW COCKTAIL BAR

Map p434 (www.69colebrookerow.com; 69 Colebrooke Row, N1; ◷5pm-midnight Sun-Thu, to 2am Fri & Sat; ⊜Angel) Also known as 'the bar with no name', this tiny establishment may be nothing much to look at, but it has a stellar reputation for its cocktails (with prices to match). The seasonal drinks menu is steeped in ambitious flavours and blends, with classic drinks for more conservative palates. It also runs cocktail masterclasses (£40).

☆ ENTERTAINMENT

North London is the home of indie rock and many a famous band started out playing in the area's grungy bars. You can be sure to find live music of some kind every night of the week. Venues such as Scala, KOKO, the Jazz Cafe, **Barfly and the Electric Ballroom are multi-purpose, with gigs in the first part of the evening (generally around 7pm or 8pm), followed by club nights around midnight. Be sure to also check out what's on at Proud Camden (p249), the Lock Tavern (p250), the Dublin Castle (p249) and the Blues Kitchen (p250).**

★CECIL SHARP HOUSE TRADITIONAL MUSIC

Map p436 (www.cecilsharphouse.org; 2 Regent's Park Rd, NW1; ⊜Camden Town) If you've ever fancied clog stamping, hanky waving or bell jingling, this is the place for you. Home to the English Folk Dance and Song Society, this institute keeps all manner of wacky folk traditions alive, with performances and classes held in its gorgeous mural-covered Kennedy Hall. The dance classes are oodles of fun; no experience necessary.

★SCALA LIVE MUSIC

Map p434 (📞020-7833 2022; www.scala-london. co.uk; 275 Pentonville Rd, N1; ⊜King's Cross St Pancras) Opened in 1920 as a salubrious golden-age cinema, Scala slipped into porn-movie hell in the 1970s only to be reborn as a club and live-music venue in the noughties. It's one of the best places in London to catch an intimate gig and a great dance space too, hosting a diverse range of club nights.

★KOKO LIVE MUSIC

Map p436 (www.koko.uk.com; 1a Camden High St, NW1; ⊜Mornington Cres) Once the legendary Camden Palace, where Charlie Chaplin, the Goons and the Sex Pistols all performed, KOKO is maintaining its reputation as one of London's better gig venues. The theatre has a dance floor and decadent balconies and attracts an indie crowd with Club NME on Friday. There are live bands almost every night of the week.

★JAZZ CAFE LIVE MUSIC

Map p436 (📞0844 847 2514; www.thejazz-cafelondon.com; 5 Parkway, NW1; ⊜Camden Town) Although its name would have you think that jazz is this venue's main staple, it's only a small part of what's on the menu. The intimate club-like space also serves up funk, hip hop, R&B and soul, with big-name acts regularly dropping in. The Saturday club night, 'I love the 80s v I love the 90s', is a long-standing favourite.

ANGEL COMEDY
COMEDY

Map p434 (www.angelcomedy.co.uk; 2 Camden Passage, N1; ◷shows 8pm; ⊖Angel) **FREE** There's free comedy every night (donations are gratefully received, however) at this great little comedy club upstairs at the Camden Head. Monday is improv night and on any other evening you might get anything from a new act to a famous name road testing new material; check the website for listings.

UNION CHAPEL
CONCERT VENUE

Map p434 (www.unionchapel.org.uk; 19 Compton Tce, N1; ⊖Highbury & Islington) One of London's most atmospheric and individual music venues, the Union Chapel is an old church that still holds services as well as concerts – mainly acoustic – and the monthly **Live At The Chapel** comedy club. It was here that Björk performed one of her most memorable concerts to a candlelit audience in 1999.

BARFLY
LIVE MUSIC

Map p436 (www.thebarflylondon.com; 49 Chalk Farm Rd, NW1; ⊖Chalk Farm) This typically grungy indie-rock venue is well known for hosting small-time artists looking for their big break. The venue is small, so you'll feel like the band is playing just for you and your mates. There are club nights most nights of the week. Jubilee on Fridays is probably the best, with a mix of live bands and DJs.

THE FORUM
CONCERT VENUE

Map p433 (www.theforumlondon.com; 9-17 Highgate Rd, NW5; tickets from £10; ⊖Kentish Town) You can find your way to the Forum – once the famous Town & Country Club – by the ticket touts that line the way from Kentish Town tube station. This art deco former cinema (built 1934) is spacious yet intimate enough for bands and comedians starting to break through (or big names a little past their prime).

ROUNDHOUSE
CONCERT VENUE

Map p436 (www.roundhouse.org.uk; Chalk Farm Rd, NW1; ⊖Chalk Farm) Built as a railway shed in 1847, this unusual round building became an arts centre in the 1960s and hosted many a legendary band before falling into near-dereliction in 1983. Its 21st-century resurrection has been a great success and it now hosts everything from big-name concerts to dance, circus, stand-up comedy, poetry slam and improvisation sessions.

ELECTRIC BALLROOM
LIVE MUSIC

Map p436 (⌨020-7485 9006; www.electricballroom.co.uk; 184 Camden High St, NW1; ⊖Camden Town) One of Camden's historic venues, the Electric Ballroom has been entertaining North Londoners since 1938. Many great bands and musicians have played here, from Blur to Paul McCartney, The Clash and U2. There are constantly changing club nights on Fridays, while on Saturdays it hosts Shake, a crowd pleaser featuring dance anthems from the '70s, '80s and '90s.

REGENT'S PARK OPEN AIR THEATRE
THEATRE

Map p436 (⌨0844 826 4242; www.openairtheatre.org; Queen Mary's Gardens, NW1; ◷May-Sep; ⊖Baker St) A popular summertime fixture in London, this 1250-seat outdoor auditorium plays host to four productions a year – usually famous plays (Shakespeare often features) and the occasional musical.

HAMPSTEAD THEATRE
THEATRE

(⌨020-7722 9301; www.hampsteadtheatre.com; Eton Ave, NW3; ⊖Swiss Cottage) The Hampstead is famed for staging new writing and taking on emerging directors. It was an early champion of Harold Pinter, which shows it knows a good thing when it sees one.

KING'S HEAD THEATRE
THEATRE

Map p434 (www.kingsheadtheatre.com; 115 Upper St, N1; ⊖Angel) This stalwart pub theatre hosts new plays and musicals, along with revivals of classics. Classical music and opera are part of the mix, too.

ALMEIDA
THEATRE

Map p434 (⌨020-7359 4404; www.almeida.co.uk; Almeida St, N1; ⊖Highbury & Islington) Housed in a Grade II–listed Victorian building, this plush theatre can be relied on for imaginative programming.

🛍 SHOPPING

Shopping in Camden Town is all about market stalls, Doc Martin boots and secondhand clothes. Islington is great for antiques, quality vintage clothes and design objects.

★**CAMDEN PASSAGE MARKET** ANTIQUES
Map p434 (www.camdenpassageislington.co.uk; Camden Passage, N1; ◷8am-6pm Wed & Sat, 11am-6pm Sun-Tue, Thu & Fri; ⊖Angel) Not to

WHICH CAMDEN MARKET?

....

Camden Market (p240) comprises four distinct market areas. They tend to sell similar kinds of things (numerous T-shirts with variations on the 'Keep Calm & Carry On' theme, for instance), although each has its own specialities and quirks.

Stables Market (Map p436; Chalk Farm Rd, NW1; ◎10am-6pm; ◉Chalk Farm) Connected to the Lock Market, the Stables is the best part of the Camden Market complex, with antiques, Asian artefacts, rugs, retro furniture and clothing.

Camden Lock Market (Map p436; www.camdenlockmarket.com; 54-56 Camden Lock Pl, NW1; ◎10am-6pm; ◉Camden Town) Right next to the canal lock, this is the original Camden Market, with diverse food stalls, ceramics, furniture, oriental rugs, musical instruments and clothes.

Camden Lock Village (Map p436; Chalk Farm Rd, NW1; ◎10am-6pm; ◉Camden Town) Stretched along the canal on the opposite side of the road from the Lock Market, this part of Camden Market is lined with stalls selling bric-a-brac. There are controversial plans to turn it into the 'Borough Market of North London' as part of a development involving the building of offices and 170 apartments in a large building backing the site.

Buck Street Market (Map p436; cnr Buck & Camden High Sts, NW1; ◎9am-5.30pm; ◉Camden Town) While it bills itself as 'The Camden Market', this little covered market isn't part of the main complex. Stalls sell mainly T-shirts, jewellery and tourist tat. It's the closest market to the station, but the least interesting.

be confused with Camden Market, Camden Passage is a pretty cobbled lane in Islington lined with antique stores, vintage clothing boutiques and cafes. Scattered along the lane are four separate market areas devoted to antique curios and whatnots. The main market days are Wednesday and Sunday. Stallholders know their stuff, so bargains are rare.

★**ANNIE'S VINTAGE COSTUME & TEXTILES** VINTAGE
Map p434 (www.anniesvintageclothing.co.uk; 12 Camden Passage, N1; ◎11am-6pm Sun-Tue, Thu & Fri 8am-6pm Wed & Sat; ◉Angel) One of London's most enchanting vintage shops, Annie's has costumes to make you look like Greta Garbo. Many a famous designer has come here for inspiration, so you might also get to do some celebrity spotting.

HARRY POTTER SHOP AT PLATFORM 9¾ CHILDREN
Map p434 (www.harrypotterplatform934.com; King's Cross Station, N1; ◎8am-10pm; ◉King's Cross St Pancras) Diagon Alley is impossible to find, so if your junior witches and wizards have come to London seeking a wand of their own, apparate the family directly to King's Cross Station instead. This little wood-panelled store also stocks jumpers sporting the colours of Hogwarts' four houses (Gryffindor having pride of place) and assorted merchandise.

TWENTYTWENTYONE GIFTS
Map p434 (www.twentytwentyone.com; 274 Upper St, N1; ◎10am-6pm; ◉Highbury & Islington) Crammed with exceedingly cool, mainly northern European design objects, this is a great spot for quirky gifts or high-quality homewares. A £45 Jan Kochanski dustpan and broom, perhaps?

GILL WING GIFTS
Map p434 (www.gillwing.co.uk; 194-195 Upper St, N1; ◎9am-6pm; ◉Highbury & Islington) Inhabiting multiple stores on Upper St, Gill Wing sells shoes (at number 192), kitchenware (at 190) and jewellery (at 182), but our favourite is its flagship gift shop. It's basically impossible to walk past without doing a double take at the colourful window full of glasses, cards, children's toys and other eclectic titbits.

EXCLUSIVO FASHION
Map p433 (2 Flask Walk, NW3; ◎10.30am-6pm; ◉Hampstead) If you've ever dreamed of owning a pair of Manolo Blahniks or a Pucci dress but have always balked at the price, Exclusivo might just be your chance. This tiny shop specialises in top-quality second-hand designer garments and accessories, and while prices remain high (£300 for a dress, for instance), they are a fraction of the original price tag.

CAMDEN & NORTH LONDON SHOPPING

WORTH A DETOUR

DILLY-DALLY AT ALLY PALLY

Alexandra Palace (www.alexandrapalace.com; Alexandra Palace Way, N22; ®Alexandra Palace) Built in 1873 as North London's answer to Crystal Palace, this grand construction sits high on a hill overlooking the city, surrounded by 196 hectares of parkland. Don't be fooled into imagining royal connections; 'Ally Pally' (as it's affectionately known) is a people's palace, used for conferences, exhibitions, festivals and the occasional rock gig and club night. Locals come to enjoy the sweeping views, whizz around the indoor ice-skating rink and to fondle veggies at the Sunday farmers market.

The building suffered the ignoble fate of burning to the ground only 16 days after opening. Encouraged by attendance figures, investors decided to rebuild and it reopened just two years later. During WWI it housed German prisoners of war and in 1936 was the scene of the world's first TV transmission – a variety show called *Here's Looking at You*. It burned down again in 1980 but was rebuilt for the second time and reopened in 1988.

HOUSMANS BOOKS
Map p434 (www.housmans.com; 5 Caledonian Rd, N1; ⊙10am-6.30pm Mon-Sat, noon-6pm Sun; ⊖King's Cross St Pancras) If you're searching for hard-to-find tomes on a progressive, radical, pacifist, feminist, socialist or communist theme, this long-standing, not-for-profit bookshop is your best bet.

🏃 SPORTS & ACTIVITIES

HAMPSTEAD HEATH PONDS SWIMMING
Map p433 (Hampstead Heath, NW5; adult/child £2/1; ⊖Hampstead Heath) Set in the midst of the gorgeous heath, Hampstead's three bathing ponds (men's, women's and mixed) offer a cooling dip in murky brown water. Despite what you might think from its appearance, the water is tested daily and meets stringent quality guidelines.

The men's and women's ponds are open year-round and are supervised by a life-guard. Opening times vary with the seasons, from 7am or 8am until 3.30pm in winter and 8.30pm at the height of summer. The men's pond is particularly popular with gay men and the lawns surrounding are a prime sunbathing and posing spot whenever the sun's out. There's also a nude sunbathing area within the changing-room enclosure.

The mixed pond closes in winter. It's the least secluded of the three and can sometimes get crowded in summer.

LORD'S SPECTATOR SPORT
(☎020-7432 1000; www.lords.org; St John's Wood Rd, NW8; ⊖St John's Wood) For cricket devotees a trip to Lord's is often as much a pilgrimage as anything else. As well as being home to Marylebone Cricket Club, the ground hosts Test matches, one-day internationals and domestic cricket finals. International matches are usually booked months in advance, but tickets for county cricket fixtures are reasonably easy to come by.

Notting Hill & West London

NOTTING HILL | WESTBOURNE GROVE | HIGH STREET KENSINGTON | EARL'S COURT | WEST BROMPTON | MAIDA VALE | SHEPHERD'S BUSH | HAMMERSMITH | PADDINGTON | BAYSWATER

Neighbourhood Top Five

1 Spending a Saturday afternoon browsing the stalls of **Portobello Road Market** (p258).

2 Sizing up the outrageous exterior floral cascade of the **Churchill Arms** (p264).

3 Taking a **boat trip** (p258) between Little Venice and Camden along Regent's Canal.

4 Raising a glass to Old Father Thames from the terrace of the **Dove pub** (p265).

5 Cosying up in a front-row double bed with a glass of vino at the **Electric Cinema** (p265).

For more detail of this area see Map p438 and p440 ➡

Lonely Planet's Top Tip

To make the best of your time at Portobello Road Market, do a one-way circuit between Notting Hill Gate and Ladbroke Rd tube stations. The flow tends to go from Notting Hill to Ladbroke Grove, but either way works fine. Follow our Notting Hill Walk (p261) for a suggested route.

✖ Best Places to Eat

➡ Potli (p262)

➡ Ledbury (p260)

➡ River Cafe (p263)

➡ Mazi (p260)

➡ Kerbisher & Malt (p262)

For reviews, see p260 ➡

♟ Best Places to Drink

➡ Troubadour (p264)

➡ Windsor Castle (p264)

➡ Churchill Arms (p264)

➡ Dove (p265)

For reviews, see p263 ➡

☉ Best Guided Tours

➡ Regent's Canal (p267)

➡ Brompton Cemetery (p258)

➡ 18 Stafford Terrace (p257)

➡ Kensal Green Cemetery (p259)

For reviews, see p257 ➡

Explore: Notting Hill & West London

Most people come to West London for three reasons: for Portobello Road Market, outstanding dining, or because they're kipping in one of the area's choice accommodation options.

West London is sight-light, but you should allow half a day for Portobello Road Market and another half day to walk along the Grand Union Canal towards Little Venice, maybe with a pint at one of the waterside pubs en route.

Some excellent restaurant and entertainment options will save those staying in the area from legging it into the West End (although it's close enough to do so if you want). For eating, Notting Hill has a great concentration of good names, but cast your net further and land superb pickings in Hammersmith and Shepherd's Bush.

For nightlife, Notting Hill and Shepherd's Bush are the most vibrant, while Kensington is home to one of the capital's most unique rooftop clubs. Other areas will be pretty quiet once the pubs have rung the 11pm bell.

Local Life

➡**Fruit and vegetable markets** Although also popular with tourists, Portobello Road Market (p258) is where many Notting Hill residents shop for their daily fruit and veg. Another good fruit and veg market is Shepherd's Bush Market (p262).

➡**Waterside strolling** Little Venice (p258) is very popular at the weekend when families go for a walk along the canal's towpaths.

➡**Affordable pampering** The Porchester Spa (p267) is run by Westminster Council and is cheaper than typical commercial spas.

Getting There & Away

➡**Underground** The west–east Central Line stops at Queensway (Bayswater), Notting Hill Gate and Shepherd's Bush. For Paddington, Westbourne Grove, and the western end of Shepherd's Bush, there's the painfully slow Hammersmith & City Line. Earl's Court and Hammersmith are on the zippy Piccadilly Line.

➡**Santander Cycles** Useful to get from one neighbourhood to another, with docking stations across West London.

⊙ SIGHTS

⊙ Notting Hill & Westbourne Grove

MUSEUM OF BRANDS, PACKAGING & ADVERTISING   MUSEUM
Map p438 (✆020-7908 0880; www.museumof-brands.com; 111-117 Lancaster Rd, W11; adult/child £7.50/3; ⊙10am-6pm Tue-Sat, 11am-5pm Sun; ⊜Ladbroke Grove) This recently relocated shrine to nostalgia is the brainchild of consumer historian Robert Opie, who has amassed advertising memorabilia and packaging since the age of 16. There are early Monopoly sets, the first appearances of Mickey Mouse and Disney, a primitive version of Cluedo, Teazie-Weazie powder shampoo, radios, TVs, and ephemera celebrating cultural/consumer icons the Fab Four, Mork & Mindy, Star Wars, Star Trek, Buzz Lightyear, Pokemon *et al*. An annual ticket is £20.

⊙ High Street Kensington

LEIGHTON HOUSE   HOUSE
Map p440 (✆Mon-Fri 020-7602 3316, Sat & Sun 020-7471 9160; www.leightonhouse.co.uk; 12 Holland Park Rd, W14; adult/child £10/6; ⊙10am-5.30pm Wed-Mon; ⊜High St Kensington) Sitting on a quiet street just west of Holland Park and designed in 1866 by George Aitchison, Leighton House was home to the eponymous Frederic, Lord Leighton (1830–96), a painter belonging to the Aesthetic movement. The ground floor is served up in an Orientalist style, its exquisite **Arab Hall** added in 1879 and densely covered with blue and green tiles from Rhodes, Cairo, Damascus, and Iznik in Turkey.

A fountain tinkles away in the centre beneath the golden dome; even the wooden latticework of the windows and gallery was brought from Damascus. A fireplace upstairs inlaid with Chinese tiles, a stuffed peacock at the foot of the stairs and peacock quills in the fireplace amplify the Byzantine mood. The house also contains notable pre-Raphaelite paintings by Burne-Jones, Watts, Millais and Lord Leighton himself.

18 STAFFORD TERRACE   HOUSE
Map p440 (✆Mon-Fri 020-7602 3316, Sat & Sun 020-7938 1295; www.rbkc.gov.uk/subsites/museums/18staffordterrace1.aspx; 18 Stafford Tce, W8; adult/child £8/3; ⊙tours 11.15am & 2.15pm Wed, 11.15am, 1pm, 2.15pm & 3.30pm Sat & Sun mid-Sep–mid-Jun; ⊜High St Kensington) Formerly known as Linley Sambourne House, 18 Stafford Terrace, tucked away behind Kensington High St, was the home of *Punch* cartoonist and amateur photographer Linley Sambourne and his wife Marion from 1875 to 1914. What you see is pretty much the typical home of a comfortable middle-class Victorian family, with dark wood, Turkish carpets and sumptuous stained glass throughout. You can visit some nine rooms, by 90-minute guided tour only.

HOLLAND PARK   PARK
Map p440 (Ilchester Pl; ⊙7.30am-dusk; ⊜High St Kensington, Holland Park) This handsome park divides into dense woodland in the north, spacious and inviting lawns by Holland House, sports fields for the beautiful game and other exertions in the south, and some lovely gardens, including the restful Kyoto Garden The park's many splendid peacocks

NOTTING HILL & WEST LONDON SIGHTS

NOTTING HILL CARNIVAL

Every year, for three days during the last weekend of August, Notting Hill echoes to the beats of calypso, ska, reggae and soca sounds of **Notting Hill Carnival** (www.thelondon-nottinghillcarnival.com). Launched in 1964 by the local Afro-Caribbean community keen to celebrate its culture and traditions, it has grown to become Europe's largest street festival (over one and a half million visitors in total) and a highlight of the annual calendar in London.

The carnival includes events showcasing the five main 'arts': the 'mas' (derived from masquerade), which is the main costume parade; pan (steel bands); calypso music; static sound systems (anything goes, from reggae, dub, funk and drum and bass); and the mobile sound systems. The 'mas' is generally held on the Monday and is the culmination of the carnival's celebrations. Processions finish around 9pm, although parties in bars, restaurants and seemingly every house in the neighbourhood go on late into the night.

Another undisputed highlight of the carnival is the food: there are dozens of Caribbean food stands and celebrity chefs such as Levi Roots often make an appearance.

are a gorgeous sight and an adventure playground keeps kids occupied. Holland House is the venue of Opera Holland Park (p266) in the summer months.

The former Commonwealth Institute, just south of the park, is being reinvented as the new Design Museum (p166).

⊙ Earl's Court & West Brompton

BROMPTON CEMETERY CEMETERY
Map p440 (www.royalparks.org.uk/parks/brompton-cemetery; Old Brompton Rd, SW5; tour £6; ⊙8am-dusk; ⊜West Brompton, Fulham Broadway) While this atmospheric 19th-century, 16-hectare boneyard's most famous denizen is suffragette Emmeline Pankhurst, the cemetery is fascinating as the possible inspiration for many of Beatrix Potter's characters. A local resident in her youth, Potter may have noted some of the names on headstones: there's a Mr Nutkin, Mr McGregor, Jeremiah Fisher, Tommy Brock – even a Peter Rabbet!

The chapel and colonnades at one end are modelled on St Peter's in Rome. Two-hour **tours** depart at 2pm every Sunday from May to August (and two Sundays a month from September to April) from the South Lodge, near the Fulham Rd entrance. The annual summer open day includes rare visits to the catacombs (see www.brompton-cemetery.org.uk for details).

⊙ Maida Vale

LITTLE VENICE CANAL
Map p438 It was Lord Byron who dreamed up this evocative phrase to describe the junction between Regent's Canal (p246) and the **Grand Union Canal** (Map p438), a confluence overseen by beautiful mansions and navigated by colourful narrow boats. The canals go back to the early 19th century when the government was trying to develop new transport links across the country.

The Grand Union Canal actually finishes up in Birmingham (you can journey much of its entire length by bicycle): horse-drawn barges were ideal to carry coal and other bulk commodities such as grain or ice. Little Venice is an important mooring point for narrow boats (many of them permanent homes), which keeps the boating spirit bubbling away.

⊙ TOP SIGHT
PORTOBELLO ROAD MARKET

Buzzing Portobello Road Market is an iconic London attraction with an eclectic mix of street food, fruit and veg, antiques, curios, collectables, vibrant fashion and trinkets. Although the shops along Portobello Rd open daily and the fruit and veg stalls (from Elgin Cres to Talbot Rd) only close on Sunday, the busiest day by far is Saturday, when antique dealers set up shop (from Chepstow Villas to Elgin Cres). This is also when the fashion market (beneath Westway, from Portobello Rd to Ladbroke Rd) is in full swing – although you can also browse for fashion on Friday and Sunday.

More upmarket, **Portobello Green Arcade** (Map p438; www.portobellodesigners.com; 281 Portobello Rd, W10; ⊜Ladbroke Grove) is home to some cutting-edge clothing and jewellery designers. Across the way, **Acklam Village Market** (Map p438; 4-8 Acklam Rd, W10; ⊙11am-5pm Sat & Sun; ⊜Ladbroke Grove) is a popular weekend street-food market with snacks from across the globe.

Continue on Portobello Rd towards Golborne Rd (famous for vintage furniture and clothes shops) and you'll hit the 'new goods' section, with kitchenware, bric-a-brac and more fruit and veg stalls – as well as secondhand goods, despite this being the 'new-goods' market.

DON'T MISS...
➡ Fashion market
➡ Designers at Portobello Green Arcade
➡ Fruit and veg stalls
➡ Antiques market

PRACTICALITIES
➡ Map p438, B4
➡ www.portobellomarket.org
➡ Portobello Rd, W10
➡ ⊙8am-6.30pm Mon-Wed, Fri & Sat, to 1pm Thu
➡ ⊜Notting Hill Gate, Ladbroke Grove

LOCAL KNOWLEDGE

LAURE PROUVOST

French-born, London-living Laure Prouvost won the 2013 Turner Prize for her installation *Wantee*. We caught up with her to get her angle on London and its art scene.

Which art work in London means the most to you and why?

That's tricky as what's on constant display is quite specific to a kind of art, painting or objects. I often go to screenings that virtually exist for a period of time; the Lux (www.lux.org.uk) is amazing for the film and video development of the artist in London. In terms of what I could see any time...I think *The Ambassadors* (Hans Holbein the Younger, 1553) in the **National Gallery** (p89) is always surprising, but also the hidden panels of **Sir John Soane's Museum** (p96). I also like the divan (couch or sofa) by Franz West as an active piece of public art at the **Whitechapel Gallery** (p215).

Which art gallery (or galleries) in London do you see as being the most progressive and exciting?

I really like Raven Row (www.ravenrow.org), the Whitechapel Gallery, the Showroom (www.theshowroom.org) and the Chisenhale Gallery (www.chisenhale.org.uk), and of course my gallery MOT International (www.motinternational.com).

Public art in London – any good?

Generally not great, but excellent to come across the John Latham book emerging from his Flat Time House (www.flattimeho.org.uk) in Peckham. There are also temporary big productions and sometimes protest banners in front of Big Ben. The **Fourth Plinth** (p105) is what I can think of in terms of public art (the quality varies I think, but that's maybe for the best).

When you down your artist's materials at the end of the day, what's your choice for dinner?

Cooking eggs from the chicken in my studio, making a big omelette and a shot of vodka in our cold studio with raspberries for desserts... Or I might go to dinner at **St John** (p202) or **Koya** (p112) for Japanese noodles or just a simple Lahmacun Turkish Pizza at **Mangal Ocakbasi** (p223) on Arcola St.

⊙ Shepherd's Bush

KENSAL GREEN CEMETERY CEMETERY
(www.kensalgreencemetery.com; Harrow Rd, W10; tours £7; ⊙9am-5pm Mon-Sat, 10am-5pm Sun, to 6pm Sun in summer; ⊜Kensal Green) For many years the most fashionable necropolis in England (you wouldn't be seen dead anywhere else), Kensal Green Cemetery accepted its first occupants in 1833, and the Gothic boneyard is the final resting place of many illustrious names, including Charles Babbage, Isambard Kingdom Brunel, Wilkie Collins, Anthony Trollope, William Makepeace Thackeray, Baden Powell and the almost comically named Dr Albert Isaiah Coffin.

Supposedly based on the Cimetière du Père-Lachaise in Paris, the cemetery is distinguished by its Greek Revival architecture, arched entrances and the outrageously ornate tombs that bear testimony to 19th-century delusions of grandeur. Two-hour **tours** of the cemetery are offered on Sundays at 2pm (from March to October; first and third Sundays per month other times) by the Friends of Kensal Green Cemetery (www.kensalgreen.co.uk). Some of these tours also visit the catacombs beneath the Anglican Chapel. The cemetery is laid out alongside the Grand Union Canal, which makes for splendid walks alongside the water.

⊙ Hammersmith

WILLIAM MORRIS SOCIETY MUSEUM
Map p440 (☎020-8741 3735; www.williammorrissociety.org; 26 Upper Mall, W6; ⊙2-5pm Thu & Sat; ⊜Ravenscourt Park) **FREE** Tucked away in the coach house and basement of Kelmscott House (William Morris' former home), this small riverside museum stages temporary exhibitions on all things William Morris. There's a downstairs shop (with a fireplace designed by Morris) and a still-working printing press (demonstrations given on Saturdays).

Short films on Morris and the house are run and you can also access a small part of the garden, although the rest of the house and the main garden are out of bounds for most of the year.

EATING

✗ Notting Hill & Westbourne Grove

ARANCINA   ITALIAN £
Map p438 (www.arancina.co.uk; 19 Pembridge Rd, W11; mains £2.80-24; ⊙8am-11pm Mon-Sat, 9am-11pm Sun; ◉Notting Hill Gate) Arancina always has a scrum of people around it thanks to the whiff of freshly baked pizza, Sicilian snacks and the cut-out orange Fiat 500 in the window. Try the *arancine* (fried balls of rice with fillings; £2.80), the creamy desserts known as *cannolo siciliano* (£2.80) or a slice of perfect pizza. There's another branch not far away at 19 Westbourne Grove.

TAQUERÍA   MEXICAN £
Map p438 (www.taqueria.co.uk; 139-143 Westbourne Grove; tacos £5-7.50; ⊙noon-11pm Mon-Thu, to 11.30pm Fri & Sat, to 10.30pm Sun; 🖥; ◉Notting Hill Gate) 🖉 You won't find fresher, limper (they're not supposed to be crispy!) tacos anywhere in London because these ones are made on the premises. Refurbished in 2015, it's a small casual place with a great vibe. Taquería is also a committed environmental establishment: the eggs, chicken and pork are free-range, the meat British, the fish MSC-certified and the milk and cream organic.

CHURCHILL THAI KITCHEN   THAI £
Map p440 (☎020-7792 1246; www.churchillarms-kensington.co.uk; 119 Kensington Church St, W8; mains £8.50; ⊙noon-10pm Mon-Sat, noon-9.30pm Sun; 🖥; ◉Notting Hill Gate) Tucked away inside the Churchill Arms' conservatory (p264), this restaurant has been cooking up excellent and highly affordable Thai cuisine for more than 15 years. With one of London's most distinctive pubs attached, you can just wander in with your pint and sit down to dine.

FISH HOUSE   FISH & CHIPS £
Map p438 (29 Pembridge Rd; mains £7-14; ⊙11.30am-10pm; ◉Notting Hill Gate) This well-placed chippie en route to Portobello Rd is frequently stuffed to the gills: all fresh fish, light and crispy batter, fine chips, jostling elbows and sunny service.

★MAZI   GREEK ££
Map p438 (☎020-7229 3794; www.mazi.co.uk; 12-14 Hillgate St, W8; mains £10-26; ⊙noon-3pm Wed-Sun, 6.30-10.30pm Mon & Tue & 6.30-11pm Wed-Sun; ◉Notting Hill Gate) Mazi has shaken up the Greek tradition along pretty Hillgate St, concocting a lively menu of modern and innovative (many of sharing size) platters in a bright and neat setting, with a small back garden (for summer months) and an all-Greek wine list. It's both small and popular, so reservations are important.

★GEALES   SEAFOOD ££
Map p438 (☎020-7727 7528; www.geales.com; 2 Farmer St, W8; 2-/3-course express lunch £9.95/12.95, mains £8.50-22.95; ⊙noon-3pm Tue-Fri, 6-10.30pm Mon-Fri, noon-10.30pm Sat, noon-9.30pm Sun; ◉Notting Hill Gate) Frying since 1939, Geales enjoys a quiet location, tucked away on the corner of Hillgate Village. The succulent fish in crispy batter is a fine catch from a menu which also runs to other British faves such as pork belly with apple sauce and crackling, and beef and bacon pie. Look out for the good-value express lunch.

ELECTRIC DINER   AMERICAN ££
Map p438 (www.electricdiner.com; 191 Portobello Rd, W11; mains from £8-19; ⊙8am-midnight Mon-Thu, to 1am Fri-Sun; 🖥; ◉Ladbroke Grove) This slender American-style diner has a long counter and red-leather booths, to amplify cinematic associations with the adjacent movie theatre. The French-American menu's breakfasts, burgers, steak frites, hot dogs, knickerbocker glories and apple crumbles are delicious, backed up by a noteworthy catalogue of draught and bottled beers.

E&O   ASIAN ££
Map p438 (www.rickerrestaurants.com/e-and-o/; 14 Blenheim Cres; mains £11-33; ⊙noon-3pm & 6-11pm Mon-Fri, noon-11pm Sat, 12.30-10.30pm Sun; 🖥; ◉Ladbroke Grove) This Notting Hill hot spot offers Asian fusion fare presented as artfully as elaborate origami. The decor is equally attractive: black-and-white minimalist. You can do dim sum (£3.50 to £8) at the bar if no tables are available in the evening (it gets busy).

★LEDBURY   FRENCH £££
Map p438 (☎020-7792 9090; www.theledbury.com; 127 Ledbury Rd, W11; 4-course set lunch £50, 4-course dinner £95; ⊙noon-2pm Wed-Sun & 6.30-9.45pm daily; 🖥; ◉Westbourne Park, Notting Hill Gate) Two Michelin stars and swooningly elegant, Brett Graham's artful French restaurant attracts well-heeled diners in jeans with designer jackets. Dishes – such

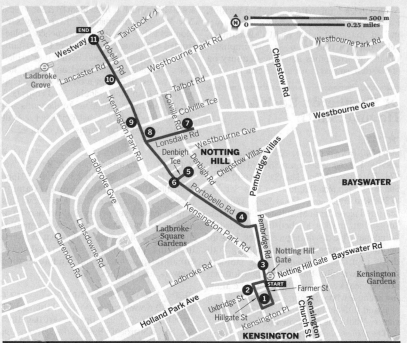

Neighbourhood Walk
Notting Hill

START NOTTING HILL GATE STATION
END PORTOBELLO GREEN ARCADE
LENGTH 1.5 MILES; TWO HOURS

From Notting Hill Gate tube station, leave the south side exit and take a left down Farmer St into **1 Hillgate Village**, with its picture-postcard painted houses. Callcott St is particularly photogenic. Loop back around and leave Hillgate St by the iconic **2 Coronet** (p265) cinema featured in the rom-com *Notting Hill*. Turn right and cross at the lights to the junction with Pembridge Rd; the tollgate – the 'gate' of Notting Hill Gate – once stood here.

Along Pembridge Rd, at the junction with Kensington Park Rd, was once the main entrance to the huge 19th-century **3 Hippodrome**. The Hippodrome vanished in the 1840s, although its layout survives in the road contours to the west. Bend into Portobello Rd and note the blue plaque high at **4 No 22**, commemorating George Orwell who lived here. Keep walking along Portobello Rd and pop into charming **5 Denbigh Terrace**, with its pastel-coloured houses. Note the steeple of

sand-coloured **6 St Peter's Church** to the west on the far side of Portobello Rd.

Continue along Portobello Rd and turn right down Lonsdale Rd to the absorbing **7 Museum of Brands, Packaging and Advertising** (p257), stuffed away down Colville Mews. Backtrack to Portobello Rd and note the **8 shop** named 'Notting Hill' at No 142 on your right: the bookshop of William Thacker (Hugh Grant) in the eponymous film (now a clothes and shoe shop). Further along Portobello Rd, stop outside the historic **9 Electric Cinema** (p265); observe the tiling by the pavement that says 'Electric House' and pop in to take a gander at the classic interior. Down further, cross Westbourne Park Rd, named after the River Westbourne, one of London's underground rivers. The blue front door at **10 280 Westbourne Park Rd**, William Thacker's flat in the film *Notting Hill*, still attracts devotees.

At **11 Portobello Green Arcade** (p258), stop to browse a clutch of invigorating designer clothes shops and quirky boutiques. Ladbroke Grove tube station is a short walk west.

as Herdwick lamb with salt baked turnips, ewe's milk and garlic shoots, or flame-grilled mackerel with pickled cucumber, celtic mustard and shiso – are triumphant. London gastronomes have the Ledbury on speed-dial, so reservations are crucial.

✗ Shepherd's Bush & Hammersmith

★POTLI   INDIAN £

Map p440 (www.potli.co.uk; 319-321 King St, W6; weekday 1-/2-course set lunch £6.95/9.95, mains £7-13.50; ⊙noon-2.45pm Mon-Sat, noon-10.30pm Sun, 6-10.30pm Mon-Thu, to 11pm Fri & Sat; 🔊; ⊜Stamford Brook, Ravenscourt Park) With its scattered pieces from Mumbai's Thieves Market, Indian market kitchen/bazaar cuisine, home-made pickles and spice mixes, plus an accent on genuine flavour, tantalising Potli deftly captures the aromas of its culinary home. Downstairs there's an open kitchen and service is very friendly, but it's the alluring menu – where flavours are teased into a rich and fully authentic India culinary experience – that's the real crowd-pleaser.

The *paneer shaslik* (Indian cottage cheese, caramelised onions and peppers) is a delectable intro, while the Kerala fish curry, with its mild yet full-flavoured accents, is a sublime choice, but the menu is a success throughout.

★KERBISHER & MALT   FISH & CHIPS £

Map p440 (www.kerbisher.co.uk; 164 Shepherd's Bush Rd, W6; mains £5.90-6.90; ⊙noon-2.30pm

& 4.30-10pm Tue-Thu, noon-10pm Fri & Sat, to 9pm Sun; 🔊; ⊜Hammersmith) 🍴 Every day save Monday is Fry Day at popular, peacock-blue-fronted Kerbisher & Malt, where the sustainably sourced, delectable, battered-or-grilled coley, haddock, pollock, cod and plaice has made waves. Served in a box to go, the chip butties (£2) and tasty double-fried chips (£2) are all good news, while white-tile walls and chunky wooden tables cast Kerbisher & Malt as a no-nonsense, but handsome, chippie.

TOSA   JAPANESE £

Map p440 (www.tosauk.com; 332 King St, W6; mains from £5; ⊙12.30-2.30pm & 6-11pm; ⊜Stamford Brook) With a welcoming flaming charcoal grill brightening its window, this simple, casual yet pretty-and-precise Japanese restaurant fixes its focus on smaller dishes, as well as delectable meat skewers, including scrummy *yakitori* (grilled chicken) and *asparamaki* (pork and aubergine) skewers, and noodles.

BUSH THEATRE CAFE & BAR   CAFE £

Map p440 (www.bushtheatre.co.uk; 7 Uxbridge Rd; mains from £2.50; ⊙9am-11pm Mon-Fri, 11am-11pm Sat; 🔊; ⊜Shepherd's Bush Market) Tread the bare wood floorboards of this roomy cafe in this erstwhile library, and grab a paperback play or two from the dense collection stuffed onto shelves. This is a great place to grab a brekkie, sink a draught beer, hang out for pre-theatre snacking or for just taking time out from the vehicular din of Shepherd's Bush.

A COOKE'S   BRITISH £

Map p440 (www.cookespieandmash.com; 48 Goldhawk Rd; mains from £4; ⊙10.30am-4.30pm Mon-Wed & Sat, to 4pm Thu & Fri; ⊜Goldhawk Rd) Fenced in by the ethnic flavours of Shepherd's Bush, rock-solid A Cooke's has been serving London pie and mash since the twilight years of Queen Vic's reign. The environment: moulded plastic furniture and Queens Park Rangers football banners. The food: honest, good-value and out-and-out London pie and mash. A Cooke's made a crucial cameo appearance in cult mod flick *Quadrophenia*.

Served in a jiffy and consumed with spoon and fork, a single pie and mash in a bowl with parsley liquor is £4, eels and mash will set you back £6. The shop is due to be sold to make way for the proposed development of adjacent Shepherd's Bush Market, but at the time of writing was still open for business.

SHEPHERD'S BUSH MARKET

Shepherd's Bush Market (Map p440; ⊙9.30am-5pm Mon-Wed, Fri & Sat, to 1pm Thu) This fruit and veg market stretches underneath the Hammersmith & City and Circle Lines between Goldhawk Rd and Shepherd's Bush tube stations. Popular with local African and Afro-Caribbean communities, it's stockpiled with mangoes, passionfruit, okra, plantains, sweet potatoes and other exotic fare. A regeneration of the market has long been waiting in the wings, but has yet to kick off.

Mr Falafel (www.mrfalafel.co.uk; Units T4-T5; falafel from £3; 11am-6pm Mon-Sat) is the place for Palestinian falafel wraps, done to a turn.

PRINCESS VICTORIA   GASTROPUB ££
Map p440 (www.princessvictoria.co.uk; 217 Uxbridge Rd, W12; mains £13.50-17.50, weekday 2-course lunch £12.50; ◉11.30am-midnight Mon-Sat, to 11pm Sun; ☎; ☒207, 607, ◉Shepherd's Bush Market) This imposing former Victorian gin palace is a quality boozer with ample elbow space. Grandly restored, the roomy interior soaks up pretty much any hubbub thrown at it. The menu is a gastronomic triumph, wine-lovers are in clover with a strong selection and at the rear is a walled herb garden.

GATE   VEGETARIAN ££
Map p440 (✆020-8748 6932; http://thegate-restaurants.com/hammersmith.php; 51 Queen Caroline St, W6; mains £13-15; ◉noon-2.30pm Mon-Fri, noon-3pm Sat & Sun, 6-10.30pm daily; ✐; ◉Hammersmith) One of London's best vegetarian restaurants, this good-looking eatery could do with better feng shui (behind the Hammersmith Apollo, off Hammersmith flyover), but the inventive menu (pan-fried broccoli-flower ravioli, aubergine schnitzel), great weekend brunches, welcoming staff, and relaxed atmosphere make the trek here worthwhile. Bookings are crucial.

SHIKUMEN   CHINESE ££
Map p440 (✆020-8749 9978; www.shikumen.co.uk; Dorsett Hotel, 58 Shepherd's Bush Green, W12; mains £8.50-19.50; ◉noon-11pm Mon-Sat, 11.30am-11pm Sun; ◉Shepherd's Bush) Named after the delightful Sino-European–styled stone gateways that line the *lilòng* lanes of Shanghai, Shikumen (pronounced shh-koo murn) serves up an eclectic range of Chinese dishes that darts about the China culinary map, from Peking duck to Sìchuān hot-and-sour soup, salted and smoked hakka-style corn-fed chicken and Cantonese dim sum. The food is excellent, but service can be slack.

RIVER CAFE   ITALIAN £££
Map p440 (✆020-7386 4200; www.rivercafe.co.uk; Rainville Rd, Thames Wharf, W6; mains from £18; ◉12.30-2.30pm & 7-9pm Mon-Sat, noon-3pm Sun; ☎; ◉Hammersmith) The Thames-side name that spawned the world-famous eponymous cookery books offers simple, precise cooking that showcases seasonal ingredients sourced with fanatical expertise; the menus change daily. Booking is essential, as it's Michelin-starred and a favourite of cashed-up local gastronomes.

✕ Paddington & Bayswater

COUSCOUS CAFÉ   MOROCCAN ££
Map p438 (7 Porchester Gardens, W2; mains £9.95-15.95; ◉noon-11.30pm; ◉Bayswater) This tiny, cosy and vividly decorated basement place excels in Moroccan-style couscous and tagines (spicy stews cooked in an earthenware dish), *pastillas* (filled savoury pastries), *brochettes* (grilled meat skewers) and slightly exaggerated service. Alcohol is served or you can BYO (no corkage fee).

🍷 DRINKING & NIGHTLIFE

🍸 Notting Hill & Westbourne Grove

EARL OF LONSDALE   PUB
Map p438 (277-281 Portobello Rd, W11; ◉noon-11pm Mon-Fri, 10am-11pm Sat, noon-10.30pm Sun; ◉Notting Hill Gate, Ladbroke Grove) Named after the bon vivant founder of the AA (Automobile Association, *not* Alcoholics Anonymous), the Earl is peaceful during the day, with a mixture of old biddies and young hipsters inhabiting the reintroduced snugs. There are Samuel Smith's ales, a fantastic backroom with sofas, banquettes, open fires and a magnificent beer garden.

Note the occasional bricked-in windows – a tax on windows introduced in 1696, resulted in windows being bricked in to avoid payment.

BEACH BLANKET BABYLON   BAR
Map p438 (www.beachblanket.co.uk; 45 Ledbury Rd, W11; ◉6pm-midnight Mon, noon-midnight Tue-Fri, 10am-midnight Sat & Sun; ☎; ◉Notting Hill Gate) This buzzing bar, decorated in baroque and rococo styles, is the place for a decadent night out. Famed for celebrity sightings, it's a hang-out for the moneyed set of the royal boroughs.

PORTOBELLO STAR   COCKTAIL BAR
Map p438 (✆020-3540 7781; www.portobellostar-bar.co.uk; 171 Portobello Rd, W11; cocktails from £6; ◉11am-11.30pm Sun-Thu, to 12.30am Fri & Sat; ☎; ◉Ladbroke Grove) Gin (and excellent cocktails) is the name of the game at the Portobello Star, a former pub given a refreshing makeover into a nifty, narrow cocktail bar. Upstairs

is *The Ginstitute*, a fascinating experience (£100) that includes a cocktail reception, a gin lecture, a 70cl bottle of Portobello Road No 171 gin and a 70cl bottle of your personally devised gin blend (and legs of rubber).

NOTTING HILL ARTS CLUB   CLUB

Map p438 (www.nottinghillartsclub.com; 21 Notting Hill Gate, W11; ◷6pm-late Mon-Fri, 4pm-late Sat & Sun; ⚑; ⊖Notting Hill Gate) London simply wouldn't be what it is without places like NHAC. Cultivating the underground music scene, this small basement club attracts a musically curious and experimental crowd. Dress code: no suits and ties.

UNION TAVERN   PUB

Map p438 (www.union-tavern.co.uk; 45 Woodfield Rd, W9; ◷noon-11pm Mon-Thu, to midnight Fri & Sat, to 10.30pm Sun; ⚑; ⊖Westbourne Park) With just the right mix of shiny gastropub, rough-and-ready local appeal, a good location on the Grand Union Canal (with waterside terrace) and a strong selection of craft beers, this pub is a great choice for a pint or two on your way to or from Portobello Road Market.

🍷 High Street Kensington

★KENSINGTON ROOF GARDENS   CLUB

Map p440 (www.roofgardens.virgin.com; 99 Kensington High St, W8; ◷club 10pm-3am Fri & Sat, garden 9am-5pm; ⚑; ⊖High St Kensington) Atop the former Derry and Toms building high above Kensington High St is this enchanting venue – a nightclub with 0.6 hectares of gardens and resident flamingos. The wow-factor comes at a premium: entry is £20 (£25 from May to September), you must register on the guest list (http://gls. roofgardens.com/) before going and drinks are £10 a pop. Dress to impress.

There are three different gardens (dating from 1938): the stunningly beautiful Spanish gardens inspired by the Alhambra in Granada; the Tudor gardens, all nooks, crannies and fragrant flowers; and the Woodlands gardens, home to ancient trees and four flamingos.

The gardens can be visited year round by the public, free of charge (although they are often hired out for private parties, so phone ahead to check); they have their own bars and often host live bands. The indoor part is the club proper where commercial dance music keeps the crowd of young socialites boogying until the early hours. Enter on Derry St.

WINDSOR CASTLE   PUB

Map p440 (www.thewindsorcastlekensington. co.uk; 114 Campden Hill Rd, W11; ◷noon-11pm Mon-Sat, to 10.30pm Sun; ⚑; ⊖Notting Hill Gate) A classic tavern on the brow of Campden Hill Rd, this place has history, nooks and charm on tap. It's worth the search for its historic compartmentalised interior, roaring fire (in winter), delightful beer garden (in summer) and affable regulars (most always). According to legend, the bones of Thomas Paine (author of *Rights of Man*) are in the cellar.

In the old days, Windsor Castle was visible from the pub, hence the name.

CHURCHILL ARMS   PUB

Map p440 (www.churchillarmskensington.co.uk; 119 Kensington Church St, W8; ◷11am-11pm Mon-Wed, to midnight Thu-Sat, noon-10.30pm Sun; ⚑; ⊖Notting Hill Gate) With its cascade of geraniums and Union Jack flags swaying in the breeze, the Churchill Arms is quite a sight on Kensington Church St. Renowned for its Winston memorabilia and dozens of knick-knacks on the walls, the pub is a favourite of both locals and tourists. The attached Churchill Thai Kitchen (p260) in the conservatory serves excellent Thai food.

🍷 Earl's Court & West Brompton

★TROUBADOUR   BAR

Map p440 (www.troubadour.co.uk; 263-267 Old Brompton Rd, SW5; ◷9am-midnight; ⚑; ⊖Earl's Court) On a compatible spiritual plane to Paris' Shakespeare and Company Bookshop, this eccentric, time-warped and convivial boho bar/cafe has been serenading drinkers since the 1950s. (Deep breath) Adele, Paolo Nutini, Joni Mitchell and (deeper breath) Jimi Hendrix and Bob Dylan have performed here, and there's still live music (folk, blues) most nights and a large, pleasant garden open in summer.

You'll be spoilt for choice with the wine list – Troubadour runs a wine club and has a wine shop (strong showing of Argentinian wines) next door. The club is open from 8pm (Tuesday to Saturday) but don't expect table reservations.

ATLAS   PUB

Map p440 (www.theatlaspub.co.uk; 16 Seagrave Rd, SW6; ◷noon-11pm Mon-Sat, to 10.30pm Sun; ⚑; ⊖West Brompton) A garrulous hubbub frequently spilling from its ivy-clad and port-coloured facade, this Victorian-era pub tempts locals, visitors, foodies and drinkers alike with a delicious wood-panelled interior, a winning Mediterranean menu, a lovely side courtyard and a fine range of beers and wines.

🍷 Maida Vale

WARRINGTON
PUB

Map p438 (www.faucetinn.com/warrington; 93 Warrington Cres, W9; ⊙8am-11pm Mon-Thu, to midnight Fri & Sat, to 10.30pm Sun; 🕾; ⊕Warwick Ave, Maida Vale) Flung up in 1857, this former high-end brothel is an ornate, art-nouveau feast of a pub, with mosaic floors, pillared portico and heaps of style. The huge saloon bar, dominated by a marble-topped hemispherical counter with a carved mahogany base and a vast stained-glass window by Tiffany, is a fabulous place to sample a range of four real ales.

Other alluring details include the imposing marble fireplace, eye-catching ceiling and magnificent porch. There's outside seating for al fresco drinking and five bedrooms (four-poster beds, roll-top baths), for overnight stays.

WATERWAY
BAR

Map p438 (www.thewaterway.co.uk; 54 Formosa St, W9; ⊙11am-11pm Mon-Fri, 10am-11pm Sat, 10am-10.30pm Sun; 🕾; ⊕Warwick Ave) Don't come here for the selection of beer or ales or the expensive nosh; this place, hard by the Grand Union Canal in Little Venice, is all about location, and it's hard to imagine a better place to while away a weekend afternoon.

🍷 Hammersmith

DOVE
PUB

Map p440 (☑020-8748 9474; www.dovehammersmith.co.uk; 19 Upper Mall, W6; ⊙11am-11pm Mon-Sat, noon-10.30pm Sun; 🕾; ⊕Hammersmith, Ravenscourt Park) Severely inundated by the epic floodwaters of 1928, this gem of a 17th-century Fuller's pub revels in historic charm and superb Thames views. Scottish poet James Thompson was reputedly inspired to write the lyrics to 'Rule Britannia' here in the 18th century. It was Graham Greene's local, Hemingway and Dylan Thomas drank here, too, and William Morris lived nearby.

To your right as you walk in is what was once listed as the smallest bar in London. If the sun comes out, fight for a spot on the lovely terrace (forget it on Boat Race day) and in winter, warm your toes by the open fire.

OLD SHIP W6
PUB

Map p440 (www.oldshipw6.co.uk; 25 Upper Mall, W6; ⊙11am-11pm Mon-Thu, 11am-midnight Fri, 9am-midnight Sat, 9am-11pm Sun; 🕾; ⊕Ravenscourt Park, Stamford Brook) With a ceiling decorated with sculls and oars, and walls hung with nautical prints, the Old Ship and its shiny, buttoned-leather sofas would hardly merit a diversion but for its terrific waterside perch, which guarantees superb al fresco Thames views from the balcony upstairs or the ground-floor terrace.

INDIE CINEMAS

If you love cinema, you're in for a treat with West London's quirky picture houses. Q&A events with directors, sofas (beds, even), alcoholic drinks permitted (nay, encouraged), and much more, this is how cinema should be. Tickets are slightly more expensive than run-of-the-mill movie houses. The magnificent **Coronet** (Map p438; www.the-print-room.org; 103 Notting Hill Gate, W8; ⊕Notting Hill Gate) is not currently running as a cinema, but as a fringe theatre, with a long-term restoration programme of its fantastic auditorium currently under way.

Electric Cinema (Map p438; ☑020-7908 9696; www.electriccinema.co.uk; 191 Portobello Rd, W11; tickets £8-22.50; ⊕Ladbroke Grove) Having notched up its first centenary a few years back, the Electric is one of the UK's oldest cinemas, updated. Avail yourself of the luxurious leather armchairs, sofas, footstools and tables for food and drink in the auditorium, or select one of the six front-row double beds! Tickets are cheapest on Mondays.

Gate Picturehouse (Map p438; ☑0871 902 5731; www.picturehouses.co.uk; 87 Notting Hill Gate, W1; tickets £8.60-12.60; ⊕Notting Hill Gate) The Gate's single screen has one of London's most charming art-deco cinema interiors, with director Q&As and a wealth of cinema clubs, including the E4 Slackers Club (students) and Silver Screen (over-60s). Cheapest tickets are on Mondays.

Dating to the 18th century, the pub is wall-to-wall with spectators during the annual Oxford and Cambridge Boat Race.

⭐ ENTERTAINMENT

O2 SHEPHERD'S BUSH
EMPIRE   CONCERT VENUE
Map p440 (www.o2shepherdsbushempire.co.uk; Shepherd's Bush Green, W12; ⊜Shepherd's Bush) Top acts (such as Mumford & Sons, Muse) and back catalogue giants (Dead Kennedys, Marc Almond) get the crowds fired up in this famous midsized venue (capacity is 2000). The downer is the fact that the floor doesn't slope, so if you're not so tall, you may not get much of a view from up the back in the stalls – it's worth paying for the balcony.

LYRIC HAMMERSMITH   THEATRE
Map p440 (☎020-8741 6850; www.lyric.co.uk; King St, Lyric Sq, W6; ⊜Hammersmith) An excellent venue that turns classics on their head, the Lyric stages a stimulating choice of productions from the highbrow to more accessible theatre.

BUSH THEATRE   THEATRE
Map p440 (www.bushtheatre.co.uk; 7 Uxbridge Rd, W12; ⊜Shepherd's Bush) This rehoused West London theatre is renowned for encouraging new talent. Its success over the past three decades is down to strong writing from the likes of Jonathan Harvey, Conor McPherson, Stephen Poliakoff and Mark Ravenhill.

OPERA HOLLAND PARK   OPERA
Map p440 (www.operahollandpark.com; Holland Park, W8; ⊜High St Kensington, Holland Park) Sit under the 800-seat canopy, temporarily erected every summer for a nine-week season in the middle of Holland Park (p257) for a mix of crowd pleasers and rare (even obscure) works. Six operas are generally performed each year.

RIVERSIDE STUDIOS   PERFORMING ARTS
Map p440 (www.riversidestudios.co.uk; Crisp Rd, W6; ⊜Hammersmith) The Riverside hosts an eclectic mix of performing arts, from circus to theatre and comedy, and also doubles as an art-house cinema. There's a popular restaurant and bar to hand, with terrace views of the Thames and Hammersmith Bridge.

🛍 SHOPPING

CERAMICA BLUE   HOMEWARES
Map p438 (www.ceramicablue.co.uk; 10 Blenheim Cres, W11; ◷10am-6.30pm Mon-Sat, noon-5pm Sun; @; ⊜Ladbroke Grove) A lovely spot for colourful, eclectic and handsome crockery, imported from more than a dozen countries. There are Japanese eggshell-glaze teacups, serving plates with tribal South African designs, gorgeous table cloths from Provence and much more.

LUTYENS & RUBINSTEIN   BOOKS
Map p438 (www.lutyensrubinstein.co.uk; 21 Kensington Park Rd, W11; ◷10am-6pm Mon, 10am-6.30pm Tue-Fri, 10am-6pm Sat, 11am-5pm Sun; ⊜Ladbroke Grove) Lutyens & Rubinstein is a fantastic, albeit compact bookshop. Established by a company of literary agents, the focus is on 'excellence in writing', as determined by customers and readers, so every book comes recommended.

NOTTING HILL BOOKSHOP   BOOKS
Map p438 (www.thenottinghillbookshop.co.uk; 13 Blenheim Cres; ◷9am-7pm Mon-Fri, 8.30am-7pm Sat, 10am-6pm Sun; ⊜Ladbroke Grove) Still milking every last drop as the inspiration behind the bookshop in Hugh Grant's and Julia Robert's monster rom-com, the former Travel Bookshop was repackaged a few years ago as a more general bookshop. The new guise did little to staunch the flow of pilgrims who pose outside for snaps. An understandable accent on travel books endures, but fiction provides equilibrium and there's a strong children's section at the rear.

BOOKS FOR COOKS   BOOKS
Map p438 (☎020-72211992; www.booksforcooks.com; 4 Blenheim Cres, W11; ◷10am-6pm Tue-Sat; ⊜Ladbroke Grove) All the recipe books from celeb and nonceleb chefs you can imagine

WESTFIELD SHOPPING CENTRE

Westfield (Map p440; http://uk.westfield.com/london; Ariel Way, W12; ◷10am-10pm Mon-Sat, noon-6pm Sun; ⊜Wood Lane) With a humongous cousin in Stratford (and one tipped for Croydon), this gigantic recession-busting shopping mecca was London's first mall. As well as the 380-odd shops that reside here (all franchises), Westfield has a raft of eateries (again, chains only), bars, a cinema, and regular events, from fashion shows to book signings.

are sold here – perfect for more adventurous cooks or for those looking for 'exotic' cookbooks. The cafe has a test kitchen where you can sample recipes at lunch and teatime.

RELLIK
VINTAGE

Map p438 (www.relliklondon.co.uk; 8 Golborne Rd; ⊙10am-6pm Tue-Sat; ◉Westbourne Park) Incongruously located opposite one of London's most notorious tower blocks – the god-awful-yet-heritage-listed concrete Trellick Tower – Rellik is a fashionista-favourite retro store. It stocks vintage numbers from the 1920s to the 1980s and, rummaging among the frippery, it's not unusual to find an Yves Saint-Laurent coat, a Chloe suit or an Ossie Clark dress.

RETRO WOMAN
VINTAGE

Map p438 (www.mgeshops.com; 20 Pembridge Rd, W11; ⊙10am-8pm; ◉Notting Hill Gate) More secondhand than vintage, but very popular, Retro Woman has racks upon racks of hand-me-down fashion and big-name designer goodies, including an astonishing selection of shoes (of Imelda Marcos proportions). There's another branch a bit further along Pembridge Rd, at No 32.

ORSINI
VINTAGE

Map p440 (76 Earl's Court Rd, W8; ⊙10.30am-6pm Mon-Sat, noon-5pm Sun; ◉Earl's Court) One of the most appealing women's vintage designer collections in town, Orsini is very small, but worth the effort to get to if you're looking for a gem. Alterations are available in-store.

ROUGH TRADE WEST
MUSIC

Map p438 (☎020-7229 8541; www.roughtrade.com/pages/about; 130 Talbot Rd, W11; ⊙10am-6.30pm Mon-Sat, 11am-5pm Sun; ◉Ladbroke Grove) With its underground, alternative and vintage rarities, this home of the eponymous punk-music label remains a haven for vinyl junkies.

BOOK & COMIC EXCHANGE
BOOKS

Map p438 (www.mgeshops.com; 14 Pembridge Rd; ⊙10am-8pm; ◉Notting Hill Gate) Stuffed with surprises, this shop is inundated with early issues of *Superboy*, *Batman*, *Justice League*, *the Flash*, *the Hulk*, *Spiderman*, *the Silver Surfer* and a host of other comic superheroes, backed up by sizeable slabs of collectable music magazines and walls densely stuffed with second-hand books.

There's an ocean of books downstairs as well, in lopsided piles, crammed into shelves and strewn across the floor. Stock is constantly reduced in price to make space for new items so there's always new literature turning up and bargains await.

HONEST JON'S
MUSIC

Map p438 (☎020-8969 9822; www.honestjons.com; 278 Portobello Rd, W10; ⊙10am-6pm Mon-Sat, 11am-5pm Sun; ◉Ladbroke Grove) Selling old-school reggae, jazz, funk, soul, dance and blues vinyl to Notting Hill's musical purists since 1974, with a large volume of CDs.

🏃 SPORTS & ACTIVITIES

★ LONDON WATERBUS COMPANY
CRUISE

Map p438 (☎020-7482 2550; www.londonwaterbus.co.uk; 58 Camden Lock Pl, NW1; adult/child one way £8.30/6.80, return £12/9.80; ⊙hourly 10am-5pm Apr-Sep; ◉Warwick Ave, Camden Town) This enclosed barge runs enjoyable 50-minute trips on Regent's Canal between Little Venice and Camden Lock, passing by Regent's Park and stopping at London Zoo. There are fewer departures outside high season – check the website for schedules.

QUEENS ICE & BOWL
SKATING

Map p438 (☎020-7229 0172; www.queensiceandbowl.co.uk; 17 Queensway; adult/child £10.50/10, skate hire £3; ⊙10am-6.45pm & 8-10.45pm daily, children's classes 4.45-5.30pm Tue & Thu; ◉Queensway) London may have a generous crop of winter-month outdoor ice rinks, but Queen's Ice Rink in Queensway is open all year. A great hit with novices and ice-skaters of all ages, the rink has been sending generations of youngsters and adults, arms whirling, around its rink for decades. There's a fun tenpin bowling alley (10am to 11pm, £7.50 per person per game) right alongside.

PORCHESTER SPA
SPA

Map p438 (Porchester Centre, Queensway, W2; admission £28; ⊙10am-10pm; ◉Bayswater, Royal Oak) Housed in a gorgeous, art-deco building, the Porchester is a no-frills spa run by Westminster Council. With a 30m swimming pool, a large Finnish-log sauna, two steam rooms, three Turkish hot rooms and a massive plunge pool, there are plenty of affordable treatments on offer including massages and male and female pampering/grooming sessions.

It's women only on Tuesdays, Thursdays and Fridays all day and between 10am and 2pm on Sundays; men only on Mondays, Wednesdays and Saturdays. Couples are welcome from 4pm to 10pm on Sundays.

Greenwich & South London

GREENWICH | WOOLWICH | LAMBETH | KENNINGTON | ELEPHANT & CASTLE | BRIXTON | BATTERSEA | DULWICH | FOREST HILL | CAMBERWELL | WANDSWORTH | VAUXHAUL

Neighbourhood Top Five

1 Taking in the 360-degree views from the statue of General Wolfe in **Greenwich Park** (p271).

2 Hanging out at fun and ever-funky **Brixton Village** (p276).

3 Exploring the **Cutty Sark's** (p273) history and admiring its golden hull from below.

4 Revisiting the horror of war and the promise of peace at the new First World War Galleries of the **Imperial War Museum** (p275).

5 Discovering the dichotomy that is **Deptford** (p283), with its Georgian architecture, state-of-the-art Laban Theatre dance academy and workaday market.

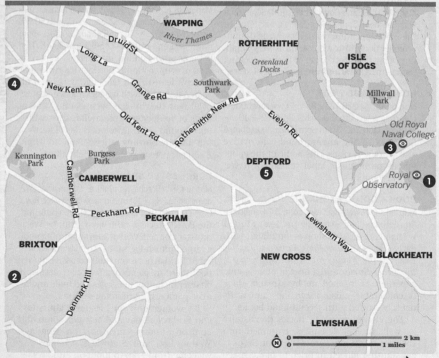

For more detail of this area see Map p442, p444 and p445 ➡

Explore: Greenwich & South London

Until recently Londoners talked as if the Thames was the huge barrier between north and south that it was in the Middle Ages. But with more attractions, better transport links and increased pedestrian areas, the allure to go south has become irresistible. Quaint Greenwich (*gren*-itch) is packed with grand architecture, while gorgeous parks and standout museums bring growing fleets of visitors. With the Royal Observatory and the fabulously renovated Cutty Sark, Greenwich should be one of the highlights of any visit to London – allow a day, particularly if you want to head down the river to the Thames Barrier.

Find time for an afternoon or a night out in edgy and artistic Brixton. Battersea and Wandsworth are home to lovely parks and a visit is ideally rounded off with a beer in a fantastic local pub. Lambeth boasts both the medieval London residence of the Archbishop of Canterbury and the incomparable Imperial War Museum with its excellent new First World War Galleries. Further afield, Dulwich and Forest Hill are home to excellent galleries and museums, while Bexleyheath and Eltham will reward day trippers with unusual architectural gems.

Local Life

➝**Hang-outs** Spending a Saturday or Sunday afternoon in the pub is time well spent in South London, particularly if you add brunch at Rivington Grill (p281) or Sunday lunch at Brunswick House; p284.

➝**Live music & clubbing** Brixton (Dogstar (p285)) and Vauxhall (Fire London; p286) swarm with London clubbers.

➝**Shopping** Funky and art-inclined Brixton Village (p276) has emerged as a vibrant and eclectic hub of local life.

Getting There & Away

➝**Underground, DLR & Train** Most areas of South London can be reached by Underground or DLR, though sometimes you have to take the train. Most sights in Greenwich can be easily reached from the Cutty Sark for Maritime Greenwich (its full name) DLR station, but a quicker way from central London is on one of the mainline trains from Charing Cross or London Bridge to Greenwich train station.

➝**Bus** From Greenwich, bus 177 or 180 is handy for the Thames Barrier and Woolwich. In Forest Hill, the P4 links the Horniman Museum and the Dulwich Picture Gallery.

➝**Boat** Thames Clipper boats run to Greenwich and Royal Arsenal Woolwich from the London Eye, Embankment and Tower Millennium piers.

➝**Cable Car** The airborne option to cross from the O2 to the Royal Docks.

Lonely Planet Top Tip

A fun way to reach Docklands from Greenwich (or vice versa) is via the foot tunnel under the Thames. From the Island Gardens park on the Isle of Dogs, enjoy the splendid view of Greenwich that Venetian artist Canaletto portrayed in his *Greenwich Hospital from the North Bank of the Thames* (1752), now in the National Maritime Museum's art collection.

✖ Best Places to Eat

➝ Angels & Gypsies (p281)
➝ Brunswick House (p284)
➝ Rivington Grill (p281)
➝ Franco Manca (p282)
➝ Chez Bruce (p282)

For reviews, see p280 ➡

🍺 Best Places to Drink

➝ Lost Angel (p286)
➝ Cutty Sark Tavern (p284)
➝ Market House (p285)
➝ Effra Hall Tavern (p285)
➝ Greenwich Union (p284)

For reviews, see p284 ➡

◉ Best Places for Music

➝ O2 Academy Brixton (p286)
➝ Chapel at Old Royal Naval College (p272)
➝ Corsica Studios (p284)
➝ O2 Arena (p286)
➝ Plan B (p285)

For reviews, see p284 ➡

GREENWICH & SOUTH LONDON

TOP SIGHT
ROYAL OBSERVATORY & GREENWICH PARK

The Royal Observatory is where the study of the sea, the stars and time converge within gorgeous Greenwich Park, London's oldest royal park. The prime meridian charts its line through the grounds of the observatory, chosen quite arbitrarily in 1884, dividing the globe into the eastern and western hemispheres. The observatory sits atop a hill within leafy and regal Greenwich Park, with its fabulous views and 74 hectares of trees and lush greenery.

Royal Observatory

Unlike most other attractions in Greenwich, the Royal Observatory contains free-access areas (Weller Astronomy Galleries, Great Equatorial Telescope) and ones you pay for (Meridian Line, Flamsteed House).

Flamsteed House & Meridian Courtyard

Charles II ordered construction of the Christopher Wren-designed **Flamsteed House**, the original observatory building, on the foundations of Greenwich Castle in 1675 after closing the observatory at the Tower of London. Today it contains the magnificent **Octagon Room** and the rather simple apartment where the Astronomer Royal, John Flamsteed, and his family lived. Here you'll also find the brilliant new **Time Galleries**, explaining how the longitude problem – how to accurately determine a ship's east-west location – was solved through astronomical means and the invention of the marine chronometer.

In the Meridian Courtyard, where the globe is decisively sliced into east and west, visitors can delightfully straddle both hemispheres, with one foot on either side of the meridian line. Every day the red **Time Ball** at the top of the Royal Observatory drops at 1pm, as it has done ever since 1833.

DON'T MISS...

→ Meridian Courtyard
→ Flamsteed House
→ Views from the statue of General Wolfe
→ Astronomy Centre

PRACTICALITIES

→ Map p445, D3
→ www.rmg.co.uk
→ Greenwich Park, Blackheath Ave, SE10
→ adult/child £9.50/5, with Cutty Sark £16.80/7.70
→ ⊙10am-5pm Oct-Jun, to 6pm Jul-Sep
→ ℝDLR Cutty Sark, ℝDLR Greenwich, ℝGreenwich

Astronomy Centre & Planetarium

The southern half of the observatory contains the the highly informative (and free) **Weller Astronomy Galleries**, where you can touch the oldest object you will ever encounter: part of the Gibeon meteorite, a mere 4.5 billion years old! Other engaging exhibits include an orrery (mechanical model of the solar system, minus the as-yet-undiscovered Uranus and Neptune) from 1780, astronomical documentaries, a first edition of Newton's *Principia Mathematica* and the opportunity to view the Milky Way in multiple wavelengths. To take stargazing further, pick up a Skyhawk telescope from the shop.

The state-of-the-art **Peter Harrison Planetarium** (Map p445; ✆020-8312 6608; www.rmg.co.uk/whats-on/planetarium-shows; adult/child £7.50/5.50; ⊠Greenwich, ⊠DLR Cutty Sark) – London's only planetarium – can cast entire heavens onto the inside of its roof. It runs at least five informative shows a day. Booking advised.

Greenwich Park

The **park** (Map p445; www.royalparks.org.uk; King George St, SE10; ⊙6am-6pm winter, to 8pm spring & autumn, to 9pm summer; ⊠Greenwich, Maze Hill, ⊠DLR Cutty Sark) is one of London's loveliest expanses of green, with a rose garden, picturesque walks, Anglo-Saxon tumuli and astonishing views from the crown of the hill near the Royal Observatory towards Canary Wharf, the financial district across the Thames. Greenwich Park hosted the 2012 Olympic Games equestrian events.

Covering 74 hectares, this is the oldest enclosed royal park and is partly the work of André Le Nôtre, the landscape architect who designed the palace gardens of Versailles. The view of central London from the statue of General James Wolfe, celebrated for his victory over the French at the Battle of Quebec in Canada in 1759, is one of the best in the city.

Ranger's House (Wernher Collection)

This elegant Georgian **villa** (EH; Map p445; ✆020-8294 2548; www.english-heritage.org.uk; Greenwich Park, Chesterfield Walk, SE10; adult/child £7.20/4.30; ⊙guided tours only at 11am & 2pm Sun-Wed late Mar–Sep; ⊠Greenwich, ⊠DLR Cutty Sark), built in 1723, once housed the park's ranger and now contains a collection of 700 works of fine and applied art (medieval and Renaissance paintings, porcelain, silverware, tapestries) amassed by Julius Wernher (1850–1912), a German-born railway engineer's son who struck it rich in the diamond fields of South Africa in the 19th century. The Spanish Renaissance jewellery collection is the best in Europe, and the rose garden fronting the house makes a visit in June even more special. Book in advance.

PRIME TARGET

On 15 February 1894, the Royal Observatory was the unexpected target of a bomb plot. The bomber – a 26-year-old French anarchist called Martial Bourdin – managed to blow his left hand off in the bungled attack and died from his wounds soon afterwards. The choice of the Royal Observatory as a target was never understood, but it was undamaged. The bombing later found literary recognition in Joseph Conrad's novel *The Secret Agent* and the anarchist appears in the TS Eliot poem *Animula* under the name Boudin.

The Greenwich meridian was selected as the global prime meridian at the International Meridian Conference in Washington DC in 1884. Greenwich became the world's ground zero for longitude and standard for time calculations, replacing the multiple meridians that had existed till then. Greenwich was assisted in its bid by the earlier US adoption of Greenwich Mean Time for its own national time zones. In any case, the majority of world trade already used sea charts that identified Greenwich as the prime meridian.

TOP SIGHT
OLD ROYAL NAVAL COLLEGE

When Christopher Wren was commissioned by King William III and Queen Mary II to construct a naval hospital here in 1692, he conceived it in two separate halves to protect the river views from the Queen's House, Inigo Jones' Renaissance masterpiece to the south. Built on the site of Palace of Placentia, where Henry VIII was born in 1491, the hospital was initially intended for sailors wounded in the victory over the French at La Hogue. In 1869 the building was converted to a college for the navy. Today it is home to the University of Greenwich and Trinity College of Music, with two main sections open to the public.

DON'T MISS...

➜ Painted Hall
➜ Concerts in the chapel
➜ Artefacts from Henry VIII's Palace of Placentia

PRACTICALITIES

➜ Map p445, C2
➜ www.ornc.org
➜ 2 Cutty Sark Gardens, SE10
➜ admission free
➜ ⊙grounds 8am-6pm
➜ ℞DLR Cutty Sark

Painted Hall

Designed as a dining hall for sailors, the **Painted Hall** (Map p445; ☑020-8269 4799) FREE in the King William Building is one of Europe's greatest banquet rooms, with 'allegorical Baroque' murals by artist James Thornhill. The magnificent ceiling mural above the Lower Hall is a feast, showing William and Mary enthroned amid symbols of the Virtues. Beneath William's feet grovels the defeated French king Louis XIV, furled flag in hand. On the west wall of the Upper Hall, George I is depicted with his family.

Off the Upper Hall to the south is the **Nelson Room**, originally designed by Nicholas Hawksmoor. In January 1806 the brandy-soaked (for embalming purposes, of course) body of the great naval hero lay in state here before his funeral at St Paul's. Today the room contains a plaster replica of the statue atop Nelson's column in Trafalgar Sq, plus other memorabilia, including lots of hospital silver.

Chapel

With its mix of ancient Greek and naval motifs, the beautiful **chapel** (Map p445; ⊙10am-5pm Mon-Sat, from 12.30pm Sun) in the Queen Mary Building is decorated in an elaborate rococo style with lots of trompe l'œil details. The eastern end of the chapel is dominated by the *Preservation of St Paul after Shipwreck at Malta* painting by the 18th-century American artist Benjamin West. The chapel is famed for its excellent acoustics and regularly hosts concerts; check the Old Royal Naval College's website for details.

Discover Greenwich

A painless introduction to this royal borough, the **Discover Greenwich** (Map p445; Pepys Building, King William Walk, SE10; ⊙10am-5pm) FREE exhibition delves into the history of Greenwich with models and hands-on exhibits, many aimed at children. It also contains artefacts from King Henry VIII's old palace, unearthed during a dig in 2005.

The Greenwich Tourist Office (p391) is also here, as is the **Old Brewery** (Map p445; www. oldbrewerygreenwich.com; Pepys Bldg, Old Royal Naval College, SE10; ⊙11am-11pm Mon-Sat, noon-10.30pm Sun).

Guided Tours

Guided tours of the Old Royal Naval College depart at noon and 2pm daily and take you behind the scenes as well as to the main sights. They cost £6 and must be booked at the Greenwich Tourist Office.

 SIGHTS

⊙ Greenwich

ROYAL OBSERVATORY   HISTORIC BUILDING
See p270.

OLD ROYAL NAVAL COLLEGE   HISTORIC
BUILDING
See p272.

QUEEN'S HOUSE   HISTORIC BUILDING
Map p445 (www.rmg.co.uk/queens-house; Romney Rd, SE10; ⊙10am-5pm; ℝDLR Cutty Sark)
FREE The first Palladian building by architect Inigo Jones after he returned from Italy is as enticing for its form as for its art collection. The Great Hall is a lovely cube shape with an elaborately tiled floor. Climb the helix-shaped Tulip Stairs up to the 1st floor, where there's a rich collection of paintings and portraits with a sea or seafaring theme from the National Maritime Museum's collection.

The house was begun in 1616 for Anne of Denmark, wife of James I, but was not completed until 1638, when it became the home of Charles I and his queen, Henrietta Maria. Don't miss the immaculately restored painted ceiling in the Queen's Presence Chamber on the 1st floor.

O2   NOTABLE BUILDING
Map p432 (www.theo2.co.uk; Peninsula Sq, SE10; ⊖North Greenwich) The 380m-wide circular O2 cost £750 million to build for the turn of the last century. Once the definitive white elephant, it has finally found its purpose as a multipurpose venue hosting big-ticket concerts, sporting events and blockbuster exhibitions. There are dozens of bars and restaurants inside and you can actually scale it with an outfit called Up at the O2 (p287).

It's located on the Greenwich Peninsula, just 10 minutes by bus from Greenwich itself and on the Jubilee line.

ST ALFEGE CHURCH   CHURCH
Map p445 (www.st-alfege.org; Greenwich Church St, SE10; ⊙11am-4pm Mon-Wed, to 2pm Thu & Fri, 10am-4pm Sat & Sun; ℝGreenwich, DLR Cutty Sark) Designed by Nicholas Hawksmoor to replace a 13th-century church and consecrated in 1718, lovely St Alfege features a restored mural by James Thornhill (whose work can also be found in the Painted Hall

TOP SIGHT
CUTTY SARK

This Greenwich landmark, the last of the great clipper ships to sail between China and England in the 19th century, is fully operational now after six years and £25 million of extensive renovations largely precipitated by disastrous fire in 2007.

The exhibition in the ship's hold tells her story as a tea clipper at the end of the 19th century (and then wool and mixed cargo). Launched in 1869 in Scotland, she made eight voyages to China in the 1870s, sailing out with a mixed cargo and coming back with a bounty of tea. As you make your way up, there are films, interactive maps and plenty of illustrations and props to get an idea of what life on board was like.

On the top deck, you can visit the crew's cramped living quarters and the officers' plush cabins. Visits end in the basement gallery located underneath the hull, which rests on a glass 'sea' design by architect Nicola Grimshow and appears to be floating. There's also an intriguing collection of figureheads below deck, one of the largest of its kind in the world.

DON'T MISS...
➜ Hull views from the basement gallery
➜ Interactive displays on the Cutty Sark's voyages
➜ Figureheads collection

PRACTICALITIES
➜ Map p445, B2
➜ ☎020-8312 6608
➜ www.rmg.co.uk/cuttysark
➜ King William Walk, SE10
➜ adult/child £12.15/6.30, with Royal Observatory £16.80/7.70
➜ ⊙10am-5pm
➜ ℝDLR Cutty Sark

GREENWICH ARCHITECTURE

Greenwich is home to an extraordinary interrelated cluster of classical buildings. All the great architects of the Enlightenment made their mark here, largely due to royal patronage. In the early 17th century Inigo Jones built one of England's first classical Renaissance homes, the **Queen's House** (p273), which still stands today. Charles II was particularly fond of the area and had Sir Christopher Wren build both the Royal Observatory and part of the Royal Naval College, which John Vanbrugh then completed in the early 17th century.

at the nearby Royal Naval College and at St Paul's Cathedral), a largely wood-panelled interior and an intriguing Thomas Tallis keyboard with middle keyboard octaves from the Tudor period. Free concerts take place at 1.05pm on Thursdays.

FAN MUSEUM   MUSEUM
Map p445 (☎020-8305 1441; www.thefanmuseum.org.uk; 12 Crooms Hill, SE10; adult/child £4/3; ☺11am-5pm Tue-Sat, noon-5pm Sun;

🚉Greenwich, 🚤Cutty Sark) This museum, entirely devoted to fans (as in the things that cool you down), has a wonderful collection of ivory, tortoiseshell, peacock-feather and folded-fabric examples, alongside kitsch battery-powered versions and huge ornamental Welsh fans. The setting, an 18th-century Georgian town house, also has an **Orangery** (Map p445; full tea £7; ☺1.45-3.45pm Tue & Sun, 12.30-4.30pm Fri & Sat), with lovely trompe l'œil murals, a fan-shaped garden and afternoon tea four days a week.

◉ Woolwich

FIREPOWER (ROYAL ARTILLERY
MUSEUM)   MUSEUM
(☎Mon-Fri 020-8312 7103, Sat 020-8312 7134; www.firepower.org.uk; Royal Arsenal, Woolwich, SE18; adult/child £5.30/2.50; ☺10am-5pm Tue-Sat; ☐177, 180, 🚉DLR Woolwich Arsenal) Loud and reeking of adrenaline, Firepower is an explosive display of artillery's evolution. The History Gallery traces artillery's development from catapults to nuclear warheads, while the multimedia, smoke-filled Field of Fire immerses you in the experience of artillery gunners from WWI to

◉ TOP SIGHT
NATIONAL MARITIME MUSEUM

Narrating the long and eventful history of seafaring Britain, this museum's highlights include **Miss Britain III** (the first boat to top 100mph on open water), the 19m-long **golden state barge** built in 1732 for Frederick, Prince of Wales, the huge **ship's propeller** and the colourful figureheads installed on the ground floor. Families will also love the **ship simulator** and the **children's gallery**.

Adults are likely to prefer the fantastic (and more serene) galleries. **Voyagers: Britons and the Sea** on the ground floor is an introduction to the collection and showcases some of the museum's incredible archives. On the 1st floor, **Traders: the East India Company and Asia** looks at Britain's 19th-century maritime trade with the East, while **The Atlantic: Slavery, Trade, Empire** explores the triangular trade between Europe, Africa and America from the 1600s to the 1850s.

On the 2nd floor, the superb **Nelson, Navy, Nation** gallery focuses on the Royal Navy during the conflict-ridden 17th century. It provides an excellent look at the legendary national hero and, through documents and memorabilia, explains Nelson's achievements and dazzling celebrity. The coat in which he was fatally wounded during the Battle of Trafalgar takes pride of place.

DON'T MISS...

➡ Frederick's golden state barge

➡ Nelson's uniform coat

➡ Miss Britain III

➡ Ship simulator

PRACTICALITIES

➡ Map p445, C2

➡ www.rmg.co.uk/national-maritime-museum

➡ Romney Rd, SE10

➡ admission free

➡ ☺10am-5pm

➡ 🚉DLR Cutty Sark

TOP SIGHT
IMPERIAL WAR MUSEUM

Fronted by a pair of intimidating 15-inch naval guns, this riveting museum is housed in what was the third home of the Bethlehem Royal Hospital, also known as Bedlam. Although its focus is on military action involving British or Commonwealth troops during the 20th century, it rolls out the carpet to war in the wider sense.

The highlight is the state-of-the-art **First World War Galleries** opened in the lower level (here floor zero) to mark the 100th anniversary of the start of the conflict in 2014. It takes a hard look at those who experienced the war both on the front line and at home. In the forecourt and the atrium above are **Witnesses to War** – everything from a Battle of Britain Spitfire and a towering German V-2 rocket to a Reuters Land Rover damaged by rocket attack in Gaza and a section of the World Trade Center in New York.

On the 1st floor, **A Family in Wartime** poignantly follows WWII through the experiences of the real-life Allpress family of Stockwell. In **Secret War** on the 2nd floor, there's an intriguing rifle through the work of the Secret Operations Executive (SOE). One of the most challenging sections is the extensive **Holocaust Exhibition** (not recommended for under 14s) on the 3rd floor.

DON'T MISS...

➡ First World War Galleries
➡ Holocaust Exhibition
➡ Spitfire
➡ Curiosities of War

PRACTICALITIES

➡ Map p444, C2
➡ www.iwm.org.uk
➡ Lambeth Rd, SE1
➡ admission free
➡ ⊙10am-6pm
➡ ⊜Lambeth North

Bosnia in a four-screen, 15-minute extravaganza. There's a Gunnery Hall packed with weapons and vehicles, while the recently reopened Cold War Gallery (guided tour only) walks you past the museum's largest material dating from 1945 to the present.

Kids will love the Camo Zone, where they can try their hand on the firing range (£1.50).

⊙ Lambeth, Kennington & Elephant & Castle

FLORENCE NIGHTINGALE MUSEUM   MUSEUM
Map p444 (✆020-7620 0374; www.florence-nightingale.co.uk; St Thomas's Hospital, 2 Lambeth Palace Rd, SE1; adult/child £7.50/3.80; ⊙10am-5pm; ⊜Westminster, Waterloo) This small but almost perfect museum looks at the life and legacy of Florence Nightingale (1820–1910), considered the founder of modern nursing. Her story is told through memorabilia and documents – don't miss her (now stuffed) pet owl Athena and the lantern she carried while visiting the wards at night. Most illuminating are her letters and, highlight of the collection, a recording of her voice made

in 1890, by which time she'd become one of the world's first modern celebrities.

Nightingale led a team of nurses to Turkey in 1854 during the Crimean War, when more soldiers were dying in the hospital than on the battlefield, and vastly improved their care. Back in London, she set up a training school for nurses at St Thomas's Hospital (where the museum is located) in 1859.

The collection is divided into several key sections: her childhood and early life as a nurse; her work in the district of Scutari (now Üsküdar) of Istanbul; and her work at St Thomas's Hospital upon her return. An audioguide is included in the admission price.

LAMBETH PALACE   HISTORIC BUILDING
Map p444 (www.archbishopofcanterbury.org/pages/visit-the-lambeth-palace-gardens-.html; Lambeth Palace Rd, SE1; ⊜Lambeth North) A gorgeous red- and fired-brick Tudor gatehouse, dating from 1495 and located beside the church of St Mary-at-Lambeth, leads to Lambeth Palace, the official London residence of the Archbishop of Canterbury. Although the palace is not open to the public, the gardens occasionally are; check the website for dates.

WORTH A DETOUR

THAMES BARRIER

This sci-fi-looking barrier is designed to protect London from flooding and, with rising sea levels and surge tides, vulnerable London is likely to become increasingly dependent on the barricade. Completed three decades ago, the barrier consists of 10 movable gates anchored to nine concrete piers, each as tall as a five-storey building. The silver roofs on the piers house the operating machinery that rotates the gates against excess water. Tested monthly, they make a glitteringly surreal sight, straddling the river in the lee of a giant warehouse.

The Thames is a tidal river, with its tide rising and falling twice a day – a difference in levels of up to 8m – and once a fortnight there's also a stronger 'spring' tide. The danger comes when the spring tide coincides with an unexpected surge, which pushes tonnes of extra water upriver. The barrier has been built to prevent that water pouring over the riverbanks and flooding nearby houses. Environmentalists are already talking about a bigger, wider damming mechanism further towards the mouth of the river on the North Sea before the current barrier comes to the expected end of its design life in about 2035.

The barrier looks best when raised, and the only guaranteed time this happens is when the mechanisms are checked once a month. For exact dates and times, check with the **Thames Barrier Information Centre** (☑020-8305 4188; www.gov.uk/the-thames-barrier; 1 Unity Way, SE18; adult/child £3.75/2.25; ☉10.30am-5pm Thu-Sun; ☒472 or 161 or, ⍰Charlton, then, ⊜North Greenwich, then, ☒472).

If you're coming from central London, take a train to Charlton from Charing Cross or London Bridge. Walk east along Woolwich Rd to Eastmoor St, which leads northward to the centre. If you're coming from Greenwich, you can pick up bus 177 or 180 along Romney Rd and get off at the Thames Barrier stop. The closest tube station is North Greenwich, from where you can pick up bus 472 or 161. Boats also travel to and from the barrier, although they don't dock here.

⊚ Brixton

The years that most shaped contemporary Brixton were the post-WWII 'Windrush' years, when immigrants arrived from the West Indies. (*Windrush* was the name of one of the leading ships that brought these immigrants to the UK.) Economic decline and hostility between the police and the black community particularly led to riots in 1981, 1985 and 1995.

Although violence returned to Brixton during the London riots of August 2011, the mood today is upbeat. Soaring property prices have sent in house hunters, and pockets of gentrification sit alongside the more run-down streets. Apart from some great restaurants and clubs, the big sights are fantastic Brixton Village – a current South London culinary and shopping magnet – and Brixton Market (p287).

BRIXTON VILLAGE   MARKET

Map p442 (www.brixtonmarket.net/brixton-village; Atlantic Rd, SW9; ☉8am-11.30pm Tue-Sun, to 6pm Mon; ⊜Brixton) This revitalised covered market has enjoyed an eye-catching renaissance in the past half-dozen years, prompted by an initiative to offer a period of free rent to outfits setting up in the dilapidated 1930s Granville Arcade. Cafes and restaurants have swarmed in as well as a host of inventively inclined shops, which happily cohabit with butchers, greengrocers and bazaars.

The 'village' is lively day and night and has a lovely, eclectic atmosphere. Shops worth popping into include **Woo Woo Boutique** (unit 97), selling vintage-inspired fashion, and **African Queen** (unit 30), piled to the rafters with colourful West African fabrics and headdresses. The village is full of lunch spots and restaurants – check out Champagne + Fromage (p282) and Honest Burgers (p282), among others.

BLACK CULTURAL
ARCHIVES   CULTURAL CENTRE

Map p442 (☑020-3757 8500; http://bcaheritage.org.uk; 1 Windrush Sq, SW2; ☉10am-6pm Tue-Sat, to 10pm every 2nd Thu) **FREE** Housed in a brand-new heritage centre in the heart of Brixton, the Black Cultural Archives puts on seminal photographic exhibitions, many in association with the V&A, and organises workshops, lectures and performances.

⊙ Battersea

BATTERSEA PARK   PARK

Map p442 (www.batterseapark.org; ⊙8am-dusk; ⊠Battersea Park) Sprinkled with sculptures by Henry Moore and Barbara Hepworth, these 50 hectares of gorgeous greenery stretch between Albert and Chelsea Bridges. To the north, the **Peace Pagoda** (Map p442), erected in 1985 by a group of Japanese Buddhists to commemorate Hiroshima Day, displays the Buddha in the four stages of his life. There are lakes and plenty of sporting facilities – rent bicycles and other pedal conveyances from **London Recumbents** (☑020-8299 6636; www.london-recumbents.co.uk; Ranger's Yard, Dulwich Park; per hr £8-15; ⊙10am-5pm).

There's also an art space called the **Pump House Gallery** (Map p442; ☑020-8871 7572; http://pumphousegallery.org.uk; ⊙11am-4pm Wed-Sun) FREE and a small **Children's Zoo** (Map p442; ☑020-7924 5826; www.batterseaparkzoo.co.uk; adult/child £8.95/6.95; ⊙10am-5.30pm Apr-Oct, to 4.30pm Nov-Mar).

BATTERSEA POWER STATION   HISTORIC BUILDING

Map p442 (www.batterseapowerstation.co.uk; ⊠Battersea Park) Its four smokestacks famously celebrated on Pink Floyd's *Animals* album cover, Battersea Power Station is one of South London's best-known monuments. Built by Giles Gilbert Scott (who also designed the power station that's now the Tate Modern, and the iconic red telephone box) in 1933, the station was snuffed out in 1983 only to enter an existential limbo for more than three decades. It's now being redeveloped as a mixed residential and commercial space.

Luck turned for the mighty brick building in 2011 when a £5 billion master plan to redevelop the site, right on the Thames, was approved. Plans include thousands of new homes, retail and corporate space and two new tube stations on the extended Northern line at Battersea Park and Nine Elms, where the new US Embassy will relocate after leaving Grosvenor Sq in Mayfair. The rebuilt chimneys, reinforced with steel, will be completed in 2016, as will the embassy and the first new homes. The total redevelopment isn't expected to be finished until 2024. Watch this space.

⊙ TOP SIGHT
HORNIMAN MUSEUM

Comprising the collection of wealthy tea merchant Frederick John Horniman, this museum is a treasure trove of discoveries, from a huge stuffed walrus and slowly undulating moon jellyfish to a nasty 17th-century torture chair from Spain and a knockout musical-instruments exhibition.

On the ground and 1st floors is the **Natural History Gallery**, with animal skeletons, pickled specimens and dusty cupboards. When the 19th-century **Apostle Clock** from Germany strikes 4pm, the saints troop out past Jesus and only Judas turns away from him. Children adore the **Hands On Base Gallery**, where you can touch, wear and play around with thousands of objects.

On the lower ground floor you'll find the **African Worlds Gallery** and the **Music Gallery**. The latter displays thousands of instruments, from Native American rattles and early English keyboards to Indonesian gamelan and Ghanaian drums. There are touch screens so you can hear what they sound like.

The **aquarium** in the basement is small but state of the art and the 6.5 hectares of hillside **gardens** (complete with views of London as far as Wembley) are magnificent.

DON'T MISS...
→ Hands On Base Gallery
→ Aquarium
→ Music Gallery
→ Gardens

PRACTICALITIES
→ ☑020-8699 1872
→ www.horniman.ac.uk
→ 100 London Rd, Forest Hill, SE23
→ museum & gardens free, aquarium adult/child £3.50/1.50
→ ⊙museum 10.30am-5.30pm, gardens 7.15am-sunset Mon-Sat, 8am-sunset Sun
→ ⊠Forest Hill

Parks & Gardens

Glance at a colour map of town and be struck by how much is olive green. London has some of the world's most superb urban parkland, most of it well-tended, accessible and a delight in any season.

Hyde Park

Perhaps London's most famous and easily accessed expanse of urban greenery, Hyde Park is astonishing for the variety of its landscapes and trees. The lovely Serpentine separates it from that other grand London park, Kensington Gardens.

Greenwich Park

Delightfully hilly, elegantly landscaped and bisected by the Meridian Line, Greenwich Park offers sweeping perspectives from its highest point. London's oldest enclosed royal park, it is home to herds of deer and some of Greenwich's top highlights.

Victoria Park

Named after its eponymous royal benefactor, Victoria Park is one of East London's most pleasant and popular parks and has recently had an expensive regeneration. In summer it becomes a venue for live music and festivals.

Richmond Park

An epic expanse of greenery down southwest, royal Richmond Park is home to herds of deer, sublime views and a fantastic collection of trees, ponds, woodland and grass. Shake off the urban fumes and immerse yourself in its wild expanses.

Kew Gardens

To fall for Kew Gardens, all you need is an eye for fine architecture, a fondness for exploration and a sense of natural curiosity. Children will adore the treetop walkway and the fantastic play zones.

1. Palm House, Kew Gardens (p294) 2. Greenwich Park (p270)
3. Fallow deer, Richmond Park (p296)

◉ Dulwich & Forest Hill

DULWICH PICTURE GALLERY　　GALLERY
(☎020-8693 5254; www.dulwichpicturegallery.org.uk; Gallery Rd, SE21; adult/child £5/free; ⊙10am-5pm Tue-Sun; ℝWest Dulwich) The world's first public art gallery, the small Dulwich Picture Gallery was designed by the idiosyncratic architect Sir John Soane between 1811 and 1814 to house nearby Dulwich College's collection of paintings by Raphael, Rembrandt, Rubens, Reynolds, Claude Lorrain, Gainsborough, Poussin, Canaletto, Van Dyck and many more. Unusually, the collector Noel Desenfans and painter Sir Peter Francis Bourgeois chose to have their mausoleums, lit by a moody *lumière mystérieuse* (mysterious light) created with tinted glass, placed among the pictures.

Go outside and look at the lantern above. It's said to be the inspiration behind Giles Gilbert Scott's iconic red telephone box.

The gallery runs fantastic temporary exhibitions (additional charge) and free guided tours of the museum depart at 3pm on Saturday and Sunday. The **cafe** (mains £5.95-14.50; ⊙9.30am-5pm Tue-Fri, 10am-5pm Sat & Sun; ☑), in a modern extension near the main entrance, is a cut above the usual museum eateries.

The museum is a 10-minute walk north along Gallery Rd, which starts almost opposite West Dulwich train station. Bus P4 conveniently links the picture gallery with the Horniman Museum (p277).

✗ EATING

Eating in South London is a treat – be it the fine dining in the restaurants of Battersea, Camberwell or Greenwich, or the eclectic market fare on offer in Brixton and Greenwich.

✗ Greenwich

GREENWICH MARKET　　MARKET £
Map p445 (www.greenwichmarketlondon.com; College Approach, SE10; ⊙9am-5.30pm; ☑; ℝDLR Cutty Sark) Perfect for snacking your way through a world atlas of food while browsing the other market stalls. Come here for delicious food to go, from Spanish tapas and Thai curries to sushi, Ethiopian

---

◉ TOP SIGHT
ELTHAM PALACE

Rayon heir Stephen Courtauld (of Courtauld Gallery fame) and his wife Virginia (Ginie) built an art-deco mansion next to a 15th-century medieval hall between 1933 and 1937. From the impressive entrance hall with its dome, African black-bean-panelled walls and huge circular carpet with geometric shapes, to the black-marble dining room with silver-foil ceiling and heavy black doors decorated with lacquered animal figures, it appears the couple had taste as well as money. A £1.7-million refurbishment has opened up areas previously closed to the public, including the decorated map room off Ginie's boudoir, where the couple plotted their extensive travels, and the basement, converted to a deluxe air-raid shelter during the Blitz.

A royal palace was built on this site in 1305 and was, for a time, the boyhood home of Henry VIII, before the Tudors decamped to Greenwich. Incorporated into the mansion, the restored Great Medieval Hall contains one of the finest hammer-beam roofs in England. The eight hectares of gardens include a rockery and moat.

Visitors view the mansion's 20 rooms on a self-paced tour with an entertaining handheld multimedia guide.

DON'T MISS
- ➡ Great Medieval Hall
- ➡ Boudoir
- ➡ Dining room
- ➡ Mah-jongg's luxury cage
- ➡ Map room

PRACTICALITIES
- ➡ www.english-heritage.org.uk
- ➡ Court Yard, Eltham, SE9
- ➡ adult/child £13/7.80
- ➡ ⊙10am-5pm Sun-Wed Apr-Sep, to 4pm Oct, to 4pm Sun Nov-Mar
- ➡ ℝEltham, Mottingham

vegetarian, French crêpes, dim sum, Mexican burritos and lots more.

GODDARDS AT GREENWICH
BRITISH £

Map p445 (www.goddardsatgreenwich.co.uk; 22 King William Walk, SE10; dishes £3.30-7.30; ⏰10am-7pm Sun-Thu, to 8pm Fri & Sat; ⓡDLR Cutty Sark) If you're keen to try that archetypal English dish, pie 'n' mash (minced beef, steak and kidney or even chicken in pastry with mashed potatoes), do so at this Greenwich institution, which always attracts a motley crowd. Jellied eels, mushy peas and 'liquor' (a green sauce made from parsley and vinegar) are optional extras.

TAI WON MEIN
CHINESE £

Map p445 (39 Greenwich Church St, SE10; mains £3.90-6.20; ⏰11.30am-11pm; ✏; ⓡDLR Cutty Sark) This great snack spot – the Cantonese moniker just means 'Big Bowl of Noodles' – serves epic portions of carbohydrate-rich noodles to those overcoming Greenwich's titanic sights.

BLACK VANILLA
ICE CREAM £

Map p445 (www.black-vanilla.com; 5 College Approach, SE10; cakes & ice creams £1.50-4; ⏰noon-7pm Tue-Sun; ⓡDLR Cutty Sark) If you want to picnic on something sweet in Greenwich Park, stop at this wonderful gelateria serving delightful (if pricey) ice cream and mountains of cupcakes. There's comfortable seating up the side staircase.

★RIVINGTON GRILL
BRITISH ££

Map p445 (✆020-8293 9270; www.rivingtongreenwich.co.uk; 178 Greenwich High Rd, SE10; mains £9.50-15.75; ⏰noon-11pm Mon-Fri, from 10am Sat & Sun; ⓡGreenwich) This younger sister of the trendy bar and grill in Hoxton is every bit as stylish, with seating on two levels overlooking a lovely long bar. The menu is very much 'British now', with truffled cauliflower, mac 'n' cheese and luxury pies rubbing shoulders with half a Devon Red with liver and onion stuffing. You'll get a warm welcome.

The full English breakfast (£11.25) at weekends is awesome.

OLD BREWERY
MODERN BRITISH ££

Map p445 (✆020-3327 1280; www.oldbrewery-greenwich.com; Pepys Bldg, Old Royal Naval College, SE10; mains cafe £7.50-13.95, restaurant £12.50-22.95; ⏰cafe 10am-5pm, restaurant 6-11pm; ♿; ⓡDLR Cutty Sark) A working brewery within the grounds of the Old Royal Naval College, with splendidly burnished 1000L copper vats at one end and a high ceiling lit with natural sunlight, the Old Brewery is a cafe serving lovely bistro fare by day and a restaurant serving a choice selection of fine dishes carefully sourced from the best seasonal ingredients by night.

It's a pub throughout the day, run by the Meantime Brewery and selling its own draught Imperial Pale Ale (brewed on-site), along with a range of more than 70 beers.

INSIDE
MODERN EUROPEAN £££

Map p445 (✆020-8265 5060; www.insiderestaurant.co.uk; 19 Greenwich South St, SE10; mains £15-23, 2/3-course set menu £20/25; ⏰noon-2.30pm Tue-Fri, to 3pm Sat & Sun, 6-10pm Tue-Sat; ⓡDLR Greenwich) With white walls, modern art and linen tablecloths, Inside is a relaxed kind of place and one of Greenwich's best restaurants. The fine food hits the mark, ranging tastily and relatively affordably from smoked haddock and chive fish cakes to roast Barbary duck and sticky toffee pudding.

✖ Kennington, Elephant & Castle & Camberwell

DRAGON CASTLE
CHINESE ££

Map p444 (✆020-7277 3388; www.dragon-castle.com; 100 Walworth Rd, SE17; mains £9.80-26.80; ⏰noon-11pm; ✏; ⊜Elephant & Castle) It's hard to imagine that one of the best non-chain Chinese restaurants in London is hidden here in deepest, darkest Kennington. The duck, pork and seafood (deep-fried crispy oysters, crab with black bean) are renowned, but come for the dim sum (noon to 4.30pm), especially at lively weekend lunchtime.

ANGELS & GYPSIES
SPANISH ££

(✆020-7703 5984; www.angelsandgypsies.com; 29-33 Camberwell Church St, SE5; tapas £4.50-12.50; ⏰7-11am & 6-10.30pm Mon-Fri, 8am-3.30pm & 6-11pm Sat, 8am-4pm & 6-10.30pm Sun; ⓡDenmark Hill, ⊜Oval, then ▣36, 185 or 436) This restaurant is run by a half-English, half-Spanish brother duo who seem to stick to their mother's way of doing things at breakfast and brunch (full English from £9) and their father's in the evening, when dinner is all about tapas, with every product lovingly sourced from Spain (ham from Salamanca, the chilli sauce a family recipe from Galicia etc).

KENNINGTON TANDOORI
INDIAN ££

Map p444 (✆020-7735 9247; www.kenningtontandoori.com; 313 Kennington Rd, SE11; mains

£6.95-14.95; ⊙noon-11pm; ♪; ⊜Kennington) This very stylish (think 1930s hurled into our very own century) local curry house is apparently a favourite of MPs from across the river, including a certain former prime minister. Particularly good are the biryani dishes and the choice of vegetarian ones (£6.95 to £9.95) is impressive.

LOBSTER POT   SEAFOOD £££

Map p444 (☎020-7582 5556; www.lobsterpotrestaurant.co.uk; 3 Kennington Lane, SE11; mains £20.50-39.50; ⊙noon-2.30pm & 7-10.30pm Tue-Sat; ⊜Elephant & Castle) This charming French-owned (well, Breton-owned) restaurant, hidden just south of Elephant & Castle, reels in diners hook, line and sinker with finely prepared fish and seafood dishes à la française (think lashings of butter and garlic). An eight-course tasting menu with/without lobster is £54.50/49.50.

✗ Brixton

★ FRANCO MANCA   PIZZERIA £

Map p442 (www.francomanca.co.uk; 4 Market Row, SW9; pizzas £4.50-6.95; ⊙noon-5pm Mon, to 11pm Tue-Sat, to 10.30pm Sun; ⊜Brixton) The Brixton branch of a chain with a difference, Franco Manca is a perennial local favourite. Beat the queues by arriving early, avoiding lunch hours and Saturday, and delight in some fine, fine pizza. The restaurant only uses its own sourdough, fired up in a wood-burning brick oven.

CHAMPAGNE + FROMAGE   FRENCH £

Map p442 (☎020-7095 8504; www.champagneplusfromage.co.uk; unit 10-11, Brixton Village, SW9; dishes £5.50-10; ⊙11am-11pm Tue-Sat, to 9pm Sun; ⊜Brixton) This charming little French shop and bistro in Brixton Village serves everything from charcuterie and cheese plates (from £6.50) to duck confit (£10). It's also a shop, a fromagerie and will deliver champagne to your door.

MAMA LAN   CHINESE £

Map p442 (www.mamalan.co.uk; unit 18, Brixton Village, SW9; dishes £4-9; ⊙noon-4pm Mon, to 10.30pm Tue-Sun; ⊜Brixton) For authentic, handmade Beijing street food – dumplings, noodles, salads and snacks – this cute-as-a-button eatery in Brixton Village is the business. We can't get enough of its beef-noodle soup, and and pork and Chinese-leaf dumplings!

ROSIE'S DELI CAFÉ   CAFE £

Map p442 (www.rosiesdelicafe.com; 14e Market Row, SW9; mains £4.50-7; ⊙9.30am-5.30pm Mon-Sat; ⊜Brixton) Park yourself on one of the mismatched wooden chairs at this much-loved Brixton cafe run by cook and author Rosie Lovell for a wholesome treat. Quiches, wraps, ciabattas, sandwiches such as Reubens and pies emerge from her kitchen, and the cakes and biscuits are fantastic.

HONEST BURGERS   BURGERS ££

Map p442 (www.honestburgers.co.uk; unit 12, Brixton Village, SW9; mains £8.50-11.50; ⊙noon-4pm Mon, to 10.30pm Tue-Thu, 11.30am-10.30pm Fri & Sat, 11.30am-10pm Sun; ⊜Brixton) This minichain deserves plaudits for its juicy and tender burgers and glorious rosemary-seasoned triple-cooked chips. It's well worth the wait for a table, which you could well have to do (it's tiny, seats around 30 and there are no bookings).

NAUGHTY PIGLETS   BISTRO ££

Map p442 (☎020-7274 7796; www.naughtypiglets.co.uk; 28 Brixton Water Lane, SW2; mains £8-17; ⊙noon-2.30pm Thu, to 3pm Fri & Sat, to 4pm Sun, 6-10pm Tue-Sat; ⊜Brixton) This wonderful Anglo-French bistro all but defines the new Brixton, a district forever reinventing itself. Expect such inventive starters as dashi, clams and chives and mains such as lamb leg with pistachio. Naughty Piglets (something to do with gastronomic greed) is small – just 30 covers – so book ahead or treat yourself to a less-rammed lunch.

✗ Battersea & Wandsworth

SANTA MARIA DEL SUR   SOUTH AMERICAN ££

Map p442 (☎020-7622 2088; www.santamariadelsur.co.uk; 129 Queenstown Rd, SW8; mains £14.50-26.50; ⊙noon-3pm & 6pm-midnight; ☒Queenstown Rd or Battersea Park) Catering to carnivores with succulent grilled meats and sausages (and some token veggie dishes). Go for one of the parrilladas (mixed grill, £47.50 to £61.80 for two) to share and finish your meal with delicious pancakes and dulce de leche and a coffee with cream and cinnamon. Booking is advised.

★ CHEZ BRUCE   FRENCH £££

(☎020-8672 0114; www.chezbruce.co.uk; 2 Bellevue Rd, SW17; 3-course menu lunch £29.50-35, dinner £47.50; ⊙noon-2.30pm Mon-Fri, to 3pm Sat &

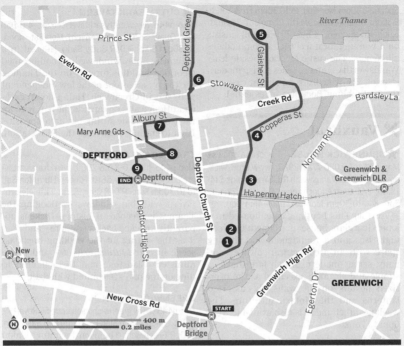

Neighbourhood Walk
Deptford in Depth

START DEPTFORD BRIDGE DLR & RAILWAY STATION
END DEPTFORD RAILWAY STATION
LENGTH 1.5 MILES, THREE HOURS

This walk explores edgy Deptford, just west of Greenwich, once an important and wealthy dockyard and shipbuilding centre, and now a district in transition, with galleries and art centres squeezing in between pie 'n' mash shops, and pubs turning into bars.

From the station walk up Deptford Church St and turn right into ❶**Creekside**, a street running parallel to Deptford Creek that's lined with galleries and artist studios with regularly changing art exhibitions, including ❷**Art Hub Gallery** and ❸**Cockpit Arts**. A short distance north is the plastic-clad ❹**Laban Theatre** (p286). The turf-covered mounds in front conceal debris cleared from the site.

Follow Copperas St to the creek then head north over Creek Rd to join Glaisher St. Just beyond the new footbridge is a ❺**statue of Peter the Great** recalling

the Russian tsar's four-month stay in 1698, when he came to Deptford to learn more about new developments in shipbuilding.

From the western end of Glaisher St walk south along Deptford Green to the late-17th-century ❻**St Nicholas Church**, which contains a memorial to playwright Christopher Marlowe, who was murdered in Deptford in a tavern brawl at the age of 29 in 1593 and may be buried here. The skull and crossbones over the lychgate entrance may have inspired the Jolly Roger pirate flag.

Running off Deptford Green, delightful ❼**Albury St** is lined with Georgian buildings that once housed Deptford's naval officers, including (it is said) Lord Nelson and Lady Hamilton. Notice the exquisite wood carvings decorating many of the doorways. To the south is the baroque ❽**St Paul's Church**, built in 1730.

Walk over to Deptford High St and, if the day is right, land in the centre of ❾**Deptford Market**, a colourful market held three days a week. Deptford railway station is just north.

Sun, 6.30-10pm Mon-Thu, to 10.30pm Fri & Sat, to 9.30pm Sun; ⓡWandsworth Common) Though Michelin-starred, Chez Bruce still insists on a winning local feel that accommodates all comers. The rustic exterior, beside leafy Wandsworth Common, belies a crisp modern interior. The wine list is an all-star cast, and the food sublime. Bookings are essential.

✕ Vauxhaul

★**BRUNSWICK HOUSE** MODERN BRITISH ££
Map p444 (✆020-7720 2926; www.brunswickhouse.com; 30 Wandsworth Rd, SW8; mains £14-18.60, 2/3-course lunch menu £16/19; ⊘noon-3pm & 6-10.30pm Mon-Sat, noon-4pm Sun; ☎; ⊜Vauxhall) This boutique cafe, housed in a lone Georgian house marooned between high-rises and a roundabout and sharing space with an architectural salvage company, serves modern British fare that's as simple and elegantly executed as the oversized posters on the walls, the assorted lanterns and the vintage furniture. The weekday lunch menu is also available from 6pm to 7pm.

COUNTER VAUXHALL ARCHES BRASSERIE ££
Map p444 (✆020-3693 9600; www.counterrestaurants.com; Arch 50, 7-11 South Lambeth Pl, SW8; mains £10-19; ⊘7am-midnight Mon-Thu, to 1am Fri, 8am-1am Sat, 8am-midnight Sun) This cavernous new kid under the arches at Vauxhall has something for everyone: bar, brasserie, cafe and breakfast nook. Food is correct if predictable (steak, chicken, pasta), but the place comes into its own at weekend brunch when the demanding denizens of the nearby gay clubs hold court.

🍷 DRINKING & NIGHTLIFE

When it comes to nightlife, South London has everything from historic boozers to flagship nightclubs – and everything in between.

📍 Greenwich

The drinking in Greenwich is top-notch, a mix of superb, historic old pubs and trendy microbreweries. A must after a day's sightseeing, even if you're not staying in the area.

★**CUTTY SARK TAVERN** PUB
Map p445 (www.cuttysarktavern.co.uk; 4-6 Ballast Quay, SE10; ⊘11am-11pm Mon-Sat, noon-10.30pm Sun; ⓡDLR Cutty Sark) Housed in a delightful bow-windowed, wood-beamed Georgian building directly on the Thames, the Cutty Sark is one of the few independent pubs left in Greenwich. Half a dozen cask-conditioned ales on tap line the bar, with an inviting riverside sitting-out area opposite. It's a 10-minute walk from the DLR station.

TRAFALGAR TAVERN PUB
Map p445 (✆020-8858 2909; www.trafalgartavern.co.uk; 6 Park Row, SE10; ⊘noon-11pm Mon-Sat, to 10.30pm Sun; ⓡDLR Cutty Sark) This elegant tavern with big windows overlooking the Thames is steeped in history. Dickens apparently knocked back a few here – and used it as the setting for the wedding breakfast scene in *Our Mutual Friend* – and prime ministers Gladstone and Disraeli used to dine on the pub's celebrated whitebait.

GREENWICH UNION PUB
Map p445 (www.greenwichunion.com; 56 Royal Hill, SE10; ⊘noon-11pm Mon-Fri, 11am-11pm Sat & Sun; ⓡDLR Greenwich) The award-winning Union plies six or seven Meantime microbrewery beers, including raspberry and wheat varieties, and a strong list of ales, plus bottled international brews. It's a handsome place, with duffed-up leather armchairs and a welcoming long, narrow aspect that leading to a conservatory and beer garden at the rear.

📍 Kennington & Elephant & Castle

CORSICA STUDIOS CLUB
Map p444 (www.corsicastudios.com; 4/5 Elephant Rd, SE17; admission £6-17.50; ⊘hours vary; ⊜Elephant & Castle) Places like Corsica Studios have given the once-rough Elephant & Castle area an edge. This not-for-profit, underground club is a well-known venue for electronic music. It's a small, intimate space with excellent sound and a mix of gigs and club nights till 3am weekdays and 6am weekends.

MINISTRY OF SOUND CLUB
Map p444 (www.ministryofsound.com; 103 Gaunt St, SE1; admission £16-22; ⊘10pm-6.30am Fri-Sun; ⊜Elephant & Castle) This legendary club-cum-enormous-global-brand (four bars, four dance floors) lost some 'edge' in the early noughties but, after pumping in top DJs, the

DANSON HOUSE & RED HOUSE

A couple of historic houses in Bexleyheath, once a village in Kent and now a typical southeast London suburb, are well worth exploring.

Red House (NT; ☎020-8304 9878; www.nationaltrust.org.uk/red-house; 13 Red House Lane, Bexleyheath, Kent DA6; adult/child £7.20/3.60, gardens only £2.20/1.20; ⊘11am-5pm Wed-Sun mid-Feb–Oct, 11am-5pm Fri-Sun Nov–late Dec; ℝBexleyheath, then 15min walk south) From the outside, Red House is reminiscent of a gingerbread house wrought in stone. It was built in 1859 by Victorian designer William Morris – of Morris wallpaper fame. The nine rooms open to the public, including two bedrooms only recently accessible after being shut up for more than a century, bear all the elements of the Arts and Crafts Movement to which Morris adhered – Gothic art here, some religious symbolism there, an art nouveau–like sunburst over there.

Furniture by Morris and the house's designer, Philip Webb, are on display, as are stained glass, paintings and murals (some only recently revealed under the wallpaper) by Edward Burne-Jones. The one-time kitchen has been converted into a lovely cafe. Entry before 1.30pm is by guided tour only.

The surrounding gardens were designed by Morris 'to clothe' the house. Don't miss the well with a conical roof, inspired by a traditional oast house used for drying hops.

Danson House (☎01322-526 574; www.dansonhouse.org.uk; Danson Park, Bexleyheath, Kent DA6; adult/child £8/free; ⊘noon-5pm Sun-Fri Apr-Oct; ℝBexleyheath, then 20min walk southwest) This Palladian villa was built by John Boyd, an East India Company director, in 1766. It was saved from demolition in 1995 and painstakingly renovated over the next decade based on mid-19th-century watercolours by Sarah Johnston.

Highlights include the dining room's reliefs and 17 wall paintings celebrating love and romance; the chinoiserie salon; the library, with a fair few 'decorative' books; the music room, with its functioning organ; the dizzying spiral staircase; and the original Victorian kitchens. The English-style garden and surrounding park are a delight and the tearoom in the one-time breakfast room serves wholesome, delicious food.

Ministry has firmly rejoined the top club ranks. Fridays is the Gallery trance night, while Saturday sessions offer the crème de la crème of house, electro and techno DJs.

🍷 Brixton

MARKET HOUSE   PUB
Map p442 (www.market-house.co.uk; 443 Coldharbour Lane, SW9; ⊘3-11pm Mon-Wed, to midnight Thu, to 3am Fri, 1pm-4am Sat, 1-11pm Sun; ℮Brixton) Brixton used to be known for its grotty pubs and rough music venues, so the designer-wallpapered, vintage-furnished, cocktail-serving Market House is something of a departure for the area – and a roaring success at that. The late (and free) opening hours on the weekend music nights are especially popular with locals.

EFFRA HALL TAVERN   PUB
Map p442 (38a Kellett Rd, SW2; ⊘5-11pm Mon-Fri, 11am-11pm Sat, noon-10pm Sun; ℮Brixton) This slightly run-down old boozer brings you closer to the heart of the Brixton Afro-Caribbean vibe than any other pub in the area, thanks to the spicy Jamaican menu and regular live jazz. The patio outback is fringed with palm trees, while the interior is all shabby Victorian splendour.

PLAN B   CLUB
Map p442 (www.planb-london.com; 418 Brixton Rd, SW9; admission £6-17.50; ⊘10pm-5am Fri & Sat; ℮Brixton) This small venue, with its minimalist warehouse-like interior, is a point on the Brixton nightlife map with a shaken-up roll call of hip hop, R&B, house and electro acts.

DOGSTAR   BAR
Map p442 (http://dogstarbrixton.com; 389 Coldharbour Lane, SW9; ⊘4-11pm Tue & Wed, to 2am Thu, to 4am Fri & Sat, noon-10pm Sun; ℮Brixton) Downstairs, this long-running local institution has a cavernous DJ and live-music bar, mobbed by a young South London crowd. The main bar is as casual as you'd expect from a converted pub – comfortable sofas, big wooden tables – so dressing to kill is not obligatory. Dogstar Comedy on Thursday.

Battersea & Wandsworth

LOST ANGEL
BAR

Map p442 (www.lostangel.co.uk; 339 Battersea Park Rd, SW11; entry weekends £5; ⏱5-11pm Tue & Wed, to midnight Thu, 4pm-2am Fri, noon-2am Sat, noon-11pm Sun; ⌖Wandsworth Rd, Battersea Park or Queenstown Rd) New home of the much-missed Lost Society on Wandsworth Rd, this fantastic bar-cum-restaurant is dedicated to delightful decadence and aristocratic glitz. There's a garden at the back where many a summer drinking session goes on. DJs and burlesque shows take over on weekends.

MASON'S ARMS
PUB

Map p442 (www.masons-arms-battersea.co.uk; 169 Battersea Park Rd, SW8; ⏱noon-11pm; ☎; ⌖Battersea Park) This lovely boozer is a favourite of Battersea residents for its winning combination of relaxed atmosphere, beer garden on sunny days (and open fire for winter blues) and fantastic food (mains £10.50 to £19.50).

Vauxhall

The opening hours of Vauxhall's gay clubs can be something of a moving target because of club nights. Check the venues' websites or gay listings for the latest information.

FIRE LONDON
GAY

Map p444 (www.firelondon.net; 39 Parry St, SW8; entry £5-15; ⏱11pm-10am Thu-Sat; ⊖Vauxhall) Regularly hosting the best gay club nights in London, Fire is an expansive, smart space under Vauxhall's railway arches. Its best-known bill is the infamous 12-hour Sunday all-nighter, Orange. Its outdoor garden is a rare thing on the clubbing scene – good to watch the sunrise!

EAGLE
GAY

(www.eaglelondon.com/; 349 Kennington Lane, Vauxhall, SE11; ⏱9pm-2am Mon-Wed, to 3am Thur & Fri, to 4am Sat, 8pm-3am Sun; ⊖Vauxhall) This fantastic place is a haven of alternative queer goings-on in muscle-bound Vauxhall. Open nightly with a different feel throughout the week with Men Inc every Friday and the legendary Horse Meat Disco on Sunday.

RVT
GAY

Map p444 (Royal Vauxhall Tavern; www.rvt.org.uk; 372 Kennington Lane, SE11; entry £5-8; ⏱7pm-midnight Mon-Thu, 9pm-3am Fri, to 2am Sat, 3pm-midnight Sun; ⊖Vauxhall) Rough around the edges to say the least, the Royal Vauxhall Tavern is the perfect antidote to the gleaming new wave of uppity gay venues now crowding Vauxhall's gay village. Saturday's Duckie, tagged 'London's Authentic Honky Tonk', is the club's signature queer performance night.

⭐ ENTERTAINMENT

★ O2 ACADEMY BRIXTON
LIVE MUSIC

Map p442 (www.o2academybrixton.co.uk; 211 Stockwell Rd, SW9; ⏱doors open 7pm most nights; ⊖Brixton) It's hard to have a bad night at the Brixton Academy, even if you leave with your soles sticky with beer, as this cavernous former-5000-capacity art-deco theatre always thrums with bonhomie. There's a properly raked floor for good views, as well as plenty of bars and an excellent mixed bill of established and emerging talent.

UP THE CREEK
COMEDY

Map p445 (www.up-the-creek.com; 302 Creek Rd, SE10; admission £5-15; ⏱7-11pm Thu & Sun, to 2am Fri & Sat; ⌖DLR Cutty Sark) Bizarrely enough, the hecklers can be funnier than the acts at this great club. Mischief, rowdiness and excellent comedy are the norm, with the Blackout open-mic night on Thursdays (www.the-blackout.co.uk, £5) and Sunday specials (www.sundayspecial.co.uk, £7). There's an after-party disco on Fridays and Saturdays.

O2 ARENA
LIVE MUSIC

(www.theo2.co.uk; Peninsula Sq, SE10; ⊖North Greenwich) One of the city's major concert venues, hosting all the biggies – the Rolling Stones, Paul Simon and Sting, Barbra Streisand, Prince and many others – inside the 20,000-capacity arena. It's also a popular venue for sporting events. The smaller Indigo at the O2 seats 2350.

LABAN THEATRE
DANCE

Map p445 (www.trinitylaban.ac.uk; Creekside, SE8; admission £6-15; ⌖DLR Greenwich) Home of the Trinity Laban Conservatoire of Music and Dance, the Laban Theatre is the largest and best-equipped contemporary dance school in Europe and presents student dance performances, graduation shows and regular shows by the resident troupe, Transitions Dance Company. Its stunning £23-million home was designed by Herzog & de Meuron, designers of the Tate Modern.

There are two ways to cross the Thames without boarding a boat or stepping on a bridge.

Reached through glass-topped domes on either side of the river, the 370m-long **Greenwich Foot Tunnel** (Cutty Sark Gardens, SE10; ⊘24hr; ⒭DLR Cutty Sark) FREE built in 1902 runs under the Thames from the Isle of Dogs to Greenwich. There are lifts – and about 100 stairs – on both sides.

Further downstream is London's airborne river-crossing option, the **Emirates Air Line** (p385) cable car. It runs between the O2 Arena and the Excel exhibition centre in Royal Docks and affords great views of Greenwich, Canary Wharf, and the Docklands.

🛍 SHOPPING

GREENWICH MARKET   MARKET
Map p445 (www.greenwichmarketlondon.com; College Approach, SE10; ⊘10am-5.30pm; ⒭DLR Cutty Sark) Greenwich may be one of the smallest of London's ubiquitous markets, but it holds its own in quality. On Tuesdays, Wednesdays, Fridays and weekends, stallholders tend to be small, independent artists, offering original prints, wholesome beauty products, funky jewellery and accessories, cool fashion pieces and so on. On Tuesdays, Thursdays and Fridays, there are also vintage, antiques and collectables.

CASBAH RECORDS   MUSIC
Map p445 (www.casbahrecords.co.uk; 320-322 Creek Rd, SE10; ⊘10.30am-6pm; ⒭DLR Cutty Sark) Funky meeting ground of old vinyl (Bowie, Rolling Stones, vintage soul) as well as CDs, DVDs and memorabilia.

RETROBATES VINTAGE   VINTAGE
Map p445 (330-332 Creek Rd, SE10; ⊘10.30am-6pm Mon-Fri, to 6.30pm Sat & Sun; ⒭DLR Cutty Sark) Each piece is individual at this lovely vintage shop, where glass cabinets are crammed with costume jewellery, old perfume bottles and straw hats, while gorgeous jackets and blazers intermingle on the clothes racks. The men's offering is unusually good for a vintage shop.

NAUTICALIA   GIFTS, SOUVENIRS
Map p445 (www.nauticalia.com; 25 Nelson Rd, SE10; ⊘10am-6pm; ⒭DLR Cutty Sark) If it's 'salty', this 'first shop in the world' (it's just over the meridian at 00°00.4' W, so can thus make that claim) will stock it – from bells and barometers to silly captain's hats. It'll have just the souvenir to take home from World Heritage–listed Maritime Greenwich.

ARTY GLOBE   GIFTS, SOUVENIRS
Map p445 (www.artyglobe.com; 15 Greenwich Market, SE10; ⊘11am-6pm; ⒭DLR Cutty Sark)

The unique fisheye-view drawings of various areas of London (and other cities, including New York, Paris and Berlin) by architect Hartwig Braun are works of art and appear on the shopping bags, place mats, notebooks, coasters, mugs and jigsaws available in this tiny shop. They make excellent gifts.

BRIXTON MARKET   MARKET
Map p442 (www.brixtonmarket.net; Electric Ave & Granville Arcade; ⊘8am-6pm Mon, Tue & Thu-Sat, to 3pm Wed; ⊖Brixton) A heady, cosmopolitan blend of silks, wigs, knock-off fashion, halal butchers and the occasional Christian preacher on Electric Ave. Tilapia fish, pig's trotters, yams, mangoes, okra, plantains and Jamaican *bullah* (gingerbread) cakes are just some of the exotic products on sale.

20 STOREY   GIFTS
Map p442 (www.20storey.com; 2a Market Row, SW9; ⊘10am-6pm Mon-Sat, from 11am Sun; ⊖Brixton) A shop with a sense of humour, 20 Storey is your essential stop for funky mugs, great cards, gadgets, posters and original books.

🏃 SPORTS & ACTIVITIES

UP AT THE O2   ADVENTURE SPORTS
(www.theo2.co.uk/upattheo2; O2, Greenwich Peninsula, SE10; weekdays/weekends from £28/35; ⊘hours vary; ⊖North Greenwich) London isn't exactly your thrill-seeking destination, but this ascent of the O2 dome is definitely not for the faint-hearted. Equipped with climbing suit and a harness, you'll scale the famous white dome to arrive at a viewing platform perched 52m above the Thames with sweeping views of Canary Wharf, the river, Greenwich and beyond.

Not suitable for children under 10 (also check height and weight restrictions).

Richmond, Kew & Hampton Court

RICHMOND | KEW | PUTNEY | BARNES | CHISWICK | TWICKENHAM | WIMBLEDON

Neighbourhood Top Five

1 Listening out for poltergeists along the galleries and vaults of majestic **Hampton Court Palace** (p290) before getting lost in the maze.

2 Plunging into the luxuriant green expanses, wooded thickets and tropical foliage of **Kew Gardens** (p294).

3 Turning your back on urban London to discover a pristine pocket of wilderness at the **London Wetland Centre** (p297).

4 Sinking a pint of beer at the historic riverside **White Cross pub** (p301) while trying to avoid being cut off by the high tide.

5 Exploring London's wild side, roaming at will around **Richmond Park** (p296).

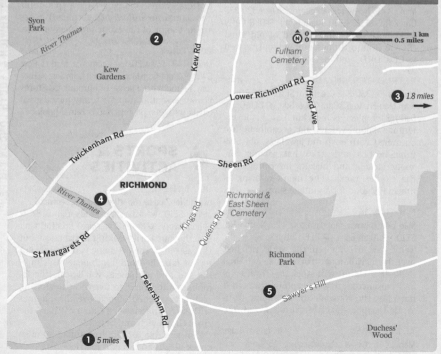

For more detail of this area see Map p446 ➡

Explore: Richmond, Kew & Hampton Court

If anywhere in London could be described as a village, Richmond – with its delightful green, riverside vistas and handsome architecture – is it. But the entire southwest from Putney to Twickenham is a refreshing alternative to central London's urban density. When the weather is fine, few London diversions can top time spent upriver by the Thames – whether exploring the major sights, walking along the riverbank or poking your head into a historic waterside pub. And if you really warm to the charms of London's green southwest, you'll also find a few lovely hotels to look after you.

You might not find yourself coming here to shop, but bring your wallet as there's no shortage of fine dining, and you'll find pubs aplenty. But it's exploration that should top your agenda, whether it be getting lost in the maze at splendid Hampton Court Palace, finding endless botanic discoveries at Kew Gardens or walking the wilds of Richmond Park.

Local Life

➡**Hang-outs** Get into the riverside pub lunch mood joining locals quaffing beer at the City Barge (p302) or White Cross (p301).

➡**Greenery** Londoners from all over town bolt down to Richmond Park (p296) and Kew Gardens (p294) for weekend great escapes.

➡**River Views** Join locals jogging by the river, walking their dogs or catching some sunshine north and south of Richmond Bridge (p296).

Getting There & Away

➡**Train & Underground** Both Kew Gardens and Richmond are on the District Line and London Overground; Richmond train station can be reached from Clapham Junction. Trains run to Hampton Court station from Waterloo. East Putney, Putney Bridge, Fulham Broadway and Chiswick Park are on the District Line.

➡**Boat** Services run several times daily from Westminster Pier to Kew and on to Hampton Court Palace (boats sometimes stop at Richmond).

Lonely Planet's Top Tip

A manageable section of the fantastic Thames Path is the 4 miles between Putney Bridge and Barnes Footbridge. Taking around 90 minutes, most of the walk is very rural and at times you will only be accompanied by birdsong and the gentle swish of the river. From the footbridge, Chiswick train station is about 0.75 miles to the northwest. For more details, see the River Thames Alliance's Visit Thames site (www.visit-thames.co.uk).

✖ Best Places to Eat

➡ Glasshouse (p301)
➡ Gelateria Danieli (p300)
➡ Chez Lindsay (p300)
➡ Orange Pekoe (p301)

For reviews, see p300 ➡

▣ Best Places to Drink

➡ White Cross (p301)
➡ White Hart (p302)
➡ City Barge (p302)
➡ London Apprentice (p302)

For reviews, see p301 ➡

◉ Best Guided Tours

➡ Kew Explorer (p295)
➡ Hampton Court Palace (p290)
➡ Richmond Park (p296)
➡ Strawberry Hill (p299)

For reviews, see p296 ➡

TOP SIGHT
HAMPTON COURT PALACE

London's most spectacular Tudor palace, this 16th-century icon concocts an imposing sense of history, from the huge kitchens and grand living quarters to the spectacular gardens, complete with a 300-year-old maze.

History of the Palace

Hampton Court Palace was built by Cardinal Thomas Wolsey in 1515 but was coaxed from him by Henry VIII just before Wolsey (as chancellor) fell from favour. It was already one of the most sophisticated palaces in Europe when, in the 17th century, Sir Christopher Wren was commissioned to build an extension. The result is a beautiful blend of Tudor and 'restrained baroque' architecture.

Entering the Palace

Passing through the magnificent main gate, you arrive first in the **Base Court** and beyond that **Clock Court**, named after its 16th-century astronomical clock. The panelled rooms and arched doorways in the **Young Henry VIII's Story** upstairs from Base Court provide a rewarding introduction: note the Tudor graffiti on the fireplace. Off Base Court to the right as you enter and acquired by Charles I in 1629, Andrea Magenta's nine-painting series *The Triumphs of Caesar* portray Julius Caesar returning to Rome in a triumphant procession.

Henry VIII's Apartments

The stairs inside Anne Boleyn's Gateway lead up to Henry VIII's Apartments, including the stunning **Great Hall**. The **Horn Room**, hung with impressive antlers, leads to the **Great Watching Chamber** where guards controlled access to the king. Henry VIII's dazzling gemstone-encrusted **crown** has been re-created – the original was melted down by Oliver

DON'T MISS...
→ Great Hall
→ Chapel Royal
→ William III's Apartments
→ Gardens and maze
→ Cumberland Art Gallery
→ Henry VIII's Crown

PRACTICALITIES
→ www.hrp.org.uk/HamptonCourtPalace
→ adult/child/family £17.50/8.75/43.80
→ ⏱10am-6pm Apr-Oct, to 4.30pm Nov-Mar
→ 🚢Hampton Court Palace, 🚆Hampton Court

Cromwell – and sits in the **Royal Pew** (open 10am to 4pm Monday to Saturday and 12.30pm to 1.30pm Sunday), which overlooks the beautiful **Chapel Royal** (still a place of worship after 450 years).

Tudor Kitchens & Great Wine Cellar

Also dating from Henry's day are the delightful Tudor kitchens, once used to rustle up meals for a royal household of some 1200 people. Don't miss the Great Wine Cellar, which handled the 300 barrels each of ale and wine consumed here annually in the mid-16th century.

Cumberland Art Gallery

The restored and recently opened Cumberland Suite off Clock Court is the venue for a staggering collection of art works from the Royal Collection, including Rembrandt's *Self-portrait in a Flat Cap* (1642) and Sir Anthony van Dyck's *Charles I on Horseback* (c 1635–6).

William III's & Mary II's Apartments

A tour of William III's Apartments, completed by Wren in 1702, takes you up the grand **King's Staircase**. Highlights include the **King's Presence Chamber**, dominated by a throne backed with scarlet hangings. During a devastating fire in 1986 which gutted an entire wing of the palace, staff were ready to cut the huge portrait of William III from its frame with knives, if necessary. The sumptuous **King's Great Bedchamber**, with a bed topped with ostrich plumes, and the **King's Closet** (where His Majesty's toilet has a velvet seat) should not be missed. Restored and reopened in 2014, the unique **Chocolate Kitchens** were built for William and Mary in around 1689.

William's wife Mary II had her own apartments, accessible via the fabulous **Queen's Staircase** (decorated by William Kent).

Georgian Private Apartments

The Georgian Rooms were used by George II and Queen Caroline on the court's last visit to the palace in 1737. Do not miss the fabulous Tudor **Wolsey Closet** with its early-16th-century ceiling and painted panels, commissioned by Henry VIII.

Garden & Maze

Beyond the palace are the stunning gardens; keep an eye out for the **Real Tennis Court**, dating from the 1620s. Originally created for William and Mary, the **Kitchen Garden** is a magnificent, recently opened re-creation.

No one should leave Hampton Court without losing themselves in the 800m-long **maze** (adult/child/family £4/2.50/12; ⊙10am-5.15pm Apr-Oct, to 3.45pm Nov-Mar), also accessible to those not entering the palace.

VISIT BY BOAT

Between April and September, the palace can be reached by boat on the 22-mile route along the Thames from Westminster Pier in central London (via Kew and Richmond), but can take up to four hours (depending on the tide). Boats (single adult/child £15/7.50) are run by **Westminster Passenger Services Association** (www.wpsa.co.uk).

Hampton Court Palace presses up against 445-hectare Bushy Park (www.royalparks.gov.uk), a semiwild expanse with herds of red and fallow deer.

HAUNTED HAMPTON COURT

With a history this old and as eventful, a paranormal dimension is surely mandatory. Arrested for adultery and detained in the palace in 1542, Henry's fifth wife, Catherine Howard, was dragged screaming down a gallery at the palace by her guards after an escape bid. Her ghost is said to do a repeat performance, uttering 'unearthly shrieks' in the Haunted Gallery leading to the Royal Pew (she must be a tireless ghost as she also haunts the Tower of London).

Hampton Court Palace

A DAY AT THE PALACE

With so much to explore and seemingly infinite gardens, it can be tricky knowing where to begin. It helps to understand how the palace has grown over the centuries and how successive royal occupants embellished Hampton Court to suit their purposes and to reflect the style of the time.

As soon as he had his royal hands upon the palace from Cardinal Thomas Wolsey, Henry VIII began expanding the **Tudor architecture** ❶, adding the **Great Hall** ❷, the exquisite **Chapel Royal** ❸, the opulent Great Watching Chamber and the gigantic **kitchens** ❹. By 1540 it had become one of the grandest and most sophisticated palaces in Europe. James I kept things ticking over, while Charles I added a new tennis court and did some serious art-collecting, including pieces that can be seen in the newly opened **Cumberland Art Gallery** ❺.

VISITBRITAIN / GETTY IMAGES ©

❼ The Maze
Around 150m north of the main bulding
Created from hornbeam and yew and planted in around 1700, the maze covers a third of an acre within the famous palace gardens. A must-see conclusion to Hampton Court, the maze takes the average visitor about 20 minutes to reach the centre.

Tudor Architecture
Dating to 1515, the heart of the palace serves as one of the finest examples of Tudor architecture in the nation. Cardinal Thomas Wolsey was responsible for transforming what was originally a grand medieval manor house into a stunning Tudor palace.

CHRIS MELLOR / GETTY IMAGES ©

Tudor Kitchens
These vast kitchens were the engine room of the palace. With a staff of 200 people, there were six spit-rack-equipped fireplaces, with roast meat always on the menu (to the tune of 8200 sheep and 1240 oxen per year).

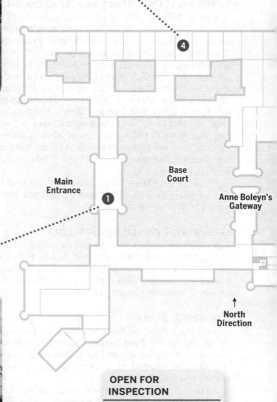

Main Entrance

Base Court

Anne Boleyn's Gateway

↑ North Direction

OPEN FOR INSPECTION

The palace was opened to the public by Queen Victoria in 1838.

After the Civil War, puritanical Oliver Cromwell warmed to his own regal proclivities, spending weekends in the comfort of the former Queen's bedroom and selling off Charles I's art collection. In the late 17th century, William and Mary employed Sir Christopher Wren for baroque extensions, chiefly the William III Apartments, reached by the **King's Staircase 6**. William III also commissioned the world-famous **maze 7**.

The Great Hall
This grand dining hall is the defining room of the palace, displaying what is considered England's finest hammer-beam roof, 16th-century Flemish tapestries telling the story of Abraham, and some exquisite stained-glass windows.

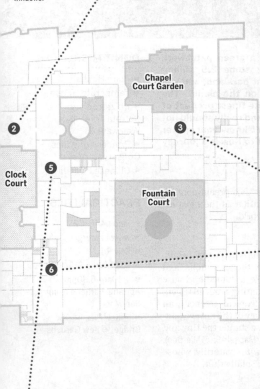

Chapel Court Garden

Clock Court

Fountain Court

Chapel Royal
The blue-and-gold vaulted ceiling was originally intended for Christ Church, Oxford, but was installed here instead; the 18th-century oak reredos was carved by Grinling Gibbons. Books on display include a 1611 1st edition of the King James Bible, printed by Robert Barker.

The King's Staircase
One of five rooms at the palace painted by Antonio Verrio and a suitably bombastic prelude to the King's Apartments, the overblown King's Staircase adulates William III by elevating him above a cohort of Roman emperors.

Cumberland Art Gallery
The former Cumberland Suite, designed by William Kent, has been restored to accommodate a choice selection of some of the finest works from the Royal Collection.

⊙ TOP SIGHT
KEW GARDENS

A staggering 24% of London is a green patchwork of domestic gardens, sprouting some 2.5 million trees. Throw in London's abundant parkland, and you have one of the greenest cities on the planet. The 121-hectare gardens at Kew are the finest product of the British botanical imagination and really should not be missed. No worries if you don't know your quiver tree from your alang-alang, a visit to Kew is a journey of discovery for all.

Botanical Collection

As well as being a public garden, Kew is a preeminent research centre, maintaining its reputation as the most exhaustive botanical collection in the world.

Palm House

Assuming you come by tube and enter via Victoria Gate, you'll come almost immediately to the enormous and elaborate 700-glass-paned Palm House, a domed hothouse of metal and curved sheets of glass dating from 1848, enveloping a splendid display of exotic tropical greenery; an aerial walkway offers a parrot's-eye view of the lush vegetation. Just northwest of the Palm House stands the tiny and irresistibly steamy **Waterlily House** (Map p446; ⊙Mar-Dec), sheltering the gigantic *Victoria cruziana* waterlily, whose vast pads can support the weight of a small adult.

Chinese Pagoda

Kew's 49.5m-tall eight-sided Chinese Pagoda (1762), designed by William Chambers (the architect of Somerset House), is one of the gardens' architectural icons. During WWII, the pagoda withstood the blast from a stick of Luftwaffe bombs exploding nearby, and was

DON'T MISS...

- ➡ Palm House
- ➡ Temperate House
- ➡ Rhizotron and Xstrata Treetop Walkway
- ➡ Princess of Wales Conservatory
- ➡ Chinese Pagoda

PRACTICALITIES

- ➡ Map p446, C2
- ➡ www.kew.org
- ➡ Kew Rd
- ➡ adult/child £15/3.50
- ➡ ⊙10am-6.30pm Apr-Aug, earlier closing Sep-Mar
- ➡ 🚢Kew Pier, 🚇Kew Bridge, ⊖Kew Gardens

also secretly employed by the Ministry of Defence to test bomb trajectories (which involved cutting holes in each floor!). Unfortunately, the pagoda is not usually open to be climbed.

Temperate House

Built in 1860 and closed for vital restoration work until 2018, the beautiful Temperate House in the southeast of Kew Gardens (north of the pagoda) is the world's largest surviving Victorian glasshouse, covering 4880 sq metres.

Rhizotron & Xstrata Treetop Walkway

In the **Arboretum** – a short walk from Temperate House – this fascinating walkway first takes you underground and then 18m up in the air into the tree canopy (a big hit with kids).

Kew Palace

Built in 1631 and the smallest of the royal palaces, adorable red-brick **Kew Palace** (www.hrp.org.uk/kew-palace; ⊙10.30am-5.30pm Apr-Sep), in the northwest of the gardens, is a former royal residence once known as Dutch House. It was the favourite home of George III and his family; his wife, Queen Charlotte, died here in 1818 (you can see the very chair in which she expired). Don't miss the recently restored **Royal Kitchens** next door.

Other Highlights

Several long vistas (**Cedar Vista**, **Syon Vista** and **Pagoda Vista**) are channelled by trees from vantage points within Kew Gardens. The idyllic, thatched **Queen Charlotte's Cottage** (Map p446; ⊙11am-4pm Sat & Sun Apr-Sep) in the southwest of the gardens was popular with 'mad' George III and his wife; the carpets of bluebells around here are a drawcard in spring. The **Marianne North Gallery** displays the botanical paintings of Marianne North, an indomitable traveller who roamed the continents from 1871 to 1885, painting plants along the way. The **Orangery** near Kew Palace contains a restaurant, cafe and shop.

Getting Around

If you want a good overview of the gardens, jump aboard the **Kew Explorer** (adult/child £4.50/1.50), which allows you to hop on and off at stops along the way.

VISITING THE GARDENS

Spring is a spectacular season to visit, but any time of the year is fine. Most visitors arrive by tube or train, but from April to October, boats run by the **Westminster Passenger Services Association** (Map p416; ☏020-7930 2062; www.wpsa.co.uk; return adult/child £18/9; ⊖Westminster) sail from Westminster Pier to Kew Pier. For eats, there's a restaurant in the 18th-century **Orangery**, the Pavilion restaurant, a cafe by Victoria Gate and the **White Peaks Cafe** (mains £3.95-8.50). Kids can explore the fun-filled Treehouse Towers (an outdoor play area) and Climbers and Creepers (an interactive botanical zone). Popular summer concerts bring music to Kew (visit the website for more info).

The angular Princess of Wales Conservatory houses plants in 10 different climatic zones – everything from a desert to a mangrove swamp. Look out for stone plants, which resemble pebbles (to deter grazing animals), carnivorous plants, gigantic waterlilies, cacti and a collection of tropical orchids.

 **SIGHTS**

⊙ Richmond & Kew

KEW GARDENS   GARDENS
See p294.

RICHMOND PARK   PARK
Map p446 (⊘7am-dusk; ⊖Richmond) At almost 1000 hectares (the largest urban parkland in Europe), this park offers everything from formal gardens and ancient oaks to unsurpassed views of central London 12 miles away. It's easy to flee the several roads slicing up the rambling wilderness, making the park perfect for a quiet walk or a picnic with the kids, even in summer when Richmond's riverside heaves. Coming from Richmond, it's easiest to enter via Richmond Gate or from Petersham Rd.

Herds of more than 600 red and fallow deer basking under the trees are part of its magic, but they can be less than docile in rutting season (September and October) and when the does bear young (May to July), so keep your distance (more than 50m) during these times. Birdwatchers will love the diverse habitats, from neat gardens to woodland and assorted ponds. Floral fans should visit **Isabella Plantation**, a stunning 16-hectare woodland garden created after WWII, in April and May when the rhododendrons, azaleas and camellias bloom.

Set in a beautiful 13-hectare garden and affording great views of the city from the back terrace, **Pembroke Lodge** (Map p446; www.pembroke-lodge.co.uk; TW10; ⊘9am-5.30pm Apr-Oct, to just before dusk Nov-Mar) was the childhood home of Bertrand Russell. The Georgian tea rooms can garnish your visit with warm scones and clotted cream from 9am to 5.30pm.

The pastoral vista from **Richmond Hill** (Map p446) has inspired painters and poets for centuries and still beguiles. It's the only view (which includes St Paul's Cathedral 10 miles away) in the country to be protected by an act of Parliament.

RICHMOND GREEN   PARK
Map p446 (⊠Richmond, ⊖Richmond) A short walk west of the Quadrant, where you'll emerge from the tube, is Richmond Green with its mansions and delightful pubs. Cross the green diagonally for the attractive remains of **Richmond Palace** (Map p446) – the main entrance and red-brick gatehouse – built in 1501. Henry VII's arms are visible above the main gate: he built the Tudor additions to the edifice, although the palace had been in use as a royal residence since 1125. Elizabeth I died here in 1603.

HAM HOUSE   HISTORIC BUILDING
Map p446 (☑020-8940 1950; www.nationaltrust. org.uk; Ham St, Ham, TW10; whole property adult/ child/family £10/5/25, garden adult/child/family £4/2/10.20; ⊘house noon-4pm Sat-Thu late Mar–mid-Nov, gardens 11am-4pm Sat-Thu Jan–mid-Feb & Nov–mid-Dec, 11am-5pm Sat-Thu mid-Feb–Oct; ☒371, ⊠Richmond, ⊖Richmond) Known as 'Hampton Court in miniature', much haunted Ham House was built in 1610 and became home to the first Earl of Dysart, unluckily employed as 'whipping boy' to Charles I. Inside it's grandly furnished; the Great Staircase is a magnificent example of Stuart woodworking. Look out for ceiling paintings by Antonio Verrio, a miniature of Elizabeth I by Nicholas Hilliard and works by Constable

---

THAMES AT RICHMOND

The stretch of the river from Twickenham Bridge to Petersham and Ham is one of the prettiest in London. The action is mostly around five-span **Richmond Bridge** (Map p446), built in 1777. It's London's oldest surviving crossing, only widened for traffic in 1937. Just before it, along one of the loveliest parts of the Thames, is tiny Corporation Island, colonised by flocks of feral parakeets. The gorgeous walk to Petersham can be crowded in nice weather; best to cut across pastoral **Petersham Meadows** (Map p446; ⊠Richmond, ⊖Richmond) – where cows still graze – and continue to Richmond Park for peace and quiet. There are several companies near Richmond Bridge, including **Richmond Bridge Boathouses** (Map p446; ☑020-8948 8270; www.richmondbridge-boathouses.co.uk; adult/child £7/3.50; ⊠Richmond, ⊖Richmond) that offer skiff hire. Alternatively, walk north from Twickenham Bridge, alongside the Old Deer Park, past the two obelisks and climb onto **Richmond Lock** (Map p446; ⊠Richmond, St Margarets, ⊖Richmond) and footbridge, dating from 1894.

TOP SIGHT
LONDON WETLAND CENTRE

One of Europe's largest inland wetland projects, this 43-hectare centre was transformed from four Victorian reservoirs in 2000 and attracts some 140 species of bird, as well as frogs, butterflies, dragonflies and lizards, plus a thriving colony of watervoles.

From the visitor centre and glass-fronted observatory, meandering paths and boardwalks lead visitors around the grounds, penetrating the reed bed, marsh, fen and watery habitats of its many residents and transients, including black swans, ducks, Bewick's swans, geese, red-crested pochards, sand martins, coots and the rarer bitterns, herons and kingfishers. Don't miss the **Peacock Tower**, a three-storey hide – and magnet for serious birders – on the main lake's eastern edge; other hides are sprinkled around the reserve, including the **Headley Discovery Hide** in the west. The wetland is also well-populated with eight different species of bats that feed on the abundant moths. A short walk north of the entrance, the wetland's family of sleek-coated **otters** are fed daily at 11am and 2pm (Monday to Friday). Free daily **tours**, which are led by knowledgable and enthusiastic staff members, are highly recommended. They depart at 11.30am and 2.30pm daily. Binoculars can be hired from the shop.

DON'T MISS...

➡ Peacock Tower
➡ Headley Discovery Hide
➡ Otter Feeding
➡ Daily Tours

PRACTICALITIES

➡ ☏020-8409 4400
➡ www.wwt.org.uk
➡ Queen Elizabeth's Walk, SW13
➡ adult/child/family £12.75/7/35.55
➡ ◔9.30am-6pm Apr-Oct, to 5pm Nov-Mar
➡ ⓇBarnes, ⊖Hammersmith then ⓠ283 (Duck Bus), 33, 72 or 209

---

and Reynolds. The grounds slope down to the Thames and lovely 17th-century formal gardens await exploration.

The garden ticket also allows you access to the below-stairs rooms. Special house tours run between December and March, while nocturnal after-hours ghost tours (£22) delve into Ham House's paranormal dimensions. Just opposite the Thames and accessible by small ferry is Marble Hill Park and its splendid mansion (p298).

◉ Putney & Barnes

PUTNEY & BARNES　　　　NEIGHBOURHOOD
Called *Putelei* in the Domesday Book of 1086, Putney is most famous as the starting point of the annual **Oxford and Cambridge Boat Race** (www.theboatrace.org). Barnes is less well known and more 'villagey' in feel. The best way to approach Putney is to follow the signs from Putney Bridge tube station for the footbridge (which runs parallel to the rail track), admiring the gorgeous riverside houses, with their gardens fronting the Thames, and thereby avoiding the tatty High St until the last minute.

◉ Chiswick

CHISWICK HOUSE　　　　HISTORIC BUILDING
(☏020-8995 0508; www.chgt.org.uk; Burlington Lane, Chiswick Park, W4; adult/child £6.10/3.70, gardens free; ◔gardens 7am-dusk, house 10am-6pm Sun-Wed Apr-Sep, to 5pm Oct; ☏; ⓇChiswick, ⊖Turnham Green) Designed by the third Earl of Burlington (1694–1753) – fired up with passion for all things Roman after his grand tour of Italy – this stunner of a neo-Palladian pavillion with an octagonal dome and colonnaded portico is a delight. The almost overpoweringly grand interior includes the coffered dome of the Upper Tribunal – left ungilded, the walls below are decorated with eight enormous paintings.

Admire the stunningly painted ceiling (by William Kent) of the **Blue Velvet Room** and look out for carvings of the pagan vegetative deity, the Green Man, in the marble fireplaces of the **Green Velvet Room**.

Lord Burlington also planned the house's original gardens, now **Chiswick Park**, surrounding the house, but they have been much altered since his time. Children will love them – look out for the stone sphinxes near the

WORTH A DETOUR

SYON HOUSE

Just across the Thames from Kew Gardens, **Syon House** (Syon Park; Map p446; www.syonpark.co.uk; Brentford, TW7; adult/child £12/5, gardens only £7/3.50; ⊙house 11am-5pm Wed, Thu & Sun mid-Mar–Oct, gardens & conservatory 10.30am-5pm daily mid-Mar–Oct; ▣237 or 267, ▨Gunnersbury, then, ⊜Gunnersbury) was once a medieval abbey named after Mt Zion. In 1542 Henry VIII dissolved the order of Bridgettine nuns who peacefully lived here and rebuilt it into a residence. (They say God had the last laugh in 1547 when Henry's coffin was brought to Syon en route to Windsor for burial and burst open during the night, leaving his body to be set upon by the estate's dogs.)

The house from where Lady Jane Grey ascended the throne for her nine-day reign in 1553 was remodelled in the neoclassical style by Robert Adam in the 18th century and has plenty of Adam furniture and oak panelling. The interior was designed on gender-specific lines, with pastel pinks and purples for the ladies' gallery, and mock Roman sculptures for the men's dining room. Guests at the house have included the great Mohawk chieftain Thayendanegea (Joseph Brant) and Gunpowder Plot–member Thomas Percy.

The estate's 16-hectare gardens, with a lake and a magnificent domed Great Conservatory (1826) were landscaped by Capability Brown. Syon Park is filled with attractions for children, including an adventure playground and an aquatic park. Children get free access during school holidays and bank holidays.

Cedar of Lebanon trees (another sphinx made of lead can be found in the Lower Tribuna). Home to a splendid 19th-century conservatory and a gateway designed by Inigo Jones, Chiswick House also has an excellent cafe.

The house is about a mile southwest of the Turnham Green tube station and 750m northeast of Chiswick train station.

HOGARTH'S HOUSE　　HISTORIC BUILDING

(☑020-8994 6757; www.hounslow.info/arts/hogarthshouse; Hogarth Lane, W4; ⊙noon-5pm Tue-Sun; ⊜Turnham Green) **FREE** Home between 1749 and 1764 to artist and social commentator William Hogarth, this small house displays his caricatures and engravings, with such works as the haunting *Gin Lane* (and the less well-known, more affirmative *Beer Street*), *Marriage-à-la-mode* and copies of *A Rake's Progress* and *The Four Stages of Cruelty*.

The low ceiling of the narrow staircase is a head-bumping reminder that the Sergeant Painter to the King was under five foot tall at full stretch. The house was bombed by the Luftwaffe in 1940, but the artist's mulberry tree survived and still flourishes in the garden (which would be a quiet retreat were it not for the roaring dual carriageway beyond the wall), accompanied by daffodils in spring. Prints and postcards are available from the downstairs shop.

FULLER'S GRIFFIN BREWERY　　BREWERY

(☑020-8996 2000; www.fullers.co.uk/brewery; Chiswick Lane South, W4; tours/with tastings £7/10; ⊙tours hourly 11am-3pm Mon-Fri; ▨Chiswick, ⊜Turnham Green) If you're a beer fiend, hop (excuse the pun) on a tour to see it being brewed up and join in a good-old tasting session (over-18s only). Informative one-hour guided tours of the brewery depart regularly on weekdays and are followed by 30-minute tutored tastes. Book in advance online; over-16s can take a nontasting tour.

⊙ Twickenham

MARBLE HILL HOUSE　　HISTORIC BUILDING

Map p446 (☑020-8892 5115; www.english-heritage.org.uk/daysout/properties/marble-hill-house; Richmond Rd, TW1; adult/child/family £6.20/3.70/16.10; ⊙park 7am-dusk, tours 10.30am & noon Sat, 10.30am, noon, 2.15pm & 3.30pm Sun Apr-Oct; ☎; ▨St Margarets, Richmond, ⊜Richmond) An 18th-century Palladian peach conceived as an idyllic escape from the hurly-burly of city life, this majestic love nest was originally built for George II's mistress Henrietta Howard and later occupied by Mrs Fitzherbert, the secret wife of George IV. The Georgian interior contains some astonishing flourishes, including the hand-painted Chinese wallpaper in the dining parlour and some delectable furniture. Entrance is only possible on one of the guided tours but you are free to visit the park.

The poet Alexander Pope had a hand in designing the park, which stretches leisurely down to the Thames. To get there from St Margarets station, turn right along

St Margarets Rd, then take the right fork along Crown Rd and turn left along Richmond Rd. Turn right along Beaufort Rd and walk across Marble Hill Park to the house. It is also easily accessible by pedestrian ferry from Ham House. It's a 25-minute walk from Richmond station.

STRAWBERRY HILL HISTORIC BUILDING

(www.strawberryhillhouse.org.uk; 268 Waldegrave Rd, TW1; adult/child £12/free; ⊙house 1.40-5.30pm Mon-Wed & noon-5.30pm Sat & Sun Mar-Oct, garden 10am-6pm daily; ℞Strawberry Hill, ⊜Richmond Station, then ☎R68) With its snow-white walls and Gothic turrets, this fantastical and totally restored 18th-century creation in Twickenham is the work of art historian, author and politician Horace Walpole. Studded with elaborate stained glass, the building reaches its astonishing apogee in the gallery, with its magnificent papier-mâché ceiling. For the full magic, join a twilight tour (£20). Last admission to the house is 4pm.

⊙ Wimbledon

WIMBLEDON COMMON COMMON

(www.wpcc.org.uk; ℞Wimbledon, ⊜Wimbledon, then ☎93) Surging on into Putney Heath, Wimbledon Common blankets a staggering 460 hectares of southwest London. An astonishing expanse of open, wild and wooded space for walking (the best mode of exploration), nature trailing and picnicking, the common has its own **Wimbledon Windmill** (www.wimbledonwindmill.org.uk; Windmill Rd, SW19; adult/child £2/1; ⊙2-5pm Sat, 11am-5pm Sun late Mar–Oct; ⊜Wimbledon), a fine smock mill (ie octagonal-shaped with sloping weatherboarded sides) dating from 1817.

The windmill, which ceased operating in 1864, contains a museum with working models on the history of windmills and milling. The adjacent **Windmill Tearooms** can supply tea, caffeine and sustenance. On the southern side of the common, the misnamed **Caesar's Camp** (Wimbledon Common, SW19; ⊜Wimbledon) is what's left of a roughly circular earthen fort built in the 5th century BC.

WIMBLEDON LAWN

TENNIS MUSEUM MUSEUM

(☎020-8946 6131; www.wimbledon.com/museum; Gate 4, Church Rd, SW19; adult/child £13/8, museum & tour £24/15; ⊙10am-5pm; ℞Wimbledon, then bus 93, ⊜Wimbledon) This ace museum details the history of tennis – from its French precursor *Jeu de paume* (which employed the open hand) to the supersonic serves of today's champions. It's a state-of-the-art presentation, with plenty of video clips and a projection of John McEnroe in the dressing room at Wimbledon, but the highlight is the chance to see Centre Court from the **360-degree viewing box**. During the championships in June/July, only those with tickets to the tournament can access the museum.

Riveting facts and figures abound: tennis clothes worn by female tennis players in 1881 weighed up to a gruelling 4.9kg! Compare this with Maria Sharapova's skimpy 2004 Ladies Singles outfit, also on display. The museum houses a cafe and a shop selling all manner of tennis memorabilia. Audioguides are available. Regular 90-minute tours of Wimbledon that take in Centre Court, No 1 Court and other areas of the All England Club also include access to the museum (best to book ahead, online or over the telephone).

BUDDHAPADIPA TEMPLE TEMPLE

(☎020-8946 1357; www.buddhapadipa.org; 14 Calonne Rd, SW19; ⊙temple 9am-6pm Sat & Sun, grounds 9am-5pm daily; ⊜Wimbledon, then ☎93) FREE Surrounded by trees in over 1.5 hectares of tranquil Wimbledon land, this delightful Thai Buddhist temple actively welcomes everyone. Accompanying its reflective Buddhist repose, a community feel permeates the temple grounds, with visitors invited in for coffee and a chat. The *wat* (temple) boasts a *bot* (consecrated chapel) decorated with traditional scenes by two leading Thai artists (take your shoes off before entering).

ⓘ WIMBLEDON TICKETS

For a few weeks each June and July, the sporting world's attention is fixed on the quiet southern suburb of Wimbledon, as it has been since 1877. Most show-court tickets for the **Wimbledon Championships** (☎020-8944 1066; www.wimbledon.com/championships/tickets) are allocated through public ballot, applications for which usually begin in early August of the preceding year and close at the end of December. Entry into the ballot does not mean entrants will get a ticket. A quantity of show court, outer court, ground tickets and late-entry tickets are also available if you queue on the day of play, but if you want a show-court ticket it is recommended you arrive early the day before and camp in the queue.

Sundays are generally the most eventful times to visit, when Dhamma talks and discussions are given in the main temple between 1pm and 2pm. The temple also holds regular meditation classes, retreats (see the website) and colourfully celebrates festivals on the Buddhist calendar. To reach the temple, take the tube or train to Wimbledon and then bus 93 up to Wimbledon Parkside. Calonne Rd leads off it on the right.

✖ EATING

✖ Richmond

★ GELATERIA DANIELI
GELATERIA £

Map p446 (☑020-8439 9807; www.gelateriadanieli.com; 16 Brewers Lane, TW9; ice cream from £2.25; ☺10am-6pm Mon-Fri, 10am-7pm Sat, 11am-7pm Sun, open later in summer; ℝRichmond, ☻Richmond) Stuffed away down delightful narrow, pinched and flagstone-paved Brewer's Lane off Richmond Green, this tiny gelateria is a joy, and often busy. The handmade ice cream arrives in some lip-smacking flavours, from Christmas pudding through pistachio, walnut and tiramisu to pinenut and chocolate, scooped into small tubs or chocolate and hazelnut cones.

STEIN'S
GERMAN £

Map p446 (☑020-8948 8189; www.stein-s.com/richmond; Richmond Towpath, TW10; mains from £4-11.40; ☺noon-10pm, to dusk in winter; 🚸; ℝRichmond, ☻Richmond) On sunny Richmond days, this popular riverside *biergarten* not far from Richmond Bridge is a natural choice for sampling the lazy Thames-side vibe as well as affordable *würstchen* (small sausages), other Bavarian specialities and a stein or two of chilled *weissbier* (white beer). Shaded by two tall yew trees and parasols, the setting is choice, and overloaded parents can rejoice at the small playground for under-fours at the back.

RICHMOND HILL BAKERY
BAKERY £

Map p446 (54 Friars Stile Rd; pastries from £1.50; ☺8am-6pm; ℝRichmond, ☻Richmond) This canine-friendly and homely bakery and cafe occupies a popular and welcoming niche along the marvellously named Friars Stile Rd, supplying Richmond Park ramblers with grade-A coffee, teas, pastries, sandwiches and cakes. Sunbathers can aim for one of the tables out front.

★ CHEZ LINDSAY
FRENCH ££

Map p446 (☑020-8948 7473; www.chez-lindsay.co.uk; 11 Hill Rise, TW10; mains £11-21.50; ☺noon-11pm Mon-Sat, to 10pm Sun; 🛜; ℝRichmond, ☻Richmond) An appetising slice of Brittany at the bottom of Richmond Hill, enduringly popular Chez Lindsay serves wholesome Breton cuisine, comfortable ambience and river views. There's an accent on seafood and house specialities include adorable galettes (buckwheat pancakes; from £3.95) with countless tasty fillings (or plain), washed down with a variety of hearty (and very dry) Breton ciders.

PIER 1
FISH & CHIPS ££

Map p446 (☑020-8332 2778; www.pier1fishandchipshop.co.uk; 11-13 Petersham Rd, TW10; mains from £8.95; ☺11.30am-11pm Mon-Sat, to 10.30pm Sun; ℝRichmond, ☻Richmond) There's little by way of charm in the white, bright and voluminous interior of Pier 1, but the fish here is what it's all about, ferried to tables by helpful waiting staff. The fish – served with chips and a small dish of mushy peas – is prodigiously sized and succulent, fried in batter or grilled.

The menu also nets a haul of non-fish dishes, from sirloins to roast chicken and vegetable lasagne.

PETERSHAM NURSERIES CAFE
MODERN EUROPEAN £££

Map p446 (☑020-8940 5230; www.petershamnurseries.com; Church Lane, off Petersham Rd, TW10; mains £19-27, 2-/3-course menu Wed-Fri £23/28; ☺cafe noon-2pm Tue-Fri, noon-3.30pm Sat & Sun, teahouse 10am-4.30pm Tue-Sat, 11am-4.30pm Sun) 🌱 In a greenhouse at the back of the fabulously located Petersham Nurseries is this award-winning cafe straight out of the pages of *The Secret Garden*. The confidently executed cuisine includes organic ingredients harvested from the nursery gardens and produce adhering to Slow Food principles. Seasonal plates range from pan-fried wild sea bass to osso buco with polenta. Booking in advance is essential.

There's also a **teahouse** for coffee, tea and cakes through the day and an Italian lunch menu. Because of local residents and council concerns about traffic increasing with the cafe's popularity, patrons are asked to walk here via the picturesque river towpath, or to use public transport.

AL BOCCON DI'VINO
ITALIAN £££

Map p446 (☑020-8940 9060; www.nonsolovinoltd.co.uk; 14 Red Lion St, TW9; set meal £45; ☺lunch from 1pm Thu-Sun, dinner from 7pm Tue-

Sun; 🚇Richmond, ⊖Richmond) This stellar Venetian restaurant is generally crammed with eager gourmands. Rather audaciously, there's neither menu nor wine list, but this adds adventurousness to the culinary occasion, as overseen by owner Riccardo Grigolo. You may get *pasta fresca ripiena* (filled pasta) or *agnello al forno* (roast lamb), depending on the availability of the freshest ingredients (and fresh they are).

Meals consist of a sequence of 10 or more courses, at a flat fee of £45 (wine is also a take-it or leave-it £25), so come with an empty tummy. Book well ahead.

✗ Kew

★GLASSHOUSE
MODERN EUROPEAN ££

Map p446 (☏020-8940 6777; www.glasshouse-restaurant.co.uk; 14 Station Pde, TW9; 2/3-course lunch Mon-Sat £24.50/29.50, 3-course lunch Sun £32.50, 3-course dinner £47.50; ◷noon-2.30pm & 6.30-10.30pm Mon-Sat, 12.30-3pm & 7-10pm Sun; 🛜🚻; 🚇Kew Gardens, ⊖Kew Gardens) A day at Kew Gardens finds a perfect conclusion at this Michelin-starred gastronomic highlight. The glass-fronted exterior envelops a delicately lit, low-key interior, where the focus remains on divinely cooked food. Diners are rewarded with a consistently accomplished menu from chef Berwyn Davies that combines English mainstays with modern European innovation.

✗ Putney & Barnes

★ORANGE PEKOE
CAFE ££

(www.orangepekoeteas.com; 3 White Hart Lane, SW13; cream tea £8.95; ◷7.30am-5pm Mon-Fri, 9am-5pm Sat & Sun; 🚇Barnes Bridge) This delightful Barnes tea shop is a consummate haven for lovers of the tea leaf. Surround yourself with all types of tea and present all your tricky leaf-related questions to the on-site tea sommelier. There's fine coffee, too, plus tasty breakfasts and cakes, ravishing all-day cream teas (scones with clotted cream, strawberry jam and a pot of tea) throughout the day and the guilty pleasure of full-on traditional afternoon teas, presented in thoroughly English fashion. Reservations recommended.

MA GOA
INDIAN ££

(www.ma-goa.com; 242-244 Upper Richmond Rd, SW15; mains £7.95-13.95; ◷6.30-10.30pm Tue-Sat, to 11pm Fri & Sat, 12.45-2.45pm & 6-10pm Sun; 🛜✐; 🚇Putney, ⊖Putney Bridge) This much-loved restaurant specialises in the subtle cuisine of Portugal's former colony of Goa on India's west coast. Winning dishes include the fantastic *achari raan* (pot-roasted lamb shank with spices) and the stir-fried *Goa chorizo*. Vegetarian options are also available, plus there's a good-value Sunday buffet lunch (£11).

ENOTECA TURI
ITALIAN ££

(www.enotecaturi.com; 28 Putney High St, SW15; mains £10.50-26.50, 2-/3-course set lunch £18.50/21.50; ◷noon-2.30pm Mon-Sat, 7-10.30pm Mon-Thu, 7-11pm Fri & Sat; 🚇Putney, ⊖Putney Bridge) The atmosphere at this stylish place is serene, the service charming, the menu enticing. Enoteca Turi devotes equal attention to the grape as to the food, which means that each dish, be it *fedelini* with clams or seared Cornish squid with beetroot gnocchi, comes recommended with a particular glass of wine (or you can pick from the huge wine selection if you have ideas of your own).

✗ Chiswick

FRANCO MANCA
PIZZA £

(☏020-8747 4822; www.francomanca.co.uk; 144 Chiswick High Rd, W4; pizzas £4.50-6.95; ◷noon-11pm Mon-Fri, 11.30am-11pm Sat-Sun; ⊖Turnham Green) Branching out from its original Brixton pizzeria, Franco Manca has brought its deliciously aromatic thin crust, sourdough pizzas (and culinary pizzazz) to Chiswick, with longer hours, more elbowroom and a selection of organic wines. Never be put off by its stark choice of six pizzas, this place is all about quality, not quantity.

🍷 DRINKING & NIGHTLIFE

🍷 Richmond & Kew

★WHITE CROSS
PUB

Map p446 (www.thewhitecrossrichmond.com; Water Lane, TW9; ◷10am-11pm; 🛜; ⊖Richmond) The riverside location and fine food and ales make this bay-windowed pub on the site of a former friary a winner. There are entrances for low and high tides, but when the river is at its highest, Cholmondeley Walk running along the Thames floods and the pub is out of bounds to those not willing to wade. Wellies are provided.

Very occasionally boats have to pick up stranded boozers: a chalkboard lists high-tide times and depths (you can also check the website). The pub dates to 1748 and was rebuilt in 1838. Quirky detail: there's a tiny working fireplace *under* the window on your right as you enter.

Putney & Barnes

WHITE HART
PUB

(www.whitehartbarnes.co.uk; The Terrace, SW13; ⊘11am-11pm Mon-Thu, 11am-midnight Fri & Sat, noon-11pm Sun; ⛉; ⬡Barnes Bridge) This riverside Young's pub in Barnes was formerly a Masonic lodge. It's huge, traditional and welcoming downstairs, but the temptation in warmer months is to head to the balcony upstairs for Thames views, or to plonk yourself down at one of the riverside tables. When Boat Race (p297) day arrives, the pub is deluged with beer-toting spectators.

Chiswick

★CITY BARGE
PUB

(www.metropolitanpubcompany.com/our-pubs/the-city-barge/; 27 Strand on the Green, W4; ⊘noon-11pm Mon-Thu, to midnight Fri, 10am-midnight Sat, 10am-10.30pm Sun; ⛉; ⊖Gunnersbury) In a line of small riverside cottages facing wooded Oliver's Island (where Cromwell is alleged to have taken refuge), this excellent pub looks straight onto the muddy Thames. Once known as the Navigators Arms, there has been a pub here since the Middle Ages (1484, to be exact), although the Luftwaffe gave it a dramatic facelift (as has a recent, attractive refurb).

There are three open fires, drinkers spill outside in clement weather and a fine gastropub menu has taken hold. A scene from the Beatles' film *Help!* was shot here, celebrated in framed photo stills.

Twickenham

LONDON APPRENTICE
PUB

Map p446 (www.thelondonapprentice.co.uk; 62 Church St, TW7; ⊘11am-11pm Sun-Thu, to midnight Fri & Sat; ⛉; ⬡Isleworth) This riverside pub (apparently unconnected with the Cornish village of the same name) trumpets a lineage dating back to Tudor days, although the building you drink in today is 18th century. Henry VIII is said to have dallied with wife-to-be number five, Catherine Howard, at the tavern's older incarnation; other regulars included smugglers and highwaymen, including Dick Turpin.

WHITE SWAN
PUB

Map p446 (www.whiteswantwickenham.com; Riverside, TW1; ⊘11am-11pm Mon-Fri, 10am-11pm Sat, 11am-10.30pm Sun; ⛉; ⬡Twickenham) This traditional pub in Twickenham overlooks a quiet stretch of the Thames from what must be one of the most English-looking streets in London. It boasts a fantastic riverside location, a great selection of beer and a loyal crowd of locals. Check the website tide chart to dine outside on the paved garden with Thames water lapping at your table.

Wimbledon

CROOKED BILLET
PUB

(www.thecrookedbilletwimbledon.com; 14-15 Crooked Billet, SW19; ⊘10am-11pm Sun-Thu, to midnight Fri & Sat; ⛉; ⊖Wimbledon) This historic Young's boozer south of Cannizaro Park, just off Wimbledon Common, is brim-full of character, with flagstone floors, open fires and a cosy village-pub personality. Drinkers collapse on the green opposite in summer, while home-cooked food, award-winning ale and seasonal drinks welcome weary ramblers and Wimbledon wayfarers. The Hand in Hand pub next door is another snug option, packed at weekends.

🏃 SPORTS & ACTIVITIES

TWICKENHAM RUGBY STADIUM
STADIUM

(✆020-8892 2000; www.rfu.com; Rugby Rd, Twickenham, TW1; tours adult/child/family £16/10/45; ⬡Twickenham, ⊖Hounslow East, then 🚌281) This is the home of English rugby union. A **museum** (✆020-8892 8877; www.englandrugby.com; adult/child £8/6; ⊘10am-5pm Tue-Sat, 11am-5pm Sun) showcases old matches in the video theatre and boasts a collection of 10,000 items of rugby memorabilia. Guided tours of the stadium take place at various times every day (except Mondays and match days) and include entry to the museum; see the website for details on times. Tickets for international matches are hard to obtain.

Day Trips from London

Windsor Castle p304

The bastion of British royalty, Windsor Castle overlooks the affluent town of Windsor, picturesquely located along the River Thames.

Oxford p307

The world's oldest university town, Oxford boasts more than three dozen prestigious (and eye-catching) colleges, but also some world-class museums.

Brighton p310

With its heady mix of seaside, seediness and sophistication, Brighton is London's favourite coastal resort – with a mock-Moghul summer palace thrown in to boot.

Cambridge p311

Awash in exquisite architecture, steeped in history and tradition and renowned for its quirky rituals, Cambridge is the quintessential English university town.

Bath p314

A cultural trendsetter and fashionable haunt for three centuries, Bath has so many architectural gems the entire city has been named a World Heritage Site.

TOP SIGHT
WINDSOR CASTLE

The world's largest and oldest continuously occupied fortress, this redoubtable mass of battlements and towers dominates the Berkshire town of Windsor, 25 miles west of London. British monarchs have holed up at Windsor Castle for more than 900 years and it's the Queen's favourite of her several official residences. One of the world's greatest surviving medieval castles, Windsor Castle's longevity and easy accessibility from London guarantee its popularity.

Some History

An earth-and-timber fortress was erected around 1080 by William the Conqueror and it was rebuilt in stone by his great-grandson, Henry II, in 1170. Edward III added a Gothic palace, while Charles II gave the state apartments a baroque makeover, creating an 'English Versailles'. George IV swept in with his team of artisans, largely creating today's palace within the castle. As a result of all this re-building, the 951-room castle displays a lively range of architectural style, from half-timbered fired brick to Gothic stonework. A disastrous fire in 1992 nearly wiped out this incredible piece of English cultural heritage – luckily the damage, though severe, was limited and a £37-million, five-year restoration returned the State Apartments to their former glory.

State Apartments

The castle area, covering more than 10 hectares, is divided into three wards. In the Upper Ward, the State Apartments

DON'T MISS...

➡ Grand Vestibule
➡ St George's Hall
➡ St George's Chapel
➡ Queen Mary's Dolls' House
➡ Changing of the Guard

PRACTICALITIES

➡ www.royalcollection.org.uk
➡ Castle Hill
➡ adult/child £19.20/11.30
➡ ◷9.45am-5.15pm Mar-Oct, to 4.15pm Nov-Feb
➡ 🚌701 or 702 from Victoria coach station, 🚉London Waterloo to Windsor Riverside, 🚉London Paddington to Windsor Central via Slough

reverberate with style and history. The crossed swords, suits of armour and banners of the **Grand Staircase** set the tone for the two-dozen-or-so rooms open to the public.

The **Grand Vestibule**, presided over by a marble statue of Queen Victoria, displays gifts and spoils from the empire, including a life-size tiger's head of gold with crystal teeth from the throne of Tipu, Sultan of Mysore. Here you'll also encounter the musket ball that killed Nelson. The **Waterloo Chamber**, commemorating the battle of that name, is filled with portraits of the great and the good by Sir Thomas Lawrence.

From here you move to the **King's Rooms** and **Queen's Rooms**. These 10 chambers are lessons in how the other half lives, with opulent furniture, tapestries, frescoed ceilings, carved panelled walls and paintings by Hans Holbein, Bruegel, Rembrandt, Peter Paul Rubens, Van Dyck and Gainsborough.

The **Queen's Guard Chamber**, bristling with pistols and swords, gives way to the fabulous **St George's Hall**, the venue of state banquets. On the ceiling the shields of the Knights of the Garter (originally from George IV's time here) were re-created after the fire of 1992. The blank shields record 'degraded' knights, who were expelled from the order for various reasons. The devastating fire began next door in the **Lantern Lobby**, a former chapel. The tour ends in the **Garter Throne Room**.

Queen Mary's Dolls' House

This astonishing creation off the North Terrace of the Upper Ward is not a toy but a work of artful miniaturisation, designed by Sir Edwin Lutyens for Queen Mary. Completed in 1924 on a 1:12 scale, an exquisite attention to detail holds sway – it has running water, flushing toilets, electric lights, tiny Crown Jewels, a silver service, vintage wine in the cellar and a fleet of six cars in the garage.

St George's Chapel

Moving westward through the Middle Ward and past the distinctive **Round Tower**, rebuilt in stone from the original Norman keep in 1170, you enter the Lower Ward. This royal chapel, begun by Edward IV in 1475 but not completed until 1528, has a superb nave fashioned in the uniquely English style of Perpendicular Gothic, with gorgeous fan vaulting and massive 'gridiron' stained-glass windows. Serving as a **royal mausoleum**, the chapel contains the tombs of 10 monarchs, including Henry VI, Edward IV, Henry VIII, Charles I, George VI and the late Queen Mother. Note the magnificent **Quire**, hung with Garter Knights' banners above the beautifully

LOCAL EATS

Little **Gilbey's** (☎01753-854921; www.gilbeygroup.com; 82-83 High St; 2/3-course menu £20.50/26.50; ⊙noon-3pm Tue-Sun, 6-10pm daily) is a British restaurant in Eton and one of the area's finest. **Cornucopia** (☎01753-833009; www.cornucopia-bistro.co.uk; 6 High St; 2/3-course menu £10/13; ⊙noon-2.30pm daily, 6-9.30pm Mon-Thu, to 10pm Fri & Sat) is a very convenient small French/Mediterranean bistro southwest of the castle. **Two Brewers** (☎01753-855426; www.twobrewerswindsor.co.uk; 34 Park St; mains £12-15; ⊙noon-2.30pm Mon-Fri, to 5.30pm Sat, to 8.30pm Sun, 6.30-10pm Mon-Thu) is a cosy 17th-century inn perched by Cambridge Gate on the edge of Windsor Great Park.

Join a free 30-minute guided tour (every half-hour) of the wards, or tour the State Apartments and chapels with a handheld multimedia guide. The State Apartments and St George's Chapel close for official functions at various times throughout the year; check the website. If the Queen is in residence, you'll see the Royal Standard, not the Union Flag, above the Round Tower.

carved 15th-century wooden stalls. St George's Chapel closes on Sunday, but time your visit well and you can attend choral evensong at 5.15pm daily (except Wednesday) throughout most of the year.

Albert Memorial Chapel

Originally built by Henry III in 1240 and dedicated to Edward the Confessor, this small and highly decorated chapel was the place of worship for the Order of the Garter until St George's Chapel snatched away that honour. After the death of Prince Albert at Windsor Castle in 1861, Queen Victoria ordered its elaborate redecoration as a tribute to her husband. A major feature of the restoration is the magnificent vaulted roof – the gold mosaic pieces were crafted in Venice. The chapel abuts St George's Chapel.

Windsor Great Park

South of the castle there is a beautiful **park** (☏01753-860222; www.windsor.gov.uk) ranging over a staggering area of 2000 hectares. The **Long Walk** is a 3-mile jaunt along a tree-lined path from King George IV Gate to the Copper Horse statue (of George III) on Snow Hill, the park's highest point. The **Savill Garden** (www. theroyallandscape.co.uk; Wick Lane, Englefield Green; adult/child £9.75/4.35; ⊙10am-6pm Mar-Oct, to 4pm Nov-Feb) is particularly lovely and located just over 4 miles south of Windsor Castle. Take the A308 out of town and follow the brown signs.

Changing of the Guard

A must for any visitor is the changing of the guard, a fabulous spectacle of pomp and ceremony that takes place in the Lower Ward or, when the Queen is in official residence, the Quadrangle in the Upper Ward. It happens daily at 11am Monday to Saturday from April to July and on alternate days the rest of the year. If you're just interested in watching the marching bands, find a spot along Sheet St, from where the guards leave Victoria Barracks at 10.45am, or along High St further north. They return along the same route an hour later.

ETON COLLEGE

A 20-minute walk over the Thames via Windsor Bridge, **Eton** (☏01753-370100; www. etoncollege.com) is arguably the world's most famous public (ie private) school, one that has educated 19 prime ministers and a host of explorers, authors and economists. Several buildings, including Lower School, date from its founding in 1440 by Henry VI. All 1300-plus boys (and it's still boys-only!) are boarders and must wear formal tailcoats, waistcoats and white collars to lessons (though the top hats went out in 1948).

Tours taking in the School Yard, Cloisters Court, Lower School, College Chapel and the Museum of Eton Life take place at various times year-round, depending on the school term and holiday times, but at the time of writing it wasn't possible to visit the school due to building work. Check the visitors tab on its website to see whether tours have resumed.

Oxford

Explore

The Victorian poet Matthew Arnold described Oxford as 'that sweet city with her dreaming spires'. These days the spires coexist with a flourishing commercial city of 150,000 people that has all the usual urban social problems. But for visitors, the superb architecture and the unique atmosphere of the three-dozen-plus colleges – synonymous with academic excellence – and their courtyards and gardens remain major attractions.

The town dates back to the early 12th century (having developed from an earlier Saxon village) and has been responsible for educating 26 British prime ministers, including Margaret Thatcher, Tony Blair and David Cameron.

The Best...

➡ **Sight** Christ Church
➡ **Place to Eat** Vaults & Garden (p310)
➡ **Place to Drink** Turf Tavern (p311)

Top Tip

There are several towers to climb in Oxford, but for the best views of the skyline and surrounding countryside, clamber up the 127 steps of the 14th-century tower of the beautiful **University Church of St Mary the Virgin** (☑01865-279111; www.university-church.ox.ac.uk; High St; adult/child £4/3; ⊙9.30am-5pm Mon-Fri, 9am-5pm Sat, 11.30am-5pm Sun Sep-Jun, 9am-6pm Mon-Sat, 11.30am-6pm Sun Jul & Aug). On Sunday the tower opens just before noon, after the morning service.

Getting There & Away

➡ **Bus Oxford Tube** (☑01865-772250; www.oxfordtube.com) and **Oxford Express** (☑01865-785400; www.oxfordbus.co.uk) buses depart every 10 to 30 minutes round the clock from London's Victoria coach station (return from £18) and can also be boarded at various other points in London, including Marble Arch, Notting Hill Gate and Shepherd's Bush. Journey time is one hour and 40 minutes.

➡ **Train** There are two trains (p381) per hour from London's Paddington station (return from £27.50, one hour).

Need to Know

➡ **Area code** 01865
➡ **Location** 59 miles northwest of London
➡ **Tourist Office** (☑01865-686430; www.visitoxfordandoxfordshire.com; 15-16 Broad St; ⊙9.30am-5pm Mon-Sat, 10am-3.30pm Sun)

◉ SIGHTS & ACTIVITIES

CHRIST CHURCH   HISTORIC BUILDING

(☑01865-276150; www.chch.ox.ac.uk; St Aldate's; adult/child £8/6.50; ⊙10am-4.15pm Mon-Sat, 2-4.15pm Sun) Founded in 1525 and now massively popular with Harry Potter fans, having appeared in several of the films, Christ Church is the largest and grandest of Oxford's colleges. The main entrance is below imposing **Tom Tower** (1681), designed by Christopher Wren and containing a seven-tonne bell called Great Tom. The bell chimes 101 times each evening at 9.05pm to sound the curfew imposed on the original 101 students.

Visitors enter further down St Aldate's through the wrought-iron gates of the War Memorial Gardens and Broad Walk. Immediately on entering is the 15th-century **cloister**, a relic of the ancient Priory of St Frideswide, whose shrine was once a focus of pilgrimage.

From here, you go up to the **Great Hall**, the college's magnificent dining room that served as the model for the Great Hall at Hogwarts, with its hammer-beam roof and imposing portraits of past scholars.

The college chapel is **Christ Church Cathedral**, the smallest in the country. To the south of the college is **Christ Church Meadow**, a leafy expanse bordered by the Rivers Cherwell and Isis (or Thames) and ideal for leisurely walking. Be advised that the Great Hall often closes between 11.40am and 2.30pm and the cathedral in the late afternoon.

MAGDALEN COLLEGE   COLLEGE

(☑01865-276000; www.magd.ox.ac.uk; High St; adult/child £5/4; ⊙1-6pm Oct-Jun, noon-7pm Jul-Sep) Set amid 40 hectares of lawns, woodlands, river walks and deer park, Magdalen (*mawd*-lin), founded in 1458, is one of the wealthiest and most beautiful of Oxford's colleges. It has a reputation as an artistic

Oxford

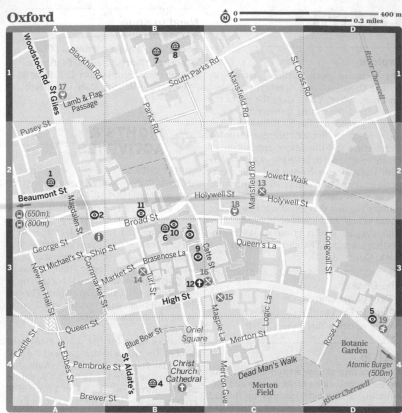

Oxford

◉ Sights

1 Ashmolean Museum	A2
2 Balliol College	A2
3 Bodleian Library	B3
4 Christ Church	B4
5 Magdalen College	D4
6 Museum of the History of Science	B3
7 Oxford University Museum of Natural History	B1
8 Pitt Rivers Museum	B1
9 Radcliffe Camera	B3
10 Sheldonian Theatre	B3
11 Trinity College	B2

12 University Church of St Mary the Virgin	B3

⊗ Eating

13 Edamame	C2
14 Missing Bean	B3
15 Quod	C3
16 Vaults & Garden	C3

◉ Drinking & Nightlife

17 Lamb & Flag	A1
18 Turf Tavern	C2

✦ Sports & Activities

19 Magdalen Bridge Boathouse	D4

college, and some of its famous students have included writers Julian Barnes, Alan Hollinghurst, CS Lewis, John Betjeman, Seamus Heaney and Oscar Wilde.

TRINITY COLLEGE   COLLEGE
(☏01865-279900; www.trinity.ox.ac.uk; Broad St; adult/child £2/1; ⊙10am-noon Mon-Fri, 2-5pm daily) Founded in 1555, this small college counts four lovely quadrangles, including

the Garden Quad designed by Christopher Wren. Its exquisitely carved chapel, perhaps the work of Grinling Gibbons, is one of the most beautiful in the city and a masterpiece of English baroque.

BALLIOL COLLEGE
COLLEGE

(☎01865-277777; www.balliol.ox.ac.uk; Broad St; adult/child £2/1; ⊙10am-5pm, to dusk in winter) Founded in 1263 Balliol College is one of the three oldest colleges in Oxford. The huge Gothic wooden doors between the inner and outer quadrangles bear scorch marks from when four Protestant clerics were burned at the stake here in the mid-16th century.

BODLEIAN LIBRARY
LIBRARY

(☎01865-287400; www.bodleian.ox.ac.uk/bodley; Catte St; tours £5-13; ⊙9am-5pm Mon-Sat, 11am-5pm Sun) The most impressive library you'll ever see, the early 17th-century Bodleian is one of the oldest public libraries in the world and one of just three copyright libraries in England. It currently holds more than 11 million printed items, 117 miles of shelving managed by a staff of 400 and has seating space for up to 2500 readers. A staggering 350,000 books and articles arrive annually.

The oldest part of the library surrounds the stunning **Old Schools Quadrangle**, which dates from the early 17th century and sports some of Oxford's odder architectural treasures, including the **Tower of Five Orders**, an ornate building depicting the five classical orders of architecture on the eastern side of the quad. On the west side is the **Divinity School**, the university's first teaching room. It is a masterpiece of 15th-century Perpendicular Gothic architecture and has a superb fan-vaulted ceiling – it featured as the Hogwarts hospital wing in the Harry Potter films.

Tours of the library last from 30 to 90 minutes; only the extended tour includes a visit to the Radcliffe Camera.

RADCLIFFE CAMERA
LIBRARY

(www.admin.ox.ac.uk/sheldonian; Radcliffe Sq) This quintessential Oxford landmark is one of the city's most photographed buildings. The spectacular circular reading room, filled with natural light, was built between 1737 and 1749 in grand Palladian style, and is protected by Britain's third-largest dome. The only way to see the interior is to join one of the extended tours (£13, 90 minutes)

of the Bodleian Library. Tours take place at 9.15am on Wednesday and Saturday and at 11.15am and 1.15pm Sunday.

SHELDONIAN THEATRE
THEATRE

(www.sheldon.ox.ac.uk; Broad St; adult/child £3.50/2.50, guided tour £8/6; ⊙10am-4.30pm daily May-Sep, 10am-4.30pm Mon-Sat Oct, Nov & Feb-Apr, 10am-3pm Mon-Sat Dec & Jan) Built in 1663 this monumental building was the first major work of Christopher Wren, at the time a professor of astronomy in Oxford. It was inspired by the classical Theatre of Marcellus in Rome and contains a fine 17th-century painting of the triumph of truth over ignorance. The Sheldonian is now used for college ceremonies, including graduation, and public concerts, but you can climb to the cupola for good views of the surrounding buildings.

ASHMOLEAN MUSEUM
MUSEUM

(www.ashmolean.org; Beaumont St; ⊙10am-5pm Tue-Sun; ◉) FREE Britain's oldest public museum (1683) is now among its finest after a £61-million makeover. Its five floors of bright, spacious galleries contain everything from Egyptian artefacts and Chinese art to European and British paintings by the likes of Michelangelo, Turner and Picasso. There's a wonderful rooftop-terrace restaurant with stunning views of the city.

PITT RIVERS MUSEUM
MUSEUM

(www.prm.ox.ac.uk; South Parks Rd; ⊙noon-4.30pm Mon, 10am-4.30pm Tue-Sun) FREE Hidden away through a door at the back of the main exhibition hall of the **Oxford University Museum of Natural History** (www.oum.ox.ac.uk; Parks Rd; ⊙10am-5pm) FREE, famous for its dinosaur and dodo skeletons, is this Aladdin's cave of explorers' booty spread over three floors and crammed with such things as blowpipes, magic charms, voodoo dolls and shrunken heads from the Caribbean, Africa and the Pacific.

MUSEUM OF THE HISTORY OF SCIENCE
MUSEUM

(www.mhs.ox.ac.uk; Broad St; ⊙noon-5pm Tue-Sun) FREE Science, art, celebrity and nostalgia come together at this fascinating museum housed in a beautiful 17th-century building. Exhibits include everything from a blackboard used by Einstein and 'wireless' equipment invented by Marconi, to the world's finest collection of historical scientific instruments.

DAY TRIPS FROM LONDON OXFORD

BRIGHTON: BY THE BEAUTIFUL SEA

With its large student population, the country's biggest gay scene outside London and working-class families down for a jolly, this city by the sea, 53 miles south of London, caters to just about everyone. In one outstretched hand Brighton offers atmospheric cafes, some excellent restaurants and the good-for-a-laugh **Brighton Pier** (www.brightonpier.co.uk; Madeira Dr), a century-old amusement centre with plenty of stomach-churning fairground rides and dingy arcades to keep you amused.

But *the* must-see site here is the **Royal Pavilion** (http://brightonmuseums.org.uk/royalpavilion; Royal Pavilion Gardens; adult/child £11.50/6.20; ⊙9.30am-5.45pm Apr-Sep, 10am-5.15pm Oct-Mar), the glittering palace and party pad of the playboy Prince Regent and later King George IV. It's one of the most opulent buildings in the country – Indian palace on the outside and over-the-top chinoiserie within – and an apt symbol of Brighton's reputation for decadence. The self-paced audioguide tour takes you through a dozen-or-so rooms, including the magnificent ground-floor **Long Gallery** with its metal bamboo staircases, the **Banqueting Room**, a blaze of red and gold infested with coiling dragons, a glorious dome and a one-tonne chandelier, and the sublime **Music Room**.

For seafood, try the long-established **English's of Brighton** (☑01273-327980; www.englishs.co.uk; 29-31 East St; mains £11-35; ⊙noon-10pm). More refined is **Riddle & Finns** (www.riddleandfinns.co.uk; 12 Meeting House Lane; mains £13.50-36.50; ⊙noon-late) in the Lanes (no bookings). **Terre à Terre** (☑01273-729051; www.terreaterre.co.uk; 71 East St; mains £15; ⊙noon-10.30pm Mon-Fri, 11am-11pm Sat, to 11am-10pm Sun; ☑) is one of the best vegetarian restaurants in the country.

National Express (p312) runs hourly buses from Victoria coach station (return from £16, two hours). There are fast trains (p381) throughout the day from London's Victoria station (return from £27, 50 minutes) and slower ones from Blackfriars, London Bridge and King's Cross (return from £16, 1¼ hours).

MAGDALEN BRIDGE BOATHOUSE   BOATING
(☑01865-202643; www.oxfordpunting.co.uk; High St; chauffered 4-person punt per 30min £25, 5-person self-punt per hr £20; ⊙9.30am-dusk Feb-Nov) The most central location to hire a punt, chauffeured or otherwise. From here you can head downstream around the Botanic Garden and Christ Church Meadow or upstream around Magdalen Deer Park. You can also hire rowboats and pedalos.

✕ EATING & DRINKING

★VAULTS & GARDEN   CAFE £
(www.thevaultsandgarden.com; University Church of St Mary the Virgin, High St; mains £6-9; ⊙10am-5pm; ☑) Set in the vaulted 14th-century Old Congregation House at the University Church, this place serves a wholesome line of soups, salads, pastas and paellas, with plenty of choice for vegetarians. It's one of the most beautiful lunch venues in Oxford, with a lovely garden overlooking Radcliffe Sq. Come early for lunch as it's a local favourite.

EDAMAME   JAPANESE £
(www.edamame.co.uk; 15 Holywell St; mains £6-8; ⊙11.30am-2.30pm Wed-Sat, noon-3.30pm Sun, 5-8.30pm Thu-Sat) The queue out the door speaks volumes about the quality of the food at this tiny joint. All light wood and friendly bustle, Edamame is the best place in town for genuine Japanese and the sushi (Thursday only 5pm to 8.30pm, £2.50 to £9) is divine. Arrive early and be prepared to wait.

ATOMIC BURGER   BURGERS £
(www.atomicburger.co.uk; 96 Cowley Rd; mains £7-11; ⊙11.30am-10.30pm) Atomic comes with the Fallout Challenge, which involves consuming a triple burger stack complete with indecent XXX-chilli hot sauce. Not keen on killing your taste buds? Try the Chuck Norris, Dead Elvis, Forrest Gump and the fries in all their incarnations, all washed down with mega shakes.

MISSING BEAN   CAFE £
(www.themissingbean.co.uk; 14 Turl St; mains £2.50-4; ⊙8am-6.30pm Mon-Fri, 9am-6.30pm Sat, 10am-5.30pm Sun) Oxford's best coffee can be found here, as well as loose-leaf teas and

smoothies for those less caffeine inclined. The fresh muffins, cakes and ciabatta sandwiches make this a great lunchtime stop.

QUOD
MODERN BRITISH ££

(☎01865-202505; www.quod.co.uk; 92 High St; mains £11-18; ⊘7am-11pm Mon-Sat, to 10.30pm Sun) Perennially popular for its smart surroundings and buzzing atmosphere, this restaurant dishes up modern brasserie-style food to the Oxford masses. The two-course weekday set lunch (£11.95) is great value and if you're caught between meals, opt for afternoon tea (£6.95 to £22.95) from 3pm to 5.30pm. The live jazz on Sundays (5pm to 7pm) is a treat.

TURF TAVERN
PUB

(www.theturftavern.co.uk; 4 Bath Pl; ⊘11am-11pm) Hidden down a narrow alleyway, this tiny medieval pub (dating from at least 1381) is one of the town's best loved – it's where former US president Bill Clinton famously 'did not inhale' while studying at University College. Home to a dozen ever-changing real ales, it's always packed with a mix of students, professionals and tourists. Plenty of outdoor seating.

LAMB & FLAG
PUB

(cnr St Giles & Lamb & Flag Passage; ⊘noon-11am Mon-Sat, to 10.30pm Sun) Though it might not be able to claim the same number of literary links as the Eagle & Child across the road, authors JRR Tolkien and CS Lewis did sup here, as did Thomas Hardy while writing *Jude the Obscure*. The pub is owned by nearby St John's College and it funds scholarships for doctoral students, so drink up!

Cambridge

Explore

It must be said: Cambridge beats Oxford as the quintessential English university town. True, Oxford has a solid record in educating political grandees, but Cambridge's reputation lies more in the scientific and technological fields. Past names to have studied and/or worked here range from Isaac Newton and Charles Darwin to the discoverers of DNA, James Watson and Francis Crick, and renowned physicist Stephen Hawking.

Founded in the 13th century, contemporary Cambridge is more compact and manageable than its rival. The centre of town lies in a wide bend of the River Cam, and the prettiest section of riverbank is the mile-long Backs, which combines lush scenery with superb views of half a dozen colleges (the other 25 colleges are scattered throughout the city).

The Best...

➡**Sight** King's College Chapel (p313)
➡**Place to Eat** Midsummer House (p314)
➡**Place to Drink** Eagle (p314)

Top Tip

Colleges close to visitors while students are preparing for and sitting exams – between early April and mid-June. Be aware that opening hours can vary from day to day, so check the college websites to avoid disappointment.

FANCY A PUNT?

Gliding along the Backs in a flat-bottomed boat called a punt is a quintessential Cambridge pastime. Punts are available from 9.30am to dusk daily March to October – they cost £20 to £25 per hour and a 45-minute chauffeured trip is £18 per person. Two recommended firms are **Granta Canoe & Punt Hire Company** (www.puntingincambridge.com; Newnham Rd) and **Scudamore's Punting Cambridge** (www.scudamores.com; Granta Pl).

Punting looks fairly straightforward, but we've landed in the drink, heels (and other bits) over head, enough times to say unequivocally that it ain't. Still, that shouldn't deter anyone who isn't afraid of getting a wee bit wet. Here's what you should do: Stand at the back of the punt and lift the pole up to one side. Tilt the pole forward. Slide the pole through your hands, and push down from the bottom of the river to propel the punt forward. Twist the pole to free it and trail it behind the punt, using it as a rudder to steer. Repeat.

Cambridge

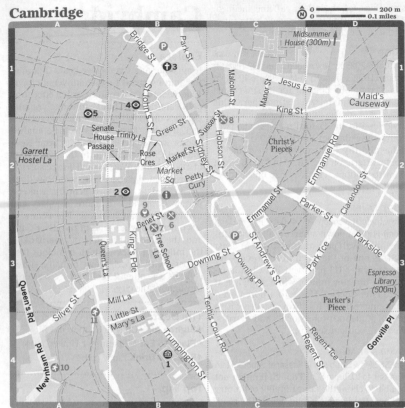

Cambridge

⊙ Sights
1 Fitzwilliam Museum..............................B4
2 King's College Chapel........................B2
3 Round Church B1
4 Trinity College B1
5 Wren Library.......................................A1

⊗ Eating
6 Pint Shop..B3
7 Smokeworks..B3
8 Stickybeaks C2

⊙ Drinking & Nightlife
9 Eagle B2

⊙ Sports & Activities
10 Granta Canoe & Punt Hire
    Company...A4
11 Scudamore's Punting
    Cambridge......................................A4

Getting There & Away
➡ **Bus National Express** (📞0871 781 8178; www.nationalexpress.com) runs hourly buses from Victoria coach station (return from £14, 2¼ hours).

➡ **Train** There are trains (p381) departing every 30 minutes from both Liverpool St (return from £16) and King's Cross (return from £17) stations. The journey takes between 50 minutes and 1¼ hours.

Need to Know
➡ **Area Code** 01223

➡ **Location** 60 miles north of London

➡ **Tourist Office** (📞0871 226 8006; www.visitcambridge.org; Peas Hill, Market Sq; ⊙10am-5pm Mon-Sat, 11am-3pm Sun Apr-Oct, 10am-5pm Mon-Sat Nov-Mar)

⊙ SIGHTS

KING'S COLLEGE CHAPEL   NOTABLE BUILDING
(☏01223-331212; www.kings.cam.ac.uk/chapel; King's Pde; adult/child £8/5.50; ⊘9.30am-3.30pm Mon-Fri, to 3.15pm Sat, 1.15-2.30pm Sun term time, 9.45am-4.30pm Mon, 9.30am-4.30pm Tue-Sun university holidays) This is one of the most sublime buildings in Europe and Cambridge's foremost tourist attraction. Begun in 1446 by Henry VI and completed around 1516, it is one of the finest examples of the Perpendicular Gothic style unique to Britain. Henry VI's successors, notably Henry VIII, added the intricate fan vaulting, elaborately carved organ screen and lofty stained-glass windows in the 1530s; the latter uncharacteristically managed to escape the iconoclastic excesses of the Civil War.

Hear the chapel's world-famous choir at evensong.

TRINITY COLLEGE   COLLEGE
(www.trin.cam.ac.uk; Trinity St; adult/child £2/1; ⊘10am-4.30pm, closed early Apr–mid-Jun) The largest and wealthiest of Cambridge's colleges, Trinity was established in 1546 by Henry VIII, whose statue peers out from the top niche of the great gateway (he's holding a chair leg instead of the royal sceptre, the result of a student prank). The **Great Court**, the largest in either Cambridge or Oxford, incorporates some fine 15th-century buildings and is the annual setting for the sprint around the quadrangle immortalised in the 1981 film *Chariots of Fire*.

Beyond the Great Court are the dignified cloisters of **Nevile's Court** and the **Wren Library** (⊘noon-2pm Mon-Fri, 10.30am-12.30pm Sat term time only), built by Sir Christopher in the 1680s. Here you can view the original AA Milne manuscript of *Winnie the Pooh* and Isaac Newton's personal effects.

FITZWILLIAM MUSEUM   MUSEUM
(www.fitzmuseum.cam.ac.uk; Trumpington St; donation requested; ⊘10am-5pm Tue-Sat, noon-5pm Sun) FREE 'The Fitz' was one of the first art museums in the UK. Its lower galleries are filled with priceless treasures from the ancient world, from splendid Egyptian sarcophagi and Greek and Roman art to porcelain from the Near and Far East. The upper galleries house paintings by Titian, Leonardo, Rubens, Rembrandt and Picasso, as well as contemporary art and changing themed exhibitions. Guided tours (£6) depart at 2.30pm on Saturday.

ROUND CHURCH   CHURCH
(www.christianheritageuk.org.uk; cnr Bridge & Round Church Sts; adult/child £2.50/free; ⊘10am-5pm Tue-Sat, 1-5pm Sun) What is officially known as the Church of the Holy Sepulchre was built by the mysterious Fraternity of the Holy Sepulchre in 1130 to commemorate its namesake in Jerusalem. Thick Norman pillars encircle an unusual circular nave, and the church's original role was as a chapel for pilgrims crossing the River Cam. It's one of only four round churches still standing in England.

✕ EATING & DRINKING

ESPRESSO LIBRARY   CAFE £
(www.espressolibrary.co.uk; 210 East Rd; mains £5-8; ⊘7am-7pm Mon-Sat, 9am-6pm Sun; ✎) This funky new cafe combines industrial-chic-meets-contemporary-art decor with a constantly changing, innovative menu, the chef's repertoire including imaginative salads and mostly vegetarian lunch mains. Come for breakfast, lunch or brunch, or savour one of its signature coffees alongside the laptop-toting clientele.

STICKYBEAKS   CAFE £
(www.stickybeakscafe.co.uk; 42 Hobson St; mains from £5; ⊘8am-5.30pm Mon-Fri, 9am-5.30pm Sat, 10am-5pm Sun; ✎) The window seats at this popular minimalist cafe with vintage touches are perfect for people-watching with coffee and cake in hand. For something more substantial, go for its chunky sandwiches with homemade chutney, hearty soups and veggie-friendly mains such as sweet-potato gratin.

PINT SHOP   MODERN BRITISH ££
(☏01223-352293; www.pintshop.co.uk; 10 Peas Hill; mains £12-21; ⊘noon-11pm Sun-Thu, to midnight Fri & Sat) An appealing patio for sipping a wide range of cocktails and craft beers. A stylish dining room serving traditional dishes with a twist (slow-cooked lamb, overnight pork belly, rib-eye with whisky butter). A bar buzzing with Cambridge's after-work crowd. Pint Shop wears many hats and we love them all. The two-course lunch is a snip at £10.

SMOKEWORKS   BARBECUE ££
(www.smokeworks.co.uk; 2 Free School Lane; mains £8-15; ⊘11.45am-10.30pm Mon-Thu, to 11pm Fri & Sat, to 9.30pm Sun) Tucked away in

a super-central nook, this dark, industrial-themed dining spot draws discerning carnivores and local hipsters with its melt-in-your-mouth ribs, wings and wonderfully smoky pulled pork. The service is friendly and prompt and its salted-caramel milkshakes come in a glass the size of the Colosseum.

★MIDSUMMER HOUSE   INTERNATIONAL £££
(☎01223-369299; www.midsummerhouse.co.uk; Midsummer Common; 5/7/10 courses £47.50/ 82.50/105; ⊗noon-1.30pm Wed-Sat, 7-9.30pm Tue-Thu, 6.30-9.30pm Fri & Sat; ☑) Served in a lovely Victoria villa on the corner of Midsummer Common near the river, chef Daniel Clifford's creative, visually striking dishes have earned him two Michelin stars. Expect the likes of roast quail with grapes and wild mushroom tortellini. Vegetarian versions of all set menus are available. Book well ahead.

EAGLE   PUB
(www.gkpubs.co.uk; Benet St; ⊗9am-11pm Mon-Sat, to 10.30pm Sun) Cambridge's most-famous watering hole has hosted many an illustrious academic in its day, including Nobel Prize–winning scientists Crick and Watson, who discussed their DNA research here. It's a cosy 17th-century pub typically packed to the heavy wooden beams with visitors coming to see the signatures left on the ceiling by US airmen who were based near Cambridge during WWII.

Bath

Explore
This delightful city of honey-coloured stone has always been renowned for its architecture – especially its elegant Georgian terraces. Nowadays, though, Bath is celebrated in equal measure for its association with the novelist Jane Austen – not so much for her actual works, but for the films based on them. Sometimes it seems the crowds just can't get enough.

The Romans established the town of Aquae Sulis in AD 43 and built an extensive baths complex and a temple to the goddess Sulis Minerva. Throughout the Middle Ages, Bath was an ecclesiastical centre and a wool-trading town, but it was not until the early 18th century that Bath and its

spas became the centre of fashionable society. Certain districts in Bath still vie with some in London as the nation's top 'des res' (desirable residences).

The Best...
→**Sight** Roman Baths
→**Place to Eat** Circus (p317)
→**Place to Drink** Star Inn (p317)

Top Tip
The Roman Baths have been off limits to bathers since 1976 for health reasons. But should you want to take the plunge in Bath's thermal waters, head for the **Thermae Bath Spa** (☑0844 888 0844; www.thermaebathspa.com; Hot Bath St; Mon-Fri £32, Sat & Sun £35; ⊗9am-9.30pm, last entry 7pm), an ultramodern shell of stone and glass sitting comfortably beside a Georgian spa building. It has steam rooms, waterfall showers and a choice of bathing venues, including an open-air rooftop pool with jaw-dropping views of Bath.

Getting There & Away
→**Bus** Bath is linked to London's Victoria coach station (return from £23, three hours) by **National Express** (☑0871 781 8181; www.nationalexpress.com) buses throughout the day.

→**Train** There are direct trains (p381) from London Paddington and Waterloo stations (return from £44, 1½ hours) at least hourly.

Need to Know
→**Area code** 01225
→**Location** 115 miles west of London
→**Tourist Office** (☑0906 711 2000, accommodation bookings 0844 847 5256; www.visitbath. co.uk; Abbey Chambers, Abbey Churchyard; ⊗9.30am-5.30pm Mon-Sat, 10am-4pm Sun)

◉ SIGHTS

ROMAN BATHS   MUSEUM
(www.romanbaths.co.uk; Abbey Churchyard; adult/ child £14/9; ⊗9am-9pm Jul & Aug, to 5pm Mar-Jun, Sep & Oct, 9.30am-5pm Nov & Dec, to 4.30pm Jan & Feb) Ever since the Romans arrived in Bath, life in the city has revolved around the three geothermal springs that bubble up near Bath Abbey. Situated alongside an

STONEHENGE

....

Britain's most iconic archaeological site, this compelling assemblage of monolithic stones has been attracting a steady stream of pilgrims, artists and tourists for the last 5000 years, yet it still remains a mystical, ethereal place. Effectively it consists of two rings and two horseshoe shapes of stones ranging in weight from six to 40 tonnes and hauled (or floated) from as far away as the Preseli Hills in Wales, 150 miles to the west, before the wheel had been invented. Is it a temple, an observatory, a solar calendar...or all three? The flashy new visitor centre, with archaeological finds, re-created Neolithic dwellings and a 360-degree projection of the stones through the ages and seasons poses as many questions as it answers. The best way to visit is to take a bus (£17, three hours, three daily) or train (£38, 1½ hours) from London Waterloo to Salisbury and join the **Stonehenge Tour** (⊘0845 0727 093; www.thestonehengetour. info; adult/child £27/17), which departs Salisbury railway station half-hourly June to August and hourly between September and May.

important temple dedicated to the healing goddess Sulis Minerva, the 2000-year-old baths form one of the best-preserved ancient Roman spas in the world. The heart of the complex is the **Great Bath** – head down to water level and along the raised walkway to see the original Roman paving.

Highlights are the vast **Temple of Sulis Minerva** with its gilded bronze head of the goddess and the 12th-century **King's Bath**, built around the original sacred spring. Take a drinking cure from the fountain by the exit.

Above the temple is the 18th-century **Pump Room**, now an elegant cafe-restaurant.

BATH ABBEY
CHURCH

(www.bathabbey.org; requested donation adult/student £2.50/1.50; ⊙9.30am-5.30pm Mon, 9am-5.30pm Tue-Fri, 9am-6pm Sat, 1-2.30pm & 4.30-5.30pm Sun) Looming above the city centre, Bath's huge abbey church was built between 1499 and 1611, making it the last great medieval church raised in England. Its most striking feature is the west facade, where angels climb up and down stone ladders, commemorating a dream of the founder, Bishop Oliver King (note the crown and olive-tree symbols).

Tower tours (adult/child £6/3; ⊙10am-5pm Apr-Aug, to 4pm Sep & Oct, 11am-4pm Jan & Feb, 11am-3pm Nov & Dec) leave on the hour from Monday to Friday and every half-hour on Saturday. They don't run on Sunday.

ROYAL CRESCENT
ARCHITECTURE

Bath is justifiably celebrated for its glorious Georgian architecture, and it doesn't get any grander than this semicircular terrace of majestic town houses overlooking

the green sweep of Royal Victoria Park. Designed by John Wood the Younger in 1775, the 30 houses appear perfectly symmetrical from the outside, but the owners were allowed to tweak the interiors to their own specifications.

THE CIRCUS
HISTORIC SITE

(The Circus) This Georgian masterpiece, built to John Wood the Elder's design in 1766, is said to have been inspired by the Colosseum. Arranged over three equal terraces, the 33 mansions overlook a garden populated by plane trees. Famous residents have included Thomas Gainsborough, Clive of India, David Livingstone and the American actor Nicholas Cage.

BATH ASSEMBLY ROOMS
HISTORIC BUILDING

(www.nationaltrust.org.uk/bath-assembly-rooms; 19 Bennett St; ⊙10.30am-5.30pm) **FREE** Opened in 1771, the city's glorious Assembly Rooms (painstakingly reconstructed after being bombed in WWII) were where fashionable Bath socialites once gathered to waltz, play cards and listen to chamber music. Rooms open to the public include the card room, tearoom and ballroom, all lit by original 18th-century chandeliers.

If you want to see how these Georgian socialites dressed, visit the **Fashion Museum** (⊘01225-477789; www.fashionmuseum.co.uk; adult/child £8.25/6.25; ⊙10.30am-5pm Mar-Oct, to 4pm Nov-Feb) in the basement.

PULTENEY BRIDGE
BRIDGE

Hovering gracefully above the rushing waters of Pulteney Weir in the River Avon, this elegant bridge is one of only a handful in the world to be lined with shops (the most famous other example is its inspiration, the

Bath

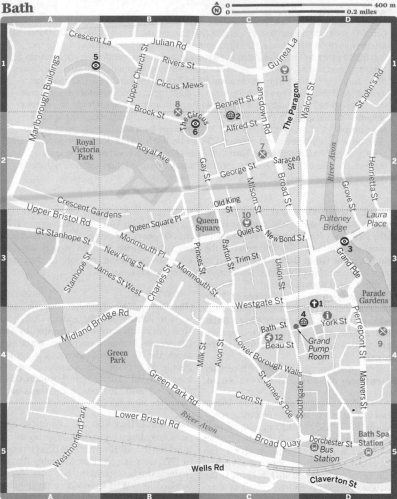

Bath

◎ **Sights**
1 Bath Abbey		D3
2 Bath Assembly Rooms		C2
Fashion Museum		(see 2)
3 Pulteney Bridge		D3
4 Roman Baths		D4
5 Royal Crescent		A1
6 The Circus		B2

✗ **Eating**
7 Adventure Cafe Bar		C2

8 Circus		B2
9 Sotto Sotto		D4

🍷 **Drinking & Nightlife**
10 Salamander		C3
11 Star Inn		C1

✦ **Sports & Activities**
Bath Abbey Tower Tours		(see 1)
12 Thermae Bath Spa		C4

Ponte Vecchio in Florence). It was built in 1773 by Scottish architect Robert Adams.

EATING & DRINKING

ADVENTURE CAFE BAR   CAFE £

(www.adventurecafebar.co.uk; 5 Princes Bldgs, George St; mains £4-8.50; ⊘8am-3am Mon-Fri, from 8.30 Sat & Sun) This cool cafe-bar, just a slipper's throw from the Assembly Rooms, offers something for everyone at most times of the day: morning cappuccino, lunchtime ciabatta and late-night beer and cocktails. Great outdoor seating in the back.

★CIRCUS   MODERN BRITISH ££

(⊠01225-466020; www.thecircuscafeandrestaurant.co.uk; 34 Brock St; mains lunch £10-14, dinner £16.50-18.50; ⊘10am-midnight Mon-Sat) Just off the namesake Circus, this bistro is one of Bath's best. The food, prepared by chef Ali Golden, is British with a continental twist: rabbit, guinea fowl, roast chicken, spring lamb, infused with herbal flavours and rich sauces. Choose the ground floor overlooking a small courtyard, or the intimate (but cramped when full) cellar. Reserve well ahead.

SOTTO SOTTO   ITALIAN ££

(⊠01225-330236; www.sottosotto.co.uk; 10 North Pde; pasta £8.50-10.75, mains £13.50-18.50; ⊘noon-2pm & 5-10pm) Bath's best Italian eatery, hidden away in a vaulted cellar, is a short walk from Bath Abbey. Ingredients are shipped in from Italy and everything is just like Mamma made, from the classic house lasagne to more elaborate offerings such as veal, grilled swordfish and sea bass in Parma ham.

STAR INN   PUB

(www.abbeyales.co.uk/www.star-inn-bath.co.uk; 23 The Vineyards, off the Paragon; ⊘noon-2.30pm & 5.30pm-midnight Mon-Thu, noon-1am Fri & Sat, noon-midnight Sun) Not many pubs are registered relics, but the Star is and still retains many of its 19th-century bar fittings. It's the brewery tap for Bath-based Abbey Ales and some ales are served in traditional jugs. You can even ask for a pinch of snuff in the 'smaller bar' at the entrance.

SALAMANDER   PUB

(⊠01225-428889; www.bathales.com/pubs/salamander.html; 3 John St; ⊘10am-midnight Mon-Thu, to 1am Fri & Sat, to 11.30pm Sun) Owned by the city bespoke brewery, Bath Ales, the Sally serves in-house beers such as amber Gem and Golden Hare and the stronger, darker Rare Hare in summer (it's Forest Hare in autumn and the porter Festivity in spring and winter). There's a dining room (mains £10 to £14) upstairs.

🛏 Sleeping

Landing the right accommodation is integral to your London experience, and there's no shortage of choice. But be aware that rooms in sought-after hotels can be booked solid. There is some fantastic accommodation about – whatever the price – but plan ahead.

Hotels

London has a grand roll-call of stately hotels and many are experiences in their own right. Standards across the top end and much of the boutique bracket are high, but so are prices. Quirkiness and individuality can be found in abundance, alongside dyed-in-the-wool traditionalism. A wealth of budget boutique hotels has exploited a lucrative niche, while a rung or two down in overall quality and charm, midrange chain hotels generally offer good locations and dependable comfort. Demand can often outstrip supply – especially on the bottom step of the market – so book ahead, particularly during holiday periods and in summer.

B&Bs

Housed in good-looking old properties, bed and breakfasts come in a tier below hotels, often promising boutique-style charm and a more personal level of service. Handy B&B clusters appear in Paddington, South Kensington, Victoria and Bloomsbury.

Hostels

After B&Bs the cheapest form of accommodation is hostels, both the official Youth Hostel Association (YHA) ones and the usually hipper, more party-orientated independent ones. Hostels vary in quality so select carefully; most offer twins as well as dorms.

Rates & Booking

Deluxe hotel rooms will cost from around £350 per double but there's good variety at the top end, so you should find a room from about £200 that offers superior comfort without the prestige. Some boutique hotels also occupy this bracket. There's a noticeable dip in quality below this price, but we have listed the best in this range. Under £100 and you're at the more serviceable, budget end of the market. Look out for weekend deals that can put a better class of hotel within reach. Rates often slide in winter. Book through the hotels' websites for the best online deals or promotional rates. Unless otherwise indicated, accommodation prices quoted include breakfast. Hostelling International (HI) members net discounts on YHA accommodation.

Apartments

If you're in London for a week or more, a short-term or serviced apartment such as 196 Bishopsgate (p325), Number 5 Maddox Street (p323) or Beaufort House (p328) may make sense; rates at the bottom end are comparable to a B&B.

Websites

LondonTown (☎020-7437 4370; www.londontown.com/hotels) Bookings.

Lonely Planet (www.lonelyplanet.com/hotels) Bookings.

YHA Central Reservations System (www.yha.org.uk/hostel/london-central) Hostels.

Lonely Planet's Top Choices

York & Albany (p330) North London Georgian elegance meets luxurious comfort.

Beaumont (p322) Art deco opulence just off Oxford St.

Hoxton Hotel (p328) Cool location, nifty looks and very cheap rooms.

Clink78 (p330) Heritage hostel and former magistrates court.

Threadneedles (p325) Fresh new look but same old impeccable service.

Best by Budget

£

Clink78 (p330) Best facilities in London, and possibly the most original.

Hoxton Hotel (p328) Outstanding value for its location and design.

££

Citizen M (p326) High-tech, innovative and intimate.

Main House (p332) All-suite hotel in a Victorian terrace house.

£££

Brown's Hotel (p323) London's oldest hotel remains top of the heap.

Nadler Soho (p324) Sleek boutique in the heart of Soho.

Best Romantic Hotels

Ritz (p324) So grand it lent its name to the English language.

Goring (p322) Delectable slice of classy, classic England.

Best Boutique Hotels

Zetter Hotel & Townhouse (p328) Sustainable two-part hotel with a mix of luxurious sleek and period interiors.

Charlotte Street Hotel (p324) London's first boutique hotel and arguably its best.

Artist Residence (p327) One of a kind hotel with personality-plus.

Best B&Bs

No 90 (p327) Excellent value in the heart of leafy Chelsea.

Barclay House (p332) Ticks every box – and a few more.

Best for Contemporary Cool

Soho Hotel (p324) Very hip, very central, with original artwork throughout.

Citizen M (p326) Tablet-controlled rooms and square beds, this is hotel 2.0.

Best for Heritage

Ritz (p324) There's only one Ritz and it reigns supreme.

Corinthia (p322) Jewel in the crown near the seat of power.

Best for Views

ME by Melia London (p323) Stunning terrace views from Foster-designed hotel.

One Aldwych (p323) Costly, but priceless, river views from the uppermost rooms.

NEED TO KNOW

Price Ranges

In our listings we've used the following codes to represent the price of an en suite double room in high season:

£ less than £100

££ £100 to £200

£££ more than £200

Reservations

➡ Book rooms as far in advance as possible, especially for weekends and holiday periods.

➡ **British Hotel Reservation Centre** (☏020-7592 3055; www.bhronline.com) has desks at airports and major train stations.

➡ **Visit London** (☏0871 222 3118; www.visitlondon offers.com) offers a free booking service with a wide range of accommodation options and has special deals and a list of gay friendly accommodation.

Tax

➡ Value-added tax (VAT; 20%) is added to hotel rooms. Some hotels include this in their advertised rates. Prices listed here include VAT.

Checking In & Out

➡ Check in is usually 2pm, though most places will let you check in earlier if your room is available or let you leave your luggage. Check out is usually between 10am and noon.

Breakfast

➡ Breakfast may be included in the room rate. Sometimes this is a continental breakfast; full English breakfast might cost extra.

SLEEPING

Where to Stay

Neighbourhood	For	Against
The West End	Close to main sights; great transport links; wide accommodation range in all budgets; good restaurants	Busy tourist areas; expensive
The City	St Paul's and Tower of London; good transport links; handy central location; quality hotels; some cheaper weekend rates	Very quiet at weekends; a business district so high prices during the week
The South Bank	Near Tate Modern, London Eye and Southbank Centre; cheaper than West End; excellent pubs and views	Many chain hotels; choice and transport limited
Kensington & Hyde Park	Excellent for South Kensington museums and shopping; great accommodation range; stylish area; good transport	Quite expensive; drinking and nightlife options limited
Clerkenwell, Shoreditch & Spitalfields	Trendy area with great bars and nightlife; excellent for boutique hotels	Few top sights; transport options somewhat limited
East London & Docklands	Markets, multicultural feel; great restaurants and traditional pubs	Limited sleeping options; some areas less safe at night
Camden & North London	Leafy; vibrant nightlife; pockets of village charm; excellent boutique hotels and hostels; great gastropubs; quiet during the week	Non-central and away from main sights
Notting Hill & West London	Cool cachet; great shopping, markets and pubs; excellent boutique hotels; good transport	Pricey; light on top sights
Greenwich & South London	Great boutique options; leafy escapes; near top Greenwich sights	Sights spread out beyond Greenwich; transport limited
Richmond, Kew & Hampton Court	Smart riverside hotels; semi-rural pockets; quiet; fantastic riverside pubs	Sights spread out; a long way from central London

🛏 The West End

GENERATOR   HOSTEL £

Map p412 (📞020-7388 7666; www.generatorhos
tels.com/london; 37 Tavistock Pl, WC1; dm/r from
£18/55; @🛜; 🔵Russell Sq) With its industrial
lines and funky decor, the huge Generator
(more than 870 beds) is one of central London's grooviest budget spots. The bar, complete with pool tables, stays open until 2am
and there are frequent themed parties. Dorm
rooms have between six and 12 beds; backing
it all up are twins, triples and quad rooms.

There is no kitchen but breakfast is provided and the large canteen serves bargain
dinners from £4.50.

YHA LONDON OXFORD STREET   HOSTEL £

Map p408 (📞020-7734 1618; www.yha.org.uk; 14
Noel St, W1; dm/tw from £18/46; @🛜; 🔵Oxford
Circus) The most central of London's eight
YHA hostels is also one of the most intimate
with just 104 beds, and excellent shared facilities, including the fuchsia kitchen and
the bright, funky lounge. Dormitories have
three and four beds and there are doubles
and twins. The in-house shop sells coffee
and beer and wi-fi is free.

RIDGEMOUNT HOTEL   B&B £

Map p412 (📞020-7636 1141; www.ridgemountho-
tel.co.uk; 65-67 Gower St, WC1; s/d/tr/q from
£54/82/108/128; @🛜; 🔵Goodge St) This old-
fashioned hotel dispenses a warmth and
consideration that can be hard to find in
London these days. About half of its 32 utili-
tarian rooms have bathrooms and there are
a number of triples and quadruples, plus a
laundry service.

GEORGE HOTEL   B&B £

Map p412 (📞020-7387 8777; www.georgehotel.
com; 58-60 Cartwright Gardens, WC1; s/tw/tr
incl breakfast from £65/90/140; @🛜; 🔵Russell
Sq) Housed in a building dating to around
1810, the George is a friendly chap, if a tad
old-fashioned. Don't expect much but with
this location, who's complaining? Cheaper
rooms share bathrooms and guests get access to the gardens in front.

FIELDING HOTEL   BOUTIQUE HOTEL ££

Map p406 (📞020-7836 8305; www.thefield-
inghotel.co.uk; 4 Broad Ct, Bow St, WC2; s/d from
£108/168; ❋🛜; 🔵Covent Garden) Hidden
away in a pedestrianised court in the heart
of Covent Garden, this pretty, 25-room hotel

(named after the novelist Henry Fielding,
who lived nearby) has been furnished to a
very high standard: bathrooms have lovely
walk-in showers, and rooms are beautifully
done up and are fully air-conditioned. The
hotel doesn't provide breakfast but the area
is full of cafes.

ACADEMY   BOUTIQUE HOTEL ££

Map p412 (📞020-7631 4115; www.theacademy-
hotel.co.uk; 21 Gower St, WC1; s/d/ste from £140/
170/190; ❋🛜; 🔵Goodge St) This beautiful,
terribly English hotel ranges through five
Georgian town houses in Bloomsbury. The 49
lovely rooms are kitted out with fluffy feather
duvets, elegant furnishings and the latest in
creature comforts. A conservatory overlooks
a leafy back garden with a fish pond, and
there's a cosy breakfast room, but no lift.

HARLINGFORD HOTEL   HOTEL ££

Map p412 (📞020-7387 1551; www.harlingford-
hotel.com; 61-63 Cartwright Gardens, WC1; s/d/
tr incl breakfast £93/124/150; 🛜; 🔵Russell Sq)
With its 'H' logo proudly sewn on the bedroom cushion, a modern interior with lashings of lavender and mauve, and green-tiled
bathrooms, this stylish Georgian 43-room
hotel in Bloomsbury is arguably the best
on a street where competition is fierce. The
welcome is always warm and the price unbeatable, but there's lots of stairs and no lift.

MORGAN HOTEL   B&B ££

Map p412 (📞020-7636 3735; www.morganhotel.
co.uk; 24 Bloomsbury St, WC1; s/d/tr incl breakfast £120/145/195; ❋@🛜; 🔵Tottenham Court
Rd) In a row of 18th-century Georgian
houses, the family-owned Morgan is distinguished by its friendliness, fine service,
breakfast fit for a king, and good value.
Decor in the rooms is somewhat dated, but
they are very clean. The larger suites (sin-
gle/double/triple £175/205/250, no air-con)
are worth the extra outlay.

AROSFA HOTEL   B&B ££

Map p412 (📞020-7636 2115; www.arosfalondon.
com; 83 Gower St, WC1; s/tw/tr/f incl breakfast
£83/128/155/185, d £135-155; 🛜; 🔵Goodge St)
The Philippe Starck furniture and modern
look in the lounge is more lavish than the
decor in the hotel's 16 rooms, with cabin-
like bathrooms in many of them. About half
have been refurbished; they are small but
remain good value. There are a couple of
family rooms; room 4 looks on to a small
garden. Prices rise on Saturdays.

JESMOND HOTEL
B&B ££

Map p412 (☑020-7636 3199; www.jesmondhotel. org.uk; 63 Gower St, WC1; s/d/tr/q incl breakfast from £70/120/155/175; @🛜; ⊖Goodge St) The rooms – nine with bathroom – at this popular, 15-guestroom hotel are basic but clean and cheerful, and there's a small, pretty garden. There's also laundry service, free wi-fi and use of the internet, plus good breakfasts for kicking off your London day.

ARRAN HOUSE HOTEL
B&B ££

Map p412 (☑020-7636 2186; www.arranhotel-london.com; 77-79 Gower St, WC1; s/d/tr/q incl breakfast £155/175/195/225, s/d/tr without bathroom £95/125/155; @🛜; ⊖Goodge St) This welcoming Georgian house B&B provides excellent value for the location. The 30 rooms range from basic singles with shared facilities to bright, well-furnished doubles with bathrooms. There is a cosy lounge at the front and gorgeous gardens at the back, perfect for a few drinks or a quiet read. Guests can use the microwave, fridge and dining room.

SEVEN DIALS HOTEL
HOTEL ££

Map p406 (☑020-7240 0823; www.sevendials-hotellondon.com; 7 Monmouth St, WC2; s/d/tr/q £95/105/130/150; 🛜; ⊖Covent Garden, Tottenham Court Rd) In a very central location, the Seven Dials is a clean, comfortable and very basic option with half of its 18 rooms facing onto charming Monmouth St; the ones at the back don't get much of a view but are quieter. TV sets are micro.

★BEAUMONT
HOTEL £££

Map p414 (☑020-7499 1001; www.thebeaumont. com; Brown Hart Gardens, W1; d/studio/ste from £395/620/1575 ; 🌼🛜; ⊖Bond St) A stylish, handsome and luxurious hotel, the 73-room Beaumont is all deco opulence. Fronted by an arresting chunk of deco-inspired stainless steel and fumed oak sculpture from Antony Gormley called *Room* (part of a £2250 per night suite), the striking white building dates from 1926. Rooms and suites are swish and elegant, with a 1920s modernist aesthetic.

★CORINTHIA
HOTEL £££

Map p416 (☑020-7930 8181; www.corinthia. com; Whitehall Place, SW1; d/ste/penthouse £425/1380/3000; 🌼🛜🌼; ⊖Embankment) With hotels from Malta to St Petersburg, the Corinthia group's jewel in its crown is this grand Victorian property in Whitehall. It's as smart as you can imagine, but never overbearing and stuffy. A stay here is a delight, from the perfect rooms to the flawless service, tempting afternoon tea and a location that ensconces you at the very heart, but just beyond the bustle, of London.

★LONDON EDITION
HOTEL £££

Map p412 (☑020-7781 0000; www.editionhotels. com/london; 10 Berners St, W1; d/ste from £375/500; 🌼🛜; ⊖Tottenham Court Rd) Step into the lobby of the London Edition and you're greeted by a stunning combination of old and new; from the revived stucco ceiling hangs an Ingo Maurer pendulum, reflecting the ornate surrounds in all directions. The 173 wood-panelled rooms are uncomplicated, with mid-century elements and faux fur throws; all are adorned by portraits of artist Hendrick Kerstens' daughter Paula.

HAZLITT'S
HISTORIC HOTEL £££

Map p408 (☑020-7434 1771; www.hazlittshotel. com; 6 Frith St, W1; s/d/ste from £216/288/660; 🌼🛜; ⊖Tottenham Court Rd) Built in 1718 and comprising four original Georgian houses, this Soho gem was the one-time home of essayist William Hazlitt (1778–1830). The 30 guestrooms have been furnished with original antiques and boast a profusion of seductive details, including panelled walls, mahogany four-poster beds, antique desks, Victorian claw-foot tubs, sumptuous fabrics and modern creature comforts.

HAYMARKET HOTEL
HOTEL £££

Map p406 (☑020-7470 4000; www.haymarkethotel.com; 1 Suffolk Pl, off Haymarket, SW1; r/ste from £336/504; 🌼🛜🌼; ⊖Piccadilly Circus) With the trademark colours and lines of hoteliers and designers Tim and Kit Kemp, the Haymarket is beautiful, with hand-painted Gournay wallpaper, signature fuchsia and green designs in the 50 guestrooms, a sensational 18m pool with mood lighting, an exquisite library lounge with honesty bar, and original artwork throughout. Just love the dog silhouettes on the chairs and bar stools.

GORING
HOTEL £££

Map p416 (☑020-7396 9000; www.thegoring. com; Beeston Pl; r/ste £430/1340; 🌼 @🛜; ⊖Victoria) Kate Middleton spent her last night as a commoner in the Royal Suite (£8400 per night) before joining the Royal Family, propelling the (refurbished) Goring into an international media glare. Glistening with chandeliers, dotted with trademark fluffy sheep and overseen by highly professional staff, this family-owned hotel is a supremely grand, albeit highly relaxed slice of England and Englishness, with a sumptuous garden.

ME BY MELIÃ LONDON   HOTEL £££

Map p406 (☑020-7395 3400; www.melia.com; 336-337 The Strand; d £285-375, ste from £525; ✳🔊; ⊖Temple, Covent Garden) The Foster + Partners–designed 157-room ME by Meliã London at the southwestern curve where the Strand meets Aldwych is all sophisticated and natty cool, and the roof bar has some of the best views in town from its al fresco terrace. All rooms – also Foster + Partners–designed – are super neat, ultra-modern and classy. Terrace rooms come with balcony.

ONE ALDWYCH   HOTEL £££

Map p406 (☑020-7300 1000; www.onealdwych. co.uk; 1 Aldwych, WC2; d £255-470, ste £465-1005; ✳🔊✦; ⊖Covent Garden) Housed in former art-nouveau newspaper offices (1907), One Aldwych is an upbeat hotel with 105 rooms, modern art throughout and a chlorine-free swimming pool. The spacious and stylish rooms are replete with raw silk curtains, natural tones, daily fresh flowers and huge bathtubs. The circular suites have fabulous views of the Strand and Waterloo Bridge.

DEAN STREET TOWNHOUSE   BOUTIQUE HOTEL £££

Map p408 (☑020-7434 1775; www.deanstreet-townhouse.com; 69-71 Dean St, W1; r £260-450; ✳🔊; ⊖Tottenham Court Rd) This 39-room gem in the heart of Soho has a wonderful boudoir atmosphere with its Georgian furniture, retro black-and-white tiled bathroom floors, beautiful lighting, Egyptian cotton sheets and luxury touches for self-pampering (Cowshed bathroom products, hairdryer *and* straighteners in every room!). 'Medium' and 'bigger' rooms have four-poster beds and antique-style bathtubs right in the room.

BROWN'S HOTEL   HOTEL £££

Map p416 (☑020-7493 6020; www.roccofortehotels.com/hotels-and-resorts/browns-hotel/; 30 Albemarle St, W1; r/ste from £460/2000; ✳🔊; ⊖Green Park) London's oldest hostelry, this landmark hotel was created in 1837 from 11 town houses. Each of the 117 rooms has been individually decorated by designer Olga Polizzi and many feature antiques and original artworks. The rest is lovely: the traditional English Tea Room is all Edwardian oak panelling and working fireplaces while the Donovan Bar has a stunning 19th century stained-glass window.

NUMBER 5 MADDOX STREET   APARTMENT £££

Map p408 (☑020-7647 0200; www.living-rooms. co.uk/hotel/no5maddoxstreet; 5 Maddox St, W1; ste £250-925; ✳🔊; ⊖Oxford Circus) Right off Regent St, this 12-suite/apartment luxury establishment will feel like your own London pad. Along with all the facilities the contemporary traveller could require, including iPod docking stations and Nespresso coffee machines, each neutrally-coloured apartment has a fully equipped kitchen, and some even get their own little balcony or patio. Rooms are on five floors but there's no lift.

No 8 is the largest apartment.

HAM YARD HOTEL   HOTEL £££

Map p408 (☑020-3642 2000; www.firmdale-hotels.com/hotels/london/ham-yard-hotel; 1 Ham Yard, W1; d £350-560, ste from £500, apt from £2000; ✳🔊; ⊖Piccadilly Circus) With 91 rooms, 24 apartments, 13 shops, a restaurant, a bar, a plethora of common areas, plus a spa, a gym, a 190-seat cinema and even a bowling alley, this hotel can literally cater to your every whim. On the southern side of Soho, it loops around a courtyard, where you can dine al fresco, and is colourfully dressed in Kit Kemp's eclectic modern British style.

Rooms continue the arty, vivid decor; each is uniquely designed, with enormous windows.

COVENT GARDEN HOTEL   BOUTIQUE HOTEL £££

Map p406 (☑020-7806 1000; www.coventgardenhotel.co.uk; 10 Monmouth St, WC2; d/ste from £318/510; ✳🔊; ⊖Covent Garden) This 58-room boutique hotel housed in a former French hospital features antiques such as the beautiful marquetry desk in the drawing room, gorgeous, bright fabrics and quirky bric-a-brac to mark its individuality. There's an excellent bar-restaurant off the lobby and two stunning guest lounges with fireplaces on the 1st floor (that come into their own in the winter), plus an honesty bar.

ROSEWOOD   HOTEL £££

Map p406 (☑020-7781 8888; www.rosewoodhotels.com/en/london; 252 High Holborn, WC1; d £380-750, ste £1140-9000; ✳@🔊; ⊖Holborn) After an £85 million refurb, the incredibly grand Pearl Assurance building (dating from 1914) now houses the stunning Rosewood Hotel. An artful marriage of period and modern styles can be found in the 262 rooms and 44 suites. British heritage is carefully woven throughout the bar, restaurant, deli, lobby and even the housekeepers' uniforms.

SOHO HOTEL
HOTEL £££

Map p408 ([📞]020-7559 3000; www.sohohotel. com; 4 Richmond Mews, off Dean St W1; r/ste from £354/540; [❄][📶]; [Ⓔ]Oxford Circus) The hip Soho has all the hallmarks of the eclectically chic duo Tim and Kit Kemp writ large over 91 individually-fashioned guest rooms, each with light-filled floor-to-ceiling windows. Colours are soft, yet vivacious and creative, and the loving attention to design extends to a stunning black cat sculpture by Fernando Botero at the entrance.

ONE LEICESTER STREET
BOUTIQUE HOTEL £££

Map p408 ([📞]020-3301 8020; oneleicesterstreet. com; 1 Leicester St, WC2; d £189-229, ste from £350; [📶]; [Ⓔ]Leicester Sq) Steps away from Leicester Sq, this hotel provides an oasis of hip tranquillity above the swirling neon of the square and the bustle of adjacent Chinatown. 'Post-supper' rooms are smallest, with an in-room bath; superior rooms are larger with separate facilities, and there's a suite on the top floor. All are white-wood panelled, in a classy minimalist style.

CHARLOTTE STREET
HOTEL
BOUTIQUE HOTEL £££

Map p412 ([📞]020-7806 2000; www.firmdale-hotels.com; 15-17 Charlotte St, W1; d/ste from £300/498; [❄][📶]; [Ⓔ]Goodge St) Presented in striking and eye-catching designs – with frequent nods to the Bloomsbury Group (original art work from Vanessa Bell and Duncan Grant) – this snazzy 52-room boutique property is a favourite of visiting media types. The Drawing Room, with its working fireplace and capacious sofas, is an inviting place to unwind. The Charlotte also has its own cinema and shows on Sunday night (£35, with three-course meal).

RITZ
LUXURY HOTEL £££

Map p416 ([📞]020-7493 8181; www.theritzlondon. com; 150 Piccadilly, W1; r/ste from £380/680; [❄][@][📶]; [Ⓔ]Green Park) What can you say about a hotel that has lent its name to the English lexicon? The 136-room Ritz has a spectacular position overlooking Green Park and is supposedly the Royal Family's home away from home (it does have a royal warrant from the Prince of Wales and is very close to the palace). All rooms have period interiors and antique furniture.

Check in about the various formal-dress/ smart-casual codes (shirt and tie) that apply in different areas of the hotel.

NADLER SOHO
BOUTIQUE HOTEL £££

Map p408 ([📞]020-3697 3697; www.thenadler. com; 10 Carlisle St, W1; s £180, d £190-320, ste £495; [❄][@][📶]; [Ⓔ]Tottenham Court Rd) In the heart of Soho, this 78-room boutique hotel is a sleek mix of creams and browns, with a good range of rooms, all with minikitchens complete with microwave and fridge. Service is polished and guests are offered discounts at nearby bars and restaurants.

RUBENS AT THE PALACE
HOTEL £££

Map p416 ([📞]020-7834 6600; www.rubenshotel. com; 39 Buckingham Palace Rd, SW1; d/ste £203/423; [@][📶]; [Ⓔ]Victoria) Opposite the grounds of Buckingham Palace, it's perhaps not surprising to find that Rubens is a favourite with visitors seeking that quintessential British experience. Rooms are monarchist chic: heavy patterned fabrics, dark wood, thick drapes and crowns above the beds.

🛏 The City

LONDON ST PAUL'S YHA
HOSTEL £

Map p418 ([📞]020-7236 4965; www.yha.org.uk/ hostel/london-st-pauls; 36 Carter Lane, EC4; dm £17-30, d £60; [@][📶]; [Ⓔ]St Paul's) This 213-bed hostel is housed in a former choirboys school in the shadow of St Paul's. Dorms have between three and 11 beds, and twins and doubles are available. There's a great lounge, licensed cafeteria (breakfast £5, dinner £6 to £10) but no kitchen – and lots of stairs (and no lift). Seven-night maximum stay. Internet £1 for 20 minutes.

HOTEL INDIGO
TOWER HILL
BOUTIQUE HOTEL ££

Map p418 ([📞]020-7265 1014; www.hotelindigo. com/lontowerhill; 142 Minories, EC3; r weekend/ weekday from £100/260; [❄][📶]; [Ⓔ]Aldgate) This branch of the US InterContinental group's boutique-hotel chain offers 46 differently styled rooms, all with four-poster beds and iPod docking stations. Larger-than-life drawings and photos of the neighbourhood won't let you forget where you are.

MOTEL ONE LONDON
TOWER HILL
HOTEL ££

Map p418 ([📞]020-7481 6420; www.motel-one. com/en/hotels/london/london-tower-hill; 24-26 Minories, EC3; s/d from £98/113; [❄][📶]; [Ⓔ]Aldgate) This almost-budget option is a welcome addition, a short hop from the Tower of London. The 290 rooms are not huge but fully equipped, with a sleek contemporary design. Some offer stunning views of the City and its iconic skyline.

THREADNEEDLES
HOTEL ££

Map p418 (☑020-7657 8080; www.hotelthread-needles.co.uk; 5 Threadneedle St, EC2; r week-end/weekday from £150/280; ❋ ☎; ❸Bank) You have to know this place is here. It's wonderfully anonymous, though once through the doorway the grand circular lobby, furnished in a vaguely art deco style and covered with a hand-painted glass dome, comes into view. The 74 rooms spread over five floors are smallish but pleasantly kitted out, all with high ceilings and dark, sleek furnishings.

GRANGE ST PAUL'S
HOTEL ££

Map p418 (☑020-7074 1000; www.grangehotels.com/hotels-london/grange-st-pauls; 10 Godliman St, EC4; r from £118; ❋ ☎ ☎; ❸St Paul's) The sheer size of the lobby atrium will have you gasping on entering this contemporary hostelry. The 460 well-proportioned rooms are fully loaded with high-tech gadgetry, and there's a 'female friendly' wing designed specifically with women in mind. Add to that a fully equipped health and fitness club and spa with a 20m swimming pool.

ANDAZ LIVERPOOL STREET
HOTEL ££

Map p418 (☑020-7961 1234; www.london.liverpoolstreet.andaz.hyatt.com; 40 Liverpool St, EC2; r weekday/weekend from £180/365; ❋ ☎; ❸Liverpool St) This is the London flagship for Hyatt's sophisticated Andaz chain. There's no reception, just black-clad staff who check you in on iPads. The 267 rooms are cool and spacious, with interesting furnishings and lighting scheme. On top of this there are five restaurants, two bars, a health club and a subterranean Masonic temple discovered during the hotel's refit in the '90s.

196 BISHOPSGATE
APARTMENT ££

Map p418 (☑020-76218788; www.196bishopsgate.com; 196 Bishopsgate, EC2; apt from £175; ❋ ☎; ❸Liverpool St) These 48 luxury serviced apartments are well equipped and in a very handy location opposite Liverpool St station. Two-bedroom and executive studios (with balcony) are also available. Guests can use the swimming pool at the Town Hall Hotel & Apartments (p330) in East London.

🛏 The South Bank

WALRUS
HOSTEL £

Map p420 (☑020-7928 4368; www.walrussocial.com; 172 Westminster Bridge Rd, SE1; dm incl breakfast £21-29.75; ☎; ❸Waterloo) This little hostel gets top marks for trying so hard (and succeeding!) at making a welcoming, individual, friendly and cosy hostel in the big smoke. The corridors and stairs are on the shabby side but the dorms (sleeping four to 22) and bathrooms are spick and span. The downside is the noise from the street and railway, but at this price...

The vintage kitchen is fun, as is the tip-top shabby-chic pub downstairs, which is just as popular with the locals as it is with hostel residents (who get 15% off all drinks).

FEW-FRILLS CHAINS

London has a number of discount hotel chains that offer clean and modern – if somewhat institutional – accommodation for reasonable rates.

➧ **Days Hotel** (☑0800 028 0400; www.daysinn.co.uk; r £70-153) Just three branches in central London.

➧ **easyHotel** (www.easyhotel.com; r from £48) Functional, with orange-moulded-plastic rooms, some without windows; five branches in central London.

➧ **Express by Holiday Inn** (☑0871 423 4876; www.hiexpress.co.uk; weekday d from £235, weekend from £115) The most upmarket of the chains listed here with more than two dozen properties in Greater London.

➧ **Premier Inn** (☑0871 527 9222; www.premierinn.com; r from £127) London's original cheap chain; in large numbers.

➧ **Travelodge** (☑0871 984 8484; www.travelodge.co.uk; r from £78) Pleasant rooms, few public facilities.

➧ **Tune Hotel** (www.tunehotels.com; r from £45) Clean, neat and pared down; pay for extras as required. Five branches in town.

Breakfast, linen and towels are all included in the price.

ST CHRISTOPHER'S VILLAGE — HOSTEL £

Map p420 (☏020-7939 9710; www.st-christophers.co.uk; 163 Borough High St, SE1; dm/r from £15.90/50; @🛜; ⊜London Bridge) This 194-bed hostel was in the midst of a serious upgrade when we visited: new bathrooms, fresh paint, new pod beds with privacy curtains, reading lights, power sockets (British and European) and USB ports, and refurbished common areas. Its two bars, Belushi's and Dugout, are perennially popular. Dorms have four to 22 beds (female dorms available); breakfast and linen are included.

The hotel has another branch (same contact details) 100m up the road: **St Christopher's Inn** (Map p420; 121 Borough High St, SE1; dm/r from £15.90/50; ⊜London Bridge), which sits above a traditional pub. The dorms are smaller and look a little tired, but it's altogether quieter than at the Village.

★CITIZEN M — BOUTIQUE HOTEL ££

Map p420 (☏020-3519 1680; www.citizenm.com/london-bankside; 20 Lavington St, SE1; r £109-199; ✴@🛜; ⊜Southwark) If Citizen M had a motto, it would be 'less fuss, more comfort'. The hotel has done away with things it considers superfluous (room service, reception, bags of space) and instead gone all out on mattresses and bedding (heavenly super king-size beds), state-of-the-art technology (everything in the room from mood-lighting to the TV is controlled through a tablet computer) and superb decor.

Downstairs, the canteen-restaurant works on a self-service basis so that you can grab a meal whenever you feel like it (breakfast at 1pm and midnight chef encouraged) and the bar-lounge is an uncanny blend of designer and homely.

BERMONDSEY SQUARE HOTEL — BOUTIQUE HOTEL ££

Map p420 (☏020-7378 2450; www.bermondseysquarehotel.co.uk; Bermondsey Sq, Tower Bridge Rd, SE1; r £99-250, ste £300-500; ✴@🛜; ⊜London Bridge, Borough) Just the ticket for Bermondsey is this hip, purpose-built, 80-room boutique hotel. Rooms are spacious and comfortable, if a little simple in decor. The pricier suites on the top floor however, with their colour themes, king-sized beds and balconies, have the wow-factor. Choose a room on the street side for great views of the city.

🛏 Kensington & Hyde Park

CHERRY COURT HOTEL — B&B £

Map p424 (☏020-7828 2840; www.cherrycourthotel.co.uk; 23 Hugh St, SW1; s/d/tr £65/75/110; ✴@🛜; ⊜Victoria) The brighly-coloured rooms may be pocket-sized but are clean and tidy at this five-floor Victorian house hotel (no lift). Rates are very attractive for this part of town. The heartfelt welcome from the Patel family is a real bonus, as is the handy breakfast basket (fresh fruit, cereal bar and fruit juice), which you can eat in or take away.

A 5% credit-card surcharge applies.

ASTOR VICTORIA — HOSTEL £

Map p424 (☏020-7834 3077; www.astorhostels.co.uk; 71 Belgrave Rd, SW1; dm/d from £19/49; @🛜; ⊜Pimlico, Victoria) This laid-back hostel has 200 beds, including four- to eight-bed dorms and a handful of twins and doubles with shared bathrooms. There are great communal facilities – two large kitchens, spacious dining areas, movie room – and nightly events (pub crawl, games night, movie night etc). The hostel only accepts guests between the ages of 18 and 35.

ASTOR HYDE PARK — HOSTEL £

Map p424 (☏020-7581 0103; www.astorhostels.com; 191 Queen's Gate, SW7; dm/d from £19/55; @🛜; ⊜Gloucester Rd, High St Kensington) Wood-panelled walls, bay windows with leaded lights, plus a 19th-century vibe and a posh address just over from the Royal Albert Hall. This hostel has 150 beds in rooms over five floors (no lift), including dorms with five to 12 beds, and a good kitchen and spacious lounge. The hostel only accepts guests between the ages of 18 and 35.

MEININGER — HOSTEL £

Map p424 (☏020-3318 1407; www.meiningerhostels.com; Baden Powell House, 65-67 Queen's Gate, SW7; dm £16-50, s/tw from £75/90; ✴@🛜; ⊜Gloucester Rd, South Kensington) In late-1950s Baden Powell House, opposite the Natural History Museum, this 48-room German-run 'city hostel and hotel' has spic-and-span rooms, most of which are dorms of between four and 12 beds, with pod-like showers. There is also a handful of private rooms. There's good security and nice communal facilities, including a bar and a big roof terrace.

★**NO 90** B&B **££**

Map p424 (☎07831 689 167; www.chelseabed-breakfast.com; 90 Old Church St, SW3; s/d from £110/130; ☜) No 90 is a rare thing: a gorgeous yet affordable B&B in the heart of leafy Chelsea. Rooms are a lovely blend of design and homey, with antique furniture and beautiful furnishings. Owner Nina St Charles has lived in the area for nearly 30 years and is a mine of information. Unusually, breakfast is not included and a two-night minimum stay applies.

LIME TREE HOTEL BOUTIQUE HOTEL **££**

Map p424 (☎020-7730 8191; www.limetreehotel.co.uk; 135-137 Ebury St, SW1; s/tr £115/220, d £175-205; @☜; ⊖Victoria) Family run for over 40 years, this beautiful Georgian town-house hotel is all comfort, British designs and understated elegance. There is a lovely back garden to catch the late afternoon rays (picnics encouraged on summer evenings). Rates include a hearty full-English breakfast. No lift.

37 TREVOR SQUARE B&B **££**

Map p424 (☎020-7823 8186; www.37trevorsquare.co.uk; 37 Trevor Sq, SW7; s/d £120/200; ☜; ⊖Knightsbridge) It's hard to believe that a place like 37 Trevor Square still exists in the real estate hotspot that is Knightsbridge. Rooms in this cosy town house are chic, homely and rather spacious, especially the lower ground double. Margaret serves breakfast in her glorious kitchen overlooking Trevor Sq. She has lived in the area for years and has plenty of tips to offer.

B+B BELGRAVIA B&B **££**

Map p424 (☎020-7259 8570; www.bb-belgravia.com; 64-66 Ebury St, SW1; d £89-209, studios £130-279; @☜; ⊖Victoria) This spiffing six-floor Georgian B&B, remodelled with contemporary flair, boasts crisp common areas and a chic lounge. The 17 rooms (some with shower, others with bath) aren't enormous but there's a further batch of studio rooms with compact kitchens at No 82 Ebury St. A pleasant courtyard garden is out back. No lift.

WINDERMERE HOTEL B&B **££**

Map p424 (☎020-7834 5163; www.windermere-hotel.co.uk; 142-144 Warwick Way, SW1; s £121-145, d £152-215; @☜; ⊖Victoria) In a sparkling-white, mid-Victorian town house (with lift and brasserie), the Windermere has 19 small, but bright, individually designed rooms, all recently refurbished. Service is exemplary and there is a full breakfast menu.

★**NUMBER SIXTEEN** HOTEL **£££**

Map p424 (☎020-7589 5232; www.firmdalehotels.com/hotels/london/number-sixteen; 16 Sumner Pl, SW7; s from £192, d £240-396; ❀@☜; ⊖South Kensington) With uplifting splashes of colour, choice art and a sophisticated-but-fun design ethos, Number Sixteen is ravishing. There are 41 individually designed rooms, a cosy drawing room and a fully stocked library. And wait until you see the idyllic, long back garden set around a fountain, or have breakfast in the light-filled conservatory. Great amenities for families.

ARTIST RESIDENCE BOUTIQUE HOTEL **£££**

Map p424 (☎020-7931 8946; www.artistresidencelondon.co.uk; 52 Cambridge St, SW1; r £180-350; ❀☜; ⊖Pimlico, Victoria) This superb boutique hotel elevates the concept of shabby chic to new heights: every piece of furniture and decor has been individually sourced and crafted, from the bare brick walls, to the reclaimed parquet floors, vintage furniture to retro Smeg fridges. All rooms have rainforest showers – for grand free-standing baths, upgrade to the suites.

BLAKES HOTEL **£££**

Map p424 (☎020-7370 6701; www.blakeshotels.com; 33 Roland Gardens, SW7; d from £384; ❀@☜; ⊖Gloucester Rd, South Kensington) Blakes oozes panache: five Victorian houses cobbled into one hotel and incomparably designed by Anouska Hempel. Each of its 47 guest rooms is elegantly decked out in a distinctive, flamboyant style: expect four-poster beds (with and without canopies), rich fabrics, plenty of Asian influences, and antiques set on bleached hardwood floors.

AMPERSAND HOTEL BOUTIQUE HOTEL **£££**

Map p424 (☎020-7589 5895; www.ampersandhotel.com; 10 Harrington Rd, SW7; s £170, d £216-360; ❀@☜; ⊖South Kensington) A light, fresh and bubbly feel fills the Ampersand. Smiling staff wear denims and waist coats rather than impersonal dark suits, the common rooms are colourful and airy, and the stylish rooms are decorated with wallpaper designs celebrating the nearby arts and sciences of South Kensington's museums.

GORE HOTEL **£££**

Map p424 (☎020-7584 6601; www.gorehotel.com; 190 Queen's Gate, SW7; r from £195; ❀☜; ⊖Gloucester Rd) With obliging staff in tails, twinkling chandeliers, walls crowded with framed portraits and prints, and enough wood-panelling to put paid to a sizeable chunk of woodland, this fantastic 50-room hotel wallows in old England charm. The suites are especially lavish (Judy Garland aficionados can sleep on her bed – shipped over from the US – in her namesake suite).

BEAUFORT HOUSE
APARTMENT £££

Map p424 (✆020-7584 2600; www.beaufort-house.co.uk; 45 Beaufort Gardens, SW3; 1-4 bed apt £440-1346; ✳☎; ⊖Knightsbridge) Run by very helpful, friendly and welcoming staff, these stylish, comfortable and fully equipped serviced apartments in a grand building on a quiet cul-de-sac off Brompton Rd are ideally located for the breathless shopping vortex of Knightsbridge. Free access to a nearby health club; no minimum stay requirement outside of high season.

KNIGHTSBRIDGE HOTEL
HOTEL £££

Map p424 (✆020-7584 6300; www.firmdale-hotels.com/hotels/london/knightsbridgehotel; 10 Beaufort Gardens, SW3; s/d/ste from £234/294/474; ✳@☎; ⊖Knightsbridge) The lovely six-floor, 44-room Knightsbridge occupies a 200-year-old house on a particularly quiet, no-through-traffic, tree-lined street. Each room is different, with elegant and beautiful interiors done in a sumptuous, subtle and modern English style. The hotel goes out of its way to cater to children with board games, London activity books, kiddy cutlery etc.

LEVIN HOTEL
HOTEL £££

Map p424 (✆020-7589 6286; www.thelevinhotel.co.uk; 28 Basil St, SW3; r from £379; ✳@☎; ⊖Knightsbridge) The luxury 12-room Levin is a bijou boutique gem. Attention to detail (US, EU, UK and Asian sockets in every room, iPhone docking stations, Nespresso coffee machines, fine linen, iPads on loan), exquisite design and highly hospitable service create a delightful stay. The continental buffet breakfast is complimentary.

ASTER HOUSE
B&B £££

Map p424 (✆020-7581 5888; www.asterhouse.com; 3 Sumner Pl, SW7; s £180, d £240-375; ✳@☎; ⊖South Kensington) The trumpcards of this Victorian town house in South Kensington are its location and the charming welcome of its hosts. The plant-filled Orangerie is an atmospheric place for breakfast but the standard of the decor is rather underwhelming for the price. Continental buffet breakfast included.

🛏 Clerkenwell, Shoreditch & Spitalfields

★HOXTON HOTEL
HOTEL £

Map p426 (✆020-7550 1000; www.hoxtonhotels.com; 81 Great Eastern St, EC2; r from £49; ✳@☎; ⊖Old St) In the heart of hip Shoreditch, this sleek hotel takes the easyJet approach to selling its rooms – book long enough ahead and you might pay just £49. The 209 recently renovated rooms are small but stylish; there are flat-screen TVs, a desk, fridge with complimentary bottled water and milk, and breakfast in a bag delivered to your door.

Try to book one of the eight 'random' rooms designed with both humour and comfort in mind.

★ZETTER HOTEL & TOWNHOUSE
BOUTIQUE HOTEL £££

Map p426 (✆020-7324 4444; www.thezetter.com; 86-88 Clerkenwell Rd, EC1; d from £222, studio £300-438; ✳☎; ⊖Farringdon) ✿ The Zetter comprises two quite different properties. The original Zetter is a temple of cool with an overlay of kitsch on Clerkenwell's main thoroughfare. Built using sustainable materials on the site of a derelict office, its 59 rooms are small but perfectly formed. The **Zetter Townhouse** (Map p426; 49-50 St John's Sq; r £222-294, ste £438-480), on a pretty square behind, has 13 rooms in a lovely Georgian pile.

At the main Zetter, the rooftop studios are the real treat, with terraces commanding superb views across the city. The rooms in the Zetter Townhouse are uniquely decorated in period style but with witty touches such as headboards made from reclaimed fairground carousels. The fantastic cocktail bar is a destination in itself.

SHOREDITCH ROOMS
BOUTIQUE HOTEL £££

Map p426 (✆020-7739 5040; www.shoreditchhouse.com/hotel; Shoreditch House, Ebor St, E2; r £150-295; ☎✖; ⊖Shoreditch High St) Part of a private members' club but with rooms available to all, Shoreditch Rooms are quite upfront here about the size of the 26 rooms, categorising them as tiny, small and small-plus. Each room is freshly decorated in a vaguely Cape Cod style, with light grey wood panelling and sparkly white linen. Internal rooms are the largest and small-plus ones have a balcony.

Guests get to use the gorgeous rooftop heated pool and gym. The sumptuous Cowshed products in the guestrooms are made at Babington House estate in Somerset.

FOX & ANCHOR

BOUTIQUE HOTEL **£££**

Map p426 (020-7250 1300; www.foxandanchor. com; 115 Charterhouse St, EC1; r £180-230, ste from £275; 🕏; ⊖Farringdon, Barbican) Characterful option in a handy location above a glorious pub, this delightful small hotel offers just six small but sumptuous rooms, each individually decorated and many with roll-top zinc bath tubs. For the ultimate luxury, choose the Market Suite, with a king-size bed and its own private rooftop terrace.

ROOKERY

HERITAGE HOTEL **£££**

Map p426 (020-7336 0931; www.rookeryhotel.com; 12 Peter's Lane, Cowcross St, EC1; s/d £222/288, ste £474-660; ❋🕏; ⊖Farringdon) This charming warren of 33 rooms has been built within a row of 18th-century Georgian houses and fitted out with period furniture (including a museum-piece collection of Victorian baths, showers and toilets), original wood panelling shipped over from Ireland and artwork selected personally by the owner. Highlights: the small courtyard garden and the two-storey Rook's Nest penthouse suite.

BOUNDARY

DESIGN HOTEL **£££**

Map p426 (020-7729 1051; www.theboundary. co.uk; 2-4 Boundary St, E2; d £240-295, ste £480-600; ❋🕏; ⊖Shoreditch High St) Terence Conran's impressive design hotel in a converted factory towers over the shops on hip Redchurch St. Each of the 17 rooms takes its theme from a particular designer or style, such as Eames, Bauhaus, Heath Robinson or Scandinavian. Mod cons are as flash as you'd expect. Rates are reduced on Sundays.

MALMAISON

BUSINESS HOTEL **£££**

Map p426 (020-7123 7000; www.malmaison-london.com; 18-21 Charterhouse Sq, EC1; r £175-400; ❋🕏; ⊖Farringdon) Facing a leafy square in Clerkenwell, this chic 97-room hotel in a converted nurses' home has been given a total refit and now revels in bold primary colours and crazy-quilt patterns. The cocktail bar in the reconfigured lobby is a centre of continental cool and the luminous subterranean restaurant a delight. Prices vary considerably and can be much cheaper at weekends.

⤷ East London & Docklands

★QBIC

DESIGN HOTEL **££**

Map p430 (020-3021 3300; https://london. qbichotels.com; 42 Adler St, E1; d £70-200; ❋🕏; ⊖Aldgate East) The 171 rooms of this hotel are based around a 'cubi', with each bed and bathroom part of a square-box design. There's a very modern feel throughout, with white tiling, neon signs, and vibrant art and textiles. Rooms are sound-insulated, mattresses excellent and rainforest showers powerful. A great continental buffet breakfast is available for less than £8.

40 WINKS

BOUTIQUE HOTEL **££**

Map p430 (020-7790 0259; www.40winks.org; 109 Mile End Rd, E1; s/d £120/195; 🕏; ⊖Stepney Green) Short on space but not on style, this two-room boutique guesthouse in Stepney Green oozes quirky charm. It is housed in an early 18th-century town house owned by a successful designer and has been used as a location for a number of fashion shoots. The rooms (the single is quite compact) are uniquely decorated with an expert's eye. Book far ahead.

AVO

BOUTIQUE HOTEL **££**

Map p430 (020-3490 5061; www.avohotel.com; 82 Dalston Lane, E8; d £79-139; ❋🕏; ⊖Dalston Junction) Occupying a little shopfront on a

SLEEPING

STUDENT DIGS

During university holidays (generally mid-March to late April, late June to September, and mid-December to mid-January), student dorms and halls of residence are open to paying visitors. Choices include **LSE Vacations** (020-7955 7676; www.lsevacations. co.uk; s/tw/tr from £45/66/89), whose eight halls include **Bankside House** (Map p420; 020-7107 5750; www.lsevacations.co.uk; 24 Sumner St, SE1; ⊖Southwark) and **High Holborn Residence** (Map p412; 020-7107 5737; www.lsevacations.co.uk; 178 High Holborn, WC1; ⊖Holborn). **King's College Conference & Vacation Bureau** (020-7848 1700; www.kingsvenues.com; s £45-55, tw £77-87) handles five residences, including the centrally-located **Great Dover St Apartments** (Map p420; 020-7407 0068; www. kingsvenues.com; 165 Great Dover St, SE1; ⊖Borough) and **Stamford St Apartments** (Map p420; 020-7633 2182; www.kingsvenues.com; 127 Stamford St, SE1; ⊖Waterloo).

rather unlovely stretch of road just down from Dalston Junction, Avo has turned what was once a newsagency into a very welcoming boutique hotel. Family-run, it has just six rooms, all with mango-wood furnishings, gleaming black-and-grey bathrooms, memory foam mattresses, iPod docks and Elemis toiletries. Double-glazing keeps things quiet.

TOWN HALL HOTEL & APARTMENTS   HOTEL £££

Map p430 (☑020-7871 0460; www.townhall-hotel.com; Patriot Sq, E2; r from £192; ❄☎✆; ⊖Bethnal Green) Set in a former Edwardian town hall (1910) and updated with art deco features in the 1930s, this 97-room hotel was the council's headquarters until 1965. The design aesthetic of the hotel combines these eras beautifully, with the addition of cutting-edge contemporary art by London-based artists. Each room has quirks from the original structure, and the apartments are extremely well equipped.

🛏 Camden & North London

★CLINK78   HOSTEL £

Map p434 (☑020-7183 9400; www.clinkhostels.com/london/clink78; 78 King's Cross Rd, WC1; dm/r from £13/50; @☎; ⊖King's Cross/St Pancras) This fantastic 630-bed hostel is housed in a 19th-century magistrates courthouse where Dickens once worked as a scribe and members of the Clash made an appearance in 1978. Rooms feature pod beds (including overhead storage space) in four- to 16-bed dormitories. There's a top kitchen with a huge dining area and the busy Clash bar in the basement.

Parts of the hostel, including six cells converted to bedrooms and a pair of wood-panelled court rooms used as a cinema and internet room, are heritage-listed. ATM and change machine conveniently in lobby.

CLINK261   HOSTEL £

Map p434 (☑020-7183 9400; www.clinkhostels.com/london/clink261; 261 Grays Inn Rd, WC1; dm/r from £13/65; @☎; ⊖King's Cross/St Pancras) A top-notch 170-bed hostel with bright, funky dorms sleeping four to 18, good bathrooms, bunk beds fitted with a privacy panel and individual lockers for valuables. There's a fabulous self-catering kitchen and cosy TV lounge in the basement.

LONDON ST PANCRAS YHA   HOSTEL £

Map p434 (☑020-7388 9998; www.yha.org.uk; 79-81 Euston Rd, NW1; dm/r from £16/65; @☎; ⊖King's Cross/St Pancras) This hostel, with 186 beds spread over eight floors, has modern, clean dorms sleeping four to six (nearly all with private facilities) and some private rooms. There's a good bar and cafe, although there are no self-catering facilities.

★YORK & ALBANY   BOUTIQUE HOTEL £££

Map p436 (☑020-7387 5700; www.gordonram-say.com/yorkandalbany; 127-129 Parkway, NW1; r from £205; ❄☎; ⊖Camden Town) Luxurious yet cosy, the York & Albany oozes Georgian charm. There are feature fireplaces in many of the rooms, antique furniture, beautiful floor-to-ceiling windows and lush bathrooms (with underfloor heating). All nine rooms have flatscreen TV and DVD player. We love the four-poster bed and sunken bathroom in room 5.

GREAT NORTHERN HOTEL   HISTORIC HOTEL ££

Map p434 (GNH; ☑020-3388 0800; www.gnhlondon.com; King's Cross Station, Pancras Rd, N1; r from £150; ❄☎; ⊖King's Cross/St Pancras) Built as the world's first railway hotel in 1854, the GNH is now a boutique hotel in a classic style reminiscent of luxury sleeper trains. Exquisite craftsmanship is in evidence everywhere. And along with two lively bars (one specialises in Japanese whiskey) and a rather unique restaurant, there's a 'pantry' on every floor from which you can help yourself to hot or cold drinks and snacks.

MEGARO   BOUTIQUE HOTEL £££

Map p434 (☑020-7843 2222; www.hotelmegaro.co.uk; Belgrove St, WC1; d £180-260, f £260-285; ❄☎; ⊖King's Cross/St Pancras) There are many things that commend the Megaro: the 49 indulgently large rooms, lovely decor, creature comforts in the rooms (espresso machine, fresh milk, rainforest showerhead), attentive service, and its excellent bar-restaurant. There is some noise from the street so if you're a light sleeper, go high or at the back.

Many rooms, including the very large family ones (202 and 302) that face the train station, have Murphy (or wall) beds to accommodate extra sleepers.

ROUGH LUXE   BOUTIQUE HOTEL £££

Map p434 (☑020-7837 5338; www.roughluxe.co.uk; 1 Birkenhead St, WC1; r £209-259; ❄☎; ⊖King's Cross/St Pancras) Half-rough, half-luxury is the strapline of this unique eight-room hotel, and the distressed interior is true to its words. Scraps of old newspaper adorn the walls, along with original works of art; the bathrooms are utterly gorgeous but the vintage 1970s TV are for show only.

The rooms are admittedly tiny but service, location and the delightful patio garden at the back more than make up for it.

ST PANCRAS RENAISSANCE LONDON HOTEL
LUXURY HOTEL £££

Map p434 (✆020-7841 3540; www.stpancrasrenaissance.co.uk; Euston Rd, NW1; d from £230; 🅿☀🛜; ⊖King's Cross/St Pancras) Housed in the former Midland Grand Hotel (1873), red-brick Victorian marvel designed by Sir George Gilbert Scott, the St Pancras Renaissance counts 245 rooms but only 38 of them are are in the original building; the rest are in an extension at the back and rather bland.

The hotel's spa is anything but bland, however, with Victorian tiling in the pool. Victoriana can also be found in abundance in the hotel bar and restaurant.

🛏 Notting Hill & West London

TUNE HOTEL
HOTEL £

Map p438 (✆020-7258 3140; www.tunehotels.com; 41 Praed St, W2; r £45-120; 🅿@🛜; ⊖Paddington) This 137-room Malaysian-owned budget hotel offers super-duper rates for early birds who book a long way in advance. The ethos is you get the bare bones – a twin or double room, the cheapest without window – and pay for add-ons (towel, wi-fi, TV) as you see fit, giving you the chance to just put a roof over your head, if that's all you need.

You don't even get a wardrobe, just hangers. Things are super hygienic, everything's clean as a whistle and staff are welcoming. Check out time is 10am.

17 HOMESTEAD RD
B&B £

Map p440 (✆020-7385 6773; www.fulhambedandbreakfastlondon.co.uk; 17 Homestead Rd, SW6; d & tw incl breakfast £95-110; 🛜; ⊖Fulham Broadway, Parsons Green) With its pristine buff-coloured carpets, this charming and completely spotless two-room B&B is housed in a Victorian terraced property. The ambience is lovingly maintained with lashings of elbow grease (and a no-shoes policy) from the friendly and welcoming owner, Fiona. Book ahead. Breakfasts are simple (muesli, toast, orange juice, tea or coffee).

Single occupancy prices are £20 cheaper than the double occupancy price and check-in time is usually after 5pm.

LONDON HOUSE HOTEL
HOTEL £

Map p438 (✆020-7243 1810; www.londonhouse-hotels.com; 81 Kensington Gardens Sq, W2; d £80-140; 🅿🛜; ⊖Bayswater) This good-value, snappy-looking hotel in a rather grand Regency-style building looks over Kensington Gardens Sq. The 102 rooms are on the small side, as are the bathrooms, but all are clean and pleasantly furnished and the setting is peaceful. The best rooms have views onto the leafy square.

MELROSE GARDENS
B&B £

Map p440 (✆020-7603 1817; www.staylondonbandb.co.uk; 29 Melrose Gardens, W6; s/tw/d incl breakfast £78/90/105; 🛜) Ideal for those seeking peace and a sedate tempo, this charming B&B is run from a typical Victorian family home. Everything is in its right place, overseen by cordial hosts Su and Martin, who are quick to dispense handy London info. The only room with its own bathroom is at the top, while the other two look out over the small garden.

STYLOTEL
HOTEL £

Map p438 (✆020-7723 1026; www.stylotel.com; 160-162 Sussex Gardens, W2; s/d/tr/q £65/95/115/135, studio/1-bedroom ste £135/175; 🅿@🛜; ⊖Paddington) The crisp industrial design – scored aluminium treads, opaque green glass, riveted stainless steel, metal bed frames – of this 40-room niche hotel is contemporary and well-priced. Elbow room is at a premium: 'stylorooms' are small, but the largely carpet-free floor surfaces help keep things dapper. The eight more spacious 'stylosuites' above the Sussex Arms around the corner are more swish.

Free tea and coffee in the lounge.

YHA EARL'S COURT
HOSTEL £

Map p440 (✆0845 371 9114; www.yha.org.uk/hostel/london-earls-court; 38 Bolton Gardens, SW5; dm £25-33, d & tw from £80; @🛜; ⊖Earl's Court) There's some lovely original tiling on the floor as you enter this fine old property on a quiet, leafy street in Earl's Court, although most other period detailing has been overlaid. Most accommodation (186 beds) is in clean, airy dormitories of between four and 10 bunk beds. There's a sense of space in the common areas; showers and toilets are clean and staff helpful.

There's a huge gravel garden out back strewn with tables, plus a good-sized kitchen, two lounges and a bright, modern cafe.

RUSHMORE — HOTEL £

Map p440 (☎020-7370 3839; www.rushmore-hotel.co.uk; 11 Trebovir Rd, SW5; s/d £69/89; ☎; ⊖Earl's Court) The gentle pastel shades, Mediterranean murals, terracotta and faux marbling of this modest hotel create a different and charming atmosphere. All 22 guest rooms are of a decent size and are impeccably clean. It's prudent to compare rooms. Four rooms on the 1st floor have balconies: Nos 11 and 12 face the street and Nos 14 and 15, the courtyard. There's no lift.

SAFESTAY HOLLAND PARK — HOSTEL £

Map p440 (☎020-3326 8471; www.safestay.co.uk; Holland Walk, W8; dm £18, tw/s from £58/£66; ☎; ⊖High St Kensington, Holland Park) This brand new place replaced the long-serving YHA hostel running here since 1958. With a bright and bold colour design, the hostel has four to eight bunk dorm rooms, twin bunk and single bunk rooms, free wi-fi in the lobby and a fabulous location in the Jacobean east wing of Holland House in Holland Park (p257).

★MAIN HOUSE — HOTEL ££

Map p438 (www.themainhouse.co.uk; 6 Colville Rd, W11; ste £120-155; ☎; ⊖Ladbroke Grove, Notting Hill Gate, Westbourne Park) The four adorable suites at this peach of a Victorian mid-terrace house on Colville Rd make this a superb choice. Bright and spacious, with vast bathrooms, rooms are also excellent value and include endless tea or coffee. Cream of the crop is the uppermost suite, occupying the entire top floor. There's no sign, but look for the huge letters 'SIX'. Minimum three-night stay.

BARCLAY HOUSE — B&B ££

Map p440 (☎020-7384 3390; www.barclayhouse-london.com; 21 Barclay Rd, SW6; r £110-168; @☎; ⊖Fulham Broadway) The two dapper, thoroughly modern and comfy bedrooms in this ship-shape Victorian house are a dream, from the Phillipe Starck shower rooms, walnut furniture, new double-glazed sash windows and underfloor heating to the small, thoughtful details (fumble-free coat hangers, drawers packed with sewing kits and maps). The cordial, music-loving owners – bursting with tips and handy London knowledge – concoct an inclusive, homely atmosphere.

Usually there is a three to four-night minimum stay.

NADLER KENSINGTON — HOTEL ££

Map p440 (☎020-7244 2255; www.thenadler.com; 25 Courtfield Gardens, SW5; s £138, tw bunk r £152, d £152-278; ✿ @☎; ⊖Earl's Court) Things – service and design – are snappy and efficient at this sure-footed hotel, and each immaculate room (including the neat bunk bed rooms) comes with a minikitchen (with microwave, minifridge and sink) and 20-inch (up to 26-inch) flat screen TV. It's well-located in a quiet street not too far from Earl's Court tube station for quick journeys to the West End.

ROCKWELL — BOUTIQUE HOTEL ££

Map p440 (☎020-7244 2000; www.therockwell.com; 181-183 Cromwell Rd, SW5; s £120-125, d £145-180, ste from £200; ✿ @☎; ⊖Earl's Court) With an understated-cool design ethos and some lovely floor tiling, things are muted, dapper and more than a tad minimalist at the 'budget boutique' 40-room Rockwell. Spruce and stylish, all rooms have shower, the mezzanine suites are peaches and the three rooms giving on to the walled garden (LG1, 2 and 3) are particularly fine.

Rooms facing Cromwell Rd are triple-glazed to stifle the roar.

SPACE APART HOTEL — HOTEL ££

Map p438 (☎020-7908 1340; www.aparthotel-london.co.uk; 36-37 Kensington Gardens Sq, W2; apt £140-190; ✿ @☎; ⊖Bayswater, Royal Oak) Light, bright, spic-and-span studio apartments with kitchenette at eye-catching rates. This neatly designed, converted 30-room Georgian building provides a handy and affordable stay not far from the Notting Hill action. The studios are not big, but for around £20 you can upgrade to a roomier double studio. There's usually a two-night minimum stay.

TWENTY NEVERN SQUARE — HOTEL ££

Map p440 (☎020-7565 9555; www.20nevernsquare.com; 20 Nevern Sq, SW5; r incl breakfast from £90; ☎; ⊖Earl's Court) Each room is different at this elegant and stylish four-floor brick hotel overlooking a lovely London square. Cosy, but not especially large, rooms are decorated with Asian-style woodwork, imposing carved-wood beds (some four-poster), venetian blinds and heavy fabrics. Some rooms have bath, others shower. There is a gorgeous conservatory where breakfast is served, and a tiny patio.

PAVILION HOTEL — HOTEL ££

Map p438 (☎020-7262 1324; www.pavilionhoteluk.com; 34-36 Sussex Gardens, W2; s £69-100, d

& tw £110, tr £130; 🕿; ⊖Edgware Rd) Those after something a little eccentric will love this self-proclaimed 'fashion, rock 'n' roll' hotel. Each room has a different garish theme in a thrift-store style. It's a little dark and makeshift but the price, great location and quirky atmosphere more than make up for it.

VANCOUVER STUDIOS   APARTMENT ££

Map p438 (📞020-7243 1270; www.vancouverstudios.co.uk; 30 Prince's Sq, W2; apt £97-350; @🕿; ⊖Bayswater) Everyone will feel at home in this appealing terrace of stylish and affordable apartments, with a restful and charming walled garden. Very well maintained rooms all contain kitchenettes but otherwise differ wildly – ranging from a tiny but well-equipped single to a spacious three-bedroom that sleeps up to six.

PORTOBELLO GOLD   INN ££

Map p438 (📞020-7460 4910; www.portobellogold. com; 95-97 Portobello Rd, W11; tw/apt incl breakfast from £60/150 ; 🕿; ⊖Notting Hill Gate) This cheerful guesthouse above a pleasant restaurant and pub has 10 rooms of varying sizes and quality of furnishings. There are several small doubles (with minuscule shower room) and a couple of new twin-bunk rooms. The four-poster suite has antique furnishings, a foldaway four-poster bed and (decorative) open-hearth fireplace, while room/maisonette No 6 boasts a roof terrace with splendid views over Portobello Rd.

LA SUITE WEST   BOUTIQUE HOTEL £££

Map p438 (📞020-7313 8484; www.lasuitewest. com; 41-51 Inverness Tce, W2; r £129-279; ❋@🕿; ⊖Bayswater) The black-and-white foyer of the Anouska Hempel-designed La Suite West – bare walls, a minimalist slit of a fireplace, an iPad for guests' use on an otherwise void white marble reception desk – presages the OCD neatness of rooms hidden away down dark corridors. The straight lines, spotless surfaces and sharp angles are accentuated by impeccable bathrooms and softened by comfortable beds and warm service.

Downstairs suites have gardens and individual gated entrances.

K + K HOTEL GEORGE   BOUTIQUE HOTEL ££

Map p440 (📞020-7598 8700; www.kkhotels. com; 1-15 Templeton Pl, SW5; s/d from £175/190; ❋🕿; ⊖Earl's Court) From the niftily designed, wide-open foyer to the joyfully huge garden with its glorious lawn, this tidy 154-room boutique hotel just round the corner from Earl's Court tube station has smallish rooms, but they are attractively presented, comfy and come with neat shower. There's a snazzy bar, helpful service throughout, soft colours and the location is great for zipping into the centre of town.

PORTOBELLO HOTEL   BOUTIQUE HOTEL £££

Map p438 (📞020-7727 2777; www.portobellohotel.co.uk; 22 Stanley Gardens, W11; s/d/feature r from £140/195/240; @🕿; ⊖Notting Hill Gate) This splendidly located, 21-room property has been a firm favourite with rock and rollers and movie stars throughout the decades. Feature rooms are presented with stylish colonial decor, four-poster beds and inviting roll-top baths; room 16 has an ample round bed, a Victorian bathing machine and a roll-call of past celebrity lodgers.

Things are simpler and rooms much smaller lower down the tariff registry, while the overall decor could do with some attention. Rooms at the back have views of the neighbouring properties' beautiful gardens, but the hotel itself has no garden.

EUROPA HOUSE   APARTMENT £££

Map p438 (📞020-7724 5924; www.living-rooms. co.uk/hotel/europa; 79A Randolph Ave, W9; 1-bed apt £199-320, 2-bed apt £250-485, 3-bed apt from £600; ❋🕿; ⊖Warwick Ave) In a wonderfully leafy area of the city, this set of apartments offers very elegant and classically attired flats, with one- and two-bed apartments and a 153 sq metre three-bed penthouse apartment on a 14-night minimum stay. Perhaps the best asset is access to the huge, enclosed communal garden.

🛏 Greenwich & South London

★SAFESTAY ELEPHANT & CASTLE   HOSTEL £

Map p444 (📞020-7703 8000; www.safestay. co.uk; 144-152 Walworth Rd, SE17; dm/d from £26/96; @🕿; ⊖Elephant & Castle) Who would have thought that the Labour Party's staid former headquarters would make such a flashy hostel? The 18th-century Georgian building has been stunningly renovated: inside, it's all purple and magenta stripes and bright lights, though the 74 rooms are more sober. Most dorms (four to eight beds) are en suite. Enormous bar/lounge with garden.

SLEEPING

ST CHRISTOPHER'S INN GREENWICH
HOSTEL £

Map p445 (☑020-8858 3591; www.st-christophers.co.uk; 189 Greenwich High Rd, SE10; dm £10-25, tw £40-55; 🛜; ℞Greenwich, ⊖Greenwich) The Greenwich branch of this successful chain of hostels has expanded next door and now counts 84 beds. It's quieter than its half-dozen more centrally located sister properties (though it is next to Greenwich DLR and train station). The hostel has a lively pub but the dorms (six to eight beds) are pretty cramped.

★ NUMBER 16
B&B ££

Map p445 (☑020-8853 4337; www.st-alfeges.co.uk; 16 St Alfege Passage, SE10; s/d £90/125; 🛜; ℞DLR Cutty Sark) One-time sweet shop, this gay-owned B&B has two well-appointed doubles and a single, individually decorated in shades of yellow, blue or green and all with bathroom. The owners do their best to make everyone – gay or straight – feel at home, with chats and cups of tea in the charming basement kitchen. Enter via Roan St.

CHURCH STREET HOTEL
BOUTIQUE HOTEL ££

(☑020-7703 5984; www.churchstreethotel.com; 29-33 Camberwell Church St, SE5; s £70-90, d £90-155, tr £160; ✱🛜; ℞Denmark Hill) 🥘 One of London's most individual boutique hotels, this vibrant 27-room establishment is a much needed shot of tequila into the hotel landscape of London. Run by a half-Spanish, half-English brother duo, the hotel brims with colour, vibrant details and Mexicana (the tiled bathrooms will perk up anyone's day). The smallest rooms share bathrooms. Very off-the-beaten track but transport links are good.

CAPTAIN BLIGH GUEST HOUSE
B&B ££

Map p444 (☑020-7928 2735; www.captainblighhouse.co.uk; 100 Lambeth Rd, SE1; s £85, d £95-115; 🛜; ⊖Lambeth North) This late-18th-century property and former home of the ill-fated commander of the mutinied *Bounty* is in a leafy corner of South London. Pros: the five fully equipped suites (complete with kitchen) are gorgeous (especially the Royal Suite and eyrie-like Crow's Nest), quiet and immaculately kept. Cons: no credit cards, a four-night minimum stay and one night's nonrefundable deposit required.

KENNINGTON B&B
B&B ££

Map p444 (☑020-7735 7669; www.kenningtonbandb.com; 103 Kennington Park Rd, SE11; d £120-150; 🛜; ⊖Kennington) With gorgeous bed linen, well-preserved Georgian features and just seven bedrooms and a suite, this lovely B&B in an 18th-century house is tasteful in every regard, from the shining, tiled shower rooms and Georgian shutters to the fireplaces and cast-iron radiators. Bathrooms on the landing are private but not en suite.

🛌 Richmond, Kew & Hampton Court

FOX AND GRAPES
PUB ££

(☑020-8619 1300; www.foxandgrapeswimbledon.co.uk; 9 Camp Rd, SW19; r incl breakfast £125; ✱🛜; ⊖Wimbledon) This popular gastropub sees the rambling Wimbledon set decamping with mud-flecked canines in tow. The location is lovely and the three modern rooms-with-shower upstairs – each one named after a Womble – can cast a roof over your head if you take to Wimbledon's semi-rural charms. Rooms include Nespresso machines, with continental breakfast included.

★ BINGHAM
BOUTIQUE HOTEL £££

Map p446 (☑020-8940 0902; www.thebingham.co.uk; 61-63 Petersham Rd, TW10; s/d £195/210; ✱🛜; ℞Richmond then bus 65, ⊖Richmond) Just upriver from Richmond Bridge, this lovely riverside Georgian town house is an enticing boutique escape from central London, with 15 very stylish and well-presented, art-deco-inspired rooms. Each room takes its name from a poem (the house holds a literary history). Riverside rooms are naturally pricier, but worth it, as roadside rooms – although deliciously devised and double-glazed – look out over busy Petersham Rd.

Further treasures are the excellent restaurant and the lounge bar where some irresistible cocktail mixing takes place.

PETERSHAM
HOTEL £££

Map p446 (☑020-8940 7471; www.petershamhotel.co.uk; Nightingale Lane, TW10; s £130, d £195, riverview d £260, riverview ste from £450; 🛜; ℞Richmond then bus 65, ⊖Richmond) Neatly perched on the slope down Richmond Hill leading across Petersham Meadows towards the Thames, the impressive four-star Petersham offers stunning Arcadian views at every turn. And its restaurant, with its voluminous windows gazing down to the river, offers some choice panoramas. The 58 rooms are classically styled but those with good river views are more expensive.

Understand London

LONDON TODAY...........................336

Has ever-expanding London become the 'Capital of Europe'?

HISTORY 338

London has been defined by waves of immigrants – from the Celts and Romans to 'New Europeans'.

ARCHITECTURE 356

From Roman remains and medieval churches to ultra-modern skyscrapers, London is a head-spinning compendium of building styles.

LITERARY LONDON 361

London is paved with poetry and prose – from Chaucer and Pepys to Dickens and TS Eliot.

THEATRE & DANCE 365

London is an audacious and compelling world leader in the performing arts.

ART & FASHION 368

London's creative pulse has nurtured generations of painters and fashion designers.

THE MUSIC SCENE 372

Few world cities come with music credentials as diverse, or as innovative, as London.

FILM & MEDIA...........................375

London has served as the iconic backdrop to an array of films and boasts a thriving media.

London Today

The 2012 Olympic legacy bequeathed a feel-good factor to London that just seems to go on and on. Tourism has increased by leaps and bounds in the past few years – aided and abetted not just by the Games but by one royal wedding and two royal births. But it's more than all that. London has reaffirmed itself over and over as a capital of new ideas, cultural dynamism and change.

Best on Film

Withnail & I (1986) Cult black comedy about two unemployed actors in 1969 Camden.

Skyfall (2012) Sam Mendes' masterful contribution to the James Bond franchise.

Bridget Jones's Diary (2001) Eponymous bachelorette seeks and (spoiler!) finds love, with London as a gorgeous backdrop.

A Royal Night Out (2015) Comedy and romance ensure when Princesses Elizabeth and Margaret step out for VE Day celebrations.

Best in Print

Journal of the Plague Year (Daniel Defoe; 1722) Defoe's classic reconstruction of the Great Plague of 1665.

White Teeth (Zadie Smith; 2000) Poignant multi-ethnic romp in post-millennial Willesden.

London Fields (Martin Amis; 1989) Gripping, dark postmodern study of London lowlife.

Oliver Twist (Charles Dickens; 1837) Unforgettable characters and a vivid depiction of Victorian London, seen through the eyes of a hapless orphan.

Sour Sweet (Timothy Mo; 1982) Vivid and moving portrayal of a Hong Kong Chinese family moving to London in the 1960s.

London (Edward Rutherfurd; 1997) Sweeping drama that brings London's epic history vividly to life.

Happy Days (May Be) Here Again

London is the world's leading financial centre for international business and commerce and the fifth-largest city economy in the world. As the economic downturn of the last decade fades into memory, the UK is increasingly a nation of two halves: London (and the southeast) and the rest of the country. The capital generates more than 20% of Britain's income, a percentage that has been rising over the last 10 years. Employment in London is rosier than the rest of the nation, with the jobless rate at just under 6%; the price of property is double the national average; and incomes are 30% higher in London than elsewhere in the country. And tourism continues to grow at 3.5% a year. But there's a flip side: 28% of Londoners are living in poverty compared with just 21% in the rest of England (as defined by having an income less than 60% of the national median).

Capital of Europe

What has become the world's most cosmopolitan place in which to live continues to lure immigrants from around the globe. Rich investors from Russia, the Middle East and China seeking a stable place to invest capital jostle for space with others looking for opportunities that are in short supply back home. Indeed, London is now France's sixth-biggest city, with upwards of 400,000 French nationals living here. According to the last census (2011), almost 37% of London's population is foreign born – with almost a quarter born outside Europe. Today an estimated 270 different ethnic groups speak 300 different languages and, despite some tensions, most get along well.

Building Boom

The huge rise in population – London is expected have 9 million inhabitants by 2020, up from 8.3 million today – has led to a building boom not seen since the end of WWII. Church spires are now dwarfed by a forest of construction cranes working to build more than 230 high-rise condos and office buildings. East London is where most of the activity is taking place these days, but the building boom is evident along the entire stretch of the Thames. East London is where most of the activity is taking place these days, but the building boom is evident along the entire stretch of the Thames. New landmark skyscrapers in the City include the 37-storey Walkie Talkie (20 Fenchurch St) and the 225m-tall Cheesegrater (Leadenhall Building), with many more on the cards or under construction south of the river. More than 50,000 new homes are needed annually over the next 20 years to keep up with demand. And just as important as housing is the proposed 15-mile-long Thames Tideway Tunnel, which would upgrade the city's sewer system from one designed in the mid 19th-century for a city with half the current population.

Forever Forward

With London's Underground trains, its buses and its roads packed to bursting point, an ambitious redesign of London's transport options is under way. To help cope with demand, the city is building miles of new lanes for cyclists, including those on Santander Cycles. Crossrail, a 73-mile railway line running east–west across Greater London, will begin operations in 2018. And even the crusty old tube has begun 24-hour operations at the weekend on certain lines.

All Change

Virtually no one foresaw the outcome of the 2015 national elections, in which the Conservative Party soundly beat Labour, gaining 28 seats and a narrow majority in parliament. It thus abandoned its coalition government with the Liberal Democrats, whose seats were reduced from 56 down to eight. The biggest winner was the Scottish National Party, which increased its seats from six to 56. What that all means to the London mayoral race in May 2016 is anyone's guess. London tends to vote on personality; often bucking the national trend (it voted Labour in the national elections). Whether any of the candidates can fill the sizeable gap left by the bouncy and often Teflon-coated outgoing mayor, Conservative Boris Johnson, remains to be seen.

population per sq km

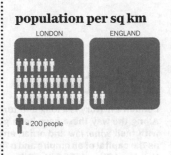

LONDON ENGLAND

≈ 200 people

if London were 100 people

60 would be white
19 would be Asian
13 would be black
5 would be mixed race
3 would be other

belief systems
(% of population)

48 Christianity
21 Non-religious
12 Islam
5 Hinduism
2 Judaism
12 Other

History

London's history is a long and turbulent narrative spanning more than two millennia. Along the way there have been good times (the arrival of the Romans, for example, with their wine, law and order, and road-building skills, and the expansion of London as the capital of an empire and a financial centre) and bad times (apocalyptic plagues, the Great Fire of 1666, the Blitz carpet bombing of WWII). But even when down on its knees, London has always been able to get up, dust itself off and move on, constantly re-inventing itself along the way.

Londinium

London was settled by the Romans, and the area, particularly the City of London, has been inhabited continuously ever since. As a result, archaeologists have had to dig deep to discover the city's past, relying more often than not on redevelopment to allow excavations.

But the Romans were not the first on the block. The Celts had arrived in Britain sometime in the 4th century BC and settled around a ford in the Thames. The river was twice as wide as it is today, and probably served as a barrier separating tribal groups.

When the Romans first visited in the 1st century BC, they traded with the Celts. In 43 AD, an invasion force led by Emperor Claudius established the port of Londinium, the first real settlement at what is now London, and used it as a springboard to capture Celtic strongholds. They constructed a wooden bridge across the Thames near today's London Bridge, and this became the focal point for a network of roads fanning out around the region.

The settlement's development as a trading centre was interrupted in 60 or 61 AD when an army led by Boudicca, queen of the Celtic Iceni tribe based in East Anglia, exacted violent retribution on the Romans, who had attacked her kingdom, flogged her and raped her daughters. The Iceni overran Camulodunum (now Colchester in Essex), which had become the capital of Roman Britannia, and then turned on Londinium, massacring its inhabitants and razing the settlement before the Romans defeated them.

They say that if you dig deep enough in the City you'll find a layer of rubble and soft red ash dating from the great conflagration brought about by Boudicca's attack on Roman Londinium.

TIMELINE

55–54 BC	AD 43	47–50
Roman Emperor Julius Caesar makes a fast-paced and badly planned visit to Britain and returns empty-handed – though the Senate declares a celebration that lasts 20 days.	The Romans invade Britain, led by Emperor Claudius; they mix with the local Celtic tribespeople and stay for almost four centuries.	A defensive fort at Londinium is built. The name Londinium was probably taken from a Celtic place name (a common Roman practice) but there is no evidence as to what it actually means.

The Romans rebuilt Londinium around Cornhill, the highest elevation north of the bridge, between 80 and 90 AD. About a century later they wrapped a defensive wall some 2.7m thick and 6m high around it. Towers were added to strengthen it, and the original gates – Aldgate, Ludgate, Newgate and Bishopsgate – are remembered as place names in today's London. By then Londinium, a centre for business and trade but not a fully fledged *colonia* (settlement), was an imposing city with a massive basilica, an amphitheatre, a forum and a governor's palace.

By the middle of the 3rd century, Londinium was home to some 30,000 people of various ethnic groups, with temples dedicated to a large number of cults. When Emperor Constantine converted to Christianity in 312, the fledgling religion became the empire's – and London's – official cult.

In the 4th century, the Roman Empire in Britain began to decline, with increasing attacks by the Picts and Scotti in the north and the Saxons, Germanic tribes originating from north of the Rhine, in the southeast. In 410, when the embattled Emperor Honorius refused them military aid, the Romans abandoned Britain, and Londinium was reduced to a sparsely populated backwater.

Hidden London (http://hidden-london.com) explores and exposes London's obscure attractions, curiosities, districts and localities to the light of day, seasoned with some fascinating historical nuggets and details. Even locals rave.

Lundenwic

What happened to Londinium after the Roman withdrawal is still the subject of much historical debate. While there is no written record whatsoever of the town from 457 to 604, most historians now think that Romano-Britons continued to live here even as Saxon settlers established farmsteads and small villages in the area.

Lundenwic (or 'London settlement') was established outside the city walls due west of Londinium and around present-day Aldwych and Charing Cross as a Saxon trade settlement. By the early 7th century the Saxons had been converted to Christianity by the pope's emissary Augustine. Lundenwic was an episcopate and the first St Paul's Cathedral was established at the top of Ludgate Hill.

This infant trading community grew in importance and attracted the attention of the Vikings in Denmark. They attacked in 842 and again nine years later, burning Lundenwic to the ground. Under the leadership of King Alfred the Great of Wessex, the Saxon population fought back, driving the Danes out in 886.

Saxon London grew into a prosperous and well-organised town divided into 20 wards, each with its own alderman, and resident colonies of German merchants and French vintners. But attacks by the Danes continued apace, and the Saxon leadership was weakening; in 1016 Londoners were forced to accept the Danish leader Knut (Canute) as king of England.

When Edward the Confessor moved his court to Westminster, the port, now the City, became the trading and mercantile centre, while Westminster became the seat of politics, administration and justice – an arrangement that continues to this day.

122	190–225	410	597
Emperor Hadrian pays a visit to Londinium and many impressive municipal buildings are constructed. Roman London reaches its peak, with temples, bathhouses, a fortress and a port.	London Wall is constructed around Londinium after outsiders breach Hadrian's Wall to the north. The wall encloses an area of just 132 hectares and is 6m high.	The Emperor Honorius decrees that the colony of Britannia should take care of its own defences, effectively ending the Roman presence in Londinium.	Ethelbert, the first English monarch to convert to Christianity, welcomes St Augustine and his missionaries to Canterbury, ensuring that city's religious supremacy.

With the death of Knut's brutal son Harthacanute in 1042, the throne passed to the Saxon Edward the Confessor, who went on to found an abbey and palace at Westminster.

The Normans

The winds of change were still blowing a quarter of a century after the Norman Conquest when the Great London Tornado of 1091 swept through town, destroying much of the original church of St Mary-le-Bow, the wooden London Bridge and countless houses.

The year 1066 marks the real birth of England as a unified nation state. After the death of Edward the Confessor in 1066, a dispute over who would take the English throne spelled disaster for the Saxon kings. Harold Godwinson, the Earl of Wessex, was anointed successor by Edward on his deathbed, but this enraged William, the Duke of Normandy, who claimed that Edward had promised him the throne. William mounted a massive invasion of England from France and on 14 October defeated Harold at the Battle of Hastings, before marching on London to claim his prize. William, now dubbed 'the Conqueror', was crowned king of England in the new Westminster Abbey on 25 December 1066, ensuring the Norman conquest was complete.

William distrusted the 'vast and fierce populace' of London, and to intimidate his new subjects as well as protect himself from them, he built 10 castles within a day's march of London, including the White Tower, the core of the Tower of London. Cleverly, he kept the prosperous merchants on side by confirming the city's independence in exchange for taxes. London soon became the principal town of England.

Medieval London

The first stone London Bridge was completed in 1209, although it was frequently too crowded to cross, and most people traversed the river on a small boat called a wherry. The current bridge dates from 1972.

The last of the Norman kings, Stephen, died in 1154, and the throne passed to Henry II of the powerful House of Plantagenet, which would rule England for the next two and a half centuries. Henry's successors were happy to let the City of London keep its independence as long as its merchants continued to finance their wars and building projects. When Richard I (known as 'the Lionheart'), a king who spent a mere six months of his life in England, needed funds for his crusade to the Holy Land, he recognised the city as a self-governing commune in return for cash.

A city built on trade and commerce, London would always guard its independence fiercely, as Richard's successor, King John, learned the hard way. In 1215 John was forced to cede to the powerful barons, and to curb his arbitrary demands for pay-offs from the city. Among those pressing him to put his seal to the landmark Magna Carta, which effectively diluted royal power, was the by-then powerful lord mayor of the City of London; the first holder of this office, Henry Fitz Aylwin, had taken office just a quarter-century before.

c 600	604	852	886
The Saxon trade settlement of Lundenwic – literally 'London settlement' – is formed to the west of the Roman site of Londinium.	The first Christian cathedral dedicated to St Paul is built on Ludgate Hill, the site of the current cathedral; fashioned from wood, it burns down in 675 and is later rebuilt.	Vikings settle in London, having attacked the city 10 years before; a period of great struggle between the kingdoms of Wessex and Denmark begins for control of the Thames.	King Alfred the Great, first king of all England, reclaims London for the Saxons and founds a new settlement within the walls of the old Roman town.

Fire was a constant hazard in the cramped and narrow houses and lanes of 14th-century London, but disease caused by unsanitary living conditions and impure drinking water from the Thames was the greatest threat to the burgeoning city. In 1348 rats on ships from Europe brought the Black Death, a bubonic plague that wiped out almost half the population of about 80,000 over the next year and a half.

With their numbers down, there was growing unrest among labourers, for whom violence became a way of life, and rioting was commonplace. In 1381, miscalculating – or just disregarding – the mood of the nation, the young Richard II tried to impose a poll tax on everyone in the realm. Tens of thousands of peasants, led by the soldier Wat Tyler and the prelates Jack Straw and John Ball, marched in protest on London. The Archbishop of Canterbury, Simon Sudbury, was dragged from the tower and beheaded, several ministers were murdered and many buildings were razed before the Peasants' Revolt ran its course and its leaders were executed.

London gained wealth and stature under the Houses of Lancaster and York in the 15th century, but the two houses' struggle for ascendancy led to the catastrophic Wars of the Roses. The century's greatest episode of political intrigue occurred during this time: in 1483 the 12-year-old Edward V of the House of York reigned for only two months before vanishing with his younger brother into the Tower of London, never to be seen again. Whether or not their uncle, Richard III – who became the next king – murdered the boys has been the subject of much conjecture over the centuries (Shakespeare would have us believe he did the evil deed). In 1674, workers found a chest containing the skeletons of two children near the White Tower, which were assumed to be the princes' remains, and they were reburied in Westminster Abbey.

Richard III didn't have long to enjoy the hot seat: he was killed in 1485 at the Battle of Bosworth by Henry Tudor, who as Henry VII became the first monarch of the eponymous dynasty. In September 2012, Richard's remains, confirmed by rigorous DNA tests, were excavated beneath a car park in central Leicester. They were ceremonially laid to rest in that city's cathedral in March 2015.

To mark the 800th anniversary of the issue of the Magna Carta in 2015 (http://magna carta800th.com), the British Library exhibited its two copies alongside those from Lincoln Cathedral and Salisbury Cathedral – the first time in history the four original surviving manuscripts were brought together in one place.

The House of Tudor

Though the House of Tudor lasted less than 120 years and three generations, it is the best-known English dynasty. London became one of the largest and most important cities in Europe during its reign, which coincided with the discovery of the Americas and thriving world trade.

Henry's son and successor, Henry VIII, was the most extravagant of the clan, instructing new palaces to be built at Whitehall and St

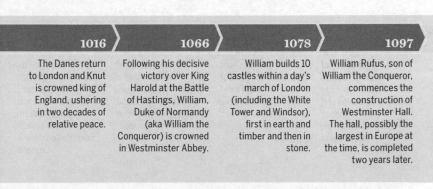

1016	1066	1078	1097
The Danes return to London and Knut is crowned king of England, ushering in two decades of relative peace.	Following his decisive victory over King Harold at the Battle of Hastings, William, Duke of Normandy (aka William the Conqueror) is crowned in Westminster Abbey.	William builds 10 castles within a day's march of London (including the White Tower and Windsor), first in earth and timber and then in stone.	William Rufus, son of William the Conqueror, commences the construction of Westminster Hall. The hall, possibly the largest in Europe at the time, is completed two years later.

James's, and bullying his lord chancellor, Cardinal Thomas Wolsey, into giving him Hampton Court.

Henry's life was dominated by the need to produce a male heir, which indirectly led to his split with the Roman Catholic Church. This occurred in 1534 after the Pope refused to annul his marriage to Catherine of Aragon, who had borne him only a daughter after 24 years of marriage. Turning his back on Rome, he made himself the supreme head of the church in England and married Anne Boleyn, the second of his six wives. He 'dissolved' (abolished) London's monasteries, seized the church's vast wealth and property, and smashed ecclesiastical culture. Many of the religious houses disappeared, leaving only their names in such areas as Whitefriars and Blackfriars (after the colour of the robes worn by Carmelite and Dominican monks).

Despite his penchant for settling differences with the axe (two of his six wives and Wolsey's replacement as lord chancellor, Thomas More, were beheaded, along with 32 other leaders and up to 72,000 others) and his persecution of both Catholics and fellow Protestants who didn't toe the line, Henry VIII remained a popular monarch until his death in 1547. The reign of Mary I, his daughter by Catherine of Aragon, saw a brief return to Catholicism, during which the queen sanctioned the burning to death of 200 Protestants at Smithfield and earned herself the nickname 'Bloody Mary'. By the time Elizabeth I, Henry VIII's daughter by Anne Boleyn, took the throne, Catholicism was a waning force, and hundreds of people who dared to suggest otherwise were carted off to the gallows at Tyburn near today's Marble Arch.

Begging was treated very harshly in 16th-century London. Henry VIII instructed that able-bodied beggars and vagabonds be whipped, beaten or even imprisoned, but such policies failed to stem the tide of vagrants.

Elizabethan London

The 45-year reign (1558–1603) of Elizabeth I is still looked upon as a 'golden age' of English history, and it was just as significant for London. During these four decades, English literature reached new and still unbeaten heights, and religious tolerance gradually became accepted doctrine, although Catholics and some Protestants still faced persecution. England became a naval superpower, having defeated the Spanish Armada in 1588, and the city established itself as the premier world trade market with the opening of the Royal Exchange by Elizabeth in 1571.

London was blooming economically and physically: in the second half of the 16th century the population doubled to 200,000. The first recorded map of London was published in 1558, and John Stow produced *A Survey of London,* the first history of the city, in 1598.

This was also the golden era of English drama, and the works of William Shakespeare, Christopher Marlowe and Ben Jonson packed new playhouses, such as the Rose (built in 1587) and the Globe (1599). Both

1170	1176	1189	1215
Archbishop of Canterbury Thomas Becket, born in Ironmongers Lane and known as Thomas of London in his lifetime, is murdered by four of Henry II's knights.	London Bridge is built in stone for the first time, although most people still cross the river by boat.	The coronation of Richard I sees a pogrom in which Jews of both sexes and all ages are killed in London.	King John signs the Magna Carta (literally 'Great Charter'), an agreement with England's barons forming the basis of constitutional law in England.

were in Southwark, a notoriously 'naughty' place at the time, teeming with stews (brothels) and bawdy taverns. Most importantly, they were outside the jurisdiction of the City, which frowned upon and even banned theatre.

When Elizabeth died without an heir in 1603, she was succeeded by her second cousin, who was crowned James I. Although the son of the Catholic Mary, Queen of Scots (not to be confused with Elizabeth's half-sister Mary), James was slow to improve conditions for England's Catholics and drew their wrath. He narrowly escaped death when the plot by Guy Fawkes and his co-conspirators to blow up the Houses of Parliament on 5 November 1605 was uncovered. The discovery of the audacious plan is commemorated on this date each year with bonfires and fireworks.

The Civil Wars & Restoration

When James I's son, Charles I, came to the throne in 1625, his intransigent personality and total belief in the 'divine right of kings' set the monarchy on a collision course with an increasingly confident parliament at Westminster and a City of London tiring of extortionate taxes. The crunch came when Charles tried to arrest five antagonistic members of parliament, who fled to the city, and in 1642 the country slid into civil war.

The Puritans (extremist Protestants) and the city's expanding merchant class threw their support behind Oliver Cromwell, leader of the Parliamentarians (or Roundheads), who battled the Royalist troops (the Cavaliers). London firmly backed the Roundheads, and Charles I was

In order to raise money to build ships and develop England's ports, Elizabeth I held the world's first national lottery in 1567, with an unheard-of top prize of £5000. Tickets cost 10 shillings and the draw took place next to old St Paul's Cathedral.

1241	1348	1455	1476
Cock Lane in Smithfields effectively becomes London's first red-light district.	Rats on ships from Europe bring the so-called Black Death, a bubonic plague that wipes out almost two-thirds of the city's residents over the following decades.	The Wars of the Roses, a series of rebellions and battles between two houses of the Plantagenet Dynasty – Lancaster (red rose) and York (white rose) – erupts and rages for three decades.	William Caxton, a prominent merchant from Kent, establishes his press at Westminster, printing nearly 100 volumes of works by the likes of Geoffrey Chaucer and the poet John Gower.

LONDON'S UNDERGROUND RIVERS

The Thames is not London's only river: many now course underground. Some survive only in place names: the Hole Bourne, Wells, Tyburn, Walbrook and Westbourne, which was dammed in 1730 to form the Serpentine in Hyde Park. The most famous of all, the Fleet, rises in Hampstead and Kenwood ponds and flows south before emptying into the Thames at Blackfriars Bridge. It had been used as an open sewer and dumping area for entrails by butchers for centuries; after the Great Fire, Christopher Wren oversaw the deepening and widening of the Fleet into a canal, but this was covered over in 1733 and the rest of the river three decades later.

defeated in 1646, although a Second Civil War (1648–49) and a Third Civil War (1649–51) continued to wreak havoc on what had been a stable and prosperous nation.

Charles I was beheaded for treason outside Banqueting House in Whitehall on 30 January 1649, famously wearing two shirts on the cold morning of his execution so as not to shiver and appear cowardly. Cromwell ruled the country as a quasi-republic for the next 11 years, during which time Charles' son, Charles II, continued fighting for the restoration of the monarchy. During this period Cromwell banned theatre, dancing, Christmas and just about anything remotely fun.

After Cromwell's death, parliament decided that the royals weren't so bad after all, refused to recognise the authority of his successor, his son Richard, and restored the exiled Charles II to the throne in 1660.

Plague & Fire

Crowded, filthy London had suffered from recurrent outbreaks of bubonic plague since the 14th century, but nothing had prepared it for the Great Plague of 1665, which dwarfed all previous outbreaks.

As the plague spread, families affected were forced to stay inside for 40 days quarantine, until the victim had either recovered or died. Previously crowded streets were deserted, the churches and markets were closed, and an eerie silence descended. To make matters worse, the mayor believed that dogs and cats were the spreaders of the plague and ordered them all killed, thus ridding the disease-carrying rats of their natural predators. By the time the winter cold arrested the epidemic, an estimated 100,000 people had perished, their corpses collected and thrown into vast 'plague pits'.

The plague finally began to wane in November 1665. But Londoners scarcely had a year to recover when another disaster struck. The city had for centuries been prone to fire, as nearly all buildings were con-

For trivia, little-known facts and endless specialist information on the history of the East End and its personalities, click on East London History at www.eastlondon-history.com.

1558	1599	1605	1613
The first detailed map of London is commissioned by a group of German merchants; a golden age of peace, art and literature begins when Queen Elizabeth I takes the throne.	The Globe opens in Southwark, alongside other London theatres such as the Rose and the Swan; most of Shakespeare's plays written after 1599 are staged here, including *Macbeth* and *Hamlet*.	A Catholic plot to blow up James I by hiding gunpowder under the House of Commons is foiled; Guy Fawkes, one of the alleged plotters, is executed the following year.	The Globe theatre catches fire and burns to the ground; it is rebuilt the following year but closed by the Puritans and demolished in 1642.

structed from wood and thatch, but the mother of all blazes broke out on 2 September 1666 in a bakery in Pudding Lane.

It didn't seem like much to begin with – the mayor himself dismissed it as 'something a woman might pisse out' before going back to bed – but the unusual autumn heat combined with rising winds meant the fire raged out of control for four days, reducing some 80% of London to ash. Only eight people died (officially at least), but most of medieval London was obliterated. The fire finally stopped at Pye Corner in Smithfield, on the very edge of London, not before destroying 88 churches, including St Paul's Cathedral, and more than 13,000 houses, leaving tens of thousands of people homeless.

Wren's London

The inferno created a blank canvas upon which master architect Christopher Wren could build his 51 magnificent new churches and cathedral. Wren's plan for rebuilding the entire city – much of it on a grid pattern – was deemed too expensive and many landlords opposed it; the familiar pattern of streets that had grown up over the centuries since the time of the Romans quickly reappeared. However, new laws stipulated that brick and stone designs replace the old timber-framed, overhanging Tudor houses and that many roads be widened. The fire accelerated the movement of the wealthy away from the City and into what is now the West End.

By way of memorialising the blaze – and rebuilding of London – the Monument, designed by Wren, was erected in 1677 near the site of the fire's outbreak. At the time, the 61m-tall column was by far the highest structure in the city, visible from everywhere in the capital.

In 1685 some 1500 Huguenot refugees arrived in London, fleeing persecution in Catholic France; another 3500 would follow. Mainly artisans, many began manufacturing luxury goods such as silks and silverware in and around Spitalfields and Clerkenwell, which were already populated with Irish, Jewish and Italian immigrants and artisans. London was fast becoming one of the world's most cosmopolitan places.

The Glorious – ie bloodless – Revolution in 1688 brought the Dutch King William of Orange to the English throne after the Catholic James II had fled to France. He relocated from Whitehall Palace to a new palace in Kensington Gardens and, in order to raise finances for his war with France, established the Bank of England in 1694.

London's growth continued unabated, and by 1700 it was Europe's largest city, with some 600,000 people. The influx of foreign workers brought expansion to the east and south, while those who could afford it headed to the more salubrious environs of the north and west.

For a real-time experience of a 17th-century blogger, click on The Diary of Samuel Pepys (www.pepysdiary.com), where a new entry written by the celebrated diarist is published daily.

HISTORY WREN'S LONDON

1649	1661	1665	1666
King Charles I is executed at Whitehall at the height of the English Civil Wars, a series of armed conflicts between Royalists and Parliamentarians.	Oliver Cromwell's body is dug up from Westminster Abbey and given a posthumous 'execution'; his head is then stuck on a spike and displayed above Westminster Hall.	The Great Plague ravages London, wiping out a fifth of the population. It was one of Europe's last outbreaks of the disease.	The Great Fire of London burns for five days, destroying the city Shakespeare had known, leaving four-fifths of the metropolis in smoking ruins.

The crowning glory of the 'Great Rebuilding', Wren's St Paul's Cathedral, opened in 1711 during the reign of the last Stuart monarch, Queen Anne. A masterpiece of English baroque architecture, it remains one of the city's most prominent landmarks.

Georgian London

Queen Anne died without an heir in 1714. Although there were some 50 Catholic relatives with stronger claims to the throne, a search was immediately launched to find a Protestant relative, since the 1701 Act of Settlement forbade Roman Catholics becoming monarch. Eventually George of Hanover, a great-grandson of James I, arrived from Germany and was crowned king of England, though he never learned to speak English.

Robert Walpole's Whig Party controlled parliament during much of George I's reign and, as 'First Lord of the Treasury', effectively became Britain's first prime minister. He was presented with 10 Downing St, which remains the official residence of the prime minister today.

London grew at a phenomenal pace during this time, and measures were taken to make the city more accessible. The Roman wall surrounding the City of London was torn down, and a second span over the Thames, Westminster Bridge, opened in 1750.

Georgian London saw a great creative surge in music, art and architecture. Court composer George Frederick Handel wrote *Water Music* (1717) and *Messiah* (1741) after settling here at age 27, and in 1755 Dr Johnson published the first English dictionary. William Hogarth, Thomas Gainsborough and Joshua Reynolds produced some of their finest paintings and engravings, and many of London's most elegant buildings, streets and squares were erected or laid out by architects John Soane, his pupil, Robert Smirke, and the prolific John Nash.

All the while, though, London was becoming ever more segregated and lawless. Indeed, King George II himself was relieved of 'purse, watch and buckles' during a stroll through Kensington Gardens. This was Hogarth's London, in which the wealthy built fine mansions in attractive squares and gathered in fashionable new coffee houses while the poor huddled together in appalling slums and drowned their sorrows with cheap gin. To curb rising crime, two magistrates, including the writer Henry Fielding, established the Bow Street Runners in 1749. This voluntary group was effectively a forerunner to the Metropolitan Police Force, which would be established in 1829.

In 1780 parliament proposed to lift the law preventing Catholics buying or inheriting property. One MP, Lord George Gordon, led a 'No Popery' demonstration that turned into the so-called Gordon Riots. A mob

For superb city views from London's most iconic piece of ecclesiastical architecture, climb the 528 stairs (no lift) to the Golden Gallery in the dome of Sir Christopher Wren's opus magnum: three-centuries-old St Paul's Cathedral.

1702	1707	1711	1759
The *Daily Courant*, London's first daily newspaper, is published in Fleet St, consisting of a single page of news.	The first-ever sitting of the parliament of the Kingdom of Great Britain occurs in London as the 1707 Act of Union brings England and Scotland together under one parliament.	Sir Christopher Wren's masterpiece St Paul's Cathedral is officially completed, 35 years after old St Paul's Cathedral was gutted in the Great Fire.	The British Museum opens to the public for the first time, housed in Montagu House in Bloomsbury and levying no admission fee to all 'studious and curious persons'.

ALBERT & THE GREAT EXHIBITION

In 1851, Queen Victoria's consort, the German-born Prince Albert, organised a huge celebration of new technology from around the world in Hyde Park. The so-called Great Exhibition was held in a 7.5-hectare iron-and-glass hothouse, a 'Crystal Palace' designed by gardener and architect Joseph Paxton using the newfangled plate glass. Some two million people flocked from around Britain and abroad to marvel at the more than 100,000 exhibits. So successful was this first world's fair that Albert arranged for the profits of £186,000 (almost £18 million today) to be ploughed into building exhibitions that eventually became the Victoria & Albert, Natural History and Science Museums. Exactly 10 years after the exhibition, the prince died of typhoid, and Victoria was so prostrate with grief that she wore mourning clothes until her death four decades later.

of 30,000 went on a rampage, attacking Irish labourers, and burning prisons, 'Papishe dens' (chapels) and several law courts. As many as 850 people died during five days of rioting.

As George III, forever remembered as the king who lost the American colonies, slid into dementia towards the end of the 18th century, his son, the Prince Regent, set up an alternative and considerably more fashionable court at Carlton House in Pall Mall. By this time London's population had mushroomed to just under a million.

Victorian London

In 1837 George III's 18-year-old granddaughter, Victoria, ascended the throne. During her long reign London would become the nerve centre of the largest and richest empire the world had ever known, covering a quarter of the globe's surface and ruling more than 500 million people.

New docks were built to facilitate the booming trade with the colonies, and railways began to fan out from the capital. The world's first underground railway opened between Paddington and Farringdon Rd in 1863 and was such a success that other lines quickly followed. Many of London's most famous buildings and landmarks were built at this time: the recently renamed Elizabeth Tower (popularly known as 'Big Ben'; 1859), Royal Albert Hall (1871) and the iconic Tower Bridge (1894).

The city, however, heaved under the burden of its vast size, and in 1858 London was in the grip of the 'Great Stink', when the population explosion so overtook the city's sanitation facilities that raw sewage seeped in through the floorboards of wealthy merchants' houses and the Houses of Parliament were draped with sheets soaked in lime chloride to allay the stench. Leading engineer Joseph Bazalgette tackled

You may worry about today's vehicle emissions, but at the end of the 19th century, 1000 tonnes of horse manure would fall on the streets of London daily. Crossing sweepers, often young boys, made meagre earnings clearing a path for pedestrians.

1812	1829	1838	1843
Charles Dickens, Victorian England's greatest novelist, is born in Portsmouth; many of his novels portray London in all its Victorian squalor.	London's first regular bus service – the horse-drawn 'omnibus' – begins, running from Paddington to Bank. The fare is 1 shilling (5p).	The coronation of Queen Victoria at Westminster Abbey ushers in a new era for London; the British capital becomes the economic centre of the world.	Connecting Rotherhithe and Wapping, Marc Isambard Brunel's Thames Tunnel, the first tunnel to be constructed under a navigable river, opens.

the problem by creating an underground network of sewers in the late 1850s.

At the same time, intellectual achievement in the arts and sciences was enormous. The greatest chronicler of the Victorian age was Charles Dickens, whose *Oliver Twist* (1837) and other works explored the themes of poverty, hopelessness and squalor among the working classes. In 1859 Charles Darwin published his seminal and immensely controversial *On the Origin of Species* here, in which he outlined the theory of evolution.

Some of Britain's most capable prime ministers served during Victoria's 64-year reign, most notably William Gladstone (four terms between 1868 and 1894) and Benjamin Disraeli (who served in 1868 and again from 1874 to 1880). And with the creation of the London County Council (LCC) in 1889, the capital had its first-ever directly elected government.

Waves of immigrants, from Irish and Jews to Chinese and Indian sepoys, arrived in London during the 19th century, when the population exploded from one million to six million people. This breakneck expansion was not beneficial to all – inner-city slums housed the poor in atrocious conditions of disease and overcrowding, while the affluent expanded to leafy suburbs.

Queen Victoria (of 'We are not amused' fame) is often seen as a dour, humourless old curmudgeon, but was an intelligent, progressive and passionate woman. She lived to celebrate her Diamond Jubilee in 1897 but died four years later at the age of 81 and was buried in Windsor. Her reign is considered the climax of British world supremacy.

From Empire to World War

Victoria's self-indulgent son Edward, the Prince of Wales, was already 60 by the time he was crowned Edward VII in 1901. London's *belle époque* was marked with the introduction of the first motorised double-decker buses in 1904, which replaced the horse-drawn versions that had plodded their trade since 1829. And a touch of glamour came in the form of luxury hotels, such as the Ritz in 1906, and department stores, such as Selfridges, in 1909. The first London Olympics were held at White City Stadium in 1908.

What became known as the Great War (or WWI) broke out in August 1914, and the first German bombs fell from zeppelins near the Guildhall a year later, killing 39 people. In all, some 670 Londoners were killed by bombs (half the national total of civilian casualties) and another 2000 were wounded.

For an upfront view of WWI and its unspeakable devastation, visit the state-of-the-art First World War Galleries (www.iwm.org.uk/exhibitions/iwm-london/first-world-war-galleries) at the Imperial War Museum, which opened to mark the centenary of the start of the conflict in 2014.

1851	1878	1884	1893
The Great Exhibition, the brainchild of Victoria's consort, Albert, who would die a decade later, opens to great fanfare in the purpose-built Crystal Palace in Hyde Park.	London's first electric lights are installed in Billingsgate Fish Market, using Yablochkov 'candles' (arc lamps).	Greenwich Mean Time is established, making Greenwich Observatory the centre of world time, according to which all clocks around the globe are set.	The world's first outdoor aluminium statue, the Shaftesbury Memorial Fountain, topped with a statue of the Angel of Christian Charity (or Eros), is unveiled in Piccadilly Circus.

RICHARD TAMES: HISTORIAN

Prolific author Richard Tames has published hundreds of books, including the seminal *A Traveller's History of London*.

Where in London is the past most palpable for you?

Well, there is big history and little history. For big history it would be Westminster Abbey stuffed with all those statues. For little history the East End, specifically the area around Brick Lane. To think the likes of Jack London and Israel Zangwill walked up and down those streets...

Which period of history most closely reflects our own?

It would have to be the late Victorian and early Edwardian periods. If you consider the time from the 1890s till 1910, along came the telephone, motorcar, powered flight and radio. They all fundamentally changed the dimensions of human experience in a way that was very difficult to work out or foresee at the time. With the information revolution we're doing exactly the same thing.

Help settle the ultimate London argument. Which is the oldest pub?

Ye Olde Mitre (p207) probably deserves the title. **Hoop and Grapes** (www.thehoopandgrapes.co.uk; 47 Aldgate High St, EC3; ⊘10am-11pm Mon-Fri; ⊜Aldgate) might claim it but it has not continuously functioned as a pub over the years. If you want to know how old a building is go downwards – no one fills in cellars. **Ye Olde Cheshire Cheese** (p155) has a wonderful array of them.

The Interwar Years

After the war ended in 1918, London's population continued to rise, reaching nearly 7.5 million in 1921. The LCC busied itself clearing slums and building new housing estates, while the suburbs spread further into the countryside.

Unemployment rose steadily, and in May 1926 a wage dispute in the coal industry escalated into a nine-day general strike, in which so many workers downed tools that London virtually ground to a halt. The army was called in to maintain order and to keep the buses and the Underground running, but the stage was set for more than half a century of industrial strife.

Intellectually the 1920s were the heyday of the Bloomsbury Group, which counted writers Virginia Woolf and EM Forster and the economist John Maynard Keynes in its ranks. The spotlight shifted westwards to Fitzrovia in the following decade, when George Orwell and Dylan Thomas raised glasses with contemporaries at the Fitzroy Tavern

1901	1908	1926	1936
Queen Victoria dies after reigning 63 years and 217 days – the longest reign in British history until Elizabeth II broke that record in September 2015.	London hosts its first Olympic Games in the now-demolished White City Stadium; a total of 22 teams take part and the entire budget is £15,000.	London all but closes shop for nine days during the General Strike, with little violence and ultimately almost no impact on trade-union activity or industrial relations.	The 'Year of Three Kings': George VI ascends the throne following the death of his father and abdication of his brother, who gave up his throne for an American divorcée.

on Charlotte St. Cinema, TV and radio arrived: the BBC aired its first radio broadcast from the roof of Marconi House on The Strand in 1922, and the first TV program from Alexandra Palace 14 years later.

The monarchy took a knock when Edward VIII abdicated in 1936 to marry a woman who was not only twice divorced but – egad! – an American. The same year Oswald Mosley attempted to lead the black-shirted British Union of Fascists on an anti-Jewish march through the East End but was repelled by a mob of around half a million at the famous Battle of Cable St.

WWII & the Blitz

Prime Minister Neville Chamberlain's policy of appeasing Adolf Hitler during the 1930s eventually proved misguided as the Führer's lust for expansion appeared insatiable. When Germany invaded Poland on 1 September 1939, Britain declared war, having signed a mutual-assistance pact with that nation a few days before. WWII had begun.

The first year of the war was one of anxious waiting for London. Some 600,000 women and children had been evacuated to the countryside and the Battle of Britain raged elsewhere, primarily around Royal Air Force bases in England, but no bombs fell to disturb the blackout in the capital. On 7 September 1940 that all came to a devastating end when the German Air Force, the Luftwaffe, dropped hundreds of bombs on the East End, killing 430 people.

The Blitz (from the German 'blitzkrieg' or 'lightning war') lasted for 57 nights, and then continued intermittently until mid-May 1941. Some Underground stations were turned into giant bomb shelters, although one bomb rolled down the escalator at Bank station and exploded on the platform, killing more than 100 people. Londoners responded with resilience and stoicism. To the great admiration and respect of the people, the royal family refused to leave London during the bombing. Buckingham Palace took a direct hit during a bombing raid early in the campaign, famously prompting Queen Elizabeth (the present monarch's late mother) to pronounce that 'Now I can look the East End in the face'. Winston Churchill, prime minister from 1940, orchestrated much of Britain's war strategy from the subterranean Cabinet War Rooms at Whitehall, and it was from here that he made his stirring wartime speeches.

London's spirit was tested again in June 1944, when Germany launched pilotless V-1 bombers (known as doodlebugs) over East London. By the time Nazi Germany capitulated in May 1945, up to a third of the East End and the City of London had been flattened, almost 30,000 Londoners killed and a further 50,000 seriously wounded.

For an idea of the scale of the devastation brought about by the Blitz on London, visit the website of the Bomb Sight project (http://bombsight.org), which has mapped the WWII bomb census between October 1940 and June 1941 for the first time.

The night of 29 December 1940 has been called the 'Second Great Fire of London', when German bombers dropped more than 100,000 bombs on London in a few hours, starting 1500 fires raging across the City and up to Islington.

1940–41	1945	1951	1952
London is devastated by the Blitz, although miraculously St Paul's Cathedral and the Tower of London escape the bombing largely unscathed.	Big Ben is illuminated again in April and full street lighting restored six months after the Blackout is downgraded to a dim-out over London; 'Victory In Europe' is declared in May.	King George VI opens the Festival of Britain marking the centenary of the Great Exhibition and aiming to lift the national mood after the destruction of WWII.	London is brought to a virtual standstill for four days in December by a thick pea-souper smog that smothers and chokes the city and leaves up to 4000 people dead.

Postwar London & the '60s

Once the Victory in Europe (VE) celebrations had died down, the nation began to confront the war's appalling toll and to rebuild. The years of austerity had begun, with rationing of essential items and the building of high-rise residences on bomb sites in areas such as Pimlico and the East End to solve the chronic housing problem. To help boost morale London hosted the 1948 Olympics (dubbed 'the austerity Games') and the Festival of Britain in 1951.

The gloom returned, quite literally, on 6 December 1952 in the form of the Great Smog. A lethal blend of fog, smoke and pollution descended, and some 4000 people died of respiratory disorders. This prompted the Clean Air Act of 1956, which introduced zones to central London where only smokeless fuels could be burned.

The current queen, Elizabeth II, was crowned in 1953 following the death of her much-loved father King George VI the year before. Rationing of most goods ended in 1954, 14 years after it had begun.

Immigrants from around the world – particularly the former colonies – flocked to London, where a dwindling population had led to labour shortages. However, despite being officially encouraged to come,

THE WORLD IN ONE CITY

London is historically made up of immigrants. Whether Roman, Viking, Anglo-Saxon, Norman, Huguenot, Irish or Jamaican, large numbers of ethnically diverse people have always been assimilated into the city. Africans are well documented to have served in the Roman army, but they first came to England in significant numbers as slaves in Elizabethan times and settled around St Giles in Soho. The first truly large influx of foreigners was in the late 17th century, when Huguenots, French Protestant refugees fleeing religious persecution at home, settled in Spitalfields and Soho. Jews have arrived over the past four centuries; their traditional areas have been the East End (particularly Spitalfields and Whitechapel) and northwest London. WWII brought Poles, Ukrainians and other Eastern Europeans to London, and today the Poles are a long-established community in Hammersmith and Shepherd's Bush.

The single biggest wave of immigration came in the 1950s, when, facing a labour shortage, the government allowed anyone born in a UK colony to have British citizenship. This brought a huge black population from the Caribbean and a large Asian diaspora from India, Bangladesh and Pakistan. The black population settled in West London and South London, while those from the subcontinent were concentrated in the East End. A third of all Londoners are now foreign-born, representing 270 different nationalities speaking 300 languages.

1953	1956	1959	1966
Queen Elizabeth II's coronation is held at Westminster Abbey, the first major event to be broadcast live around the world on TV; many English families buy their first television.	Red Routemaster double-decker buses make their first appearance in London and instantly become a city icon.	The Notting Hill Carnival is launched by Claudia Jones to promote better race relations following the riots of 1958 when white and Afro-Caribbean communities clashed.	England beat Germany to win the World Cup at Wembley – possibly the greatest day in the history of British sport and one seared into the consciousness of every schoolchild.

new immigrants weren't always welcomed on the streets as was proved in the Notting Hill race riots of 1958.

Some economic prosperity returned in the late 1950s, and Prime Minister Harold Macmillan told Britons they'd 'never had it so good'. London became the place to be during the 1960s, when the bottled-up creative energy of the postwar era was spectacularly uncorked. London found itself the epicentre of cool in fashion and music: the streets were awash with colour and vitality, the iconic Mini car (1959) became a British icon and the Jaguar E-type (1961) was launched to adoring crowds.

Social norms underwent a revolution: the introduction of the contraceptive pill, the decriminalisation of homosexuality, and the popularisation of drugs such as marijuana and LSD through the hippy movement created an unprecedented permissive and liberal climate. Popular music in the mid-to-late 1960s became increasingly linked with drug use, political activism and a counter-cultural mindset. The Beatles recording at Abbey Rd and the Rolling Stones performing free in front of half a million people in Hyde Park were seminal moments. Carnaby St and the King's Rd were the most fashionable places on earth, and pop-culture figures from Twiggy and David Bailey to Marianne Faithfull and Christine Keeler became the icons of the new era.

> For a fascinating review of the social, musical and cultural history of 20th-century London, take a look at Another Nickel in the Machine (www.nickelinthemachine.com), covering everything from suffragettes and Charlie Chaplin's homecoming to vintage Bowie.

The Punk Era

London returned to the doldrums in the harsh economic climate of the 1970s. The city's once-important docks never recovered from the loss of empire, the changing needs of modern container ships and poor labour relations, disappearing altogether between 1968 and 1981. Shipping moved 25 miles east to Tilbury, and the Docklands declined to a point of decay, until they were rediscovered by property developers a decade later. In 1973 a bomb exploded at the Old Bailey (the Central Criminal Court), signalling the arrival on English soil of the Irish Republican Army (IRA) and its campaign for a united Ireland.

Post-1960s music became more formulaic as glam rock ruled, despite the blossoming of London legends Marc Bolan and David Bowie. Economic stagnation, cynicism and the superficial limits of disco and glam rock spawned a novel London aesthetic: punk. Largely white, energetic, abrasive and fast, punk transformed popular music and fashion in one stroke as teenagers traded in denim bell-bottoms for black drainpipes, and long hair for spiked Mohicans. The late 1970s were exhilarating times for London youth as punk opened the door for new wave, a punchy mod revival and the indulgent new romantics.

Meanwhile, torpor had set into Britain's body politic. Seen as weak and in thrall to the all-powerful trade unions, the brief and unremark-

1979	1981	1984	1987
Margaret Thatcher is elected prime minister. Her policies will transform Britain beyond recognition – part vital modernisation, part radical right-wing social policy.	Brixton sees the worst race riots in London's history; Lord Scarman, delivering his report on the events, puts the blame squarely on 'racial disadvantage that is a fact of British life'.	The Thames Barrier, designed to protect London from flooding during high tides and storm surges, is officially opened by the Queen.	A fire, probably started by a dropped match or cigarette, at King's Cross Underground station causes the deaths of 31 people.

able Labour premiership of James Callaghan (1976–79) was marked by crippling strikes in the late 1970s, most significantly the 'Winter of Discontent' of 1978–79.

The Thatcher Years

In 1979 the Conservative leader Margaret Thatcher became the UK's first female prime minister. In power for all of the 1980s and embarking on an unprecedented program of privatisation, Margaret Thatcher – aka the 'Iron Lady' – is arguably the most significant of Britain's post-war leaders. While her critics decry her approach to social justice and the large gulf that developed between the haves and have nots during her time in power, her defenders point to the massive modernisation of Britain's trade-union-dominated infrastructure and the vast wealth creation her policies generated.

In the beginning, her monetarist policy sent unemployment skyrocketing; an inquiry following the Brixton riots of 1981 found that an astonishing 55% of men aged under 19 in that part of London were jobless. Meanwhile the Greater London Council (GLC), under the leadership of 'Red' Ken Livingstone, proved to be a thorn in Thatcher's side. County Hall, which faces the Houses of Parliament across the Thames, was hung with a giant banner recording the number of unemployed in the capital and goading the prime minister to do something about it. Thatcher responded in 1986 by abolishing the GLC, leaving London the only European capital without a unified central government.

While poorer Londoners suffered under Thatcher's significant trimming back of the welfare state, things had rarely looked better for the business community. Riding a wave of confidence partly engendered by the deregulation of the stock exchange in 1986 (the so-called Big Bang), London underwent explosive economic growth. Property developers proved to be only marginally more discriminating than the Luftwaffe, though some outstanding modern structures, including the Lloyd's of London building went up.

Like previous booms, the one of the late 1980s proved unsustainable. As unemployment started to rise again and people found themselves living in houses worth much less than they had paid for them, Thatcher introduced a flat-rate poll tax. Protests around the country culminated in a 1990 march on Trafalgar Sq that ended in a fully fledged riot. Thatcher's subsequent resignation after losing a confidence vote in Parliament brought to an end this divisive era in modern British history. Her successor, the former Chancellor of the Exchequer, John Major, employed a far more collective form of government.

Though it is now a few years old, *The Iron Lady* (2011), starring Meryl Streep, remains a very watchable biopic of the late Margaret Thatcher. It seamlessly traces the former prime minister's life and career from politically astute grocer's daughter to grieving widow suffering from dementia. Thatcher died two years after the film's release.

1990	1997	2000	2003
Britain erupts in civil unrest, culminating in the poll tax riots in Trafalgar Sq; the deeply unpopular tax is ultimately Thatcher's undoing and she resigns in November.	Labour sweeps to victory after almost two decades of Conservative government. Tony Blair's centrist 'New Labour' party wins a majority of 179 in the House of Commons.	Ken Livingstone is elected mayor of London as an independent, despite the Labour government's attempts to shoehorn its own candidate into the job.	London's congestion charge is introduced by Livingstone, creating an outcry that grows more muted as traffic flow improves.

In 1992, to the amazement of most Londoners, the Conservatives were elected for a fourth successive term in government, without the inspiring leadership of Thatcher. The economy went into a tailspin shortly after, and the IRA detonated two huge bombs, one in the City in 1992 and another in the Docklands four years later. The writing was on the wall for the Conservatives, as the Labour Party re-emerged with a new face.

Blair's Britain

The shock of the new has traditionally knocked London sideways and the Millennium Dome on the Greenwich Peninsula failed to impress when it opened in 2000. Designed by Richard Rogers and sometimes mockingly referred to as the Millennium Tent, the dome eventually triumphed when rebranded as the 02 in 2007. It is now one of the the world's most successful live-entertainment venues.

Desperate to return to power after almost two decades in opposition, the Labour Party selected the telegenic Tony Blair to lead it. The May 1997 general election overwhelmingly returned a Labour government to power, but it was a much changed 'New Labour' party, one that had shed most of its socialist credo and supported a market economy, privatisation and integration with Europe.

Most importantly for London, Labour recognised the legitimate demand the city had for local government, and created the London Assembly and the post of mayor. Former leader of the GLC Ken Livingstone stood as an independent candidate and won easily. Livingstone introduced a successful congestion charge to limit private vehicles in central London and sought to bring London's backward public transport network into the 21st century.

London's resurgence as a great world city seemed to be going from strength to strength, culminating in its selection to host the Olympic Games in 2012. London's buoyant mood was, however, shattered the very next morning when extremist Muslim terrorists detonated a series of bombs on the city's public transport network, killing 52 people. Triumph turned to terror, followed quickly by anger and then defiance. Just two weeks later the attempted detonation of several more bombs on London's public transport system sent the city into a state of severe unease, which culminated in the tragic shooting by the Metropolitan Police of an innocent Brazilian electrician, Jean Charles de Menezes, mistaken for one of the failed bombers.

Enter Boris

Ken Livingstone's campaign to get a third term as London mayor in 2008 was fatally undermined when the Conservative Party fielded maverick MP and popular TV personality Boris Johnson as its candidate. Even more of a populist than Livingstone, Eton-educated Johnson, portrayed by the media as a gaffe-prone toff, actually proved to be a deft political operator and surprised everyone by sailing past Livingstone to become the first Conservative mayor of London.

2005	2008	2010	2011
A day after London is awarded the 2012 Olympics, 52 people are killed by extremist Islamic terrorists in a series of suicide bombings on London's transport network on 7 July.	Boris Johnson, a Conservative MP and journalist famed for both his gaffes and wonderful turns of phrase, beats Ken Livingstone to become London's new mayor.	Labour is defeated in the general elections, which results in a hung Parliament and a Conservative–Liberal Democrat coalition government with David Cameron as prime minister.	A demonstration against alleged police brutality in Tottenham on 6 August turns into a riot and episodes of mass looting which spread to numerous boroughs and towns across the UK.

Johnson was popularised in the media as an almost eccentric, odd-ball figure, with his wild mop of blond hair, shapeless suits and in-your-face eagerness. It was a persona Londoners warmed to. He disagreed with Livingstone on many issues, but continued to support several of his predecessor's policies, including the congestion charge and the expansion of bicycle lanes. A keen cyclist himself, Boris is forever associated with the bicycle hire scheme sponsored by Barclays and now Santander Bank and nicknamed 'Boris Bikes' (though Livingstone proposed it first). Johnson pledged to replace Livingstone's unloved 'bendy buses' with remodelled Routemasters, which were introduced on some routes in 2012.

Johnson's first mayoral term coincided with London's transformation for the 2012 Olympic Games. Neglected areas of the recession-hit city were showered with investment and a vast building program in East London took shape. The era also saw a transferral of government power from the lacklustre Labour Party under Gordon Brown's leadership to a Conservative-Liberal Democrat coalition government with fellow Etonian David Cameron as prime minister and Nick Clegg deputy prime minister.

London's Year

The year 2012 promised to be London's year, and few people – at home or abroad – were disappointed.

A four-day holiday in June marked the Queen's Diamond Jubilee – the 60th anniversary of her ascension to the throne. As celebratory and joyous as the Jubilee was, it was but a prelude to *the* London event of the year: the all-singin', all-dancin' Olympics and Paralympics that welcomed some 15,000 athletes competing in almost 50 sports for 800 medals. Over the course of 29 days there were many expected highs (Britain took 65 Olympic and 120 Paralympic medals, to rank third in each games) and some surprising ones (London's transport system did not just cope but excelled). But nothing quite came close to Danny Boyle's Olympics Opening Ceremony, in which the world was treated to an extravagant potted history of London and the UK. For many, most memorable was the finale, when 'James Bond' (in the form of actor Daniel Craig) jumped out of a helicopter into the Olympic Stadium accompanied by a Queen impersonator.

Relive all the the excitement of the 2012 Olympic Games by logging onto the official London 2012 site (www.london 2012.com).

2012	2013	2014	2015
Boris Johnson narrowly beats Ken Livingstone to win his second mayoral election; London hosts the 2012 Olympics and Paralympics.	The Shard, at 310m/1016ft the tallest building in the European Union, opens to the public; MPs vote in favour of legalising gay marriage.	The southern half of the Olympic site opens to the public as Queen Elizabeth Olympic Park, followed by the Aquatics Centre, Velodrome and ArcelorMittal Orbit.	The Conservatives defeat Labour in the general election, emerging with a narrow majority and abandoning their coalition government with the Liberal Democrats.

Architecture

Unlike many other world-class cities, London has never been methodically planned. Rather, it has developed in an organic (read haphazard) fashion. London retains architectural reminders from every period of its long history, but they are often hidden: part of a Roman wall enclosed in the lobby of a modern building near St Paul's Cathedral, say, or a galleried coaching inn dating to the Restoration and tucked away in a courtyard off Borough High St. This is a city for explorers. Bear that in mind and you'll make discoveries at virtually every turn.

Laying the Foundations

London's architectural roots lie within the walled Roman settlement of Londinium, established in AD 43 on the northern banks of the River Thames, on the site of today's City of London. Few Roman traces survive outside museums, though a Temple of Mithras, built in AD 240 and excavated in 1954, will be relocated to the eastern end of Queen Victoria St in the City when the Bloomberg headquarters are completed at Walbrook Sq in 2016. Stretches of the Roman wall remain as foundations to a medieval wall outside Tower Hill tube station and in a few sections below Bastion Highwalk, next to the Museum of London.

The Saxons, who moved into the area after the decline of the Roman Empire, found Londinium too small, ignored what the Romans had left behind and built up their communities further up the Thames. Excavations carried out during renovations at the Royal Opera House in the late 1990s uncovered extensive traces of the Saxon settlement of Lundenwic, including some houses of wattle and daub. All Hallows-by-the-Tower, northwest of the Tower of London, shelters an important archway, the walls of a 7th-century Saxon church and a Roman pavement. St Bride's, Fleet St, has a similar pavement.

With the arrival of William the Conqueror in 1066, the country received its first example of Norman architecture with the White Tower, the sturdy keep at the heart of the Tower of London. The church of St Bartholomew-the-Great at Smithfield also has Norman arches and columns supporting its nave. The west door and elaborately moulded porch at Temple Church (shared by Inner and Middle Temple), the undercroft at Westminster Abbey and the crypt at St-Mary-le-Bow are other outstanding examples of Norman architecture.

The London Festival of Architecture (www.london festivalof architecture. org/) is an annual month-long event in June celebrating the capital's buildings with a range of events, walks, talks, tours and debates.

Medieval London

Enlarged and refurbished in the 13th and 14th centuries by the 'builder king' Henry III and his son, Edward I, or 'Longshanks', Westminster Abbey is a splendid reminder of the work of master masons in the Middle Ages. Perhaps the finest surviving medieval church in the city is the 13th-century church of St Ethelburga-the-Virgin near Liverpool St station, heavily restored after Irish Republican Army (IRA) bombings in 1993. The 15th-century Church of St Olave, northwest of Tower Hill, is one of the City's few remaining Gothic parish churches, while the crypt at the largely restored Church of St Etheldreda, north of Holborn

Circus, dates from about 1250. Southwark Cathedral includes some remnants from the 12th and 13th centuries.

Secular medieval buildings are even more scarce, although the ragstone Jewel Tower, opposite the Houses of Parliament, dates from 1365, and much of the Tower of London goes back to the Middle Ages. Staple Inn in Holborn dates from 1378, but the half-timbered shopfront facade (1589) is mostly Elizabethan, and heavily restored in the mid-20th century. Westminster Hall was originally built in 1199; the hammer-beam roof came 300 years later. The great Medieval Hall (1479) at Eltham Palace also has a splendid hammer-beam roof.

A Trinity of Architects

The finest London architect of the first half of the 17th century was Inigo Jones (1573–1652), who spent a year and a half in Italy and became a convert to the Renaissance architecture of Andrea Palladio. His *chefs d'œuvre* include Banqueting House (1622) in Whitehall and Queen's House (1635) in Greenwich. Often overlooked is the much plainer church of St Paul's in Covent Garden, which Jones designed in the 1630s.

The greatest architect to leave his mark on London was Christopher Wren (1632–1723), responsible for St Paul's Cathedral (1711). Wren oversaw the building (or rebuilding) of more than 50 churches, many replacing medieval churches lost in the Great Fire, as well as the Royal Hospital Chelsea (1692) and the Old Royal Naval College, begun in 1694 at Greenwich. His English baroque buildings and churches are taller and lighter than their medieval predecessors, with graceful steeples taking the place of solid square medieval towers.

Nicholas Hawksmoor (1661–1736) was a pupil of Wren and worked with him on several churches before going on to design his own masterpieces. The restored Christ Church (1729) in Spitalfields, St George's Bloomsbury (1731), St Anne's, Limehouse (1725), and St George-in-the-East (1726) at Wapping are among the finest of his half-dozen London churches.

Georgian Manners

Among the greatest exponents of classicism (or neo-Palladianism) was Robert Adam (1728–92), whose surviving work in London includes Kenwood House (1779) on Hampstead Heath and some of the interiors of Apsley House (1778) in Hyde Park Corner.

Adam's fame has been eclipsed by that of John Nash (1752–1835), whose contribution to London's architecture can almost compare to that of Christopher Wren. Nash was responsible for the layout of Regent's Park and its surrounding crescents. To give London a 'spine', he created Regent St as an axis from the new Regent's Park south to St James's Park. This project also involved the formation of Trafalgar Sq, and the development

A lovely row of four houses at 52-55 Newington Green, N16, make up London's oldest surviving brick terrace houses. Predating the Great Fire of London, they were built in 1658.

OPEN SESAME

If you want to see the inside of buildings whose doors are normally shut tight, visit London on the third weekend in September. That's when the charity **Open House London** (☎020-7383 2131; www.openhouselondon.org.uk) arranges for owners of some 850 (at last count) private and public buildings to let the public in free of charge. Major buildings (eg the Gherkin, City Hall, Lloyd's of London, Royal Courts of Justice, BT Tower) have participated in the past; the full program becomes available in August. Maggie's Culture Crawl, an architectural night walking tour, wends its way through the city over the same weekend. **Open City** (☎020-3006 7008; www.open-city.org.uk; tours £24.50-35.50) offers architect-led tours year-round.

of the Mall and the western end of The Strand. Nash refashioned the old Buckingham House into Buckingham Palace (1830) for George IV.

Nash's contemporary John Soane (1753–1837) was the architect of the Bank of England, completed in 1833 (though much of his work was lost during the bank's rebuilding by Herbert Baker during 1925–39), as well as the Dulwich Picture Gallery (1814). Robert Smirke (1780–1867) designed the British Museum in 1823; it's one of the finest expressions of the so-called Greek Revivalist style.

A 'Gothick' Rethink

In the 19th century the highly decorative neo-Gothic style, also known as Victorian High Gothic or 'Gothick', became all the vogue. Champions were the architects George Gilbert Scott (1811–78), Alfred Waterhouse (1830–1905) and Augustus Pugin (1812–52). Scott was responsible for the elaborate Albert Memorial (1872) in Kensington Gardens and the 1872 Midland Grand Hotel (later St Pancras Chambers and now once again a hotel). Waterhouse designed the flamboyant Natural History Museum (1881), while Pugin worked from 1840 with the designer Charles Barry (1795–1860) on the Houses of Parliament after the Palace of Westminster burned down in 1834. The last great neo-Gothic public building to go up in London was the Royal Courts of Justice (1882), designed by George Edmund Street.

The emphasis on the artisanship and materials necessary to create these elaborate neo-Gothic buildings led to the so-called Arts and Crafts movement of which William Morris (1834–96) was the leading exponent. Morris' work can be seen in the Green Dining Room of the Victoria & Albert Museum and his Red House in Bexleyheath.

Flirting with Modernism

Relatively few notable public buildings emerged from the first 15 years of the 20th century, apart from Admiralty Arch (1910) in the Edwardian baroque style of Aston Webb (1849–1930), who also designed the 1911 Queen Victoria Memorial in front of Buckingham Palace. County Hall, designed by Ralph Knott in 1909, was not completed until 1922. More modern imagination is evident in commercial design, for example the superb art-nouveau design of Michelin House on Fulham Rd, dating from 1911.

In the period between the two World Wars, English architecture was barely more creative, though Edwin Lutyens (1869–1944) designed the Cenotaph (1920) in Whitehall as well as the impressive 1927 Britannic House, now with modern additions and called Alphabeta, in Moorgate. Displaying the same amount of Edwardian optimism is the former Port of London Authority (1922) designed by Edwin Cooper and now an apartment block and hotel.

Designed by US architect Harvey Wiley Corbett (1873–1954), Bush House, at the southern end of Kingsway and until recently the home of the BBC World Service, was built between 1923 and 1935. The delicious curves of the Daily Express Building (1932, Ellis Clarke with Owen Williams) at 120 Fleet St are a splendid example of art deco grace. Two other art deco classics are St Olaf House, an office block on Tooley St and fronting the Thames designed by HS Goodhart-Rendel in 1928, and 55 Broadway (1929), a listed block above St James's tube station designed by Charles Holden and headquarters of London Underground until 2015.

Postwar Reconstruction

Hitler's bombs during WWII wrought the worst destruction on London since the Great Fire of 1666 and the immediate postwar problem was

Situated above St James's Underground station, 55 Broadway was highly controversial when it opened in 1929, not the least for its pair of sculptures *Day* and *Night* by Jacob Epstein. The generous anatomy of the figures caused an outcry and Epstein had to snip 4cm from the penis of the smaller figure, *Day*.

a chronic housing shortage. Low-cost developments and ugly high-rise housing were thrown up on bomb sites and many of these blocks still scar the horizon today.

The Royal Festival Hall, designed by Robert Matthew (1906–75) and J Leslie Martin (1908–99) for the 1951 Festival of Britain, attracted as many bouquets as brickbats when it opened as London's first major public building in the modernist style. Even today, hardly anyone seems to have a good word to say about the neighbouring National Theatre, a brutalist structure by Denys Lasdun (1914–2001) begun in 1966 and finished a decade later.

The 1960s saw the ascendancy of the workaday glass-and-concrete high-rises exemplified by the mostly unloved Centre Point (1967) by Richard Seifert (1910–2001). But the once-vilified modernist tower has now been listed by English Heritage, meaning that it cannot be altered for the most part. The 1964 BT Tower, formerly known as the Post Office Tower and designed by Eric Bedford (1909–2001), has also received listed status.

Little building was undertaken in the 1970s apart from roads, and the recession of the late 1980s and early 1990s brought much development and speculation to a standstill. Helping to polarise traditionalists and modernists still further was Prince Charles, who described a proposed (and never built) extension to the National Gallery as being like 'a monstrous carbuncle on the face of an elegant and much loved friend'.

London's smallest house – 3ft wide at its narrowest point – is 10 Hyde Park Pl, now part of Tyburn Convent. Despite being such a small target, it was damaged by a German bomb during WWII.

Postmodernism Lands

London's contemporary architecture was born in the City and the revitalised Docklands in the mid-1980s. The City's centrepiece was the 1986 Lloyd's of London, Richard Rogers' 'inside-out' masterpiece of ducts, pipes, glass and stainless steel. Taking pride of place in the Docklands was Cesar Pelli's 244m-high One Canada Sq (1991), commonly known as Canary Wharf and easily visible from central London. But London's very first postmodern building (designed in the late 1980s by James Stirling but not completed until 1998) is considered to be No 1 Poultry, a playful shiplike City landmark faced with yellow and pink limestone. The graceful British Library (Colin St John Wilson, 1998), with its warm red-brick exterior and wonderfully bright interior, initially met a very hostile reception but has now become a popular landmark.

At the end of the 1990s, attention turned to public buildings, including several new landmarks. From the disused Bankside Power Station (Giles Gilbert Scott, 1947–1963), the Tate Modern (Herzog & de Meuron, 1999) was refashioned as an art gallery that scooped international architecture's most prestigious prize, the Pritzker. The stunning Millennium Bridge (Norman Foster and Anthony Caro, 2000), the first new bridge to cross the Thames in central London since Tower Bridge went up in 1894, is much loved and much used. Even the white-elephant Millennium Dome (Richard Rogers), the class dunce of 2000, won a new lease of life as the O2 concert and sports hall.

For a good look at how London's built environment looks and will look in future visit New London Architecture (and don't miss the ever-updated scale model).

Today & Tomorrow

Early in the millennium such structures as the 2002 glass 'egg' of City Hall and the ever-popular, ever-present 2003-built 30 St Mary Axe – or 'the Gherkin' – gave the city the confidence to continue planning more heady buildings.

By the middle of the noughties London's biggest urban development project ever was under way: the 200-hectare Olympic Park in the Lea River Valley near Stratford, where most of the events of the 2012 Summer Olympics and Paralympics would take place. But the park would offer few architectural surprises, with the exception of of Zaha Hadid's stunning

BROKEN GLASS & RAZOR SHARP

Londoners have a predilection for nicknaming new towers – whether built or planned – and many of them go on to replace the original name. Here are some of the popular ones, inspired, of course, by the building's shape and form:

→ **Hubble-Bubble** (p221) A shisha, or water pipe, is what Mayor Boris Johnson imagined the 115m-tall tangle-of-metal called the ArcelorMittal Orbit, the centrepiece of the Olympic Park, to be when he first saw it.

→ **Cheese Grater** (Leadenhall Building; 122 Leadenhall St, EC3) Finally opening in mid-2014, this recession-delayed 48-storey, 225m-tall tower in the form of a stepped wedge faces architect Richard Rogers' other icon, the Lloyd's of London building.

→ **Gherkin** (p146) The 180m-tall bullet-shaped tower that seems to pop up at every turn has also been known as the Swiss Re Tower (after its first major tenants), Cockfosters (after its architect, Norman Foster), the exotic (or erotic) pickle, the suppository etc.

→ **Shard** (p164) This needle-like 87-storey tower by Italian architect Renzo Piano (who originally dismissed tall buildings as 'statements of arrogance') is one mother of a splinter you wouldn't want to tussle with. At 310m, it is the EU's tallest building. Views from the top floors are awesome.

→ **Stealth Bomber** (p135) French architect Jean Nouvel's office block and shopping mall next to St Paul's was built to bring new life to the City, especially at weekends. Its nickname, only occasionally used, comes from its distinctive low-slung design.

→ **Walkie Talkie** (p147) This 37-storey, 160m-tall tower bulges in and bulges out, vaguely resembling an old-fashioned walkie talkie. It's probably the least popular new building from the outside as it dominates the skyline.

→ **Razor** (Strata; 8 Walworth Rd, SE1) This 43-storey, turbine-topped tower (officially the Strata building) rising 148m over Elephant & Castle in South London, resembles an electric razor. It's one of the tallest residential buildings in London.

Aquatics Centre and the ArcelorMittal Orbit, a zany public work of art with viewing platforms designed by the sculptor Anish Kapoor.

Although the 2008 recession undermined for several years what was the most ambitious building program in London since WWII, an improved economic climate at the start of the following decade saw those buildings under construction completed and 'holes in the ground' filled in with the start of new structures.

Topped out in 2010 were the 230m-tall Heron Tower in the City, then London's third-tallest building, and the very distinctive Strata (148m) south of the river with three wind turbines embedded in its roof. But nothing could compare with the so-called Shard, at 310m the EU's tallest building, completed in 2012. The glass-clad upturned icicle, dramatically poking into Borough skies and visible from across London, houses offices, apartments, a five-star hotel, restaurants and, on the 72nd floor, London's highest public viewing gallery. Not as high but twice as pleasant are the restaurants and cafe-bar in the jungle-like Sky Garden on levels 35 to 37 of the newly redeemed building called the Walkie Talkie.

Economic recovery in the middle of the 21st century's second decade and the rise in population largely through immigration sparked a building boom unseen since the reconstruction of London after WWII. Indeed, at the time of writing some 230 buildings of more than 20 storeys were in the pipeline. South London, in particular, is or will soon be one giant building site, especially around Blackfriars (52-storey One Blackfriars, Ian Simpson), Vauxhall (50-storey Vauxhall Square, Allies & Morrison) and Nine Elms (twin-towered One Nine Elms, Kohn Pedersen Fox). Brave new world or 'Gotham City' on the wrong side of the pond? Only time will tell.

Literary London

For more than six centuries, London has been the setting for works of prose. Indeed, the capital has been the inspiration for the masterful imaginations of such eminent wordsmiths as Shakespeare, Defoe, Dickens, Thackeray, Wells, Orwell, Conrad, Eliot, Greene and Woolf (even though not all were native to the city, or even British).

The Middle Ages & Renaissance

It's hard to reconcile the bawdy portrayal of London in Geoffrey Chaucer's *Canterbury Tales* with Charles Dickens' bleak hellhole in *Oliver Twist*, let alone Daniel Defoe's plague-ravaged metropolis in *Journal of the Plague Year* with Zadie Smith's multi-ethnic romp *White Teeth*. Ever-changing, yet somehow eerily consistent, London has left its mark on some of the most influential writing in the English language.

Chaucerian London

The first literary reference to London appears in Chaucer's *Canterbury Tales,* written between 1387 and 1400: the 29 pilgrims of the tale gather for their trip to Canterbury at the Tabard Inn in Talbot Yard, Southwark, and agree to share stories on the way there and back. The inn burned down in 1676; a blue plaque marks the site of the building today.

Shakespearian London

Born in Warwickshire, William Shakespeare spent most of his life as an actor and playwright in London around the turn of the 17th century. He trod the boards of several theatres in Shoreditch and Southwark and wrote his greatest tragedies, among them *Hamlet, Othello, Macbeth* and *King Lear,* for the original Globe theatre on the South Bank. Although London was his home for most of his life, Shakespeare set nearly all his plays in foreign or imaginary lands. Only *Henry IV: Parts I & II* include a London setting – a tavern called the Boar's Head in Eastcheap.

18th-Century London

Daniel Defoe was perhaps the first true London writer, both living in and writing about the city during the early 18th century. He is most famous for his novels *Robinson Crusoe* (1719–20) and *Moll Flanders* (1722), which he wrote while living in Church St in Stoke Newington. Defoe's *Journal of the Plague Year* is his most absorbing account of London life, documenting the horrors of the Great Plague during the summer and autumn of 1665, when the author was a young child.

Dickensian & 19th-Century London

Two early 19th-century Romantic poets drew inspiration from London. John Keats, born above a Moorgate public house in 1795, wrote 'Ode to a Nightingale' while living near Hampstead Heath in 1819 and 'Ode on a Grecian Urn' reportedly after viewing the Parthenon frieze in the British Museum the same year. William Wordsworth discovered

> Built in 1567, the half-timbered Old Curiosity Shop (13–14 Portsmouth St, WC2) may have been the inspiration for Charles Dickens' eponymous novel. His close friend and biographer, John Forster, did live at nearby 57–58 Lincoln's Inn Fields.

THE BLUE PLAQUES SCHEME

You won't be in London long before you'll start noticing round, very blue plaques placed outside various buildings, which identify them as the homes or workplaces of the great and the talented. The very first plaque was put up in 1867, identifying the birthplace of the poet Lord Byron at 24 Holles St, W1, off Cavendish Sq. Since then a large percentage – some 25% of the 850 in place – have honoured writers and poets. These include everything from the offices of publisher Faber & Faber at 24 Russell Sq, where TS Eliot worked, to the Primrose Hill residence of Irish poet and playwright WB Yeats at 23 Fitzroy Rd, NW1 (where, incidentally, the US poet Sylvia Plath committed suicide in 1963). The minimum requirements for selection are that candidates must have been dead for at least two decades or have been born 100 years before, and be known to the 'well-informed passer-by'.

inspiration for the poem 'Upon Westminster Bridge' while visiting London in 1802.

Charles Dickens was the definitive London author. When his father and family were interned at Marshalsea Prison in Southwark for not paying their debts, the 12-year-old Charles was forced to fend for himself on the streets. That grim period provided a font of experiences on which to draw. His novels most closely associated with London are *Oliver Twist,* with its gang of thieves led by Fagin in Clerkenwell, and *Little Dorrit,* whose hero was born in the Marshalsea. The house in Bloomsbury where he wrote *Oliver Twist* and two other novels now houses the expanded Charles Dickens Museum (p99).

Sir Arthur Conan Doyle (1858–1930) portrayed a very different London, his pipe-smoking, cocaine-snorting sleuth, Sherlock Holmes, coming to exemplify a cool and unflappable Englishness. Letters to the mythical hero and his admiring friend, Dr Watson, still arrive at 221b Baker St, where there's a museum to everyone's favourite Victorian detective (p110).

London at the end of the 19th century appears in many books, but especially those of Somerset Maugham. His first novel, *Liza of Lambeth,* was based on his experiences as an intern in the slums of South London, while *Of Human Bondage* provides a portrait of late-Victorian London.

Top Literary Sites

Shakespeare's Globe

Charles Dickens Museum

Keats House

Carlyle's House

Sherlock Holmes Museum

British Library

20th-Century Writing

American Writers & London

Of the Americans who wrote about London at the turn of the century, Henry James, who settled here, stands supreme with his *Daisy Miller* and *The Europeans. The People of the Abyss,* by socialist writer Jack London, is a sensitive portrait of poverty and despair in the East End. St Louis–born TS Eliot moved to London in 1915, where he published his poem 'The Love Song of J Alfred Prufrock' almost immediately and moved on to his ground-breaking epic 'The Waste Land', in which London is portrayed as an 'unreal city'.

Interwar Developments

Between the World Wars, PG Wodehouse depicted London high life with his hilarious lampooning of the English upper classes in the Jeeves stories. Quentin Crisp, the self-proclaimed 'stately homo of England', provided the flipside, recounting in his ribald and witty memoir *The Naked Civil Servant* what it was like to be openly gay in sexually repressed pre-war London. George Orwell's experience of living as a beggar in London's East End coloured his book *Down and Out in Paris and London* (1933).

The Modern Age

The End of the Affair, Graham Greene's novel chronicling a passionate and doomed romance, takes place in and around Clapham Common just after WWII, while *The Heat of the Day* is Elizabeth Bowen's sensitive, if melodramatic, account of living through the Blitz.

Colin MacInnes described the bohemian, multicultural world of 1950s Notting Hill in *Absolute Beginners,* while Doris Lessing captured the political mood of 1960s London in *The Four-Gated City,* the last of her five-book *Children of Violence* series. She also provided some of the funniest and most vicious portrayals of 1990s London in *London Observed.* Nick Hornby, nostalgic about his days as a young football fan in *Fever Pitch* and obsessive about vinyl in *High Fidelity,* found himself the voice of a generation.

Before it became fashionable, Hanif Kureishi explored London from the perspective of ethnic minorities, specifically young Pakistanis, in his best-known novels *The Black Album* and *The Buddha of Suburbia.* He also wrote the screenplay for the groundbreaking film *My Beautiful Laundrette.* Author and playwright Caryl Phillips won plaudits for his description of the Caribbean immigrant's experience in *The Final Passage,* while Timothy Mo's *Sour Sweet* is a poignant and humorous account of a Chinese family in the 1960s trying to adjust to English life.

The decades leading up to the turn of the millennium were great ones for British literature, bringing a dazzling new generation of writers to the fore. Martin Amis *(Money, London Fields),* Julian Barnes *(Metroland, Talking it Over),* Ian McEwan *(Enduring Love, Atonement),* Salman Rushdie *(Midnight's Children, The Satanic Verses),* AS Byatt *(Possession, Angels & Insects)* and Alan Hollinghurst *(The Swimming Pool Library, The Line of Beauty)* all need little introduction to keen readers.

The sternly modernist Senate House (1937) on Malet St in Bloomsbury contained offices of the Ministry of Information, where George Orwell worked during WWII. It is thought to have been the inspiration for the Ministry of Truth in his classic dystopian 1949 novel *Nineteen Eighty-Four.*

LITERARY LONDON 20TH-CENTURY WRITING

LITERARY READINGS, TALKS & EVENTS

To catch established and budding authors, attend the monthly **Book Slam** (www. bookslam.com; admission £6; ⊙from 6.30pm last Thu of month) – 'London's leading literary shindig' – usually held from 6.30pm on the last Thursday of the month at various clubs around London. Guests have included Nick Hornby, Hanif Kureishi and Will Self, and the event features readings, poetry, comedy and even live music. Check the website for dates and venues.

Covent Garden's **Poetry Café** (☑020-7420 9888; www.poetrysociety.org.uk; 22 Betterton St, WC2; ⊙11am-11pm Mon-Fri, from 7pm Sat; ◉Covent Garden) is a favourite for lovers of verse, with almost daily readings and performances by established poets, open-mic evenings and writing workshops.

Both the **British Library** (p232) and the **Institute of Contemporary Arts** (p102) have excellent talks and lectures every month, with well-known writers from all spectrums.

Bookshops, particularly **Waterstones** (www.waterstones.com), **Foyles** (p127) and the **London Review Bookshop** (p127), often stage readings. Some major authors also now appear at the **Southbank Centre** (p171). Many such events are organised on an ad-hoc basis, so keep an eye on the listings in the freebie *Time Out* or any of the weekend newspaper supplements, including the *Guardian Guide* distributed with Saturday's paper.

Millenium London

Helen Fielding's *Bridget Jones's Diary* and its sequel, *Bridget Jones: The Edge of Reason*, launched the 'chick lit' genre, one that transcended the travails of a young single Londoner to become a worldwide phenomenon. *Enfant terrible* and incisive social commentator Will Self's *Grey Area* is a superb collection of short stories focusing on skewed and surreal aspects of the city. *The Book of Dave* is his hilarious story of a bitter, present-day London cabbie burying a book of his observations, which are later discovered and regarded as scripture by the people on the island of Ham (Britain in the distant future is an archipelago due to rising sea levels).

Peter Ackroyd names the city as the love of his life. *London: the Biography* is his inexhaustible paean to the capital, while *The Clerkenwell Tales* brings to life the 14th-century London of Chaucer, and his more recent *The Canterbury Tales: A Retelling* renders Chaucer's timeless tales in lucid, compelling modern English. *Thames: Sacred River* is Ackroyd's fine monument to the muck, magic and mystery of the river through history.

Iain Sinclair is the bard of Hackney, who, like Ackroyd, has spent his life obsessed with and fascinated by the capital. His acclaimed and ambitious *London Orbital,* a journey on foot around the M25, London's mammoth motorway bypass, is required London reading, while *Hackney, That Rose-Red Empire* is an exploration of what was once one of London's most notorious boroughs and is now increasingly trendy.

A larger-than-life statue of John Betjeman gazing up in wonder above the departures hall at St Pancras International Station recalls the former poet laureate's campaign in the 1960s to save the Victorian High Gothic structure.

Current Scene

Home to most of the UK's major publishers and its best bookshops, London remains a vibrant place for writers and readers alike. But the frustrating predominance of several powerful corporations within publishing can occasionally limit pioneering writing.

This state of affairs has, however, stimulated an exciting literary fringe, which, although tiny, is very active and passionate about good writing. London still has many small presses where quality and innovation are prized over public relations skills, and events kick off in bookshops and in the back rooms of pubs throughout the week.

Back in the mainstream, the big guns of the 1980s, such as Martin Amis, Ian McEwan, Salman Rushdie and Julian Barnes, are still going strong, although new voices have broken through in the last decade – indeed, there have been some outstanding new London writers in recent years, from Monica Ali, who brought the East End to life in *Brick Lane,* and Zadie Smith, whose *NW* was shortlisted for the Women's Prize for Fiction in 2013, to Jake Arnott's intelligent Soho-based gangster yarn *The Long Firm* and Gautam Malkani's much-hyped *Londonstani.*

'Rediscovered' author Howard Jacobson, variously called the 'Jewish Jane Austen' and the 'English Philip Roth' won the Man Booker Prize in 2010 for *The Finkler Question,* the first time the prestigious award had gone to a comic novel in a quarter of a century. Literary titan and huge commercial success Hilary Mantel, author of *Wolf Hall,* won the same award for her historical novel *Bring up the Bodies* two years later.

Every bookshop in town has a London section, where you will find many of these titles and lots more.

Literary Pubs

George Inn (South Bank)

Museum Tavern (West End)

French House (West End)

Prospect of Whitby (East End & Docklands)

Dove (Notting Hill & West London)

Fitzroy Tavern (West End)

Theatre & Dance

London has more theatrical history than almost anywhere else in the world, and it's still being made nightly on the stages of the West End, the South Bank and the vast London fringe. No visit to the city is complete without taking in a show, and a mere evening walk amongst the theatre-going throngs in the West End is an electrifying experience. If dance tops your list, take your pick from the capital's various and varied world-class companies.

Theatre
Dramatic History

Elizabethan Period

Very little is known about London theatre before the Elizabethan period, when a series of 'playhouses', including the Globe, were built on the south bank of the Thames and in Shoreditch. Although the playwrights of the time – Shakespeare, Christopher Marlowe (*Doctor Faustus, Edward II*) and Shakespeare's great rival, Ben Jonson (*Volpone, The Alchemist*) – are now considered timeless intellectual geniuses, theatre then was a raucous popular entertainment, where the crowd drank and heckled the actors. The Puritans responded by shutting the playhouses down after the Civil War in 1642.

Restoration

Three years after the return of the monarchy in 1660, the first famous Drury Lane theatre was built and the period of 'restoration theatre' began, under the patronage of the rakish Charles II. Borrowing influences from Italian and French theatre, Restoration theatre incorporated drama (such as John Dryden's *All For Love*, 1677) and comedy. The first female actors appeared (in Elizabethan times men played female roles), and Charles II is recorded as having had an affair with at least one, Nell Gwyn.

Victorian Period

Despite the success of John Gay's *The Beggar's Opera* (1728), Oliver Goldsmith's farce *She Stoops to Conquer* (1773) and Richard Sheridan's *The Rivals* and *The School for Scandal* (also in the 1770s) at Drury Lane, popular music halls replaced serious theatre during the Victorian era. Light comic operetta, as defined by Gilbert and Sullivan (*HMS Pinafore, The Pirates of Penzance, The Mikado*), was all the rage. A sea change only arose with the emergence at the end of the 19th century of such compelling playwrights as Oscar Wilde (*An Ideal Husband, The Importance of Being Earnest*) and George Bernard Shaw (*Pygmalion*).

The 20th Century

Comic wits, including Noël Coward (*Private Lives, Brief Encounter*), and earnest dramatists, such as Terence Rattigan (*The Winslow Boy, The Browning Version*) and JB Priestley (*An Inspector Calls*), followed.

London's Best Theatres

Shakespeare's Globe (South Bank)

National Theatre (South Bank)

Old Vic (South Bank)

Donmar Warehouse (West End)

Royal Court Theatre (Kensington & Hyde Park)

Young Vic (South Bank)

Regent's Park Open Air Theatre (Camden & North London)

Barbican (The City)

Bush Theatre (West London)

Hampstead Theatre (North London)

However, it wasn't until the 1950s and 1960s that English drama yet again experienced such a fertile period as the Elizabethan era.

Perfectly encapsulating the social upheaval of the period, John Osborne's *Look Back in Anger* at the Royal Court Theatre in 1956 heralded a rash of new writing, including Harold Pinter's *The Homecoming*, Joe Orton's *Loot*, Tom Stoppard's *Rosencrantz and Guildenstern are Dead* and Alan Ayckbourn's *How the Other Half Loves*. During the same period many of today's leading theatre companies were formed, including the National Theatre.

Though somewhat eclipsed by the National Theatre, today's Royal Court Theatre (p194) retains a fine tradition of new writing. In the past decade it has nurtured such talented playwrights as Jez Butterworth *(Mojo, The Night Heron)*, Ayub Khan-Din *(East Is East)*, Conor McPherson *(The Weir, Shining City)* and Joe Penhall *(Dumb Show)*.

Current Scene

London remains a thrilling place for theatre lovers. Nowhere else, with the possible exception of New York, offers such a diversity of high-quality drama, first-rate musical theatre and such a sizzling fringe. Whether it's Hollywood A-listers gracing tiny stages and earning Equity minimum for their efforts, or lavish West End musicals, London remains an undisputed theatrical world leader and innovator.

West End & Off West End

While the West End's 'Theatreland' gets most of the attention, some of London's hottest theatre tickets are for a trio of innovative venues south of the river: the National Theatre (p171), the Old Vic (p172) and the Young Vic (p172). Other innovative off–West End theatres include the Royal Court Theatre (p194) in Chelsea, the Bush Theatre (p266) in Shepherd's Bush and the Hampstead Theatre (p252). Many successful off–West End plays eventually make their way to the West End for a longer theatrical run.

In recent years, the mainstream West End has re-established its credentials, with extraordinary hits by the likes of Donmar Warehouse (p126), while the smarter end of the fringe continues to shine with risky, controversial and newsworthy productions.

Big names can often be seen treading Theatreland's hallowed boards – think Bradley Cooper playing *The Elephant Man* at the Haymarket Theatre Royal, Helen Mirren followed by Kristen Scott Thomas playing the Queen in *The Audience* at the Apollo Shaftesbury, or Imelda Staunton belting it out in *Gypsy* at the Savoy Theatre.

There's something for all dramatic tastes in London, from contemporary political satire to creative reworking of old classics, and all shades in between. Recent productions that have won critical acclaim include the children's musical *Matilda*, the adaptation of Mark Haddon's novel *The Curious Incident of the Dog in the Night-Time*, Sam Mendes' version of *Charlie and the Chocolate Factory*, and *Sunny Afternoon*, based on the life of Ray Davies from the Kinks.

Shakespearean Offerings

Shakespeare's legacy is generously honoured on the city's stages, most notably by the Royal Shakespeare Company (RSC) and at the Globe theatre. The RSC stages one or two of the bard's plays in London annually, although it has no London home (its productions are based in Stratford-upon-Avon and usually transfer to the capital later in their run).

Shakespeare's Globe (p171) on the South Bank attempts to re-create an Elizabethan open-air theatre experience. Its new indoor Sam Wa-

If innovation and change are too much for you, drop by St Martin's Theatre, where the same production of *The Mousetrap* has been running since 1952! Or there's the monolithic musicals that show no sign of letting up anytime soon: *Phantom of the Opera, Les Miserables, Billy Elliot* et al.

namaker Playhouse is a unique place to savour Shakespeare's words, with an intimate candle-lit atmosphere. Shakespeare's plays remain at the core of the Globe's programming, but other classic and contemporary plays do get a look-in.

Children's Theatre

If you've got junior culture vultures in tow, make sure to scan the theatre listings for kid-friendly West End smashes such as *Matilda* and *Charlie and the Chocolate Factory*, both of which just happen to be adaptations of books by Roald Dahl.

It's also worth checking out what's on at the **Little Angel Theatre** (www.littleangeltheatre.com) in Islington, which specialises in puppetry, and the **Unicorn Theatre** (www.unicorntheatre.com) in Southwark, which stages productions for infants, children and young adults.

Dance

Whether contemporary, classical or crossover, London will have the right moves for you. As one of the world's great dance capitals, London's artistic environment has long created and attracted talented choreographers with both the inspiration and aspiration to fashion innovative productions.

London's most celebrated choreographer is award-winning Matthew Bourne (*Play Without Words, Edward Scissorhands, Dorian Gray, Oliver!, Cinderella,* an all-male *Swan Lake*), who has been repeatedly showered with praise for his reworking of classics. Another leading London-based talent is Wayne McGregor, who worked as movement director on *Harry Potter and the Goblet of Fire* and is a Professor of Choreography at the acclaimed Trinity Laban Conservatoire of Music and Dance in Greenwich.

The Place in Bloomsbury was the original birthplace of modern British dance and is the home of the edgy Richard Alston Dance Company. The revamped Sadler's Wells (p210) – the birthplace of English classical ballet in the 19th century – continues to deliver exciting programming covering many styles of dance. Its roster of 16 'associate artists' include such luminaries as Matthew Bourne, Russell Maliphant, Sidi Larbi Cherkaoui, Wayne McGregor, Crystal Pite, Nitin Sawhney, Christopher Wheeldon and Sylvie Guillem.

Covent Garden's Royal Opera House (p124) is the impressive home of London's leading classical-dance troupe, the world-famous Royal Ballet. The company largely sticks to the traditional, but more contemporary influences occasionally seep into productions. Contemporary fairytale *Raven Girl* was a 2013 collaboration between Wayne McGregor and Audrey Niffenegger, author of the award-winning novel *The Time Traveler's Wife*.

One of the world's best companies, the **English National Ballet** (www. ballet.org.uk), is a touring ballet company. You may be fortunate enough to catch it at one of its various venues in London – principally at the London Coliseum.

For more cutting-edge work, the innovative **Rambert Dance Company** (☎020-8630 0600; www.rambert.org.uk) is the UK's foremost contemporary dance troupe. It is arguably the most creative force in UK dance and its autumn 2013 move from Chiswick to purpose-built premises in Doon St (behind the National Theatre) in the far more creative milieu of the South Bank has made it that much more accessible.

Another important venue for experimental dance is the Barbican (p155), which is particularly good at presenting new works exploring the intersection of dance, theatre and music.

Even if you've heard that a hot new play is completely sold out for months ahead, its often possible to secure a ticket via standby lists and the like. See our Entertainment overview (p56) for tips on securing hard-to-get or discounted tickets.

THEATRE & DANCE DANCE

Consult London's *Time Out* for weekly theatrical listings.

Art & Fashion

When it comes to both visual art and fashion, London has traditionally been overshadowed by other European capitals. Yet many of history's greatest artists have spent time in London, including the likes of Monet and Van Gogh, and in terms of contemporary art and cutting-edge street fashion, there's a compelling argument for putting London at the very top of the European pack.

Art

Holbein to Turner

It wasn't until the rule of the Tudors that art began to take off in London. The German Hans Holbein the Younger (1497–1543) was court painter to Henry VIII, and one of his finest works, *The Ambassadors* (1533), hangs in the National Gallery. A batch of great portrait artists worked at court during the 17th century, the best being Anthony Van Dyck (1599–1641), who painted *Charles I on Horseback* (1638), also in the National Gallery. Charles I was a keen collector and it was during his reign that the Raphael Cartoons, now in the Victoria & Albert Museum, came to London.

Local artists began to emerge in the 18th century, including landscapist Thomas Gainsborough (1727–88); William Hogarth (1697–1764), whose much-reproduced social commentary, *A Rake's Progress* (1733), hangs in Sir John Soane's Museum; and poet, engraver and watercolourist William Blake (1757–1827). A superior visual artist to Blake, John Constable (1776–1837) studied the clouds and skies above Hampstead Heath, sketching hundreds of scenes that he'd later match with subjects in his landscapes.

JMW Turner (1775–1851), equally at home with oils and watercolours, represented the pinnacle of 19th-century British art. Through innovative use of colour and gradations of light he created a new atmosphere that seemed to capture the wonder, sublimity and terror of nature. His later works, including *Snow Storm – Steam-boat off a Harbour's Mouth* (1842), *Peace – Burial at Sea* (1842) and *Rain, Steam and Speed – the Great Western Railway* (1844), now in the Tate Britain and the National Gallery, were increasingly abstract, and although widely vilified at the time, later inspired the Impressionist works of Claude Monet.

Popular art classes are held at the Dulwich Picture Gallery and other museums and galleries around London.

The Pre-Raphaelites to Hockney

The brief but splendid flowering of the Pre-Raphaelite Brotherhood (1848–54) took its inspiration from the Romantic poets, abandoning the pastel-coloured rusticity of the day in favour of big, bright and intense depictions of medieval legends and female beauty. The movement's main proponents were William Holman Hunt, John Everett Millais and Dante Gabriel Rossetti; artists Edward Burne-Jones and Ford Madox Brown were also strongly associated with the movement. The Pre-Raphaelites are well represented at Tate Britain, with highlights including Millais' *Mariana* (1851) and *Ophelia* (1851–52), Rossetti's *Ecce*

Ancilla Domini! (The Annunciation, 1849–50) and John William Waterhouse's *The Lady of Shalott* (1888).

In the early 20th century, cubism and futurism helped generate the short-lived Vorticists, a modernist group of London artists and poets, centred on the dapper Wyndham Lewis (1882–1957), that sought to capture dynamism in artistic form. Sculptors Henry Moore (1898–1986) and Barbara Hepworth (1903–1975) both typified the modernist movement in British sculpture (you can see examples of their work in the grounds of Kenwood in Hampstead Heath).

After WWII, art transformed yet again. In 1945, the tortured, Irish-born painter Francis Bacon (1909–92) caused a stir when he exhibited his *Three Studies for Figures at the Base of a Crucifixion* – now on display at the Tate Britain – and afterwards continued to spook the art world with his repulsive yet mesmerising visions. Also at the Tate Britain is Bacon's *Triptych – August 1972*, painted in the aftermath of his partner George Dyer's suicide.

Australian art critic Robert Hughes once eulogised Bacon's contemporary, Lucian Freud (1922–2011), as 'the greatest living realist painter'. Freud's early work was often surrealist, but from the 1950s the bohemian Freud exclusively focused on pale, muted portraits – often nudes, and frequently of friends and family (although he has also painted the Queen).

Also prominent in the 1950s was painter and collage artist Richard Hamilton (1922–2011) whose work includes the cover design of the Beatles self-titled 1968 album (the legendary 'White Album'). London in the swinging 1960s was perfectly encapsulated by pop art, its vocabulary best articulated by the brilliant David Hockney (b 1937). Hockney gained a reputation as one of the leading pop artists (although he rejected the label) through his early use of magazine-style images, but after a move to California, his work became increasingly naturalistic. Two of his most famous works, *Mr and Mrs Clark and Percy* (1971) and *A Bigger Splash* (1974), are displayed at the Tate Britain.

Gilbert & George were quintessential English conceptual artists of the 1960s. The Spitalfields odd couple are still at the heart of the British art world, having now become a part of the establishment. In recent years they've been awarded honorary doctorates by East London, Plymouth and the Open University.

Brit Art

Despite its incredibly rich collections, Britain had never led, dominated or even really participated in a particular artistic epoch or style. That all changed in the twilight of the 20th century, when 1990s London became the beating heart of the art world.

Brit Art sprang from a show called *Freeze*, which was staged in a Docklands warehouse in 1988, organised by artist and showman Damien Hirst and largely featuring his fellow graduates from Goldsmiths' College. Influenced by pop culture and punk, this loose movement was soon catapulted to notoriety by the advertising guru Charles Saatchi, who bought an extraordinary number of works and came to dominate the scene.

Brit Art was brash, decadent, ironic, easy to grasp and eminently marketable. Hirst chipped in with a cow sliced into sections and preserved in formaldehyde; flies buzzed around another cow's head and were zapped in his early work *A Thousand Years*. Chris Ofili provoked with *The Holy Virgin Mary,* a painting of the black Madonna made partly with elephant manure; brothers Jake and Dinos Chapman produced mannequins of children with genitalia on their heads; and

---

London's Greatest Paintings

Self-Portrait with Two Circles, by Rembrandt van Rijn (1665, Kenwood House)

················

Fighting Temeraire, by JMW Turner (1839, National Gallery)

················

A Bar at the Folies-Bergère, by Edouard Manet (1882, Courtauld Gallery)

················

Sunflowers, by Vincent Van Gogh (1888, National Gallery)

················

Three Studies for Figures at the Base of a Crucifixion, by Sir Francis Bacon (1945, Tate Britain)

················

The Seagram Murals, by Mark Rothko (1958, Tate Modern)

Since 1999, the Fourth Plinth Project (p105) in Trafalgar Sq has offered a platform for novel, and frequently controversial, works by contemporary artists.

LONDON ARTISTS TODAY

London continues to generate talent across a range of artistic media, keeping critics on their toes. These are some of the biggest-name artists working in contemporary London:

Antony Gormley This sculptor is best known for the 22m-high *Angel of the North*, beside the A1 trunk road near Gateshead in northern England.

Anish Kapoor An Indian-born sculptor working in London since the 1970s. His **ArcelorMittal Orbit** (p221) towers over Queen Elizabeth Olympic Park.

Marc Quinn *Self* is a sculpture of the artist's head made from his own frozen blood, which Quinn recasts every five years. It can be seen – in all its refrigerated glory – at the National Portrait Gallery.

Chantal Joffe This London-based artist is well known for her naive, expressionist portraits of women and children.

Laure Prouvost French-born but London-based Prouvost (p259) works mainly in film, collage and installation art.

Banksy The anonymous street artist whose work is a worldwide phenomenon probably hails from Bristol, but you'll find many of his most famous works on London's streets.

Marcus Harvey created a portrait of notorious child-killer Myra Hindley, made entirely with children's hand-prints, whose value skyrocketed when it was repeatedly vandalised with ink and eggs by the public.

The areas of Shoreditch, Hoxton, Spitalfields and Whitechapel – where many artists lived, worked and hung out – became the epicentre of the movement, and a rash of galleries moved in. For the 10 years or so that it rode a wave of publicity, the defining characteristics of Brit Art were notoriety and shock value. It's two biggest names, Damien Hirst and Tracey Emin, inevitably became celebrities.

Some critics argued the hugely hyped movement was the product of a cultural vacuum, an example of the emperor's new clothes, with people afraid to criticise the works for fear they'd look stupid.

Beyond Brit Art

On the fringes of Brit Art are a lot of less-stellar but equally inspiring artists exploring other directions. A highlight is Richard Wilson's memorable installation *20:50* (1987; now a permanent installation at the Saatchi Gallery) – a room filled waist-high with recycled oil. Entering down the walkway, you feel as if you've just been shot out into space. In Douglas Gordon's most famous work, *24 Hour Psycho* (1993), the Scottish video artist slowed Alfred Hitchcock's masterpiece so much it was stripped of its narrative and viewed more like a moving sculpture. Gary Hume first came to prominence with his *Doors* series: full-size paintings of hospital doors, which can be seen as powerful allegorical descriptions of despair – or just perfect reproductions of doors.

The biggest date on the art calendar is the controversial Turner Prize at the Tate Britain. Any British artist under the age of 50 is eligible to enter, although there is a strong preference for conceptual art.

The high point on the London fashion calendar is London Fashion Week (www.londonfashionweek.co.uk), held in February and September each year. The main venue is Somerset House.

Fashion

The British fashion industry has always been about younger, directional and more left-field designs. London fashion focuses on streetwear and the wow factor, with a few old reliables mingling with hot new designers, who are often unpolished through inexperience, but bursting with talent and creativity. As a result, London is exciting in a global sense and nobody with an interest in street fashion will be disappointed.

London's has weathered a tough decade economically that saw its status as an international fashion centre dip, but the city has returned to the heart of the fashion universe, boasting a bright new firmament of young stars.

London's Who's Who

The biggest names in London fashion are internationally famous and need little introduction. They include punk maven Vivienne Westwood, menswear designer Paul Smith and ethical fashionista Stella McCartney, who has transcended the connection to her famous father (former Beatle, Sir Paul) to become world famous in her own right. Born and living in London, McCartney was Team GB's Olympic creative director and in 2013 she was voted one of the UK's 100 most powerful women.

Other big international names include Christopher Bailey (chief creative at Burberry), Sarah Burton (royal wedding dress designer and creative director at Alexander McQueen) and Phoebe Philo (creative director at Céline).

With his witty designs and eclectic references, St Martin's graduate Giles Deacon took London fashion by storm with his own label, Giles. Gareth Pugh is also someone to look out for, another St Martin's alumnus who took the underground club fashions of Shoreditch and transposed them for the shop floor. Other Brit stars making a buzz are Erdem Moralıoğlu, Henry Holland, Jonathan Saunders and Christopher Kane.

London Fashion Abroad

The influence of London's designers continues to spread well beyond the capital. The 'British Fashion Pack' still work at, or run, many of the major Continental fashion houses. Houses such as Alexander McQueen retain design studios in London, and erstwhile defectors to foreign catwalks, such as Luella Bartley and Matthew Williamson, have returned to London to show their collections.

Fame & Celebrity

With its eccentricity when compared to the classic feel of the major Parisian and Milanese houses or the cool street-cred of New York designers, the London fashion spirit was best exemplified by Isabella Blow. This legendary stylist discovered Alexander McQueen, Stella Tennant and Sophie Dahl (among many others) during her career at *Vogue* and *Tatler*. Blow sadly committed suicide in 2007. A further shock for the industry was the tragic suicide of Alexander McQueen in 2010 at the age of 40.

British fashion's 'bad girl' Kate Moss has been in and out of the news since the start of her career – for both her sense of style and Top Shop clothes line and her off-runway antics. The fashion world thrives on notoriety but John Galliano's much-publicised arrest in 2011 for an anti-Semitic diatribe against a couple in a Paris cafe was a nadir for Dior's chief designer, who was consequently dropped by the fashion house. Despite these tragic losses and moments of scandal, London retains all the innovative ingredients for exhilarating developments in fashion, today and tomorrow.

Where to go for...

High street fashion Oxford St, Westfield Stratford City

New designers & hip boutiques Shoreditch, Spitalfields

Luxury brands Mayfair, Knightsbridge

Traditional men's tailoring Savile Row (Mayfair), Jermyn St (Piccadilly)

High-end department stores Knightsbridge, Piccadilly, Oxford St

Vintage Spitalfields, Camden Passage in Islington, Dalston

Rock, goth, punk & alternative looks Camden Town

Outlet stores Hackney

Gems & jewellery Hatton Garden

The Music Scene

Drawing upon a deep and often gritty reservoir of talent, London's modern music scene is one of the city's greatest sources of artistic power, and a magnet for bands and hopefuls from all musical hemispheres. Periodically a world leader in musical fashion and innovative soundscapes, London blends its homegrown talent with a continuous influx of styles and cultures, keeping currents flowing and inspiration percolating.

The Swinging '60s

At around the same time that the Beatles were laying down their first recordings with George Martin at Abbey Road Studios in St John's Wood, a group of London lads were stepping on stage together for the first time at the Marquee Club in Oxford St. An R&B band with frequent trajectories into blues and rock and roll, the Rolling Stones quickly set up as a more rough-edged counterpoint to the cleaner boy-next-door image of Liverpool's Fab Four.

In the musical explosion that followed, there was one band that chronicled London life no other. Hailing from Muswell Hill in North London, the Kinks started out with a garagy R&B sound not dissimilar to the Stones, but eventually began to incorporate elements of the Victorian music hall tradition into their music while liberally seeding their lyrics with London place names.

The Who, from West London, attracted attention to their brand of gritty rock by smashing guitars on stage, propelling TVs from hotel windows and driving cars into swimming pools. Struggling to be heard above the din was inspirational mod band the Small Faces, formed in 1965 in East London.

Jimi Hendrix came to London and took guitar playing to unseen heights before tragically dying in a flat in the Samarkand Hotel in Notting Hill in 1970. In some ways, the swinging '60s ended in July 1969 when the Stones famously staged their free concert in Hyde Park in front of more than 250,000 liberated fans.

London Songs – 1960s

Play With Fire (The Rolling Stones)

Eight Miles High (The Byrds)

The London Boys (David Bowie)

Waterloo Sunset (The Kinks)

The '70s

A local band called Tyrannosaurus Rex had enjoyed moderate success throughout the '60s. In 1970, they changed their name to T.Rex, frontman Marc Bolan donned a bit of glitter and the world's first 'glam' band had arrived. Glam encouraged the youth of uptight Britain to come out of the closet and be whatever they wanted to be. Baritone-voiced Brixton boy David Jones (aka David Bowie) then altered the rock landscape with his astonishing *The Rise and Fall of Ziggy Stardust and the Spiders from Mars* in 1972, one of the decade's seminal albums. Genre-spanning Roxy Music blended art rock and synth pop into a sophisticated glam sound.

Back at the rock face, a little band called Led Zeppelin (formed in 1968) were busy cultivating the roots of heavy metal. And 17-year-old Farok Bulsara changed his name to Freddie Mercury and led Queen to become one of the greatest rock-and-roll stars of all time. British-

London Songs – 1970s

Do the Strand (Roxy Music)

London Boys (T.Rex)

Baker Street (Gerry Rafferty)

(I Don't Want to Go to) Chelsea (Elvis Costello)

London Calling (The Clash)

American band Fleetwood Mac left blues for pop rock and stormed the charts in the US as well as in Britain; their landmark *Rumours* became the fifth-highest-selling album in history.

Punk's unexpected arrival kicked in the complacent mid-'70s commercial-rock edifice. Few saw it coming but none could miss it. The Sex Pistols were the most notorious of a wave of bands that began pogoing around London in 1976.

Fellow Londoners The Clash harnessed the raw anger of the time into a collar-grabbing brand of political protest that would see them outlast their peers, treading the fine line between angry punks and great songwriters. The disillusioned generation finally had a plan and a leader in frontman Joe Strummer; *London Calling* is a spirited call to arms.

Punk cleared the air and into the oxygen-rich atmosphere swarmed a gaggle of late '70s acts. The Damned sought out an innovative niche as Goth punk pioneers. The Jam deftly vaulted the abyss between punk and mod revivalism (lead singer and 'Modfather' Paul Weller followed up with a hugely successful solo career after sophisti-pop hits with The Style Council) and Madness put the nutty sound on the London map. New Wave and the New Romantics quickly shimmied into the fast-changing music scene... And before London knew it, the '80s had arrived.

The '80s

Guitars disappeared, swiftly replaced by keyboard synthesisers and drum machines. Fashion and image became indivisible from music. Thin ties, winklepickers, velcro-fastening white sneakers, spandex, densely-pleated trousers and make-up dazzled at every turn. Big hair was big. Overpriced, oversexed and way overdone, '80s London was a roll-call of hair-gelled pop: Spandau Ballet, Culture Club, Bananarama and Wham!. Wham!'s Georgios Panayiotou changed his name to George Michael and gained massive success as a solo artist.

While the late '80s brought blond boy band Bros and the starlets of the Stock Aitken Waterman hit factory (including Londoners Mel & Kim and Samantha Fox), relief had already been assured from up north with the arrival of The Smiths and their alternative rock innovations. In the closing years of the decade, fellow Mancunians the Stone Roses and the Happy Mondays devised a new sound that had grown out of the recent acid-house raves. Dance exploded in 1988's summer of love, with Soul II Soul, dilated pupils and a stage set for rave anthems such as the KLF's mighty *What Time is Love?* A generation was gripped by dance music and a new lexicon ruled: techno, electronica, hip hop, garage, house and trance.

The '90s

The early 1990s saw the explosion of yet another scene: Britpop, a genre broadly defined as a punky take on The Beatles. A high-profile battle between two of the biggest bands, Blur from London and Oasis from Manchester, drew a line in the musical sand.

Weighing in on the London side were the brilliant Suede and Elastica, not to mention Sheffield defectors to the capital, Pulp (with their irrepressible lead man, Jarvis Cocker). Skirting around the edges, doing their own thing, were Radiohead (from Oxford, close enough to London).

But other musical styles were cooking. London's Asian community made a big splash in the early 21st century, with Talvin Singh and Nitin Sawhney fusing dance with traditional Indian music, and Asian Dub Foundation bringing their unique brand of a mix of rapcore, dub, dancehall and ragga, and political comment to an ever-widening audience.

London Songs – 1980s

Driving in my Car (Madness)

Electric Avenue (Eddy Grant)

West End Girls (Pet Shop Boys)

London Girl (The Pogues)

London (The Smiths)

London Songs – 1990s

Piccadilly Palare (Morrissey)

Black Boys on Mopeds (Sinéad O'Connor)

Parklife (Blur)

Mile End (Pulp)

Babylon (David Gray)

THE MUSIC SCENE THE '80S

Arguably the most world-wide fame in this period was taken by the London-based boy and girl bands Take That, All Saints, East 17 and the then-ubiquitous Spice Girls. Their enduring popularity is reflected in the reunions of some of these bands two decades later and the Spice Girls' appearance in the London Olympics closing ceremony in 2012, which cemented them as an inherent part of British music culture.

As Britpop ebbed in the late '90s, other currents were flowing into town, and drum 'n' bass and electronica found an anthem-packed sound with DJs such as Goldie and London band Faithless seeing out the millennium.

The Noughties

London band Coldplay – melodic rockers led by falsetto front man Chris Martin – first made a big splash in the UK at the dawn of the new century, before finding international fame. After six best-selling albums, their position as one of the world's biggest rock bands appears unshakeable.

Just as The Strokes did Stateside, Pete Doherty and Carl Barât of The Libertines renewed interest in punky guitar music following its post-Britpop malaise. Their 2002 debut single *What a Waster* created a huge splash and their first album *Up The Bracket* went platinum. Doherty went on to form Babyshambles and Barât released albums with Dirty Pretty Things and The Jackals, but fans were overjoyed when The Libertines reunited for live gigs in 2015.

Fronted by eponymous Alison, Goldfrapp brought a seductive and sensual electronica to the fore on the albums *Black Cherry* and *Supernature,* before abruptly departing in a mystical pastoral-folk direction on the band's much-applauded *Seventh Tree* (2008). The band then backpedaled with 2010's *Head First* as Goldfrapp rediscovered 1980s synthpop.

The decade also saw the rise of grime and its successor genre, dubstep – two indigenous London musical forms born in the East End out of a fusion of hip-hop, drum 'n' bass and UK garage. Dizzee Rascal and Kano are the best-known rappers working in the genre.

Other London noughties talents include the bellowing Florence + the Machine, quirky West London singer-songwriter Lily Allen, and extraordinary but tragic (she passed away in July 2011, aged just 27) Southgate chanteuse Amy Winehouse.

London Music Today

While it's never really lost its position at the top rung of popular music creativity, the London sound is once again riding a wave of international commercial success.

With her second album, Tottenham-born soulster-songwriter Adele won not just the nation's hearts but spent 10 weeks at number one in the US album charts with *21* (2011). Other Londoners at the helm of the new British invasion of the US include indie folk-rock ensemble Mumford & Sons, rapper Tinie Tempah, and angel-faced soul singer Sam Smith, who took out four Grammys in 2015 for his debut *In The Lonely Hour*.

Meanwhile London band The xx have been busy creating their own genre of stripped back electronic pop, Brixton-based Jessie Ware has won the hearts of soul and electro-loving audiences worldwide, and the ethereal singer James Blake won critical acclaim for his soulful post-dubstep sound.

London Songs – 2000s

Tied Up Too Tight (Hard-Fi)

Me & Mr Jones (Amy Winehouse)

LDN (Lily Allen)

Warwick Avenue (Duffy)

Dirtee Cash (Dizzee Rascal)

London Songs – 2010s

The City (Ed Sheeran)

Under the Westway (Blur)

Ill Manors (Plan B)

Dirty Boys (David Bowie)

All Under One Roof Raving (Jamie xx)

Film & Media

The UK punches well above its weight in its standing on the international film scene, but London is far from the glittering hub of the film industry that it might be, despite notable celluloid triumphs. Nonetheless, the city forms the backdrop to a riveting array of films. The nation's media sphere has had its share of crises in recent years but there's still a wide variety of newspapers and magazines filling the shelves of London newsagencies.

London & Film

The Local Cinematic Industry

Londoners are proud of their hometown, but few see it as being at the forefront of the film industry. Despite frequent originality and creative novelty, British films can be hit and miss, certainly at the box office. Commercial triumphs include Oscar-winners *The King's Speech* (2010) and *The Queen* (2006), and further back the classics *Four Weddings and a Funeral* (1994) and *Shakespeare in Love* (1998), but a frustrating inconsistency persists, despite the disproportionate influence of Brits in Hollywood.

Film fans nostalgically dwell on the golden – but honestly rather brief – era of Ealing comedies, when the London-based Ealing Studios turned out a steady stream of hits. Between 1947 and 1955 (after which the studios were sold to the BBC), it produced enduring classics such as *Passport to Pimlico*, *Kind Hearts and Coronets*, *Whisky Galore*, *The Man in the White Suit*, *The Lavender Hill Mob* and *The Ladykillers*. This was also the time of legendary film-makers Michael Powell and Emeric Pressburger, the men behind *The Life and Death of Colonel Blimp* and *The Red Shoes*.

Today the industry finds itself habitually stuck in a deep groove of romantic comedies, costume dramas and gangster pics, while setting periodic benchmarks for horror. Producers, directors and actors complain about a lack of adventurousness in those holding the purse strings, while film investors claim there are not enough scripts worth backing.

Recently, however, there has been a run of notable British films based on real events, including the Stephen Hawking biopic *The Theory of Everything* (2014), the Alan Turing biopic *The Imitation Game* (2014), the fictionalised royal family romp *A Royal Night Out* (2015) and *Pride* (2014), which tells the true story of gay activists supporting striking miners in the 1980s.

Where Brits are at the very top of the world is in the field of acting, with British stars taking out numerous Oscars in recent years, including Eddie Redmayne, Dame Helen Mirren, Sir Daniel Day-Lewis, Colin Firth, Kate Winslet, Christian Bale, Tilda Swinton and Rachel Weisz. Other notable names include Dame Judi Dench, Dame Maggie Smith, Sir Ian McKellen, Benedict Cumberbatch, Ewan McGregor, Ralph Fiennes, Jude Law, Liam Neeson, Hugh Laurie, Keira Knightley and Emily Watson.

Outdoor cinema is rolled out in London in the warmer months at Somerset House's Film4 Summer Screen (p107), where films can be enjoyed in a sublime setting.

Well-known British directors include Steve McQueen *(12 Years a Slave)*, Tom Hooper *(The King's Speech)*, Danny Boyle *(Slumdog Millionaire)*, Ridley Scott *(Blade Runner, Alien, Thelma & Louise, Gladiator, Black Hawk Down)* and Sam Mendes *(American Beauty)*.

London on the Screen

Get the low-down on British films, as well as films made in London and the UK, at the London Film Museum (p105).

From the impressions of an interwar Harley St in *The King's Speech* (2010) to the seedy South Kensington and Earl's Court of Roman Polanski's *Repulsion* (1965), London remains a hugely popular location to make films. That most die-hard of New Yorkers, Woody Allen, has made *Match Point, Scoop, Cassandra's Dream* and *You Will Meet a Tall Dark Stranger* in the capital over the past decade.

The city's blend of historic and modern architecture works massively to its advantage: Ang Lee's *Sense and Sensibility* (1995) retreated to historic Greenwich for its wonderful parkland and neoclassical architecture. Merchant Ivory's costume drama *Howard's End* (1992) and the biopic *Chaplin* (1992) feature the neo-Gothic St Pancras Station, while David Lynch's *The Elephant Man* (1980) took advantage of the moody atmosphere around the then-undeveloped Shad Thames. *Withnail & I* (1987) remains a quintessential classic of offbeat British comedy, partly set in Camden. Camden also features prominently in spy romp *Kingsman: The Secret Service* (2014), as does Savile Row and Kennington's Black Prince pub.

London also serves as an effective backdrop to the horror genre and dystopian cinema. Danny Boyle's shocking *28 Days Later* (2002) haunted viewers with images of an entirely deserted central London in its opening sequences, scenes rekindled in the gore-splattered sequel *28 Weeks Later* (2006). Much of Stanley Kubrick's controversial and bleak *A Clockwork Orange* (1971) was filmed in London, while Alfonso Cuarón's *Children of Men* (2006) forged a menacing and desperate vision of a London to come. Further dystopian visions of a totalitarian future London coalesce in James McTeigue's *V for Vendetta* (2005).

Other parts of town to look out for include the eponymous West London neighbourhood in *Notting Hill* (1999) and the Dickensian backstreets of Borough that feature in such polar opposites as chick-flick *Bridget Jones's Diary* (2001) and Guy Ritchie's gangster-romp *Lock, Stock and Two Smoking Barrels* (1998). Smithfield conveys a certain bleak glamour in *Closer* (2004) and Brick Lane finds celluloid fame

---

BEST CINEMATIC FESTIVALS

A host of London festivals ranging across the film spectrum entertains cinema enthusiasts, from the popcorn crowd to arthouse intelligentsia, and various shades in between.

➡ **London Film Festival** (www.bfi.org.uk/lff) Held in October; the highlight of London's many festivals celebrating cinema.

➡ **Raindance Festival** (www.raindance.co.uk) Europe's leading independent filmmaking festival. It's a terrific celebration of independent, nonmainstream cinema from across the globe, screening just before the London Film Festival.

➡ **Portobello Film Festival** (www.portobellofilmfestival.com) Held in September; features largely independent works by London film-makers and international directors. It's the UK's largest independent film competition and it's free to attend.

➡ **BFI Flare: London GLBT Film Festival** (www.bfi.org.uk/flare) One of the best of its kind with hundreds of gay and lesbian films from around the world shown over a fun fortnight in March at BFI Southbank.

in its namesake drama (2007). Farringdon and other parts of town north of the Thames provide the backdrop to David Cronenberg's ultra-violent *Eastern Promises* (2007), while Crouch End and New Cross Gate are overrun by zombies in the hilarious *Shaun of the Dead* (2004).

Mike Newell's moving drama *Soursweet* (1988) follows the travails of a newly married Hong Kong couple moving to London in the 1960s. Sam Mendes' well-received *Skyfall* puts London into action-packed context in James Bond's spectacular 2012 outing, while awkward British monster movie *Attack the Block* (2011) sees a south London council-estate gang fighting off an alien invasion. British director Terence Davies' critically acclaimed dramatic adaption of Terence Rattigan's *The Deep Blue Sea* (2011) conjures up a tragic portrait of post-WWII London.

The urban environment's capacity to isolate people in one of the world's most densely populated cities forms the background of Carol Morley's poignant *Dreams of a Life* (2011), a moving examination of the life of Joyce Vincent, a sociable 38-year-old woman whose dead body lay undiscovered for three years in her North London flat.

Media

Television

When it comes to televisual output, London plays with a stronger hand than it does in film: a huge amount of global TV content originates in Britain, from the *Teletubbies* and *Top Gear* to the extraordinary films of the BBC natural history unit, to cutting-edge comedy and drama across the channels (including smash hits such as *Downton Abbey*, *Doctor Who* and *Call the Midwife*). British TV shows adapted to localised versions garnering huge followings include *Who Wants to Be a Millionaire?*, *The X Factor* and *MasterChef*. There are five free-to-air national TV stations: BBC1, BBC2, ITV1, Channel 4 and Five. Publicly owned broadcaster the BBC has the advantage of being commercial free.

> Set in Poplar in the East End of London in the 1950s, the period drama *Call the Midwife* has been the BBC's most successful TV series of recent years, having been sold to almost 200 territories. It's made an international celebrity out of much-loved British comedian Miranda Hart, whose own sitcom *Miranda* ended in 2015 after three madcap seasons.

Newspapers

National newspapers in England and London are almost always financially independent of any political party, although their political leanings are quite obvious. There are two broad categories of newspapers, most commonly distinguished as broadsheets (or 'qualities') and tabloids (the distinction is more about content than physical size).

Daily Papers

The main London newspaper is the centre-right *Evening Standard,* a free tabloid published between Monday and Friday and handed out around mainline train stations, tube stations, retailers and stands. *Metro* (published Monday to Friday) is a skimpy morning paper designed to be read in 20 minutes, littering tube stations and seats, giving you an extra excuse to ignore your fellow passengers.

Readers are extremely loyal to their paper and rarely switch from one to another. Liberal and middle-class, *The Guardian* has excellent reporting, an award-winning website and a progressive agenda. A handy small-format entertainment supplement, the *Guide,* comes with Saturday's paper. Dubbed the 'Torygraph', the right-wing *Daily Telegraph* is the unofficial Conservative party paper, and fogeyish perhaps, but with first-rate foreign news coverage. *The Times* is a stalwart of the British press, despite now being part of Australian mogul Rupert Murdoch's media empire; it's a decent read with a wide range of articles and strong foreign reporting. Not aligned with any political party, *The Independent* is a left-leaning serious-minded tabloid with a focus on lead stories that other papers ignore. The *Financial Times* is a heavyweight business paper with a fantastic travel section in its weekend edition.

For sex and scandal over your bacon and eggs, turn to the *Mirror*, a working class and Old Labour tabloid; *The Sun* – the UK's bestseller – a gossip-hungry Tory-leaning tabloid legendary for its sassy headlines; or the lowbrow *Daily Star*. Other tabloid reads include the midlevel *Daily Express* and the centre-right *Daily Mail*.

Sunday Papers

Most dailies have Sunday stablemates, and (predictably) the tabloids have bumper editions of trashy gossip, star-struck adulation, fashion extras and mean-spirited diatribes. *The Observer,* established in 1791, is the oldest Sunday paper and sister of *The Guardian,* with a great Sunday arts supplement *(The New Review).* The *Sunday Telegraph* is as serious and politically blue as its weekly sister paper, while *The Sunday Times* is brimful of fashion and scandal and probably puts paid to a rainforest per issue (but most of it can arguably be tossed in the recycling bin upon purchase).

Magazines

An astonishing range of magazines is published and consumed in London, from celebrity gossip to ideological heavyweights.

Political magazines are particularly strong. The satirical *Private Eye* has no political bias and lampoons everyone equally, although anyone in a position of power is preferred. The excellent weekly *The Economist* cannot be surpassed for international political and business analysis. Claiming to be Britain's oldest running magazine, the right-wing weekly *The Spectator* is worshipped by Tory voters, but its witty articles are often loved by left-wingers, too. The *New Statesman* is a stalwart left-wing intellectual news magazine.

A freebie available from tube stations, big museums and galleries, *Time Out* is the listings guide par excellence and great for taking the city's pulse, with strong arts coverage, while the *Big Issue,* sold on the streets by the homeless, is not just an honourable project, but a damned fine read.

London loves celebrities with *Heat, Closer* and *OK!* the most popular purveyors of the genre. US import *Glamour* is the queen of the women's glossies; *Marie Claire, Elle* and *Vogue* are regarded as the thinking-woman's glossies. The smarter men's magazines include *GQ* and *Esquire,* while less edifying reads are the so-called 'lads' mags': *FHM, Loaded, Maxim* and *Nuts.* A slew of style magazines are published here, including *i-D,* an übercool London fashion and music gospel, and rival *Dazed & Confused.*

New Media

London's new media scene is of its nature a disparate and nefarious beast. All of the major print publications have an online presence, but some other useful websites and blogs to seek out include: **Londonist** (www.londonist.com), particularly for it's 'Things To Do' tab; **Urban 75** (www.urban75.com), an outstanding community website, with a counter-cultural edge; **London On The Inside** (www.londontheinside.com), for its opinions about what's so-hot-right-now; and **London Eater** (www.london-eater.com), one of the better food blogs.

If you're on Twitter and you're not following actor, intellect and fabulous Londoner Stephen Fry (@stephenfry), you really should be. It should come as no surprise that One Direction (@onedirection) is the most followed Twitter handle in London, then Harry Potter star Emma Watson (@EmWatson) and BBC Breaking News (@BBCBreaking). *The Economist* (@TheEconomist) tops the publications, while Arsenal (@Arsenal) is the favoured football club of London's twitterati.

As with the tele, BBC Radio is commercial-free: BBC London (94.9 FM) is largely a talk-fest, Radio 4 (93.5 FM) has news, Radio 2 (88.8 FM) has adult-orientated music and frivolity, and Radio 1 has youth-focussed pop. Capital FM (95.8 FM) is Radio 1's commercial equivalent. Then there's Xfm (104.9 FM) for indie music, Kiss (100 FM) for dance and Classic FM (100.9 FM).

Survival Guide

TRANSPORT 380

ARRIVING IN LONDON . . 380
Heathrow Airport 380
Gatwick Airport 381
Stansted Airport 381
Luton Airport 382
London City Airport 382
Train 382
Bus 382

GETTING AROUND
LONDON 382
London Underground . . . 383
Bus 383
Bicycle 384
Taxi 384
Boat 385
Car & Motorcycle 385
Cable Car 385

TOURS 385
Air Tours 386
Boat Tours 386
Bus Tours 386
Specialist Tours 386
Walking Tours 386

DIRECTORY A–Z 387
Customs
Regulations 387
Discount Cards 387
Electricity 387
Emergency 387
Internet Access 387
Legal Matters 387
Medical Services 388
Money 389
Opening Hours 389
Post 389
Public Holidays 390
Safe Travel 390
Taxes & Refunds 390
Telephone 390
Time 391
Toilets 391
Tourist
Information 391
Travellers with
Disabilities 391
Visas 392
Women Travellers 392

Transport

ARRIVING IN LONDON

Most people arrive in London by air, but an increasing number of visitors coming from Europe let the train take the strain, while buses from across the Continent are a further option.

The city has five airports: Heathrow, which is the largest, to the west; Gatwick to the south; Stansted to the northeast; Luton to the northwest; and London City in the Docklands.

Most transatlantic flights land at Heathrow (average flight time from the US East Coast is between 6½ and 7½ hours, 10 to 11 hours from the West Coast; slightly more on the return).

Visitors from Europe are more likely to arrive at Gatwick, Stansted or Luton (the latter two are used exclusively by low-cost airlines such as easyJet and Ryanair). Most flights to continental Europe last from one to three hours.

An increasingly popular form of transport is the Eurostar – the Channel Tunnel train – between London and Paris or Brussels. The journey lasts 2¼ hours to Paris and less than two hours to Brussels. Travellers depart from and arrive in the centre of each city.

Flights, cars and tours can be booked online at lonelyplanet.com.

Heathrow Airport

Some 15 miles west of central London, **Heathrow** (LHR; www.heathrowairport.com; ☎) is the world's busiest international airport and counts four terminals (numbered 2 to 5), including the totally revamped Terminal 2.

Each terminal has currency-exchange facilities, information counters and accommodation desks.

Left-luggage Facilities are in each terminal and open 5am (5.30am at T4) to 11pm. The charge per item is £5 for up to two hours, £10 for up to 24 hours, up to a maximum of 90 days.

Hotels There are four international-style hotels that can be reached on foot from the terminals, and another 20 or so nearby. The **Hotel Hoppa** (www.nationalexpress.com/wherewego/airports/heathrow-hotel-hoppa.aspx; adult/child £4.50/free) bus links nearby hotels with the airport's terminals, running every 15 to 30 minutes from 4am to midnight.

Train

Three Underground stations on the Piccadilly line serve Heathrow: one for Terminals 2 and 3, another for Terminal 4, and the terminus for Terminal 5. The Underground, commonly referred to as 'the tube' (one way £5.10, from central London one hour, every three to nine minutes) is the cheapest way of getting to Heathrow. It runs from just after 5/5.45am from/to the airport to 11.45pm/12.30am (and all night Friday and Saturday, with reduced frequency). Buy tickets at the station.

Heathrow Express (www.heathrowexpress.com; one way/return £21.50/35) This high-speed train whisks passengers from Heathrow Central station (serving Terminals 2 and 3) and Terminal 5 to Paddington in just 15 minutes. Terminal 4 passengers should take the free interterminal shuttle train available to Heathrow Central and board there. Trains run every 15 minutes from just after 5am in both directions to between 11.25pm (from Paddington) and 11.40pm (from the airport).

Heathrow Connect (www.heathrowconnect.com; adult £10.10) Travelling between Heathrow and Paddington station, this modern passenger-train service departs every 30 minutes and makes five stops en route. The journey takes about 30 minutes. The first trains leave Heathrow at around 5.20am (7am Sunday) and the last service is just before midnight. From Paddington, services leave between approximately 4.45am (6.30am Sunday) and just after 11pm.

Bus

National Express (www.nationalexpress.com) coaches (one way from £5.50, 35 to 90 minutes, every 30 minutes to one hour) link the Heathrow Central Bus Station with Victoria coach station. The first bus leaves the Heathrow Central Bus station (at Terminals 2 and 3) at 4.20am, with the last departure just after 10pm. The first bus leaves Victoria at 7.30am, the last just before midnight.

At night, the **N9 bus** (£1.50, 1¼ hours, every 20 minutes) connects Heathrow with central London, terminating at Aldwych.

Taxi

A metered black-cab trip to/from central London will cost between £45 and £85 and take 45 minutes to an hour, depending on traffic and your departure point.

Gatwick Airport

Located some 30 miles south of central London, **Gatwick** (LGW; www.gatwickairport.com; ☎) is smaller than Heathrow. The North and South Terminals are linked by a 24-hour shuttle train, with the journey time about three minutes. There are left-luggage facilities in both terminals, open 5am to 9pm. The charge is £9 per item for 24 hours (or part thereof), up to a maximum of 90 days.

Train

National Rail (www.nationalrail.co.uk) has regular train services to/from London Bridge (30 minutes, every 15 to 30 minutes), London King's Cross (55 minutes, every 15 to 30 minutes) and London Victoria (30 minutes, every 10 to 15 minutes). Fares vary depending on the time of travel and the train company, but allow £10 to £20 for a single.

Gatwick Express (www.gatwickexpress.com; one way/return £19.90/34.90) This dedicated train service links the station near the South Terminal with Victoria station in central London every 15 minutes. From the airport, there are services between 4.30am and 1.35am. From Victoria, they leave between 3.30am and just after 12.30am. The journey takes 30 minutes.

Bus

National Express (www.nationalexpress.com) coaches (one way from £5, 80 minutes to two hours) run throughout the day from Gatwick to Victoria Coach station. Services leave hourly around the clock.

EasyBus (www.easybus.co.uk) runs 19-seater minibuses to Gatwick every 15 to 20 minutes on two routes: one from Earl's Court/West Brompton and from Waterloo (one way from £4.95). The service runs from 3am to 11pm daily. Journey time averages 75 minutes.

Taxi

A metered black-cab trip to/from central London costs around £100 and takes just over an hour. Minicabs are usually cheaper.

Stansted Airport

Stansted (STN; www.stanstedairport.com; ☎) is 35 miles northeast of central London in the direction of Cambridge.

Train

The **Stansted Express** (☎0845 850 0150; www.stanstedexpress.com; single/return £19/32) rail service (one way/return £23.40/32.80, 45 minutes, every 15 to 30 minutes) links the airport and Liverpool St station. From the airport, the first train leaves at 5.30am, the last at 1.30am (12.30am on Saturday). Trains depart Liverpool St station from 4.10am to just before 11.30pm.

Bus

National Express (www.nationalexpress.com) coaches run around the clock, offering well over 100 services per day. The A6 runs to Victoria coach station (one way from £12, 85 minutes to more than two hours, every 20 minutes) via North London. The A9 runs to Liverpool St station (one way from £10, 60 to 80 minutes, every 30 minutes).

EasyBus (www.easybus.co.uk) runs services to Baker St and Old St tube stations every 15 minutes. The journey (one way from £4.95) takes one hour from Old St, 1¼ hours from Baker St.

CLIMATE CHANGE & TRAVEL

Every form of transport that relies on carbon-based fuel generates CO_2, the main cause of human-induced climate change. Modern travel is dependent on aeroplanes, which might use less fuel per kilometre per person than most cars but travel much greater distances. The altitude at which aircraft emit gases (including CO_2) and particles also contributes to their climate-change impact. Many websites offer 'carbon calculators' that allow people to estimate the carbon emissions generated by their journey and, for those who wish to do so, to offset the impact of the greenhouse gases emitted with contributions to portfolios of climate-friendly initiatives throughout the world. Lonely Planet offsets the carbon footprint of all staff and author travel.

Terravision (www.terravision. eu) Coaches link Stansted to both Liverpool St train station (bus A51, one way/return from £8/14, 55 minutes) and Victoria coach station (bus A50, one way/return from £9/15, 75 minutes) every 20 to 40 minutes between 6am and 1am.

Taxi

A metered black-cab trip to/ from central London costs around £130. Minicabs are cheaper.

Luton Airport

A smallish airport 32 miles northwest of London, **Luton** (LTN; www.london-luton.co.uk) generally caters for cheap charter flights and discount airlines.

Train

National Rail (www.national-rail.co.uk) services (one way from £14, 35 to 50 minutes, every six to 30 minutes, from 7am to 10pm) run from London Bridge and London King's Cross stations to Luton Airport Parkway station, from where an airport shuttle bus (one way £1.60) will take you to the airport in 10 minutes.

Bus

EasyBus (www.easybus.co.uk) minibuses run between Victoria coach station and Luton (one way from £4.95) every half-hour round the clock. Another route links the airport with Liverpool St station (buses every 15 to 30 minutes).

Green Line Bus 757 (www. greenline.co.uk; one way/ return £10/15) Buses to/from Luton (75 to 90 minutes) run to/from Victoria Coach station, leaving approximately every half-hour round the clock.

Taxi

A metered black-cab trip to/ from central London costs about £110.

London City Airport

Its proximity to central London, which is just 6 miles to the west, as well as to the commercial district of the Docklands, means **London City Airport** (LCY; www. londoncityairport.com; ☎) is predominantly a gateway airport for business travellers. You can also now fly to New York from here.

Train

The **Docklands Light Railway** (DLR; www.tfl.gov. uk/dlr) stops at the London City Airport station (one way £2.80 to £3.30). The journey to Bank takes just over 20 minutes, and trains go every eight to 10 minutes from just after 5.30am to 12.15am Monday to Saturday, and 7am to 11.15pm Sunday.

Taxi

A metered black-cab trip to or from the City/Oxford St/Earl's Court costs about £25/35/50.

Train

Main national rail routes are served by InterCity trains, which are neither cheap nor particularly punctual. Check **National Rail** (www.national-rail.co.uk) for timetables and fares.

Eurostar (www.eurostar.com) The high-speed passenger-rail service links St Pancras International Station with Gare du Nord in Paris (or Bruxelles Midi in Brussels), with between 14 and 16 daily departures. Fares vary enormously, from £69 for the cheapest return to upwards of £300 for a fully flexible return at busy periods.

Eurotunnel (www.eurotunnel. com) High-speed shuttle trains transport cars and bicycles between Folkestone in England and Coquelles (5km southwest of Calais) in France. Services

run round the clock – up to four times an hour during the day but hourly from 1am to 6am. Booking online is cheapest: day-overnight return fares start at £46 and two- to five-day excursion fares from £110. Prices include a car and passengers.

Bus

Eurolines (www.eurolines. com; Colonnades Shopping Centre, 115 Buckingham Palace Road, SW1; ◷9am-5.30pm Mon-Sat, to 4.30pm Sun) Has buses operated by National Express to continental Europe leaving from Victoria coach station (164 Buckingham Palace Rd, SW1; ⊖Victoria).

Megabus (www.megabus.com) Operates no-frills, airline-style seat pricing; large route network.

National Express (www. nationalexpress.com) National coach company with the most comprehensive network, including many direct routes to airports. Comfortable and generally reliable.

GETTING AROUND LONDON

Public transport in London is extensive, often excellent and always pricey. It is managed by **Transport for London** (www.tfl.gov.uk), which has a user-friendly, multilingual website with a journey planner, maps, detailed information on every mode of transport in the capital and live updates on traffic.

The cheapest way to get around London is with an **Oyster Card** or a UK contactless card (foreign-card holders should check for contactless charges first). Paper tickets still exist and, although day-travel cards cost the same on paper as on Oyster or contactless card, using paper singles or returns is substantially more expensive than using an Oyster.

OYSTER CARD & CONTACTLESS CARDS

The Oyster Card is a smart card on which you can store credit towards 'prepay' fares, as well as Travelcards valid for periods from a day to a year. Oyster Cards are valid across the entire public-transport network in London. All you need to do when entering a station is touch your card on a reader (which has a yellow circle with the image of an Oyster Card on them) and then touch again on your way out. The system will then deduct the appropriate amount of credit from your card, as necessary. For bus journeys, you only need to touch once upon boarding.

The benefit lies in the fact that fares for Oyster Card users are lower than standard ones. If you are making many journeys during the day, you will never pay more than the appropriate Travelcard (peak or off peak) once the daily 'price cap' has been reached.

Oyster Cards can be bought (£5 refundable deposit required) and topped up at any Underground station, travel information centre or shop displaying the Oyster logo. To get your deposit back along with any remaining credit, simply return your Oyster Card at a ticket booth.

Contactless cards (which do not require chip and pin or a signature) can now be used directly on Oyster Card readers and are subject to the same Oyster fares. The advantage is that you don't have to bother with buying, topping up and then returning an Oyster Card, but foreign visitors should bear in mind the cost of card transactions.

The tube, DLR and Overground network are ideal for zooming across different parts of the city; buses and **Santander Cycles** (p67) are great for shorter journeys.

Left-luggage facility **Excess Baggage** (www.left-baggage.co.uk) operates at London's main train stations: St Pancras, Paddington, Euston, Victoria, Waterloo, King's Cross, Liverpool St and Charing Cross. Allow £10 per 24-hour slot.

London Underground

The London Underground ('the tube'; 11 colour-coded lines) is part of an integrated transport system that also includes the Docklands Light Railway (DLR; a driverless overhead train operating in the eastern part of the city) and Overground network (mostly outside Zone 1 and sometimes underground). Despite the never-ending upgrades and 'engineering works' requiring weekend closures, it is overall the quickest and easiest way of getting around the city, if not the cheapest.

The first trains operate from around 5.30am Monday to Saturday and 6.45am Sunday. The last trains leave around 12.30am Monday to Saturday and 11.30pm Sunday.

Additionally, selected lines (the Victoria and Jubilee lines, plus most of the Piccadilly, Central and Northern lines) run all night on Fridays and Saturdays to get revellers home, with trains every 10 minutes or so.

During weekend closures, schedules, maps and alternative route suggestions are posted in every station, and staff are at hand to help redirect you.

Fares

➡ London is divided into nine concentric fare zones.

➡ It will always be cheaper to travel with an Oyster card or a Contactless card than a paper ticket.

➡ Children under the age of 11 travel free; 11 to 15 year-olds are half-price if registered on an accompanying adult's Oyster Card (register at Zone 1 or Heathrow tube stations).

➡ If you're in London for a longer period and plan to travel every day, consider a weekly or even a monthly Travelcard.

➡ If you're caught without a valid ticket, you're liable for an on-the-spot fine of £80. If paid within 21 days, the fine is reduced to £40. Inspectors accept no excuses.

Bus

London's ubiquitous red double-decker buses afford great views of the city but be aware that the going can be slow, thanks to traffic jams and dozens of commuters getting on and off at every stop.

There are excellent bus maps at every stop detailing all routes and destinations served from that particular area (generally a few bus stops within two to three minutes' walk, shown on a local map). See our handy key bus-routes map.

Bus services normally operate from 5am to 11.30pm.

Night bus

More than 50 night-bus routes (prefixed with the letter 'N') run from around 11.30pm to 5am.

There are also another 60 bus routes operating 24 hours; the frequency decreases between 11pm and 5am.

Oxford Circus, Tottenham Court Rd and Trafalgar Sq are the main hubs for night routes.

TUBE, DLR & OVERGROUND FARES

Zone	Cash single	Oyster/contactless peak single	Oyster/contactless off-peak single	Cap (Oyster/contactless day travel card)
Zone 1 only	£4.80	£2.30	£2.30	£6.40
Zone 1 & 2	£4.80	£2.90	£2.30	£6.40
Zone 1-3	£4.80	£3.30	£2.80	£7.50
Zone 1-4	£5.80	£3.90	£2.80	£9.20
Zone 1-5	£5.50	£4.70	£3.10	£10.90
Zone 1-6	£6	£5.10	£3.10	£11.70

Night buses can be infrequent and stop only on request, so remember to ring for your stop.

Fares

Cash cannot be used on London's buses. Instead you must pay with an Oyster Card, Travelcard or a contactless payment card. Bus fares are a flat £1.50, no matter the distance travelled. If you don't have enough credit on your Oyster Card for a £1.50 bus fare, you can make one more bus journey. You must then top up your credit before you can use your Oyster Card again.

Children under 11 travel free; 11 to 15 year-olds are half-price if registered on an accompanying adult's Oyster Card (register at Zone 1 or Heathrow tube stations)

Bicycle

Tens of thousands of Londoners cycle to work every day, and it is generally a good way to get around the city, although traffic can be intimidating for less confident cyclists. The city has tried hard to improve the cycling infrastructure, however, opening new 'cycle superhighways' for commuters and launching **Santander Cycles** (p67), which is particularly useful for visitors.

Hire

London Bicycle Tour (☎020-7928 6838; www.

londonbicycle.com; 1 Gabriel's Wharf, 56 Upper Ground, SE1; tour incl bike from £23.95, bike hire per day £20; ◉Southwark, Waterloo, Blackfriars) Three-hour tours begin in South Bank and take in London's highlights on both sides of the river; a night ride is also available. You can also hire traditional or speciality bikes, such as tandems and folding bikes, by the hour or day.

On Your Bike (☎020-7378 6669; www.onyourbike.com; The Vaults, Montague Close, SE1; 1-day hire £18; ⊙7.30am-7.30pm Mon-Fri, 10am-6pm Sat, 11am-5pm Sun; ◉London Bridge) Rentals cost £18 for the first day, £10 for subsequent days, £45 per week. Prices include hire of helmet and lock. A deposit (via credit card) is required and you will need to show ID. It also offers a suite of bike-servicing options.

Bicycles on Public Transport

Bicycles can be taken on the Overground, DLR and on the Circle, District, Hammersmith & City and Metropolitan tube lines, except at peak times (7.30am to 9.30am and 4pm to 7pm Monday to Friday). Folding bikes can be taken on any line at any time, however.

Taxi

Black Cabs

The **black cab** is as much a feature of the London

cityscape as the red double-decker bus. Licensed black-cab drivers have 'The Knowledge', acquired after rigorous training and a series of exams. They are supposed to know 25,000 streets within a 6-mile radius of Charing Cross/Trafalgar Sq and the 100 most visited spots of the moment, including clubs and restaurants.

➡ Cabs are available for hire when the yellow sign above the windscreen is lit; just stick your arm out to signal one.

➡ Fares are metered, with the flagfall charge of £2.40 (covering the first 310m during a weekday), rising by increments of 20p for each subsequent 168m.

➡ Fares are more expensive in the evenings and overnight.

➡ You can tip taxi drivers up to 10% but most Londoners simply round up to the nearest pound.

➡ Apps such as **Hailo** (www.hailocab.com) or **Black Cabs App** (www.blackcabsapp.com) use your smartphone's GPS to locate the nearest black cab to you. You only pay the metered fare.

Minicabs

➡ Minicabs, which are licensed, are cheaper (usually) competitors of black cabs.

➡ Unlike black cabs, minicabs cannot legally be hailed on the street; they must be hired by phone or directly from one of the minicab offices (every high street has at least one and most clubs work with a minicab firm to send revellers home safely).

➡ Don't accept unsolicited offers from individuals claiming to be minicab drivers – they are just guys with cars.

➡ Minicabs don't have meters; there's usually a fare set by the dispatcher. Make sure you ask before setting off.

➡ Your hotel or host will be able to recommend a reputable minicab company in the neighbourhood; every Londoner has the number of at least one company. Or phone a large 24-hour operator such as **Addison Lee** (☑020-7407 9000; www.addisonlee.com).

➡ Apps such as **Uber** (www.uber.com) or **Kabbee** (www.kabbee.com) allow you to book a minicab in double-quick time.

Boat

There are a number of companies operating along the River Thames. Only **Thames Clippers** (www.thamesclippers.com; adult/child £6.50/3.25) really offers commuter services, however. It's fast, pleasant and you're almost always guaranteed a seat and a view.

Boats run every 20 minutes from 6am to between 10pm and 11pm. The route goes from London Eye Millennium Pier to Woolwich Arsenal Pier, serving the London Eye, Tate Modern, Shakespeare's Globe, Borough Market, Tower Bridge, Canary Wharf, Greenwich and the O2.

Discounts apply for pay-as-you-go Oyster Card holders (£6.44) and Travelcard holders (paper ticket or on an Oyster Card; £4.75).

Car & Motorcycle

As a visitor, it's very unlikely you'll need to drive in London. Mayors Ken Livingstone (2000–08) and Boris Johnson (2008–2016) have done

everything in their power to encourage Londoners to get out of their car and into public transport (or on their bikes!) and the same disincentives should keep you firmly off the road: the congestion charge, extortionate parking fees, traffic jams, high price of petrol, fiendishly efficient traffic wardens and wheel clampers and so on.

If you get a parking ticket or your car gets clamped, call the number on the ticket. If the car has been removed, ring the free 24-hour service called **TRACE** (Tow-Away Removal & Clamping Enquiries; ☑0845 206 8602) to find out where your car has been taken to. It will cost you a minimum of £200 to get your vehicle back on the road.

Driving
ROAD RULES

➡ Get a copy of the *The Highway Code* (www.gov.uk/highway-code), available at Automobile Association (AA) and Royal Automobile Club (RAC) outlets, as well as some bookshops and tourist offices.

➡ A foreign driving licence is valid in Britain for up to 12 months from the time of your last entry into the country.

➡ If you bring a car from continental Europe, make sure you're adequately insured.

➡ All drivers and passengers must wear seatbelts, and motorcyclists must wear a helmet.

CONGESTION CHARGE

London has a congestion charge in place to reduce the flow of traffic into its centre. For full details log on to www.tfl.gov.uk/roadusers/congestioncharging.

The congestion charge zone encompasses Euston Rd and Pentonville Rd to the north, Park Lane to the west, Tower Bridge to the east and Elephant & Castle and Vauxhall Bridge Rd to the south. As you enter the zone, you will see a large white 'C' in a red circle.

If you enter the zone between 7am and 6pm Monday to Friday (excluding public holidays), you must pay the £11.50 charge (payable in advance or on the day) or £14 on the first charging day after travel to avoid receiving a fine (£130, or £65 if paid within 14 days).

You can pay online, at newsagents, petrol stations or any shop displaying the 'C' sign.

Hire

There is no shortage of car-rental agencies in London. Book in advance for the best fares, especially at weekends.

The following rental agencies have several branches across the capital:

Avis (www.avis.co.uk) International franchise with plenty of branches and vehicle choices.

easyCar (www.easycar.com) Good-value car rental from the Easy brand.

Hertz (www.hertz.com) Good offers and choice of vehicles.

Cable Car

The **Emirates Air Line** (www.emiratesairline.co.uk; 27 Western Gateway, E16; one way adult/child £4.50/2.30, with Oyster Card or Travelcard £3.40/1.70; ⊙7am-9pm Mon-Fri, 9am-9pm Sat & Sun, closes 8pm Oct-Mar; ⍟DLR Royal Victoria, ⊜North Greenwich) is a cable car linking the Royal Docks in East London with North Greenwich some 90m above the Thames. The journey is brief, and rather pricey, but the views are stunning.

TOURS

From erudite to eccentric, tours on offer to see the sights are legion in London. Bus tours, although not particularly cool, are good for those who are short on time. Those with special interests – Jewish London, birdwatching, pop music – might consider hiring their own guide.

Air Tours

Adventure Balloons
(☎01252-844222; www.adventureballoons.co.uk; Winchfield Park, London Rd, Hartley Wintney, Hampshire RG27) Weather permitting, there are weekday morning London flights (£210 per person) shortly after dawn from late April to mid-August. The flight lasts one hour, but allow four to six hours, including take-off, landing and recovery. See website for meeting points.

London Helicopter
(☎020-7887 2626; www.thelondonhelicopter.com; London Heliport, Bridges Ct, Battersea, SW11) Panoramic flights over London lasting 12/18 minutes (per person £150/200) depart daily throughout the day. Call or book online.

Boat Tours

Travelcard holders get one-third off all boating fares listed here (London RIB Voyages excluded). Boat services cruise along the Thames in central London but also go as far as the Thames Barrier and Hampton Court.

Circular Cruise
(☎020-7936 2033; www.crownrivercruise.co.uk; adult/child one way £9.90/4.95, return £13.15/6.58; ⊙11am-6.30pm late May–early Sep, to 5pm Apr, May, Sep & Oct, to 3pm Nov-Mar) Vessels travel east from Westminster Pier to St Katharine's Pier near the Tower of London and back, calling at Embankment, Festival and Bankside Piers. You can travel just one way, make the return trip or use the boat as a hop-on/hop-off service to visit sights on the way. Tours depart half-hourly late May to early September, every 40 minutes the rest of the year.

London RIB Voyages
(☎020-7928 8933; www.londonribvoyages.com; Boarding Gate 1, London Eye, Waterloo Millennium Pier, Westminster Bridge Rd, SE1; adult/child £42/22.95; ⊙hourly 10am-6pm) Feel like James Bond – or David Beckham en route to the 2012 Olympic Games – on this high-speed inflatable boat that flies down the Thames at 30 to 35 knots. RIB also does a Captain Kidd–themed trip between the London Eye and Canary Wharf for the same price.

Thames River Services
(www.thamesriverservices.co.uk; adult/child one way £12.25/6.13, return £16/8) These cruise boats leave Westminster Pier for Greenwich, stopping at the Tower of London. Every second service continues on from Greenwich to the Thames Barrier (one way adult/child £14/7, return £17/8.50, hourly 11.30am to 3.30pm) but does not land there, passing the O2 along the way. From Westminster it's a two-hour round trip to Greenwich, three hours to the Thames Barrier.

Thames River Boats
(☎020-7930 2062; www.wpsa.co.uk; Westminster Pier, Victoria Embankment, SW1; Kew adult/child one way £12/6, return £18/9, Hampton Court one way £15/7.50, return £22.50/11.25; ⊙10am-4pm Apr-Oct) These boats go upriver from Westminster Pier to the Royal Botanic Gardens at Kew (1½ hours, four per day) and on to Hampton Court Palace (another 1½ hours, 11am sailing only), a distance of 22 miles. It's possible to get off the boats at Richmond, but it depends on the tides; check before you sail.

Bus Tours

The following companies offer commentary and the chance to get off at each sight and rejoin the tour on a later bus. Tickets are valid for 24 hours.

Big Bus Tours (www.bigbustours.com; adult/child £32/13; ⊙every 20min 8.30am-6pm Apr-Sep, to 5pm Oct & Mar, to 4.30pm Nov-Feb) Informative commentaries in eight languages. The ticket includes a free river cruise with City Cruises and three thematic walking tours (Royal London, film locations, mysteries). Good online booking discounts available.

Original Tour (www.theoriginaltour.com; adult/child £30/15; ⊙8.30am-8.30pm) A hop-on-hop-off bus service with a river cruise thrown in as well as three themed walks: Changing of the Guard, Rock 'n' Roll and Jack the Ripper. Buses run every five to 20 minutes; you can buy tickets on the bus or online.

Specialist Tours

Guide London (Association of Professional Tourist Guides; ☎020-7611 2545; www.guidelondon.org.uk; half/full day £150/240) Hire a prestigious Blue Badge Tourist Guide, know-it-all guides who have studied for two years and passed a dozen written and practical exams to do their job. They can tell you stories behind the sights that you'd only hear from them or take you on a themed tour – from royalty and the Beatles to parks and shopping. Go by car, public transport, bike or on foot.

Walking Tours

London Walks (☎020-7624 3978; www.walks.com; adult/child £10/free) A huge choice of themed walks, including Jack the Ripper, the Beatles, Sherlock Holmes and Harry Potter. Check the website for the schedule – there are walks every day.

Directory A–Z

Customs Regulations

The UK distinguishes between goods bought duty-free outside the EU and those bought in another EU country, where taxes and duties will have already been paid.

If you exceed your duty-free allowance, you will have to pay tax on the items. For European goods, there is officially no limit to how much you can bring but customs use certain guidelines to distinguish between personal and commercial use.

Discount Cards

Of interest to visitors who want to take in lots of paid sights in a short time is the **London Pass** (www.londonpass.com; 1/2/3/6 days £52/71/85/116). The pass offers free entry and queue-jumping to all major attractions and can be altered to include use of the Underground and buses. Check the website for details. Child passes available too.

Electricity

230V/50Hz

Emergency

Dial ☎999 to call the police, fire brigade or ambulance in the event of an emergency.

Internet Access

Virtually every hotel in London now provides wi-fi free of charge (only a couple of budget places have it as an add-on).

A number of hotels (and especially hostels) also provide guest computers and access to a printer (handy to print your boarding pass).

A huge number of cafes, and an increasing number of restaurants, offer free wi-fi to customers, including chains such as Starbucks, Costa and Pret a Manger, as well as McDonald's. Cultural venues such as the Barbican or the Southbank Centre also have free wi-fi.

Open-air and street wi-fi access is available in areas across London, including Oxford St, Trafalgar Sq, Piccadilly Circus, the City of London and Islington's Upper St. Users have to register but there is no charge.

Most major train stations, airport terminals and even some Underground stations also have wi-fi, but access isn't always free.

Legal Matters

Should you face any legal difficulties while in London, visit a branch of the Citizens Advice Bureau (www.citizens-advice.org.uk), or contact your embassy.

Driving Offences

The laws against drink-driving are very strict in the UK and treated seriously. Currently the limit is 80mg of alcohol in 100mL of blood. The safest approach is not to drink anything at all if you're planning to drive.

It is illegal to use a hand-held phone (or similar devices) while driving.

IMPORT RESTRICTIONS

ITEM	DUTY-FREE	TAX & DUTY PAID
Tobacco	200 cigarettes, 100 cigarillos, 50 cigars or 250g tobacco	800 cigarettes, 400 cigarillos, 200 cigars, 1kg tobacco
Spirits & liqueurs	1L spirit or 2L of fortified wine (eg sherry or port)	10L spirit, 20L fortified wine
Beer & wine	16L beer & 4L still wine	110L beer, 90L still wine
Other goods	Up to a value of £390	n/a

Drugs

Illegal drugs of every type are widely available in London, especially in clubs. Nonetheless, all the usual drug warnings apply. Cannabis was downgraded to a Class C drug in 2004 but reclassified as a Class B drug in 2009 following a government rethink. If you're caught with pot today, you're likely to be arrested. Possession of harder drugs, including heroin and cocaine, is always treated seriously. Searches on entering clubs are common.

Fines

In general you rarely have to pay on the spot for an offence. The exceptions are trains, the tube and buses, where people who can't produce a valid ticket for the journey when asked to by an inspector can be fined there and then. No excuses are accepted, though if you can't pay, you'll be able to register your details (if you have some sort of ID with you) and be sent a fine in the post.

Medical Services

EU nationals can obtain free emergency treatment (and, in some cases, reduced-cost healthcare) on presentation of a **European Health Insurance Card** (www.ehic. org.uk).

Reciprocal arrangements with the UK allow Australians, New Zealanders and residents and nationals of several other countries to receive free emergency medical treatment and subsidised dental care through the **National Health Service** (NHS; ☏111; www.nhs.uk). They can use hospital emergency departments, GPs and dentists. For a full list click on 'Services near you' on the NHS website.

Visitors staying 12 months or longer, with the proper documentation, will receive care under the NHS by registering with a specific practice near their residence.

Travel insurance is advisable for non-EU residents as it offers greater flexibility over where and how you're treated and covers expenses for an ambulance and repatriation that will not be picked up by the NHS.

Dental Services

For emergency dental care, visit the NHS website or call into **University College London Hospital** (☏020-3456 7890, 0845 155 5000; www.uclh.nhs.uk; 235 Euston Rd, NW1; ⊖Warren St, Euston).

Note that many travel-insurance schemes do not cover emergency dental care.

Hospitals

A number of hospitals have 24-hour accident and emergency departments. However, in an emergency just call ☏999 and an ambulance will normally be dispatched from the hospital nearest to you.

Charing Cross Hospital (☏020-3311 1234; www. imperial.nhs.uk/charingcross; Fulham Palace Rd, W6; ⊖Hammersmith) The name is misleading – this hospital is actually near Hammersmith.

Chelsea & Westminster Hospital (☏020-3315 8000; www.chelwest.nhs.uk; 369 Fulham Rd, SW10; ☒14 or 414, ⊖South Kensington, Fulham Broadway) Large hospital in Chelsea.

Guy's Hospital (☏020-7188 7188; www.guysandstthomas. nhs.uk; Great Maze Pond, SE1; ⊖London Bridge) One of central London's busiest hospitals, near London Bridge.

Royal Free Hospital (☏020-7794 0500; www.royalfree.nhs.uk; Pond St, NW3; ℞Hampstead Heath, ⊖Belsize Park) North London's largest hospital.

Royal London Hospital (☏020-3416 5000; www.barts-health.nhs.uk; Whitechapel Rd, E1; ⊖Whitechapel) Very busy hospital in East London.

St Thomas' Hospital (☏020-7188 7188; www. guysandstthomas.nhs.uk; Westminster Bridge Rd, SE1; ⊖Waterloo, Westminster) Large hospital across the Thames from Westminster.

University College London Hospital (☏020-3456 7890, 0845 155 5000; www. uclh.nhs.uk; 235 Euston Rd, NW1; ⊖Warren St, Euston) One of central London's busiest hospitals.

Pharmacies

The main pharmacy chains in London are Boots and Superdrug; a branch of either – or both – can be found on virtually every high street.

The **Boots** (📞020-7734 6126; www.boots.com; 44-46 Regent St, W1; ⏲8am-midnight Mon-Fri, 9am-midnight Sat, 12.30-6.30pm Sun; 🚇Piccadilly Circus) in Piccadilly Circus is one of the biggest and most centrally located and has extended opening times.

Money

Although it is a member of the EU, the UK has not adopted the euro and has retained the pound sterling (£) as its unit of currency.

One pound sterling is made up of 100 pence (called 'pee', colloquially).

Notes come in denominations of £5, £10, £20 and £50, while coins are 1p ('penny'), 2p, 5p, 10p, 20p, 50p, £1 and £2.

Unless otherwise noted, all prices are in pounds sterling.

ATMs

ATMs are everywhere and will generally accept Visa, Master-Card, Cirrus or Maestro cards, as well as more obscure ones. There is almost always a transaction surcharge for cash withdrawals with foreign cards. There are nonbank-run ATMs that charge £1.50 to £2 per transaction. These are normally found inside shops and are particularly expensive for foreign-bank cardholders. The ATM generally warns you before you take money out that it will charge you but be vigilant.

Also, always beware of suspicious-looking devices attached to ATMs. Many London ATMs have now been made tamper-proof, but certain fraudsters' devices are capable of sucking your card into the machine, allowing the fraudsters to release it when you have given up and left.

Changing Money

The best place to change money is in any local post office branch, where no commission is charged.

You can also change money in most high-street banks and some travel agencies, as well as at the numerous bureaux de change throughout the city.

Compare rates and watch for the commission that is not always mentioned very prominently. The trick is to ask how many pounds you'll receive in total before committing – you'll lose nothing by shopping around.

Credit & Debit Cards

Londoners live off their debit cards, which can also be used to get 'cash back' from supermarkets. Card transactions and cash withdrawals are generally subject to additional charges for foreign cardholders; check with your provider.

➡ Credit and debit cards are accepted almost universally in London, from restaurants and bars to shops and even by some taxis.

➡ American Express and Diners Club are far less widely used than Visa and MasterCard.

➡ Contactless cards and payments (which do not require a chip and pin or a signature) are increasingly widespread (watch for the wi-fi like symbol on cards and in shops). Transactions are limited to a maximum of £30.

Tipping

Many restaurants add a 12.5% 'discretionary' service charge to your bill. It's legal for them to do so but this should be clearly advertised.

In places that don't include a service charge, you are expected to leave 10% extra unless the service was unsatisfactory. A tip of 15% is for extraordinary service.

You never tip to have your pint pulled or wine poured in a pub.

Some guides and/or drivers on Thames boat trips will solicit you – sometimes rather forcefully – for their commentary. Whether you pay is up to you but it is not required.

You can tip taxi drivers up to 10% but most people just round up to the nearest pound.

Opening Hours

The following table summarises standard opening hours. Reviews will list exact times for each venue.

Sights	10am-6pm
Banks	9am-5pm Mon-Fri
Shops	9am-7pm Mon-Sat, noon-6pm Sun
Restaurants	noon-2.30pm & 6-11pm
Pubs & bars	11am-11pm

Post

The **Royal Mail** (www.royalmail.co.uk) is no longer the humdinger it once was but is generally very reliable.

Postcodes

The unusual London postcode system dates back to WWI. The whole city is divided into districts denoted by a letter (or letters) and a number. For example, W1, the postcode for Mayfair and Soho, stands for 'West London, district 1'. EC1, on the other hand, stands for 'East Central London, district 1'. The number a district is assigned has nothing to do with its geographic location, but rather its alphabetical listing in that area. For example, in North London N1 and N16 are right next to each other as are E1 and E14 in East London.

Public Holidays

Most attractions and businesses close for a couple of days over Christmas and sometimes Easter. Places that normally shut on Sunday will probably close on bank-holiday Mondays.

New Year's Day 1 January

Good Friday Late March/April

Easter Monday Late March/April

May Day Holiday First Monday in May

Spring Bank Holiday Last Monday in May

Summer Bank Holiday Last Monday in August

Christmas Day 25 December

Boxing Day 26 December

School Holidays

These change from year to year and often from school to school. As a general rule, however, they are as follows:

Spring half term One week in mid-February

Easter holidays One week either side of Easter Sunday

Summer half term One week in late May/early June

Summer holiday Late July to early September

Autumn half term One week in late October/early November

Christmas holidays Roughly 20 December to 6 January

Safe Travel

London is a fairly safe city for its size, so exercising common sense should keep you secure.

If you're getting a cab after a night's clubbing, make sure you go for a black taxi or a licensed minicab firm. Many of the touts operating outside clubs and bars are unlicensed and can therefore be unsafe.

Pickpocketing does happen in London, so keep an eye on your handbag and wallet, especially in bars and nightclubs, and in crowded areas such as the Underground.

Taxes & Refunds

Value-added tax (VAT) is a sales tax of up to 20% levied on most goods and services except food, books and children's clothing. Restaurants must, by law, include VAT in their menu prices, although VAT is not always included in hotel room prices, so always ask when booking to avoid unpleasant surprises at bill time.

It's sometimes possible for visitors to claim a refund of VAT paid on goods. You're eligible if you live outside the EU and are heading back home, or if you're an EU citizen and are leaving the EU for more than 12 months.

Not all shops participate in what is called either the VAT Retail Export Scheme or Tax Free Shopping, and different shops will have different minimum purchase conditions (normally around £75 in any one shop). On request, participating shops will give you a special form (VAT 407). This must be presented with the goods and receipts to customs when you depart the country. (VAT-free goods can't be posted or shipped home.) After customs has certified the form, you can sometimes get a refund on the spot, otherwise the form gets sent back to the shop, which then processes your refund (minus an administration or handling fee). This can take up to 10 weeks.

Telephone

British Telecom's famous red phone boxes survive in conservation areas only (notably Westminster). Some people use them as shelter while using their mobile phones.

Some BT phones still accept coins, but most take phonecards (available from retailers, including most post offices and some newsagents) or credit cards.

Useful phone numbers (charged calls) include:

Directory Enquiries (International) ☑118 505

Directory Enquiries (Local & National) ☑118 118, ☑118 500

International dialing code ☑00

Operator (International) ☑155

Operator (Local & National) ☑100

Premium rate applies ☑09

Reverse Charge/Collect Calls ☑155

Special rates apply ☑084 and ☑087

Toll-free ☑0800

Calling London

London's area code is 020, followed by an eight-digit number beginning with 7 (central London), 8 (Greater London) or 3 (non-geographic).

You only need to dial the 020 when you are calling London from elsewhere in the UK or if you're dialling from a mobile.

To call London from abroad, dial your country's international access code (usually 00 but 011 in Canada and the USA), then 44 (the UK's country code), then 20 (dropping the initial 0), followed by the eight-digit phone number.

International Calls & Rates

International direct dialling (IDD) calls to almost anywhere can be made from nearly all public telephones. Direct dialling is cheaper than making a reverse-charge (collect) call through the international operator.

Many private firms offer cheaper international calls than BT. In such places you phone from a metered booth and then pay the bill. Some cybercafes and internet shops also offer cheap rates for international calls.

International calling cards with stored value (usually £5, £10 or £20) and a PIN, which you can use from any phone by dialling a special access number, are usually the cheapest way to call abroad. These cards are available at most corner shops.

Note that the use of Skype may be restricted in hostels and internet cafes because of noise and/or bandwidth issues.

Local & National Call Rates

Local calls are charged by time alone; regional and national calls are charged by both time and distance.

Daytime rates apply from 7am to 7pm Monday to Friday.

The cheap rate applies from 7pm to 7am Monday to Friday and again over the weekend from 7pm Friday to 7am Monday.

Mobile Phones

The UK uses the GSM 900 network, which covers Europe, Australia and New Zealand, but is not compatible with CDMA mobile technology used in the US and Japan (although some American and Japanese phones can work on both GSM and CDMA networks).

If you have a GSM phone, check with your service provider about using it in the UK and enquire about roaming charges.

It's usually better to buy a local SIM card from any mobile-phone shop, though in order to do that you must ensure your handset from home is unlocked.

Time

Wherever you are in the world, the time on your watch is measured in relation to the time at Greenwich in London – Greenwich Mean Time (GMT). British Summer Time, the UK's form of daylight-saving time, muddies the water so that even London is ahead of GMT from late March to late October.

Paris	GMT +1
New York	GMT -5
San Francisco	GMT -8
Sydney	GMT +10

Toilets

It's now an offence to urinate in the streets. Train stations, bus terminals and attractions generally have good facilities, providing also for people with disabilities and those with young children. You'll also find public toilets across the city, some operated by local councils, others automated and self-cleaning. Most now charge 50p.

Tourist Information

Visit London (⌨0870 156 6366; www.visitlondon.com) Visit London can fill you in on everything from tourist attractions and events (such as the Changing of the Guard and Chinese New Year parade) to river trips and tours, accommodation, eating, theatre, shopping, children's London, and gay and lesbian venues. There are helpful kiosks at **Heathrow Airport** (Terminal 1, 2 & 3 Underground station; ⊙7.30am-7.30pm), **King's Cross St Pancras Station** (⊙8.15am-6.15pm),

Liverpool Street Station (⊙7.15am-7pm Sun-Thu, to 9pm Fri & Sat), **Piccadilly Circus Underground Station** (⊙8am-7pm Mon-Fri, 9.15am-6pm Sat & Sun) and **Victoria Station** (⊙7.15am-8pm Mon-Sat, 8.15am-7pm Sun). Local tourist offices include the following:

City of London Information Centre (www.visitthecity.co.uk; St Paul's Churchyard, EC4; ⊙9.30am-5.30pm Mon-Sat, 10am-4pm Sun; ☏; ⊖St Paul's) Tourist information, fast-track tickets to City attractions and guided walks (adult/child £7/6).

Greenwich Tourist Office (⌨0870 608 2000; www.visitgreenwich.org.uk; Pepys House, 2 Cutty Sark Gardens, SE10; ⊙10am-5pm; ⊟DLR Cutty Sark) Has a wealth of information about Greenwich and the surrounding areas. Free daily guided walks leave at 12.15pm and 2.15pm.

Travellers with Disabilities

For travellers with disabilities, London is an odd mix of user-friendliness and downright disinterest. New hotels and modern tourist attractions are legally required to be accessible to people in wheelchairs, but many historic buildings, B&Bs and guesthouses are in older buildings, which are hard to adapt.

Transport is equally hit and miss, but slowly improving:

➜ Only 66 of London's 270

PRACTICALITIES

Weights & Measures

The UK uses a confusing mix of metric and imperial systems.

Smoking

Forbidden in all enclosed public places nationwide. Most pubs have some sort of smoking area outside.

VISA REQUIREMENTS

COUNTRY	TOURISM	WORK	STUDY
European Economic Area	X	X	X
Australia, Canada, New Zealand, USA	X (for stay of up to 6 months)	√	√
Other nationalities	√	√	√

tube stations have step-free access; the rest have escalators or stairs.

➡ The above-ground DLR is entirely accessible for wheelchairs.

➡ All buses can be lowered to street level when they stop; wheelchair users travel free.

➡ Guide dogs are universally welcome on public transport and in hotels, restaurants, attractions etc.

Transport for London (www.tfl.gov.uk) publishes the *Getting Around London* guide, which contains the latest information on accessibility for passengers with disabilities. Download it from the website.

The following organisations can provide helpful information before you travel:

Disability Rights UK (☎020-7250 8181; www.disabilityrightsuk.org) This is an umbrella organisation for voluntary groups for people with disabilities. Many wheelchair-accessible toilets can be opened only with a special Royal Association of Disability and Rehabilitation (Radar) key, which can be obtained via the website or from tourist offices for £4.50.

Royal National Institute for the Blind (☎020-7388 1266; www.rnib.org.uk) The UK's main charity for people with sight loss.

Action on Hearing Loss (☎0808 808 0123, textphone 0808 808 9000; www.actiononhearingloss.org.uk) This is the main organisation working with deaf and hard of hearing people in the UK. Many ticket offices and banks are fitted with hearing loops to help the hearing-impaired; look for the ear symbol.

Visas

Immigration to the UK is becoming tougher, particularly for those seeking to work or study. The following table indicates who will need a visa for what, but make sure you check the website of the **UK Border Agency** (www.gov.uk/check-uk-visa) or with your local British embassy or consulate for the most up-to-date information.

Visa Extensions

Tourist visas can be extended as long as the total time spent in the UK is less than six months, or in clear emergencies (eg an accident, death of a relative). Contact the **UK Visas and Immigration Contact Centre** (☎0300 123 2241; ☺9am-4.30pm Mon-Fri) for details.

Women Travellers

Female visitors to London are unlikely to have many problems, provided they take the usual big-city precautions. Don't get into an Underground carriage with no one else in it or with just one or two men. And if you feel unsafe, you should take a taxi or licensed minicab.

Apart from the occasional wolf whistle and unwelcome body contact on the tube, women will find male Londoners reasonably enlightened. Going into pubs alone may not always be a comfortable experience, though it is in no way out of the ordinary.

Marie Stopes International (☎0845 300 8090; www.mariestopes.org.uk; 108 Whitfield St, W1; ☺8am-4pm Mon-Wed, 11am-5pm Fri; ⊖Warren St) provides contraception, sexual-health checks and abortions.

Behind the Scenes

SEND US YOUR FEEDBACK

We love to hear from travellers – your comments keep us on our toes and help make our books better. Our well-travelled team reads every word on what you loved or loathed about this book. Although we cannot reply individually to your submissions, we always guarantee that your feedback goes straight to the appropriate authors, in time for the next edition. Each person who sends us information is thanked in the next edition – the most useful submissions are rewarded with a selection of digital PDF chapters.

Visit **lonelyplanet.com/contact** to submit your updates and suggestions or to ask for help. Our award-winning website also features inspirational travel stories, news and discussions.

Note: We may edit, reproduce and incorporate your comments in Lonely Planet products such as guidebooks, websites and digital products, so let us know if you don't want your comments reproduced or your name acknowledged. For a copy of our privacy policy visit lonelyplanet.com/privacy.

OUR READERS

Many thanks to the travellers who used the last edition and wrote to us with helpful hints, useful advice and interesting anecdotes:
Cornelia Pabijan, Denise Heijstek, Elena Delfino, Elinor McKenzie, Fabio Baldi & Monica Ramazzotti, Maggie Terp, Mariana Banus, Mihnea Anastasiu, Rob McDonald, Sara Ward.

AUTHOR THANKS

Peter Dragicevich

Many thanks to Tim Benzie, Paul Joseph, Lucille Henry, Kerri Tyler and Tasmin Waby for your unstinting dedication to helping me eat and drink my way around East and North London.

Steve Fallon

A million thanks to fellow authors Emilie Filou, Damian Harper and Peter Dragicevich for their advice and suggestions along the way. Fellow Blue Badge Tourist Guides – too many to name – were also of great help. As always, I'd like to state my admiration, gratitude and great love for my partner, Michael Rothschild.

Emilie Filou

Big thanks to team London (Steve, Damian, Peter and James) for their collaboration and tips. Thank you to my lovely friends Catherine and Nikki who chipped in with recommendations and made eating and drinking so much more fun. Thanks as usual to chief critic and husband extraordinaire Adolfo for his company on weekend outings; and for the first time, thank you to our daughter, Sasha, who came along for (some of!) the ride aged just six months!

Damian Harper

Many thanks to all the following for their help and suggestions for this book: Laure Prouvost, Giles Bird, Alan Kingshott, Joanna Freeman, Laura Teale, Ian Franklin, Jim Peake and Paul Collins. Thanks also to my co-authors for all their help, and gratitude once more to Daisy, Tim and Emma.

ACKNOWLEDGEMENTS

Cover photograph: The Shard and Tower Bridge/Richard Boll/Getty. The Shard is designed by Renzo Piano.

THIS BOOK

This 10th edition of Lonely Planet's *London* guidebook was researched and written by Peter Dragicevich, Steve Fallon, Emilie Filou and Damian Harper. The previous edition was written by Emilie Filou, Steve Fallon, Damian Harper and Vesna Maric. This guidebook was produced by the following:

Destination Editor
James Smart
Product Editors Katie O'Connell, Kathryn Rowan
Senior Cartographer
Mark Griffiths
Book Designer
Wibowo Rusli
Senior Editors Andi Jones, Karyn Noble
Assisting Editors Andrew Bain, Judith Bamber, Justin Flynn, Carly Hall, Victoria Harrison, Kellie

Langdon, Luna Soo, Amanda Williamson
Cover Researcher
Naomi Parker
Illustrators Javier Zarracina, Michael Weldon
Thanks to Sasha Baskett, Brendan Dempsey, Ryan Evans, Katherine Marsh, Wayne Murphy, Kirsten Rawlings, Diana Saengkham, Sally Schafer, Ellie Simpson, Lyahna Spencer, Angela Tinson, Lauren Wellicome

See also separate subindexes for:

✗ **EATING P398**

🍷 **DRINKING & NIGHTLIFE P400**

☆ **ENTERTAINMENT P401**

🛍 **SHOPPING P401**

🏃 **SPORTS & ACTIVITIES P402**

🛏 **SLEEPING P402**

Index

18 Stafford Terrace 257
20 Fenchurch St 147
30 St Mary Axe 146

A
Abbey Road Studios 238
Abney Park Cemetery 247
accommodation 19, 318-34,
   see also Sleeping *subindex*
activities 65-7
airports 380-2
Albert Memorial 186-7
Alexandra Palace 254
All Hallows by the Tower 146
All Saints 99
All Souls Church 100
Apsley House 186
ArcelorMittal Orbit 221
architecture 28, 274, 356-60
Arsenal Emirates Stadium
   241-2
art 259, 368-70
Ashmolean Museum
   (Oxford) 309
Auld Shillelagh 247

B
Balliol College (Oxford) 309
Bank of England Museum 147
Bankside
   drinking & nightlife 170
   food 167
   sights 164
Banqueting House 107
Barbican 149-50
Bath 314-17, **316**
Bath Abbey (Bath) 315
Bath Assembly Rooms
   (Bath) 315
bathrooms 391
Battersea 277, **442**
   drinking & nightlife 286
   food 282, 284
   sights 277

Sights 000
Map Pages **000**
Photo Pages **000**

Battersea Park 277
Battersea Power Station 277
Bermondsey 166, 167,
   169, 170
Bethnal Green
   drinking & nightlife 225-6
   food 222-3
   sights 216
Bevis Marks Synagogue 146
Big Ben 87, **3**
Black Cultural Archives 276
Bloomsbury **412**
   drinking & nightlife 120-1
   food 111
   shopping 128
   sights 98-100
boat races 65
boat travel 385
Bodleian Library (Oxford) 309
Borough Market 162, **45, 162**
Brick Lane Great Mosque 201
Brighton 310
Brighton Pier (Brighton) 310
British Library 39, 232-3, **232**
British Museum 7, 17, 81-4,
   6-7, 81, 82, 83, 82-3
Brixton **442**
   drinking & nightlife 285
   food 282
   sights 276-7
Brixton Village 276, **36**
Broadcasting House 100
Brompton Cemetery 258
Brompton Oratory 185-6
Brunel Museum 166
BT Tower 97
Buckingham Palace 85-6, **85**
Buddhapadipa Temple
   299-300
Bunhill Fields 200
Burlington Arcade 100
bus travel 382, 383-4
business hours 45, 53, 389

C
cable car 385
Cambridge 311-14, **312**
Camden 73, **436**
   accommodation 330-1

drinking & nightlife 231,
   249-50
entertainment 251-2
food 231, 245
highlights 10, 230, 232-4
shopping 252-4
sights 238, 240
sports & activities 254
transport 231
Camden Market 240, **11**
Canonbury Square 243
Carlyle's House 189
car travel 385
cell phones 18, 391
cemeteries 27
Cenotaph 107-8
Central Criminal Court
   (Old Bailey) 150-1
Changing of the Guard 38, **3**
Charles Dickens Museum 99
Charterhouse 199
Chelsea 188-9, 192
Chelsea Flower Show 30
Chelsea Old Church 189
Chelsea Physic Garden 189
children, travel with 33-5
Chinatown
   drinking & nightlife 121-2
   food 112-16
   shopping 128, 130-1
   sights 102-4
Chiswick 297-8, 301, 302
Chiswick House 297-8
Christ Church (Oxford) 307
Christ Church Spitalfields 201
churches 28
Churchill War Rooms 95, **95**
Circus, the (Bath) 315
City Hall 166
City, the 72, 152-3, **418**
   accommodation 324-5
   drinking & nightlife 135,
      153, 155
   entertainment 155
   food 135, 152-3
   highlights 134, 136-45
   shopping 155
   sights 136-52
   transport 135
   walks 154

Clapham **442**
Clarence House 101
Clerkenwell 73, **426**
   accommodation 328-9
   drinking & nightlife 197,
      207-8
   entertainment 210-11
   food 197, 201-2, 204
   highlights 196
   shopping 211-12
   sights 198-200
   transport 197
climate 19
Columbia Road Flower
   Market 216
costs 18, 45, 319, 384,
   387, 390
County Hall 164
Covent Garden **406**
   drinking & nightlife 122-3
   food 116-18
   shopping 131-2
   sights 104-6
Covent Garden Piazza
   104-5, **21**
cricket 65-6
Crystal, the 220
culture 27, 336-7
currency 18
customs regulations 387, 388
Cutty Sark 273
cycling 66, 67, 384

D
Dalston 216-17, 223, 226
Dalston Eastern Curve
   Gardens 217
dance 367
Danson House 285
Dennis Severs' House 200
Deptford 283, **283**
Design Museum 166
disabilities, travellers with 391
drinking 52-5, **53, 54**
   see also Drinking &
   Nightlife *subindex, indi-*
   vidual neighbourhoods
Dr Johnson's House 151-2
Dulwich Picture Gallery
   280, **40**

INDEX E-M

E

Earl's Court 258, 264-5, **440**
East London 73, **430**
  accommodation 329-30
  drinking & nightlife 214, 225-7
  entertainment 227-8
  food 214, 222-5
  highlights 213
  shopping 228-9
  sights 215-17, 219-21
  sports & activities 229
  transport 214
  walks 218, **218**
economy 336-7
electricity 387
Elephant & Castle 275, 281-2, 284-5
Eltham Palace 280
emergencies 387
Emirates Air Line 220-1, 287
entertainment 56-60, *see also* Entertainment *subindex, individual neighbourhoods*
Estorick Collection of Modern Italian Art 243-4
Eton (Windsor) 306
Euston 235-7, 244-5, 248-9
events 29-32

F

Fan Museum 274
Faraday Museum 102
fashion 370-1
Fashion & Textile Museum 166
Fenton House 240
festivals 29-32
film 336, 375-7
Firepower (Royal Artillery Museum) 274-5
Fitzrovia
  drinking & nightlife 120-1
  food 111-12
  shopping 128
  sights 98-100
Fitzwilliam Museum (Cambridge) 313
Florence Nightingale Museum 275
food 10, 44-51, **10**, **44**, **47**, **49**, **46**, *see also* Eating *subindex, individual neighbourhoods*
football 65
Fourth Plinth Project 17, 105

Sights 000
Map Pages 000
Photo Pages **000**
---

free attractions 38-9
Freud Museum 241
Fulham Palace 188
Fuller's Griffin Brewery 298

G

gay travellers 68-9
Geffrye Museum 198
Golden Boy of Pye Corner 150
Golden Hinde 164
Granary Square 236-7
Great Exhibition, the 347
Great Fire of London 344-5
Green Park 102
Greenwich 73, **445**
  accommodation 333-4
  drinking & nightlife 269, 284
  entertainment 286
  food 269, 280-1
  highlights 268, 270-2
  shopping 287
  sights 270-4
  sports & activities 287
  transport 269
Greenwich Foot Tunnel 287
Greenwich Park 270-1, **278**
Guards Museum 102
Guildhall 148-9
Guildhall Galleries 149
Guy Fawkes Night 32

H

Hackney 217, 219, 224, 227
Hackney City Farm 216
Hackney Museum 217
Ham House 296-7
Hammersmith 259, 262-3, 265
Hampstead **433**
  drinking & nightlife 250
  food 246
  sights 240-1
Hampstead Heath 242
Hampton Court 12, 73, 288, 334
Hampton Court Palace 290-3, **12**, **290**, **292**, **293**, **292-3**
Handel House Museum 110
Henry VIII 341-2
Highgate 241, 250, **433**
Highgate Cemetery 243
Highgate Wood 241
history 28, 338-55
HMS Belfast 165
Hogarth's House 298
Holborn 108-10, 118, 123-4
Holborn Viaduct 151
holidays 390
Holland Park 257-8

Horniman Museum 277
Horse Guards Parade 107
horse racing 66
House Mill 221
House of Illustration 237
Houses of Parliament 38, 87-8, 98, **87**
Hunterian Museum 109-10
Hyde Park 73, **13**, **182**, **424**
  accommodation 326-8
  drinking & nightlife 175, 193
  entertainment 194
  food 175, 189, 192
  highlights 12, 174, 176-84
  shopping 194-5
  sights 176-89, 186-8
  transport 175

I

ice skating 66
Imperial War Museum 17, 275, **42**
Inns of Court 106
Institute of Contemporary Arts 102
internet access 21, 387
Isle of Dogs 219-20, 225, **432**
Islington **434**
  drinking & nightlife 250-1
  food 247-8
  sights 242-4
itineraries 24-5

J

Jewish Museum London 238, 240

K

Keats House 241
Kennington 275, 281-2, 284-5
Kensal Green Cemetery 259
Kensington 73, **424**
  accommodation 326-8
  drinking & nightlife 175, 193
  entertainment 194
  food 175, 189, 191-3
  highlights 174, 176-84
  shopping 194-5
  sights 176-89
  transport 175
  walks 190, **190**
Kensington Gardens 12, 186
Kensington Palace 187
Kenwood House 241
Kew 73, **446**
  drinking & nightlife 289, 301-2

food 289, 301
  highlights 288
  sights 296-7
Kew Gardens 294-5, **278-9**, **294**
King's College Chapel (Cambridge) 313
King's Cross **434**
  drinking & nightlife 248-9
  food 244-5
  sights 235-7
King's Cross Station 236
King's Road 188
Knightsbridge 185-6, 189, 191

L

Lambeth Palace 275
language 18
Leadenhall Market 147, **3**
Leake Street Graffiti Tunnel 164
legal matters 387-8
Leicester Square
  drinking & nightlife 122-3
  food 116-18
  shopping 131-2
  sights 104-6
Leicester Square 105
Leighton House 257
lesbian travellers 68-9
literature 336, 361-4
Little Venice 258
Lloyd's of London 146-7
local life 36-7
London Bridge 164-5, 167, 170
London Bridge Experience & London Tombs 165
London Canal Museum 237
London Central Mosque 238
London Dungeon 163
London Eye 14, 161, **14**, **161**
London Fields 217
London Film Museum 105
London Sea Life Aquarium 164
London Transport Museum 105, **35**
London Underground 17, 383, 384
London Wetland Centre 297
London Zoo 234, **234**
Lord's 238

M

Madame Tussauds 109
Magdalen Bridge Boathouse (Oxford) 310
Magdalen College (Oxford) 307-8
Mansion House 148

Marble Arch 187
Marble Hill House 298-9
Marx Memorial Library 199-200
Marylebone
  drinking & nightlife 124
  food 118-19
  shopping 132
  sights 110
Mayfair **414**
  drinking & nightlife 124
  food 119-20
  shopping 132-3
  sights 110
measures 391
medical services 388-9
Michelin House 186
Mile End Park 219
Millennium Bridge 164
mobile phones 18, 391
money 18, 21, 45, 319, 389
Monument 148
motorcycle travel 385
Mudchute 220, **33**
Museum of Brands, Packaging & Advertising 257
Museum of London 151
Museum of London Docklands 220
Museum of the History of Science (Oxford) 309
museums & galleries 40-3
music 27, 228, 248, 372-4

N
National Army Museum 189
National Gallery 7, 38, 89, **7, 26, 89, 90-1**
National Maritime Museum 274
National Portrait Gallery 93, **93**
National Theatre 163-4, 171
Natural History Museum 16, 33, 180-1, **16, 180**
New London Architecture 99
No 2 Willow Road 240-1
No 10 Downing Street 106
North London 73, **433, 434, 436**
  accommodation 330-1
  drinking & nightlife 231, 248-51
  entertainment 251-2
  food 231, 244-8
  highlights 230, 232-4
  shopping 252-4
  sights 232-44
  sports & activities 254
  transport 231
  walks 239

Notting Hill 73, **438**
  accommodation 331-3
  drinking & nightlife 256, 263-4
  entertainment 266
  food 256, 260, 262
  highlights 255
  shopping 266-7
  sights 257
  sports & activities 267
  transport 256
  walks 261, **261**
Notting Hill Carnival 15, 31, 257, **14**

O
O2 273
Old Operating Theatre Museum & Herb Garret 165
Old Royal Naval College 272
Old Truman Brewery 201
opening hours 45, 53, 389
Oxford 307-11, **308**
Oxford and Cambridge Boat Race 297
Oyster Card 383

P
parks & gardens 27
Petersham Meadows 296
Petrie Museum of Egyptian Archaeology 99
Photographer's Gallery 104
Piccadilly Circus 103
Pimlico 192-3
Pitt Rivers Museum (Oxford) 309
plague, the 341, 344
planning
  budgeting 18, 38, 45, 387
  children, travel with 33-5
  festivals & events 29-32
  first time visitor 20-1
  itineraries 24-5
  local life 36-7
  London basics 18
  London's neighbour-hoods 72-5
  repeat visitors 17
  travel seasons 19
  websites 18
politics 337
Pollock's Toy Museum 99
population 337
Portobello Road Market 258
postal services 389
Postman's Park 150
Primrose Hill 238
public holidays 390
pubs 9, **8** see also Drinking & Nightlife subindex
Pulteney Bridge (Bath) 315

Q
Queen Elizabeth Olympic Park 17, 221
Queen's Chapel 102
Queen's House 273

R
Radcliffe Camera (Oxford) 309
Ragged School Museum 219
Rasa 247
Red House 285
Regent Street 104
Regent's Canal 246
Regent's Park 237-8
religion 337
Richmond 73, **446**
  accommodation 334
  drinking & nightlife 289, 301-2
  food 289, 300-1
  highlights 288
  sights 296-7
Richmond Bridge 296
Richmond Bridge Boathouses 296
Richmond Green 296
Richmond Lock 296
Richmond Park 296, **279**
Ridley Road Market 216
River Westbourne 185
rivers & canals 27-8
Roman Amphitheatre 149
Roman Baths (Bath) 314-15
Rotherhithe 166, 170-1
Round Church (Cambridge) 313
Roupell St 163
Royal Academy of Arts 101
Royal Albert Hall 185, 194, **56**
Royal College of Music Museum 185
Royal Courts of Justice 108
Royal Crescent (Bath) 315
Royal Exchange 148
Royal Hospital Chelsea 188-9
Royal Observatory 270-1, **270**
Royal Opera House 105, 124 **57**
Royal Pavilion (Brighton) 310

S
Saatchi Gallery 39, 188
safety 390
Savill Garden (Windsor) 306
Science Museum 184, **41, 184**
Serpentine Gallery 182-3
Shakespeare's Globe 160, 171-2, **59, 75, 160**

Shard 17, 164, **5, 71**
Sheldonian Theatre (Oxford) 309
Shepherd's Bush 259, 262-3, **440**
Sherlock Holmes Museum 110
shopping 61-4, see also Shopping subindex, individual neighbour-hoods
Shoreditch 73, **426**
  accommodation 328-9
  drinking & nightlife 197, 208-10
  entertainment 210-11
  food 197, 205-6
  highlights 196
  shopping 211-12
  transport 197
  walks 202-3, **203**
Sir John Soane's Museum 17, 96, **96**
Smithfield Market 150
smoking 391
soccer 65
Soho
  drinking & nightlife 121-2
  food 112-16
  shopping 128, 130-1
  sights 102-4
Somerset House 107, **74**
South Bank, the 73, **420**
  accommodation 325-6
  drink 157
  drinking & nightlife 169-71
  entertainment 171-2
  food 157, 166-7, 169
  highlights 156, 158-62
  shopping 173
  sights 158-66
  transport 157
  walks 168, **168**
South Kensington
  food 189, 191
  sights 185-6
South London 73, 333-4, **442, 444**
Southbank Centre 163, 171
Southwark 164, 167, 170
Southwark Cathedral 165
Spencer House 102
Spitalfields 73, **426**
  accommodation 328-9
  drinking & nightlife 197, 210
  food 197, 206-7
  highlights 196
  sights 200-1
  walks 202-3, **203**
sports 65-7
Square of Bloomsbury 98-9
St Alfege Church 39, 273-4

INDEX EATING

St Anne's Limehouse 219
St Augustine's Tower 217
St Bartholomew-the-Great 150
St Bride's, Fleet Street 152
St Clement Danes 108-9
St George-in-the-East 217
St George's, Bloomsbury 99-100
St George's Town Hall 217
St Giles-in-the-Fields 103
St James's **416**
 drinking & nightlife 120
 food 110-11
 shopping 126-8
 sights 100-2
St James's Palace 101
St James's Park 100
St James's Piccadilly 100-1
St John's Gate 198-9
St John's Priory Church 199
St John's, Smith Square 97-8
St Katharine Docks 215
St Lawrence Jewry 149
St Martin-in-the-Fields 39, 106, **26**
St Mary-le-Bow 148
St Mary's Church 243
St Olave's 146
St Pancras Station & Hotel 235-6
St Paul's Cathedral 142-4, 147, **142**, **144**
Stoke Newington 247
Stonehenge 315
Strand, the 108-10, 123-4
Strawberry Hill 299
St Stephen Walbrook 148
Supreme Court 97
Sutton House 217
Syon House 298

T
Tate Britain 92, **92**
Tate Modern 9, 39, 158-9, **8**, **75**, **158**
taxes 390
taxis 384-5
telephone services 18, 390-1
Temple Church 39, 152, **38**
Thames Barrier 276
Thames, the 74-5
Thatcher, Margaret 353-4
theatre 12, 365-7, **13**
time 18, 391

Sights 000
Map Pages **000**
Photo Pages **000**

tipping 21, 45
toilets 391
tourist information 18, 391
tours 385-6
Tower Bridge 145, **5**, **145**
Tower Hamlets Cemetery Park 219
Tower of London 9, 38, 136-41, **9**, **136**, **138**, **139**, **141**, **138-9**
Trafalgar Sq 17, 94
train travel 17, 382, 383, 384
travel to London 19, 380-2
travel within London 22-3, 382-5
Trinity College (Cambridge) 313
Trinity College (Oxford) 308-9
Trinity Square Gardens 146
Trooping the Colour 30
tube, the 17, 383, 384
Two Temple Palace 109
Tyburn Convent 187-8

V
V&A Museum of Childhood 216
Victoria & Albert Museum 11, 38, 176-9, **11**, **176**, **178**, **179**, **178-9**
Victoria Park 219
View Tube 221
Viktor Wynd Museum of Curiosities, Fine Art & Natural History 219
visas 18, 392

W
walks 28
 City, the 154, **154**
 Deptford 283, **283**
 East London 218, **218**
 Kensington 190, **190**
 North London 239, **239**
 Notting Hill 261, **261**
 Shoreditch 202-3, **203**
 South Bank, 168, **168**
 Spitalfields 202-3, **203**
 West End, 129, **129**
Wallace Collection 108
Warner Bros Studios 17, 237
Waterloo 163-4, 166-7, 169
weather 19
websites 18, 318
weights 391
Wellcome Collection 236
Wellington Arch 185
Wesley's Chapel 200
West End, the 72, **406**, **408**, **412**, **414**, **416**
 accommodation 321-4

drinking & nightlife 77, 120-4
 entertainment 124-6
 food 77, 110-20
 highlights 76-7, 78-96
 shopping 126-8, 130-3
 sights 78-96, 97-110
 transport 77
 walks 129, **129**
West London 73, **438**, **440**
 accommodation 331-3
 drinking & nightlife 256, 263-6
 entertainment 266
 food 256, 260, 262-3
 highlights 255
 shopping 266-7
 sights 257-9
 sports & activities 267
 transport 256
Westbourne Grove 257, 260, 263-4
Westminster 97-8, 110-11, 126-8
Westminster Abbey 15, 78-80, **15**, **78**
Westminster Cathedral 97
White Cube Bermondsey 166
Whitechapel 215-16, 222, 225
Whitechapel Bell Foundry 216
Whitechapel Gallery 215
Whitechapel Road 215
William Morris Gallery 244
William Morris Society 259
Wimbledon 30, 66
Wimbledon Common 299
Wimbledon Lawn Tennis Museum 299
Windsor Castle (Windsor) 304-6, **304**
Windsor Great Park (Windsor) 306
women travellers 392

✕ EATING
10 Greek St 115

A
A Cooke's 262
A Little of What You Fancy 223
Abeno 111
Addis 245
Al Boccon di'Vino 300-1
Albion 206
Allpress Espresso 205
Anchor & Hope 167
Andina 205-6
Andrew Edmunds 114
Angels & Gypsies 281

Arabica Bar & Kitchen 167
Arancina 260
Arbutus 116
Atomic Burger (Oxford) 310

B
Baiwei 113
Balthazar 117
Baltic 167
Baozi Inn 114
Bar Boulud 191
Bar Shu 114
Barnyard 112
Barrafina 115
Bistrotheque 224
Black Vanilla 281
Blackfoot 204
Bó Drake 115
Bocca di Lupo 115
Bone Daddies Ramen Bar 113
Brasserie Chavot 120
Brasserie Zedel 114
Brawn 222
Breakfast Club, the 114
Briciole 119
Brick Lane Beigel Bake 206
Brunswick House 284
Burger & Lobster Soho 115
Busaba Eathai 111
Bush Theatre Cafe & Bar 262

C
Café Below 152
Cafe Murano 110-11
Cafe Spice Namasté 222
Camino Monumento 153
Canela 117
Cantina Laredo 118
Caravan 204, 244-5
Casse-Croûte 169
Cây Tre 205
Ceviche 113
Champagne + Fromage 282
Chez Bruce 282, 284
Chez Lindsay 300
Chilango 247
Chiltern Firehouse 119
Chin Chin Labs 245
Churchill Thai Kitchen 260
Circus (Bath) 317
City Social 153
Climpson & Sons 224
Clove Club 206
Coach & Horses 201-2
Comptoir Gascon 202
Corner Room 222
Cornucopia (Windsor) 305
Counter Cafe 224-5
Counter Vauxhall Arches 284
Couscous Café 263

D

Dabbous 112
Daylesford Organic 193
Delaunay 117
Dinner by Heston
  Blumenthal 191
Dirty Burger 245
Dishoom 116
Diwana Bhel Poori House
  244
Dragon Castle 281
Drawing Room Café 188
Duck & Waffle 152-3
Duke's Brew & Que 223

E

E Pellicci 222
Eagle 204
Edamame (Oxford) 310
Electric Diner 260
Ember Yard 119
Empress 224
English's of Brighton
  (Brighton) 310
Enoteca Turi 301
E&O 260
Eyre Brothers 206

F

F Cooke 224
Fernandez & Wells 114
Fifteen 205
Fino 112
Fish House 224, 260
Folly 153
Food For Thought 117
Foodilic 244
Formans 225
Foyer at Claridge's 120
Franco Manca 111-12,
  282, 301

G

Gallery Cafe 222
Galvin Café à Vin 206
Galvin La Chapelle 206-7
Gate 263
Gauthier Soho 115
Geales 260
Gelateria Danieli 300
Gelupo 113-14
Gilbey's (Windsor) 305
Glasshouse 301
Goddards at Greenwich 281
Golden Hind 118
Grain Store 244
Great Queen Street 117
Green Papaya 224
Greenhouse 119
Greenwich Market 280-1
Gymkhana 119

H

Hackney Pearl 225
Hakkasan Hanway Place 112
Hawksmoor 207
Hawksmoor Seven Dials 117
HKK 206
Honest Burgers 113, 282
Hunan 193

I

Iberia 246-7
Inn the Park 111
Inside 281

J

J Sheekey 117
Jose 169

K

Kanada-Ya 118
Karpo 245
Kennington Tandoori 281-2
Kerbisher & Malt 262
Kêu! 205
Kipferl 248
Kolapata 222
Konditor & Cook 166-7
Koya 112-13

L

La Fromagerie 119
Lady Ottoline 111
Lardo 224
L'Atelier 223
Launceston Place 191
Laxeiro 222-3
Le Boudin Blanc 120
Ledbury 260, 262
L'Eto 191
Lima 112
Little Bay 204
Little Georgia 224
Loafing 224
Lobster Pot 282
Locanda Locatelli 118
Look Mum No Hands! 204

M

M Manze 167, 169
Ma Goa 301
Magazine 192
Mama Lan 282
Mangal Ocakbasi 223
Manna 245
Market 245
Mazi 260
Medcalf 202
Medlar 192
Midsummer House
  (Cambridge) 314
Mildred's 113

Min Jiang 192
Miyama 153
Modern Pantry 204
Momo 119
Monocle Cafe 118
Morito 202
Moro 204

N

Namaaste Kitchen 245
National Dining Rooms 116
Naughty Piglets 282
Nobu 120
Nordic Bakery 113
North Sea Fish Restaurant
  111
Nude Espresso 206

O

Ognisko 191
Old Brewery 281
Orange Pekoe 301
Orangery 192
Orchard 111
Ottolenghi 247-8
Ozone Coffee Roasters 205

P

Painted Heron 192
Palomar 114
Perkin Reveller 153
Petersham Nurseries
  Cafe 300
Pied-à-Terre 112
Pier 1 300
Pimlico Fresh 192-3
Pint Shop (Cambridge) 313
Pitt Cue Co 115
Pollen Street Social 115
Polpo 113, 201
Poppies 206
Portrait 116
Potli 262
Princess of Shoreditch 205
Princess Victoria 263
Prufrock Coffee 201

Q

Quod (Oxford) 311

R

Rabbit 192
Ragam 112
Rib Room 191
Richmond Hill Bakery 300
Riddle & Finns (Brighton)
  310
River Cafe 263
Rivington Grill 281
Rock & Sole Plaice 116-17
Roka 112
Roots at N1 246

Rosa's 206
Rosie's Deli Café 282
Roti Chai 118
Rotorino 223
Rules 117

S

Santa Maria del Sur 282
Shepherd's Bush Market
  262
Shikumen 263
Shoreditch Grind 204
Shoryu 116
Skylon 167
Smokehouse 248
Smokeworks (Cambridge)
  313-14
Sông Quê 204-5
Sotto Sotto (Bath) 317
Spuntino 113
St John 202
St John Bread & Wine 202
Stag 246
Stein's 300
Sugar 111

T

Tai Won Mein 281
Taquería 260
Tayyabs 222
Terre à Terre (Brighton) 310
The Gun 225
Tibits 119
Tom's Kitchen 189, 191
Tosa 262
Towpath 223
Trullo 248
Two Brewers (Windsor) 305

U

Union Street Cafe 167

V

V&A Café 189
Vincent Rooms 110

W

Wahaca 116
Wallace 116
Watch House 167
Wells Tavern 246
White Swan 153
Wild Honey 120
Wine Library 153
Woodlands 246
Wright Brothers 207

Y

Yalla Yalla 118
Yauatcha 115
Yipin China 248
Yoobi 114

INDEX DRINKING & NIGHTLIFE

York & Albany 245

Z

Zucca 169
Zuma 191

🍸 DRINKING & NIGHTLIFE

5CC 208
6 St Chad's Place 249
40 Maltby Street 170
69 Colebrooke Row 251
93 Feet East 210
333 Mother 208

A

Adventure Cafe Bar (Bath) 317
Anglesea Arms 193
Anspach & Hobday 171
Ape & Bird 122
Artesian 124
Atlas 264-5

B

Bar Pepito 249
Barrio North 251
Beach Blanket Babylon 263
Bethnal Green Working Men's Club 226
Big Chill House 249
Blackfriar 155
Blues Kitchen 250
Book Club 209
Booking Office Bar & Restaurant 249
Bradley's Spanish Bar 121
BrewDog 209
BrewDog Camden 250
Bridge 208
Buddha Bar 193
Bull, the 250-1

C

Callooh Callay 209
Camino 249
Captain Kidd 225
Cargo 209-10
Carpenter's Arms 225
Castle, the 251
Cat & Mutton 227
Churchill Arms 264
City Barge 302
Corsica Studios 284
Counting House 155
Crooked Billet 302

Sights 000
Map Pages **000**
Photo Pages **000**

Cross Keys 123
Cutty Sark Tavern 284

D

Dalston Roof Park 226
Dalston Superstore 226
Dandelyan & Rumpus Room 170
Dog and Duck 122
Dogstar 285
Dove 265
Dove Freehouse 227
Draft House 123-4
Drayton Arms 193
DreamBagsJaguarShoes 209
Drink, Shop & Do 248
Dublin Castle 249
Duke of Wellington 122
Duke's Bar 120

E

Eagle 286
Eagle (Cambridge) 314
Earl of Lonsdale 263
Edge 122
Edinboro Castle 250
Effra Hall Tavern 285
Egg LDN 249
Espresso Library (Cambridge) 313
Euston Tap 248
Experimantal Cocktail Club 121

F

Fabric 207
Farr's School of Dancing 226
Fire London 286
Fitzroy Tavern 121
Flask Tavern 250
Four Corners Cafe 169
Fox & Anchor 207
French House 122
Freud Bar 123

G

Galvin at Windows 124
Garden Gate 250
George Inn 170
Golden Heart 210
Gordon's Wine Bar 123
Grapes, the 227
Greenwich Union 284
Guinea 124

H

Happiness Forgets 208
Hawksmoor 210
Heaven 123
Holborn Whippet 123

Holly Bush 250
Horse & Groom 210

I

Indo 225

J

Jamaica Wine House 155
Jerusalem Tavern 207

K

Kensington Roof Gardens 264
King's Arms 169
Ku Klub Lisle St 123

L

Lab 121
Lamb 120-1
Lamb & Flag (London) 122
Lamb & Flag (Oxford) 311
Lock Tavern 250
London Apprentice 302
London Cocktail Club 121
Lost Angel 286

M

Macbeth 208
Madison 155
Market House 285
Mason's Arms 286
Mayflower 170-1
Ministry of Sound 284-5
Missing Bean (Oxford) 310-11
Museum Tavern 121

N

Netil360 227
Nightjar 208
Notting Hill Arts Club 264

O

Oblix 170
Old Blue Last 209
Old Ship 227
Old Ship W6 265-6

P

Palm Tree 227
People's Park Tavern 227
Phene 193
Plan B 285
Polski Bar 124
Pond Dalston 226
Portobello Star 263-4
Princess Louise 123
Prospect of Whitby 225
Proud Camden 249
Public House 251
Punch Bowl 124

Purl 124

Q

Queen of Hoxton 209
Queen's 249
Queen's Arms 193
Queen's Larder 121

R

Rake 170
Red Lion 208
Rhythm Factory 225
Rivoli Bar 120
Royal Inn on the Park 227
Royal Oak 226
RVT 286

S

Sager + Wilde 226
Salamander (Bath) 317
Satan's Whiskers 226
Scootercaffe 169
Seven Stars 123
She Soho 122
Ship 155
Sky Pod 153, 155
Skylon 169
Southwark Brewing Company 171
Spaniard's Inn 250
Star Inn (Bath) 317
Stickybeaks (Cambridge) 313

T

Tea and Tattle 121
Ten Bells 210
Terroirs 123
The Nest 226
Three Kings 207-8
Tomtom Coffee House 193
Trafalgar Tavern 284
Troubadour 264
Turf Tavern (Oxford) 311

U

Union Tavern 264

V

Vaults & Garden (Oxford) 310
Village 122
Vinoteca 208
Viva 226

W

Warrington 265
Waterway 265
White Cross 301-2
White Hart 302
White Lyan 208

White Swan 227, 302
Windsor Castle 264
Wine Pantry 170
Woolpack 170
Worship St Whistling Shop 208-9

X
XOYO 209

Y
Yard 122
Ye Olde Cheshire Cheese 155
Ye Olde Mitre 207

Z
Zetter Townhouse Cocktail Lounge 207
Zuma 193

☆ **ENTERTAINMENT**
100 Club 126
606 Club 194
Almeida 252
Amused Moose Soho 126
Angel Comedy 252
Arcola Theatre 228
Barbican 155
Barfly 252
BFI IMAX Cinema 172
BFI Southbank 172
Borderline 125
Bush Theatre 266
Cadogan Hall 194
Cafe Oto 228
Cecil Sharp House 251
Ciné Lumière 194
Comedy Cafe Theatre 211
Comedy Store 125
Curzon Soho 125
Donmar Warehouse 126
Electric Ballroom 252
Electric Cinema 211, 265
Forum, the 252
Gate Picturehouse 265
Genesis 228
Hackney Empire 228
Hampstead Theatre 252
ICA Cinema 126
Jazz Cafe 251
King's Head Theatre 252
KOKO 251
Laban Theatre 286
London Coliseum 126
Lyric Hammersmith 266
National Theatre 163-4, 171
O2 Academy Brixton 286
O2 Arena 286
O2 Shepherd's Bush Empire 266

Old Vic 172
Opera Holland Park 266
Passing Clouds 228
Pizza Express Jazz Club 125
Place 125
Prince Charles 125
Regent's Park Open Air Theatre 252
Rio Cinema 228
Riverside Studios 266
Ronnie Scott's 125
Roundhouse 252
Royal Albert Hall 185, 194, **56**
Royal Court Theatre 194
Royal Opera House 105, 124, **57**
Sadler's Wells 210-11
Scala 251
Shakespeare's Globe 160, 171-2, **59**, **160**
Soho Theatre 125
Southbank Centre 163, 171
Union Chapel 252
Up the Creek 286
Vortex Jazz Club 228
Wigmore Hall 125-6
Wilton's 227-8
Young Vic 172

🛍 **SHOPPING**
20 Storey 287

A
Abercrombie & Fitch 132-3
Absolute Vintage 212
Agent Provocateur 130
Algerian Coffee Stores 130
Annie's Vintage Costume & Textiles 253
Arty Globe 287

B
Backyard Market 210
Bang Bang Clothing Exchange 128
Beatles Store 132
Benjamin Pollock's Toy Shop 132
Bermondsey Market 173
Berwick Street Market 118
Beyond Retro 131, 229
Blade Rubber Stamps 128
Blitz London 211
Book & Comic Exchange 267
Books for Cooks 266-7
Boxpark 211
Brick Lane Market 210
British Red Cross 194-5
Brixton Market 287
Broadway Market 228-9, **62**

Browns Focus 133
Buck Street Market 253
Burberry 133
Burberry Outlet Store 229

C
Cadenhead's Whisky & Tasting Shop 132
Cambridge Satchel Company 131
Camden Lock Market 253
Camden Lock Village 253
Camden Market 240, 253, **11**
Camden Passage Market 252-3
Casbah Records 287
Cath Kidston 132
Ceramica Blue 266
Conran Shop 194
Craft Central 212

D
Darkroom 128
Daunt Books 127
Do Shop 132
Dover Street Market 133

E
E.C.One 212
Exclusivo 253

F
Folk 128
Fortnum & Mason 127
Foyles 127

G
Gay's the Word 128
Gill Wing 253
Gina 133
Gosh! 127
Greenwich Market 287

H
Hamleys 131
Harold Moore's Records 130
Harrods 194, **61**
Harry Potter Shop at Platform 9¾ 253
Harvey Nichols 195
Hatchards 127
Hatton Garden 212
Honest Jon's 267
House of Hackney 211
Housmans 254

J
James J. Fox 128
James Smith & Sons 128
John Lewis 133

John Sandoe Books 195
Jo Loves 195
Joy 128

K
Karen Millen 132

L
Labour & Wait 212
Liberty 131
Limelight Movie Art 195
Lina Stores 131
London Review Bookshop 127
Lovely & British 173
Lulu Guinness 195
Lutyens & Rubinstein 266

M
Magma 212
Maltby Street Market 173
Marylebone Farmers Market 118
Molton Brown 131
Monmouth Coffee Company 131
Monocle Shop 132
Mulberry 133

N
National Theatre Gift Shop 173
Nauticalia 287
Neal's Yard Dairy 131
Notting Hill Bookshop 266

O
Old Spitalfields Market 211, **49**
Orsini 267

P
Paul Smith 132
Paxton & Whitfield 128
Penhaligon's 126
Peter Harrington 133
Phonica 130
Pickett 195
Postcard Teas 133
Present 211-12
Pringle of Scotland Outlet Store 229

R
Ray's Jazz 130
Reckless Records 130
Rellik 267
Retro Woman 267
Retrobates Vintage 287
Rippon Cheese 195
Rough Trade East 211
Rough Trade West 267

S

Selfridges 133
Shanghai Tang 195
Silver Vaults 155
Sister Ray 130
Skoob Books 127
Slightly Foxed on Gloucester Road 195
Sounds of the Universe 130
South Bank Book Market 173
Southbank Centre Shop 173
Stables Market 253
Stanford's 127
Start 212
Stella McCartney 133
Sting 132
Sunday UpMarket 210

T

T2 195
Tatty Devine 212
Taylor of Old Bond Street 128
Ted Baker 131-2
Topshop 130
Traid 229
twentytwentyone 253

U

Urban Outfitters 130

W

Waterstones 127
Watkins 131
Westfield 266
Westfield Stratford City 229

🏃 SPORTS & ACTIVITIES

Granta Canoe & Punt Hire Company (Cambridge) 311
Hampstead Heath Ponds 254
Lee & Stort Boats 229
Lee Valley VeloPark 229
London Aquatics Centre 229
London Fields Lido 229
London Waterbus Company 267
Lord's 254
Porchester Spa 267
Queens Ice & Bowl 267
Scudamore's Punting (Cambridge) 311

Sights 000
Map Pages **000**
Photo Pages **000**

Twickenham Rugby Stadium 302
Up at the O2 287

🛏 SLEEPING

17 Homestead Rd 331
37 Trevor Square 327
40 Winks 329
196 Bishopsgate 325

A

Academy 321
Ampersand Hotel 327
Andaz Liverpool Street 325
Arosfa Hotel 321
Arran House Hotel 322
Artist Residence 327
Aster House 328
Astor Hyde Park 326
Astor Victoria 326
Avo 329-30

B

Bankside House 329
Barclay House 332
B+B Belgravia 327
Beaufort House 328
Beaumont 322
Bermondsey Square Hotel 326
Bingham 334
Blakes 327
Boundary 329
Brown's Hotel 323

C

Captain Bligh Guest House 334
Charlotte Street Hotel 324
Cherry Court Hotel 326
Church Street Hotel 334
Citizen M 326
Clink78 330
Clink261 330
Corinthia 322
Covent Garden Hotel 323

D

Days Hotel 325
Dean Street Townhouse 323

E

easyHotel 325
Europa House 333
Express by Holiday Inn 325

F

Fielding Hotel 321
Fox & Anchor 329
Fox and Grapes 334

G

Generator 321
George Hotel 321
Gore 327-8
Goring 322-3
Grange St Paul's 325
Great Dover St Apartments 329
Great Northern Hotel 330

H

Ham Yard Hotel 323
Harlingford Hotel 321
Haymarket Hotel 322
Hazlitt's 322
High Holborn Residence 329
Hotel Indigo Tower Hill 324
Hoxton Hotel 328

J

Jesmond Hotel 322

K

Kennington B&B 334
King's College Conference & Vacation Bureau 329
K + K Hotel George 333
Knightsbridge Hotel 328

L

La Suite West 333
Levin Hotel 328
Lime Tree Hotel 327
London Edition 322
London House Hotel 331
London St Pancras YHA 330
London St Paul's YHA 324

M

Main House 332
Malmaison 329
ME by Meliã London 323
Megaro 330
Meininger 326
Melrose Gardens 331
Morgan Hotel 321
Motel One London Tower Hill 324-5

N

Nadler Kensington 332
Nadler Soho 324
No 90 327
Number 5 Maddox Street 323
Number 16 334
Number Sixteen 327

O

One Aldwych 323

One Leicester Street 324
Pavilion Hotel 332-3
Petersham 334
Portobello Gold 333
Portobello Hotel 333
Premier Inn 325

Q

Qbic 329

R

Ridgemount Hotel 321
Ritz 324
Rockwell 332
Rookery 329
Rosewood 323
Rough Luxe 330-1
Rubens at the Palace 324
Rushmore 332

S

Safestay Elephant & Castle 333
Safestay Holland Park 332
Seven Dials Hotel 322
Shoreditch Rooms 328
Soho Hotel 324
Space Apart Hotel 332
St Christopher's Inn Greenwich 334
St Christopher's Village 326
St Pancras Renaissance London Hotel 331
Stamford St Apartments 329
Stylotel 331

T

Threadneedles 325
Town Hall Hotel & Apartments 330
Travelodge 325
Tune Hotel 325, 331
Twenty Nevern Square 332

V

Vancouver Studios 333

W

Walrus 325-6
Windermere Hotel 327

Y

YHA Earl's Court 331-2
YHA London Oxford Street 321
York & Albany 330

Z

Zetter Hotel & Townhouse 328

London Maps

Sights

- Beach
- Bird Sanctuary
- Buddhist
- Castle/Palace
- Christian
- Confucian
- Hindu
- Islamic
- Jain
- Jewish
- Monument
- Museum/Gallery/Historic Building
- Ruin
- Sento Hot Baths/Onsen
- Shinto
- Sikh
- Taoist
- Winery/Vineyard
- Zoo/Wildlife Sanctuary
- Other Sight

Activities, Courses & Tours

- Bodysurfing
- Diving
- Canoeing/Kayaking
- Course/Tour
- Skiing
- Snorkelling
- Surfing
- Swimming/Pool
- Walking
- Windsurfing
- Other Activity

Sleeping

- Sleeping
- Camping

Eating

- Eating

Drinking & Nightlife

- Drinking & Nightlife
- Cafe

Entertainment

- Entertainment

Shopping

- Shopping

Information

- Bank
- Embassy/Consulate
- Hospital/Medical
- Internet
- Police
- Post Office
- Telephone
- Toilet
- Tourist Information
- Other Information

Geographic

- Beach
- Hut/Shelter
- Lighthouse
- Lookout
- Mountain/Volcano
- Oasis
- Park
- Pass
- Picnic Area
- Waterfall

Population

- Capital (National)
- Capital (State/Province)
- City/Large Town
- Town/Village

Transport

- Airport
- Border crossing
- Bus
- Cable car/Funicular
- Cycling
- Ferry
- Metro station
- Monorail
- Parking
- Petrol station
- Taxi
- Train station/Railway
- Tram
- Tube station
- Other Transport

Note: Not all symbols displayed above appear on the maps in this book

Routes

- Tollway
- Freeway
- Primary
- Secondary
- Tertiary
- Lane
- Unsealed road
- Road under construction
- Plaza/Mall
- Steps
- Tunnel
- Pedestrian overpass
- Walking Tour
- Walking Tour detour
- Path/Walking Trail

Boundaries

- International
- State/Province
- Disputed
- Regional/Suburb
- Marine Park
- Cliff
- Wall

Hydrography

- River, Creek
- Intermittent River
- Canal
- Water
- Dry/Salt/Intermittent Lake
- Reef

Areas

- Airport/Runway
- Beach/Desert
- Cemetery (Christian)
- Cemetery (Other)
- Glacier
- Mudflat
- Park/Forest
- Sight (Building)
- Sportsground
- Swamp/Mangrove

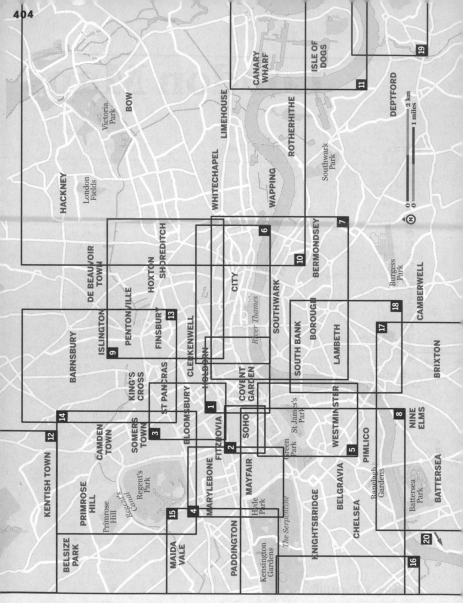

MAP INDEX

1 West End: Covent Garden (p406)

2 West End: Central (p408)

3 West End: Bloomsbury (p412)

4 West End: Mayfair (p414)

5 West End: St James's (p416)

6 The City (p418)

7 The South Bank (p420)

8 Kensington & Hyde Park (p424)

9 Clerkenwell, Shoreditch & Spitalfields (p426)

10 East London (p430)

11 Isle of Dogs (p432)

12 North London: Hampstead & Highgate (p433)

13 North London: Islington & King's Cross (p434)

14 North London: Camden (p436)

15 Notting Hill & West London (p438)

16 West London: Shepherd's Bush & Earl's Court (p440)

17 South London: Brixton, Clapham & Battersea (p442)

18 South London (p444)

19 Greenwich (p445)

20 Richmond & Kew (p446)

WEST END: COVENT GARDEN *Map on p406*

◉ Top Sights p78

1 National Gallery............ B7
2 National Portrait
  Gallery B6
3 Sir John Soane's
  Museum E2
4 Trafalgar Square.......... B7

◉ Sights p97

5 Courtauld Gallery..........E5
6 Covent Garden Piazza.. D4
7 Fourth Plinth Project.... B7
8 Gray's Inn......................G1
9 Hunterian Museum.......F3
10 Inner Temple H4
11 Leicester Square.......... A6
12 Lincoln's Inn..................F2
13 London Film
  Museum D5
14 London Transport
  Museum D5
15 Middle Temple..............G4
16 Royal Courts of
  Justice G4
17 Royal Opera House.......C4
18 Somerset House...........E5
19 St Clement Danes.........F4
20 St Giles Church B3
21 St Martin-in-the-
  Fields B6
22 St Paul's Church C5
23 Staple Inn......................G1
24 Strand............................C6
25 Temple Church H4
26 Twinings.........................G4
27 Two Temple Place G5

⊗ Eating p110

28 Baiwei A5
29 Balthazar.......................D4
30 Baozi Inn A5
31 Canela............................B4
32 Cantina Laredo..............B4
  Counter .... (see 33)
33 Delaunay E4
34 Dishoom........................ B5
35 Food for Thought..........B4
36 Great Queen Street D3
37 Hawksmoor Seven
  Dials B4
38 J Sheekey B5
39 Kanada-Ya...................... B3
40 National Dining
  Rooms A7
41 Orchard D1
  Portrait ....(see 2)
42 Rock & Sole Plaice........C3
43 Rules...............................C5
44 Wahaca...........................C6

◎ Drinking & Nightlife p120

45 Ape & Bird...................... A4
46 Cross Keys.....................C3
47 Freud Bar B3
48 Gordon's Wine Bar........ C7
49 Heaven C7
50 Holborn Whippet............D1
51 Ku Klub Lisle St A5
52 Lamb & Flag...................C5
53 Polski Bar......................D2
54 Princess Louise.............D2
55 Seven Stars G3
56 Terroirs...........................C6

◉ Entertainment p124

57 Donmar Warehouse B4
58 London Coliseum.......... B6
59 Poetry Café....................C3
60 Royal Opera House.......D4

◎ Shopping p126

61 Apple Store....................C5
62 Benjamin Pollock's
  Toy Shop D5
63 Cambridge Satchel
  Company......................C5
64 Do Shop..........................C3
65 Forbidden Planet...........B3
66 Karen Millen...................C4
67 Molton Brown................D4
68 Monmouth Coffee
  Company......................B3
69 Neal's Yard Dairy B3
70 Paul Smith......................C4
71 Poste Mistress...............B4
72 Stanford's B5
73 Stanley Gibbons........... D5
74 Ted Baker........................C4
75 Watkins...........................B6

◎ Sleeping p321

76 Covent Garden
  Hotel B3
77 Fielding Hotel.................D4
78 Haymarket Hotel........... A7
79 ME by Meliã
  London E5
80 One Aldwych.................. E5
81 Rosewood E2
82 Seven Dials Hotel......... B3

WEST END: COVENT GARDEN

Key on p405

WEST END: COVENT GARDEN

See map p412

British Museum

Montague St

Bloomsbury Square

Procter St

Bloomsbury St

Bedford Ave

Great Russell St

Little Russell St

Bloomsbury Way

Barter St

Southampton Pl

Southampton Row

Catton St

50

41

53

Great Russell St

New Oxford St

Museum St

High Holborn

New Oxford St

54

Holborn

Tottenham Court Rd

New Oxford St

Shaftesbury Ave

Bucknall St

Grape St

Newton St

Stukely St

St Giles High St

New Compton St

Endell St

Shorts Gdns

Drury La

Macklin St

Parker St

Great Queen St

Wild Ct

20

39

65

47

42

59

COVENT GARDEN

36

Wild St

Charing Cross Rd

Shaftesbury Ave

82

76

64

46

Shelton St

Drury La

77

Greek St

69

68

57

31

35

Neal St

Long Acre

Bow St

Crown Ct

Kemble St

Russell St

See map p408

Earlham St

West St

71

37

Langley St

Neal St

Covent Garden

66

60

Wellington St

Catherine St

45

SOHO

Shaftesbury Ave

32

Mercer St

Long Acre

70

74

James St

17

6

67 **29**

34

Rose St

72

Floral St

63

61

Covent Garden Market

14 **13**

Lisle St

30

28

51

Cranbourn St

52

Garrick St

King St

22

62

Covent Garden

Tavistock St

Exeter St

Leicester Sq

New Row

Henrietta St

Southampton St

The Strand

Bear St

38

St Martin's La

Bedfordbury

Bedford St

43

73

Carting La

Leicester Sq

11

75

44

Chandos Pl

Agar St

Adam St

Savoy Pl

Irving St

58

William IV St

24

John Adam St

Victoria Embankment

OrangeSt

National Portrait Gallery

2

56

Victoria Embankment Gardens

Whitcomb St

St Martin's St

40

National Gallery

1

21

Duncannon St

78

7 **4**

Villiers St

49

48

Pall Mall

Trafalgar Square

Charing Cross

Cockspur St

Trafalgar Sq

See map p416

Craven St

Embankment

ST JAMES'S

Victoria Embankment

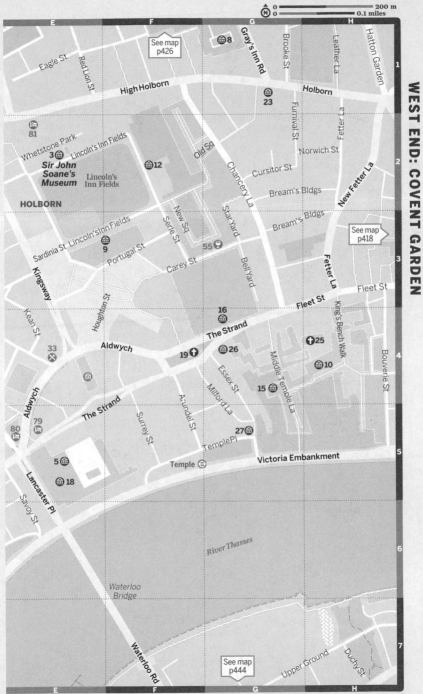

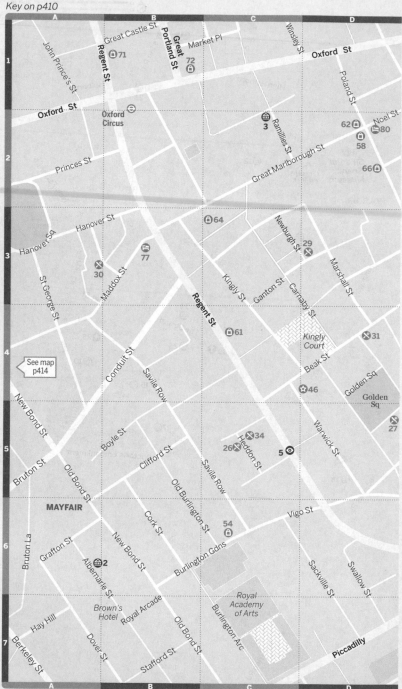

WEST END: CENTRAL

MAPS

Regent St

Oxford St

John Prince's St

Great Castle St

71

Great Portland St

Market Pl

72

Winsley St

Oxford St

Poland St

Noel St

62

80

58

66

Princes St

Ramillies St

3

Great Marlborough St

Hanover St

Hanover Sq

30

Maddox St

77

64

Newburgh St

29

Kingly St

Ganton St

Carnaby St

Marshall St

St George St

Regent St

61

Kingly Court

31

Conduit St

Savile Row

Beak St

Golden Sq

46

Golden Sq

Warwick St

27

See map p414

New Bond St

Boyle St

Clifford St

Heddon St

34

26

5

Bruton St

Old Bond St

Savile Row

MAYFAIR

Bruton La

Grafton St

New Bond St

Cork St

Old Burlington St

Vigo St

54

Burlington Gdns

Sackville St

Swallow St

2

Albemarle St

Brown's Hotel

Royal Arcade

Royal Academy of Arts

Hay Hill

Dover St

Old Bond St

Stafford St

Burlington Arc

Piccadilly

Berkeley St

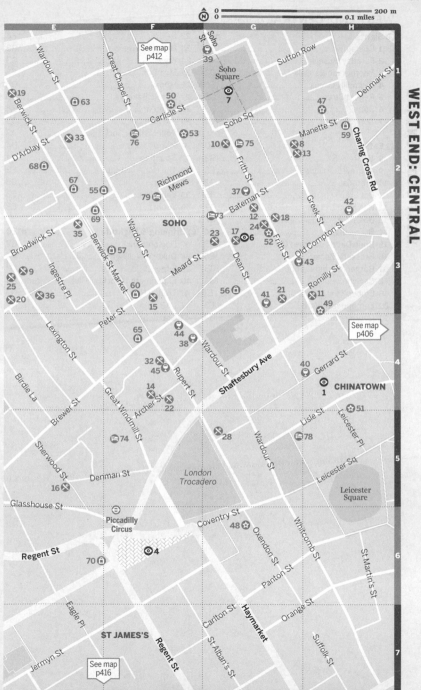

WEST END: CENTRAL *Map on p408*

◎ **Sights** **p97**
1 Chinatown..H4
2 Faraday Museum................................A6
3 Photographers' Gallery...............C2
4 Piccadilly Circus...............................F6
5 Regent Street....................................C5
6 Soho..G3
7 Soho Square.......................................G1

✕ **Eating** **p110**
8 10 Greek St...G2
9 Andrew Edmunds.........................E3
10 Arbutus..G2
11 Bar Shu...H3
12 Barrafina...G2
13 Bó Drake...G2
14 Bocca di Lupo...................................F4
15 Bone Daddies Ramen Bar.......F3
16 Brasserie Zédel.............................E5
17 Burger & Lobster Soho............G3
18 Ceviche..G3
19 Ember Yard...E1
20 Fernandez & Wells......................E3
21 Gauthier Soho...................................G3

22 Gelupo...F4
23 Honest Burgers...............................G3
24 Koya...G3
25 Mildreds...E3
26 Momo..C5
27 Nordic Bakery...................................D5
28 Palomar...G5
29 Pitt Cue Co...D3
30 Pollen Street Social...................A3
31 Polpo..D4
32 Spuntino..F4
33 The Breakfast Club......................E2
34 Tibits...C5
35 Yauatcha...E3
36 Yoobi..E3

◎ **Drinking & Nightlife** **p120**
37 Dog and Duck...................................G2
38 Duke of Wellington.....................F4
39 Edge..G1
40 Experimental Cocktail Club....H4
41 French House.....................................G3
42 LAB...H2
43 She Soho..G3

44	Village	F4
45	Yard	F4

⭐ **Entertainment**   **p124**
46	Amused Moose Soho	D4
47	Borderline	H1
48	Comedy Store	G6
49	Curzon Soho	H3
50	Pizza Express Jazz Club	F1
51	Prince Charles	H4
52	Ronnie Scott's	G3
53	Soho Theatre	F2

🛍 **Shopping**   **p126**
54	Abercrombie & Fitch	C6
55	Agent Provocateur	F2
56	Algerian Coffee Stores	G3
57	Berwick Street Market	F3
58	Beyond Retro	D2
59	Foyles	H2
60	Gosh!	F3
	Grant & Cutler	(see 59)
61	Hamleys	C4
62	Harold Moore's Records	D2

63	Joy	E1
64	Liberty	C3
65	Lina Stores	F4
66	Phonica	D2
	Ray's Jazz	(see 59)
67	Reckless Records	E2
68	Sister Ray	E2
69	Sounds of the Universe	E2
70	Sting	E6
71	Topshop	B1
72	Urban Outfitters	B1

🛏 **Sleeping**   **p321**
73	Dean Street Townhouse	G2
74	Ham Yard Hotel	F5
75	Hazlitt's	G2
76	Nadler Soho	F2
77	Number 5 Maddox Street	B3
78	One Leicester Street	G5
79	Soho Hotel	F2
80	YHA London Oxford Street	D2

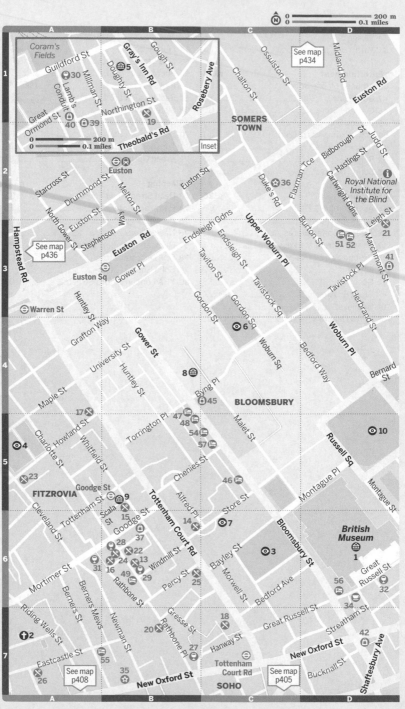

0   200 m
0   0.1 miles

Coram's Fields

Guildford St
Gray's Inn Rd
Gough St
30
5
Lamb's Conduit St
Doughty St
Millman St
Great Ormond St
Northington St
40   39
19
Theobald's Rd

0   200 m
0   0.1 miles

Inset

See map p434

Roseberry Ave
Chalton St
Ossulston St
Midland Rd
Euston Rd

SOMERS TOWN

Starcross St
Drummond St
Melton St
Kew
Euston Sq
Duke's Rd
36
Flaxman Tce
Bidborough St
Hastings St
Judd St
Cartwright Gdns
Royal National Institute for the Blind

Euston

North Gower St
Euston St
Stephenson
Euston Rd
Gower Pl
Endsleigh Gdns
Endsleigh St
Upper Woburn Pl
Burton St
Leigh St
51   52
21

See map p436

Euston Sq

Taviton St
Gordon St
Tavistock Sq
Marchmont St
41

Hampstead Rd

Warren St
Huntley St
Grafton Way
Gordon Sq
6
Woburn Sq
Bedford Way
Tavistock Rd
Herband St
Woburn Pl

University St
Gower St
Bernard St
8
Byng Pl
45
BLOOMSBURY

Maple St
Huntley St
Howland St
17
Torrington Pl
47
48
54
57
Malet St
10
Russell Sq

4
Charlotte St
Whitfield St
Chenies St
46
Montague Pl
Montague St

23
FITZROVIA
Goodge St
9
Scala St
15
Goodge St
Tottenham Court Rd
Alfred Pl
14
Store St
7
3
Bloomsbury St

Cleveland St
28
22
24   13
Windmill St
Bayley St
British Museum
1
Great Russell St

31
16
49
29
Percy St
25
Morwell St
Bedford Ave
56
32

Mortimer St
Berners St
Rathbone St
Gresse St
20
Rathbone Pl
27
18
Hanway St
Great Russell St
34
Streatham St
42
Shaftesbury Ave

2
Riding Wells St
Berners Mews
Newman St
Eastcastle St
55
35
New Oxford St
Tottenham Court Rd
SOHO
New Oxford St
Bucknall St

26
See map p408
See map p405

◎ **Top Sights** **p81**
1 British Museum D6

◎ **Sights** **p98**
2 All Saints A7
3 Bedford Square C6
4 BT Tower A5
5 Charles Dickens Museum B1
6 Gordon Square C4
7 New London Architecture .. C6
8 Petrie Museum of Egyptian
   Archaeology B4
9 Pollock's Toy Museum B5
10 Russell Square D5
11 St George's, Bloomsbury E7

✕ **Eating** **p111**
12 Abeno E6
13 Barnyard B6
14 Busaba Eathai B6
15 Dabbous B5
16 Fino B6
17 Franco Manca A4
18 Hakkasan Hanway Place C7
19 Lady Ottoline B1
20 Lima B7
21 North Sea Fish Restaurant . D3
22 Pied-à-Terre B6
23 Ragam A5
24 Roka B6
25 Sagar B6
26 Yalla Yalla A7

🍷 **Drinking & Nightlife** **p120**
27 Bradley's Spanish Bar B7
28 Draft House B6

29 Fitzroy Tavern B6
30 Lamb A1
31 London Cocktail Club A6
32 Museum Tavern D6
33 Queen's Larder E5
34 Tea and Tattle D6

✿ **Entertainment** **p124**
35 100 Club B7
36 Place C2

🛍 **Shopping** **p126**
37 Bang Bang Clothing
   Exchange B6
38 Blade Rubber Stamps E6
39 Darkroom A2
40 Folk A1
41 Gay's the Word D3
42 James Smith & Sons D7
43 London Review Bookshop ... E6
44 Skoob Books E3
45 Waterstones C4

🛏 **Sleeping** **p321**
46 Academy C5
47 Arosfa Hotel B4
48 Arran House Hotel B5
49 Charlotte Street Hotel B6
50 Generator E3
51 George Hotel D3
52 Harlingford Hotel D3
53 High Holborn Residence E7
54 Jesmond Hotel C5
55 London Edition A7
56 Morgan Hotel D6
57 Ridgemount Hotel C5

WEST END: MAYFAIR

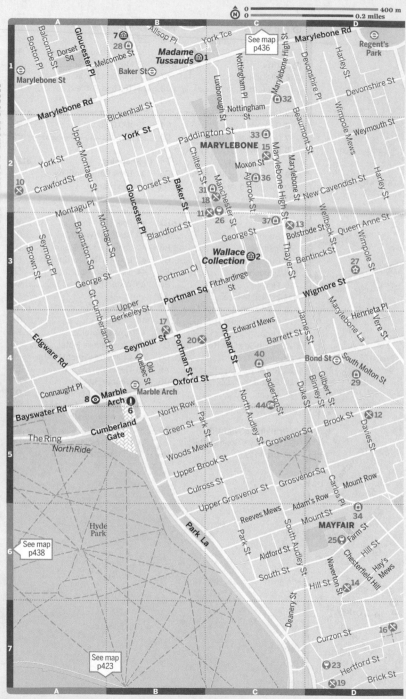

See map p436

See map p438

See map p423

Marylebone Rd

Regent's Park

Madame Tussauds 1

Baker St

MARYLEBONE

Wallace Collection 2

Wigmore St

Oxford St

Marble Arch

Cumberland Gate

Hyde Park

Park La

MAYFAIR

◎ **Top Sights** **p78**
1 Madame Tussauds B1
2 Wallace Collection C3

◎ **Sights** **p97**
3 All Souls Church................... E3
4 Broadcasting House............. E2
5 Handel House Museum........ E4
6 Marble Arch B4
7 Sherlock Holmes Museum .. B1
8 Tyburn Tree memorial
    plaque............................... A4

✖ **Eating** **p110**
9 Brasserie Chavot E5
10 Briciole A2
11 Chiltern Firehouse C2
12 Foyer at Claridge's.............. D5
13 Golden Hind C3
14 Greenhouse D6
15 La Fromagerie C2
16 Le Boudin Blanc D7
17 Locanda Locatelli................ B4
18 Monocle Cafe C2
19 Nobu D7
20 Roti Chai.............................. B4
    Wallace.......................... (see 2)
21 Wild Honey.......................... E5

🍷 **Drinking & Nightlife** **p120**
22 Artesian............................... E3

23 Galvin at Windows .... D.
24 Guinea E5
25 Punch Bowl.......................... D6
26 Purl C2

🎭 **Entertainment** **p124**
27 Wigmore Hall........................ D3

🛍 **Shopping** **p126**
28 Beatles Store........................ B1
29 Browns Focus D4
30 Burberry E5
31 Cadenhead's
    Whisky &
    Tasting Shop C2
32 Cath Kidston C1
33 Daunt Books......................... C2
34 Gina D6
35 John Lewis............................ E4
36 Marylebone
    Farmers Market C2
37 Monocle Shop C3
38 Mulberry E5
39 Postcard Teas E4
40 Selfridges............................. C4
41 Shepherds E7
42 Stella McCartney E5
43 Vivienne Westwood............. E5

🛏 **Sleeping** **p321**
44 Beaumont.............................. C4

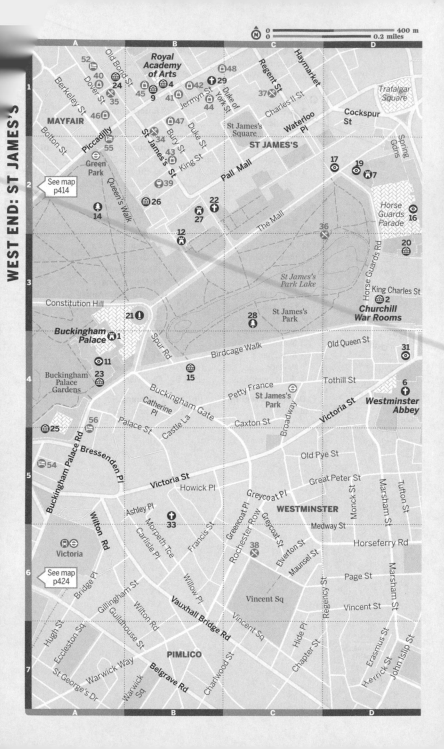

0
0   400 m
                                          0.2 miles

A **B** **C** **D**

Berkeley St

52
40 24
Dover St Old Bond St
35
46

MAYFAIR

Bolton St

Piccadilly
55

Green
Park

See map
p414

14

Royal
Academy
of Arts

45 9 4
41
Jermyn St 42
44

47
34
Bury St Duke St
43
King St

St James's St

39

26

12

Queen's Walk

Spur Rd

48
29

Regent St

Haymarket

Duke of York St
St James's
Square

ST JAMES'S

Pall Mall

22
27

37
Charles II St

Waterloo Pl

Cockspur
St

Spring Gdns

Trafalgar
Square

17
19 7

16

The Mall

Horse
Guards
Parade

36

20

St James's
Park Lake

Horse Guards Rd

King Charles St

Constitution Hill

21

Buckingham
Palace

1

11
23

Buckingham
Palace
Gardens

25

54

56

Buckingham Palace Rd

Bressenden Pl

Palace St
Castle La

Catherine
Pl

Buckingham Gate

15

Birdcage Walk

28

St James's
Park

Petty France
St James's
Park

Caxton St

Victoria St

Broadway

Old Queen St

Tothill St

31

Churchill
War Rooms

6

Westminster
Abbey

Victoria St
Howick Pl

Ashley Pl

Morpeth Tce
Carlisle Pl

Wilton Rd

Victoria

See map
p424

Bridge Pl

Gillingham St

Hugh St
Eccleston Sq
St George's Dr

PIMLICO

Warwick Way

Wilton Rd

Guildhouse St

Warwick
Sq

Charlwood St

Vauxhall Bridge Rd

Belgrave Rd

33

Francis St

Willow Pl

Vincent Sq

Greycoat Pl
Greycoat Pl
Greycoat St
Rochester Row

WESTMINSTER

Medway St

38

Elverton St
Maunsel St

Vincent Sq

Hide Pl

Chapter St

Regency St

Old Pye St

Great Peter St

Monck St

Page St

Vincent St

Horseferry Rd

Marsham St

Tufton St

Marsham St

Erasmus St
Herrick St
John Islip St

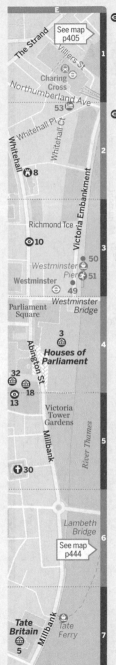

⊙ Top Sights p78
1 Buckingham Palace..............A4
2 Churchill War Rooms..........D3
3 Houses of Parliament..........E4
4 Royal Academy of Arts.......B1
5 Tate Britain..........................E7
6 Westminster Abbey............D4

⊙ Sights p97
7 Admiralty Citadel................D2
8 Banqueting House...............E2
9 Burlington Arcade...............B1
10 Cenotaph...........................E3
11 Changing of the Guard.........A4
12 Clarence House...................B3
13 College Garden...................E5
14 Green Park.........................A2
15 Guards Museum.................B4
16 Horse Guards Parade..........D2
House of Commons......(see 3)
House of Lords..............(see 3)
17 Institute of
Contemporary Arts..........D2
18 Jewel Tower.......................E4
19 National Police
Memorial.........................D2
20 No 10 Downing Street.........D3
21 Queen Victoria Memorial.....B3
22 Queen's Chapel...................B2
23 Queen's Gallery...................A4
24 Royal Arcade......................A1
25 Royal Mews.......................A5
26 Spencer House....................B2
27 St James's Palace................B2
28 St James's Park...................C3
29 St James's Piccadilly...........B1
30 St John's, Smith Square......E5
31 Supreme Court...................D4
32 Westminster Abbey
Museum..........................E4
33 Westminster Cathedral........B5

⊗ Eating p110
5th View......................(see 48)
34 Cafe Murano.......................B1
Cellarium......................(see 6)
35 Gymkhana.........................A1
36 Inn the Park........................D3
37 Shoryu...............................C1
Smith Square Cafe &
Restaurant................(see 30)
38 Vincent Rooms....................C6

⊙ Drinking & Nightlife p120
39 Dukes Bar..........................B2
Rivoli Bar.....................(see 55)

⊙ Entertainment p124
ICA Cinema..................(see 17)

⊙ Shopping p126
40 Dover Street Market............A1
41 Fortnum & Mason................B1
42 Hatchards...........................B1
43 James J. Fox.......................B2
44 Paxton & Whitfield..............B1
45 Penhaligon's......................B1
46 Peter Harrington.................A1
47 Taylor of Old Bond Street....B1
48 Waterstones.......................B1

⊙ Sports & Activities p386
49 Guided Tour........................E3
50 Thames River Boats............E3
51 Westminster Passenger
Services Association........E3

⊙ Sleeping p321
52 Brown's Hotel......................A1
53 Corinthia...........................E2
54 Goring...............................A5
55 Ritz..................................A2
56 Rubens at the Palace..........A5

THE CITY

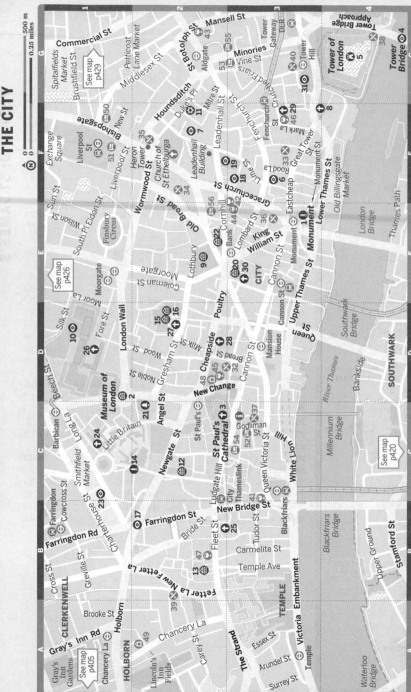

0 500 m
0 0.25 miles

See map p429

See map p426

See map p405

See map p420

Spitalfields Market
Commercial St
Petticoat Lane Market
Brushfield St
Middlesex St
Houndsditch
Bishopsgate
New St
Wormwood St
Old Broad St
Liverpool St
Heron Tower
Church of St Ethelburga
Leadenhall Building
Sun St
Wilson St
South Pl
Finsbury Circus
Eldon St
Moorgate
London Wall
Coleman St
Lothbury
Moorgate
Bank
Poultry
Cheapside
Mansion House
Museum of London
Beech St
Silk St
Fore St
Noble St
Wood St
Gresham St
Milk St
Bread St
New Change
St Paul's Cathedral
Ludgate Hill
St Paul's
Angel St
Newgate St
Little Britain
Smithfield Market
Long La
Charterhouse St
Cowcross St
Farringdon
Farringdon Rd
Cross St
Greville St
Brooke St
Gray's Inn Gardens
Gray's Inn Rd
Chancery La
HOLBORN
CLERKENWELL
Lincoln's Inn Fields
Chancery La
Carey St
The Strand
Essex St
Arundel St
Surrey St
Victoria Embankment
Temple
TEMPLE
Fetter La
New Fetter La
Fleet St
Bride La
Tudor St
Carmelite St
Temple Ave
New Bridge St
Blackfriars
Queen Victoria St
Godliman St
White Lion Hill
Upper Thames St
Cannon St
Queen St
Cannon St
King William St
Gracechurch St
Lombard St
Cornhill
Bank
Lime St
Leadenhall St
Fenchurch St
Crutched Friars
Aldgate
St Botolph St
Mansell St
Minories
Vine St
Tower Hill
Tower Gateway
Tower of London
Tower Bridge
Tower Bridge Approach
Mark La
Great Tower St
Monument St
Lower Thames St
Old Billingsgate Market
Eastcheap
Monument
Fish St Hill
Thames Path
London Bridge
River Thames
Southwark Bridge
Millennium Bridge
Blackfriars Bridge
Waterloo Bridge
Bankside
SOUTHWARK
Stamford St
Upper Ground
Duke's Pl
Mitre St
Leadenhall St
Fenchurch St
Rood La
CITY
Monument
Bishopsgate
Exchange Square
Moor La
Barbican
Farringdon St
Blackfriars
Thameslink
City

43 55
53
40
31 8
29 46 33
11 7
19 18 6
34
56 42 44 1
22 36
9 20 30
35 51 50
10 26
15 16 27
24 14 21 12 45 48 32 28
23 17 13 47 39 49
25 41 52 54 37 3
4 5 38

THE CITY

◎ Top Sights   p136
1 Monument E3
2 Museum of London D1
3 St Paul's Cathedral C2
4 Tower Bridge G4
5 Tower of London G4

◎ Sights   p146
6 20 Fenchurch St F3
7 30 St Mary Axe F2
8 All Hallows by the Tower F3
9 Bank of England Museum E2
10 Barbican D1
Barbican Gallery .... (see 10)
11 Bevis Marks Synagogue F2
12 Central Criminal Court (Old Bailey) C2
Curve .... (see 10)
13 Dr Johnson's House B2
14 Golden Boy of Pye Corner C2
Great Hall .... (see 15)
15 Guildhall D2
16 Guildhall Galleries & Roman Amphitheatre D2
17 Holborn Viaduct B2
18 Leadenhall Market F3
19 Lloyd's of London F2
20 Mansion House E3
21 Postman's Park C2
22 Royal Exchange E2
23 Smithfield Market C1
24 St Bartholomew-the-Great C1
25 St Bride's, Fleet Street B2
26 St Giles' Cripplegate D1
27 St Lawrence Jewry D2
28 St Mary-le-Bow D2
29 St Olave's F3
30 St Stephen Walbrook E3
31 Trinity Square Gardens G3

◎ Eating   p152
32 Bea's of Bloomsbury D2
Café Below .... (see 28)
33 Camino Monumento F3
34 City Social F2
Cloister Cafe .... (see 24)
Crypt Café .... (see 3)
35 Duck & Waffle F2
36 Folly E3
37 Miyama C3
38 Perkin Reveller G4
Restaurant at St Paul's .... (see 3)
39 White Swan B2
40 Wine Library G3

◉ Drinking & Nightlife   p153
41 Blackfriar C3
42 Counting House F3
43 Hoop and Grapes G2
44 Jamaica Wine House E3
45 Madison D2
46 Ship .... (see 6)
Sky Pod .... (see 6)
47 Ye Olde Cheshire Cheese B2

◎ Entertainment   p155
Barbican .... (see 10)

◉ Shopping   p155
48 One New Change D2
49 Silver Vaults A2

◉ Sleeping   p324
50 196 Bishopsgate F1
51 Andaz Liverpool Street F1
52 Grange St Paul's C3
53 Hotel Indigo Tower Hill G3
54 London St Paul's YHA C3
55 Motel One London Tower Hill G3
56 Threadneedles E2

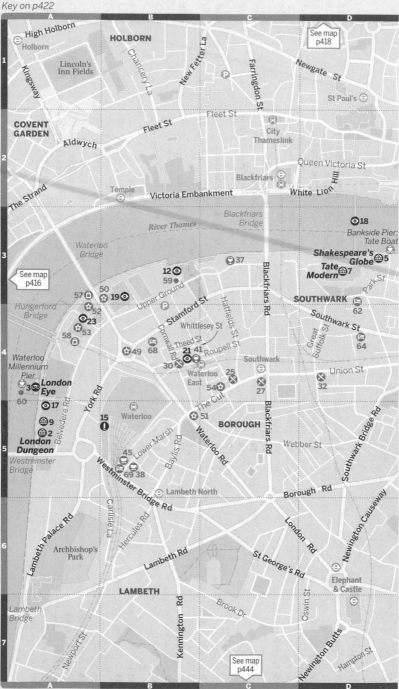

THE SOUTH BANK

A **B** **C** **D**

1

Holborn
High Holborn

HOLBORN

Lincoln's
Inn Fields

Chancery La

New Fetter La

Farringdon St

Newgate St

St Paul's

2

**COVENT
GARDEN**

Aldwych

Fleet St

Fleet St

Fleet St

City
Thameslink

Blackfriars

Queen Victoria St

The Strand

Temple

Victoria Embankment

White Lion Hill

Blackfriars
Bridge

River Thames

Ⓞ18

Bankside Pier;
Tate Boat

3

Waterloo
Bridge

Ⓞ37

12 Ⓞ
59 ●

**Shakespeare's
Globe** Ⓞ5

**Tate
Modern** ☉7

Blackfriars Rd

SOUTHWARK

62

See map
p416

57 🔒
58 🔒

50
19 Ⓞ

52
★
23 Ⓞ
53 ★

Hungerford
Bridge

Upper Ground

Stamford St

Whittlesey St

Theed St

Hatfields St

Southwark St

Great Suffolk St

Park St

64

4

Waterloo
Millennium
Pier

3
60

**London
Eye**

Ⓞ17

York Rd

Belvedere Rd

49 68

Cornwall Rd

21 41
30 Ⓞ

Roupell St

Waterloo
East

Southwark

25

27

Union St

32

**London
Dungeon**

Westminster
Bridge

9
2

15

Waterloo

54

The Cut

51

BOROUGH

Waterloo Rd

Blackfriars Rd

5

60

Lower Marsh

Baylis Rd

Webber St

Southwark Bridge Rd

45
69 38

Lambeth North

Borough Rd

London Rd

6

Lambeth Palace Rd

Archbishop's
Park

Hercules Rd

Carlisle La

Westminster Bridge Rd

Lambeth Rd

St George's Rd

Newington Causeway

Elephant
& Castle

LAMBETH

Kennington Rd

Brook Dr

Oswin St

7

Lambeth
Bridge

Newport St

See map
p444

Newington Butts

Hampton St

See map
p418

A **B** **C** **D**

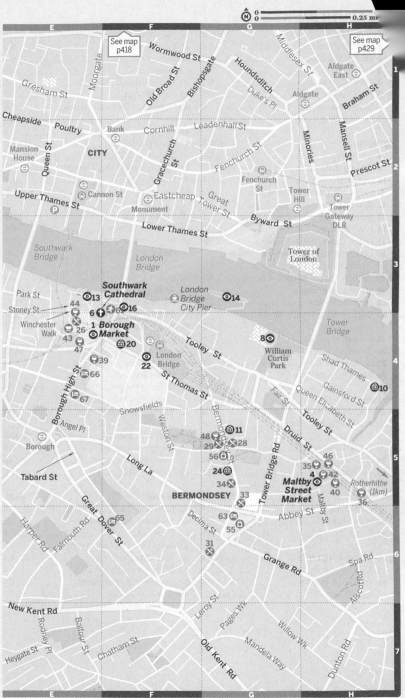

0.25 mi

See map
p418

See map
p429

Wormwood St

Moorgate

Old Broad St

Bishopsgate

Houndsditch

Middlesex St

Aldgate
East

Gresham St

Duke's Pl

Aldgate

Braham St

Cheapside

Poultry

Bank

Cornhill

Leadenhall St

Queen St

Gracechurch St

Fenchurch St

Minories

Mansell St

Prescot St

Mansion
House

CITY

Cannon St

Eastcheap

Great Tower St

Fenchurch
St

Tower
Hill

Tower
Gateway
DLR

Upper Thames St

Monument

Lower Thames St

Byward St

Southwark
Bridge

London
Bridge

Tower of
London

Park St

13

Southwark
Cathedral

London
Bridge
City Pier

14

Stoney St

44

6

62

16

Tower
Bridge

Winchester
Walk

26

1 Borough
Market

8

Shad Thames

43

Tooley St

William
Curtis
Park

Gainsford St

47

20

London
Bridge

10

39

22

St Thomas St

Queen Elizabeth St

66

Borough High St

Snowsfields

Weston St

Bermondsey St

Fair St

Tooley St

67

Angel Pl

Druid St

Borough

48

11

46

Long La

29

28

35

42

Tabard St

56

24

4

40

Rotherhithe
(1km)

34

Maltby
Street
Market

36

BERMONDSEY

33

Tower Bridge Rd

Maltby St

Abbey St

Great Dover St

65

Decima St

63

55

Harper Rd

Falmouth Rd

31

Grange Rd

Spa Rd

Alscot Rd

New Kent Rd

Heygate St

Rodney Pl

Balfour St

Chatham St

Leroy St

Old Kent Rd

Pages Wk

Willow Wk

Mandela Way

Dunton Rd

Top Sights   p158

1 Borough Market E4
2 London Dungeon A5
3 London Eye A4
4 Maltby Street Market H5
5 Shakespeare's Globe D3
6 Southwark Cathedral E3
7 Tate Modern D3

◉ Sights   p163

8 City Hall G4
9 County Hall A5
10 Design Museum H4
11 Fashion & Textile Museum G5
12 Gabriel's Wharf B3
13 Golden Hinde E3
14 HMS Belfast G3
15 Leake Street Graffiti Tunnel B5
16 London Bridge Experience & London
    Tombs F3
17 London Sea Life Aquarium A5
18 Millennium Bridge D3
19 National Theatre B3
20 Old Operating Theatre Museum &
    Herb Garret F4
21 Roupell St B4
22 Shard F4
23 Southbank Centre A4
24 White Cube Bermondsey G5

✖ Eating   p166

25 Anchor & Hope C4
26 Arabica Bar & Kitchen E4
27 Baltic C4
28 Casse-Croûte G5
29 Jose G5
30 Konditor & Cook B4
31 M Manze G6
    Skylon .... (see 53)
32 Union Street Cafe D4
33 Watch House G5
34 Zucca G5

◉ Drinking & Nightlife   p169

35 40 Maltby Street H5
36 Anspach & Hobday H5
    Aqua Shard .... (see 22)

37 Dandelyan & Rumpus Room C3
38 Four Corners Cafe B5
39 George Inn E4
40 Jensen H5
41 King's Arms B4
42 Little Bird Gin H5
43 Monmouth Coffee Company E4
    Oblix .... (see 22)
44 Rake E3
45 Scootercaffe B5
    Skylon .... (see 53)
46 Southwark Brewing Company H5
47 Wine Pantry E4
48 Woolpack G5

◉ Entertainment   p171

49 BFI IMAX Cinema B4
50 BFI Southbank B3
    National Theatre .... (see 19)
51 Old Vic B5
52 Queen Elizabeth Hall A4
53 Royal Festival Hall A4
    Shakespeare's Globe .... (see 5)
    Southbank Centre .... (see 23)
54 Young Vic C4

◉ Shopping   p173

55 Bermondsey Market G6
56 Lovely & British G5
    National Theatre Gift Shop .... (see 19)
57 South Bank Book Market A3
58 Southbank Centre Shop A4

◉ Sports & Activities   p386

59 London Bicycle Tour B3
60 London RIB Voyages A4
61 On Your Bike F3

◉ Sleeping   p325

62 Bankside House D3
63 Bermondsey Square Hotel G6
64 Citizen M D4
65 Great Dover St Apartments F6
66 St Christopher's Inn E4
67 St Christopher's Village E4
68 Stamford St Apartments B4
69 Walrus B5

◎ Top Sights — p176
1 Apsley House.................F3
2 Hyde Park D2
3 Kensington Palace........A2
4 Natural History
    Museum C4
5 Science Museum C4
6 Victoria & Albert
    Museum C4

◎ Sights — p185
7 Albert Memorial B3
8 Brompton Oratory........C4
9 Carlyle's House D7
10 Chelsea Old Church......C7
11 Chelsea Physic
    Garden.........................E7
12 Diana, Princess of
    Wales
    Memorial
    Fountain....................C2
13 Diana, Princess of
    Wales
    Memorial
    Playground A2
14 Holocaust Memorial
    Garden........................E3
15 Italian Gardens..............C1
16 Kensington
    Gardens......................A2
17 King's Road...................D6
18 Michelin House.............D5
19 National Army
    Museum E6
20 Peter Pan Statue..........C2
21 Rose Garden.................E3
22 Royal Albert Hall B3
23 Royal College of
    Music Museum..........B4
24 Royal Hospital
    Chelsea.......................E6
25 Saatchi Gallery..............E5
26 Sensational
    Butterflies C4

27 Serpentine Galleries.....C3
28 Serpentine Sackler
    Gallery C2
29 Speakers' Corner..........E1
30 The Arch.......................C2
31 Tyburn Convent D1
32 Wellington Arch.............F3

✕ Eating — p189
33 Bar Boulud E3
34 Daylesford Organic.......F5
35 Dinner by Heston
    Blumenthal E3
36 Hunan F5
37 Launceston Place A4
38 L'Eto............................D4
    Magazine............. (see 28)
39 Medlar C7
40 Min Jiang A3
41 Ognisko C4
42 Orangery A2
43 Painted Heron C7
44 Pimlico Fresh................G5
45 Rabbit D6
46 Rib Room......................E4
47 Tom's Kitchen D6
    V&A Café.................(see 6)
48 Zuma.............................D3

◎ Drinking & Nightlife — p193
49 Anglesea Arms.............C6
50 Buddha Bar...................D3
51 Drayton Arms B6
52 Phene...........................D7
53 Queen's Arms...............B4
54 Tomtom Coffee
    House F5
    Zuma...................(see 48)

◎ Entertainment — p194
55 Cadogan Hall E5
56 Ciné Lumière C5
    Royal Albert Hall . (see 22)
57 Royal Court Theatre E5

◎ Shopping — p
58 British Red Cross..........
    Conran Shop.........(see 18)
59 Harrods D4
60 Harvey Nichols E3
61 Jo Loves F5
62 John Sandoe Books......E5
63 Limelight Movie Art C7
64 Lulu Guinness...............E5
65 Pickett E5
66 Rippon Cheese..............G5
67 Shanghai Tang E3
68 Slightly Foxed on
    Gloucester
    Road...........................B5
69 T2 ....E5

◎ Sports & Activities — p183
70 Serpentine
    Boathouse..................D2
71 Serpentine Lido.............C2
    Serpentine
    Solar Shuttle
    Boat ....(see 70)

◎ Sleeping — p326
72 37 Trevor Square D3
73 Ampersand Hotel..........C5
74 Artist Residence............G5
75 Aster House..................C5
76 Astor Hyde Park............B3
77 Astor Victoria H5
78 B+B Belgravia................F5
79 Beaufort House.............D4
80 Blakes...........................B6
81 Cherry Court Hotel G5
82 Gore B3
83 Knightsbridge Hotel......D4
84 Levin Hotel....................D3
85 Lime Tree Hotel.............F5
86 Meininger B4
87 No 90...........................C6
88 Number Sixteen............C5
89 Windermere Hotel G5

KENSINGTON & HYDE PARK

See map p438

See map p440

Bayswater Ⓢ

Queensway Ⓢ

BAYSWATER

Inverness Tce

Bayswater Rd

Lancaster Tce

Lancaster Gate

31 🏳

The Ring

15

Buck Hill Walk

20

30

28

2 Hyde Park

13

16

42

Kensington Palace Green

3 Kensington Palace

Budge's Walk

Round Pond

Lancaster Walk

Kensington Gardens

Serpentine Rd

70

The Serpentine

27

12

71

Rotten Row

40

The Flower Walk

7

Kensington Gore

50

76 82

22

53

Queen's Gate Tce

23

Exhibition Rd

41

72

48

84

KNIGHTSBRIDGE

Trevor Sq

Brompton Rd

59

83 79

Ansdell St

Douro Pl

St Alban's Gve

37

Gloucester Rd

Queen's Gate

Queen's Gate Tce

Elvaston Pl

5 Science Museum

Natural History Museum

86

4

26

8

6 Victoria & Albert Museum

38

Cromwell Rd

Gloucester Rd

56

73

South Kensington

18

EARL'S COURT

Collingham Rd

Harrington Gdns

Wetherby Gdns

68

Gloucester Rd

Queen's Gate

SOUTH KENSINGTON

75

88

Onslow Sq

CHELSEA

Donne Pl

Walton St

Cadogan St

51

80

Roland Gdns

Drayton Gdns

Cranley Gdns

Selwood Tce

49

Cranley Pl

Fulham Rd

Chelsea Sq

Old Church St

87

Manresa Rd

Sydney St

Cale St

47

45

17

King's Rd

Flood St

Smith Tce

Old Brompton Rd

Redcliffe Gdns

Westgate Tce

Finborough Rd

Cathcart Rd

Fawcett St

Redcliffe Rd

Park Walk

Beaufort St

The Vale

Beaufort St

Old Church St

Paultons Sq

63

58

10

Cheyne Walk

9

52

Oakley St

Bramerton St

Brompton Cemetery

Fulham Palace (1.5mi)

39

43

606 Club (500m)

Albert Bridge

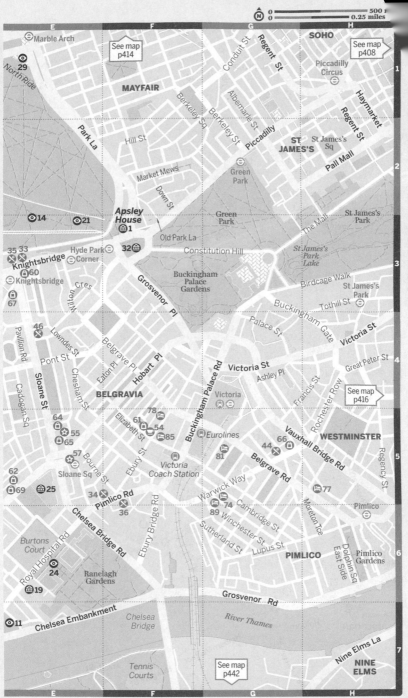

Marble Arch

29
North Ride

See map
p414

MAYFAIR

Conduit St

Regent St

Piccadilly
Circus

SOHO

See map
p408

Haymarket

Hill St

Park La

Berkeley Sq

Berkeley St

Albemarle St

Piccadilly

Regent St

ST
JAMES'S

St James's
Sq

Pall Mall

Market Mews

Down St

Green
Park

14

21

Apsley
House
1

Old Park La

Green
Park

Constitution Hill

The Mall

St James's
Park

35 33
Knightsbridge
60
Knightsbridge
67

Hyde Park
Corner

32

St James's
Park
Lake

St James's
Park

Buckingham
Palace
Gardens

Birdcage Walk

Buckingham Gate

Tothill St

Willow Cres

Grosvenor Pl

Palace St

Victoria St

Great Peter St

46
Pavilion Rd

Lowndes St

Pont St

Chesham St

Belgrave Pl

Eaton Pl

Hobart Pl

Buckingham Palace Rd

Victoria St

Ashley Pl

Francis St

Rochester Row

See map
p416

Cadogan St

Sloane St

BELGRAVIA

Elizabeth St

78
61 54
85

Victoria

Eurolines

Vauxhall Bridge Rd

66

WESTMINSTER

64
55
65

57
Sloane Sq

Bourne St

Ebury St

81

44

Belgrave Rd

Regency St

62
69

25

34
36

Pimlico Rd

Victoria
Coach Station

Warwick Way

74
89

Cambridge St

Winchester St

77

Pimlico

Chelsea Bridge Rd

Ebury Bridge Rd

Sutherland St

Lupus St

PIMLICO

Dolphin Sq
East Side

Pimlico
Gardens

Burtons
Court

Royal Hospital Rd

24

19

Ranelagh
Gardens

Grosvenor Rd

11

Chelsea Embankment

Chelsea
Bridge

River Thames

Tennis
Courts

See map
p442

Nine Elms La

NINE
ELMS

0   500 m
0   0.25 miles

CLERKENWELL, SHOREDITCH & SPITALFIELDS

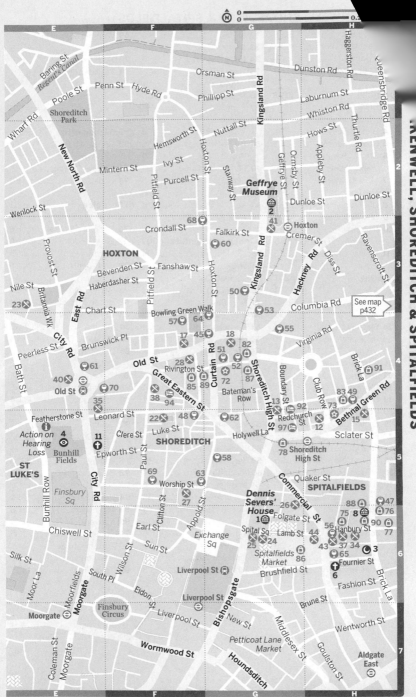

See map p432

E F G H

0
0   0.2

HOXTON

ST LUKE'S

SHOREDITCH

SPITALFIELDS

Geffrye Museum
2

Dennis Severs' House
1

Action on Hearing Loss
4

Bunhill Fields

Finsbury Sq

Finsbury Circus

Spitalfields Market

Petticoat Lane Market

Liverpool St

Moorgate

Aldgate East

Regent's Canal

Shoreditch Park

Kingsland Rd

New North Rd

City Rd

Old St

Bishopsgate

Commercial St

Brick La

Bethnal Green Rd

CLERKENWELL, SHOREDITCH & SPITALFI...

ights **p198**

ennis Severs'
House G6
Geffrye Museum G2

◎ **Sights** **p198**
3 Brick Lane Great
Mosque.......................H6
4 Bunhill Fields E5
5 Charterhouse C6
6 Christ Church
Spitalfields H6
7 Marx Memorial
Library B5
8 Old Truman Brewery H6
9 St John's Gate C5
10 St John's Priory
Church.........................C5
11 Wesley's Chapel.............E5

✖ **Eating** **p201**
Albion.................... (see 92)
12 Allpress Espresso H5
13 Andina G5
14 Blackfoot.......................B4
15 Brick Lane Beigel
Bake.............................H5
16 Caravan A4
17 Cây Tre F4
18 Clove Club......................G4
19 Coach & Horses A5
20 Comptoir Gascon..........B6
21 Eagle A5
22 Eyre Brothers F5
23 Fifteen E3
24 Galvin Café à Vin G6
25 Galvin La Chapelle G6
26 Hawksmoor G5
27 HKK.................................F5
28 Kêu!.................................F4
29 Little Bay A5
30 Look Mum No
Hands! D5
Medcalf................. (see 33)
31 Modern Pantry B5

32 Morito A4
33 Moro A4
34 Nude Espresso H6
35 Ozone Coffee
Roasters......................E4
36 Polpo..............................C6
37 Poppies...........................H6
38 Princess of
Shoreditch F4
39 Prufrock Coffee.............A6
Rosa's .... (see 37)
40 Shoreditch Grind...........E4
41 Sông Quê.......................G3
42 St John C6
43 St John Bread & Wine ..H6
44 Wright Brothers H6

◎ **Drinking & Nightlife** **p207**
45 333 Mother G4
46 5CC A4
47 93 Feet East...................H5
48 Book Club.......................F5
49 BrewDog H4
50 Bridge.............................G3
51 Callooh Callay................G4
52 Cargo G4
53 DreamBags-
JaguarShoes...............G3
54 Fabric..............................C6
Fox & Anchor....... (see 93)
55 George & Dragon G4
56 Golden Heart H6
57 Happiness Forgets........ F4
Hawksmoor .... (see 26)
58 Horse & Groom G5
59 Jerusalem Tavern B6
60 Macbeth G3
61 Nightjar..........................E4
62 Old Blue Last G5
63 Queen of Hoxton F5
64 Red Lion G4
65 Ten Bells.........................H6
66 Three Kings....................B5
67 Vinoteca C6
68 White Lyan F3

69 Worship St Whistling
Shop.............................F5
70 XOYO E4
71 Ye Olde Mitre B7
Zetter
Townhouse
Cocktail Lounge (see 99)

◎ **Entertainment** **p210**
72 Comedy Cafe
Theatre........................G4
73 Electric Cinema.............H5
74 Sadler's Wells B3

◎ **Shopping** **p211**
75 Absolute Vintage...........H6
76 Backyard Market..........H6
77 Blitz London...................H6
78 Boxpark..........................G5
79 Craft Central..................C5
80 E.C.One A4
81 Hatton Garden...............B6
82 House of Hackney.........G4
83 Labour & Wait................H4
84 Magma............................A6
85 Mr Start F4
86 Old Spitalfields
Market G6
87 Present...........................G4
88 Rough Trade East H5
89 Start................................G4
Start Menswear... (see 85)
90 Sunday UpMarket.........H6
91 Tatty Devine H4

◎ **Sleeping** **p328**
92 Boundary G5
93 Fox & Anchor.................C6
94 Hoxton Hotel F4
95 Malmaison C6
96 Rookery C6
97 Shoreditch Rooms........G5
98 Zetter Hotel &
Townhouse B5
99 Zetter Townhouse B5

◉ Top Sights   p215
1 Whitechapel Gallery B5

◉ Sights   p215
2 ArcelorMittal Orbit.........F2
3 Blind Beggar C5
4 Columbia Road Flower
    Market B4
5 Dalston Eastern Curve
    Gardens...................... H2
6 East London Mosque.... B5
7 Emirates Air Line.......... H6
8 Fieldgate St Great
    Synagogue.................. B5
9 Hackney City Farm B3
10 Hackney Museum C2
11 House Mill F4
12 London Fields B2
13 Mile End Park............... D4
14 Queen Elizabeth
    Olympic Park E2
15 Ragged School
    Museum D5
16 Ridley Road Market H2
17 St Anne's Limehouse ... E6
18 St Augustine's Tower C1
19 St George-in-the-East.. B6
20 St George's Town Hall.. C6
21 St Katharine Docks....... B6
22 Stadium........................F2
23 Sutton House C1
24 The Crystal H6
25 Tower Bridge
    Exhibition A6
26 Tower Hamlets
    Cemetery Park E4
27 Tower House B5
28 Trinity Green
    Almshouses............... C5
29 V&A Museum of
    Childhood................... C4
30 Victoria Park................. D3
31 View Tube F3
32 Viktor Wynd Museum
    of Curiosities,
    Fine Art & Natural
    History...................... B3

33 Whitechapel Bell
    Foundry B5
34 Whitechapel Road......... B5
    William Booth
    Statue .... (see 28)

⊗ Eating   p222
35 A Little of What You
    Fancy G3
36 Bistrotheque................ C3
37 Brawn B4
38 Cafe Spice Namasté..... B6
39 Climpson & Sons........... B3
    Corner Room......(see 105)
40 Counter Cafe E2
41 Duke's Brew & Que A3
42 E Pellicci.......................B4
43 Empress C3
44 F Cooke B3
45 Fish House C3
46 Formans....................... E2
47 Gallery Cafe C4
48 Green Papaya............... C2
49 Hackney Pearl E2
50 Kolapata.......................C5
51 Lardo C2
52 L'Atelier.......................G1
53 Laxeiro.........................B4
54 Little Georgia B3
55 Loafing......................... D3
56 Mangal Ocakbasi.......... H1
57 Rotorino G3
58 Tayyabs........................ B5
59 Towpath A3

⊗ Drinking & Nightlife   p225
60 Bethnal Green
    Working Men's
    Club............................ B4
61 Captain Kidd C7
62 Carpenter's Arms B4
63 Cat & Mutton B3
    Dalston Roof Park(see 84)
64 Dalston Superstore G1
65 Dove Freehouse B3
66 Farr's School of
    Dancing H2
67 Indo............................. B5

68 Netil360 ....
69 Old Ship.........................
70 Palm Tree...................... D
71 People's Park Tavern ... D2
72 Pond Dalston G2
73 Prospect of Whitby....... C6
74 Rhythm Factory B5
75 Royal Inn on the Park ... D3
76 Royal Oak..................... B4
77 Sager + Wilde A3
78 Satan's Whiskers C4
79 The Grapes D6
80 The Nest.......................H1
81 Viva H1
82 White Swan................... D6

◉ Entertainment   p227
83 Arcola Theatre.............. G2
84 Cafe Oto H2
85 Copper Box Arena E2
86 Genesis........................ C5
87 Hackney Empire............ C2
88 Passing Clouds............. G3
89 Rio Cinema................... G2
90 Vortex Jazz Club G2
91 Wilton's........................ B6

◉ Shopping   p228
92 Beyond Retro B4
93 Beyond Retro H1
94 Brick Lane Market......... B5
95 Broadway Market B3
96 Burberry Outlet Store .. C2
97 Pringle of Scotland
    Outlet Store C1
98 Traid............................ G2

◉ Sports & Activities   p229
99 Lee & Stort Boats..........F2
100 Lee Valley VeloPark.......F1
101 London Fields Lido........ B2

◉ Sleeping   p329
102 40 Winks C5
103 Avo H2
104 Qbic............................. B5
105 Town Hall Hotel &
    Apartments................ C3

EAST LONDON

See Enlargement

DALSTON

Dalston
Kingsland

Cecilia Rd

Ridley Rd

Hackney
Downs

Dalston La

Hackney
Central

18

23

Homerton High St

HOMERTON

Kenworthy Rd

Morning La

97

96

Homerton

Ball's Pond
Rd

De Beauvoir Rd

Dalston
Junction

Graham Rd

Forest Rd
Richmond Rd

87

51 **10**

101

Chatham Pl

HACKNEY

Kenton Rd

Cassland Rd

Well St

Victoria Park Rd

71

DE BEAUVOIR
TOWN

Downham
Rd

59 **41**

Haggerston Rd

Middleton Rd
Albion Dr

Queensbridge Rd

12

London
Fields

London
Fields

Well St

Laurston Rd

Victoria Park Rd

43

45

55

75

Grove Rd

30

Hertford
Union Canal

Old Ford Rd

48

Haggerston

Dunston Rd

Broadway
Market

39

95 **63**

Mate St

68

Kingsland Rd

Whiston Rd

Hackney Rd

Hoxton St

77

53
76
37

9

Goldsmith's Row

54

44 **65**

32

36

Regent's Canal

Old Ford Rd

Roman Rd

BOW

Cambridge
Heath

105 **47**

78

Cambridge Heath Rd

29

70

Grove Rd

Hoxton

4

Columbia Rd

Gosset St

60

BETHNAL
GREEN

Bethnal Green Rd

42

Bethnal
Green

Bethnal
Green

Old St

Shoreditch
High St

Cheshire
St

62

92

Vallance Rd

Stepney
Green

Mile End Rd

13

Mile
End

**MILE
END**

Mile
End
Park

Commercial St

Brick La

94

WHITECHAPEL

Whitechapel

67

3

28

86 **102**

Stepney Green

15

See map
p426

Liverpool St

Whitechapel
Gallery

74

6 **27**

Whitechapel
Rd

50

Stepney Way

STEPNEY

Whitehorse Rd

LIMEHOUSE

69

Commercial
Rd

Bishopsgate

Middlesex St

Aldgate
East

1 **34**

33 **8**

58

New Rd

104

Stepney Way

82

Limehouse
DLR

Aldgate

Mansell St

Alie St

38

Ellen St

Cannon St Rd

Commercial Rd

Shadwell
DLR

Cable St

79

Narrow St

Fenchurch St

Tower
Gateway DLR

91

20

19

The Highway

The Highway

73

Rotherhithe
Tuhnel

Salter Rd

Tower
Hill

East Smithfield

25

21

Ensign St

WAPPING

Wapping

River Thames

ROTHERHITHE

Tower
Bridge

Wapping High St

Green
Bank

61

Tooley St

Rotherhithe

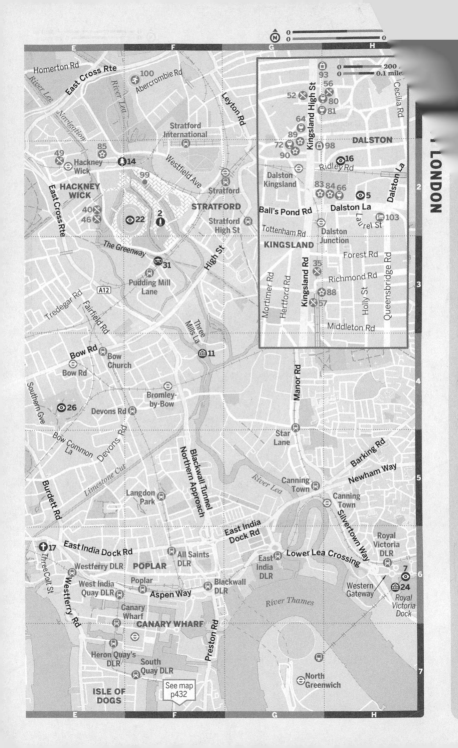

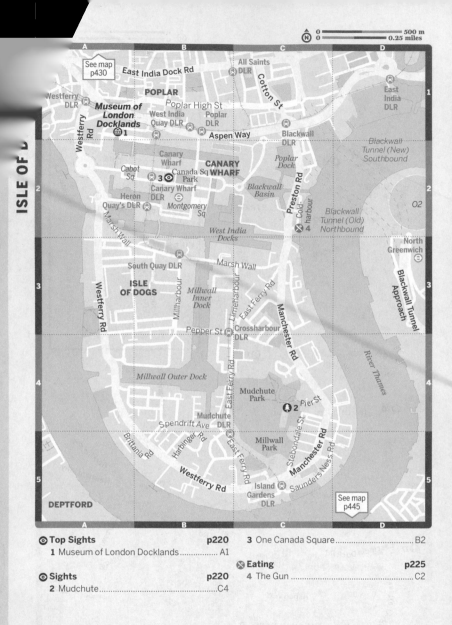

ISLE OF

See map p430

East India Dock Rd

POPLAR

All Saints DLR

Cotton St

Westferry DLR

Museum of London Docklands 1

Poplar High St

West India Quay DLR

Poplar DLR

Aspen Way

Blackwall DLR

East India DLR

Westferry Rd

Canary Wharf

Canada Sq Park

Cabot Sq.

3

CANARY WHARF

Poplar Dock

Blackwall Tunnel (New) Southbound

Canary Wharf DLR

Heron Quay's DLR

Montgomery Sq

Blackwall Basin

Preston Rd

Coldharbour

Blackwall Tunnel (Old) Northbound

O2

West India Docks

4

North Greenwich

Marsh Wall

South Quay DLR

ISLE OF DOGS

Millharbour

Millwall Inner Dock

Marsh Wall

East Ferry Rd

Manchester Rd

Blackwall Tunnel Approach

Westferry Rd

Limeharbour

Pepper St

Crossharbour DLR

River Thames

Millwall Outer Dock

East Ferry Rd

Mudchute Park

2

Pier St

Mudchute DLR

Spendrift Ave

Stebondale St

Millwall Park

Manchester Rd

Brittania Rd

Harbinger Rd

East Ferry Rd

Saunders Ness Rd

Westferry Rd

Island Gardens DLR

Saunders Ness Rd

See map p445

DEPTFORD

◎ **Top Sights**   **p220**
   1 Museum of London Docklands................. A1

◎ **Sights**   **p220**
   2 Mudchute... C4

3 One Canada Square................................. B2

⊗ **Eating**   **p225**
   4 The Gun.. C2

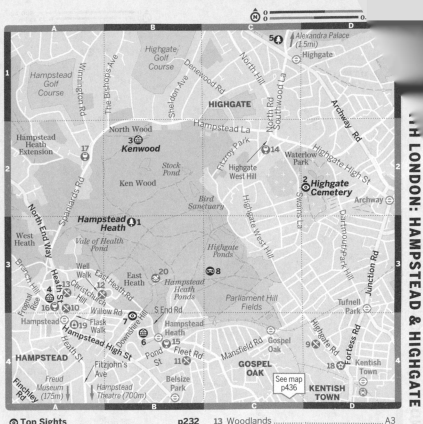

◎ **Top Sights**   **p232**
1 Hampstead Heath B3
2 Highgate Cemetery D2
3 Kenwood B2

◎ **Sights**   **p235**
4 Fenton House A3
5 Highgate Wood C1
6 Keats House B4
7 No 2 Willow Road......................................B4
8 Parliament Hill..C3

✖ **Eating**   **p244**
9 Dirty Burger...D4
10 Gaucho..A3
11 Stag..B4
12 Wells Tavern..A3

13 Woodlands A3

◎ **Drinking & Nightlife**   **p248**
14 Flask Tavern..C2
15 Garden Gate..B4
16 Holly Bush A3
17 Spaniard's Inn A2

✪ **Entertainment**   **p251**
18 The Forum..D4

🛍 **Shopping**   **p252**
19 Exclusivo..A4

✪ **Sports & Activities**   **p254**
20 Hampstead Heath
    Ponds B3

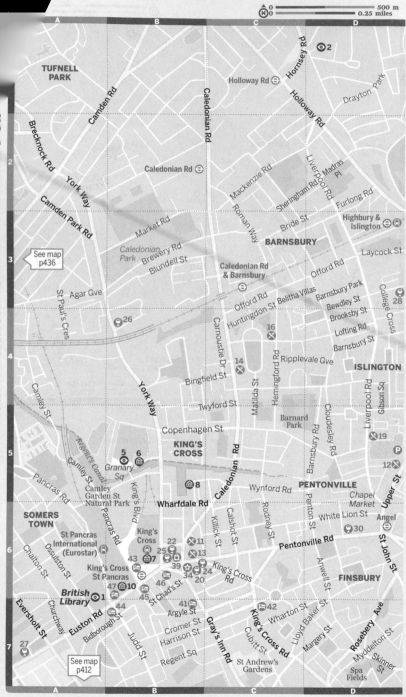

⦿ Top Sights   p232
1 British Library A6

⦿ Sights   p235
2 Arsenal Emirates Stadium... D1
3 Canonbury Square E3
4 Estorick Collection of
  Modern Italian Art............. E3
5 Granary Square.................... B5
6 House of Illustration B5
7 King's Cross Station B6
8 London Canal Museum B5
9 St Mary's Church E4
10 St Pancras Station &
   Hotel B6

⊗ Eating   p244
11 Addis................................. B6
   Caravan .... (see 5)
12 Chilango D5
13 Foodilic B6
   Grain Store .... (see 5)
14 Iberia.................................. C4
   Karpo .... (see 45)
   Kipferl .... (see 37)
15 Ottolenghi.......................... E4
16 Roots at N1 .... C4
17 Smokehouse......................... E3
18 Trullo E2
19 Yipin China......................... D5

◉ Drinking & Nightlife   p248
20 6 St Chad's Place................. B6
21 69 Colebrooke Row E5
22 Bar Pepito B6
23 Barrio North........................ E5
24 Big Chill House B6

Booking Office Bar
  & Restaurant .... (see 47)
25 Camino................................ B6
   Drink, Shop & Do .... (see 39)
26 Egg LDN.............................. B4
27 Euston Tap A7
28 Public House D3
29 The Bull E5
30 The Castle........................... D6

⊛ Entertainment   p251
31 Almeida E4
32 Angel Comedy...................... E5
33 King's Head Theatre............. E4
34 Scala.................................. B6
35 Union Chapel....................... E3

⊞ Shopping   p252
36 Annie's Vintage
   Costume & Textiles........... E5
37 Camden Passage
   Market E5
38 Gill Wing E3
   Harry Potter Shop
   at Platform 9¾ .... (see 7)
39 Housmans B6
40 twentytwentyone................. E4

⊟ Sleeping   p330
41 Clink261 .... B7
42 Clink78 .... C7
43 Great Northern Hotel B6
44 London St Pancras YHA B7
45 Megaro B6
46 Rough Luxe.......................... B6
47 St Pancras Renaissance
   London Hotel B6

See map
p426

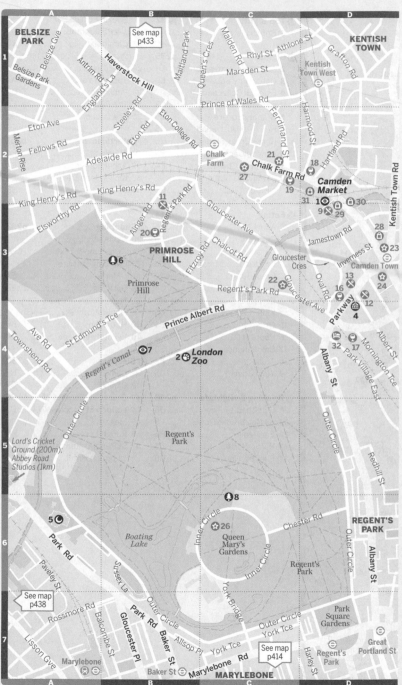

See map p433

A **B** **C** **D**

1

BELSIZE PARK

KENTISH TOWN

Belsize Park Gardens

Belsize Gve

Antrim Rd

England's La

Haverstock Hill

Maitland Park

Queen's Cres

Maiden Rd

Rhyl St

Athlone St

Grafton Rd

Kentish Town West

Marsden St

2

Eton Ave

Fellows Rd

Merton Rise

Steele's Rd

Eton Rd

Eton College Rd

Adelaide Rd

Prince of Wales Rd

Ferdinand St

Harmood St

Hartland Rd

Kentish Town Rd

Chalk Farm

Chalk Farm Rd

21

27

18

19

Camden Market

31 1 30

9 29

King Henry's Rd

King Henry's Rd

Elsworthy Rd

Ainger Rd

Regent's Park Rd

11

20

Gloucester Ave

Jamestown Rd

28

3

PRIMROSE HILL

6

Primrose Hill

Fitzroy Rd

Chalcot Rd

Gloucester Cres

Inverness St

Camden Town

23

24

Oval Rd

13

16

Parkway

12

4

Regent's Park Rd

22

Gloucester Ave

4

Ave Rd

Townshend Rd

St Edmund's Tce

Prince Albert Rd

Regent's Canal

7

2 London Zoo

Albany St

32

17

Park Village East

Mornington Tce

Albert St

5

Lord's Cricket Ground (200m); Abbey Road Studios (1km)

Outer Circle

Regent's Park

Outer Circle

Redhill St

5

REGENT'S PARK

6

Park Rd

Paveley St

Boating Lake

Inner Circle

8

26

Queen Mary's Gardens

Chester Rd

Inner Circle

Regent's Park

Outer Circle

Albany St

See map p438

Rossmore Rd

Lisson Gve

Sussex La

Park Rd

Gloucester Pl

Balcombe St

Outer Circle

Allsop Pl

York Bridge

York Tce

Outer Circle

York Tce

Park Square Gardens

7

Marylebone

Baker St

Marylebone Rd

MARYLEBONE

Harley St

Regent's Park

Great Portland St

A **B** **C** **D**

◎ **Top Sights** p2

1 Camden Market..................................... E
2 London Zoo.. B4
3 Wellcome Collection........................... F6

◎ **Sights** p235

4 Jewish Museum London...................... D4
5 London Central Mosque...................... A6
6 Primrose Hill.. B3
7 Regent's Canal.................................... B4
8 Regent's Park...................................... C6

✖ **Eating** p244

9 Chin Chin Labs..................................... D3
10 Diwana Bhel Poori House.................... E6
11 Manna.. B3
12 Market.. D3
13 Namaaste Kitchen............................... D3
York & Albany.............................. (see 32)

🍷 **Drinking & Nightlife** p248

14 Blues Kitchen....................................... E4
15 BrewDog Camden................................ E3
16 Dublin Castle....................................... D3
17 Edinboro Castle................................... D4
18 Lock Tavern... D2
19 Proud Camden..................................... C2
20 Queen's.. B3

🎭 **Entertainment** p251

21 Barfly... C2
22 Cecil Sharp House............................... C3
23 Electric Ballroom................................ D3
24 Jazz Cafe... D3
25 KOKO.. E4
26 Regent's Park Open Air Theatre......... C6
27 Roundhouse... C2

🛍 **Shopping** p252

28 Buck Street Market............................. D3
29 Camden Lock Market........................... D3
30 Camden Lock Village........................... D2
31 Stables Market.................................... D2

🛏 **Sleeping** p330

32 York & Albany...................................... D4

NORTH LONDON: CAMDEN TOWN

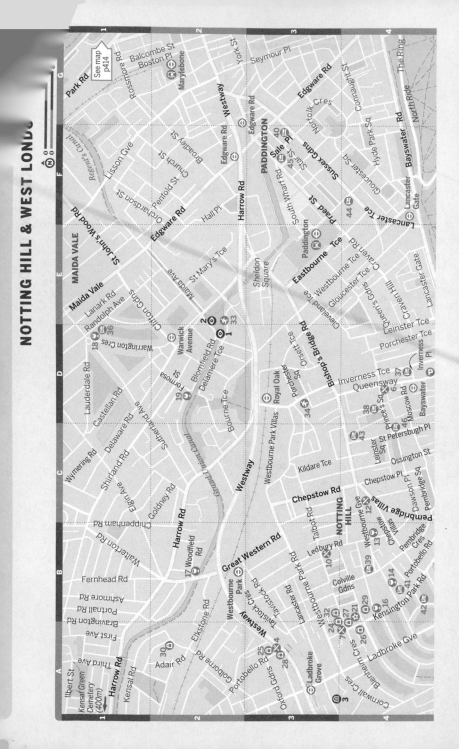

NOTTING HILL & WEST LOND

See map p414

G
Park Rd
Rossmore Rd
Balcombe St
Boston Pl
Marylebone
York St
Seymour Pl

Regent's Canal
Lisson Gve
Edgware Rd
Westway
Edgware Rd
Edgware Rd

F
St John's Wood Rd
Orchardson St
Penfold St
Broadley St
Church St
Hall Pl
Harrow Rd
PADDINGTON
Edgware Rd
Norfolk Cres

Edgware Rd
St Mary's Tce
Maida Ave
Sale Pl
Star St
Sussex Gdns
40
45
South Wharf Rd
Praed St
44
Bayswater Rd
North Ride
The Ring
Connaught St
Hyde Park Sq
Gloucester Sq
Lancaster Gate

E
MAIDA VALE
Maida Vale
Lanark Rd
Randolph Ave
Clifton Gdns
Paddington
Sheldon Square
Eastbourne Tce
Westbourne Tce
Cleveland Tce
Gloucester Tce
Craven Rd
Leinster Tce
Lancaster Gate
Lancaster Tce
Craven Hill
Queen's Gdns

D
Lauderdale Rd
Castellain Rd
Warrington Cres
18
36
Warwick Avenue
Blomfield Rd
Delamere Tce
Formosa St
19
Bourne Tce
2
33
1
Royal Oak
Bishop's Bridge Rd
Porchester Sq
Orsett Tce
Porchester Tce
34
Inverness Tce
Queensway
6
37
Bayswater
Moscow Rd
46
Prince's Sq
38
43
St Petersburgh Pl
Inverness Pl
Porchester Tce

C
Wymering Rd
Delaware Rd
Shirland Rd
Elgin Ave
Goldney Rd
Sutherland Ave
Grand Union Canal
Harrow Rd
Westway
Westbourne Park Villas
Kildare Tce
Chepstow Rd
NOTTING HILL
Westbourne Gve
12
Chepstow Pl
Dawson Pl
Pembridge Sq
Ossington St
Leinster Sq
Chepstow Villas
Pembridge Villas

B
Fernhead Rd
Walterton Rd
Chippenham Rd
Woodfield Rd
17
Harrow Rd
Great Western Rd
Talbot Rd
Ledbury Rd
Lancaster Rd
10
13
39
NOTTING HILL
Westbourne Gve
Colville Gdns
16
29
Pembridge Cres
Pembridge Rd
14
41
Portobello Rd
Kensington Park Rd
42

A
Ilbert St
First Ave
Third Ave
Kensal Green Cemetery (400m)
Harrow Rd
Kensal Rd
Bravington Rd
Portnall Rd
Ashmore Rd
Adair Rd
30
Golborne Rd
Elkstone Rd
Westbourne Park
Westbourne Park Rd
Tavistock Rd
Tavistock Cres
Oxford Gdns
25
28
24
32
4
Ladbroke Grove
27
21
26
Blenheim Cres
Cornwall Cres
Ladbroke Gve
3

Ladbroke Square Gardens

Lansdowne Rd

Clarendon Rd

Portland Rd

See map p440

Ladbroke Rd

Holland Park Ave

Ladbroke Rd

Holland Park

Kensington Pl

Notting Hill Gate

Pembridge Rd

Notting Hill Gate

Kensington Church St

Bayswater Rd

Queensway

The Broad Walk

Kensington Gardens

The Long Water

Lancaster Walk

Buck Hill Walk

The Broad Walk

Hyde Park

See map p424

⊙ Sights   p257
1 Grand Union Canal D2
2 Little Venice E2
3 Museum of Brands,
   Packaging &
   Advertising A3

⊗ Eating   p260
4 Acklam Village Market A3
5 Arancina C5
6 Couscous Café D4
7 E&O A4
   Electric Diner .... (see 21)
8 Fish House C5
9 Geales C5
10 Ledbury B3
11 Mazi C5
12 Taqueria C4

⊙ Drinking & Nightlife   p263
13 Beach Blanket Babylon B4
14 Earl of Lonsdale B4
15 Notting Hill Arts Club C5
16 Portobello Star B4
17 Union Tavern B2
18 Warrington D1
19 Waterway D2

⊙ Entertainment   p266
20 Coronet C5
21 Electric Cinema B4
22 Gate Picturehouse B3

⊙ Shopping   p266
23 Book & Comic Exchange C5
   Books for Cooks .... (see 24)
24 Ceramica Blue A3
25 Honest Jon's A3
26 Lutyens & Rubinstein A4
27 Notting Hill Bookshop A4
28 Portobello Green Arcade A3
29 Portobello Road Market B4
30 Rellik A2
31 Retro Woman C5
32 Rough Trade West B3

⊙ Sports & Activities   p267
33 London Waterbus
   Company E2

34 Porchester Spa D3
35 Queens Ice & Bowl D5

⊙ Sleeping   p331
36 Europa House D1
37 La Suite West D4
38 London House Hotel D4
39 Main House B4
40 Pavilion Hotel F3
41 Portobello Gold B4
42 Portobello Hotel B4
43 Space Apart Hotel C4
44 Stylotel F4
45 Tune Hotel F3
46 Vancouver Studios C4

WEST LONDON: SHEPHERD'S BUSH & EARL'S COURT

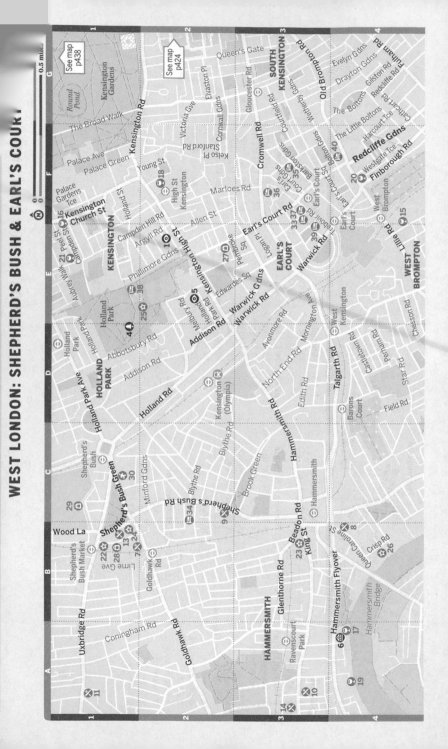

0.5 miles

See map p438

See map p424

Round Pond

Kensington Gardens

The Broad Walk

Palace Ave

Palace Green

Palace Gardens Tce

Kensington Church St

KENSINGTON

Aubrey Walk

Peel St

Campden St

Campden Hill Rd

Argyll Rd

Phillimore Gdns

Holland St

Holland Park

HOLLAND PARK

Holland Park Ave

Holland Park

Holland Park Rd

Abbotsbury Rd

Addison Rd

Addison Rd

Holland Rd

Young St

High St Kensington

Kensington High St

Allen St

Marloes Rd

Melbury Rd

Addison Rd

Edwardes Sq

Pembroke Sq

Warwick Gdns

Warwick Rd

Kensington (Olympia)

Blythe Rd

Blythe Rd

Brook Green

Queen's Gate

Elvaston Pl

Victoria Gve

Cornwall Gdns

Kelso Pl

Stanford Rd

Gloucester Rd

Cromwell Rd

Courtfield Rd

Wetherby Gdns

SOUTH KENSINGTON

Old Brompton Rd

Evelyn Gdns

Drayton Gdns

Gilston Rd

The Boltons

The Little Boltons

Redcliffe Gdns

Westgate Tce

Finborough Rd

Redcliffe Rd

Cathcart Rd

Harcourt Tce

Fulham Rd

Earl's Court Rd

Earl's Court Gdns

Barkston Gdns

Earl's Court

Earl's Court Sq

Bolton Gdns

Earl's Court

EARL'S COURT

Logan Pl

Nevern Pl

Warwick Rd

West Kensington

West Brompton

WEST BROMPTON

Lillie Rd

North End Rd

Avonmore Rd

Mornington Ave

Talgarth Rd

Hammersmith Rd

Edith Rd

Barons Court

Castletown Rd

Perham Rd

Chesson Rd

Star Rd

Field Rd

Wood La

Shepherd's Bush Market

Lime Gve

Shepherd's Bush Green

Goldhawk Rd

Uxbridge Rd

Coningham Rd

Goldhawk Rd

Minford Gdns

Shepherd's Bush Rd

Shepherd's Bush

Glenthorne Rd

Beadon Rd

King St

HAMMERSMITH

Hammersmith

Ravenscourt Park

Hammersmith Flyover

Queen Caroline St

Crisp Rd

Hammersmith Bridge

Map labels: BARNES, Wetland Centre, River Thames, Rainville Rd, FULHAM, Fulham Palace Rd, Munster Rd, Dawes Rd, Disbrowe Rd, Brecon Rd, Lillie Rd, Dalford St, Prothero Rd, Fabian Rd, Racton Rd, Hatton Rd, Waham Gve, Farm La, Fulham Broadway, Seagrave Rd, Ifield Rd, Fulham Rd, King's Rd, Lillie Rd, Hortensia Rd, Gunter Gve, Fernshaw Rd, Edith Gve, Lamont Rd

⊙ Sights p257
1 18 Stafford Terrace E2
2 Brompton Cemetery F5
3 Chelsea Football Club F5
4 Holland Park D1
5 Leighton House E2
6 William Morris Society A4

✕ Eating p260
7 A Cooke's B1
Bush Theatre Café & Bar ...... (see 22)
Churchill Thai Kitchen .... (see 16)
8 Gate B4
9 Kerbisher & Malt C2
10 Potli A3
11 Princess Victoria A1
12 River Café C5
13 Shikumen B1
14 Tosa A3

⚑ Drinking & Nightlife p263
15 Atlas F4
16 Churchill Arms F1
17 Dove A4
18 Kensington Roof Gardens F2
19 Old Ship W6 .... A4
20 Troubadour F4
21 Windsor Castle E1

✪ Entertainment p266
22 Bush Theatre B1
23 Lyric Hammersmith B3
24 O2 Shepherd's Bush Empire B1
25 Opera Holland Park E2
26 Riverside Studios B4

⊞ Shopping p266
27 Orsini E2
28 Shepherd's Bush Market B1
29 Westfield C1

✪ Sports & Activities p267
30 Fitness First E1

⚏ Sleeping p331
31 17 Homestead Rd E5
32 Barclay House E5
33 K + K Hotel George F3
34 Melrose Gardens C2
35 Nadler Kensington F3
36 Rockwell F3
37 Rushmore F3
38 Safestay Holland Park E1
39 Twenty Nevern Square E3
40 YHA Earl's Court F4

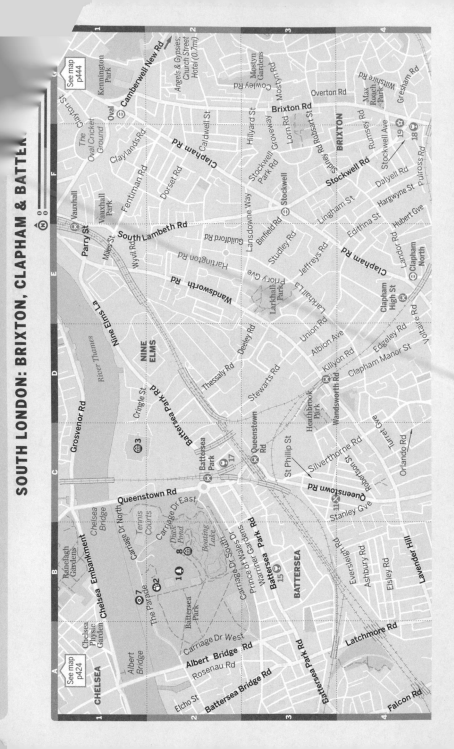

LONDON: BRIXTON, CLAPHAM & BATTERSEA

⊙ Sights   p276
1 Battersea Park........................... B2
2 Battersea Park Children's Zoo...... B2
3 Battersea Power Station.............. C1
4 Black Cultural Archives.............. G5
5 Brixton Village.......................... G5
6 Brixton Windmill........................ F6
7 Peace Pagoda............................ B1
8 Pump House Gallery.................... B2

⊗ Eating   p282
9 Asmara..................................... G5
10 Champagne + Fromage............ (see 5)
    Franco Manca......................... (see 21)
    Honest Burgers...................... (see 5)
    Mama Lan.............................. (see 5)
    Naughty Piglets...................... G6
    Rosie's Deli Café.................... (see 21)
11 Santa Maria del Sur................. C3
12 Satay Bar............................... F5

⊙ Drinking & Nightlife   p285
13 Dogstar................................. G5
14 Effra Hall Tavern..................... G5
15 Lost Angel.............................. B3
16 Market House.......................... G5
17 Mason's Arms......................... C2
18 Plan B................................... F4

☆ Entertainment   p286
19 O2 Academy Brixton................. G4

⊙ Shopping   p287
20 20 Storey............................... G5
21 Brixton Market........................ G5

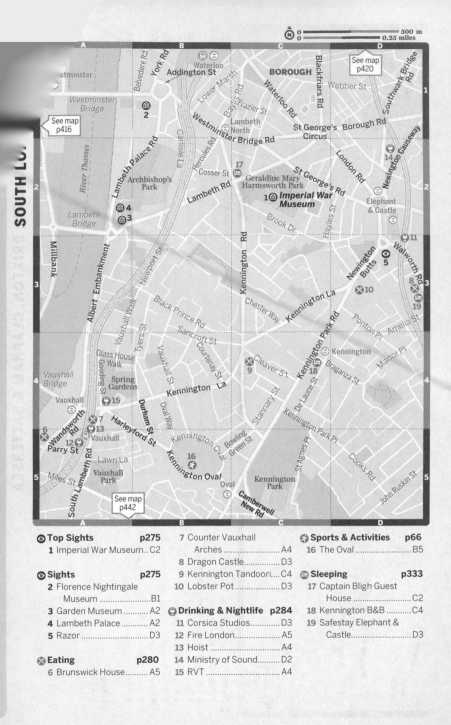

SOUTH LONDON

◉ Top Sights   p275
1 Imperial War Museum.. C2

◉ Sights   p275
2 Florence Nightingale
    Museum B1
3 Garden Museum A2
4 Lambeth Palace A2
5 Razor D3

✕ Eating   p280
6 Brunswick House A5

7 Counter Vauxhall
    Arches A4
8 Dragon Castle D3
9 Kennington Tandoori C4
10 Lobster Pot D3

◉ Drinking & Nightlife   p284
11 Corsica Studios D3
12 Fire London A5
13 Hoist A4
14 Ministry of Sound D2
15 RVT A4

✪ Sports & Activities   p66
16 The Oval B5

🛏 Sleeping   p333
17 Captain Bligh Guest
    House C2
18 Kennington B&B C4
19 Safestay Elephant &
    Castle D3

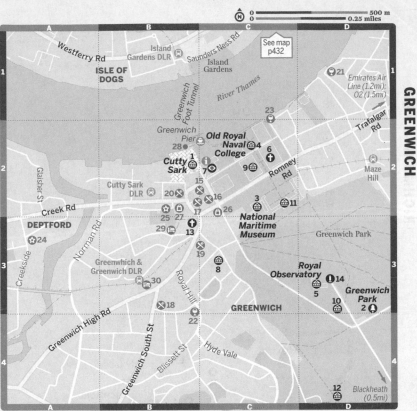

0 500 m
0 0.25 miles

See map
p432

GREENWICH

⊙ Top Sights **p270**
1 Cutty Sark B2
2 Greenwich Park D3
3 National Maritime
    Museum C2
4 Old Royal Naval
    College C2
5 Royal Observatory D3

⊙ Sights **p273**
6 Chapel at Old Royal
    Naval College C2
7 Discover Greenwich C2
8 Fan Museum C3
9 Painted Hall C2
10 Peter Harrison
    Planetarium D3
11 Queen's House C2
12 Ranger's House
    (Wernher
    Collection) D4

13 St Alfege Church B3
14 Statue of General
    Wolfe D3

✗ Eating **p280**
15 Black Vanilla C2
16 Goddards at
    Greenwich C2
17 Greenwich Market B2
18 Inside
    Old Brewery .... (see 7)
19 Rivington Grill C3
20 Tai Won Mein B2

◐ Drinking & Nightlife **p284**
21 Cutty Sark
    Tavern D1
22 Greenwich Union B3
    Old Brewery .... (see 7)
    Orangery .... (see 8)
23 Trafalgar Tavern C1

◑ Entertainment **p286**
24 Laban Theatre A3
25 Up the Creek, ... B2

◖ Shopping **p287**
Arty Globe .... (see 17)
Casbah
    Records .... (see 27)
Greenwich
    Market .... (see 17)
26 Nauticalia C2
27 Retrobates Vintage B2

◉ Sports & Activities **p386**
28 Thames River
    Services B2

◰ Sleeping **p334**
29 Number 16 .... B3
30 St Christopher's
    Inn Greenwich B3

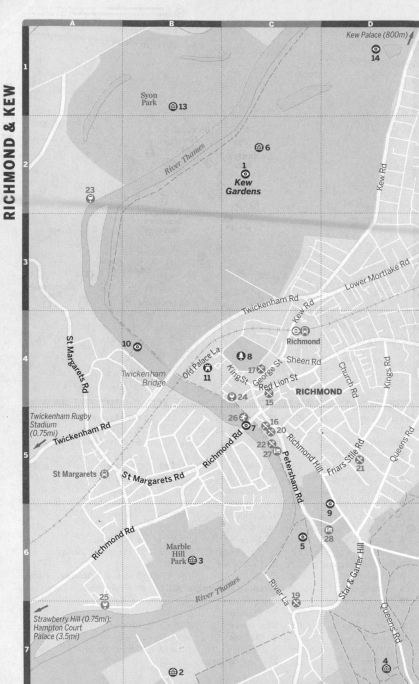

Kew Palace (800m)

14

Syon Park
13

6

1
Kew Gardens

River Thames

23

Lower Mortlake Rd

Twickenham Rd

Kew Rd

Kew Rd

10

St Margarets Rd

Twickenham Bridge

Old Palace La

Richmond

8

17 George St
Sheen Rd

King St

11

Red Lion St

24

15

RICHMOND

Church Rd

Kings Rd

26
7

16
20

22
27

Richmond Rd

Richmond Hill

Petersham Rd

Friars Stile Rd

Queens Rd

21

Twickenham Rugby
Stadium
(0.75mi)
Twickenham Rd

St Margarets

St Margarets Rd

9

Richmond Rd

5

28

Marble
Hill
Park   3

River Thames

River La

Star & Garter Hill

Queens Rd

25

19

Strawberry Hill (0.75mi);
Hampton Court
Palace (3.5mi)

4

2

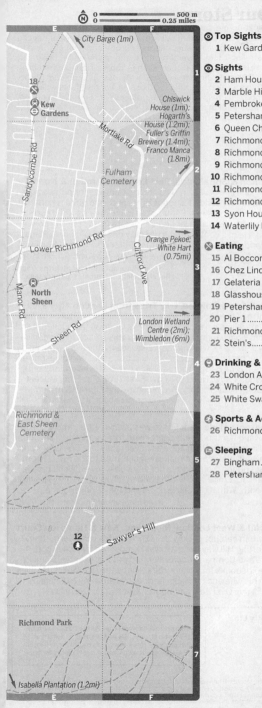

◎ **Top Sights** p294

1 Kew Gardens C2

◎ **Sights** p296

2 Ham House B7
3 Marble Hill House B6
4 Pembroke Lodge D7
5 Petersham Meadows C6
6 Queen Charlotte's Cottage C2
7 Richmond Bridge C5
8 Richmond Green C4
9 Richmond Hill D6
10 Richmond Lock B4
11 Richmond Palace Remains B4
12 Richmond Park E6
13 Syon House B1
14 Waterlily House D1

◎ **Eating** p300

15 Al Boccon di'Vino C4
16 Chez Lindsay C5
17 Gelateria Danieli C4
18 Glasshouse E1
19 Petersham Nurseries Cafe C7
20 Pier 1 .... C5
21 Richmond Hill Bakery D5
22 Stein's C5

◎ **Drinking & Nightlife** p301

23 London Apprentice A2
24 White Cross C4
25 White Swan A7

◎ **Sports & Activities** p296

26 Richmond Bridge Boathouses C5

◎ **Sleeping** p334

27 Bingham C5
28 Petersham D6

Our Story

A beat-up old car, a few dollars in the pocket and a sense of adventure. In 1972 that's all Tony and Maureen Wheeler needed for the trip of a lifetime – across Europe and Asia overland to Australia. It took several months, and at the end – broke but inspired – they sat at their kitchen table writing and stapling together their first travel guide, *Across Asia on the Cheap*. Within a week they'd sold 1500 copies. Lonely Planet was born.

Today, Lonely Planet has offices in Franklin, London, Melbourne, Oakland, Beijing and Delhi, with more than 600 staff and writers. We share Tony's belief that 'a great guidebook should do three things: inform, educate and amuse'.

Our Writers

Peter Dragicevich

Clerkenwell, Shoreditch & Spitalfields, East London, Camden & North London After a dozen years reviewing music and restaurants for publications in New Zealand and Australia, London's bright lights and loud guitars could no longer be resisted. Like all good Kiwis, Peter got to know the city while surfing his way between friends' flats all over London before finally putting down roots in North London. He has contributed to literally dozens of Lonely Planet titles, including *Walking in Britain*, *England*, *Wales* and *Great Britain*. Peter also wrote Drinking & Nightlife Overview, Entertainment Overview, Shopping Overview, Theatre & Dance, Art & Fashion, Music and Film.

Read more about Peter at: https://auth.
lonelyplanet.com/profiles/peterdragicevich

Steve Fallon

The City, Greenwich & South London, Day Trips from London After a full 15 years living in the centre of the known universe – East London – Steve cockney-rhymes in his sleep, eats jellied eel for brekkie, drinks lager by the bucketful and dances round the occasional handbag. As always, for this edition of *London* he did everything the hard/fun way: walking the walks, seeing the sights, taking (some) advice from friends, colleagues and the odd taxi driver and digesting everything in sight. Steve is a qualified London Blue Badge Tourist Guide (www.steveslondon.com). Steve also wrote Welcome to London, What's New, Need to Know, First Time, For Free, Museums Overview, Gay Overview, Sleeping, London Today, History, Architecture and Literary London.

Read more about Steve at: https://auth.
lonelyplanet.com/profiles/SteveF

Emilie Filou

South Bank, Kensington & Hyde Park Emilie was born in Paris, where she lived until she was 18. Following her three-year degree and three gap years, she found herself in London, fell in love with the place and never really left. She now works as a journalist specialising in Africa and makes regular trips to the region from her home in northeast London. You can see her work on www.emiliefilou.com; she tweets at @EmilieFilou. Emilie also wrote London's Top 16, Getting Around, Top Itineraries, If You Like, Month by Month, With Kids, Like a Local and the Survival Guide.

Read more about Emilie at: https://auth.
lonelyplanet.com/profiles/EmilieFilou

Damian Harper

West End, Notting Hill & West London, Richmond, Kew & Hampton Court Born off the Strand within earshot of Bow Bells (favourable wind permitting), Damian grew up in Notting Hill way before it was discovered by Hollywood. A onetime Shakespeare and Company bookseller and radio presenter, Damian has been authoring guidebooks for Lonely Planet since the late 1990s. He lives in South London with his wife and two kids, frequently returning to China (his second home). Damian also wrote the Eating Overview and Sports & Activities Overview.

Published by Lonely Planet Publications Pty Ltd
ABN 36 005 607 983
10th edition – Feb 2016
ISBN 978 1 74321 856 3
© Lonely Planet 2016   Photographs © as indicated 2016
10 9 8 7 6 5 4 3 2 1
Printed in China